Electric Eden

Unearthing Britain's Visionary Music

Rob Young

ff

faber and faber

First published in Great Britain in 2011
by Faber and Faber Ltd
Bloomsbury House
74–77 Great Russell Street
London WC1B 3DA
This paperback edition first published in 2011

Printed in England by CPI Bookmarque, Croydon

A CIP record for this book
is available from the British Library

ISBN 978–0–571–23753–1

2 4 6 8 10 9 7 5 3 1

Rob Young has worked at *The Wire* magazine since 1993, including five years as editor. He is the author of *Rough Trade* and *Warp*, and editor of *Undercurrents: The Hidden Wiring of Modern Music* and *The Wire Primers: A Guide to Modern Music*. He has contributed to publications including *Uncut*, The *Guardian*, *Sight & Sound*, *Frieze* and *Art Review*. He lives in London.

Further praise for *Electric Eden*:

'In the face of British folk's sprawling diversity, Young's greatest achievement is to locate a real sense of continuity, a unifying flow that underpins decades, if not centuries, of artistry . . . Prepare to wander down countless previously unpondered highways and byways. And prepare to consider Britain's satisfyingly strange and surprisingly hardy indigenous musical heritage afresh. A treat.' Phil Harrison, *Time Out* Book of the Week *****

'Consistently absorbing . . . After decades of opportunistic reportage, the modern publisher's catalogue positively crawls with big, serious and thoroughly well-intentioned books about "English pop". This is one of the best.' D J Taylor, *Independent*

'This year's most lushly poetic music book . . . takes the reader on a ramble through the evolution of English folk music from the druids up to the electronic pulses of the Noughties.' Helen Brown, *Daily Telegraph*

'An eye-opening account of modern British music's conversation with the rural. It has been too easy to knock this kind of music out of embarrassment more than anything else, but this epic book will hopefully redress this tendency.' Jeremy Deller, *Observer*

'Here is a masterpiece . . . nothing less than a magical exploration of transcendent twentieth-century British 'folk' music and the folk imagination . . . a book that, like the subject itself, redraws the map of cultural Britain, awakening long-dormant protectors, radical spirits and utopian dreamers. Like the revered and forgotten texts Young himself unearths, *Electric Eden* possesses the power to haunt and enchant for many years to come.' Andrew Male, *Caught by the River*

'Moving from the folk revival of the early twentieth century onto what the author calls "Albion-centric, historically resonant folk-rock" of the 60s and 70s, music fans will enjoy comprehensive analyses of Fairport Convention, Comus, Nick Drake and many others. Where Young takes more esoteric flight is when he convincingly works such disparate concepts as the free festival scene, Bagpuss and The Wicker Man into his meditations on an agrarian past that survives in the imagination. Fascinating.' Ian Harrison, *Q*

'*Electric Eden* makes a persuasive case for folk-rock's essentially liberating nature, and ingeniously links it with the utopian dreams of Britishness of earlier generations of twentieth-century folk-revivalists.' Ludovic Hunter-Tilney, *Financial Times*

'A passionately researched, carefully written and compulsively readable map of the leys and songlines of an oral culture with its roots in pre-Roman times and its branches in the charts . . . Young's grasp of context is enviable, his knowledge encyclopaedic . . . *Electric Eden* constructs a new mythography out of old threads, making antiquity glow with an eerie hue. It can sit proudly on any bookshelf beside Alan Lomax's *The Land Where Blues Began*, Greil Marcus's *Invisible Republic*, Nick Tosches' *Where Dead Voices Gather* or Jon Savage's *England's Dreaming*. If Mr Young never writes another word, he can count this epic book as the fruit of a beautiful labour.' Peter Murphy, *Sunday Business Post*

CALIBAN: Be not afeard. The isle is full of noises,
Sounds, and sweet airs, that give delight, and hurt not.
Sometimes a thousand twangling instruments
Will hum about mine ears; and sometimes voices,
That, if I then had wak'd after long sleep,
Will make me sleep again; and then, in dreaming,
The clouds methought would open and show riches
Ready to drop upon me, that, when I wak'd,
I cried to dream again.

> William Shakespeare, *The Tempest* (1610–11)

The Nature of my Work is Visionary or Imaginative;
it is an Endeavour to Restore what the Ancients calld the
Golden Age.

> William Blake, *A Vision of the Last Judgment* (1810)

Contents

Contents

III Poly-Albion

The Silver Chain

He rises and begins to round
He drops the silver chain of sound,
Of many links without a break . . .
George Meredith, *The Lark Ascending* (1895)

As I rode out on a hot, bright, early-May day of birdsong and blossom, cycling over London's Blackfriars Bridge in the early evening, with the dazzling sky vaulting above the silver chain of the Thames, it felt as though the wheel of the year had decisively rolled forwards on its compulsive journey from spring to summer. It had been a day for forward planning, daydreaming, letting it all hang out. Almost in defiance of the light, I was on my way to a place where the murk was king. Glancing to my right as I sped across the bridge, I could see my destination: the BFI Cinema, a recently refitted extension to the Southbank's post-war brick-and-concrete palace of culture.

The screening was a specially conceived, one-off event, co-organised by the British Film Institute and the English Folk Dance and Song Society. A kinetic parade of films and fragments culled from their joint archives: artless step-dancers and toothless drinkers in Norfolk and Suffolk pubs; the whirling, randy Obby Oss of Padstow in Cornwall, filmed in mesmerising Technicolor in the early 1950s by Alan Lomax and Peter Kennedy; an episode of a long-forgotten 1980s Channel Four documentary series, *The Future of Things Past*, catching the nation's superstitions and unaccountable rituals before they are lost altogether to the digital age. There's a brutality to much of them: the smashed limbs and dislocated spines of the cheese-rollers; the tortuous, sweaty ordeal of the Scottish Burryman, plastered all day with prickly burrs; the heat rashes suffered by carriers of blazing tar barrels at Lewes each November. A world, a Britain, vanished and foreign to all but the eldest gathered in tonight's audience. The local and parochial made strange. Customs to which few, nowadays, are actually accustomed at all.

And then the projection screen becomes a window on an even more distant past. For here's the only known moving footage of Cecil Sharp, the folklorist and collector indelibly associated with the origins of the past century's folk revival, skipping and twirling and enjoying a merry roister-doister with his assistants, Maud and Helen Karpeles, and the moustachioed George Butterworth, the English composer of pastoral music. Shot in 1912, their country dances and morris exercises are divided into short segments of film, totalling no more than five minutes. The footage flickers, blinks: almost breaks down into its constituent still frames. These images, held for decades deep in the archive rooms of Cecil Sharp House, are preserved on Kinora spools, a long-dead motion-picture medium. The Kinora was the British adaptation of the Lumière brothers' pioneering 'cinématographe'. Each spool was effectively a paper or celluloid flick book, bound onto a wheel and whirled through a lightbox at approximately twelve frames per second. Until the Kinora factory burned down in 1914, this primitive projector was a popular form of high-tech Edwardian home entertainment.

The Kinora spools are silent, of course. Filmed two years before the outbreak of the First World War, they date from long before the advent of the film soundtrack. In 1982, financed by a grant from the Sheffield Morris Ring, they were transferred faithfully to film stock, simply to prolong their life and to extend it beyond the extinct Kinora device. It's a reminder that Cecil Sharp was a creature of the pre-phonographic era: while his contemporary Percy Grainger hauled

A film still from the only existing footage of folklorist Cecil Sharp (left), performing a country dance with Maud Karpeles, Helen Karpeles and George Butterworth, 1912.

a cumbersome wax-cylinder recording device around the English countryside to record village labourers reciting old folk songs, Sharp's own song-collecting was all transcribed by hand in notebooks. But Butterworth, Sharp and the Karpeles sisters must have been dancing to *something* on the day these images were preserved. So, here at the BFI, the event's curators have arranged for a fiddle player, Laurel Swift, to stand beside the screen and play jigs that match the dance moves. It only lasts three minutes at most, but there's something about this recital that triggers an indescribable reverie, as music present stretches through the screen's shining portal to touch, however briefly, a set of actions nearly a century old. There's Sharp, in his specs and loose-fitting flannel suit, prancing in this corner of a garden with abandoned, joyous innocence. It's a full eighteen years before the posthumous building of the house that still bears his name and contains his legacy. And here's vigorous, twenty-nine-year-old Butterworth, composer of English idylls, songs romantic and rueful, a year away from completing his rich orchestral tapestry of folk tunes, *The Banks of GreenWillow*. In four years' time, his blazered torso and jigging, cricket-trousered legs will be prone and lifeless in the mud of the Somme. But they dance as if the music from the fiddle in front of us, alive and resonant, is bubbling just out of camera range in this secret garden. The illusion becomes absolute, to the point where it is unclear whether the music is driving the picture, or the image is guiding the music. Perhaps, I find myself thinking, this is the nearest thing to time travel it's possible to experience. This alchemy of live music and ancient film creates a conduit, a wormhole, a charmed shortcut through the huge block of elapsed time. In this moment, I feel like a guest in the Edenic corner of England depicted in these historic vignettes. And conversely, the two-dimensional dancers momentarily become guests in our own time.

And then the lights go up.

It was *music* that cast that magic spell, dispersing time for an instant in the cinema gloom. One of the germinal ideas for this book was to locate and understand an undercurrent of music in Britain that, to my ears at least, is concerned at a root, instinctive level with a form of imaginative time travel. A significant portion of Britain's cultural identity is built on a succession of golden ages. The medieval Land of Cockayne was a land of plenty and laziness, balm to the oppressed feudal labourer. Gerrard Winstanley, the activist of the English Revolution, reclaimed common land as a slice of God-given Paradise for his Digger comrades. William Blake cast his visionary faculties back to a pre-lapsarian era in which none of his present woes – industrialism, poverty, urban blight – existed. The early twentieth century saw the salvage of the Tudor and Elizabethan eras, recast as 'Merrie England', a perpetual springtime of courtliness, artistic treasures and clearly stratified society. In my own time, the nostalgia industry operates at fever pitch, often promoting an anachronistic hybrid of artefacts from both my grandparents' and my parents' generations – 'Boys'

Own' adventure stories, vintage confectionery, Regency costume dramas – as well as my own youthful memories of the 1970s.

Britain's literature, poetry, art and music abounds in secret gardens, wonderlands, paradises lost, postponed or regained. Avalon, Xanadu, Arden, Prospero's island, Tír-na-nÓg, Middle-earth, Narnia, Elidor, Utopia, the New Atlantis, Erewhon, the Perfumed Garden: fictive domains that subtly swap the present for alternative speculations. British music accumulates a powerful charge when it deals with a sense of something unrecoupable, a lost estate. One of the most vivid indicators of the changes affecting the nation is marked upon its physical terrain. I wanted to grasp how British musicians and composers have drawn on an idea of folk, alongside a literary (or cinematic) sense of nostalgia and connection with the landscape, all of which feeds into an encompassing expression of Britain that Blake, at least, called 'visionary'. His definition of 'Vision or the Imagination' was 'a Representation of what Eternally Exists, Really & Unchangeably. [. . .] The Nature of Visionary Fancy, or Imagination, is very little known [. . .] yet the Oak dies as well as the Lettuce, but Its Eternal Image & Individuality never dies, but renews by its seed . . .'[1] The image of the organic transmission of an ever-changing same was replicated, almost word for word, by Cecil Sharp, in his attempts to define the passage of folk music through time. The 'Visionary Music' invoked in this book's title refers to any music that contributes to this sensation of travel between time zones, of retreat to a secret garden, in order to draw strength and inspiration for facing the future.

This music is the sound of an *Electric* Eden, one that has always been required to interface with the modern world. My first intention was to write a history of British folk-rock's high-water mark (Pentangle, Fairport Convention, Nick Drake, Sandy Denny, Incredible String Band et al.) – music born out of the battle between progressive push and nostalgic pull. Even in the late

1960s, folk purists were coming on like the children's television wizard Catweazle, ever suspicious of modern-day 'electrickery' when folk songs were recast in rock idioms. But electrification comes in many forms. For the early-twentieth-century composers such as Vaughan Williams and Holst, there were thunderbolts of inspiration from oriental mysticism, angular modernism and the body blow of the Great War, as well as input from the rediscovered folk tradition itself. For the second wave of folk revivalists such as Ewan MacColl and A. L. Lloyd in the 1950s, the vital spark was communism's dream of a post-revolutionary New Jerusalem. For their younger successors in the 1960s, who thronged the folk clubs set up by the old guard, the lyrical freedoms of Dylan and the unchained melodies of psychedelia created the conditions for folk-rock's own golden age, a brief Indian summer and fruitful autumn that lasted from around 1969 to 1972. Breakthroughs in contemporary music – modal jazz, world musics from Jamaica to India, the period-instrument movement – all had an impact. Four decades on, even that progressive period has become just one more era ripe for fashionable emulation and pastiche. The idea of a folk tradition being exclusively confined to oral transmission has become a much looser, less severely guarded concept. Recorded music and television, for today's metropolitan generation, are where the equivalent of folk memories are seeded.

A well is only good while it's in use. Untouched, the water at the bottom will stagnate and become poisoned. *Electric Eden* is not so much about the source singers and players, guardians of the well of folk tradition. It's really the story of people who have slaked their thirsts at the well, treating it as an oasis from which to refresh their own art. At certain times, many of its champions have selectively cherry-picked from the entire folk canon: MacColl privileging workers' and industrial songs; The Watersons collecting pagan, seasonal music; Shirley Collins and Ashley Hutchings focusing on agricultural and pastoral material from southern England. Interest in folk music and other buried aspects of national culture tends to be reawakened at moments when there's a perceived danger of things being lost for ever. Of the two historical landmarks that continue to permeate the British collective unconscious, the Industrial Revolution gave birth to the Romantic movement in literature and art, and the huge losses to the working population sustained during the First World War altered the constitution of society, reshaping the equilibrium between country and city. In the late 1960s and early 70s, fear of annihilation, technological progress, and a vision of alternative societies filtered through popular and underground culture, conspiring to promote the ideal of 'getting back to the garden'. 'Folk' is only one of many ingredients in the mix during these charged moments. Neither Nick Drake nor Kate Bush nor Talk Talk sang old folk songs, but their music resonates with Romantic yearning for an intense communion with nature and the desire to reclaim a stolen innocence. In a quest for a workable religious experience, Gustav Holst sought enlightenment in Hindu mythology, while The Incredible String Band folded psychedelics into a cocktail of visionary and Beat poetry. Faerie magic and Celtic lore infused the orchestral music of Arnold Bax and John Ireland, as much as the cosmic folk-rock of Donovan and Marc Bolan's Tyrannosaurus Rex. The Tudor-influenced work of Vaughan Williams and Peter Warlock, and the medieval instrumental textures employed by John Renbourn, Pentangle and Shirley and Dolly Collins, present a beguiling form of sonic time travel. In telling these artists' stories, I wanted above all to keep these undercurrents in focus: silver chains that bind more than a century of music into a continuum.

It's important to remember, though, that the links in the chain of tradition have been forged by revolutionaries. The great age of folkloric retrieval is synchronous with the age of Karl Marx. 'Folk' in Britain has always been contested territory. No longer does the word refer solely to particular songs and melodies attached to the ancient lore of the land; nor to techniques of singing, instrumentality and delivery; nor to a music's sense of belonging to small, often rural communities, or even a nation. Folk still includes these preserved traditions, but it is also applied to areas of contemporary music, to writers of new, personal songs such as John Martyn and Roy Harper. Cecil Sharp wanted folk music taught in schools to inculcate national identity. Ewan MacColl intended it as a tool to stir up a workers' revolution. Nowadays it's become as much a signifier of texture and aesthetics as an indicator of ingrained authenticity – as in such descriptive terms as 'acid folk', 'free folk', even the ungainly 'folktronica'. Folk manages to occupy fashionable and unfashionable status simultaneously. Just as the radical floral wallpapers of William Morris – an outspoken Victorian socialist – now cover middle-class lounges, so the radical intentions of many folk historians and revivalists have led to a music commonly regarded as parochial and conservative. I wanted to get to the bottom of why, and when, its less appealing traits began to be taken as typical. While there has always been someone ready to poke fun at folk singers and morris dancers, the mockery only really turned hostile in the late 1970s, by which time most utopian dreams, hangovers from the 1960s, were falling permanently out of reach. Clichés of the folkie, finger in ear and quaffing real ale, persist. And yet, newspaper columns periodically rejoice, folk is hip again, influencing artists, clothing and furniture designers, celebrated at music festivals and on TV documentaries, reissued on countless major and specialist record labels. Folk is a sonic 'shabby chic' that contains elements of the uncanny and eerie, as well as an antique veneer, a whiff of Britain's pagan ancestry. The very obscurity and anonymity of folk music's origins open up space for rampant imaginative fancies. The idea of folk still seems unstable, volatile: there's an ongoing chemical reaction that hasn't yet subsided.

It's difficult to envisage a time when these internal arguments will cease to define and invigorate Britain's cultural life. If it is to thrive, and not stagnate, it will continue to need the friction between conservation and progression, city and country, acoustics and electricity, homespun and visionary, familiar and uncanny. As the most immediately audible signifier of changing times, the acoustic/electric debate has always stimulated controversy in the musical realm. Concepts of tradition and authenticity – acoustic guitars versus Fender Strats – too frequently shore up Luddite agendas. But critics (and musicians) who reject electrification on principle are working from a fundamentally erroneous idea of what tradition means. The village folk singers visited in the Edwardian age by Cecil Sharp and Percy Grainger sang their songs with no accompaniment at all, so guitars – whether classical, steel-strung acoustic or a Fender Telecaster – or a piano or synthesizer for that matter, are all equally outrageous, equally 'inauthentic'. The adoption of 'folk' by the 1960s generation helped to unearth a resource, and an idea of national music, that might well have lain unheard, as Americanised popular music took full hold. Instead, electricity applied to the British visionary continuum produced some of the most exciting music of the age, one that reached its most progressive forms precisely when the tussle between acoustics and electricity was being enacted within the fabric of the music itself. As Dave Swarbrick, fiddle player with Fairport Convention, observed in the mid-1970s: 'If you're singing about a bloke having his head chopped off, or a girl fucking her brother and having a baby and the brother getting pissed off and cutting her guts open and stamping on the baby and killing his sister – now that's a fantastic story by any standards, whether told in a pub or on Broadway. Having to work with a storyline like that with acoustic instruments wouldn't be half as powerful or potent, dramatically, as saying the same things electrically. Because when you deal with violence, when you deal with someone slashing with a sword, say, there are sounds that exist electrically – with electric bass, say –

that can very explicitly suggest what the words are saying.'²

Paradise is a kind of false-memory syndrome, a clinging refusal to let go of an illusory golden age. Elements are periodically amputated along the way in order to prevent aspects of the culture from becoming gangrenous, but when things are killed off, the voices of these ghost memories tend to linger. The British imagination seems peculiarly well attuned to their uncanny cries.

I left the cinema and strolled along the Embankment, letting the evening chill descend into my bones. A man in a twin-oared sculling boat slipped past me upriver, wrapped in thick layers of clothing and with a bulging rucksack nestling between his knees, looking for all the world as though he was setting out to seek the source of the Thames. I thought about my own quest to open the rusty gate and unearth the secret garden of Britain's visionary music. Unlike a river, I knew that there would be no single spring from which all else flows, and I expected to find many tributaries to explore along the way. So I decided to begin with a pilgrim of the pavement, in the late 1960s' diamond days, whose journey along the entire length of the British mainland embodies the dreams, the illusions, the music and the redrawn map of Albion that make up Electric Eden.

I

Music from Neverland

I

The Inward Exodus

The battered Austin, its fifty years clearly legible in rust and mud flecks, slowed to a halt, the motor spluttering on its empty fuel tank. The doors spread their wings and two of its three occupants emerged onto the country road, taking stock of their position among the hedgerows before rolling up their sleeves to push the vehicle, while the third, a slight female, took hold of the wheel in the driver's seat. As the tyres bit against the rough tarmac and the car began to move off, one of them, Robert, caught sight of something glinting behind the thorny hedgerow. He called to his friend John to stop pushing for a moment, and to his girlfriend Vashti to apply the handbrake. She climbed out of the car and together they vaulted the gate.

It was a Gypsy caravan, or more accurately, an old baker's delivery cart, constructed from tin sheets covered with fading brown paint. A curved roof crowned it, and its wheels, which looked as if they had been taken off a vintage motor car, were mounted on a buckling chassis. How many miles had this unroadworthy jalopy already travelled? The three friends could not tell, but they set off down the short path in search of its owner. He was soon found: a Gypsy, or as he himself styled it, a Romany, sitting with his pots and pans and keeping his horse, Bess, company.

His wandering life appealed to Robert Lewis and Vashti Bunyan at just that moment in their lives. Until their friend John James's car had run out of petrol, they had been fleeing from their last home, a camp in a clearing in some Kentish woods, where they had been living for several months among piles of home-made wooden

Pilgrims' progress: Vashti Bunyan, her dog Blue, horse Bess and Robert
Lewis on the road to Skye, 1969.

stools and tables, log fires, bivouacs and hammocks. The clearing
was decorated with Lewis's giant sheet paintings, part of the art
diploma he was enrolled in at Ravensbourne College of Art, near
Chislehurst on the fringes of south-east London. The land was just
at the back of the college, and in 1967, with a few weeks to go
before his time was up, Lewis strung up a bivouac under a giant
rhododendron, hung more sections of canvas between trees and
bushes, and began executing a series of paintings in the outdoors.
In the late spring, his girlfriend Vashti resigned her post as an
assistant in a veterinary practice in Hammersmith, picked up a
blanket, a pillow, her guitar and her dog Blue, and boarded a bus
bound for Chislehurst. Was he pleased to see her or did he fear that
the introduction of a live-in partner in his woodland idyll would
jeopardise his diploma prospects? Whatever his initial feelings, the
pair made a little haven of their forest home, constructing rude
furniture from felled branches and logs and singing Vashti's simple
songs around the campfire in a small and picturesque clearing. As
Lewis daubed his canvases, Bunyan sat on his mildewed mattress

Vashti Bunyan's drawing of herself and Robert Lewis camping in woods near Ravensbourne College, 1967. Note approaching bailiffs.

with her feet on a patch of threadbare carpet and sewed curtains for their rudimentary bush dwelling by the light of an oil lamp. 'We made a little heaven in the wood,' she said many years later.

But the spell in the sylvan paradise did not last more than a few weeks. A banishing god appeared in the form of a suited Bank of England official, representing the true owners of the land, flanked by two policemen to enforce the eviction. They clutched a summons Robert Lewis had previously received – for taking a pillion passenger on his motorbike without a licence – and the wonk from the bank added an admonishing lecture about the breakdown of civil order if everybody suddenly decided to go and live in their wood. Frogmarched to the edge of the forest, they telephoned John James with news of their plight, and after some minutes his Austin came rattling around to pick them up.

Her name – and it's her real one – is almost too perfect. Vashti comes from the Old Testament's Book of Esther: a Persian queen banished for refusing to dance in front of her husband's guests. The Bunyan family have never proved any lineage to the seventeenth-century author of *The Pilgrim's Progress*, but the name is richly evocative of quests in search of paradise. Bunyan herself was no stranger to the milieu of the music business. On a trip to New York when she was eighteen, she found a copy of *The Freewheelin' Bob Dylan* and became hooked on the singer's music, and quickly developed an intense desire to become a successful pop singer. She won a place at the Ruskin School of Drawing in Oxford, but spent a whole term skiving off her lectures, instead teaching herself to play the guitar, writing songs and becoming lost in a world of music. When she tried to pass off this non-attendance as a different and valid form of art, her supervisors were not amused and in 1964 she was slung out.

The following year, she met Rolling Stones manager Andrew Loog Oldham through an actress friend of her mother's. The svengali was practically the same age and soon developed a crush on Vashti, but could not bring himself to declare it.[1] He signed her up to fill the gap left by Marianne Faithfull, who had just left his stable, giving her a song written by Mick Jagger and Keith Richards, 'Some Things Just Stick in Your Mind', as her first single on the Decca label. 'I wanted to be a pop singer,' she admitted later. 'There was no way Andrew Oldham took this innocent folk singer and tried to mould her into a pop singer, that wasn't what happened at all. I was ready and willing . . .' She was a female singer with her own songbook, which, she recalls, was unusual. 'There weren't many female singers who wrote their own songs. Whenever I knocked on doors, they were looking for people in sequins and ballgowns, not a skinny art student with an old jumper with holes in it and a guitar slung over her shoulder.' Vashti, however, fought against the standard practice of women singers singing other (men's) songs, and the B-side of that first single contained a composition of her own, 'I Want to Be Alone'.

Perhaps that song expressed a sentiment that made her unfit for massive pop stardom. In 1966, apparently shaking her head one day and looking at the predominantly sad tenor of the songs she was writing (or stung by the comments of others), she and her friend Jenny Lewis came up with a throwaway tune called 'Seventeen Pink Sugar Elephants'. A Canadian producer, Peter Snell, surfaced out of nowhere and bought her out of her contract with Oldham's Immediate label, hoping to sprinkle his own stardust on her. The poet Alasdair Clayre had begun sending lyrics for her to set to music, and her 'Pink Sugar Elephants' tune fitted the words of a piece of his called 'Train Song'. When this found its way onto a single, it received almost no airplay and failed to puncture the charts. Some months later, Immediate co-founder Tony Calder managed to sweet-talk Vashti back to the studio, which proved to be a waste of time, commercially speaking. 'Winter Is Blue', despite its recording session being filmed by Peter Whitehead for his hip documentary *Tonite Let's All Make Love in London*, and eventually re-recorded by Oldham himself, never came out; neither did 'Coldest Night of the Year', sung by Vashti with the boy duo Twice As Much; nor her own 'I'd Like to Walk Around Inside Your Mind', which Oldham complained needed a string section and more dramatic production, only no one could be bothered. That was Vashti's Summer of Love; the following year, 1968, she dropped into a spiral of depression during which she walked away from the metropolitan music business. 'That was the nosedive time, when I realised that I had to get out of London.'

She had encountered Robert Lewis in 1965 when, driving through the Suffolk countryside in the middle of the night, she picked him up as he was hitch-hiking. They kept in touch but it wasn't until two years later that she discovered he was camping in the woods in the grounds of his art college.

Which is how they found themselves marooned halfway home with a broken-down car, with an open future, staring transfixed at this house on wheels, their minds whirring with new possibilities. Two weeks later they came up with the money to buy the cart and the horse from its Romany owner down there in the field. The cash was lent to them by Donovan Leitch, whose reputation as the Grand Vizier of the British hippy folk scene was at its height. One of Robert's college friends knew Donovan, and they began hanging out with the singer and his circle. Once the cart was purchased, they repaired to the singer's small cottage in Essex to make it roadworthy.

Donovan's success after the Dylan-influenced singles such as 'Catch the Wind', 'Colours' and 'Universal Soldier' was in part due to some steerage by his new producer/svengali Mickie Most, who had urged the young artist to trick out his acoustic folkiness with generous helpings from the new palette of psychedelic colours creeping into pop production in the wake of such records as The Beatles' *Revolver* and The Kinks' *Face to Face*. In 1965 he was still immersed in the Woody Guthrie/Dylan knock-off protest folk of his first LP, *What's Bin Did and What's Bin Hid*, while on his second, *Fairytale*, he began to inch towards a more bucolic mode with the inclusion of 'Jersey Thursday' and 'Summer Day Reflection Song'. At the time Bunyan got to hang out with him, Donovan was rich on the proceeds of his third LP, *Sunshine Superman*, a UK compilation culled from the US releases

And Clett makes three: Donovan surveys his newly
purchased Isle of Skye fiefdom, 1968.

Sunshine Superman and *MellowYellow*. From a landowner named Donald MacDonald, he had just purchased three remote Scottish islands, Isay, Mingay and Clett, near Skye's north-west Vaternish peninsula, where he and his friend/'manager' Gypsy Dave intended to set up a 'Renaissance community' of artists, musicians and poets in a row of tumbledown shepherds' cottages. In tandem with this dreamy project, he released the double album *A Gift from a Flower to a Garden* in 1967, which included a languid slice of Highlands picturesque, 'Isle of Islay' (another song, 'And Clett MakesThree', dates from the same period, but was never officially released). *A Gift* comprised two LPs clasped in a box: one with electric pop songs, the other a series of acoustic fairy tales. These benignly stoned odes fondly and naively imagined a long-lost, bucolic Avalon where like minds of a forever-young Flower Generation might gather in peace, singing, dancing, smoking, making love and contemplating the universe in a guilt-free environment. Its sleeve included a photo of Donovan in Rishikesh, India, where he had just been staying with The Beatles and other celebrity truth-seekers on a high-profile creative retreat under the tutelage of the Maharishi MaheshYogi.

He flew back high as a magic carpet with a pipe-load of Eastern mysticism and a newly piqued interest in Celtic medievalism and Victoriana, manifested in songs such as 'Guinevere', 'Legend of a Child Girl Linda' and 'Season of the Witch'. As well as odes to the grooviness of his London pop set – 'Sunny Goodge Street', 'Hampstead Incident', 'Sunny South Kensington' – the LP waved a rallying freak-flag for British hippies with its laidback anthems such as 'Epistle to Dippy' and 'Preachin' Love'. Now, with his purchase of a faraway island kingdom, Donovan was planning to use his status as counter-cultural guru to convert this pipe dream into a living experiment.

His international fame was at its zenith. He had just featured on the cover of the inaugural issue of *Rolling Stone*, and this Glasgow-born youth was styling himself 'the last of the English minstrels'[2] in interviews. He had attempted to escape the mounting legal wranglings over his music by fleeing to a Greek island, but the exile had not worked, and now he declared he was seeking 'a place where the twentieth century had never existed'.[3]

His latest music, though, was nothing if not supremely cosmopolitan, eclectic and outward-looking. He had employed a wide variety of musicians from mingled disciplines: Phil Seamen's jazz drumming, Jack Bruce's hard-rock bass, etc., and a trailer-load of unusual ethnic instruments, including the obligatory-for-the-age Indian sitars and tablas. Scorned by 'serious' folk fans and viewed uneasily by the likes of his one-time mentor Bob Dylan, Donovan seemed to want to wish all the attention away just at the moment he had reached his artistic and financial peak.

This, then, was the artist who bought his own stab at Wonderland, the pied piper whose master plan was to sail off to his private fiefdom singing Lewis Carroll's line 'Won't you join the dance?', and who put up the money for potential acolytes like Vashti Bunyan and Robert Lewis to make the pilgrimage. But Vashti and Robert planned to make it as much about the journey as the destination.

The USA, its entire coast-to-coast extent traversed and mapped in the space of two centuries, is the place where the wide open road has taken on a vibrant cultural currency. Trail songs of the nineteenth century gave way to a host of 'freight train' songs in the blues/Depression era; while rock 'n' roll's thrusting, insistent beat, arriving in Jack Kerouac's dust clouds, has proved the perfect medium for evoking the sensation of freewheeling travel down the horizon-seeking highways of the American interior. Steppenwolf's 'Born to Be Wild', the soundtrack of *Easy Rider* and later songs such as Lynyrd Skynyrd's 'Freebird' are perfect for slamming on the car stereo and putting foot to the floor, or better still, setting the cruise control for the heart of the sun and kicking back with a jazz Woodbine. The exhilaration of driving itself complements the pulse and throb of rock. On the European mainland, Kraftwerk bequeathed a small tradition of 'transport music' in 'Autobahn', 'Trans-Europe Express' and 'Tour de France': time-and-motion music celebrating efficiency and tamed technological energy. Neu!, another German group formed in the early 1970s, refined a motorik groove and drone-guitar riff cocktail that conveyed a vivid sense of eating up the kilometres.

But the land mass of the British Isles is not large enough to have generated a culture of the open road. Leaving aside such one-off terrace chants as Tom Robinson's '2-4-6-8 Motorway', the culture of British travel is more commonly linked to the sense of a quest, a journey undertaken for purposes of knowledge or self-restoration. In that sense, the British road is a road to the interior, of the imagination rather than a physical coverage of distance. Its poetic energy is supplied by lanes, forest spurs and hillside tracks, not motorways and slip roads. A large proportion of its highways, from its smallest bridleways to the main road arteries, have been in place for centuries: Roman roads, such as the A10 that begins at Liverpool Street in the heart of the City of London and leads directly north for eighty miles, connecting Cambridge and King's Lynn, have been in use for two millennia. Thus, they have accumulated all the fear that would have accompanied long-distance travel in the Dark and Middle Ages, when roads cut through ancient forests, when there were many fewer towns and sheltering posts along the route. Yet still the British traveller seeks out the unfamiliar. Take a look at the shelves of any bookshop section on British travel: you will find very few devoted to exploring its A-roads and motorways. All rambling efforts are focused on byways, lanes, hidden walks, undiscovered villages, forgotten churches, ruined walls and weathered stones: the buried treasures of the British landscape. To wander there, solitary and unchecked, is an experience increasingly difficult to find, but it is the dream of most of those who walk on Britain's soil – Vashti Bunyan included. There is the sense that one wants the landscape, and the history it contains, all to oneself.

The antiquarian impulse in British travel can be identified almost as far back in history as you care to look: from the Tudor chronicler John Leland, entrusted with a mission from Henry VIII to delve into as many ancient libraries as he could find around the land in order to unearth unknown facts about England (published as *The Laborious Journey and Search for England's Antiquities*), to the epic cross-country trek made by the poet John Clare in 1841.[4] Enlightenment antiquarian William Stukeley's *Itinerarium Curiosum* (*Curious Journey*), including his pioneering 1724 survey of the Avebury stone circle, found its echo in the twentieth century with Alfred Watkins's *The Old Straight Track*, published in 1925. Watkins claimed to have discovered a complex system of 'leys' criss-crossing the English landscape, aligned through focal points such as churches, wells, prehistoric mounds and long barrows. As the much later mystic geographer John Michell commented in his introduction to a 1970s edition of Watkins's book, 'for many . . . *The Old Straight Track* awoke as it were the memory of a half familiar truth'.[5]

Crucially, Watkins's book points out how easy it is for the reader to take part in the survey of ley lines, simply by taking a map and ruler and rambling out into almost any part of the British countryside: antiquarianism for weekend rovers. 'The clear, modest style . . . invoke[s] the same *genius terrae britannicae* from the red Herefordshire earth that inspired [his] mystic predecessors, Traherne and Henry Vaughan,' Michell continues. 'There would be no poetry without heretics.'

'Land Art' technically originated in the 1960s/early 70s work of Americans such as Robert Smithson, Walter de Maria and James Turrell: an abandonment of the gallery system to embrace large-scale work that might involve a journey. Among the first to pick up on the Land Art movement in Britain were the London psychedelic-lightshow projector Mark Boyle and the Bristol-based artist Richard Long, who began exhibiting in 1968 – the year of Vashti Bunyan's walk – with pieces such as *A Line Made by Walking*.

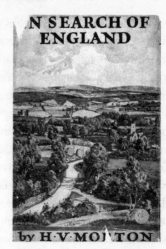

Journeys through inter-war England: Alfred Watkins, *The Old Straight Track* (1925);
H. V. Morton, *In Search of England* (1927).

Long's forays into the landscape, first in Britain, then overseas, sometimes involved fashioning small marker sculptures of grass, sticks or stones. His forensic interest in nature appears drawn away from the city by the same magnetism that attracted the late-1960s counter-culture.

Britain's literature brims with accounts of journeys in which movement combines with the unlocking of memory to create a sensation of inward/vertical rather than forward/lateral travel. H. V. Morton's *In Search of England* (1927) and J. B. Priestley's *English Journey* (1934) are just two examples of inter-war surveys of the sociocultural landscape. More recently, Iain Sinclair has made a career of the seer-like ability to view 'the past inside the present', identifying the friction points where the tectonic plates of history and the present moment rub up against each other, whether in the East End of London or around the perimeter of the capital in his masterly survey of the M25 motorway, *London Orbital*. Michael Hulse's lyrical translation of W. G. Sebald's *The Rings of Saturn*

(1995), a novel which describes a meditative journey through the rural county of Suffolk, captures the peculiarly English facility for letting modern cladding fall out of sight and zoning in on the surviving traces of antiquity (all the more remarkable since Sebald, though a long-time English resident, was German). Both these authors are adept at springing out the hermetic and esoteric histories lying latent in the landscape.

In 1998 the rock musician Julian Cope completed an eight-year 'pre-millennial odyssey', visiting and cataloguing more than 300 prehistoric sites in the British Isles. *The Modern Antiquarian* acted as the first 'Gazetteer' to collect and analyse so many in a single publication and with such doggedness. In the early 1990s, following a run of five solo albums for Island Records, Cope was kicked off his label for delivering the career-shifting *Jehovahkill*, which featured images of the Callanish stone circle on its cover and inflammatory sleeve notes that called for a pagan revolution of the mind to combat the 'straight-lined' Roman thinking of the imperialist authorities. At the same time, Cope relocated from south London to a remote farm on the Marlborough Downs, where he spent the 1990s setting up an autonomous self-publishing base from which he could disseminate his music and writing, both of which continued prolifically, as if uncorked by his rural liberation. Simultaneously embodying rock's righteous conscience and furious rites, Cope's redrawing of Albion fuses the passion of the antiquarian with the experimental spirit of rock, couched in a powerful advocacy for the primacy of land and freedom. He is merely a recent example of a desire to reconnect with the wilderness that has periodically transported composers and musicians in Britain since the late nineteenth century.

While Donovan and Gypsy Dave shuttled back and forth in a Land Rover, Bunyan and Lewis planned a grand tour of Britain: to walk

its length from Kent in the south, along the roads and lanes of
England and over the Scottish Highlands, singing their merry songs
on village greens and attracting new young idealists to join their
roving band. After slapping a coat of green paint onto the metal
sides of the cart and making other repairs to deem it roadworthy,
they shoed up the black horse Bess and set out in July 1968.

The couple were on the road for the next two summers,
spending winter 1968–9 holed up in the Lake District. They didn't
reach their final destination on Skye until almost a year and a half
after they had begun. It was not entirely a rural ride: they stuck to
the main road, the A6, which led from London via the Midlands up
to the north-west (this was before the age of the motorway). 'We
learned our lesson in Derby,' says Vashti, 'because we thought we'd
go round the edge, the ring road, and it took us ages. The horse
was getting tired, it was very industrial and we couldn't find any
green to put her on. In the end we had to stop on a rubbish dump
behind the Rolls Royce factory. And there was a traveller family
there who looked after us, brought us fish and chips – this sort of
thing would happen all the time.'

The pilgrimage was not entirely as they had imagined it. The
handful of extra friends who set out with them soon dropped
out when the colder weather set in – and their hopes of singing
on the village greens turned out to be naive, as they were usually
moved along by local police any time they started tuning up in
public. As self-elected nomads in a land of castle-dwellers, they
found they needed constantly to negotiate and plead for their
own presence. Suspicion and hostility greeted them from town to
town. Children might run out to watch their strange procession,
even jump on for a ride, but terrified parents would snatch them
back, evidently assuming their offspring would be kidnapped.
This was still an England of relative rural immobility; fear and
mistrust of travellers was the norm. 'Someone would phone up
the village ahead and say, "Lock up your chickens,"' she recalls.

'We went through this little village, and a whole lot of kids got really excited, running along by the side of the wagon and asking us what we were doing. And this one little kid said, "Can you give me a ride?" So he got up onto the front of the wagon. And we went through the middle of the village and by the time we got to the other end this absolutely terrified parent came to pick his child up off the wagon – he really did think we were stealing his child. And I realised from then on we had to be really careful. If that had happened to me I would have been terrified as well, but it never occurred to me, we were just giving this little boy a ride along the street.'

Just as she had found doors closing to her as a prospective singer in London, so she was finding a similar attitude prevailing on the roads of late-1960s Britain. But in spite of the difficulties, Bunyan and Lewis pressed on doggedly, and she found the muse again. While Lewis kept his diary, Vashti's songs were mysteriously being written – often frail wisps of things, or autobiographical road songs like 'Jog Along Bess' that were little more than extensions of their exhortations to the horse. With a flavour of nursery rhymes, Beatrix Potter's animal tales and Donovan's benign self-mythology, Bunyan's songs most of all resembled lullabies, charms to ward off danger and dread in the midst of adversity. 'I think the most jiggedy-joggedy songs were written in the worst bits of industrial England,' she says, 'where it was really horrible to be going through. Like the outskirts of Manchester, where there were a whole lot of children in the street without shoes.'

The harshest winter months were spent in the Lake District. There they met a couple from the Netherlands with musical connections who heard Vashti singing some of her travelling songs and offered to arrange some concerts in Holland for her around Christmas.

So the walk was broken off over Christmas, with the wagon

parked in the Lake District while Vashti and Robert took the boat to the Netherlands. Any hopes she may have entertained that this tour might help reactivate her career were dashed, though, as the venues were really a succession of tiny pubs and bars. Loud conversations drowned out the fragility of Vashti's music, which required the dead stillness of an attentive audience. In one bar in Ghent she broke down in tears and fled.

Later that evening, though, she discovered that an acquaintance, Derroll Adams, coincidentally lived in an apartment above that very bar. Adams was a banjo player from Portland, Oregon, who had come over to Europe along with Ramblin' Jack Elliott, exerting a powerful influence on the emerging folk-blues scene of the late 1950s and early 1960s in London by injecting a little Americana into the predominant mix of medieval balladry and workers' songs. Adams had not made as much of a name for himself as Elliott, and had recently suffered a heart attack, from which he was convalescing. But there was one English pop figure whom he had made a kind of protégé in the mid-1960s: none other than Donovan, and Vashti and Robert had met him while they were repairing their wagon. Suddenly it seemed to Vashti that this Dutch trip was no longer a red herring but a continuation of the journey she had begun months before with Donovan's own encouragement and cash. They went upstairs to pay their respects, and were greeted by a man who had not picked up his banjo for weeks. When Lewis asked him to play something for them, he agreed only if they would reciprocate, so he was treated to one of Vashti's songs. She remembers it: 'He said, "What are you doing?" I said, "I'm not doing anything." He said, "You have to let people hear these songs, you mustn't hide your light."'

She abandoned the tour then and there, and sped home across the English Channel. The song 'Diamond Day' came to her on the train from Dover to London. A friend urged her to take her music to the producer, manager and entrepreneur Joe Boyd, who was intrigued enough to offer to record an album once she had reached her Scottish destination.

'He gave me a five-pound note and a copy of The Incredible String Band's *Wee Tam and The Big Huge* – which I never played because I didn't have a record player – and we had dinner with The String Band that night.' The group, managed at the time by Boyd, were in the full exotic flush of their success. 'I'd always wanted to dress like my idea of the Romany Gypsy – the long stuff and the coins and the jangly beads and scarves and silks – and of course I could only approximate with what I could find,' remembers Vashti. 'But that night we walked in and there were these people dressed in these clothes that I would have killed for! They were bedecked with the most beautiful clothes from India, and from all the places they'd been to, and they were just like gods – not from the idea that they were stars, but just from the way they were dressed – they were from another planet. I didn't say a word all night.' The pilgrimage had suddenly acquired a new focus.

By the end of the 1960s The Incredible String Band had become something of a cult among fans and critics – one broadsheet writer even squealed that the group 'now rival the Beatles in being the most important influence in song-writing'.[6] Robin Williamson and Mike Heron's otherworldly sense of naif, pixie-esque abandon had been developed as a result of a hermetic lifestyle lived out since late 1966 at Temple Cottage, Balmore, a tiny settlement just north of Glasgow. An indication of The String Band's self-image at the time can be gleaned from their spoken introduction at their first London gig, in November 1966 at the Royal Albert Hall. 'We're songwriters and players,' announced Williamson, 'and prophets from the North, and also Seers Extraordinary by appointment to the Wonder of the Universe.'

The Incredible String Band at Glen Row cottages, Peeblesshire, 1971. Left to right:
Robin Williamson, Malcolm Le Maistre, Mike Heron, Licorice McKechnie.

Their visionary mystique, already in place months before the galvanising events that brought the psychedelic counter-culture onto the world stage – the release of *Sgt Pepper's Lonely Hearts Club Band* and the Monterey Pop Festival – was borne out by the fertile mulch of their music: riddling, pagan poetry, multi-instrumental sorcery and complex song structures extending and intertwining with the organic logic of root and twig.

Shortly afterwards, the whole roadshow was transplanted to a farmhouse deep in West Wales. Lying near a hamlet called Velindre, within striking distance of Newport Bay on the Pembrokeshire coast and the imposing prehistoric cromlech of Pentre Ifan, Penwern farm had lain empty since the 1930s. Over the course of summer 1968, the house was first occupied by members of Stone Monkey, a performance/dance troupe previously notorious for their shows accompanying the likes of Pink Floyd and Soft Machine at that psychedelic Mecca, London's UFO Club; then Williamson and his girlfriend Licorice. The String Band were at critical and commercial boiling point, yet still chose to dwell amid this maze of tiny country lanes rather than hold court in the rock 'n' roll palace of the capital. The residence at Penwern lasted for a year and a half, punctuated by the group's frequent touring during 1969 (which included a damp squib of a performance at Woodstock). It marked the point at which their music began to lose the spontaneous vibrancy and visionary lyricism of their first period – the next album to follow was 1969's lacklustre *Changing Horses* – but their one achievement at the farmhouse was the filming of the short movie *The Pirate and the Crystal Ball*. This was a series of costumed tableaux which the company pitched into, making outfits and sets and lighting, and enlisting the cooperation of a BBC TV crew who had arrived to make a straight documentary. Shot at Penwern itself, the local coastline and the mysterious Pentre Ifan stones, the romp has the gleeful naivety of a school pantomime, and was eventually incorporated into the overexposed, grainy colour film *Be Glad for the Song Has No Ending*, which ended up as part chronicle of the group and their hangers-on, part wyrd hallucinatory fable.

'*Always looking for a Paradise Island*,' Robin Williamson sings on 'Ducks on a Pond', from *Wee Tam*, '*Help me find it everywhere.*' After the eighteen-month interlude at Penwern, the String Band brood went in search of a new nest. In the summer of 1969, the incumbent Lord Glenconner (aka the Hon. Colin Tennant) advertised the vacancy of a row of former labourers' cottages on his sprawling Scottish estate, making them available for use by artists. Mike Heron saw the advert and applied for residency for the group and the Stone Monkey dancers. Collectively, these mummers, troubadours, freakish hangers-on, dogs and a clutch of lost souls arrived in October of that year and planned to develop a musical 'pantomime' entitled *U*, which they had been invited to premiere at the Fillmore East in New York in 1970. Living in a row of eight semi-detached artesan houses in the shadow of the laird's baronial 'mock-Gothic Dracula castle', they rehearsed in a 'freezing back room behind a barn-yard', according to the *Guardian*'s Robin Denselow, who visited to research an article in 1970.[7] Surrounded by thousands of acres of rolling countryside, forest and a loch, the group and their entourage were free to live a bohemian, unconventional lifestyle. 'A wispy girl dressed scantily as a mermaid sits eating oatcakes; a farmer rounding up his sheep ignores her,'[8] observed the bemused journalist. The cottages were customised by each inhabitant, often with little respect for the antique character of the place – Williamson's pad was painted midnight blue; the phrase 'The thousand mile journey begins with one step' was inscribed above a doorway. Mike Heron decked out his cottage in psychedelic orange, yellow and purple hues. Malcolm Le Maistre's living-room ceiling was painted entirely in Humbrol model-aeroplane gold paint. When they weren't lounging like mughals in their cramped palaces, strumming their ouds and tapping their tablas, these self-appointed lairds of the manor strode around the glen, practising archery, scything the grass, collecting firewood and rambling with pantheistic bent.

This was the group introduced to Vashti Bunyan by Joe Boyd at the end of 1968, while she was still halfway through her own pilgrimage. The rigours of the road ensured she remained isolated from the growing folk-rock scene Boyd was helping to nurture in London. 'If I'd thought any more of my musical career, which I didn't,' she says, 'I would have investigated what kind of music he was producing; I would have listened to The String Band; I would have found out who Fairport Convention were; I would have found out what Nick Drake was doing; but I knew nothing of any of them.' She headed back to Cumbria, from where, in early

March 1969, she and Robert resumed the wagon walk from where they had left off. Increasingly, they realised they were witnessing a rural Britain that was teetering on the brink of extinction in the 'white heat of technology' promised by Harold Wilson in his famous 1963 speech. The itinerant couple existed in a pauper's economy that sounds like something out of a fairy tale: working-class children in Manchester with no shoes; generous, mysterious Gypsies who would supply them with food and advise their brethren up the road of the couple's approach. 'We had no money at all, we knocked on doors and did odd jobs and dug gardens,' recalls Vashti. 'We had a sack of brown rice that we started off with. People would give us stuff, a dozen eggs here, a bunch of apples there, and we kept going on incredibly little. The main expense was shoes for the horse, and we'd have to find blacksmiths along the way – but we always did. We painted farms, collected scrap metal and weighed it in at the next yard, and that was it.' Their northward meander through Scotland was driven by an idealistic and, as she now admits, naive dream of a perfect life at the other end. '*Travelling towards a Hebridean sun / To build a white tower in our heads begun,*' wrote Robert in verses which eventually appeared in Vashti's 'Hebridean Sun'. The travellers passed by several of the country's scenic landmarks. 'The best time, there was a big long hill going up towards Glen Coe, a long moor, and it was constantly just slightly uphill, mile after mile, day after day, and then suddenly getting to the top of Glen Coe and seeing the road going away in front of us, and we just rode on the wagon all the way down – no cars in the way, nothing! The horse really loved to trot, and go as fast as she could, like she was trying to get away from something herself. But when she was going uphill or when it was flat then we would walk. And then going downhill we would get up on the front of the wagon and fly with her.' At the south-western end of Loch Ness, a speeding car ran into the rear of the wagon. The damage was repairable, but they managed to secure a substantial insurance payout from a loss adjuster who recognised the value of the 1908 Morris wheels attached to the cart.

By that time the end of their journey was in sight. Pressing eastwards now to Skye, they arrived at Donovan's island encampments one day in late summer to find that the Sunshine Superman had already flown his rainy nest. Up, up and away to the more controllable climate of Los Angeles. Of those devotees that remained, 'Everyone had either established themselves and taken what houses were available, or gone away,' Vashti remembers. Local talk extolled the virtues of the tiny Hebridean island of Berneray, pincered between the larger islands of Harris and North Uist. With Bess in tow, they boarded the ferry from Uig to Lochmaddy on Uist, and walked the few miles of bleak, flat road to where it runs out on a spit of land above Port Nan Long. From there, a cramped ferry supplied the only connection with Berneray. It was a short crossing – shepherds often rowed over, with their sheep swimming at their side.

Berneray is an island of only a few square kilometres, with a single road connecting its three settlements, and at that time it had no trees. The only vertical lines, in fact, were the newly installed rows of electricity and telegraph poles, which were conduits for social changes in that remote spot. Televisions replaced home-made entertainment and brought metropolitan idioms into these crofters' cottages; electric heat, light and stoves replaced domestic tasks that had previously taken up a large part of most islanders' days. These comforts were embraced by the inhabitants, an end to age-old hardships. As Vashti and Robert reached the end of the road, the sky tipped down the first of the late September rains. They sheltered in the doorway of a turf-roofed 'black house', a stone dwelling hewn in the style typical of the area. This was Ferry Cottage, and it became their home until the following spring. It was sold to them by a family for £150 – the money they had gained from their insurance claim. The karma seemed right – they initially misheard the name as 'Fairy Cottage', and a neighbour told them it had once belonged to the MacAskills, a famous Scottish musical family. One week later, they discovered they hadn't quite got what they thought they had paid for. The ancient laws of the crofting community can have the wiliest lawyers wrenching their hair out; on Berneray, property 'ownership' was limited to the (turf) roof over their heads, not the stone walls, or the floor, nor the draughts through same. Meanwhile, their troubles were compounded by the fact that they had been forced to leave Bess back on Uist, across the water. Each crofter was allotted grazing rights for a total of two cows, and, they were informed, not only did one horse equal two cows, but no boats would be large enough to bring the horse across in any case. Bess was stabled by a sympathetic family just across the strait, but they were forced to keep shuttling back and forth in order to feed and groom her.

Bess was not the only problem looming over their new life. Small, unspoken signs indicated that the other island dwellers did not consider them welcome. No drivers stopped their vehicles to give them lifts, even when they were visibly struggling with sacks of potatoes. Conversations switched rapidly from English to Gaelic whenever they entered shops. Vashti and Robert's idealistic project to live a life of rustic simplicity was at odds with the modernising trend on Berneray. 'Screening out modernity is exactly what we were doing,' Vashti confirms. 'Even the food I bought, I would try to buy in plain paper packages rather than the packet – I got quite obsessive about rejecting the modern world in the end. Even bits of old horse harness that you could start to put the pieces together and get a real idea of what it had been like . . . It was before the upsurge of little antique shops – finding something like an old smoothing iron and finding out how things used to be done. Even quite late on, doing stupid things like putting an old kitchen range in the farmhouse we eventually ended up getting . . . most people would be pulling things out and putting in something modern. We took out the modern and put in an old, smoky black range. So yes, we got completely fixated on old versus new. And the Hebrides people just couldn't understand it. They were throwing things out, anything that remotely reminded them of the bad old days – and that's what we were looking for.'

Finally, her neighbour, an eighty-three-year-old widow called Wally Dix, made efforts to befriend the couple, and the community began to unfreeze. Another woman who lived nearby introduced Vashti to the joys of potato harvesting. 'Everybody would have a little patch, and this lovely woman had me help her hook out the potatoes with this . . . it looked like a little sickle, but it was just a round piece of pointed wire on the end. You're on your hands and knees with a big canvas apron, crawling along putting them into a sack, and talking and singing and having a lovely time. Although some people the other end of the island had a tractor, there were still a whole lot of people doing it as it had been done for centuries. I knew that over the next three or four years that was going to disappear, so I felt very lucky to get to do that.' Wally Dix and her tiny circle of friends were the only islanders who showed them any sympathy, their company, their songs and stories a necessary comfort in the face of the spartan lifestyle they had chosen. 'I think the dream was so strong that it kept me going, really,' confesses Vashti. 'And compared to the journey, living in an old thatched house with the roof falling in – cobwebs falling in your porridge from sooty rafters – was wonderful. To have a roof at all was fantastic.'

Donovan was not the only rock star to have invested in tumbledown property in a distant corner of Scotland. In January 1966 Paul McCartney purchased High Park Farm, a large, remote estate on the Kintyre peninsula. This tax break came with the added benefit of providing a much-needed hideaway from the worst excesses of

Beatlemania. The land lay in a desperately calm Scottish wilderness, the three dilapidated farm buildings high on a slope yet almost invisible from the road, and came complete with its own loch and easy access to the pale sands of Machrihanish Bay to the west.

The nearest settlement, Campbeltown, lies a little way to the east, and the stunning vista of the Mull, made famous by the Wings song of 1977 – at the time the biggest-selling pop single in British history – is around fourteen miles south of the site. When McCartney first brought his new girlfriend Linda Eastman to the farm in November 1968, the Manhattan heiress's daughter was nonplussed by the condition of the living quarters. Apart from buying some used furniture and a primitive stove in Campbeltown, McCartney had neglected the interior decoration and was sleeping on a bed crudely fashioned from old potato boxes. But its very wildness helped dissuade any journalists or photographers from camping out in hopes of cornering the couple, especially in the winter months. A gentle evocation of their long drives, inspired by their first stay in Scotland, was the song 'Two of Us', recorded in January 1969, which opened The Beatles' *Let It Be*. The best line, about memories being longer than the road that stretches ahead, already suggests a shared secret existence developing in parallel with McCartney's high-profile rock career. And the ballad 'The Long and Winding Road', on the same LP, is the B842 from Kintyre to Campbeltown rendered in treacle. At this character-building hideaway, McCartney and Linda (now his wife, following their marriage in March 1969) regrouped in April 1970, shortly after McCartney had made his first public statement that he would be leaving The Beatles. One week later, his first solo LP, *McCartney*, came out, much of it written and recorded at home in London the previous year. Its sleeve featured many grainy shots of the Beatle and his family living an outdoors life, with McCartney reinvented as a proto-'New Man': cradling his young family; arm-deep in sheep muck; petting a donkey. For the first time in public, Paul sported a straggly beard, displaying a new ruggedness that was a direct result of his isolation on the farm, and in one image he's shown as quite the handyman, standing in a window of the farmhouse and taking a hammer and chisel to the frame. The McCartneys saw out much of the remainder of 1970 well away from the public and media gaze at High Park Farm, and the adjoining Low Ranadran Farm, which he purchased in January. 'I'd had a little four-track studio put in there,' McCartney said, 'so I was able to demo and experiment and make bits and pieces of music.'[9]

Here they co-wrote a large chunk of the material that eventually appeared on *Ram* (1971), whose sleeve shows a black-and-white photo of McCartney in a short-sleeved shirt, seizing the horns of a sheep in a wooden pen. He was, at the same time, wresting control of his life and career again after a period of post-Beatles depression that had caused him to exist for a while as a near alcoholic. For Linda McCartney, recalling it for a documentary film some years later, the farm was a place for 'Getting back to natural life – we have horses and sheep and we plant our own vegetables, and it's the only place we can go that is very natural, in this unnatural world . . . It really is a matter of getting back into life again.'[10] At this point, their simple life was partly forced upon them: Paul's assets were largely frozen while Apple was in receivership and The Beatles' acrimonious break-up was being processed through the courts. But Linda still characterised it as a kind of willed Eden: '[Paul said], Let's get away and go back to the beginning.'[11] The Scottish interlude also provided opportunities for self-education. Linda introduced Paul to vegetarianism and the exhilarations of horse riding. Cannabis was cultivated in pots. (In March 1973 the couple were fined £100 for marijuana possession by the local Campbeltown court, Paul quipping to reporters shortly after emerging, 'We got a load of seeds in the post, and five of them came up illegal.')

That summer of 1971, husband and wife hatched their group

Wings, inviting Denny Laine and Denny Seiwell to the farm to write new material. The sleeve of *Wild Life*, released at the climax of that summer, shows the Wings foursome in bucolic, relaxed mood, dangling their toes into a stream from their perch on an overhanging tree branch.

High Park Farm has remained in McCartney's possession, a fact not lost on the local tourist industry to this day. In the immediate aftermath of The Beatles' glittering career, the impact of this countryside retreat upon one of the most famous rock artists in the world effectively allowed him to make the transition to the next phase of his career. But although he was almost alone up in his farmhouse, he was not the only musician deriving inspiration from a retreat. And of all these musical nature-seekers, none were as unnoticed as Vashti Bunyan.

Back on Berneray, Vashti Bunyan's neighbour Wally Dix turned out to be a living repository of ancient song. Entertaining them in her cottage, she would sing to them in Gaelic, and Vashti would respond with selections from the book of songs she had now begun to fill with her own handwritten verses. Now that the journey was done and a handful of songs written, she kept her date with Joe Boyd. Recording sessions were booked at Sound Techniques, the southwest London recording studio Boyd used for all his Witchseason artists, and in November Vashti's friend Christopher Sykes arrived in his Morris Minor to pick up her and Robert. The trip did not start auspiciously: he managed to reverse over and ruin her guitar, so she had to borrow another one in London. But by this time she had bigger things on her mind: she had just discovered that she was pregnant. The fourteen songs she recorded over a six-week period in late 1969 are intimate chamber pieces. Tentatively sung in a tremulous, whispering voice, they have the soothing quality of lullabies and take a fresh delight in natural scenery and the waxing and waning of the seasons. 'I was pregnant while I was recording the songs,' she explains, 'and I desperately wanted babies, children . . . But I think the lullaby part of it was probably my way of comforting myself. They are quite "rocky": it's partly walking pace, but it is partly harking back to the comfortingness of childhood songs. That's the only explanation I have for it.' 'Glow Worms' is sung as if by someone huddling close to a single candle in the darkness, trying to ward off harm and blot out the cold and wet. 'The happier songs were written in the more dire places,' she says, 'as a way to keep the dream alive really, to make myself keep believing I was doing the right thing.' 'Rose Hip November' is full of anticipation for her unborn son Leif: *'Gold landing at our door, / Catch one Leif and fortune will surround you.'* And Vashti adapted one of the songs she had learnt from her Berneray neighbours, which became 'Iris's Song for Us'.[12] With its English/Gaelic verses and Gaelic-style fiddle by The Incredible String Band's Robin Williamson, it provided appropriate closure to the album. Boyd brought Williamson in, along with violinist Dave Swarbrick and guitarist Simon Nicol from Fairport Convention, while Robert Kirby, the former undergraduate friend of Nick Drake who had just embroidered the superb string fantasias on Drake's *Five Leaves Left* LP, touched his arranger's wand to 'Diamond Day', 'Swallow Song' and 'Rainbow River'. 'I hated the "Gaelic song",' she laughs, 'because I had another version of it . . . It was my own fault, because we'd been living in the Hebrides for three months and made a very good friend of our neighbour, the most wonderful character. She had translated these words into Gaelic for me, and found a Gaelic tune that would fit. I just knew that if I didn't use it she would be so upset, and we were going to be her neighbours for the future. She was a fierce old woman, but an absolute sweet hen, and I adored her, but I didn't like that tune, and I didn't like singing in Gaelic, and I felt that my accent was terrible.'

Painfully aware of their precarious situation in Scotland, she was wary of grafting 'folksy' elements onto the music as a fashionable gesture without a deeper understanding of the form. 'When we got into the studio and Robin Williamson came along with a fiddle and played over "Jog Along Bess", it wasn't what I had in mind. Although I'd come down from the Hebrides and was very keen on fiddle playing, I didn't particularly see it having a place on the album. What Robert Kirby did was more what I had in mind, more a sort of classical association rather than folk. If I'd known what kind of a band Fairport Convention were, if I'd known what kind of a player Robin was, or Dave Swarbrick, if it had been up to me to choose or plan this thing . . . but I just went in and sang, and I didn't have any great ambition any more. This was something I was doing because the opportunity was there. I'd just found out I was pregnant; I was about to go to the Hebrides and make my life up there; we were still fighting to get the horse over to the island . . . we had other considerations at that time.' Her friends John James and Christopher Sykes added piano and dulcichord to the record, and James's painting for the sleeve – a bevy of cows, dogs

Vashti Bunyan, *Just Another Diamond Day* (1970).

and a horse converging on a colour photo of Vashti in an apron and headscarf, greeting the dawn in the doorway of their thatched croft – created a memorably rustic image. By mid-December 1969 *Just Another Diamond Day* was finished. But the bad omens continued as soon as they returned to Berneray that winter. Vashti was not the only one carrying a baby: Bess had given birth to a foal, which promptly caught pneumonia and died the following day.

Vashti and Robert were seized with guilt: all those weeks exhausting Bess as she pulled them and their wagon up and down the steep Highlands, not knowing she was pregnant. In addition, letters they had sent to a local lawyer in the hope of resolving the issue of their cottage freehold remained unanswered. They began to realise there were too many invisible forces ranged against them, and that their dream of a permanent life on the island might not be achievable after all. Finally, Boyd licensed *Just Another Diamond Day* to Philips Records, who took a whole year to manufacture and distribute the album. It eventually trickled into shops at the tail end of 1970. 'I didn't get the [test] acetate until probably August or September,' Vashti recalls, 'and by that time I had my baby, and the world goes away.'

Inevitably, album sales were hope-crushingly small – in the low hundreds. Boyd did his best to give her the right connections. During 1970 he tried to turn her and his even more reclusive and diffident artist, Nick Drake, into a songwriting team. ('It wasn't a very productive afternoon,' she says of her attempts to goad the unworldly, cripplingly shy Drake into action.) She was commissioned to write a song for American folk star Judy Collins, but just couldn't come up with a closing line. As they said farewell to Berneray in April 1970 – abandoning their trusty wagon to be used as a chicken shed on North Uist – Bunyan, Lewis and baby returned to the nomadic life, this time in an ancient, unlicensed Volkswagen with a pram strapped to the roof. Eventually they wound up back in London living off the charity of friends. The demands of her newborn effectively barred her from going on tour to promote the album. Boyd offered her a choice: stay in the capital and attempt a last fling at promoting the album with some gigs, or go back to Scotland and live in the bosom of The Incredible String Band in a house that had become vacant at Glen Row, with Boyd picking up half the tab. It didn't take long for them to make up their minds, and within a few days their Volkswagen was crunching down the driveway of the Glen Estate. They stayed for around five months, until the lure of potentially cheap property in Ireland – at Kinvara in Galway – took them away, followed later by a Glen Row resident called Lizzie McDougall, who was engaged to bring Bess after them.

At that point Vashti Bunyan dropped off the radar, lost to musical history for the next three decades, chasing and never quite finding the perfect place to settle her family. 'We kept travelling by horse and wagon, which was entirely stupid. By the time we got there, of course, the price would go up beyond our reach. That kept happening. We walked across Ireland. We stayed there a year, with a bigger wagon that did have a stove in it. From then on I couldn't play my guitar or listen to the sound of my own voice, because it reminded me of *Diamond Day*, which had been so roundly ignored. And although it was partly my fault, it was also that the world didn't want to hear what I had to say at all.'

That was not quite true. Only a few hundred copies of *Just Another Diamond Day* even existed, but during the 1980s and 90s it became a much-treasured rarity among record collectors. Inevitably, bootleg copies began turning up on pirate CDs. In the mid-1990s Vashti had moved to Edinburgh after bearing two more children and parting company with Robert Lewis. The slow process of reconnecting with the buried musician inside her began when she Googled herself and discovered that *Diamond Day* had become an expensive collector's item. Correspondence with her record company resulted in her coming in contact with Paul

Lambden, a folk enthusiast overseeing Boyd's Warlock Publishing catalogue, which owned the rights to Vashti's music. After several years, Lambden eventually located the master tapes in a London warehouse and set up his own small reissue imprint, Spinney, to release it in 2000. Vashti, who hadn't even kept a copy of the original LP, was reunited with her music at the CD remastering. 'I'd only heard it on ropey old record players or tapes that had been taped from tapes of tapes, so to hear the master tapes through big speakers, that was when I realised, "Ah! This is what Joe did," because I'd never been able to hear what a wonderful job he made of it and how beautifully he'd produced it. It had taken that long for the penny to drop.'

Now that *Diamond Day* had officially returned to the public domain, it reached new ears, further afield than it ever could have in 1970. In 2003 Vashti received a letter and hand-drawn artwork from Devendra Banhart, a young singer-songwriter based in San Francisco. The letter professed undying admiration for the record, but Banhart himself claimed to be unsure of the worth of his own music and asked Vashti directly for advice on whether he should carry on. She sent an encouraging note back, and Banhart ended up persuading his friend Gary Held to license a US release for *Diamond Day* on his label DiChristina, while Vashti contributed vocals to Banhart's 2004 album *Rejoicing in the Hands*. The poignancy of Vashti's story and the gentle but determined nature worship audible in her songs struck a deep chord with Banhart and his West Coast circle, which included artists such as Joanna Newsom, Currituck Co., Vetiver and Brightblack Morning Light, all mostly younger than Vashti's own children. Twisted psychedelia and folk-rock roots curled deep under the surface of their musics, but these merely fed an approach that was distinctly contemporary rather than aping the past. In quick succession her appearance with Banhart was followed by invitations to collaborate with British artists Glen Johnson of Piano Magic, former Cocteau Twins bassist Simon

Raymonde, electronic musician Kieran Hebden of Four Tet, and Animal Collective. The latter were signed to Brighton independent label FatCat, which coaxed a new record out of her by putting her in touch with Max Richter, a producer and composer in Edinburgh. *Lookaftering*, clad in a painting of a vigilant hare by her daughter Whyn, was unveiled in the autumn of 2005; her new batch of songs could almost have been an addendum to the *Diamond Day* sessions of thirty years before – only the lyrics were occasionally tempered by sorrow and regret, the patina of greater experience. Joanna Newsom, Devendra Banhart, Adem and others contributed to the recording, and a circle was closed when Robert Kirby agreed to play trumpet and trombone on one track. Vashti embarked on a world tour the following year and even appeared on stage with Donovan at a BBC concert in 2006. 'Diamond Day' soundtracked a cinema advertisement for a mobile-phone company. Her music, practically inaudible when originally written, was rehabilitated to the extent that she had now become a central totem in the latest of many revivals and reinventions of 'folk' culture in Britain and beyond. In a very different musical economy from the 1960s, she had picked up the pilgrim trail once again and found the niche success she had sought as a teenage songwriter.

In hindsight, Vashti Bunyan's still, small voice of calm, and her bold improvised trek over Britain from ankle to head, serves as a powerful symbol of the wider panorama of non-mainstream rock and folk in that snapshot period of English music, 1969–71. It's a snapshot that reveals many of the contradictory impulses that shape the British artistic imagination: craving the freedom and peace of a countryside that is always already shaped and manicured; nostalgia for a golden, bucolic, pre-technological age, yet 'improving' tradition with new instruments, exotic flavours and electricity; needing to explore and incorporate a historical dimension while

44

simultaneously 'writing over' the past. Most importantly, this musical energy existed not in the traditional geographic locations of the British rock scene – London, Manchester, Liverpool, Birmingham, Glasgow. Instead, it flowed from zones far more remote: the dual landscape/dreamscape of Britain's interior.

Viewed as a camera obscura snapshot, British music at the dawn of the 1970s looks like an inward exodus, with musicians in pursuit of rural tranquillity. The McCartneys on Kintyre. Donovan on Skye. The Incredibles practising archery at Glen Row. Fairport Convention in the sepia tint of the endless Sunday afternoon at Farley Chamberlayne. Caravan, Soft Machine and Kevin Ayers hothousing their organic jazz rock tendrils in Canterbury. Pink Floyd basking in the lysergic sun over Grantchester Meadows. Robert Plant and Jimmy Page climbing the stairway at Bron-Yr-Aur. Traffic lynching John Barleycorn in Berkshire bliss at Aston Tirrold. Heron a few miles down the road, setting up mics in the meadows of Appleford. Tim Hart and Maddy Prior celebrating summer solstice in St Albans, then birthing Steeleye Span with Ashley Hutchings in Winterbourne Stoke. Bert Jansch getting quietly drunk at his Ticehurst cottage. Danny Thompson lording over his Suffolk manor house. John and Beverley Martyn settling into Hastings Old Town. Dave Cousins of The Strawbs musing on Branscombe's sparklebright beach. Shelagh McDonald in Bristol, about to fall into a life of mysterious vagrancy in the Scottish Highlands. The doomed Nick Drake, abandoning north London for the safety of his parents' idyllic Tanworth-in-Arden. Albion's underground tribes, following the leys to the ancient power centres of Glastonbury and Stonehenge. Vashti Bunyan's wagon, rusting in the salt spray of North Uist.

Where does it begin, this internal exodus into the green? We will return to these people, their times and their dreams. But first, we must follow the Thames's silver chain back through time to where the song is sprung.

2

An Orgy on the Green

Forget six counties overhung with smoke,
Forget the snorting steam and the piston stroke,
Forget the spreading of the hideous town,
Think rather of the pack-horse on the down.
    William Morris, 'Prologue', *The Earthly Paradise* (1868–70)

I am like a psychical researcher who has actually seen a ghost,
for I have been among the more primitive people of England
and have noted down their songs . . .
    Ralph Vaughan Williams (1912)[1]

To reach 26 Upper Mall in Hammersmith, south-west London, you sneak through a narrow passageway, squeeze past a homely little public house called The Dove, and emerge into a rounded forecourt. There's no through road for traffic, so this widened area in front of the immaculately proportioned townhouse lies still, peaceful, undisturbed by the rush-hour hum. The house's three tiers of sash windows look out upon the River Thames. Looking to the left, a short walk up the towpath you can see the green-and-gold painted struts of Hammersmith Bridge. In the opposite, westward direction, the horizon remains low: bushy treetops shading a jumble of Georgian facades. The khaki water streams towards you, having flowed for 200 miles from its source in the Cotswolds. In front of the house, colourful barges and wherries crush against the wharf like ducks squabbling over breadcrumbs.

This building is known as Kelmscott House, and it was once the London residence of the Victorian artist, designer, poet, environmentalist and committed socialist William Morris. Inside, his sumptuous, tapestried interiors are long gone: the main part of the house is now privately owned and modernised, but the William Morris Society still operates from basement rooms beneath its attached coach house. In the back garden, in 1816, a former owner of the house, Francis Ronalds, once dug trenches to bury Britain's first electric telegraph cable: eight miles of wire coil encased in fragile glass tubes. Sixty years later, William Morris plotted his extended garden with as much care as one of his intricate tapestries. Now the land has been drastically foreshortened, and the A4 ceaselessly roars through the space where Morris sowed his seeds.

But the view in front is largely unchanged since he wrote his novel *News from Nowhere* here in the late 1880s. And it is this panorama – the Thames glittering in June morning sunbeams –

Kelmscott House, Hammersmith: the London residence of
William Morris. Photograph taken *c.*1900.

that greets Morris's protagonist, Guest, upon waking at the start of the novel. He dives in for a morning dip, but soon realises that the great iron Hammersmith Bridge has been replaced with a bridge of stone arches more beautiful than those in Florence; the smoke-belching factories that once lined the riverbank are gone; and the usual noise of hammering and riveting has ceased. The first character Guest meets, a waterman who rows him upriver in a sculling boat, wears an outfit that 'would have served very well as a costume for a picture of fourteenth-century life'.[2]

Even though much of what's now called science fiction originated in Britain, the British mind – or perhaps more accurately, the Anglo-Saxon mind – can't seem to help envisioning the future as, to some extent, shaped like the past. For the past is what Guest encounters as he is guided through a London that has had its centres 'greened' with huge areas of wild parkland and forest following the 'great clearing of houses in 1955', and then sculls further and further upriver, through the Home Counties to Oxford, where he rematerialises back in his own time. Through lengthy conversations with a variety of unctuously hospitable characters, he discovers that he has arrived in the late twenty-first century, and English society exists with no government (the Houses of Parliament are now a 'Dung Market'), no formal education, no currency, no interest in history. Crime is treated as a disease and poverty is non-existent – the foulest slums have been transformed into lush, fertile meadows. The picture of Morris's ideal society, painted on a broad canvas like a Brueghel town panorama, is based on a vanished vision of medieval courtesy and artisanship, with ownership, law and violence consensually abolished. The economy of arts and crafts underpins this bucolic utopia, exchanged via a non-competitive barter system.

There is no doubt that Morris's novel – written in the first person – is an outpouring of his most fervently held views of the state of the nation and his dreams of an altruistic future. Its geographical

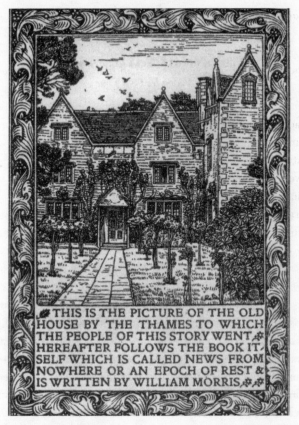

THIS IS THE PICTURE OF THE OLD HOUSE BY THE THAMES TO WHICH THE PEOPLE OF THIS STORY WENT. HEREAFTER FOLLOWS THE BOOK ITSELF WHICH IS CALLED NEWS FROM NOWHERE OR AN EPOCH OF REST & IS WRITTEN BY WILLIAM MORRIS.

Frontispiece of Morris's *News from Nowhere* (1890), based on his medieval Oxfordshire retreat, Kelmscott Manor.

trajectory joins the dots between Morris's real-life dwelling places. Guest begins the book standing outside Kelmscott House and ends at a feast in a large country manor in Oxfordshire which is the spitting image of Morris's Kelmscott Manor near Lechlade, an Elizabethan country house whose first stones were laid in 1570. Morris was one of the most outspoken political commentators of the late Victorian era. Already famous for his workshops in which

William Morris: artist, designer, writer, socialist and
imaginative time-traveller, photographed in 1889.

he designed and printed tapestries, curtains and wallpapers with
exquisite designs based on organic forms, he was invited by Queen
Victoria to decorate the armoury and tapestry rooms of St James's
Palace. Increasingly he began building a soapbox from the stout
timbers of his fame. In 1883 he threw a middle-class audience at
the Oxford Union into flapping consternation by openly declaring
himself a socialist during a talk on 'Art and Democracy'.

News from Nowhere is a novel without direct precedent in English
literature; a curious blend of future time travel, medieval romance
and miniature odyssey. For Morris, projecting back to the life and
art of the Middle Ages could show post-industrial society 'where
lies the hope for the future, and not in mere empty regret for the
days which can never come again'.[3] In the novel, the political and
commercial guts of London have been torn out, replaced by huge
open spaces of common parkland. It is Morris's symbolic revenge
on a city he both despised and thrived in. In his own life, while he
delighted in creating a quasi-medieval modus vivendi at Kelmscott

Manor, he was an early adopter who used state-of-the-art weaving and dyeing technology, photographic plates to aid reproduction of his patterns, and electrotyped ornaments. Technology could be a servant, not a master of mankind, and Morris would have had little truck with any art that explored mechanics or technology for its own sake. As one critic has perceptively pointed out, in the novel 'the adoption of handicraft techniques is portrayed as a product, not of economic backwardness, but of reflective choice'.[4]

The novel recounts how, in the rush to abandon all the trappings of modern life in an occasionally violent revolution (the mechanics of which are discussed at sometimes painful length in the book), handicrafts came to be practised by all members of society, which is organised around the pleasure and satisfaction of completing a job well done. This democratisation leads to a general coarsening of quality, but this is a feature – familiar from medieval carving and painting – dear to Morris's own aesthetic heart. Music makes its own appearance in the book: certain female characters erupt spontaneously into song on occasion, generally when they are in a state of elation, and at one point someone tries to persuade Guest to come and hear 'Welshmen' singing – an entertainment he speedily but graciously declines.

News from Nowhere describes cities transformed, not wiped out (an exception is Manchester, which has disappeared from the face of the land – no doubt a piece of wishful thinking on Morris's part). As the same commentator puts it: 'the ideal city – which was neither medieval nor contemporary . . . but of a type which has not yet existed – formed a recurring theme in his later lectures. Morris once described his goal as making "the town a part of the country and the country a part of the town". The aim was not one of uniformity, but rather of weakening the starkness of the contrast.' The book's sentiments chime with the section of Samuel Butler's *Erewhon* (1872) entitled 'The Book of the Machines', which strikes against mechanical materialism and Darwinism. Morris was also inspired to write his novel after reading Edward Bellamy's *Looking Backward* (1888). Bellamy, an American, posits his hero Julian West waking up in a socialist America of the year 2000, in which the state's private corporations have been erased in favour of a national business syndicate: 'the one capitalist in place of all other capitalists'. *Looking Backward*'s version of sedate socialism spoke to a middle class unnerved by recent Depressions and mass strike actions, and it sold hundreds of thousands of copies worldwide. The English edition appeared in 1889, and William Morris seized on it immediately. In an impassioned review in the Socialist League journal *The Commonweal*, Morris castigated its lack of interest in the past; its idea that, to achieve a socialist utopia, history and art must be eradicated. Above all, he loathed Bellamy's elevation of 'the industrious *professional* middle-class man of today' (Morris's italics) and his descriptions of machinery designed to make labour bearable. In this review, Morris makes a crucial distinction: some form of work is unavoidable for any future society, but the important matter is to make it less painful, to the point where work itself is a pleasurable activity. This is how Morris idealised the feudal Middle Ages as a time of innocence and play: 'the childhood of the world'.[5]

Morris was by no means the only British writer in his day to imagine the future in terms of the past. In 1885 Richard Jefferies published *After London, or Wild England*, an adventure story which begins with a vivid depiction of the country after some unspecified 'conflagrations' have wiped out civilisation and returned mankind to a life of barbarity in an untended wilderness. Jefferies found fame with a string of novels in which he observantly chronicled nature, wildlife and pre-mechanical agriculture in such books as *The Life of the Fields* and the memoir/reverie *The Story of My Heart*. *After London*'s apocalyptic scenario provided the excuse to reimagine the landscape as it might have been before any human intervention: England as Eden. Jefferies almost forensically imagines, element by element, the wilding of the landscape if left unfarmed and unmanaged: the gradual throttling of crops by weeds and brambles; the formation of swamps and lakes as man-made drainage systems clog up; and the springing up of trees, uncropped grass, briars and thorn bushes. After dealing with the flora, he moves on to the fauna: mice and rats overrun the untended crops, in turn feeding a growing population of owls, birds of prey, weasels and foxes. He moves up the food chain to describe domestic cats and dogs becoming feral, herds of deer and horses running amok. The story develops into more of a traditional adventure, but the opening chapters unconsciously portray Paradise restored.

Fast-forwarding into the distant future (the year 802,701, to be precise), the Time Traveller of H. G. Wells's *The Time Machine* (1899) encounters the Eloi, a society inhabiting the 'ruinous splendour' of a Thames Valley that has many of the hallmarks of Arcadia and the mythical Land of Cockayne.[6] The Eloi have no historical memory and no natural inquisitiveness, but they are uniformly clothed and eat and sleep together in huge stone palaces. One of the most disconcerting features of the landscape that strikes the Time Traveller is the lack of individual houses or cottages, 'such characteristic features of the English landscape'. There are no hedges, no signs of agriculture or property ownership: 'the whole earth had become a garden'. 'Communism,' he mutters to himself at one point. Here again the English Future is Eden Attained. (The rest of *The Time Machine* is a critique of such a view: this Upper World is one of 'feeble prettiness', at the mercy of the mechanical Under-world of the savage Morlocks.)

This tendency in British speculative fiction is typical of the imaginative quirk that might be called 'the antiquarian eye'. It is a mental trick comparable to the way the makers of period films and costume dramas are required to compose shots in order to exclude modern features such as TV aerials, power cables and other anachronisms. When I walk along a street in an English town, or in one of the older quarters of London, I find myself unconsciously screening out the more contemporary developments, trying to reconstruct an image of how the place might have once looked – focusing on, say, the eighteenth- and nineteenth-century buildings rather than the steel-and-glass additions. Britain is a place with an exceptionally strong will towards conservation, but the desire to preserve pockets of antiquity creates deep fissures in the surface of modernity: the woodwormy gate that leads into a secret garden, the still, timeless air of an ancient chapel, the medieval timbered pub nestling between a mobile-phone shop and Marks and Spencer. Two of the UK's most popular tourist attractions are literal time capsules: the 'lost gardens' of Heligan in Cornwall, a romantically neglected jungle overgrown with exotic blooms; and the house at Tyntesfield in north Somerset, a High Victorian estate untouched for decades and opened up for the first time in 2004. The *Grand Meaulnes*-like lost domain – the preserved house or garden that acts as a portal to earlier ages – is particularly common in children's literature. From *The Secret Garden* (Frances Hodgson Burnett, 1909) to *Tom's Midnight Garden* (Philippa Pearce, 1958), these concealed places offer lacunae in which the concerns and frustrations of daily life are utterly forgotten and supernatural experiences may occur.

An empire in its pomp has no need of artistic subtleties, and even less use for melancholia. As the British imperial project thundered towards the close of the nineteenth century, culminating in the ignominious Boer War of 1899–1902, it left its impoverished social margins riddled with neglect. This in turn opened the floodgates for legions of charitable workers and revolutionaries hungry for reform. Morris's coterie at the time included many radical thinkers and agitators whose thoughts were directed towards an improved sense of nationhood at the close of the nineteenth century. In 1877 he had put his fervent interest in conservation into practice by founding the Society for the Protection of Ancient Buildings. The previous year, Miranda Hill had formed the Kyrle Society, a philanthropic organisation dedicated to encouraging the working-class poor to appreciate art and books, and to increase their experience of open spaces. In 1877 it was rapidly expanding into many cities outside London. Morris was a supporter of the Society's London branch, and took a special interest in its Open Spaces Committee. Hill's elder sister, Octavia, is better known as one of the founders of the National Trust. In the 1870s and 80s Octavia was a classic Victorian philanthropist, who worked as a housing reformer and teacher and was also, like Morris, a member of the Commons Preservation Society. She strove to provide access to nature, open spaces and the arts for deprived children. 'Think,' she urged in a lecture entitled 'Colour, Space, and Music for the People', 'those of you who have had any country life as children, how early the wild flowers formed your delight; remember, those of you who can, what the bright colour of flag, or dress, or picture was; recall the impression of concerted music when first its harmonies reached you; live over again the glad burst out of doors into any open space where you could breathe and move freely . . .'[7] In 1895 her formidable energy was funnelled into a venture, with Canon H. D. Rawnsley and Sir Robert Hunter, to save England's disappearing historic buildings and beautiful areas of nature for the benefit of the nation. All three were alarmed at the impact of uncontrolled industrialisation, which was wiping out the countryside, demolishing buildings with no regulation and systematically obliterating physical tokens of what they considered the nation's heritage. This victory was secured by private means, for Hill and her associates had little faith in the state's willingness to protect its heirlooms. 'The leaders and the led,' declaimed Morris in 1884, 'are incapable of saving so much as half a dozen commons from the grasp of inexorable Commerce.'[8]

William Morris's circle was not without music of its own. He was acquainted with Arnold Dolmetsch, the Swiss-Frenchman almost singlehandedly responsible for triggering off the Early Music revival which, in the late twentieth century, swelled into a flood of 'period instrument' ensembles. His son Carl's name is familiar to anyone who grew up learning the recorder at school – the Dolmetsch descant recorder has been a staple of music education since the 1950s. In the month before Morris's death, Dolmetsch brought an Elizabethan virginals to Kelmscott House and moved the old man to tears with his rendition of a pavane and galliard by William Byrd. In the mid-1890s the Hammersmith Socialist Society held weekly Sunday-night meetings at Morris's riverside abode, featuring lectures followed by general discussion, and sometimes contributions from the Socialist Choir, including Morris's own song, 'March of the Workers'. In late 1895 the twenty-one-year-old composition student Gustav Holst began attending these meetings at Kelmscott House. This was a decisive moment in Holst's early life: at exactly the same time as his induction into the world of organised socialism, he met his future wife, Isobel Harrison, another HSS member, and also struck up a lifelong, highly influential friendship with Ralph Vaughan Williams, who, like Holst, was studying composition under Hubert Parry and Charles Villiers Stanford at the Royal College of Music. That autumn, they were both taking part in the College's production of Purcell's *Dido and Aeneas*, revived for the first time in 200 years.

Holst occasionally brought Vaughan Williams to meetings at Kelmscott House over the following year. The two young musicians had entered illustrious company, as these gatherings were often attended by some of the era's most progressive artists and radical opinion-formers, including George Bernard Shaw, Oscar Wilde, H. G. Wells and William Butler Yeats. William Morris himself died in October 1896, by which time Holst was frequently chairing and recording minutes at the Society's meetings. The Society

'Don't you think we ought to victimise Elgar?' Gustav Holst and Ralph
Vaughan Williams take a break in the Malvern Hills, *c.* 1914.

continued to assemble, and in 1897 Holst was formally invited to
conduct the Hammersmith Socialist Choir. His involvement lasted
several years, during which time he introduced a mixed repertoire
that included Thomas Morley, Purcell, Mozart and Wagner. Seated
behind a harmonium installed on a cart, Holst directed the singing
during the Society's street demonstrations.

The intense friendship and artistic exchanges between Holst
and Vaughan Williams were among the most significant forces
propelling British music-making towards a new dawn. The concept
of British music was a primordial soup waiting for an electrical
spark. Its twentieth-century reanimation flows directly from this
concentration of radical politics, speculative utopianism and rural
conservationism, all supported by a coterie of powerful national
figures who shared, in Alfred Tennyson's words, 'the passion of the
past'.

Compared to the lush groves of nineteenth-century European
classical and Romantic music, Britain's musical landscape
throughout the Victorian era was a wasteland. Looking back

from the 1920s, Holst called the historical course of English music 'a fitful flare – sometimes an explosion of musical energy followed by a long period of darkness . . . At the next explosion English musicians have either forgotten their forefathers or they disapprove of them.'[9] The most popular composer of the late nineteenth century was Arthur Sullivan, whose comic operettas with W. S. Gilbert, such as *HMS Pinafore* and *The Mikado*, furnished thousands of Victorians with light entertainment, catchy tunes and the occasional gentle brush with the exotic souvenirs of Britain's imperial conquests in China and Japan. But otherwise there was little in British composition that could compete with the big guns on the Continent. Leading Victorian composers such as Parry and Stanford unswervingly located the next wave of English music in the same Teutonic evolutionary chain that led from Bach to Schumann to Brahms (they didn't approve of Wagner). No wonder the word got out that certain German commentators were calling Britain '*das Land ohne Musik*' – the land without music. And yet, at the century's close, the great powers of Middle European music had become '*faisandés*' – a French word meaning overripe, corrupt, decadent – blooming into their late-autumn sunset, with the atonal winter heralding the blizzard of Viennese serialism in the early 1920s. The influential, radical chromaticism and total art of Wagner had bloated into the massive, opulent symphonics of Brahms, Bruckner and Mahler, and the decadent operatics of Strauss and Verdi.

In contrast, the music of Western Europe, Scandinavia and the Balkans was turning on a different cycle, and awakening to a fresh spring. France was where the soundworld was altering most audibly. Picking up from Wagner's tonal inventions but translating them to a more impressionistic, spacier idiom, Claude Debussy and Maurice Ravel brought a sensuousness and a legerdemain that signalled a mercurial future for European sound. In Norway, which gained full statehood in 1905, Nils Gade and Edvard Grieg had attained the status of national composers by searching out and incorporating the country's dispersed folk tunes. Other Nordic symphonists such as Carl Nielsen (Denmark) and Jean Sibelius (Finland) were breaking down the symphonic form's traditional narrative drive with atmospheric effects derived from an intense communion with nature. Spain's Enrique Granados, Isaac Albéniz and Manuel de Falla squeezed the zest of Iberian folk musics into the French cocktail. And in England, too, conditions were perfect for the green shoots of renewal to poke through turf that had long been muddied by years of confusion and loss of public faith.

Outside the music academies, a vernacular music tradition had been quietly preserved. Carl Engel, a German musicologist living in London, observed in 1866: 'Although the rural population of England appear to sing less than those of most other European countries, it may nevertheless be supposed that they also, especially in districts somewhat remote from any large towns, must still preserve songs and dance tunes of their own inherited from their forefathers.'[10] In his later essay collection *The Literature of National Music*, Engel added that England lagged behind countries like Germany, Russia and France in preserving its national songs, and even expressed the hope that English musicians might be persuaded to 'spend their autumnal holidays' encountering folk songs at first hand. There was no antipathy in Engel's comments; he was engaged in a comparative study of many of the world's national musics and was merely comparing the status of England's folk music in national life with that of the German people's music (*Volksmusik*). But half a century later, and ten years before the start of the First World War, the German writer Oscar Schmitz fitted a poisoned barb to Engel's observations when he published a book entitled *Das Land Ohne Musik* (*The Land Without Music*). Music is only mentioned on two of its 300 pages, but Schmitz's core argument was a perceived lack of musicality, in a symbolic sense, in the Anglo-Saxon soul. 'The English are the only cultured nation without their own music (except popular melodies),' he wrote. 'This does not mean that they have less sensitive ears, but that their life overall is much poorer for it. To have music inside yourself, no matter how little, means to possess fluidity, to slip one's moorings, to feel the world as a flow . . .'[11]

Holst, Vaughan Williams and their fellow students at the Royal College of Music were pitched headlong into this scramble for the future of music in Britain. Their tutors Parry (director of the Royal College) and Stanford commanded influential positions in the nation's musical life. As a composer, Parry was drawn to the visionary Romantic poetry of Percy Bysshe Shelley and William Blake. His immortal setting of Blake's *Jerusalem*, written in 1916, has of course permeated the consciousness of almost everyone born in the British Isles since it was written in 1916, and has been adopted as a kind of unofficial alternative national anthem. By 1900 English music was in the throes of a resurgence, swept forward on the overlapping waves of Edward Elgar and Frederick Delius. Elgar's *Pomp and Circumstance* marches and triumphalist setting of 'Land of Hope and Glory' are perfect examples of the kind of patriotic froth that firebrand Vorticist Wyndham Lewis decried as 'splurging and bombinating'; more than a century later they continue to trigger conspicuous jingoism at the Last Night of the Proms. Although certain aspects of his music did touch on the vision of Albion (notably the cantata *Caractacus*), Elgar's bluff Old World patriotism has come to represent a view of English music that has tarnished the more nuanced composers who trailed in his immediate wake. Even Holst and Vaughan Williams distanced themselves from their internationally respected forebear: 'Don't you think we ought to victimise Elgar?' Holst cheekily suggested in a 1903 letter to his friend.[12]

Delius is an altogether different case, a figure whose music is a product of the Romantic sunset yet at the same time holds out the promise of the approaching spring. Born in 1863, Delius was a cosmopolitan free spirit who had spent time in the Appalachian mountains of the eastern United States, trudged the mountain tracks of Norway, and befriended Paul Gauguin, August Strindberg, Edvard Munch and Knut Hamsun in Paris. By 1900 he was living in rustic seclusion in the French countryside in a villa at Grez-sur-Loing, near Fontainebleau, writing a music which glowed with the rapt new tonal atmospheres of Debussy and Ravel. His writing for orchestra produced rhapsodic pieces with a stillness at their centre. *Brigg Fair* (1907) was a verdant 'English rhapsody' containing a folk-song tune passed to him by Percy Grainger. His country isolation focused his attention on the changing of the seasons and the natural cycle: 'March of Spring' from *North Country Sketches* (1913–14) depicts sap rising, leaves unfurling, the gradual awakening of Nature from its winter slumber. The harmonic web is divided into separate strands of melody, suggesting the complex interweaving of a root system. In the short, evocative orchestral paintings *Summer Night on the River* (1911) and *On Hearing the First Cuckoo in Spring* (1912), much of the melodic weight is transferred to the 'lighter' tonalities of the flute, clarinet and upper strings, and his preferred mode was the tone poem rather than the symphonic development favoured by Elgar, with all its baggage of psychic dramatisation. This music was the inverse of imperial rhetoric. His biographer, the composer Peter Warlock, nailed Delius's ambitions in purple tones: 'For Delius, as for Traherne or Blake and many another mystic, Heaven is but the world transfigured and interpreted by spiritual vision . . . And those who see, in all the manifestations of Nature, a fullness, a richness and loveliness that would for very excess break through the barriers of time and change and overflow into the Infinite may well deride the materialist's heaven of harps and glass which those have feigned who never saw the world aright.'[13]

His music rarely reaches the crushing crescendos of a Mahler or an Elgar. The exception came in the monumental choral panoply of *A Mass of Life* (1904–5), whose gigantic forces can be compared to Mahler's Eighth Symphony. *A Mass of Life* has been mysteriously neglected in the British repertoire, perhaps because its visionary setting of Nietzsche's *Also Sprach Zarathustra*, and its uncompromising atheism, are so at odds with the verities of classical music's middlebrow audience. Warlock dubbed him a religious composer for an atheistic age, 'one who, instead of writing anthems and services, turns to Nature (and even Nietzsche) for his inspiration; and yet most irreligion is . . . a misconception of the very nature of religion, a confusion of ideas which is of the same order as the credulity of the sense in regard to the sun's apparent motion round the earth'.[14] The *Mass* enacts the supremacy of humankind, as it conquers Time and gains entrance to Eternity. Nietzsche's *Zarathustra* continues an ancient line of heretical, Gnostic thought that begins with the hermetic philosophy of Hermes Trismegistus and was later channelled by William Blake. 'He is a pantheistic mystic whose vision has been attained by an all-embracing acceptation, a "yea-saying" to life,' gushed Warlock, writing while Delius was still alive. 'Such a mind has become so profoundly conscious of the life of all nature that it has begun to perceive the great rhythms of life itself.'[15]

Ultimately there is more of the melancholy of sunset than the hope of spring in the Delian corpus, but there is a solemnity and a reverence for nature at its heart. In Delius's life can be found a foreshadowing of the pattern of retreat, countryside immersion and innovation that recurs throughout the ensuing century. Although his villa was near Paris, he largely kept himself cloistered away and never bothered to make connections with the city's vibrant musical life. The Delian mode of relaxed but reverent pastoral timelessness would become one of the two dominant models for the wider English music revival of the early twentieth century. The other was the resurgence of folk music, without which that rebirth is inconceivable, and which began, appropriately enough, with a man called England, in an English country garden.

'Cecil Sharp was sitting in the vicarage garden talking to Charles Marson and to Mattie Kay, who was likewise staying at Hambridge, when he heard John England quietly singing to himself as he mowed the vicarage lawn. Cecil Sharp whipped out his notebook and took down the tune; and then persuaded John to give him the words. He immediately harmonised the song ['The Seeds of Love']; and that same evening it was sung at a choir supper by Mattie Kay, Cecil Sharp accompanying. The audience was delighted; as one said, it was the first time that the song had been put into evening dress.'[16]

The incident recounted above took place in 1903 in a Somerset village and sent Cecil Sharp out across Britain, and ultimately America, on a quest to reclaim England's dispersed national folk songs and dances, and to understand their origins. His research was conducted at grass-roots level. Instead of dry musicological

The man who inadvertently triggered the twentieth-century folk-song revival: John England in his garden at Hambridge, Somerset.

study, he was prepared to commit hours, days, months knocking on cottage doors or popping into pubs, pushing flagons of ale at ageing villagers to coax out the folk songs locked in their memories. While his methods have lately been called into question, along with his more extreme prescriptions for the role of folk music within a national culture,[17] Sharp is undeniably the lynchpin and catalyst of the greater proportion that is considered British folk music in modern times, and the English Folk Dance and Song Society (EFDSS) – a 1932 coalition between the Folk-Song Society (inaugurated in 1898) and the English Folk Dance Society he set up in 1911 – is still headquartered in a building bearing his name.

But Cecil Sharp had not yet been seduced by folk music when the first of these societies was founded. Born in south London in 1859, he sought his early advancement in Australia. He spent most of his twenties working in Adelaide, first as a bank clerk and legal assistant, then as joint director of the town's School of Music, where he conducted the Adelaide Philharmonic and had two light operas performed at the local Theatre Royal. In 1892, having made an indelible mark on the music world of South Australia, he returned to England, where he continued to teach and compose. On Boxing Day 1899 he happened to see a morris-dance group, properly known as a 'side', at Headington Quarry in Oxfordshire. Fascinated by this rarely seen display of six men dressed in white shirts and flannels, with ribboned, flowery hats and sets of bells mounted on leather straps bound around their calves, Sharp instinctively noted down several of the tunes from the group's concertina player, William Kimber, whose father had been foreman of the Headington side. The sheer otherness of the display entranced him – it seemed to appear from the darkest, least conspicuous corners of English provincial life, and to be innately understood by the people who practised it. Ballads had survived the Puritan revolution of the seventeenth century; sword dances were faded relics of chivalric rituals. And yet, beyond that, no one could tell him where these traditions came from. He was pulled bodily into the mystery.

Sharp was not the first to fall under the spell of this music. Among the Folk-Song Society's founders were Alice Gomme (daughter of eminent folklorist Sir Laurence Gomme), eccentric scholar and folk historian Sabine Baring-Gould and a poet and songwriter of Scots origin called Lucy Broadwood.[18] When Sharp looked into the roots of the terminology of this strange shadow culture which had survived decades of neglect, he discovered that the first use of the word 'folklore' did not occur until 22 August 1846, in a letter to the *Athenaeum* magazine by one W. J. Thoms. Laurence Gomme supplied its first official definition: 'The science which treats of the survivals of archaic belief and customs in modern ages.' The 'science' aspect is striking, but Sharp took up the mantle, exploring the anatomy of the surviving limbs of a thriving culture with a surgeon's precision. The term 'folk music' did not appear in all English dictionaries even up to 1889, when the *Century Dictionary* gave the following definition: 'A song of the people; a song based on a legendary or historical event, or some incident of common life, the words and generally the music of which have originated among the common people, and are extensively used by them.'

Sharp examined folk song forensically, as a product of the 'common people' – i.e. the peasantry that just about still existed at his time of writing – distinct from songs, popular or otherwise, composed by the educated. He defined the common people as 'those whose mental development has been due not to any formal system of training or education, but solely to environment, communal association, and direct contact with the ups and downs of life. It is necessary that a sharp distinction should be drawn between the un-educated and the non-educated. The former are the half or partially educated, i.e. the illiterate. Whereas the non-educated, or "the common people", are the unlettered, whose faculties have undergone no formal training whatsoever . . .'[19] These unlettered people, Sharp observed, used to be evenly distributed between town and country, but at the beginning of the twentieth century, due to improved education, were confined to remoter rural regions. The arts and songs they preserved had remained out of reach of the rest of the country at large; the true definition of folk song was therefore country song, not town song or art song. But Sharp particularly highlighted the contrast between the spontaneity of the untrained musician and the conscious exercise of compositional intelligence on the part of the educated.

From 1903, when he heard John England sing 'The Seeds of Love', until 1906, Sharp beat the bounds of the county of Somerset with his notebook and pencil, methodically collecting songs from an ever-widening circle of singers and musicians who would delve deep into their collective memory banks. He was more thorough than the majority of his predecessors, often returning to the same

Cecil Sharp collecting the song 'The Golden Glove' from Edwin Clay, Brailes, Warwickshire, 1910.

individual again and again to check for lyrical or melodic variations. His five-volume *Folk-Songs from Somerset*, published between 1904–9, bore the fruits of this research, but at the same time he had been thinking deeply about the wider implications and context for his discoveries. These he set out in *English Folk-Song: Some Conclusions* (1907), which lays out the territory and the issues at stake in considerable detail but in accessible language. It is a curiously readable tract, ranging from descriptions of his methods out in the field to explosive declarations of his love of folk music and a final chapter that moves into more problematic waters, as it looks to the future of English folk music by calling for its widespread introduction into the nation's schoolrooms. 'Our system of education is . . . too cosmopolitan,' he writes, 'it is calculated to produce citizens of the world rather than Englishmen.'[20] In fact, this was not so much blind nationalism: Sharp observed the way other European countries had a much more relaxed and integrated relationship with their own folk music, and simply felt that England had a great deal of catching up to do. Inescapably, these are sentiments from the heart of the Edwardian age, in which duty and patriotic pride were governing norms, and a reaction against more sinister forms of propagandist nationalism and attempts to discredit British culture (as with Schmitz's *The Land Without Music*, published three years earlier).

In Sharp, there is none of William Morris's longing for a vanished past. Folk songs are only of interest, and of practical use, in the present and future. He contrasts the way German *Volkslieder* had penetrated that country's national life with the state of affairs in Britain, where the folk song 'comes to us destitute of association, unlinked with the past; like an ancient building newly restored, with its walls scraped and cleaned and stripped of their moss and fern'.[21]

For Sharp, folk songs existed in constant transformation, a living example of an art form in a perpetual state of renewal. 'One man sings a song, and then others sing it after him, changing what they do not like'[22] is the most concise nutshelling of his conclusions on the origins. Don't seek the 'original' copy, insisted Sharp; focus on the transformations themselves – for they are the substance of the song. He conceded that most songs probably had a sole author in the indistinct past, but unlike in high culture, the 'original' is not the authentic prototype; instead, it should be thought of as the equivalent of a composer's first draft – 'the source from which it is sprung'.[23] Every subsequent iteration becomes more 'real', more 'definitive'. The anonymity and artlessness particularly appealed to Sharp. 'The unconscious music of the folk has all the marks of fine art; that it is wholly free from the taint of manufacture, the canker of artificiality; that it is transparently pure and truthful, simple and direct in its utterance.'[24] Unlike art music, rooted in individual consciousness, folk is a product of the group mind over an immeasurable time span. Songs have come to express the taste and consensus of a community: any personal traits or quirks have long since been washed smooth. The singers that Sharp encountered were living conduits through which the music flowed – a source that's surprisingly inexhaustible. 'You never know when you have got to the bottom of a singer's memory.'[25]

The oldest of songs are the great narrative ballads. These tales are sketched in bold strokes, with repeated refrains for easy comprehension and orientation by a listening audience. Minor elaborations advance the narrative by gradual degrees. The corpus of British ballads was already established by Professor Francis J. Child, an American scholar whose massive treasury of romances, supernatural experiences, historical events and folk heroes, morality tales and riddles, *The English and Scottish Popular Ballads*, was published in ten volumes between 1882–98. This was the scholarly version of standards such as 'The False Knight upon the Road', 'The Cruel Mother', 'Twa Corbies', 'The Two Magicians', 'Tam Lin' and 'Sir Patrick Spens'. But there was a crucial difference between Child and Sharp: Child's ballads had been collected from the comfort of his New England writing desk. He sent out thousands of letters to universities, schools, churches and other organisations around the country – 2,500 to Scotland alone – soliciting the lyrics to any ballads that were known to the recipients or their communities. Child never heard the ballads leaping from the throats of the yeomen and women that Sharp encountered on his trails. There is no way of authoritatively dating any of this material, Sharp admitted, but he compared each rendition of a ballad to an acorn falling from an oak tree. Each acorn is the produce of the new season's growth; the song is re-sown with each utterance. The most ancient ballads of all were rolled up into compilations which we know as the great European epics: Homer's *Odyssey* and *Iliad*, the Scandinavian Sagas and Eddas, the German *Nibelungenlied*, Spain's *El Cid*, the Welsh *Mabinogion*, Britain's Arthurian legends. Many of these old yarns are steeped in the supernatural and contain marvellous or magical events – as in 'Tam Lin', where a prince is gripped in a protective embrace by his lover, pregnant with his child, as the Queen of the Fairies turns him into a snake, a lion and a red-hot iron bar.

With the arrival of the printing press in the Middle Ages, oral transmission of these epics was gradually replaced by paper, marginalising the illiterate. Correspondingly, there was a demand for them to be broken up again into easily digestible chunks. That was where the minstrels and troubadours came in: travelling around the land, seeding their music within communities, and then moving on, transforming it by repetition. These shortened ballads from around the fifteenth and sixteenth centuries are largely what Child preserved. Their pre-epic form, conjectured to date from around the ninth and tenth centuries, are all but lost, though their stories and characters survive.

In Sharp's account, the 'song' was the 'lineal descendant' of the ballad. Songs express more personal and subjective elements than ballads, as they are closer to the life and current interests of the individual singing them. Common themes include the Lover; the Rover or Wanderer; sea songs, such as sailors' tales of adventure; outlaw songs; executioners' songs; songs that accumulate detail (such as 'The Twelve Days of Christmas' or 'The House that Jack Built'); carols, which occupy a position midway between a ballad and a hymn; and wassails, May Day songs and any songs which celebrate dates unrecognised in the Christian calendar – these are survivors from pre-Christian, pagan times.

'The twentieth-century collector is a hundred years too late,' lamented Sharp elsewhere in his book. The widespread publication of broadsides in the early nineteenth century had a further distorting influence on the corpus of folk song. Broadsides were pamphlets with garbled, singalong versions of folk lyrics pumped out by literary hacks and distributed for quick cash around city book stalls, taverns and cafes. Due to their popular appeal, it's these versions that many of Sharp's source singers were probably blaring out – with much of the earlier detail excised. On that point, Sharp did not have a spotless record either. A Victorian by upbringing, he was unsettled by the frequently coarse or bawdy content and snipped out the more explicit verses – although this may have had more to do with his intention that the songs would be learnt by rote by schoolchildren. 'The folk-song editor', he wrote in self-justification, 'has perforce to undertake the distasteful task of modifying noble and beautiful sentiments in order that they may suit the minds and conform to the conventions of another age, where such things would not be understood in the primitive, direct and healthy sense.'[26]

In the final chapter of *English Folk-Song: Some Conclusions*, 'The Future of Folk-Song', Sharp shifts to a prescription for the wellbeing of the nation itself. The Board of Education, he suggests, should recommend the incorporation of folk song and dance into school music lessons. 'When every English child is, as a matter of course, made acquainted with the folk-songs of his own country, then, from whatever class the musician of the future may spring, he will speak in the national musical idiom.' Although the idea of a nation speaking or singing with a unified voice may appear sinister in the light of twentieth-century fascism, Sharp innocently wanted England to catch up with the rest of Europe, which, he believed, had achieved successful musical economies through the inoculation of the people with the music of the folk from birth, something England had ceased to do. For Sharp, as for Vaughan Williams, patriotism was about loving the land of one's birth, and did not spill over into the desire to inflict that country's customs on other unwilling nations. Although Sharp's recommendations were never fully implemented to the extent he proposed, a succession of British composers recognised his fieldwork as providing the vital nutrition their music needed. As Sharp put it, prophetically, at the end of his book, 'There is nothing so fertile as virgin soil.'

Around the turn of the century, Vaughan Williams found folk music harder and harder to ignore, and became increasingly persuaded that its dying form must be preserved as a national cultural asset. He was fortunate, then, that Australian composer and song collector Percy Grainger was his near neighbour in Chelsea. Grainger was an equally enthusiastic folk-song hunter, the first in Britain to use state-of-the-art wax-cylinder recorders on his field trips.[27] Vaughan Williams met Cecil Sharp in 1900, and Lucy Broadwood two years later. As it turned out, Broadwood's family had been neighbours and friends of Vaughan Williams's parents near the family home in Leith Hill, Surrey, and Ralph was familiar with her uncle John Broadwood's recently republished collection of *Sussex Songs*.[28] His research at the turn of the century fed into a series of lectures on folk music, which he delivered at adult-education classes in Bournemouth in 1902, peppering them with musical examples

A gallery of early folk-song collectors. Clockwise from top left: Cecil Sharp,
the Rev. Sabine Baring-Gould, Francis J. Child, George Butterworth,
Ralph Vaughan Williams, Lucy Broadwood.

and extracts. The extent to which he recognised that England's music culture lagged behind the European mainland came out in a lecture entitled 'Are We a Musical Nation?', in which he said, 'When England has its municipal-aided music, so that every town of decent size possesses its own permanent orchestra as is the case in Germany . . . with increased musical activity our composers will grow. Until the good time comes, the protest against foreign music . . . is futile.'[29] The final instalment of the course was called 'The Importance of Folk Song', in which he demonstrated how earlier folk tunes had impacted on the familiar hymns of the church songbook.

The pilgrim is one who walks the land with a sense of righteous purpose. In the early 1900s the idea of English music was associated with an idea of spiritual mission. Throughout his life, Vaughan Williams revered *The Pilgrim's Progress*, the Christian allegory by one of the seventeenth century's foremost Dissenters, John Bunyan, and continually tinkered with his opera version right up to its eventual 1951 premiere. The one-act opera *The Shepherds of the Delectable Mountains* (1921), based on an extract from Bunyan's text, was another product of fifteen years' pondering. Among other composers, Sir Granville Bantock wrote a choral *Pilgrim's Progress* (1938), and George Dyson wrote a cantata called *The Canterbury Pilgrims* (1930). The British music revival of the early twentieth century is driven by the founding metaphor of a small but dedicated set of individuals, each undertaking their separate journeys towards the grail – Sancta Civitas, Celestial City, New Atlantis – of a new music for a new society in which all have an equal stake.

Anglican church congregations spent most of the twentieth century singing from the same hymn book: *The English Hymnal*. Little did they know, as they pounded out the lusty lines of 'To Be a Pilgrim', that they were singing to the tune of an atheist who later in life drifted into a cheerful agnosticism. The man who commissioned

Vaughan Williams to compose new music for the church's *Hymns Ancient and Modern* in 1904 was the Reverend Percy Dearmer, the radical vicar of St Mary's Church in Primrose Hill, and a socialist who, like William Morris, had his face turned towards medieval England. For his modernised *English Hymnal*, Vaughan Williams – and Holst, who assisted his efforts – reintroduced elements of Gothic-era music to the church service, a process which acted as a training exercise in methods of seamlessly integrating ancient and modern elements into new compositions. Vaughan Williams called the existing hymn book 'elaborate, unmetrical, aloof plainsong'. 'We must remember', he reminded lecture audiences, 'that the parish church probably stood in what would now be the public square which would be the great meeting place for the people. These pagan ceremonies with their accompanying music would be going on at the very church door making the struggle for existence between the two visible and audible to all.'[30]

The more colourful and memorable tunes of the pre-Cromwell age were infinitely preferable to Vaughan Williams, and his own *Hymnal* attempted to arrive at a Christian music from the angle of pre-Christian folk song. In so doing, the composer also shrewdly recognised that the church pews held a captive audience for his folk revivalism, thus injecting it into an established, functioning auditorium for (free) public recital and bypassing the mechanics of concert-hall production and the gauntlet of music criticism.

Under the auspices of the Folk-Song Society, Vaughan Williams continued his lectures around the country. After one such gathering in 1903 in Brentwood, Essex, he was invited to a tea given by the vicar at Ingrave, where he was introduced to an elderly labourer called Charles Pottipher. Mr Pottipher, he was told, had a stock of folk tunes in his head which Vaughan Williams might be interested to hear. Pottipher thought his songs too coarse for the present company, but Vaughan Williams was bidden to visit him at home the following day, where he ground out a song called 'Bushes and

A. E. Housman, whose *A Shropshire Lad* (1896) was a poetic
beacon to many Edwardian pastoral composers.

Briars'. It touched the composer to the core; he later reported
that he felt he had known this song all his life.

So it was that, at the same time as Sharp was out in the field,
Vaughan Williams was also embarking on song-collecting trips with
zeal. From 1904 he began to stuff his notebooks with transcriptions
harvested from his bicycle trips around the lanes of Essex, Norfolk,
Wiltshire and Yorkshire. He was accompanied on many of these
trips by George Butterworth, a nineteen-year-old composer with
a growing interest in England's indigenous music. Butterworth
would go on to be strongly associated with musical settings of
poems by A. E. Housman, whose lyrics exerted a profound pull
on so many young composers of his generation. Published in 1896,
A Shropshire Lad featured none of the high rhetorical versification
of contemporaries like Arnold, Browning or Tennyson. There was
nothing complex about its vignettes of rural village life, but the
undertow of melancholy and the proximity of despair and death
(Housman described his poems as 'morbid secretions') ensured

sentimentality was kept at bay. Butterworth's orchestral suite *A Shropshire Lad* (1912) paid explicit homage; the previous year, he had set six songs from the cycle to music. Four years later, slim volumes of Housman's poetry were among the reading matter handed out to British infantrymen in the trenches of Flanders, while the thirty-one-year-old Butterworth had succumbed to a sniper's bullet.

In an age of rapid and unstoppable change, nostalgia and revivalism often flourish: they offer the solace of permanence and stability in a world whose certainties seem to be slipping away. British innovation is habitually shadowed by restoration; the Victorian mania for building schools, factories, churches and municipal buildings was couched in the architectural vernacular of medieval Gothic. Vaughan Williams, to a lesser extent Holst, and the younger composers of the English pastoral school envisioned exactly what Morris had achieved in *News from Nowhere*: a future for British music woven with rich threads from its past. The touchstones for Vaughan Williams and Holst – and those of their circle and a significant proportion of the next wave of composers after the First World War – were the previous golden ages of English music: sixteenth-century Tudor polyphony; the style of English-language setting which they admired in Henry Purcell; a love of metaphysical poetry and Romantic visionaries like William Blake and Walt Whitman.[31]

One of Vaughan Williams's most frequently performed string orchestra pieces, the magisterial *Fantasia on a Theme by Thomas Tallis* (premiered in 1910), bloomed out of this period. Tallis (c. 1505–85) is the jewel in the crown of the Elizabethan choral composers, whose extravagant, soaring polyphonic flights find their echo down the centuries in Vaughan Williams's opulent string-writing, which glides serenely out of the dock like a gigantic galleon. The piece is a symbolic bridge, travelling across time to connect vital moments in the genesis of a national music: 'English antiquarianism becomes a form of alchemy', as one modern writer puts it.[32]

Vaughan Williams's pastoral compositions brought metaphysics, mysticism and rapture, transcending English music's parochial characteristics. The poets and writers he admired and set to music were not Establishment figures but dissidents, visionaries and outsiders: Blake, Whitman and Housman, of course; Elizabethan metaphysical poets such as John Donne, George Herbert and Richard Crashaw; the Old Testament prophets; and St John of the Revelation. Pieces like *Toward the Unknown Region* (1906), *On Wenlock Edge* (1909), the *Five Mystical Songs* (1911) and, late in his life, the *Ten Blake Songs* (1957) open up a musical dialogue with English mystical thought: his resonant string vibrations tether intangibles to the roll and yaw of the landscape. Writing for the voice unlocked Vaughan Williams's most primitive instincts – 'it is hardly possible for an artist to be untrue to himself . . . when he writes for the human voice', he wrote.[33] His *Sea Symphony* (1910) uses the free verse of Whitman to meditate on the ineffable and unknowable, while examining the idea of Britain as an island.

While revising the English hymn book, Vaughan Williams was also creating the first of his orchestral pieces that explicitly referenced folk song. *In the Fen Country* (1904) is a tentative beginning, with melodies in a folk-esque style, but the *Norfolk Rhapsody* (1906) quotes tunes he had scribbled down from trawlermen in King's Lynn. *Hugh the Drover*, an opera completed just before the outbreak of war, contains themes drawn from morris dances, pagan Maying ceremonies and folk songs, using a musical vernacular designed to have a similar common appeal as John Gay's *Beggar's Opera* (1728). One sequence, in which the character of Hugh is attacked by villagers who have been whipped into a patriotic frenzy, clearly shows Vaughan Williams had no desire for the blossoming 'national music' movement to be hijacked by darker associations with nationalism or racial pride.

Ralph Vaughan Williams's life straddled a colossal stretch of music history, from Wagner's last years to the modernist age of Cage, Boulez, Stockhausen and rock 'n' roll. He lived long enough to participate in a second folk-music revival, co-writing *The Penguin Book of English Folk Songs* with A. L. Lloyd (1958). He survived the Second World War and died, aged eighty, in 1958 in a palatial residence in Regent's Park. He had a 'good war', premiering the darkened, rolling valleys of his Fifth Symphony in the midst of it, and following the victory celebrations with his tumultuous, harrowing Sixth (1948). A patriot to the extent that he loved the land and poetry of Britain, and a believer in 'nationalism as a spiritual force in art', Vaughan Williams remained an agnostic and egalitarian who passionately believed in 'a united Europe and a world federation'. As far as a celebrated composer could at the time, he kept the Establishment at arm's length.[34] But he was a socialist in all but name to the end of his life. His massive corpus of music is an example of how a national music can reflect a native consciousness without recourse to rabble-rousing or xenophobia. Indeed, there is the sense in Vaughan Williams that a universal music is only achievable via a thorough immersion in the immediate life of the locality. 'If the roots of your art are firmly planted in your own soil and that soil has anything to give you, you may still gain the whole world and not lose your own souls.'[35] The most succinctly realised version of this view comes with his well-known piece for violin and orchestra, *The Lark Ascending* (1914). This is classic pastoralism, inspired by a George Meredith poem: the violin becomes the lark, hovering and chirruping above the rolling green downs evoked by the orchestral writing. The freedom impulse and the groundedness of nation/community/home: pulling against one another, but ultimately co-existing in exquisite harmony.

From their first meeting at the Royal College in 1895 until

Holst's death in 1934, Vaughan Williams's partnership with Gustav Holst involved a perpetual round of consultation and trial, mutual critique and appreciation. Both grew up in Gloucestershire, but there were marked differences in their ancestry: Vaughan Williams's family was aristocratic, rich and successful (his father a clergyman, his mother descended from pottery magnate Josiah Wedgwood; Ralph's great-uncle was Charles Darwin). Vaughan Williams was Cambridge-educated, while Holst, two years his junior, struggled to make ends meet as a music student in the early 1890s (aside from Elgar, Holst was the first significant English composer not to have a private income). They quickly became friends, inaugurating a tradition of 'field days', during which they would review and constructively criticise each other's latest compositional efforts. Leading up to the turn of the century, their 'Tea Shop Set', which met at Wilkins' cafe in South Kensington and included John Ireland and the black composer Samuel Coleridge-Taylor, debated such motions as 'The Socialism of William Morris', 'The Philosophy of Schopenhauer', 'Open Air Music' and – Vaughan Williams's proposal – 'The Moderate Man is Contemptible', which gives some indication of his characteristically benign contrarianism. They discussed literature; Thomas Hardy's *The Return of the Native*, set on a Dorset heath that hummed and moaned with sound, was a particular favourite.

Vaughan Williams hooked Holst up with Cecil Sharp, who asked the composer to provide piano parts for the unaccompanied lyrics the folklorist had collected. Sharp is the dedicatee of Holst's *Somerset Rhapsody* (1906–7), and the piece is founded on a sheep-shearing song called 'It's a Rose-Bud in June'; Holst himself conducted its premiere at a lecture given by Sharp in Bath. It's one of several landscape pieces that mark the maturation of Holst's music: the 'Elegy' movement of his *Cotswolds Symphony* (1900) was *in memoriam* William Morris, who died in October 1896. Later works adopted folk-song themes: the 'Intermezzo' of the *St Paul's*

Suite (1913), a *Suite No.* 2 for military band (1911), *Six Choral Folk-Songs* (1916) and the opera about Shakespeare's Falstaff, *At the Boar's Head* (1924).[36] 'Like most people who come under the spell of folk-music,' wrote his daughter Imogen, 'he was soon saturated in the sound of the Dorian and Æolian modes, and for a time he found that open fifths and flattened sevenths were a necessary part of his life . . . Folk-songs finally banished all traces of Wagner from his work.'[37]

The 1890s threw up important breakthroughs in anthropology, with the publication of J. G. Frazer's monumental study *The Golden Bough* at the beginning of the decade. Holst's stepmother Mary Thorley Stone had been a follower of theosophy, and Gustav avidly read Frazer's *Silent Gods and Sun-Steeped Lands* (1896) and other works on world music and oriental mythology, becoming one of the first English musicians actively to incorporate Indian and Asian philosophy into his art. He spent the first years of the decade learning Sanskrit so that he could create his own reliable translations of Hindu and oriental texts such as the *Rig Veda* and *Bhagavad Gita*. His 'Sanskrit' compositions from the early years of the twentieth century are some of the most curious and unplaceable experiments in the English canon – if they are included in that canon at all. Over the years of writing the opera *Sita* (1899–1906), symphonic poem *Indra* (1903), *Hymns from the Rig Veda* (1907–8), chamber opera *Savitri* (1908), *The Cloud Messenger* (1910) and *Two Eastern Pictures* (1911), Holst cautiously introduced exotic textures and broke away from the conventional orchestration instilled in him at the Royal College. To modern ears, used to thinking of 'Eastern influences' as a sitar sample or a guest tabla drummer, these pieces will not sound especially 'oriental'. But for Holst, the moral underpinning of Hindu mythology gave his work a philosophical grounding in the concept of Unity, a universal interconnectedness of being and matter which he also found in his reading of Walt Whitman, and which found its correlative in the unity of musical performer and audience. 'What of being awakened at night by a thunderstorm and not knowing if one is oneself or the thunder?' he wrote in an essay on mysticism. 'Of reaching an indescribable state of existence where sound and colour are one?' Of the intimate, telepathic interactions of chamber-music performers, he believed, 'The ocean receives the drop of water, but the drop of water receives the consciousness of the ocean.'[38]

His most renowned work, the massive orchestral suite *The Planets*, dates from the savage heart of the First World War. Premiered shortly before the Armistice, on 29 September 1918, the heavenly bodies it describes are astrological rather than astronomical. Holst was indoctrinated into the mysteries of the zodiac in the company of his friend Clifford Bax on a holiday in 1913, and spent the next three years assembling the suite that would guarantee him fame beyond his own lifetime. As brother of the more famous Arnold, Clifford Bax was himself a composer, and both he and Holst became obsessed with casting birth charts for their contemporaries. Most of *The Planets*, which brought Holst a fame he was hardly psychologically or physically equipped to deal with, was written in the tranquillity of a cottage in rural Essex.

Holst was a prodigious rambler, and first visited the village of Thaxted while hiking in Essex in around 1914. On a hill overlooking the village he discovered a 300-year-old cottage, which he and his wife Isobel subsequently rented as a weekend and holiday retreat. Unlike Vaughan Williams, who volunteered for military service and went out to France as an ambulanceman aged forty-two, the sickly Holst was medically unfit for war. He spent longer and longer at Thaxted, in between his teaching posts at St Paul's School and Morley College in London; the huge church interior started him thinking about his music in spatial terms, and he found an affinity with the church's vicar, Conrad Noel, a socialist who brought a dash of unconventional, even counter-cultural behaviour to Thaxted's genteel village calm. Noel's worship included folk dances on the green, floral processions with burning incense, and a visibly left-wing agenda that saw him flying a red flag from the spire on May Day. Unusually for the time, he spliced plainchant recitals and medieval music into his daily service, and acknowledged folk song as the common man's birthright. Here was a wide-open mind with interests musical and political close to Holst's own, and the composer was soon acquainted with Noel's patron, Daisy, Countess of Warwick, a former aristocrat who had almost married Queen Victoria's youngest son Leopold but had recanted, become an admirer of George Bernard Shaw's radicalism and joined the Fabian Society. At her grand house, Easton Lodge, she cultivated a leftist think tank amid her monkeys and exotic pets, with house guests including Shaw, future Labour leader Ramsay MacDonald, trade unionist Manny Shinwell and, on one occasion, Charlie Chaplin. H. G. Wells rented a house on the Easton estate, and later, in the 1930s, Holst himself became one of her tenants.

St Mary's happened to be one of the largest country churches in the south of England, and Holst was transfixed by the architectural scale and the acoustic space. He yearned to fill it with sounds of his choosing, and with Conrad Noel devised the idea for an annual Thaxted music festival at Whitsun. The first such event, in 1916, unleashed a torrent of emotion in the buttoned-up music teacher. He imported his students from London to perform the repertoire, and Thaxted was deluged with music fourteen hours a day. The total immersion in music practice electrified Holst. 'It was a feast – an orgy,' he wrote to a friend. 'Four whole days of perpetual singing and playing, either properly arranged in the church or impromptu in various houses or still more impromptu in ploughed fields during thunderstorms, or in the train going home . . . The reason why we didn't do more is that we were not capable mentally or physically of realising heaven any further. It has been a revelation to me.'[39] Even in the midst of war, the first Whitsun Festival shines

Gustav Holst and performers in St Mary's, Thaxted,
at the first Whitsun Festival, 1916.

out as the moment English music lost its inhibitions and erupted into a cascade of spontaneous music-making. In this remote village, Holst created a four-day temporary autonomous zone, an orgy of colour, music and movement on the village green during which William Morris's desire for an art that would fill all corners of life and spill over into common experience was realised.

'I've learnt what "classical" means,' Holst wrote to Vaughan Williams after a visit to the Parthenon in Athens in 1919. 'It means something that sings and dances through sheer joy of existence.'[40] At subsequent Whitsun events, Holst was reminded of the importance of dance in mystic ritual, and he became increasingly drawn towards the Gnostic variety of religious experience hinted at in the Greek *Apocrypha*, nearly half a century before the discovery of the Dead Sea scrolls. His *Hymn of Jesus*, completed in 1917, contains his most sustained visionary music: a subdued, reverent introduction is followed by a choral section that sets a text from the *Apocrypha*'s *Acts of John*, used at the suggestion of Conrad Noel.

The piece uses experimental techniques that toy with time and space: the choir is instructed to be separated into two masses which fling calls and responses from side to side; the music itself is marked by motifs sung in parallel but at different speeds. This is the first known setting of any of the Gnostic scriptures, and the text still had no English translation, so the words in the score are Holst's own translation from the Greek,[41] including the lines: '*The Heav'nly Spheres make music for us . . ./ All things join in the dance! . . ./Ye who dance not, know not what we are knowing . . .*' The pagan ecstasy of this work seems saturated with the vivid experience he had later at the Parthenon: 'It seemed to sing to me in the sunlight,' he wrote on another occasion.[42]

By 1924 – incidentally, the year of Cecil Sharp's death – Holst's fevered creativity and rapid fame dragged him to the brink of a nervous breakdown. His sight and hearing were badly deteriorated; he could barely recognise the faces of his friends and family; noises became agonising; his conducting arm felt 'like a jelly overcharged with electricity'.[43] His new, larger residence in Thaxted's town square, The Steps, was the scene of his convalescence, or 'vegetation', as he put it. His daughter Imogen's description of the house suggests total communion with the English countryside: 'The garden was shut in by an old red brick wall that held the sunlight. Beyond the garden wall green fields rising to the windmill, and if you looked high enough you could see the tall grey spire of the church stretching towards the sky. The only sounds were the arguments of the swallows at the end of the garden, and the clamour of the ducks on the other side of the wall. In the early morning there would be the delicious smell of newly baked bread, and in the evening the still more delicious smell of smoke from innumerable wood fires.'[44] Late in life, Holst had arrived at his Earthly Paradise, and from this tranquil bower another new composition, with words by John Keats, took root of its own accord. 'It has been wonderful to sit all day in the garden and watch the [*Choral Symphony*] grow up alongside of the flowers and vegetables,' Holst wrote, 'and then to find that all is done!'[45]

Despite his poor health, Holst remained an inveterate walker, and he spent the last decade of his life merrily rambling around the Cotswolds, Suffolk, Dorset and the South Downs. In the summer of 1927 he met the eighty-seven-year-old Thomas Hardy and was given a personal tour of the fictional terrain of 'Egdon Heath', north of Weymouth, which acts as the ruthless, wild backcloth to *The Return of the Native*. The two hit it off: Holst was delighted to hear how Hardy had first heard *The Planets* on a gramophone belonging to T. E. Lawrence, author of *The Seven Pillars of Wisdom*, when his Tank Corps division were on an exercise nearby. Holst revisited Hardy's novel and found it coursing with sound, acoustic effects and music. It is the world Cecil Sharp sought to retrieve through his song-collecting excursions: morris dancers and mummers crop up in the action, and the landscape itself is repeatedly described in terms of acoustic hallucinations. Holst's astringent orchestral piece *Egdon Heath*, completed shortly after visiting Hardy, captures the novelist's eerie atmospheres and weight of foreclosing tragedy.

Holst's final years before his death, following stomach surgery in May 1934, included a walk along the Pilgrim's Way from London to Canterbury in preparation for some incidental music for a play by John Masefield and, in 1930, a return to the banks of the Thames in *Hammersmith*, a portrait of the area he remembered from the heady student years attending Morris's socialist pow-wows, underscored by the river that, as in *News from Nowhere*, flows on, unnoticed and unconcerned, echoing Holst's lasting belief that music was 'a condition of eternity'.[46]

The Great War churned up the turf of the British music revival as surely as it had muddied the pastures of Northern Europe. By 1918, out of seven who joined up, only three of Vaughan Williams's musician friends remained. George Butterworth was dead; the bipolar Ivor Gurney, wounded and gassed in 1917, suffered a nervous breakdown, driven crazy with love for a military nurse. Hubert Parry, that Establishment buttress who had taught many of these composers, was also gone. Cecil Sharp had become something of a nemesis to the English Folk Dance Society, whose earlier members had really only wanted to amuse themselves in the parlour with these quaint songs, not foist them upon a national prospectus. In the post-war climate of Depression, mass influenza, hunger and death, the Edwardian folk-song craze looked like so much drawing-room fluff for a generation of dinosaurs.

As the oldest of the musicians posted to the front, Vaughan Williams fared best on the surface of it, throwing himself into writing a new symphony. His first two had referenced London and the sea, but the third, known as the *Pastoral*, was intended specifically as an act of national healing. It's easy to hear it as the reconstructed picture of England's rolling landscapes in the mind of a soldier watching as France's verdant pastures and agricultural lands are silenced of birdsong and bombed into a bloody muck. It internalised a longing for home that prompted Gurney to write devout lines from the trenches: 'Strengthen Thou in me / The love of men here found . . . That, out of difficult ground, / Spring like flowers in barren deserts, or / Like light, or a lovely sound.'[47]

In these circumstances, the landscape that is recalled in Vaughan Williams's *Pastoral Symphony* is cast in a transfigured light – the unearthly glow of a Samuel Palmer orchard or the pre-lapsarian paradise of the Elizabethan Arcadian poets. Just as William Morris could only imaginatively apply his altruism to a future vision that aped the past, so Vaughan Williams's musical progressiveness ended up fenced in by the promise of Paradise. England as Eden – a key subtext of Gerald Finzi's supremely melancholy *Dies Natalis* (1924–39), evoking the first perceptions of a newborn child – is unchanging, debarred from its own progressive energies.

Holst's and Vaughan Williams's advocacy of new music in Britain held up a beacon to the section of their own generation, and the next, who ignored serialism and the most extreme forms of atonalism. The continental avant-garde of Stravinsky, Schoenberg and the Italian Futurists grabbed the headlines, but the British composers of the same period remained on an island of their own making. The Great War was significant in one sonic respect: for the first time ever, the sound of heavy artillery could be heard on English shores, across a hundred miles of Channel. In terms that suggested the very foundation stones of the Albion myth were being shaken, Hardy commemorated the moment in his poem 'Channel Firing':

> That night, your great guns, unawares,
> Shook all our coffins as we lay,
> And broke the chancel window-squares,
> We thought it was the Judgment Day [. . .]
>
> Again the guns disturbed the hour,
> Roaring their readiness to avenge,
> As far inland as Stourton Tower,
> And Camelot, and starlit Stonehenge.[48]

That was the first time any noise had travelled across the body of water separating the British Isles from mainland Europe. It intensified the realisation of how close the protective spell that had been cast over the island since 1066 had come to being broken. And over the islands, this 'land of lost content', the zephyr of nature mysticism continued to breathe, as if trying to weave the magic back.

3

The Island Spell

Come, heart, where hill is heaped on hill:
For there the mystical brotherhood
Of sun and moon and hollow and wood
And river and stream work out their will;
And God stands winding His lonely horn,
and time and the world are ever in flight . . .

W. B. Yeats, 'Into the Twilight', from *The Celtic Twilight* (1893)

'O Mole! the beauty of it! The merry bubble and joy, the thin, clear, happy call of the distant piping! Such music I never dreamed of, and the call in it is stronger even than the music is sweet! . . .'

The Mole, greatly wondering, obeyed. 'I hear nothing myself,' he said, 'but the wind playing in the reeds and rushes and osiers.'

Kenneth Grahame, *The Wind in the Willows*, Chapter VII: 'The Piper at the Gates of Dawn' (1908)

Paddy Flynn was 'a little bright-eyed old man, who lived in a leaky and one-roomed cabin in the village of Ballisodare'.[1] His stories, tumbling out of him with all the shape-shifting magic of Irish mythology, were retold by William Butler Yeats in *The Celtic Twilight* (1893), a collection of mainly prose meditations and folk tales set in 'the commonwealth of faery'. Yeats proclaimed his attraction to these stories was because they dared 'to mix heaven, hell, purgatory, and faeryland together, or even to set the heads of beasts to the bodies of men, or to thrust the souls of men into the heart of rocks'.[2]

Although the word Faery's similarity to 'fairy' has meant that it's difficult to hear it without the impression of effeminate tweeness, the notion of Faery has older and more malicious origins. 'Faerie', which appears in English for the first time in Edmund Spenser's epic poem *The Faerie Queen* (1590), mythologising the reign of Elizabeth I, was the land of the fae (medieval French for magical creatures). Throughout subsequent iterations in poetry and literature, the land of Faerie or Faery is a realm of enchantment accessed only by mortals who have been transported there or tricked into bondage or a pact with supernatural forces, as in the hero of the ballad 'Tam Lin'. Such characters, like visionary artists, are held in suspension between the earthly and spiritual realms.

The land of Faery was an attractive proposition to the late Victorian and Edwardian sensibility. The painter Richard Dadd's disturbing miniatures of tiny elfin folk gambolling among blades of grass and daisies are enduring images of the Victorian era, while the Tinkerbell of J. M. Barrie's *Peter Pan* (1904), the illustrations of children's books and Grimm's fairy tales by Arthur Rackham, the paintings of Joseph Noel Paton and Sidney Sime, and the fake photography of minuscule, winged, nubile humanoids taken by the young Elsie Wright and Frances Griffiths in 1917 at Cottingley point towards the more benign, whimsical image of the fairy that prevailed from the Edwardian period onwards. In Ireland, though, storytelling tradition has preserved the more malevolent aspect of the world of Faery, in the form of the Sídhe (pronounced 'shee'). Also known as the Fair Folk, these supernatural beings must be pacified with regular offerings and sacrifices, otherwise they enter the human dimension to wreak mischief and havoc on earth. The Sídhe are inextricably linked with the landscape, from ancient mounds and hills (the origin of the word itself) to the fairy rings found on expanses of grassland, which the spirits are said to guard jealously. Apparitions of the Sídhe are usually associated with the transitional times of day: dawn, dusk and twilight.

Such moments – the first glimmer of dawn sunbeams,

lengthening shadows, star-glitter permeating the darkening sky, 'a perilous pagan enchantment haunting the midsummer forest'[3] – saturate the music of Arnold Bax, the principal figure in what is sometimes referred to as the Celtic Twilight movement in British music, when the land without music was transformed into a sonorous Neverland. Born into an affluent London family, Bax was permitted the luxury of indulging artistic whims during his teens and pursuing a musical interest centring on his exposure to Wagner's *Tristan und Isolde*. The young Bax was radicalised by his uncle, a socialist philosopher and a friend of the late William Morris (the two had collaborated on writing a song called 'All for the Cause'). Cecil Sharp was among Bax's music teachers at the Hampstead Conservatory, but the nineteen-year-old Arnold's doors of perception were kicked open by Yeats's poetry. In 1902, together with his brother Clifford, he took a trip to Dublin to locate the source of this stream of inspiration. The Baxes met up with Yeats, who inducted them into the brotherhood that habitually gathered at the home of George Russell. A mystical poet who published under the pseudonym Æ, Russell was also a critic, painter, theosophist and vociferous champion of Irish nationalism, which sought to defend the Republic of Ireland against British sovereignty.[4] Bax's exposure to this potent admixture of mysticism and radical politics fuelled much of his conflicted relationship with his own home country for the rest of his life, making him distinctly uncomfortable with, for example, his 1942 appointment as Master of the King's Musick.

But it was Ireland's mercurial folklore that supplied Bax with the dominant voice in his compositions. Beginning with *Cathaleen-na-Hoolihan* (1905), written three years after encountering Yeats, the list of his tone poems (spanning the years 1909–31) reads like the contents of an Arts and Crafts compendium of decadent fairy tales: *In the Faery Hills*, *Rosc-catha*, *Spring Fire*, *Nympholept*, *The Garden of Fand*, *November Woods*, *Tintagel*, *The Happy Forest*,

The Tale the Pine Trees Knew. A sensualist and erotic adventurer (in 1910 he pursued a Ukrainian girl he was infatuated with from St Petersburg to Kiev), Bax created lush, richly foliated sound-forests that attempted to conjure up a sense of narcotic abandon and the intoxicating conjunction of myth and landscape. *In the Faery Hills* (1909) takes its cue from a section in Yeats's *Wanderings of Oisin* in which the Sídhe force a troubadour to sing them a song. Aware of their reputation as festive types, Oisin launches into his most joyous ditty. To the Sídhe, it still sounds like the most depressing dirge they've ever heard, so they toss his harp into a pool and whisk him away to show him how to party like it's AD 99. Bax claimed to have been 'possessed by Kerry's self'[5] while writing it.

In the passage from *The Celtic Twilight* called 'A Visionary', Yeats might have been describing Bax himself: 'This spiritual eagerness draws to him all those who, like himself, seek for illumination or else mourn for a joy that has gone.' The composer bestowed the title *Into the Twilight* on another piece from 1908 in honour of his friendship with the poet, stating that it 'seeks to give a musical impression of the brooding quiet of the Western Mountains at the end of twilight, and to express something of the sense of timelessness and hypnotic dream which veils Ireland at such an hour'.

Since his reappearance in the Romantic poetry of Keats, Shelley and Wordsworth, the Great God Pan had become a modern icon in European literature and art, heralding an abiding artistic interest in the Arcadian age and the recurrence of primal urges at the heart of the civilised world. Algernon Swinburne's poem *Atalanta in Calydon*, a slice of 'Naughty Nineties' decadence, transfixed many artists of its time, including Bax and Sir Granville Bantock. The persistence of Pan provided a welcome anarchic rupture in the rigid social conventions of the final years of Victoria's reign. The Horned One even made a cameo appearance in Kenneth Grahame's children's classic *The Wind*

The Great God Pan materialises in Kenneth Grahame's *The Wind in the Willows* (1908): one of many examples of the pagan resurgence.

in the Willows (1908), in a hallucinatory chapter whose title, 'The Piper at the Gates of Dawn', would be appropriated sixty years later as part of Syd Barrett's psychedelic juvenilia. At the same time, Pan cavorted into Europe's classical-music canon as well: Debussy's *Printemps* (1887), *Prelude à l'après-midi d'un faune* (1894), *Danses sacrées et profanes* (1904) and *Syrinx* (1913), Ravel's *Daphnis et Chloë* (1909) and Stravinsky's *The Rite of Spring* (1913) all contain prominent roles for flutes, piccolos and harps – instrumental textures redolent of classical antiquity. Britain's contribution includes Bantock's choral ballet *The Great God Pan* (1920) and *Pagan Symphony* (completed 1927), both painting fantastical sound pictures of frisky nymphs and satyrs, and brimming with the energy of eternal delight.

Stoke Bishop, the area of Bristol where I spent my childhood, is full of road names quaintly suggestive of pagan antiquity: Roman Way, Julian Road (as in Julius Caesar), Druid Hill, Druid Stoke Avenue, Coombe Dingle, Ivywell Road, Rockleaze Road ('leaze', suggesting leys, is a common suffix in Bristolian street names). A Mariners Drive leads up from the remains of a Roman harbour. When I looked at the history of the area, though, I found that many of these gnarly monikers were imposed on the area on either side of the First World War, when the district expanded rapidly and many of the houses and local amenities were built. It's a small indication of the feeling in the air in the immediate post-Great War years, of restoration in the vernacular of a comfortingly ancient, leafy rural past. Just as the composers of this period homed in on the Tudor and Elizabethan age, in architecture too the Victorian 'Gothick' revival gave way to a reductionist 'Tudorbethan' style, with herringbone brickwork, tall clustered chimneys, black-and-white half-timbered facades and mullioned leaded windows. Carried into the twentieth century by the likes of Edwin Lutyens, 'mock-Tudor' semi-detached housing became the defining feature of suburban spread in southern England, allowing families to feel they owned a miniaturised stately home of their own.[6] Appropriately, the Public Hall at Shirehampton, near the areas of Bristol mentioned above and another product of the Edwardian period of construction, was the venue for the 1920 world premiere of Vaughan Williams's *The Lark Ascending*.

Bristol's Folk House Cafe is a small community centre hidden behind the shopfronts of Park Street, a steep thoroughfare that connects the university tower with the Council House and Cathedral. In 1920–1 the Folk House was briefly utilised by Rutland Boughton, a composer originally from Birmingham, to run the Bristol Festival School 'for the collective and individual study of music'.[7] In fact, the 200 or so pupils were being trained – in singing, drama, dance, gesture and 'eurhythmics' – for a very specific goal: the realisation of Boughton's idealistic dream of founding a national music institution to rival Wagner's Bayreuth in the town of Glastonbury. Boughton – communist, vegetarian and suffragette sympathiser – conceived the idea of putting on music dramas in outdoor rural locations before the war, and had already been collaborating on a monumental operatic cycle based on the life of King Arthur with a librettist, Reginald Ramsden Buckley. Wagner was the role model: they admired his invocation of a 'German oversoul' to synthesise his operas from the sprawling collections of stories that made up the Ring of the Nibelung legend. After war was declared, such views could no longer profitably be held, and Boughton and Ramsden looked to the Arthurian stories, already enshrined in Malory's *Le Morte d'Arthur* and Tennyson's *Idylls of the King*, as 'national scriptures', engraved with essential qualities that could be mapped onto the 'British oversoul': 'Merlin as Britain's Isaiah, Galahad her Parsifal, Arthur her [arche]type of Manhood'.[8] The pair completed two operas, *The Birth of Arthur* and *The Round Table*, before permanently falling out in 1915.

These works were developed and performed at an extraordinary community venture, the first Glastonbury Festival, beginning in 1914. Boughton and his common-law wife Christina Walshe won the trust of the local artistic community and hoped to build a state-of-the-art amphitheatre in the town. In the event, despite the patronage of the Clark family (the famous shoe-manufacturing dynasty, based in nearby Street) and the public advocacy of George Bernard Shaw, they only scraped enough private funding to put on regular concerts at Glastonbury's rather poky Assembly Rooms. Their productions were typically British examples of making-do with the limitations of a cramped space and budget. Dispensing with lavish operatic scenery, Walshe painted impressionistic line-art backdrops, and developed a method of staging that used the chorus as singers, dancers and scenery (the battlements of Camelot castle, for instance, were delineated by four stout yeomen). Accompaniment came not from an orchestra, but a single piano.

If Canterbury, the locus of pilgrimage, is the official capital of the Church of England, Glastonbury has long been its heathen obverse. The enormous Tor, or earthen mound, that dominates its topography, topped with a lonely ruined tower, has exerted a magnetic pull on alternative pilgrims drawn by the local legends of the first English Christian church, the alleged hiding place of the Holy Grail, secreted somewhere by Joseph of Arimathea, and its supposed conjunction of ley lines and earth energies. The writer and occultist Dion Fortune, a Glastonbury resident in the early 1920s, believed the Tor to be a 'Hill of Vision' at the centre of a 'gateway to the Unseen' – a spiritual-architectural complex sheltering the slumbering spirit of Albion.[9]

Boughton settled in Glastonbury in order to create his own conditions for carrying out his dreams, building a musical Jerusalem far from the metropolis. Music performed outdoors, in the unpredictable acoustics of the open air, always appealed to him, and the summer schools he ran in order to make money placed emphasis on communal activities such as games, picnics and pilgrimages to romantic and historic local beauty spots. The Glastonbury Festival continued until 1927, a valuable platform for new British music and an experimental base for new ideas and crazes to be worked through. One of Boughton's most regularly performed works – which still holds the record for the longest first run of any opera in history – was *The Immortal Hour* (1914), a musical version of a Celtic-tinged 'psychic drama' written by one Fiona Macleod (the alter ego of mystic poet William Sharp),

A scene from Rutland Boughton's opera *The Immortal Hour* (1914), the main attraction at the earliest Glastonbury Festivals.

who, it was claimed, lived in contemplative isolation on a far-off Hebridean island. A vogue for ancient Greek culture gave rise to a separate Festival of Greek Drama and Boughton's opera *Alkestis* (1922). But the Arthurian cycle lay at the heart of the annual events, and the fact of their being performed at the ancient king's supposed burial site added an appropriate frisson. The festival began to lose momentum in the mid-1920s and was wound up in 1927. It left its mark on British musical life: the Festival Players made several tours of the country, and *The Immortal Hour* was rapturously received in London and Germany. Boughton effectively committed professional suicide, though, by outing himself as a communist in the late 1920s, and lived the rest of his life in seclusion in the Forest of Dean.

Something of the flavour of the conflicting claims upon the soul of Glastonbury at the time can be gleaned from John Cowper Powys's 1932 novel, *A Glastonbury Romance*, in which an idealistic mayor who tries to turn the town into a centre for Grail worship gets caught in the crossfire between a group of anarchists and Marxists who have formed a commune and the profitable designs of a local business tycoon. At the beginning of the 1970s Glastonbury's peculiar energies were rediscovered by the hippy movement, kicking off an event that has grown into a huge annual pop festival, a temporary city that appears for three days and then vanishes. The Hill of Vision shows no sign of shutting its eyes.

In the heart of London, between the meat markets of Smithfield and the cultural oasis of the Barbican Centre, lies the twelfth-century Church of St Sepulchre, famous for its stained-glass windows commemorating British musicians, including the composer John Ireland. In the tall, arched John Ireland Memorial Window, four roundels contain emblems outlining the haunts of a very private composer's mental landscape: a castle from Jersey; the tower of St

Luke's Church in Chelsea, where Ireland was an organist; Maiden Castle, an ancient fortification in Dorset; and Rock Mill, the windmill in West Sussex where he spent his final years. A holy boy, and cattle from Harry Watt's film *The Overlanders* (1946), which Ireland soundtracked, hover in the centre, enigmatic sigils. Above a profile of Ireland's face – looking somewhat overcome by this blazing tribute – in a whirl of vivid greens, mauves and gilt, St John the Divine clambers above his golden eagle towards a vision of a New Jerusalem.

John Ireland, who led an outwardly quiet and uneventful life, revelled in the hidden dimensions of the English landscape: his internal radar seemed biologically tuned in to the spirit of place. While waiting for a train to Deal at Charing Cross station in London one day in 1906, Ireland made a chance purchase that would zap his future music with a powerful charge. As his biographer vividly describes it, the book 'caught his casual eye and held it as if two contacts had fused together'.[10] Unlike any of the usual travellers' potboilers, Sidney Sime's drawing on the jacket of Arthur Machen's *The House of Souls* depicted a black mannequin with gigantic eyes, flamboyant antlers and a pot belly, adopting the lotus position in what looks like a field of fungi. Its skinny arms end in sinuously elongated fingers, upraised as if in supplication or surrender. Ireland bought the book on sight and was introduced to Machen's eerie, occult narrative, where the surface of everyday life could suddenly admit beings from extreme antiquity: terra cognita reverts to incognita in the blink of an eye. In *The House of Souls* a young girl with a vivid imagination and an interest in fairies is initiated by her nurse into a pagan witch cult and is eventually found dead, possibly after Pan is summoned by the coven's 'scarlet ceremonies'. The following year Ireland lapped up Machen's next book, *The Hill of Dreams*, in which an aura of unnameable evil lingers around an ancient Roman hill fort. The main character becomes so fixated on the place that he is subsumed into a

First edition of Arthur Machen's *The House of Souls* (1906).

perpetual hallucination in which he only sees figures from old times. It provoked in Ireland 'a world of hidden, forbidden beauty connected with Nature . . . now entirely overlaid by science and civilization'.[11]

No one who had not read Machen's fiction could properly understand his music, Ireland once declared. The Welsh writer's supernatural prose recalls Symbolists such as H. P. Lovecraft, Algernon Blackwood, Alfred Lord Dunsany and Arthur Symons: connoisseurs of the weird and uncanny. Machen, like Yeats, Aleister Crowley and *Dracula* author Bram Stoker, was a member of the Golden Dawn, a secret society dedicated to exploring Hermetic philosophy and magic. Ireland's compositions contain several explicit dedications to Machen, including the *Legend* for piano and orchestra (1933), which was triggered by a vision that assailed him while walking on Harrow Hill on the Sussex Downs, where he was living in the nearby village of Ashington. The site is richly layered in ancient history, containing Neolithic flint mines and the remains of a Bronze Age settlement, while later in the Middle Ages a leper colony stood on the same spot, alongside a church with a small spyhole cut in the wall known as the 'lepers' squint'. The opening and closing pages of *Legend*'s score depict the priest's weekly trudge up the rugged Lepers' Way to conduct the service. But after just over a minute the strings and brass pick up the pace and a cymbal crash wipes the screen and transforms the scene; the piano picks out slightly queasy, halting dance steps. The passage recreates an incident when, alone on the hill, Ireland was settling down to his picnic lunch. He became aware that a group of children had begun dancing in front of him, only their feet made no sound, no shouts issued from their lips, and they were dressed in clothes apparently handed down from an earlier era. His eyes darted away for an instant, and when he looked back the children had vanished. He duly informed Machen about this vision by letter, and received a one-line postcard in reply: 'So you've seen them too!'

From 1907–14 Ireland took long annual summer holidays in the Channel Islands. His eight-shilling boat fare conveyed him to the genteel but relatively undeveloped resorts of Jersey, where there was still no traffic and where he could explore the miles of bare, wide sandy beaches and savour the ancient dolmens and burial mounds being excavated in the interior. Music like *The Forgotten Rite* (1913) and the piano suites *Decorations* (also 1913) and *Sarnia* (1940) were directly inspired by the Channel Islands, and their geographical position midway between Britain and France is symbolically paralleled in the style, which has sympathies with the tonal impressionism of Ravel and Debussy, as well as their pantheistic overtones.

Ireland's bittersweet reflectiveness was ideally suited to smaller-scale chamber and solo piano music, much of it steeped in antiquarian melancholy, with watercolour tranquillity giving way to nocturnes where revelling spirits come out to create black magic. *Decorations* contains three short sections: 'The Island Spell', which arrived almost fully formed while Ireland was bathing in the sea at Jersey; 'Moon-Glade'; and 'The Scarlet Ceremonies', whose winding, incantatory melodies recall the evocative soundworld of Debussy's *Preludes*. In the score, the first two movements are prefaced by quotations from Arthur Symons; the last by a passage from Machen's *The White People*: 'Then there are the Ceremonies, which are all of them important, but some are more delightful than others: there are the White Ceremonies, and the Green Ceremonies, and the Scarlet Ceremonies. The Scarlet Ceremonies are the best . . .'[12] In filleting out these lines from Machen's prose, Ireland gestures towards what, as a gay man, he was forced to conceal: the ecstasy of physical love. He would often allude to his (male, younger) lovers by citations from classical literature or Housman's *A Grecian Lad*, one of several of the poet's works that Ireland set to music. He kept a statuette of Pan as a goat god on his piano, a reminder of the pagan association with rapacious lust. *The Forgotten Rite* (1913), which comes out of the same period of creativity, conjures up Pan mischievously disrupting a solemn, churchy atmosphere. 'I am far from repelled by an admixture of the occult and magic, of a genuine kind,'[13] he wrote to one correspondent in typically understated style.

Sarnia, completed after Ireland had spent a year living on Guernsey,[14] is closely connected to the pagan origins of Guernsey's store of prehistoric burial chambers and rock monuments, imagining the kind of rites and jamborees that might have occurred round the tumbled stones such as Le Trépied. The score for the first part, 'Le Catioroc', contains a passage from *De Situ Orbis*, a text by Roman writer Pomponius Mela dating from 50 BCE: 'All day long, heavy silence broods, and a certain hidden terror lurks there. But at nightfall gleams the light of fires; the chorus of Ægipans [fauns] resounds on every side: the shrilling of flutes and the clash of cymbals re-echo the waste shores of the sea.' That mini-narrative encapsulates the motion of many of Ireland's pieces, as a calm surface is overrun by more mysterious elemental forces, beings or visions.

Ireland ended up living permanently in the Weald of West Sussex, in a converted windmill overlooking Chanctonbury Ring, an ancient hill fort topped by a circle of trees reputed to have been used by a witch coven in the seventeenth century.[15] The landscape of the south of England also exerted its effect on pieces such as the 1923 *Cello Sonata* (referencing The Devil's Jumps at the remote Treyford Hill), and *Mai-Dun* (1920–1), which took him to the Iron Age hill fort of Maiden Castle in Dorset, scene of a brutal massacre in 43 CE by Roman legions under Vespasian, when they besieged the native Britons holding it, thus ending a continuous occupation of 800 years. The extent of the battle was not known until seventeen years after Ireland's composition, when archaeologists

Hill of dreams: Maiden Castle, Dorset, the Iron Age fortress that inspired John Ireland's *Mai-Dun*, photographed in the 1930s.

fully excavated the site, but he seems to have innately understood the scale of the attack: *Mai-Dun* is a violent, martial soundscape of swords crashing against shields, stones whizzing from slings and blaring clarions. John Ireland remains a lesser-known figure in twentieth-century English music, but his quiet, determined response to the psychogeography of Britain's pre-Christian national terrain is unparalleled in these inter-war years.

'I have never been able to understand the sentiment of patriotism, the love of empire: it has always seemed to me so empty and intangible an idea . . . so supremely unimportant as regards the things that matter – which are all the common heritage of humanity, without distinction of race or nationality . . .'[16] So wrote one opinionated young pup, starting out a career as a music critic in London, just after the Great War's outbreak. Philip Heseltine, then aged twenty, would shortly become the British music scene's answer to Wyndham Lewis. As a writer, bombardiering critic and – under the alias Peter Warlock – composer, his brash voice resounded throughout the national music discourse of the inter-war years. His transcriptions of 570 songs in original manuscript played a huge role in the archaeology of English Early and Renaissance Music; he published nine books and an enormous amount of articles and reviews; as Peter Warlock, he left a small but exquisite body of work, including more than one hundred songs and a handful of jewels for chamber orchestra and piano.

He developed an early infatuation with the music of Frederick Delius, and eventually wrote his biography in 1923. Any musician who found themselves championed by Heseltine the critic could count themselves fortunate; his praise was missionary and worshipful, but his tongue could be exceptionally sharp. 'A rather uncomfortable rhinoceros with flabby legs' was how he once described the music of Vaughan Williams. He shared many cultural interests with Vaughan Williams, but that fellow feeling couldn't stop him calling Ralph 'one of those for whom mysticism means mistiness and vacuity rather than exceptional clarity of vision'[17] (he later retracted this view).

As a conscientious objector, Heseltine evaded conscription into the army – his medical examiner reported an 'inability to micturate when mentally excited'. But the psychological effects of the backdrop of conflict, and the constant threat of air raids on the capital, took their toll. Always a volatile personality, in 1915 he was enduring depression and mood swings, and he became notorious for riotous, unconventional public behaviour, often fuelled by alcohol: stripping naked in public, flamboyant displays of acrobatic dancing, riding his motorbike at high speed through village high streets. London became a 'charnel house', a 'great cesspool' from which he had to escape in order to channel his 'impotent rage against the barbarous conditions of human life in this the 20th century'.

Around 1915 he was part of an artistic circle that met at London's Cafe Royal which included Jacob Epstein, Augustus John, Aldous Huxley and D. H. Lawrence. Already a disciple of Nietzsche, Heseltine was electrified by his meeting with Lawrence, who encouraged him to 'overcome this great flux of disintegration, further analysis, self analysis'.[18] The novelist was preparing to set up a utopian community in Florida, and Heseltine was shortlisted to take part, and even tried to persuade Delius to abandon his French country retreat and come on board. Among many stalled entrepreneurial ventures, he attempted to publish Lawrence's novel *The Rainbow* privately, before violently quarrelling with him and appearing as a less than sympathetic character in *Women in Love* (he also appears in Huxley's *Antic Hay* and a story by Jean Rhys, among others).

Heseltine was a master of the Monty Pythonesque pseudonym;

his invented names for himself included Huanebango Z. Palimpsest, Apparatus Criticus and Rab Noolas ('saloon bar' reversed). In November 1916 he signed himself 'Peter Warlock' in an issue of *The Music Student* magazine; he used the name – signifying wizard, magus, enchanter and scoundrel – on all his musical compositions until the end of his life. It also resonated with his growing interest in the theory and practice of magic. He roomed at the Dublin house of spirit medium and automatic writer Hester Dowden in 1917, where he was exposed to divination, Tarot reading, astrology and seances, and hungrily read such magickal tomes as Madame Blavatsky's *The Secret Doctrine*, Eliphas Levi's *History of Transcendental Magic* and James Morgan Pryse's *The Apocalypse Unsealed* (a commentary on the Revelation of St John that provided Yeats's introduction to the occult). During this year in Ireland he also retreated to a tiny windswept island off the west coast, where he devoted himself to studying Celtic languages such as Welsh, Manx, Breton and Cornish. The seclusion also freed up his artistic voice, and he composed ten of his most celebrated songs in the space of a fortnight: perfectly formed short settings of late medieval and Elizabethan verses with wistful melodies whose whiff of the antique is tempered with a spray of contemporary atonality. Of his writing at this time, he told a correspondent how his occult experiences had allowed an enchanted communion with his art: 'I have already received very definite and detailed communications *concerning music* from sources which the unheeding world call supernatural: and that there is unlimited power behind these sources.'[19]

Warlock's capacity for self-education was stupendous. Earlier, he had put in the hours at the British Library, poring over the scores of the Tudor polyphonists Byrd, Gibbons, Tomkins and Farnaby; his pioneering analytical work chimed with the interests of Vaughan Williams and Holst, and his book *The English Ayre* (1926) went a long way towards restoring Elizabethan music to the

Composers of the Celtic twilight: (clockwise from top left) Rutland Boughton, John Ireland, Peter Warlock, Ernest J. Moeran.

English repertoire. Having been initially critical of the folk-song revival, Warlock followed the Celtic route back into traditional music, and his settings of ancient song form the bedrock of his lasting reputation as a composer. Yet he was broad-minded enough to recognise the importance of European avant-garde composers such as Bartók, Berg and Schoenberg.

Warlock's unchained critical dagger blooded most of the musical fraternity, and after crossing the line once too often, he was fired as editor of his own journal, *The Sackbut*. He decamped to his mother's house in Wales, where he transcribed a mass of

Elizabethan music and wrote his Delius biography. In 1925 he transplanted his rowdy persona to the peaceful Kent village of Eynsford, with another of Britain's pastoral composers, Ernest J. Moeran.

Their residence lasted three years, during which time they managed to scandalise the village. Warlock had a manservant, Hal Collins (actually a Maori called Te Akua), who would fill up on stout and break into tribal dances around the huge bonfires Warlock loved to ignite in the garden. Warlock was seen riding his motorbike in the nude, and the many visitors to the house – including Arnold Bax, Augustus John, Constant Lambert and Lord Berners – would often end up stripping off too; some even wandered naked into local shops to collect food, or were pushed around the streets in a wheelbarrow. Warlock's girlfriend Barbara Peache was also in attendance, and the couple provoked scandal by indulging in threesomes with local girls. The house where they stayed was on the main road through town, with a chapel next door and the Five Bells pub conveniently opposite. Faced with the choice between virtue or vice in such close proximity, they chose the last every time, frequently staggering back to their cottage with a huge earthenware jug filled from the pub's beer taps. On Sunday mornings, raucous sea shanties and folk songs would issue from the house in an attempt to drown out the hymns being sung in the neighbouring chapel. And on more than one occasion one or other member of the household managed to run their car into a ditch or hedgerow.[20]

In the years immediately before Eynsford, Warlock had made a degree of peace with certain aspects of the pastoral school, going on folk-collecting trips with Moeran and dedicating his *Three Carols* (1923) to Vaughan Williams. He had also increased his capacity for drinking and experimented with cannabis and cocaine, at the time available from chemists' shops.[21] During the three years in Kent, Warlock appeared to be living through an adolescence put on hold since leaving Eton in 1912. Moeran, known to the company as Jack, spent much of the time in depression.

The son of an Irish father and East Anglian mother, Moeran grew up in the remote Norfolk village of Bacton-on-Sea, where he discovered the fishermen's folk-singing sessions in the local pub while still a schoolboy. Hearing Vaughan Williams's *Norfolk Rhapsody* in 1913, based around the songs carousel by King's Lynn fishermen, had a strong impact. Independently from Cecil Sharp and Vaughan Williams, Moeran collected more than 150 songs from the region, and later from the west coast of Ireland, and 'discovered' one of the most prolific sources of folk tunes, Harry Cox of Great Yarmouth, who went on to become a celebrated face of the traditional folk revival, recording more than 200 songs and appearing frequently on television until his death in 1971. Moeran remained suspicious of the 'bourgeoisation' of folk, impatient with 'those who set about the teaching of folk-songs in schools, or the organising of garden fêtes etc . . . Well-intentioned as these efforts may be, they evolve something quite apart from the art of those who have it in their very bones, handed down from father to son.'[22] Another alumnus of Parry and Stanford's Royal College, after the war Moeran studied composition with John Ireland, and his first-hand exposure to folk music – which Warlock approved of – was later funnelled into such works as his two orchestral *Rhapsodies*, the cello and violin concertos, and most of his piano music. *Two Legends* (1924) includes 'A Folk-Story' and 'Rune', in which he tried to evoke 'old forgotten far-off things and battles long ago'.[23] Moeran's sonic landscapes are punctuated with the eruptions of folk dances and tunes, like the pagan dances on Egdon Heath in Hardy's *Return of the Native*. He was not solely a pastoralist: like his contemporaries William Walton and Constant Lambert, he also enlivened some of his music with jazz harmonics.

At Eynsford, while Warlock managed to keep working through bouts of prolonged mental blockage, Moeran's output ran down to a near standstill – a three-year 'lost weekend' that all but annihilated his fragile sense of artistic self-belief. A chunk of shrapnel remained lodged close to his brain, an injury sustained in the war which was most likely responsible for his continuing bouts of illness and black moods. Meanwhile, Warlock transcribed many Elizabethan lute songs and wrote a good deal of his own there; he also composed his best-known work, the *Capriol Suite*, a vigorous piece of mock Tudor for chamber string ensemble based on old French dances; and published *The English Ayre* and a biography of turbulent Italian Renaissance composer Carlo Gesualdo.

After abandoning the village in 1928, Warlock crashed and burned out in London. In a climate of looming economic depression, and confronted by the smoking remains of the bridges he had burnt with his vituperative journalism, he found work opportunities drying up and his own creative energies reduced to selling carols, written in drunken stupors, to the Christmas editions of daily newspapers. His last significant contract was organising a festival for the old expat Delius on home turf in 1929. Then, in the kitchen of his Chelsea basement flat in December 1930, he gassed himself to death. The last song he wrote, 'The Fox', is one of the most chilling in the entire canon of English song. The text, written by his friend and drinking partner, the poet Bruce Blunt, describes a stuffed animal's head mounted behind the bar at a pub of the same name in Hampshire. Warlock – whose own facial features had a touch of the Reynard – wrote the arrangement in eighteen hours while still inebriated. He weirdly merges with the plight of the animal, which mocks onlookers even in its humiliated, stuffed-and-mounted condition. Warlock's more than one hundred songs, including his desolate 'Corpus Christi Carol' (1919), suffused with fugitive childlike memory, and his devastatingly crepuscular setting of Yeats's poem *The Curlew* for voice and string quartet (1920–2), are as significant within the lexicon of English vocal music as those of John Dowland and Henry Purcell. A later writer described Warlock's 'ebullience of the willow-herb that grows on ruined bomb-sites,'[24] a phrase that encapsulates the artistic scavenging of the composer-critic: his work cuts to the essence of his English inheritance.

After Warlock's death, Moeran's work entered a distinctly different phase. He was drawn towards Ireland and in 1938 made a home in Kenmare, County Kerry, inhaling from the pot of Celtic legend that had blown the mind of his friend Arnold Bax. The evocative landscapes of his *Symphony in G Minor* (1938) are permanently clouded over with heavy ambience; *Lonely Waters*, composed in the mid-1920s, is based on a fragment of song from the Norfolk Broads, which speak of the waters as a refuge *'where no one they shall me find'*. It could be a watchword for Moeran's life, in which he was repeatedly drawn to out-of-the-way locations, from the west of Ireland to the hilly folds of Herefordshire – one of his favourite romantic walks with his wife Peers was across Hergest Ridge, made famous in the mid-1970s by Mike Oldfield's ambient follow-up to *Tubular Bells*. Unlike, say, Vaughan Williams, Moeran was hardly a public figure; he held no academic office, producing his music at his own pace from a private reserve of deep sorrow, buffeted by outdoor winds, darkling storm clouds and the changeable climates of the British and Irish coastlines. He once said that his ideal situation would be a job minding a signal box at a remote railway junction crossed by two trains a week. He died in 1950 in appropriately solitary circumstances, toppling off the end of a pier at Kenmare during a violent storm.

The classical-music establishment likes to present the British music renaissance as a genteel village green, a sedate, controlled environment where dressing in Sunday best is required. But even before the Great War, the gentle, unchanging patterns of the past were already being torn up by the encroachments of a folk-inspired, mystical, socialist breed of national consciousness. After it, a flock of pagan, rural composers subtly flouted conventions and conducted a riotous orgy of sound on this hallowed ground. But it was a ground that was vanishing even as the music flourished – without warning, the joyous spring that Holst had witnessed at Thaxted turned inexorably to summer, waned, and the harvest was gathered in.

Benjamin Britten's *War Requiem*, commissioned to inaugurate the rebuilt Coventry Cathedral in 1962, was a sinewy memorial to Britain's Second World War dead, with its Wilfred Owen poems conveying a new generation's disgust with war that would have been foreign to the Elgar of *The Spirit of England*, dedicated in 1917 to 'the memory of our Glorious Men'. Britten's vocal settings of Baudelaire, Blake, Keats, Michelangelo, Rimbaud and Shelley place him squarely in the visionary continuum; he took Holst's interest in orientalism a stage further by adapting South-East Asian and Japanese aesthetics into works like *Prince of the Pagodas* (1956) and *Curlew River* (1964); and his colonisation of the secluded marshes of Snape for his Aldeburgh Festival on the East Suffolk coast fits the pattern set by Rutland Boughton in creating an autonomous zone in rural retreat. His folk-song settings remain popular, but hearing them sung in the extraordinary voice of his colleague and lover, Peter Pears, shows just how far such material had become distorted from its source when rewired as art music. In any case, in the grey, exhausted Britain of the late 1940s and early 50s there was no mood for a solemn national music – American popular music was providing more immediate pleasures. The post-war folk revival would renegotiate its position as a music of grass-roots politics and social protest.

The mourning of late summer as it reaches its autumnal tipping point; the pining for faded youth or lost love; the elegy for the fallen in war; otherworldly dimensions glimpsed but not touched; and the yearning for a distant home: British music is uniquely attuned to these moments and sentiments, for it is finally this sense of loss, of achievement slipping away like sand in a glass, that is at the heart of the British experience over the course of the twentieth century.

In the years before the Great War, Britain's railway network, far from accelerating the decline of agricultural and rural communities, worked in perfect harness with them. In 1902 the national horse population numbered three and a half million, pulling more than a million horse-drawn vehicles – the numbers were actually boosted by the need to transport goods from rail depots and local stations to their final delivery points. By the late 1920s the latter figure had collapsed to less than 50,000 as cars and lorries took over and the road network slowly etched its way in bolder lines across the landscape. The figures paint a graphic picture of massive modernisation and demographic change, but Britain's self-image as a rural Arcadia remained unaltered. In 1926 the government was headed by a Conservative prime minister, Stanley Baldwin, whose book, *On England*, appealed to an ageless notion of the British oversoul. A typical passage rhapsodises about 'the tinkle of the hammer on the anvil of the country smithy, the corncrake on a dewy morning, the sound of the scythe against the whetstone, and the sight of a plough team coming over the brow of a hill, the sight that has been seen in England since England was a land, and may be seen in England long after the Empire has perished and every works in England has ceased to function, for centuries the one eternal sight of England'.[25] Just as William Morris conceived of his socialist Earthly Paradise, the Tory Baldwin insisted on seeing the packhorse on the down, even as the down was being girdled by a bypass or capped with a new suburban housing project. His English soundscape was fading for ever.

In the slow drift towards war in the 1930s, 'national music' devotees and rival cosmopolitan claims to modernity began to engage in light skirmishes. In his counter-blast 'study of music in decline', *Music Ho!* (1934), Constant Lambert fired a broadside at 'the admirably meant endeavours of William Morris and his followers to combat the products of those dark satanic mills with green and unpleasant handwoven materials while its heartiness conjures up the hideous *faux bonhomie* of the hiker, noisily wading his way through the petrol pumps of metroland, singing obsolete sea shanties'.[26] For the post-Second World War baby-boom generation, the antiquarian eye would have to open even wider, and turn in a different direction to catch the fading twilight.

4

The Iron Muse

The secret of these hills was stone, and cottages
Of that stone made,
And crumbling roads
That turned on sudden hidden villages.

Now over these small hills, they have built the concrete
That trails black wire;
Pylons, those pillars
Bare like nude giant girls that have no secret.

From Stephen Spender, 'The Pylons' (1933)

I'm a rambler, I'm a rambler from Manchester way,
I get all my pleasure the hard moorland way.
I may be a wage slave on Monday,
But I am a free man on Sunday.

From Ewan MacColl, 'The Manchester Rambler' (1932)

You ascend the stairs to the top room of the Princess Louise on High Holborn, central London, where the dark wallpaper's elaborate floral pattern is shrouded in a nebulous fug of cigarette smoke, the windows bubble with condensation and the air reeks of ale-soaked carpet, sour breath and armpits. The audience is mostly young, between school-leaving age and their mid-twenties, and many have brought along acoustic and Spanish guitars.

The room's collective eyes are turned on the fellow with the polo neck and trim beard, sitting athwart a reversed chair, elbow on the seat back, hand half-cupped over his right ear to sharpen the focus of his pitch as, unaccompanied, he recounts the fate of

Lord Randall or the tragedy of an exploding coal mine. Although clearly not born to singing, his voice has an enthusiast's heartiness, its nasal overtones teetering unstably between Scottish and Lancastrian accents.

This picture is from somewhere in the mid-1950s, and it is being reproduced in dozens of similar folk clubs around Britain. It is an image of the folk singer and his milieu that has endured long after such gatherings have all but dispersed, and yet the post-war club format was invented with a defined social and political agenda, and as a conscious reaction against previous manifestations of folk music. How did it begin, and what were the driving forces behind the small handful of individuals responsible?

The brown envelopes marked KV-2/23175-2176 and KV 2/2701, held in the National Archives at Kew, south-west London, contain police Special Branch files on two individuals whose movements, telephone calls and mail were monitored during the 1950s. The documents include current residential addresses, records of phone taps, carbon copies of letters, memos from a

A. L. Lloyd (left) and Ewan MacColl at Ballads and Blues, late 1950s.

mole at the BBC, applications for visitors' visas to countries behind the Iron Curtain, copies of applications to join the Communist Party, and notes by intelligence officers who were shadowing their targets through London's streets. The files relate to the American ethnographic expert and broadcaster Alan Lomax, and the man with the finger in his ear at the Princess Louise: dramatist, actor, playwright and musician James 'Jimmie' Miller – or Ewan MacColl, as he is better known.

It's incredible to think that, at the height of the Cold War, national security was so threatened by a pair of folklorists that taxpayers' money was being expended on such vigorous surveillance. But folk music has been struggling with competing ideologies since the 1930s. That decade's political priorities and economic privations made the maypole dances and faery fables of Cecil Sharp's generation appear increasingly irrelevant, the effete leisure pursuit of a privileged class. The search for English identity in its folk history and rural base was, in addition, turning down alarming paths. Around 1926 Rolf Gardiner, youth-culture leader, early environmentalist and writer, began appearing at folk events across Britain and Europe with his Travelling Morrice dance troupe and publicly criticising the vision of folk promulgated by Sharp and his colleagues. Gardiner held the morris to be a form of earth magic connecting cosmos to soil via the body, and that it should remain a display of solely masculine virility (the elemental energies would be disrupted by the participation of females). He embraced the many alternatives to the Scouting movement of the 1920s, and until 1925 he had been 'Gleemaster' of the Kibbo Kift, an organisation which taught young men outdoor survival skills with a neo-pagan twist. He later joined the less savoury English Mistery and English Array organisations, whose far-right orientation gave them credence with Oswald Mosley's British Union of Fascists. His admiration for Germany's 1930s Wandervogel – infiltrated by the Hitler Youth – compounded the fascist taint. His membership of Kinship in Husbandry, a private think tank set up in 1941, aligned him with Conservative politicians and right-wing rural revivalists but led to the formation of the present-day Soil Association. Gardiner (whose son is the period-instrument conductor John Eliot Gardiner) tempered his racial interpretations of folk ritual once the full extent of the Nazi project was revealed, but the damage was done.

In the late 1920s and early 30s folk music was also beginning to look elitist, reactionary and supportive of cultural feudalism. Cecil Sharp's books were taken as gospel by members of the Folk-Song Society and the English Folk Dance Society; repertoire was almost exclusively confined to his own published transcriptions of songs and dances; and the insularity caused a blindness to new developments and a sense of internal decay. Sharp's followers and fans enshrined folk song as a lingering reminder of an irrevocably lost pre-industrial England. But change was on the way.

After Sharp's death in 1924, he was replaced as director of the English Folk Dance Society by Douglas Kennedy, who had been a member of Sharp's demonstration team since 1911 and was married to the sister of Sharp's loyal assistant, Maud Karpeles.[1] Kennedy spent the first years of his appointment raising funds to build the Society's national headquarters. Six years later, in 1930, William Kimber – concertina player with the Headington Quarry morris, who had so totally captured Sharp's imagination back in 1899 – laid the foundation stone of Cecil Sharp House in Camden Town, north London. Not long afterwards, in 1932, Kennedy invited the Folk-Song Society to merge with the English Folk Dance Society, creating the English Folk Dance and Song Society (EFDSS). Kennedy's tenure bridged the divide between the old guard's patrician distrust of proletarian membership and the necessity of appealing to a younger generation. After the

Second World War, he overhauled EFDSS strategy. This included the introduction of American square dancing and the setting up of folk festivals in Stratford-upon-Avon, Sidmouth, Whitby, Chippenham and Holmfirth. In the two years immediately after the war membership increased by 20 per cent.

Kennedy's policies were intended to answer the questions, increasingly asked in the immediate post-war years, of who are the 'folk' anyway, and who owns their music? When Cecil Sharp and the Edwardian revivalists rambled out on their collecting trips, they effectively treated their informants as journalists do their interviewees: as free information. Sharp was happy to profit from selling his own publications of music, lyrics and dances, but there was no mechanism in place to remunerate the country folk whose memories had furnished the source material.[2] Some read this as a malicious form of internecine cultural theft: we must take these dying songs away from those who cannot look after them and preserve them from any further harm.

Folk music was, after all, first and foremost the People's Music: harboured and preserved in the common mind through the decades and centuries, and sung and danced without the 'permission' of the cultural elite or the scrutiny of a trendsetting media. Where Sharp, Vaughan Williams et al. viewed folk as the music of *a* people (i.e. a nation, a race), for the new generation it was the music of *the* people. The working life of the rural population had merely been transposed to an industrial population; the song tradition of the agricultural trade might be dying, but a parallel tradition was very much alive, which Sharp and his cronies had totally ignored. This was the vast, still active canon of music which came to be known as industrial music: songs of the coal mine, weaving loom, conveyor belt, blast furnace, fishing trawler, road and railway. The dreams, desires, loves, fears, pain, deprivation and tragedy of working people were reflected in these songs as much as the ballads of yore, and it was a tradition still in the process of being created.

The uprooting from village and field to the city and terrace was the source of Britain's blues. Armed with a hammer and sickle, singer and folklorist A. L. Lloyd hit the nail on the head and cut to the quick on page one of his monumental study of folk song: 'The mother of folklore is poverty.'[3]

Until the Second World War, these voices were inaudible to the nation at large. Slowly, via the tape recorder, documentary, actuality recording and revolutionary Marxism fused with the folk-music scene to reorientate the debate.

'The microphone', wrote British film producer John Grierson in 1934, introducing the readers of *Sight and Sound* to the new art of talking pictures, 'can get about in the world. By doing so, it has the same power over reality as the camera had before it. It has the power to bring to the hands of the creative artist a thousand and one vernacular elements, and the million and one sounds which ordinarily attend the working of the world.'[4] It was Grierson who, in another film review, coined the modern usage of the word 'documentary'. In a 1926 review of *Moana*, an ethnographic portrait of Polynesian islanders by director Robert Flaherty, Grierson wrote of the film's 'documentary value'; subsequent usage converted the adjective to a noun.[5] *The Drifters*, which Grierson directed in 1929, was a rugged biography of North Sea herring fishermen. Working for the GPO (General Post Office) Film Unit, Grierson produced such landmark documentaries as *Industrial Britain* (1933), *Coal Face* (1935) and, most famously, *Night Mail* (1936). These promoted images of British industry, with superimposed musical soundtracks and commentaries that dignified or wryly undercut the action. *Night Mail* montaged a text commissioned from W. H. Auden, clenched, atmospheric music composed by the young Benjamin Britten, and location recordings of locomotives at full steam. Part actuality and part scripted, these films reflected new economic and social priorities, as competition was stepped up alongside the new, leaner economies of Germany, the United States and the Soviet Union. For Grierson, they also represented a higher art form than fictional movies: 'We believe that the materials and the stories thus taken from the raw can be finer (more real in the philosophic sense) than the acted article.'[6] In 1939 Grierson moved across the Atlantic and established the National Film Board of Canada, an organisation renowned for its nature, industrial and public-information output.[7]

The more experimental GPO alumnus Humphrey Jennings expunged voice-over altogether in favour of an associative flow of images. Jennings was a prime mover in the 1930s Mass Observation project, a census of national consciousness recording the fleeting thoughts of thousands of British citizens on a huge range of subjects, including motorists' gestures and shouts, beard-trimming styles and the 'cult of the aspidistra'. When the GPO unit was subsumed into the Ministry of Information and rebranded the Crown Film Unit during the Second World War, Jennings was pressed into service making films designed to brace the nation's mettle and preserve hope and a sense of community, as in *Listen to Britain* (1942), and revealing beauty even in the face of calamity, as in the heroic portrayal of Blitz firefighters in *Fires Were Started* (1943). Pitched on a sliding scale between propaganda and an observational eye bordering on rapture, these films strain against the leash of their obligation to show 'reality'.

Jennings's *Diary for Timothy* (1946) was cast as a letter to a newborn baby setting out on life during the post-war reconstruction of Britain. Although much of the time, the camera was panning over the green fields, quaint villages and rolling meadows of an idealised rural landscape, Britain's slow recovery in the post-war austerity years was driven by a metropolitan, not an agricultural, economy. The aftermath to the devastating total war in Alexander Korda's film of H. G. Wells's *Things to Come*

(1936) embodied this mismatch between national self-image and economic reality, envisioning a city-state rebuilt underground, with the deathless image of rolling fields and rural stability as an overlay while, underneath, gigantic robots assembled subterranean condominiums for the ultra-hygienic technologised society of the future.

The spectre of modernity was unveiled to the British public in 1951, at the Festival of Britain on the newly constructed South Bank in London, at which the purposeless Skylon sculpture cast its bomb-shaped shadow over displays of labour-saving consumer durables. The shadow was very real: it was too soon after the war to believe that the future was bright, and the new science fiction – John Wyndham's *The Day of the Triffids*, published in the Festival of Britain year – imagined intelligent vegetation executing a whiplash Blitzkrieg on a blinded Britain.

Alfred Watkins had published his study of leys in 1925, but twentieth-century progress was fast replacing his tracery of divinely aligned power spots with the electricity grid and the rail network. Both these spiderwebs of modernity reinforced the city as the focus of power and work. Only 20 per cent of British households still didn't have electricity by 1945, and these were all situated in outlying rural zones.

In 1928 Britain's first electricity pylon was erected just outside Edinburgh. The steel structure was skeletal and vaguely anthropomorphic, with six arms to carry the three-phase cables across large tracts of terrain. Most of today's pylons are variations on the original design by Sir Reginald Blomfield, the architect responsible for remodelling London's Regent Street as a curving neoclassical terrace. Blomfield was a fervent horticulturalist whose 1892 book *The Formal Garden in England* had reintroduced the idea of gardening as stiff-upper-lip horticulture; among other opinions, he claimed to despise the ornamented fancies of William Morris's organic tapestries. In 1953 a new crop of National Grid power stations was rolled out (including the one at Bankside in London, now Tate Modern), and the electrification of Britain was accelerated with the imposition of a 'supergrid', carried by the newly designed PL1 pylons that are still the dominant model fifty years later. Britain's open fields and moors had become parade grounds for an army of steel wicker men.

With its speed, noise and precision engineering, the railway was another evocative symbol of modernity. But the series of British Transport Films produced by the Transport Commission from 1949, and screened in theatres nationwide, was intended to inspire the public to buy a ticket to Arcadia Junction and reconnect with the landscape and history that city life obscured. The Hereford Three Counties show and the Cotswold villages depicted in *The Heart of England* (1954), the vibrant human tapestry on the Blackpool seafront in *Holiday* (1957), or Cornwall's weird juxtapositions of balmy coastlines, Arthurian ruins and prehistoric relics in *West Country Journey* (1953) confirmed the beauty, wonder, mystery and hospitality of the nation's hinterlands and seasides. The Transport Films were steered by Edgar Anstey, yet another alumnus of Grierson's documentary school. The mannered commentaries contain the unspoken assumption that the viewer's pleasure-seeking urge is underpinned by an interest in local history. 'Our land is very old,' runs a typical voice-over. 'We have lost its origins. Our fields grow neat, our hands grow smooth, forgetting their rough and hard beginnings. But on Dartmoor the spirit of our island seems to heave itself out of the bracken and we find in the weathered rock its strong and enduring character.'[8]

The films utilised the talents of various British composers, including Elizabeth Lutyens, Humphrey Searle, Doreen Carwithen and Edward Williams. Vaughan Williams, who lived around the corner from the film unit's headquarters in Marylebone, wrote

a score for *The England of Elizabeth* (1957), a pageant of England's
Tudor legacy. Yet despite valiant attempts to depict the thunder and
sparks of the steam age – by E. J. Moeran in parts of his *Symphony
in G*, and Britten in *Night Mail* – classical orchestration seemed an
unwieldy medium to represent the new technological era. During
the war Britten's pacifist exile in the United States opened up a
nostalgic yearning for the distant roots of British music, and he
began setting folk songs – sixty-eight in total – to be sung by his
partner Peter Pears, of which the most famous is his 'Foggy Foggy
Dew'. Writing for an American readership in 1941, he discreetly
joined and advanced the debate about the role of folk music in
British life. Praising swing and the American spiritual above all
other folk forms, Britten argued that their beauty and value derived
precisely from their *hybridity*, not their ethnic purity. 'What we
call folk-music is no product of a primitive society . . . the whole
conception of folk-song as a germ from which organized music
grew may prove to be a false one,' he wrote. In an accompanying
list of contemporary composers with whom Britten felt most
kinship, Vaughan Williams is conspicuously absent.[9]

But the popular ear was less and less attuned to such musical
subtlety. You had to work hard to appreciate the way a piano could
approximate the noise of a locomotive – as Britten tried to do in
Winter Words (1953), his settings of Thomas Hardy's poetry, which
included several poems referencing trains – and besides, there
were now more dynamic, visceral forces abroad within modernist
music. If the parental generation of the 1950s was enjoying its
post-war comedown to the saccharine strains of popular vocalists
like Alma Cogan, Perry Como and Frankie Laine, or the syrupy
muzak of Mantovani, their adolescent children were scouring the
airwaves for a more challenging alternative. And they found it in
the first of the great youthquakes to rock the British Isles.

'Rock Island Line' is the one skiffle song everybody knows. It
kept its singer, the young Lonnie Donegan, in the Top Twenty for

eight months in 1956. Originally a convict worksong collected in
1934 by John Lomax in Arkansas, when skiffled up it *sounds* like a
train: the chug and chuff of the pistoning strings, combined with
the furious thimble-frottage on the washboard, place you right next
to the track as a loco steams past. Skiffle seemed peculiarly suited
to the rail: Chas McDevitt and Nancy Whiskey's 'Freight Train'
(1957) was another huge hit. But Donegan, formerly a member
of Chris Barber's and Ken Colyer's jazz ensembles, was the tip of
the iceberg: the skiffle craze was a mass grass-roots response to the
influx of American music, a DIY phenomenon that conscripted an
army of thousands brandishing acoustic guitars, washboards and
tea-chest basses. Skiffle's accelerated swing rhythms and domestic
equipment – kazoos, harmonicas, comb and paper – placed music-
making in the hands of the amateur, as well as opening up a conduit
for the dust-bowl and rust-belt blues and folk poetry of Woody
Guthrie and Lead Belly to be siphoned into British ears. Among
the mid-1950s skiffle ranks were some of the most prominent
figures in the coming revolutions in folk, rock and jazz in the next
decade: John Lennon, Mick Jagger, Jimmy Page, Van Morrison,
Graham Nash, Dave Pegg. More significantly, skiffle popularised
'industrial songs': the side of folk music that Cecil Sharp and co.
had almost entirely overlooked.

Between the end of the war and 1958 many loosely connected
threads began to draw together, woven into the loom of a second
folk revival. During that time several crucial individuals converged
on London, wrapped inexorably around the shuttle. Chief among
these were singer and broadcaster Ewan MacColl; musician and
member of the distinguished American folk dynasty Peggy Seeger;
singer and Marxist folk historian A. L. Lloyd; folklorist and
archivist Alan Lomax; and researcher/broadcaster Peter Kennedy.
Their efforts transformed the role of folk music in contemporary
life, colonising as many spaces as possible, from the smallest
back-room folk club to the potentially massive reach of radio and

television, and introducing a contemporary industrial sensibility to the corpus of folk.

🙚

Eastbridge is little more than a scattering of cottages at the end of a Suffolk country lane so narrow that cars beep warning blasts at every blind corner. It feels like a remote and secluded corner of the planet: here, the roads diminish to lanes and then small footways to the crumbling coastline of East Anglia. The central feature of this hamlet is its pub, The Eel's Foot, a hostelry that seems half embedded in the soil, with a small outdoor terrace and barely room inside for more than fifty patrons. Nowadays it's the kind of place where the few regulars treat it more like an alternative family living room than a public house.

How different this snug room would have seemed in the 1930s. There were weekly singers' nights, led by regulars like Velvet and Jumbo Brightwell, and 'Mr Goddard', with Philip Lumpton, master of ceremonies, bashing a table with a gavel to announce the next singer's turn. Those who declined to take part were expected to drop sixpence in a jar to buy ale for the other souls who stood up and sang a folk song, spun a yarn or squeezed a tune out of a spluttering accordion.

One evening in early 1939, A. L. (Leslie) Morton, Marxist author of *A People's History of England* and *The English Utopia*, who lived in the nearby town of Leiston, brought his friend A. L. Lloyd to one such event, convinced he would enjoy the spectacle. Lloyd was amazed at the vitality on display, and later persuaded a producer friend of his at the BBC, Francis Dillon, to record the lively jamboree. The pair turned up on 13 March 1939 in a car loaded with recording gear. The result of their labours, *Saturday Night at the Eel's Foot*, was broadcast on 21 July: the first time authentic traditional singers – not classically trained interpreters or arrangers – had been heard on national radio. The little pub became an English folk-music landmark, and a series of recordings made there – including another BBC programme hosted by E. J. Moeran – was released commercially.

Albert Lancaster Lloyd (1908–82) was the closest thing Britain had to an Alan Lomax. His short, plump build, eternal good nature and fondness for alcohol were summed up in Ewan MacColl's thumbnail sketch: 'a walking toby jug'.[10] Like Lomax, Bert Lloyd was a communist, blacklisted from working with the BBC during the war and for several years afterwards. Born in London, he was exceptionally well travelled, having sought his fortune sheep-shearing in Australia as a sixteen-year-old in the 1920s, and later as a roving correspondent for *Picture Post*. He fell in with left-wing artists and intellectuals in the cafes and bookshops of Soho and Hampstead in the mid-1930s, and was introduced to a circle that included Dylan Thomas and A. L. Morton. He gained some experience as a radio documentary-maker just before the war, including a portrait of mariners' daily lives (*Voice of the Seamen*) and a six-part analysis of the rise of Nazism called *The Shadow of the Swastika*, broadcast in the early months of the war. All this time, his real enthusiasm was studying the origins of folk music, and years of research bore fruit with the publication of a long pamphlet entitled *The Singing Englishman* in 1944. Although he later disowned some of the book's unfounded assertions, it was effectively the first attempt to survey the totality of British folk music since Cecil Sharp's *English Folk-Song: Some Conclusions* nearly half a century before. Not only did it attempt to restore the erotic and explicit aspects of many familiar songs, but it was also implicitly critical of the current curators of the folk legacy, the EFDSS.

Lloyd respected Cecil Sharp's achievements, and loved the rural songs and magical ballads of the Sharp canon, but he disagreed with the current Society's methods of preserving their legacy and thought there was too great an emphasis on 'clodhopping bumpkin folderol' and on dances by 'prancing curate[s] in cricket flannels'.

He saw how its middle-class membership had ignored workers' songs and disdained recording technology, preferring to transcribe in stave-paper notebooks. He was astounded to discover that there were only two commercially available records (comprising four songs in total) of native British folk song in existence.[11] Surely, he reasoned, the tradition would be better served if people could hear and learn songs orally, via recordings of those who remembered them, rather than via tasteful drawing-room dilutions of the same material?

By the mid-1940s Lloyd was already acutely aware of the vitality of the new folk renaissance in America. *Corn on the Cob* (1945), his published collection of forty-three songs from the American revival, was largely drawn from the repertoire of the radical Almanac Singers and contained many songs later popularised by Pete Seeger and the Weavers. Its mixture of criminal ballads such as 'Frankie and Johnny', 'John Hardy' and 'Stackalee', prison and protest songs, and the rootless pioneer folk music of lumberjacks, railroad workers, cowboys and hobos highlighted a mercurial sense of freedom in the reactivated American folk identity. In the same year, Lloyd wrote articles comparing negro spirituals with equivalent songs recorded by white singers. He identified pentatonic scales and structures common to both, which suggested Anglo-Celtic roots, but in the mouths of black singers they had taken on the function of cries for freedom and civil liberty. Such thinking suggested to Lloyd ways in which the British tradition might become useful to a revolutionary political agenda.

The legend of Robin Hood is well known even outside British shores. With its origins in medieval minstrelsy, it is central to the mythology of England: Robin, clad in Lincoln green, hides invisibly in his forest dwelling, using cunning and daring to defeat the Sheriff of Nottingham, dictatorial barons, corrupt monks, even John, the surrogate king. Lloyd's essay 'The Revolutionary Origins of English Folk-Song'[12] identified a continuous anti-authoritarian strain in English folk song dating back to the fourteenth-century social upheavals in the aftermath of the Black Death. The ritual nature of 'John Barleycorn', 'Jolly Old Hawk' and 'The Derby Ram', and the sacrificial elements and destructive energy in 'The Cutty Wren', for example, he suspected derived from witch cults, frequently breeding grounds of rebellion and non-conformity. Much later, the machine-wreckers of the late eighteenth and early nineteenth centuries, including the Luddites of 1811–13, who trashed their industrial weaving looms in anti-mechanistic rage, left their own small body of folk songs. Lloyd was keen to emphasise these qualities of revolutionary agitation in music that celebrated a world turned upside down.

Despite his critical stance towards the EFDSS, in 1947 Lloyd was invited to lecture on the history of American folk song at Cecil Sharp House. He discovered that Douglas Kennedy loved the music of Burl Ives, and was open to the introduction of American-style music to the Society's activities. Working from within, and with access to the Society's library, Lloyd suddenly found himself well placed to exert his influence on the folk scene. During the 1950s he made field recordings for Topic Records, the label most closely associated with socially conscious and radical folk music. It had existed since 1939, when it was set up to release music by the Workers' Music Association Singers. Through the 1950s Topic sponsored rousing Red anthems by Soviet and Eastern European singers and choirs, and released music by Pete Seeger, Woody Guthrie and Paul Robeson, Ramblin' Jack Elliott, Ewan MacColl and Peggy Seeger, while Lloyd went out a-roving with his tape recorder to capture the country's traditional folk singers on tape. Topic's enthralling and historic discography, which eventually amassed to around 120 LPs of music, helped to propel the likes of Margaret Barry, Michael Gorman, William Kimber, George Maynard, Walter Pardon and Jeannie Robertson into relative stardom, with nationwide concert tours and television appearances.

The
Penguin
Book of
English
Folk
Songs

EDITED BY
R. Vaughan
Williams
AND
A. L. Lloyd

3/6

First edition of *The Penguin Book of English Folk Songs*, edited
by A. L. Lloyd and Ralph Vaughan Williams, 1958.

Another result of Lloyd's involvement with the EFDSS was
the 1958 publication of *The Penguin Book of English Folk Songs*, a
slim but user-friendly compendium of representative material.
The book was a collaboration with Ralph Vaughan Williams and
contained greenwood balladry ('The Banks of Green Willow',
'Robin Hood and the Pedlar'), tragic lovers' laments ('As Sylvie
Was Walking', 'Death and the Lady'), courting songs ('Salisbury
Plain', 'The Streams of Lovely Nancy'), shanties old and new
('Jack the Jolly Tar', 'A Sailor's Life', 'The Greenland Whale
Fishery') and supernatural ballads ('John Barleycorn', 'The Grey
Cock'). All were drawn from the EFDSS archives, but Lloyd's

presence is most strongly felt in the inclusion of so many maritime and fishermen's songs. Lloyd first came to Vaughan Williams's attention in 1948, when the composer awarded him first prize in a singing competition at Cecil Sharp House. The book was one of old Ralph's final projects: he died on 26 August 1958, and the volume represents a respectful handshake between the last surviving link to the William Morris circle and the modern, proselytising Marxist generation that followed.

Peter Kennedy had folk revivalism in his blood. As the twenty-five-year-old son of Douglas Kennedy and Helen Karpeles, Peter joined the staff of the EFDSS in 1948, and brought a documentarist's dynamic to the Society's practice. Part of his father's modernisation involved the creation of regional branches, and Peter was sent first to the north-east and then to the West Country in 1950. During both postings he unearthed previously unknown dances and songs, and began documenting local musicians with a Scophony-Baird reel-to-reel tape recorder. In particular he recognised the crucial role of Britain's travellers as keepers of musical legacies, and infiltrated Gypsy and Romany communities. On the other end of the scale, he vividly remembered once staying at the country abode of Lady Trevelyan, wife of G. M. Trevelyan, author of *English Social History*, the classic account of the centuries since the Middle Ages from the perspective of the common man. The gatepost of the driveway on one side was carved with the royal crown; on the other was a hammer and sickle.[13] Such was an earlier age's conflation of heritage and progressive thought.

Together with his friend John Hasted, Kennedy ran the small London Reel Club. As an early fan of American folk music, Hasted became enamoured of the guitar and banjo accompaniments he heard in the music of Pete Seeger's Almanac Singers. Guitars were scarce in Britain in the late 1940s, and certainly were never used to accompany traditional folk music. The jug band that Kennedy formed with Hasted and Redd Sullivan, which performed at Cecil Sharp House, was one of the first in the country to feature a guitar, and was therefore an even earlier incarnation of skiffle than Lonnie Donegan's.

Kennedy's tireless work uncovering Britain's folk music had its most visible platform via his radio productions for the BBC. The Corporation recognised the importance of the countryside and its people as a way of bolstering British identity in the arid and

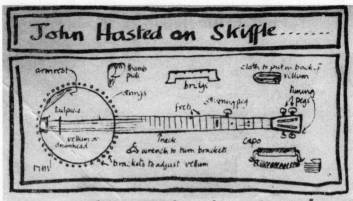

Yanks go home: flyer advertising John Hasted's pioneering
London skiffle sessions, 1957.

confused aftermath of war. The year 1950 was when *The Archers* – part soap opera, part didactic agricultural magazine, set in a Malvern-esque village – began its record-breaking run. But despite building a library of recordings of traditional singing (beginning in 1935, when a group of singers were recorded at the Oxford St Giles Fair), BBC broadcasts of folk music were non-existent until the weekly *Country Magazine*, which helped keep the metropolitan population in touch with their 'country cousins' from the rural heartland during the lean years of the war, began inviting country folk into the studio to trawl their memories for stories and songs. The programme's postbag was so besieged with listeners' letters, offering their own contributions, that a whole new series was created entitled *The Postman Brings Me Songs*.

Peter Kennedy was steeped in the documentary mindset. As a teenager, just before the outbreak of war, he had holidayed on the set built in the early 1930s by director Robert Flaherty off Ireland's west coast for *Man of Aran,* his great documentary about local herring fishers. In 1951 he took a film crew down to Padstow, Cornwall, to shoot the arcane Obby Oss procession – a May Day fertility ceremony in which a randy equine effigy cavorts through the streets – producing *Oss, Oss, Wee Oss*, a remarkable eighteen-minute ethnographic film that makes Cornwall seem as exotic as the Congo. In 1957 he assisted on Leslie Daiken's film cataloguing children's rhymes and games in the bombed ruins of Camden Town, *One Potato, Two Potato*. In 1953 Kennedy was given his own radio series, *As I Roved Out*, which showcased a weekly catch by correspondents trawling the isles for new folk music. He worked in collaboration with his counterparts Seamus Ennis, an Irish broadcaster and uilleann piper; Scottish poet and song collector Hamish Henderson; and Sussex folk singer Bob Copper. Just as Humphrey Jennings's Mass Observation project opened up aspects of working-class life, for the first time the voices of 'ordinary' folk were being heard on national radio, instead of their music being mediated and interpreted by 'educated' singers.

As I Roved Out became a popular fixture on BBC radio, with fifty-three episodes broadcast between 1953–8. Nineteen fifty-three also saw the appearance on television of *Song Hunter: Alan Lomax*, an eight-part folk magazine show in which the American presented a mixture of traditional singers and musicians such as Harry Cox, Charlie Wills, Michael Gorman and Margaret Barry, and the likes of Ewan MacColl, Isla Cameron and Seamus Ennis, as well as showing Kennedy's Padstow footage. Kennedy researched and co-presented the show, which was produced by the young David Attenborough.[14]

Folk music slowly seeped into many corners of BBC output. By 1960 the thrice-weekly TV current-affairs show *Tonight* included a regular spot in which folk and calypso singers interpreted a topical news item in song. Kennedy booked the musicians for this slot, including Jimmie MacGregor and Robin Hall, Rory and Alex McEwan, and Cy Grant – gentle popularisers of an easily digestible, catchy acoustic style delivered with a wink and a stuck-on grin.

Alan Lomax was a bear of a Texan who arrived in Britain in 1950 on the pretext of recording folk singers and musicians for an LP series on Columbia Records. He stayed for eight years, a thunderbolt of energy who set Britain's folk revival ablaze. Like Peter Kennedy, Lomax came from solid ethnomusicological stock. His father John Lomax, Assistant Curator at the Library of Congress in Washington, was given his first wax-cylinder recorder in 1933 by none other than the widow of Thomas Edison, the machine's inventor. Alan accompanied John on the fateful July 1933 visit to the Angola State Penitentiary in Louisiana, where they chanced upon Huddie Ledbetter, aka Lead Belly, the treasurer of a massive store of worksongs, blues hollers and saga-length narrative ballads. In 1937 Alan took over his father's job, promptly extending the remit of the Library's music-collecting duties to reflect his own interest in the 'living lore' of the urban streets, the nightlife blues of the dance hall, the poker saloon, the pool table. For Lomax, this was living, breathing 'folklore in the making', while the songs he had found among chain gangs in the prisons and plantations of the deep South had survived by mere good fortune. Surveying the music of the Mississippi Delta in 1941, he was as interested in what the poor black families had in their record collections and which acetates were stacked in the bar-room jukeboxes as what music they had locked up in their heads. Lomax was a voracious collector of music, and continued to make recordings of 'race' songs, hillbilly, honky-tonk piano and jazz (courtesy of Jelly Roll Morton), and folk and protest songs, from Woody Guthrie to militant union supporter Aunt Molly Jackson.

As a communist, Lomax played an instrumental part in aligning America's ongoing folk-music surge with left-wing activism. Some initial work had been done during the First World War by none other than Cecil Sharp, accompanied by his faithful assistant Maud Karpeles. Sharp's findings in the Appalachian mountains in 1916–17[15] diverted the flow of song 'down from the mountain' – the hillbilly stomps, coarse bluegrass banjo and ukulele fingerpicking, and recognisable Child ballads, frozen into different forms by their isolation in the Virginia hills. Like Darwin discovering the isolated lizards of Galapagos, Sharp assumed the songs he found in the Appalachians and down the eastern seaboard, preserved by 'people [who] are just English of the late eighteenth or early nineteenth century . . . [who] speak English, look English, and their manners are old-fashioned English',[16] and who were unaffected by, for example, the vulgarising broadside glut of the early nineteenth century, were more authentic survivors of the folk-song canon.[17]

Two decades later, as part of the New Deal intended to shore up the damage caused by the Depression, the folk-loving President Roosevelt green-lit unprecedented investment in American arts and culture, which included grants to the Library of Congress to document and preserve America's indigenous music. Overshadowing the entire American folk movement was the Seeger clan, overseen by the patriarch, Charles Seeger, an ethnomusicologist, teacher and composer who ran a number of community-development projects involving music. His son, Pete Seeger, was born to his first wife Constance in 1919. After divorcing Constance in 1927, Charles married Ruth Crawford Seeger, one of the more interesting minor American composers, who harnessed modernism and Scriabin's orchestral ravishment to the folk tradition. She gave birth to two more children, Mike (in 1933) and Peggy (1935). The Seegers were already acquainted with the Lomaxes, as Ruth had supplied the transcriptions for several of John's publications of folk songs.

In 1940 Alan Lomax introduced Pete Seeger – by now a respected singer and activist in his own right – to Woody Guthrie, the itinerant singer who combined radicalism with a love of America's wide open spaces, adapting the songs he encountered on his wanderings to his own ends. With that handshake came the alliance of Seeger, a product of America's educated musicological elite, with the gritty son of the Midwestern dustbowl: the tuning fork of the nation banging against its loose bedrock. Cumulatively, the effect on America's cultural life was the association of folk and blues with protest and radical politics during the rise of McCarthyite terror. Lomax put together The Almanac Singers with his sister Bess, Seeger, Guthrie and Josh White, who would later earn the distinction of being the first black blues singer to visit Britain professionally, in 1950. After the war Lomax involved himself in People's Songs, an organisation dedicated to promoting topical songs for use by trade unions, civil-rights activists and anyone with a liberal/left-wing agenda. In 1948 he was the music director for a presidential campaign by the Progressive Party leader, Henry Wallace. All this involvement couldn't help but flash up a red light on the radar screens of Senator Joe McCarthy and his anti-communist inquisition. Lomax's name appeared in

Red Channels, McCarthy's 1950 blacklist of Reds involved in the entertainment world. Time for a sharp exit.

The Land of Cockayne is one of the oldest English utopias, even pre-dating Thomas More. For the feudal and downtrodden peasant class of the Middle Ages, troubadours singing of Cockayne offered a compensatory vision of unimaginable plenty without effort; where unending physical and gastronomic pleasure was on tap and no punishment was meted out for laziness. 'The Big Rock Candy Mountain', a song originally collected in the 1930s by John Lomax, updates Cockayne for the Great Depression's discontents. Fittingly, the song as recorded by Burl Ives in 1949 was one of the first singles in the new American 'folk guitar' idiom to hit the big time back in the Old Country. The hobo's paradise where '*there ain't no short-handled shovels, no axes, saws, or picks . . . Where you sleep all day, where they hung the Turk that invented work*' is a post-industrial iteration of utopia that sounded mighty fine to a grey, sombre Britain licking its war wounds.

The success of Ives's single alerted many British ears to the musical revolution happening in America. In that year Herman Grisewood, controller of the BBC's highbrow Third Programme, hoped to persuade Alan Lomax to make a programme about white spirituals. The American postponed his arrival in England until the following year, so the BBC blacklisting was lifted from Bert Lloyd, who presented a selection of hymns from the Sacred Harp Singing Convention in Alabama. When Lomax finally arrived off the boat at Southampton, he instantly became embroiled in the country's musical life. His documentary instinct had been revived by Columbia Records' invention, in 1948, of the thirty-three rpm long-playing record. Suddenly a record could hold up to fifty minutes of music, a format Lomax found perfect: now, a collection of songs could be properly curated and would make sense heard as a body of twelve to sixteen tracks, rather than the three- or four-song seventy-eights. This innovation dovetailed neatly with a rapid hike in the resources available for gathering disappearing world cultures. UNESCO's International Folk Music Council was instigated in 1947; Moses Asch founded the Folkways label in 1948;[18] and following a chance meeting with Columbia Records boss Goddard Lieberson in 1949, Lomax persuaded the company to bankroll the *Columbia World Library of Folk and Primitive Music*, an encyclopedic survey of the world's native musics, planned as an eventual forty-LP series, comprising field recordings which Lomax proposed to assemble himself. It was this project, in fact, which provided the excuse for him to slip the clutches of the McCarthy hearings: his first stops were Ireland and Scotland on a trip he originally intended to last only a year.

Just as it took America's surviving music to teach the British about the riches of their own indigenous music, so in the 1950s it was an American, a self-described 'musical Columbus in reverse',[19] who exerted a unifying and galvanising effect on musical life in the United Kingdom. In the course of his eight-year stay, Lomax produced more than thirty radio and television programmes for the BBC, drawing on his recordings of hundreds of folk singers the length and breadth of the isles. And like the impulsive hero of a ballad, his parting gesture was to whisk his young lover and assistant – a young, impoverished folk singer called Shirley Collins – off to the southern states of America in 1959 on a historic journey that would profoundly inform her own approach to interpreting English folk song through the 1960s and 70s.

Lomax was hypnotised by the power of phonography. He was, of course, concerned with preserving vanishing traditions for its own sake: 'What was once an ancient tropical garden of immense colour and variety is in danger of being replaced by a comfortable but sterile and sleep-inducing system of cultural super-highways,' he prophesied.[20] To stave off that gruesome future, the domestic hi-fi could act as the megaphone of democracy, a potentially subversive way of infiltrating the Western mind with the suffering of the underclass. With his microphone and Magnecord tape recorder, Lomax could take the 'vital reality' of forgotten and oppressed voices in the remotest cotton fields and the roughest town neighbourhoods and inject them into any home with a record deck. In the future, he wrote at the time, 'Our epoch may not be known by the name of a school of composers or of a musical style. It may well be called the period of the phonograph or the age of the golden ear, when, for a time, a passionate aural curiosity overshadowed the ability to create music.'[21] When Mr Golden Ears's *Columbia World Library* series was complete, we'd all be able to hang out in mankind's pad.

Inspired by the skiffle explosion, Lomax occasionally turned his hand to music-making while in London. His own skiffle group, The Ramblers, embodied his own thoughts on the reason the music had captured the British imagination: 'These young people *felt* themselves to be in a prison – composed of class-and-caste lines, the shrinking British Empire, the dull job, the lack of money – things like these. They were shouting at these prison walls, like so many Joshuas at the walls of Jericho.'[22] And like Joshua, the other members of Lomax's Ramblers – Ewan MacColl, Pete Seeger's half-sister Peggy and Shirley Collins – wanted to preside over a revolution that would shake the world's foundations.

In 1953, at Stratford in London's bombed-out East End, a drama collective from Manchester took up a new permanent residence at the local Theatre Royal. The Theatre Workshop's roots lay in the Workers' Theatre Movement of the late 1920s and early 30s. They were just beginning to make a name for themselves after seven years of hard graft round the theatre circuit, and had achieved some notoriety with a piece called *Uranium 235*, written by founder member Ewan MacColl.

Peggy Seeger and Ewan MacColl, early 1960s.

MacColl was reluctant for the group to make the move to London. He felt he and his comrades had spent seven years slogging round Wales, Scotland and the north of England, and were only now beginning to establish a solid audience base. To attempt a new life in an outlying district of the capital, with its sophisticated metropolitan audience and its cynical, West End-fixated press, was suddenly to become small fish again. But the truth was, as a veteran of over twenty years' standing, by 1953 he was tired of the whole theatrical world and unconvinced of its ability to exact the kind of social and political change he desired.

MacColl had been embroiled in hard-left politics since leaving school at fourteen. Born in 1915 to Scottish parents living in the slums of the working-class town of Salford, Greater Manchester, Jimmie Miller, as he was then known, joined the Young Communist League in 1929, the year of the massive stock-market crash that triggered the Depression of the early 1930s. After a string of unproductive and dispiriting temporary jobs, he found himself out of work in 1931 and, with seven other unemployed actors, formed the political theatre troupe The Red Megaphones. From the flatbeds of coal wagons in the streets they spewed out anti-war songs, anti-Tory sketches and rowdy Marxist guignol, usually to indifferent audiences going about their daily business. He met and married the actress Joan Littlewood in 1933, and they worked together in subsequent groups Theatre of Action and Theatre Union, denied state funding and scraping a pittance playing to minuscule audiences at mission halls, miners' welfare benefits and damp, freezing theatres with no electricity and water trickling down the walls.

Their work reached its apex with a piece called *Last Edition*, a 'living newspaper'. It was a radical format for its time, a burlesque revue performed on a stage that semi-enclosed the audience and which critiqued recent and unfolding events by including a documentary-style voice-over to introduce telling facts and statistics. So powerful was its effect that, after five performances, Miller and Littlewood were arrested and charged with breaching the peace. It was 1940: a 'newspaper' in the hands of the working classes, portraying 'the deception and betrayal of a nation', was an unacceptable danger to the propaganda effort.

Miller was conscripted into the army in 1940 but had deserted by the end of that year, and spent the rest of the war in hiding from the military police. After VE Day he changed his name to Ewan MacColl to evade prosecution, came in from the cold and regrouped with the newly formed Theatre Workshop. By now seasoned performers, their repertoire consisted of established playwrights such as Lorca and material penned by cast members, principally MacColl. For the historical panorama of *Johnny Noble*, a sound system was built consisting of six turntables, all simultaneously cross-faded in a Futurist montage of factory sirens, ship engines, explosions and machine-gun fire. *Uranium 235* was a historical pageant and atomic-age morality play, with the figure of

Death as a puppet master (played by MacColl) spiriting off various heretical personages from the history of science, such as Giordano Bruno, Paracelsus, Marie Curie and Albert Einstein.

In the pastoral songbook of the Edwardians, the most recent news item was the Napoleonic Wars. MacColl was poised to become the architect of a new revolution in British folk music, one that was informed by his focus on the tribulations of the present-day folk and the influence of contemporary political factors. One of MacColl's final acts before abandoning the north was to visit the region's engine sheds and factory canteens, collecting the songs that made up his book *The Shuttle and Cage*. Published in 1954 and later released as a Topic ten-inch, it patched together songs from the factories, mines and railway lines of the past 200 years, such as 'The Wark of the Weavers', 'The Blantyre Explosion', chronicling a Scottish mining disaster of 1877, and railway songs like 'Moses of the Mail', 'Cosher Bailey's Engine' and 'Poor Paddy Works on the Railway'. As well as songs he'd collected, MacColl included several written by himself, such as 'Champion at Keeping 'Em Rolling', which he wrote for a 1949 radio documentary about truck drivers. 'Cannily, Cannily', another MacColl original made popular in its recorded version by Isla Cameron, was a lullaby intended to soothe a train driver's baby. The introduction to *The Shuttle and Cage* laid out the new conditions in which folk music was to be regarded: 'There are no nightingales in these songs, no flowers – and the sun is rarely mentioned, their themes are work, poverty, hunger and exploitation. They should be sung to the accompaniment of pneumatic drills and swinging hammers, they should be bawled above the hum of turbines and the clatter of looms for they are songs of toil, anthems of the industrial age . . .

'If you have spent your life striving desperately to make ends meet; if you have worked yourself to a standstill and still been unable to feed the kids properly, then you will know why these songs were made. If you have worked in a hot pit, wearing nothing but your boots and felt that the air you were breathing was liquid fire, then you will know why these songs were made. If you have crouched day after day in a twelve-inch seam of coal with four inches of water in it, and hacked with a small pick until every muscle in your body shrieked in protest – then you will know why these songs were made.'[23]

MacColl's first prominent action was in 1932, when he wrote the song 'Manchester Rambler' following an organised mass trespass on Kinder Scout in the Peak District, and his wanderings over the hills and dales near Manchester in the 1930s formed a strong counterpoint to his urban agitation. For the urban worker, trapped in the city with the necessity to attend the workplace five days a week, the countryside offered escape, release, liberty; space to imagine a future better world. In an extraordinary passage from his autobiography, MacColl recalled how 'The return to Salford after those magical Sundays and weekends was in no way depressing. We were returning to the political struggle refreshed and determined to destroy capitalism. The political battles were, in their own way, just as exhilarating as finding one's way by compass across a moor shrouded in mist, or working out a route on a rock face . . . There were the branch meetings, district meetings, conferences, education classes – they were like the bracken-covered braes which led to the high plateaux from which one could see the hazy peaks of the final goal: the end of capitalism and the beginning of a new form of society based upon all mankind's needs, the needs of all men and women, not just the privileged few. This was a vision which was just as exciting as any mountain vista.'[24]

The Second World War forced a rapprochement between the country and the city in ways previously unknown. Domestic agriculture became increasingly important, and there was greater traffic between the urban and rural as city Land Girls tilled the soil and country-dwelling workers were conscripted to labour in munitions factories. The interdependence of both was recognised.

MacColl's canon of industrial music was not only about a vision of society transformed by modern engineering and cutting-edge technology, but as much about the preservation of age-old customs, dignities, hopes and fears. To descend into a typical mineshaft in Wales or Yorkshire in the late 1940s or early 50s was to witness inefficient mining techniques essentially unchanged since the Middle Ages, as men crawled from the shaft bottom along cramped tunnels to begin work at the coalface, where they swung picks and sledgehammers at the black seam while lying on their sides, with no face masks to filter the carbon dust. Industrial music was as much about the preservation of entrenched methods as a celebration of progress.

'In a sense,' Ewan MacColl once said, 'all folk-songs are forgeries.'[25] MacColl's dramatist's instinct told him all songs were subject to individual readings and interpretations, and as an oral survival, the folk canon must have been subjected to hundreds and thousands of these rereadings over the passage of time. What was more important than preserving a bogus notion of authenticity was 'dissipating the aura of preciousness and sanctity with which nineteenth century folk-lorists shrouded popular music'.[26] Within months of arriving in London, MacColl acquired a platform to do just that.

In 1953 the BBC gave him his own radio series, *Ballads and Blues*, transmitted on Sunday evenings in six half-hour episodes. He and various guests including Alan Lomax, Bert Lloyd, Humphrey Lyttelton, Seamus Ennis and Guyanese calypso artist Cy Grant performed a song selection intended to 'demonstrate that Britain possessed a body of songs that were just as vigorous, as tough and as down-to-earth as anything that could be found in the United States'.[27] In eclectic shows with themes such as 'The Singing Sailormen' and 'Song of the Iron Road', MacColl, Isla Cameron and Bert Lloyd handled the British songs; Seamus Ennis supplied the Celtic connection; Lomax, Big Bill Broonzy and Jean Ritchie tackled the blues and American folk; and Humphrey Lyttelton's jazz band and Cy Grant added a dash of swing and calypso to the pot.

MacColl's club of the same name, opened in 1957 at the Princess Louise pub in central London, was soon copied across the capital and throughout the nation's cities and towns, laying the groundwork for the live network that would germinate the folk and folk-rock impulses of the next two decades. At a typical recital MacColl and his regulars – Dominic Behan, Fitzroy Coleman, Harry Cox, Seamus Ennis, Bert Lloyd, Peggy Seeger – would

BALLADS & BLUES

invites you to :

'THE HOOTENNANY'

S U N D A Y S   7.15 P.M.

PRINCESS LOUISE. HIGH HOLBORN. LONDON W.1.
(Holborn Tube)

SUNDAY 9TH MARCH: EWAN MacCOLL.   FITZROY COLEMAN, DEAN GITTER,
DOMINIC BEHAN.   BOB CLARKE.   BRUCE TURNER.

* * * * * * * *

SUNDAY 16TH MARCH: EWAN MacCOLL.   FITZROY COLEMAN. DEAN GITTER.
A. L. LLOYD.   BRUCE TURNER.

A section of the programme will be from the
Ballad of John Axon , including many new
songs about railway workers.

SUNDAY 23RD MARCH: EWAN MacCOLL.   FOTZROY COLEMAN.   DEAN GITTER.
& the Co.

with: SAM LARNER, BOB ROBERTS, & ARTHUR WEEMS,
some of the finest of all our country
singers – from East Anglia.

Handbill for Sunday Hootenannies at MacColl's Ballads and Blues club, 1957.

trade folk songs, a mix of country and industrial songs, English and Scottish ballads, children's street songs, industrial songs, sea shanties, broadside ballads and material written by MacColl in the folk idiom. A special guest would play a set, and the pattern would be repeated after an interval.

In 1956 Alan Lomax persuaded Peggy Seeger – twenty years old, and an accomplished five-string banjoist – to come to Britain and join his group The Ramblers. She was introduced to MacColl in Lomax's flat in March of that year, and soon began a relationship that never ceased until MacColl's death more than three decades later.[28] Her fits of giggles on hearing Cockneys or Liverpudlians attempting Lead Belly and Woody Guthrie songs alerted MacColl to the inauthenticity of his project. It was the year of the Suez calamity: Britain's imperial pretensions and its government's conspiracies with America were laid bare for the world to ridicule. The project to harness the will of the working class developed a new feverish urgency.

In 1961 Ballads and Blues became the Singer's Club, and a new doctrinaire atmosphere reigned. MacColl is often accused of encouraging parochialism by insisting on musicians confining their repertoire to their own place of origin. His own set lists were more eclectic: he was equally interested in Child ballads, nursery rhymes and miners' songs, and he slipped in his own compositions too. These were by no means universally political: his most famous composition, 'The First Time Ever I Saw Your Face' – which won Roberta Flack a Grammy in 1972 after her cover version appeared in the film *Play Misty for Me* – commemorated his love for Peggy Seeger. The dictatorial view of MacColl largely stems from his Critics Group, instigated in 1964 as a masterclass for would-be singers, in which MacColl and Seeger could pass on their years of expertise.

'It wasn't that we were hostile to so-called "foreign" songs,' he clarified in his autobiography. 'On the contrary, we were eager to attract foreign performers to the club. Our problem was English,

Dominic Behan
Enoch Kent
A.L.Lloyd
Ewan MacColl
Peggy Seeger
the resident singers welcome you to

THE SINGER'S CLUB

7-30 p.m. Every Sunday at
the PINDAR of WAKEFIELD
Grays Inn Road (Kings Cross)
membership 2s 6d admission 4s

Flyer for the Singer's Club, 1961. Controversially, performers were
only permitted to sing 'in a language they could understand'.

Scots, Welsh, Irish and American performers singing songs whose
idiom, whose language, they did not understand, hence mishandling
the songs . . . So the resident singers of Ballads and Blues decided
on a policy: that from now on residents, guest singers and those
who sang from the floor should limit themselves to songs which

were in a language the singer spoke or understood.'[29] This was a rule that applied within the confines of the club, not necessarily a prescription which MacColl would have applied outside it. After all, he himself wrote his own songs, had hits even, and on radio, television and elsewhere outside of his own milieu sang songs from all over the place. Peggy Seeger clarifies the Critics Group's position: 'We would try in the Ballads and Blues to sing songs of our own culture and in a language that we spoke. So no one would be pronouncing wrong, or getting the stresses wrong . . . That irritated people. We said, "This is for our own club" – we didn't say everybody should do this. But it turned out that once we started singing English songs, you had to know how to sing them – you couldn't do it with heavy guitar accompaniments, some songs hadn't been accompanied for years, decades, centuries probably. So you had a huge unaccompanied body of songs, and people were putting American accompaniments on them – heavy stuff, banjos and guitars, and the songs were virtually undergoing an immediate folk process without the gradualness of the folk process. And the songs . . . didn't sound English any more. So what we tried at the Ballads and Blues was to merely say: on *this* platform, you sing songs in a language you understand and from a culture that you come from. You should have a good time singing the songs, but from the platform it was different – this is what people miss. All we were doing was saying, for this platform, you are an interpreter of a very valuable heritage. If you ruin it, or change it too quickly, it will disappear, it will lose its specialness.'

On 9 February 1957 a freight train smashed into the rear of a second train in north Derbyshire. The driver, a fifty-six-year-old Stockport man called John Axon, was killed instantly in the collision. Instead of leaping to safety as soon as his brakes failed, he heroically clung onto the side of his cab, hoping to wrestle it

back under control further down the line, to avert any further loss of life. He was posthumously awarded the George Cross medal for bravery. A year and a half later, on 2 July 1958, the usually measured radio ambience of the BBC Home Service was rent by a full twenty seconds of catastrophic noise, tearing metal and thundering debris. Recreated in the BBC studios, the explosion occurred towards the climax of an hour-long tribute to Axon and the unsung lives of his fellow railway workers. *The Ballad of John Axon* was the first of a series created by MacColl, Seeger and BBC producer Charles Parker that shone the microphone like a searchlight into obscure or overlooked sectors of British society: fishermen, teenagers, motorway builders, miners, polio sufferers, even the nomadic travelling community. Gathered on the spot, their oral histories were reworked as intelligent and dynamic folk anthropology, attuned to their era's nuanced tug-of-war between conservatism and progress. The eight programmes, broadcast by the BBC between 1958–64, were experiments conducted on the wireless, splicing spoken word, field recordings, sound effects, traditional folk song and newly composed material into audio essays that verged on the hypnotic. They were given a name that elegantly fused tradition and modernity: radio ballads.

Until the mid-1950s standard BBC practice in making radio documentaries involved researchers visiting members of the public – 'actuality characters' – and talking to them, perhaps even recording them, then returning to headquarters and working out a script based on their testimonies. The original subjects would then be revisited and presented with the scripted version of their own words. That's the reason such programmes sound so stilted to modern ears: members of the public are almost always speaking a scriptwriter's distillation of their spontaneous thoughts.

When MacColl and Charles Parker drove up to Stockport in the autumn of 1957 with an EMI Midget tape recorder in their weekend bags, they planned to interview Axon's widow and his colleagues for information, then turn their findings into a dramatic reconstruction featuring actors and musicians. In fact, they stayed in the area for around a fortnight and ended up with more than forty hours of voices and location recordings. The material, they agreed, was too good to tamper with.

Educated at public school and Cambridge, a Tory and an active Christian, Parker should have been a classic BBC company man. But at the Corporation he was an outsider, frustrated with his colleagues' lack of inspiration and bureaucracy that stunted innovation. The world view he had been born with simply could not withstand the things he saw and heard during his partnership with MacColl and Seeger, which forced him to confront labouring communities who amazed him with unexpected articulacy and lyricism. In later years, pointing at his portable tape recorder, he would attest that this little machine had taught him socialism.

Unable to rewrite actuality, MacColl proposed that the programme take the form of a depiction of Axon's last journey, embellished with voices of his fellow railwaymen, the noises of the railway itself and a selection of songs whose lyrics, cadences and rhythms were suggested by the sounds and stories they had collected on tape: the actuality driving the narrative. Bert Lloyd had been involved in the production of a 'ballad opera' in 1947, *Johnny Miner*, which dramatised the life of a coal worker's family. *The Ballad of John Axon* advanced the form a significant stage further, with a mixture of traditional tunes, American folk-blues motifs and even a hint of calypso. Peggy Seeger returned from a long tour in the Soviet Union when the script was half finished and helped MacColl write accompaniments to many of his songs (she would take a larger role in the later radio ballads, as musical director and collecting much of the spoken matter). Parker then assembled a small instrumental ensemble in the studio, recorded the music, and then, in what appears to have been an epiphanic forty-eight-hour frenzy of tape splicing, edited the final programme together.

THE BALLAD OF JOHN AXON

by

Ewan MacColl   and   Charles Parker

————— ————

SEQUENCE A

OPENING ANNOUNCEMENT:

(Not recorded)

This is the BBC Home Service from the Midlands –

ORCHESTRA:

Fast solo banjo intro: into

NARRATOR:
(sings)

1st verse Narrative Ballad to banjo accompaniment

"John Axon was a railwayman

To steam trains born and bred,

He was an engine driver

At Edgeley loco shed.

For forty years he followed

And served the iron way;

He lost his life upon the track

One February day.

ORCHESTRA:

Banjo alone goes behind:-

ANNOUNCER:

MINISTRY OF TRANSPORT AND CIVIL AVIATION

10th July 1957

Page one of Ewan MacColl and Charles Parker's original script for the
first of their groundbreaking BBC radio ballads.

The Ballad of John Axon opens with MacColl singing: '*John Axon was a working man . . .*' A plummy radio announcer's voice interrupts occasionally to supply factual information. From this 'official' position we delve right down into the nitty-gritty of daily life on the railways, with reminiscences about the hardships and elations of working with steam engines, and testimonials to the good character of Axon himself from fellow workers and his widow. It tells the tragedy of an ordinary working man thrown into an emergency which required a burst of heroism: a ballad for the technological age. And the whole thing is woven together around MacColl and Seeger's contemporary folk music: a mainly bluegrass-flavoured banjo accompaniment, plus the odd lapse into jazz arrangements, all of which support Axon's canonisation as a British equivalent of Casey Jones. Throughout, the iron horses rattle down the line, whistling shrilly. At one point a chugging engine metamorphoses into a huffing harmonica; while the moment when the steam brake fails is a harsh, chilling shriek of metallic agony. The broadcast was favourably received and excited a good deal of comment at the time, as well as being entered for that year's Prix d'Italia. The BBC duly commissioned further programmes.

The subsequent radio ballads took MacColl, Parker and Seeger on a snapshot survey of various cross-sections of British life. *Song of a Road* (1959), about the construction of the M1 motorway, was an uncomfortable marriage of factual documentary and location reportage; they hadn't quite got the balance right between the 'official version' and the story on the ground. Chalking that one up to experience, they cut out all objective narration and let the material tell its own story.

MacColl remained most satisfied with the third ballad, *Singing the Fishing* (1960), which contrasted the herring industry in East Anglia (where old methods were dying out) with the new fishing centre of north-east Scotland (where trawlermen cut through the North Sea in the latest diesel-driven boats and lifted thousands of fish every day). In Great Yarmouth, the octogenarian Sam Larner, a veteran seaman since 1892, poured out reminiscences by the bucketload: songs, shanties and mariners' cant, falling into a kind of memory-trance as the long hours of interviewing transported him back into his younger self. MacColl later remembered that as Larner regressed into his memories, his vernacular and vocabulary became more biblical, rich, rhyming and uncensored. The history of Yarmouth's declining industry was all there in Larner's head to be unlocked; he had seen the ages of sail and steam come and go, and known days when the docksides weren't big enough to hold the day's catch. Another voice describes the exhilaration of the moment the herring net is landed on deck, illustrated with the squishy thump itself.

The technical set-up of *Singing the Fishing* achieved a new level of inventiveness, involving much more of a 'live' feel as tape and gramophone operators spun in the voices and sound effects, becoming members of the musical ensemble and allowing the musicians in the studio to work very closely with the speech rhythms on the tape extracts. It was this programme, MacColl stated, that 'taught us that in actuality could be found the subject matter for songs, usages, turns of expression, rhythms, pulses, idioms, all the elements out of which songs can be fashioned . . . Finally, we had learned to trust the actuality and to allow it to shape the entire work.'[30]

On *The Big Hewer* (1961) MacColl was in his element, taking listeners down into the electrically lit underworld of the coal mine. Over the clank and grind of the mining cage and the roar of the drill, we hear stories hoisted from the pits by miners from Yorkshire, Northumberland and Wales. The legendary 'Campbell', the 'big hewer' of mining lore, hangs over the piece like a delving demiurge.

The time needed to gather actuality recordings, the weeks of poring through and editing the tapes, musicians' rehearsal and session fees, etc., meant the radio ballads guzzled BBC money. Getting the programmes into a finished state led to heartburn for

Parker and questions at the top of the BBC about whether the required budget justified the results. *The Body Blow* (1962), on the psychology of living with pain, was produced quickly and cheaply in an effort to save the series from the BBC accountants' axe. But if anything the programmes' increasing sophistication and scope were going to need more resources, not cutbacks.

'It's like a big dustbin lid covering the sky,' says Dot, a Salford girl barely out of school, during the soundtrack to *On the Edge*, the radio ballad exposing the fears and dreams of teenagers aged fourteen to twenty. She's speaking in 1962, the year of the Cuban missile crisis, about the Bomb and its looming umbrella of fear casting a shadow over her future. Far from the groovy carefree world depicted in movies like Cliff Richard's *Summer Holiday*, MacColl and co. found a gloomy generation facing uncertain futures, dead-end jobs and uncomprehending adults telling them to pull their socks up. Their parents had weathered a world war but their psychic defences were not braced to withstand the 1960s youthquake. Progressive views on sex, marriage and capitalism are aired: the owners of these voices were the beatniks and hippies of the near future. As it is, they inhabit a world seemingly without clear channels (feminism, Vietnam, underground culture) for their confusion, anger and altruism. 'Their language is still akin to the language of the traditional ballads,' wrote MacColl in his autobiography, 'and as in their "with it" vocabulary, so in their passionate hopes and fears, these young people are the legitimate heirs of Lord Randall, of Burd Ellen and Young Tamlane – and, for that matter, of Hamlet.'

The Travelling People, the final radio ballad, broadcast in 1964, was the most ambitious of all, grappling with the vilified nomadic population of Britain. The programme did not flinch from including the negative sentiments of the 'not in my backyard' brigade: one gentleman is heard to call them 'misfits . . . the maggots of society'. The soundworld is particularly rich and evocative of difference: the travellers' words are surrounded by the outdoor ambience in which they dwell – birdsong, horses' hooves, the rush of road traffic. The voices of 'respectable' society speak in the dead air of cushioned interiors. Parker's editing skills reach a new level of finesse, so a succession of phrases like 'They call us the wild ones/ The pilgrims of the mist/ Romanies, Gypsies, diddikais, mumpers, travellers/ Nomads of the road/ Blackfaced diddies/ . . . In Carlisle, they call you porters, dirty porters this, dirty porters that . . .' whizz past in a kaleidoscope of lexicographic plurality and regional accents. Its conclusion – comparing Britain's treatment of its nomads to the Nazi pogroms – is shocking, but is borne out by the words of Labour councillor Harry Watton, who is heard to say, 'One must exterminate the impossibles.' It is a bitter, troubling conclusion to the radio ballads.[31]

In the post-war years it was the patronage of the political left that put folk music back in the public eye. Britain became a favoured refuge of renegade 'anti-American' artists. In 1961 Peggy Seeger's half-brother Pete fell victim to an anti-communist sedition probe and was blacklisted by conservatives. Granted leave to tour Britain in late 1961, Seeger was feted by an audience of 4,000 at the Royal Albert Hall and by a committee of prominent musicians and artists including MacColl, Paul Robeson, Benjamin Britten, Sean O'Casey and Doris Lessing. Writing at the end of his life, MacColl recalled that by placing himself at the centre of the folk revival, he 'hoped to arrest the plasticization of the popular culture. We hoped that these songs would help English, Irish, Scots and Welsh workers to assert their national and class identity. Then, again, it was necessary to preserve this highly specialised treasure of social and political information against the day when the workers came into their own.'[32]

People versus the Bomb: a 1960 *Sing!* magazine cover
reflects folk's grassroots politicisation.

In the mid-1950s newspapers began to run hostile articles
about folk clubs, calling them clandestine recruiting shops for
young Marxists. With no hard evidence for their accusations, the
reports petered out. Still, in their efforts to reposition a hybrid
British/American folk music as the dominant idiom of popular
song in Britain, MacColl, Seeger, Lomax, Lloyd and the rest
briefly had command of the voice of protest in the UK. At the
Campaign for Nuclear Disarmament's Ban the Bomb marches on
the Aldermaston nuclear weapons research centre in Berkshire,
beginning in Easter 1958, it was MacColl compositions such as
'Song of Hiroshima', 'Join in the Line' and 'That Bomb Has Got
to Go!' (with Peggy Seeger) that captured the mood, printed on

songsheets supplied by *Sing* magazine and distributed among the marchers. They viewed the British folk song as a conduit to the hearts and minds of working people. They saw the encroachment of pop music – rock 'n' roll, artists as minor deities, and the hit factories of Tin Pan Alley – as the harbingers of an art culture in thrall to consumerism. They saw a people denied access to its own folk-music heritage by an upper-middle-class elite. They saw post-war listeners steered towards the easily digestible pleasures of variety shows and American musicals. Their return to the bare bones of music-making, and a local repertoire, supplied a wholefood diet to combat the sugary confections of Broadway and the West End. And by vigorously promoting an art form based on traditional songs to which copyright didn't apply, and by not signing any long-term recording deals, they worked against the grain of the musical economy.

There's a photo, taken on 22 December 1962 by Brian Shuel, showing Bert Lloyd, MacColl and the Singer's Club audience listening tolerantly as the twenty-one-year-old Bob Dylan takes the floor, dressed in the peaked cap and sheepskin jacket he wore on the sleeve of his debut album. Although Dylan hugely admired MacColl's Topic recordings, MacColl was always distrustful of the younger singer. And from MacColl's point of view, he had good reason. By setting up a dialogue between British and American roots musics, he had unwittingly opened a Pandora's box. For with the influx of American culture came exposure to the freewheeling philosophy of the Beat writers, the liberation theory of modern jazz, the populist rhythms and electricity of rock 'n' roll, and a redefined notion of youth culture based on affluence, leisure, self-exploration and sexual freedom. The younger members of MacColl's audiences would fall under the spell of Dylan's expanded-mind poetry and pledge to speak in their own words, rather than those handed down via the oral tradition. The much-hoped-for revolution would take place not on the streets, but in the head.

II

Electric Eden

5

Songs for Swingin' Survivors

A uniformed policeman seizes the guitar's neck, thrusts his gloved fingers through the strings to grasp the circular sound hole, wrenches its strap over its owner's head. After a short tussle for possession, the guitar lies snapped on the pavement, kicked and stomped in the crush of protestors streaming down Whitehall. The crowd has been squeezed out of the crush in Trafalgar Square, where they have been chanting 'One, two, three four! We won't fight in Eden's war!' It is the afternoon of Sunday 4 November 1956, the most significant anti-government demonstration Britain has seen since the close of the Second World War. The nation, together with France, is about to enter into military action in North Africa, ostensibly as peacekeepers in the military assault Israel has just launched against Egypt. In fact, the whole scenario has been cooked up by Prime Minister Anthony Eden in order for Britain to reclaim control of the strategically priceless Suez Canal, recently nationalised by the incoming Egyptian leader, Nasser. The crisis is a crucial downturn in the fortunes of Eden's Conservative government, and a decisive factor in middle England switching its support towards a more liberal base even as Eden's successor Harold Macmillan takes over.

John Hasted looks down at the remains of his guitar. It is, or was, a Martin six-string, purchased around eight years ago. It took him nearly a year simply to obtain it when he went searching in the late 1940s, because guitars – models with a front panel that was entirely flat rather than curved, and with a round sound hole, not violin-style f-holes – were almost impossible to buy in the United Kingdom. Even Spanish guitars for playing classical music were rare, available only on import from Madrid. Hasted wanted a guitar like the one brandished by his hero Woody Guthrie, not the weedy-sounding round-bodied acoustic guitars that were used as low-level accompaniment instruments in crowd-pleasing dance bands. The vibrant, cheese-cutting twang of Guthrie's steel-string guitar amply justified the legend he had famously painted on its face: 'This machine kills fascists'.

We have encountered Hasted in the previous chapter, as a friend of and fellow jug-band player with BBC folklorist Peter Kennedy. An Oxford physics graduate and dedicated left-wing activist, he was a member of the Workers' Music Association and, from 1948, ran the WMA's Topic Singers and London Youth Choir. Hasted had been a chorister at Oxford, but he was captivated by a Pete Seeger Almanacs recording he heard as early as 1946, smuggled back from America by a friend in the merchant navy. Hasted singlehandedly introduced Almanacs material into the repertoires of his radical choirs, and his fan mail to Seeger yielded a set of written instructions for playing guitar and banjo by return post. It was this positive response from Hasted's new hero that set him off on his quest to buy himself a guitar. By the beginning of the 1950s he had made contact with Bert Lloyd and formed the 'British Almanacs', The Ramblers. He ran Britain's first folk club, The Good Earth, in Soho's Gerrard Street, and founded *Sing* magazine in 1954, which he filled with tips on playing guitar and three-string bass – the skiffle movement's very own 'how-to' guide.

So the ubiquitous image of the folkie strumming an acoustic guitar is an invention of the late 1950s and early 60s. Before prescient listeners like John Hasted began learning guitar, the instrument was practically unknown as an accompaniment to European popular and folk song. Cecil Sharp's published

John Hasted (left) and Steve Benbow, British early-adopters of the guitar.

arrangements were intended for communal singing by schoolchildren or choirs, backed by a piano. But the songs had been collected from singers who performed the material unembellished and a cappella, reserving the right to drift off key and out of metric whack. The 'purists' howling down Dylan and others in the mid-1960s for using an electric guitar to sing folk were harping on a false premise: they should have been demanding him to stop using a guitar altogether.

If Egypt was the wheel on which Britain's butterfly empire was finally broken, at the same time North African influences caused two important players to jump-start a legion of imitators back home. Around 1954 a twenty-one-year-old south Londoner named Steve Benbow was posted to Egypt for his National Service. The last days of British joint sovereignty in Egypt produced long, tedious, uneventful days, and Benbow – billeted in a tin hut near Lake Timsah on the Suez Canal – bought himself a guitar to while

away the hours. He developed a particular fondness for Greek
styles, and his self-taught dabblings with Burl Ives and Jimmie
Rodgers tunes, picked up on Forces' Radio, were put to use when
he returned to London in 1955. There, he gave informal concerts
playing a mixture of folk songs, jazz standards and easily digested
pop tunes. By 1957 he was also sitting in with a trad-jazz group
led by trombonist Dave Kier, a friend of Ewan MacColl, who
recruited Benbow to his cause by inviting him to the International
Youth Festival in Moscow and booking him for a recording session
for his Topic album *Barrack Room Ballads* (1958). Benbow also
partnered Bert Lloyd on his 1957 Topic EP *Bold Sportsmen All*,
and Lloyd helped Benbow add a sheaf of folk tunes to his song
portfolio. One of Benbow's favourite tunes, learnt on the shores
of the Suez Canal, was a Greek *rembetika* song called 'Misirlou'.
Rembetika is a harsh folk form peculiar to Greece, the product of
the country's nineteenth-century social underclass, often dealing
with grief, passion, loss, crime, alcohol and drugs. 'Misirlou'
means 'Egyptian Girl' – its derivation denoting that the heroine
is Muslim rather than Christian – and the song is an erotic hymn
to miscegenation, about a love that breaks both faith and racial
taboos. Benbow's subsequent work, often a kind of pop-folk lite
with orchestras and muzaky orchestral arrangements, earned him
plenty of TV and radio airtime in the late 1950s and into the 60s:
for many of those watching, his appearances began to cement the
image of man, guitar and gentle folk music for the first time.

Nine years younger than Steve Benbow, Davy Graham had
miscegenation and a nomadic spirit wired into his genes. His father
was a Scot from the Isle of Skye, his mother from Georgetown
in British Guyana. Born in Hinckley, Leicestershire, the teenage
Graham took up the guitar around 1956, entranced by the skiffle
revolution and by the exotic Greek timbre he heard in Benbow's
guitar playing. Graham included 'Miserlou' (*sic*) on his first album,
1963's *The Guitar Player*, by which time he had walked the walk,

visiting Greece, Morocco, Paris and the Côte d'Azur in pursuit of a seductive array of sounds. As early as 1959, when Ken Russell filmed him singing 'Cry Me a River' in front of dilapidated urban brickwork for the BBC arts documentary *Hound Dogs and Bach Addicts: The Guitar Craze*, an astounding technique was well formed.

'Angi', Graham's most famous composition, first appeared on *3/4 AD*, a 1961 Topic EP split with blues guitarist Alexis Korner. Based around a deceptively easy four-chord sequence, the plucking right hand appears to do the work of a jazz trio, the thumb maintaining a steady bass pulse while the rest of the fingers tweak out the tune's ruminative syncopations. Combined with blues-derived note-bending and hammer-ons on the fretboard, the guitar was transformed into a sophisticated percussion palette, the opposite of Lonnie Donegan's workmanlike chug. And the track '3/4 AD' itself was a barely disguised duet version of Miles Davis's 'All Blues', from 1959's groundbreaking *Kind of Blue*. Graham was fishing far outside the customary waters trawled by musicians of his generation, and his net was spread wide enough to include jazz, Indian and North African scales, folk-blues, popular song and Celtic airs. He was riding the waves of a tsunami that was in the process of washing through and destabilising the very structure of music itself: modality.

Modal music was one of the century's great liberating moments. Up to the end of the 1950s jazz players habitually performed improvised versions of what were essentially pop songs, constructed from horizontal sequences of chords. When bop musicians began writing from a *scale* of notes instead, it led to a kind of disciplined freedom where every chord corresponding to the scale, or 'mode', was allowed in. The results were comparable to older forms, especially Hispanic and Arabic musics – which Miles explored immediately following *Kind of Blue*, on 1960's *Sketches of Spain* – as well as Indian and oriental musics. Playing modally meant that a motif could be shifted upwards and downwards across harmonic keys, like the marker on a slide rule. The immediate effect was that soloists could now roam across a broader range of available notes without sounding out of tune. Modal music hovers ambiguously between harmony and discord.

Davy Graham discovered the modal bop of Miles Davis, Charles Mingus and Lennie Tristano during his late teens. Almost instantaneously, his steel strings began to act as lightning conductors, transistorising an unprecedented mix of 'folk, blues and beyond' (the title of his second album, recorded for Decca in 1964), including jazz, flamenco, English folk songs, Indian ragas, Persian love songs, Elizabethan lute song and Irish airs. 'Also, incidentally, he studies the Koran and reads Henry Miller,' breezed one sleeve note: here was the roving minstrel as intellectual traveller, presenting the world on a six-string.[1]

Such musical hybridity was rapidly replacing hardened generic boundaries, necessitating a reaction within the folk community. In 1959 Pete Seeger noted that 'a new problem looms, to threaten disaster. Today's citizens who love folk music are being thrown in contact with not one or two or three, but dozens and hundreds of traditions. Which to follow? . . . for good or bad, young people today who like folk music are combining various traditions together at a faster rate than the world has ever seen before. Some hybrids flourish so like weeds, that one fears for the very existence of other forms, just as the English sparrow has driven other birds from our parks. In many countries American popular music is looked upon in this way.'[2] In the event, Graham's multicultural vision spread through the folk-blues scene like a supervirus.

Like Miles Davis, Graham often used to turn his back on his audiences. This was primarily between songs, while he was retuning his guitars. For Graham, in the early 1960s, was privy to a secret alternative tuning system known as DADGAD, which he was reluctant to share with any rival guitarists in the crowd. He began using it around 1962–3, on a trip to the bohemian Beat capital

Tangier, where he spent six months and earned his keep by working in a snack booth selling hash cakes to locals. The raw Gnaoua trance music preserved in Morocco's town squares and remote Rif mountain villages stretched back thousands of years, and Graham was hypnotised by the oud, a large Arabic lute which resembles a bisected pear (the word 'lute' itself derives from the Arabic 'al-ud') and has been identified in Mesopotamian wall paintings 5,000 years old. The paradigm of Eastern music, defining its difference from the West, is the maqam, which uses a microtonal system that blasts open the Western eight-note octave into fifty-three separate intervals. DADGAD is not one of the tunings commonly used on the eleven-string oud, but Graham found that tuning a Western guitar that way made it easier to slip into jam sessions with Moroccan players. The configuration allows scales and chords to be created without too much complicated fingering; its doubled Ds and As and open strings often lead to more of a harp-like, droning sonority than the conventional EADGBE. The compound effect of fusing open tunings with modality electrified a generation of British guitarists.

For aspiring folk progressives of 1965 the essential record to spin on the Dansette was *Folk Roots, New Routes*. Released on Decca, the album featured Davy Graham's nimble technique in partnership with the remarkable voice of Shirley Collins. The pair were brought together by Collins's husband at the time, Austin John Marshall, whose sleeve notes accurately described the album's tapestry of sources: 'Negro blues-lore has been woven into the great Anglo-Appalachian love-knot. The soul-searching sonorities of Thelonious Monk are cheek by jowl with expansive British traditional themes and New Delhi has been builded in Cecil Sharp's green and pleasant land.' As well as solo showcases for Graham's guitar adaptation of 'Blue Monk' and Collins's five-string banjo rendition of 'The Cherry Tree Carol', Graham rewires Appalachian folk songs such as 'Nottamun Town' and 'My Dearest Dear', and on 'Pretty Saro', relocates a ballad of

Davy Graham and Shirley Collins listen to a playback of their
pathfinding *Folk Roots, New Routes* LP, 1964.

profound loneliness to the timeless calm of an Arabic courtyard,
while Collins's voice wafts upwards and disperses into a bleached
white cupola. His accompaniment to the traditional 'Reynardine'
sweetens and salts the text with a conjuror's sleight of hand. *Folk
Roots, New Routes* earned the disapprobation of Ewan MacColl's
Critics Group, but its hip, coolly delivered repertoire helped
reconnect the folk songbook with musical forms from an antiquity
beyond the Industrial Revolution, and implied many unseen
destinations for the music's future travels.

London in the winter of 1960 was beginning to offer new types
of space for young people to assemble in. With the opening of
the Moka in Soho, the coffee bar had arrived: an informal venue
particularly conducive to gatherings of slumming beatniks and

guitar-slingers. Soho became the London equivalent of New York's Greenwich Village, with Russell Quaye's Skiffle Cellar at 49 Greek Street opening in May 1958. South-west of Soho, at another coffee bar on the Old Brompton Road in Earl's Court, a Canadian couple with communist sympathies, Mike and Sheila van Bloemen, were running a club called the Troubadour, where folk and blues musicians competed for aural supremacy against the frothing Gaggias. Shirley Collins had briefly worked there as a waitress; now she joined a rotating clique of artists including Martin Carthy, Alex Campbell and itinerant Americans Ramblin' Jack Elliott, Derroll Adams – former railroading compadres of Woody Guthrie – and even Bob Dylan, all of whom blew a dash of tumbleweed into the heart of south-west London.

Martin Carthy, a teenage guitarist and singer who had grown up in Hampstead, north London, had begun attending Ballads and Blues and other folk clubs on the recommendation of his schoolfriend Joe Lloyd (Bert Lloyd's son). He was impressed with the subtle fingerpicking style of blues artesans such as Big Bill Broonzy, Mance Lipscomb and Elizabeth Cotten. In 1958 he witnessed a three-hour marathon at MacColl's club where the proceedings were effectively handed over to Norfolk fisherman Sam Larner for the night. Carthy – who had been working as an assistant stage manager at various London theatres and had ambitions to become an actor – instantly became a convert to the cause of English folk song, and in 1961 joined a group called The Thamesiders with Redd Sullivan, Marian Gray and Pete Maynard, who played an eclectic mix, from traditional songs to American blues, gospel, jazz and calypso. The group ran their own club, the King and Queen, near Goodge Street in central London. It was there, in the cold, harsh December of 1962, that Bob Dylan – midway through recording *The Freewheelin' Bob Dylan* LP – heard Carthy's versions of the ballads 'Lord Franklin' and 'Scarborough Fair', prompting him to reinterpret them within months as 'Bob Dylan's Dream' and 'Girl from the North Country'.[3]

Dylan was in England in December 1962 and January 1963 to take part in a BBC television play, *Madhouse on Castle Street*. The action takes place in a boarding house in which one of the lodgers locks himself in his attic room, threatening to stay there until he dies, unless the world changes. The play's director, Philip Saville, spotted Dylan in New York in 1962, and he was cast alongside David Warner as a pair of young male roommates, Lennie and Bobby. Evan Jones's script captured a moment in British culture when it hovered on the brink of a choice. The boarding house was a metaphor for what Britain had become during the 1950s: a place where the alienated inhabitants cling to false totems and outmoded beliefs rather than embracing change. Castle Street was deliberately named to evoke the old saw about 'an Englishman's home'. In 1963 the British were faced with the stark choice: innovate or stagnate. Move on from the greyness of post-war Britain, or become irrevocably mired in self-pity and memories of vanished glories. Lennie and Bobby represent angry young men posing questions with no clear answers. Five songs by Dylan ran through the play as a commentary, including the recently written 'Blowin' in the Wind'. The most remarkable of them was 'The Ballad of the Gliding Swan', adapted by Evan Jones from a much older Border ballad. A parade of horrific vignettes of murder, loneliness and mutation are described, as the '*swan on the river goes gliding by*'.[4]

Ewan MacColl's left-wing orthodoxy, his Singer's Club and Critics Group, came increasingly to look like petulant gestures, as if they had effectively shut themselves away in the room at the top, holding their breath until the revolution came. Gliding by with their heads in the air, while their younger audience were waking up to the fact that they didn't need to follow leaders.

Les Cousins, the 1959 *nouvelle vague* film directed by Claude Chabrol, deftly played on the tensions between the newly divergent metropolitan and provincial cultures, as a green law student comes up from the country to stay among his cousin's fashionable, sexually liberated bohemian set in Paris. The basement club at 49 Greek Street in Soho, also named Les Cousins (but pronounced the English way, 'Lez Cuzzens'), was discovered in 1965 in a fashion – if you believe the legend – that recalled a scene from Chabrol's movie. Les Bridger, a folk scenester and mediocre singer, staggered inebriated down a flight of stairs and crashed through a door to find a group of female students, for whom he promised to sing a selection of his songs. A club was born, setting itself up as the rowdy, unconventional alternative to the studious cultural Calvinism of existing folk clubs. Its proprietor, Andy Matthews – the son of the family that owned the Greek restaurant on the ground floor – tricked the small space out in what now seems like an ironic gesture towards the preoccupations of many older folk songs: a wagon wheel and a fishing net. The Greek Street basement had been the site of the previously mentioned Skiffle Cellar, which had shut down in 1960. When the Cousins opened its doors on 16 April 1965, its laidback atmosphere instantly provided a number of disparate spirits currently inhabiting London with a natural habitat and a place to lay their hats.

Wandering was a common theme in the folk-pop crossovers of the first half of the 1960s. Group names of the time –The Ramblers (twice), The Drifters, The Wayfarers, The Searchers – indicate that a freewheeling, restless spirit was abroad. As well as Davy Graham's explorations of the Mediterranean and North Africa, an assortment of raggle-taggle British folkies were roaming around France, Spain and beyond, singing for their supper and occasionally bumping into each other dossing in parks or crashing on various floors. The nomadic life was a newly desirable alternative to the manifest destiny of full-time work, marriage, parenthood and

Davy Graham/Alexis Korner, *3/4 AD* (1962); Davy Graham and Shirley Collins,
Folk Roots, New Routes (1965); Bert Jansch, *It Don't Bother Me* (1965).

conventionalism. Wandering musos such as Clive Palmer, Wizz
Jones, Donovan, Mac MacLeod, John Renbourn and Mick Softley
all came from a generation whose parents had withdrawn into
comfortable borders in the aftermath of the war, and they were
now on a quest for enlightenment, trying to 'catch the wind' of
the intuitive, impulsive, irrational side of life. They were British
hippies *avant la lettre*, their songs mixing political engagement with
cynicism, sexual freedom with romantic devotion, traditional
songs with self-penned numbers, distrust of the Establishment
with, in many cases, a powerful desire for commercial success.

April 1965, then, marked the beginning of a new epoch for
the new breed of singer-songwriters in Britain. As well as Collins
and Graham's *Folk Roots, New Routes*, in that year there appeared
Donovan's *What's Bin Did and What's Bin Hid* and *Fairytale*; John
Renbourn's self-titled first album; Mick Softley's *Songs for Swingin'
Survivors*; *Martin Carthy*, a collection of folk songs with violinist
Dave Swarbrick; Jackson C. Frank's *Jackson C. Frank*; and *Bert Jansch*,
the debut by the fastest-rising star of them all.

Jansch, who was born in Glasgow in 1943, had recently arrived
in London after making his name in Edinburgh. Spellbound by the
blues finger-style of Brownie McGhee at a gig at the city's Howff
club in 1960, he had dedicated his plentiful spare time to perfecting
his own guitar technique, taking lessons from Archie Fisher, a folk

minstrel whose popular versions of Scottish traditional music were leavened with occasional curveballs such as sitars and recorders. Jansch took to hanging out at the Howff coffee bar by day – a silent, black-polo-necked presence plucking away at his six-string. One of the main promoters in Edinburgh was a woman called Jill Doyle (also known as Jill Guest, following her marriage to Roy Guest, folk impresario and manager of such groups as The Watersons), who happened to be Davy Graham's half-sister. Through her, Jansch heard (and wore out) a copy of Graham's *3/4 AD* EP, retuned his guitar to DADGAD and proceeded to pick apart 'Angi''s clockwork secrets. In a couple of years, when it was included on his first album (as 'Angie'), Jansch would become, if anything, more closely identified with the tune than Graham himself.

The other influence on Jansch at that time was Anne Briggs, a Nottinghamshire singer who encountered the guitarist during a trip to Edinburgh in 1960. Like Shirley Collins, Briggs straddles two eras of folk music, bridging the period from the late-1950s industrial repertoire to the star-kissed folk-pastoralia of the late 1960s. Yet she remained focused on the purity of the songs themselves and, again like Collins, made her voice into a passive aeolian resonator to let the old songs emerge relatively unadorned. In 1962 she took part in Centre 42, a left-wing multi-arts festival put together by playwright Arnold Wesker to take radical culture to the provinces.[5] Briggs was co-opted to make regular 'interventions' in factory canteens and working people's pubs, popping up to belt out impromptu folk-song renditions to bemused and understandably hostile audiences.

Briggs and Jansch became intimate, briefly as lovers, then as friends and writing partners. Briggs's own recorded output was sparse: two songs on Topic's *Iron Muse* compilation; *The Hazards of Love* (a solo Topic EP, 1963); four songs on Bert Lloyd's compilation of bawdy folk, *A Bird in the Bush* (1966); and a five-year silence broached in 1971 with the release of the a cappella *Anne Briggs*

(Topic) and the guitar/vocal LP *The Time Has Come* (CBS). All the while, though, she seemed content to act as an invisible catalyst, sprinkling traditional songs and her own compositions among more prominent artists like gold dust. With Jansch she co-wrote 'Go Your Way, My Love' and 'Wishing Well', which appeared respectively on his LPs *Nicola* (1967) and *Birthday Blues* (1969). Their musical exchanges at this time, though informal, were mutually beneficial: he made her more confident in using guitar as a less formal accompaniment; she introduced and helped him to get inside the structure of many British traditional songs, including 'Blackwater Side', which would become a keystone in the repertoire of folk-rock.

When the Howff closed down in early 1962, the centre of Edinburgh's folk scene shifted to Archie Fisher's regular night at the Crown Bar on Museum Street. It was here that errant banjo player Clive Palmer fetched up in 1962, after hitch-hiking from Kent, and was introduced to Robin Williamson – a bohemian folkie who was Bert Jansch's flatmate at the time. Palmer decided to stay on in Scotland and joined Williamson and Jansch in their apartment. While the Palmer/Williamson partnership formed the nucleus of the first Incredible String Band line-up, Palmer's tales of musical bounty in the south of England impelled Jansch to seek his fortune there.

Jansch moved down to London, with Williamson, in January 1963, where his career rocketed. His insouciant angst and shy, unprepossessing stage manner struck a chord at the capital's edgy folknik pow-wows. That September Jansch made a pilgrimage to Morocco, in the footsteps of his hero Davy Graham; exactly a year later, at freelance producer Bill Leader's flat-cum-studio in North Villas, Camden Town, he recorded *Bert Jansch* – for Transatlantic, a label whose owner, Nat Joseph, was muscling in on the folk scene after several years issuing sex-education and poetry LPs. Despite containing several of his most celebrated songs – 'Strollin' Down the Highway', 'Needle of Death' and his take on 'Angie' – *Bert Jansch* is something of a false start, more rooted in American folk-blues, although subsumed into Jansch's formidable style. 'His left hand dances delicately along the fret board, like a spider on an electric grid,' gushed Keith de Groot's sleeve notes, 'while his right seems to grow another five fingers, as it swings to and fro across the chords like syncopated crinoline.' Over the records that followed, he continually surpassed himself. The first to free itself from the transatlantic influence was 1966's *Jack Orion*, with its open-tuning arrangements of traditionals such as 'The Waggoner's Lad', 'Nottamun Town', 'Pretty Polly', 'Henry Martin', 'Blackwaterside' and even Ewan MacColl's 'The First Time Ever I Saw Your Face'. The ten-minute title track was a semi-improvised but utterly transfixing ramble across the fretboard. By the end of 1965 he had been anointed the London folk-blues scene's de facto king.

At the poky palace of Les Cousins, where the folk monarchy held court, audiences of no more than 150 were routinely treated to mythically revelatory performances. The club never got around to applying for a liquor licence, so patrons consumed tea and sandwiches in a haze of hash smoke, straining to hear the soloists over percussive effects from the cash register. The crowd was mostly made up of Davy Graham's other vagrant disciples: John Renbourn, another Transatlantic protégé; Wizz Jones, pursuing his country-tinged duo with Pete Stanley; young keepers of the revivalist flame such as Anne Briggs, Martin Carthy, Dave Swarbrick, The Watersons, The Young Tradition and Toni and Dave Arthur; legions of youthful, guitar-toting, romantic troubadours – Alex Campbell, Keith Christmas, Sandy Denny, Donovan, Julie Felix, Roy Harper, Jo Ann Kelly, Alexis Korner, Trevor Lucas, John Martyn, Ralph McTell, Mick Softley, Al Stewart, Robin

Williamson and Clive Palmer's embryonic Incredible String Band
. . . It attracted a significant American clientele, too, made up of
expat residents and people passing through: Derroll Adams, Joan
Baez, Sandy Bull, Champion Jack Dupree, 'Spider' John Koerner,
Stefan Grossman, Arlo Guthrie, Paul Simon and Art Garfunkel
(who copped 'Scarborough Fair' wholesale from Martin Carthy
and copyrighted it as their own). Maverick inventor/producer
Ron Geesin stuck his head round the door, as did Jimmy Page, then
a Tin Pan Alley session musician, Jimi Hendrix, Pete Townshend of
The Who, popping up the road from the Marquee Club, and Nick
Drake, on odd nights away from Cambridge University. A whole
lot of folk songs got sung down in that basement, and in hundreds
of similar spaces around the country, but plenty of new, original
music was heard alongside them.

If the casually applied dexterity of Graham, Renbourn and
Jansch epitomised the Les Cousins ethic, its theme-tune writer
was the American singer Jackson C. Frank. Frank came into a small
fortune of $100,000 when he was twenty-one, a compensation
payout following a school fire disaster that left much of his
body permanently scarred. Embracing the itinerant life of the
wandering folkie, he hopped on an ocean liner to Britain and,
he later claimed, had written his signature tune, 'Blues Run the
Game', by the time he disembarked at Southampton. The song
instantly captivated the London scene, becoming as much of a
standard as 'Angi'.

It's appropriate that the song was written midway across the
Atlantic, for its scarred understatement and youthful cynicism
mark it as part of the same world as that inhabited by Bert Jansch.
The pain of the unhomed, the essential sadness of the unrooted
life, would become an important and recurring theme for British
folk-rockers, including Frank's girlfriend at the time, Sandy Denny,
then an eighteen-year-old trainee nurse. Denny was present at the
recording session for 'Blues Run the Game' at the CBS Studios

on New Bond Street, along with Paul Simon (producing), Art Garfunkel (making the tea) and Al Stewart (playing occasional guitar). It was she who sent out for a bottle of whisky to soothe the chronically shy, anxious singer, who insisted on recording behind a screen of acoustic baffles. Frank's perpetual self-doubt and low self-esteem were transmitted to the equally self-critical Denny, while providing emotional fodder for many of her own later compositions.

John Renbourn harboured no such timidity. Born in London in 1944, he was encouraged to explore the medieval and Elizabethan lute tradition by his classical guitar teacher. He was drawn, by way of skiffle, to the American blues picking of Elizabeth Cotten, Brownie McGhee and Ramblin' Jack Elliott while studying at Kingston College of Art, which at that moment was a breeding ground for as many upcoming musicians as artists – undergraduates included Eric Clapton, Sandy Denny and members of The Yardbirds. Renbourn's beatnik credentials were as impeccable as his art-school grounding: in the early 1960s he lived in a barge on the Thames and followed the European busking trail, even writing a bluesy eulogy to the National 7 highway through France to St Tropez.

In the summer of 1962, in the middle of a hitch-hiking trail around the west of England, he was drinking in a pub in Torquay, Devon – a town with a sizeable beatnik presence – when in walked a young man three years his senior named Keith MacLeod, usually known as Mac. The two got talking, and Renbourn learned that some days previously Mac MacLeod had arrived in Devon from his home town of St Albans, north of London, where he was involved in a folk-club scene spread between a cluster of towns in Bedfordshire and Hertfordshire.

He had been on a scooter journey to St Ives in Cornwall with his friend John Lock (later one of Donovan's roadies), but they had run out of money and, hence, fuel on the clifftops of Torquay, where they bedded down for a night outdoors. Lock abandoned MacLeod the next morning, but MacLeod stayed on, sleeping rough for a few more nights, then picking up menial work in a hotel and checking in to the local YMCA. Renbourn struck up a friendship with this reckless, itinerant character, and for the rest of that summer the pair played as a duo around folk clubs in Devon and Cornwall.[6]

Hertfordshire was already one of the most influential hotbeds of the new folk movement outside of Soho. Lying on the fringes of London's green belt, the county's satellite towns – St Albans, Luton, Aylesbury, Hatfield, Hemel Hempstead – were close enough to the capital for judicious record shopping, yet far enough away to breed their own unique characteristics and personalities. Herts heads keen for a lungful of marijuana and subterranean entertainment would gather at The Cock in St Albans and wallow in music such as Ramblin' Jack Elliott's 1961 Topic album, a big favourite with MacLeod and his friends. Down the road from The Cock brooded The Peahen, where a more traditional, MacColl-style folk-revival club was held; this gave the Cock regulars something to define themselves against.

When they began to appear, the rebellious spirit of Bob Dylan's first albums likewise touched a chord with folks such as Mick Softley, who ran a similar establishment, The Spinning Wheel, in Hemel Hempstead. Softley is one of the most unjustly forgotten figures in the British 1960s folk boom, a free spirit with a lion's mane of hair. Pete Frame, the rock-family-tree expert who opened the Luton Folk Club at the Dolphin Coffee Bar in January 1965, recalled Softley's 'amazing songs filled with laughter, barefeet and spilled beer. It seemed like he'd rolled any troubles he may have had into a ball, and simply cast them to the winds – everywhere he went he saturated the place with laughter.'[7] As early as 1959 Softley hitched through France to the Pyrenees, and spent time

Preacher of discontent: Mick Softley, 1965.

living in the jejune cultural *galère* of Paris. When his attempts to break into literary circles failed, he became a street musician and began meeting the other British ramblers – Alex Campbell, Wizz Jones, Clive Palmer et al. He would make a reasonable living at this game for a good three years, returning to Hemel Hempstead in 1964 to run The Spinning Wheel, which, in his own words, was 'really wild – the best folk club England's ever had without a doubt. It was to be open to 3 or 4 in the morning, with everyone jugging it up, sweating like hell.'[8]

Volatile, unpredictable and sensitively tuned to injustice – his mother had been an assistant to suffragette heiresses Sylvia and Christabel Pankhurst – Softley absorbed Dylan's oblique protest music more thoroughly than most of his contemporaries. Softley's first album, *Songs for Swingin' Survivors* (Columbia), produced by Donovan's management team of Peter Eden and Geoff Stephens, is one of the three great solo folk albums released in Britain in 1965, alongside Bert Jansch's second, *It Don't Bother Me*, and *John Renbourn*. On the sleeve of the Renbourn debut the guitarist adopts what he later called the 'folk-singer-on-the-rubbish-dump' stance, leaning on the headstock of his Scarth acoustic in front of a dilapidated street hoarding. But Softley went much further: he had himself photographed in the putrid vapours rising from the Two Tree Island rubbish dump in Essex; all that's left to ramble around are the steaming remains of civilisation. It was an apocalyptic image illustrating the record's anti-war themes. In a voice whose croak suggests more years than Softley's twenty-four, his evocation of a nuclear winter on 'After the Third World War Is Over' makes Ewan MacColl's Aldermaston march songs of five years earlier sound almost vaudeville. 'And the War Drags On' is the first British song explicitly to comment on the Vietnam War and evoke the nightmare of '*Cities full of people burning, screaming, shouting out loud*' in a nuclear attack. The song became Softley's best-known work, as it was included by the nineteen-year-old Donovan − another St Albans personality − on his *Universal Soldier* EP.

It was Donovan who hooked Softley up with Columbia for his first record deal, but Softley nurtured a deep distrust of the music industry throughout his career. He effectively dropped out of performing or recording until the end of the 1960s, electing to run a home-brewery shop and foam-rubber market stall on the outskirts of Hemel Hempstead, and satisfy a voracious appetite for women whose passions he aroused in his mobile 'fornicatorium' − the white van pictured on the cover of his album *Sunrise* (1970). All the while he honed a critical stance that preserved the social consciousness of a Woody Guthrie while sponging up more and more elements of late-1960s cosmic fantasy and science fiction. But financial hardship in the early 1970s saw him off the scene for good, and he ended up living a reclusive life in Northern Ireland, publishing occasional small-press volumes of poetry.[9]

For his part, Mac MacLeod was also destined to be pop's nearly man, his ensuing career frustratingly interwoven with that of his old friend Donovan. Back in St Albans at the end of 1965, he was in a shortlived duo with Maddy Prior, a nineteen-year-old daughter of a BBC scriptwriter who had been curiously exploring the contrasting universes of the Peahen and Cock. Just when things might have started moving, he resolved to try his luck in Scandinavia, and began a period of living in Copenhagen, where he formed Hurdy Gurdy in 1967 with a Danish drummer and bassist, playing in the cutting-edge hard-rock style recently pioneered by Cream. The trio rented a cottage near Bude in Cornwall in early 1968, practising a set that included 'Hurdy Gurdy Man', the song Donovan had written especially for them in hopes of scoring a hit single. Donovan had conceived it as an ethereal hippy idyll arranged with harpsichords, flutes and a celestial choir. Hurdy Gurdy played the song like a kick in the solar plexus, with fuzz guitars and jabbing riffs. The group took a short break, only to find that in their absence Donovan had recorded his own hit version in the hard-edged vein they had played him on his lawn at Little Berkhamsted a few weeks before, with Jimmy Page on guitar and John Bonham on drums.[10]

MacLeod subsequently turned down an offer to join folk-rock group America, and scraped a living roadying for Kevin Ayers while rehearsing, but never recording, an avant-garde jamming

Anne Briggs, *The Hazards of Love* EP (1964); John Renbourn, *John Renbourn* (1965); Mick Softley, *Songs for Swingin' Survivors* (1965).

group called Amber in Notting Hill. MacLeod's story remains a tantalising series of unfulfilled possibilities.

The stories of men like Mick Softley and Mac MacLeod are typical, though, of the rapid reinventions of so many artists who began the 1960s as monochrome neo-bluesmen and were overtaken by the technicolour dreamscape of the psychedelic era. Because, after Davy Graham and Shirley Collins's *Folk Roots, New Routes*, blues ceased to run the game: the next hand would be dealt by a local dealer. As the second half of the 1960s began, any number of guitarists could crank out 'Angi' or bawl a version of 'Blowin' in the Wind'. The trick was to look beyond these diminishing returns. For the rest of the decade Collins and others – including her sister Dolly, The Watersons, Peter Bellamy and The Young Tradition, Martin Carthy – focused on what was endemic to British, or even specifically English, folk culture, transforming the way traditional material could be presented. To reach these folk roots, they took a new route through the wildwood of the pagan ritual year.

6

Variations on a Theme of Albion

What are the songs really about?
Let's start with Adam and Eve.

A. L. Lloyd, sleeve notes to The Watersons'
Frost and Fire (1965)

By the mid-1960s folk and pop music were enjoying a closer relationship than ever before. And yet their original etymology reveals a huge divide. The Latin root of 'pop' – '*populus*' – confirms its links to the rigid social order of the Roman Empire, a city-based civilisation whose tastes and collective morale were bolstered by enormous public-entertainment spectacles such as gladiatorial combat and comedic dramas. A population is an organised urban mass, a people regulated by civic laws and socialised patterns of ownership and living. Pop is the culture of imperial socialisation, of institutionalised religion, consensus and commerce.

But 'folk' represents something potentially more anarchic. The word is much older than the Latin, and derives from '*Volk*' in ancient Teutonic/Scandinavian. The ancient Germanic races of Northern Europe constituted a heathen peasantry consisting of villagers and vagrants. The rule of law was a more relativist concept than in the early democracies; land was subject to seizure by whichever chieftain could raise the most brutal brigand army.

The *Volk*'s playground was the *Wald*: the forest that looms with such powerful, murky force in so many European myths and fairy tales. The Teutonic root word of '*Wald*' – '*walthus*' – is an ancestor of both 'wood' and 'wild'. Seen from its Germanic perspective,

Membership card for the Troubadour club, south-west London, early 1960s.
The folk revival and medievalism have always been closely linked.

then, the word 'folk' feels inextricably wedded to Northern
Europe's barbarous, wooded interior. The Roman Empire cleared
away much of the forest during its European campaigns, but the
Nordic wildness survives in any English place name ending with
'-wald', '-wold' or '-weald'. Other curiosities survive, too; things
of which we have only a limited understanding. By the second half
of the twentieth century folk culture in Britain had become a kind
of cargo cult, a jumble of disassociated local customs, rituals and
superstitions: uncanny relics of the distant, unknowable Britain of
ancient days. Why, for instance, do sword dancers lock weapons in
magical shapes such as the pentagram or the six-pointed star, led by
a man wearing a fox's head? What is the straw bear plodding round
the village of Whittlesey in Cambridgeshire every January? Why
do a bunch of Nutters black up their faces and perform a coconut
dance in several Lancashire villages? What possesses people to
engage in the crazed 'furry dance', singing the 'Hal-An-Tow' song,
on 6 May at Helston in Cornwall? Why do beribboned hobby horses
canter round the streets of Padstow and Minehead every May Day,
with attendant 'Gullivers' lunging at onlookers with a giant pair of

pincers? The persistence of such rites, and the apparent presence of codes, occult symbolism and nature magic in the dances, mummers' plays and balladry of yore, have provided a rich compost for some of the outgrowths of folk in the 1960s and afterwards. Even to dip a toe into the world of folklore is to unearth an Other Britain, one composed of mysterious fragments and survivals – a rickety bridge to the sweet grass of Albion. As Bert Lloyd mentioned, 'To our toiling ancestors [these customs] meant everything, and in a queer irrational way they can still mean much to us.'[1]

The conception of folk music as a carrier of secret knowledge was not new. In 1952 Folkways released a crimson, cloth-bound box set of six LPs, *Anthology of American Folk Music*, which, from its colour-coded design down to its carefully graded track sequence, seemed guided by a higher thought system. Its compiler was Harry Smith, a highly idiosyncratic American folklorist, occultist and experimental film-maker whose spread of talents made him comparable to a Renaissance polymath. Since his teenage years, when he used a portable tape machine to record the songs of Native Americans, Smith became obsessed with collecting examples of folk art, such as painted eggshells, woven Seminole blankets, string figures and even paper aeroplanes. For Smith, these crafts and ornaments, preserved through centuries of domestic life, acted as time machines, handing down ancient numeric and geometric patterns from generation to generation. Collecting them together manifested the interconnectedness of human cultures at root level.

Harry Smith ascribed the same qualities of preservation to folk music, and during the 1930s and 40s amassed a huge store of records, often salvaging old shellac and seventy-eights discarded by libraries and households. In doing so he saved many hundreds of folk, blues and roots recordings from extinction. Eighty-four of these were channelled into his Folkways *Anthology*, which has come to seem as definitive as it is quixotic. Smith presented the set as a memory theatre, dividing the tracks thematically into Ballads, Social Music and Songs, and using an alchemical colour code to align each with an element: water, fire and air.[2] The box's lid was stamped with a reproduction of the celestial monochord engraving from Elizabethan hermetic philosopher Robert Fludd's *History of the Macrocosm and Microcosm* (1617), a diagrammatic representation of Pythagorean musical theory, in which the notes of the octave are mapped onto the paths of the sun, moon and planets – the building blocks of the 'music of the spheres'.

Beyond the untempered, occult significance of the lo-fi hissy hollers, ecstatic gospel, ragged-trousered hillbilly hoedowns and mournful field blues, Appalachian ballads and slave arhoolies compiled on the *Anthology*, Smith's careful shepherding of the material was part of a plan to craft a magical talisman that would engineer social change. This was not necessarily the Marxist humanism of Alan Lomax and Ewan MacColl, but revolution on a more mythopoeic level. He was reading Plato's *Republic* at the time, and noted the Greek philosopher's references to music as a potent agent of challenge to the ruling status quo.[3]

In the sceptical intellectual climate of post-war Britain, folk music's ritual and magical properties were seldom placed in the foreground as openly as on Smith's *Anthology*. The Edwardian folk revivalists tended to characterise their songs and folk customs as a window on an Arcadian golden age, when happy workers plied their feudal existence in deference to the lords and ladies of the manor. In the 1960s Bert Lloyd believed you didn't have to be a mystic or a sentimentalist to understand that song traditions connected to nature, which determined the people's economic fortunes, would persist among the labouring population. And yet Lloyd was equally unwilling to let go of the idea that certain surviving traditions were the residue of primeval myths.

As Ralph Vaughan Williams recognised when he remade *The English Hymnal*, liturgical music is the principal means by which the folk interface with their god. There is a convincing argument that the earliest church music in Britain, plainsong, was not an entirely brand-new invention, but was grafted onto songs and ritual chants that were already deeply embedded in the collective consciousness.[4] The 'response' form, in which the song adopts the form of a lone voice asking a question that is answered by a chorus, is commonly found in folk songs as well as the Gregorian plainchant of the eighth and ninth centuries.

Writing plainsong down involved using an esoteric notation system, with notes corresponding to letters, which in turn represented deities, stars, gods and goddesses, trees, etc. This magical system, its origins fogged by time, formed the long-dead compost from which contemporary folk music has grown. The symbolic factors remain dyed into the music, like a stain in the wood. 'The folk-memory does not retain conscious ritualism, or intellectualised secrecy,' comments one folk historian, 'but works as in a dream. In this way, despite a tough oral memory, the spirit of the nature rites is still present.'[5]

The Roman invasion of Britain in 43 CE imported the full pantheon of pagan gods and goddesses. In 313 the emperor Constantine adopted Christianity as the official religion of the new Holy Roman Empire. In the ensuing trickle-down across Europe, Christianity emerged in the British Isles as one cult among many – a largely Celtic brew of beliefs seasoned by the sporadic invasions of the Angles, Saxons and Jutes. Missionaries kept returning to Britain's Celtic fringes – Cornwall, Wales, Ireland – but inland, where it was more perilous for them to penetrate, the divine family tree became gnarled and tangled, with the pagan gods twisted around the Christian Trinity as an ivy binds itself to an oak. The story of the death of Christ was, in any case, mystically aligned with the older religion, with its depiction of a sacrificed saviour king and the ritual consumption of body and blood. Paganism may have rejected the pantheon of state-sanctioned gods, but it grafted itself firmly onto the Christian gospel.

Once, when Cecil Sharp was collecting songs in Langport, Somerset, the vicar of the local parish church informed him that the use of wooden vessels for Holy Communion was expressly forbidden. The use of wood for the ritual consumption of Christ's blood carried too strong an echo of the rite's supposedly pre-Christian, pagan origins. Pagans worshipped the trees because wood was a magical substance, feeding the fires that cooked their food, supplying materials to make weapons and construct shelter. In the world's earliest agricultural societies, fertility and the perpetuation of natural cycles – the rising and setting of the moon and sun, the recurrence of spring, the ebb and flow of rivers and sea tides, the growth and ripening of crops – were sacred because they were vital to survival.

The gods controlling these cycles needed to be appeased with sacrifices. At first, the leader of the pack, the king himself, was slaughtered before his vital energies began to die off, and a new healthy replacement was appointed in his place. Over time, slaves or captives were slain instead. In ancient Britain, the Roman occupiers banned human sacrifice so the ritual changed: animals – goat, ram, wren – took starring roles in the sacrificial spectacle. The royal sacrifice mutated into a harvest cult, where the dying king symbolised the end of the waning year and the appointment of the new ruler the beginning of the waxing year, after the winter solstice when the days begin to grow longer again. The cycle of birth, growth and death was synchronised with the turning of the stars, planets, moon and sun. Finally, the sacrifice was simply enacted in public art forms more familiar to modern sensibilities, such as dance, tragic drama, opera and the ballad.

The early English church got properly established between 597, when St Augustine splashed down on the Kent coastline on a papal mission to convert the Britons, and the late ninth century, when the first of many Danish Viking raids took place on the holy island of Lindisfarne in the North Sea. The pagan Norsemen applied a particularly destructive zeal to the monasteries and churches springing up across Britain. It was Alfred of Wessex, the king who vanquished this last band of marauders, who finally settled on Christianity as the desirable religion of his people. William the Conqueror was an enthusiastic builder of churches and monasteries, but even by the time he and his invading armies arrived from Normandy in 1066, Britons' national psyche – their customs, culture and language – had already been shaped by almost 900 years of wrestling for possession between competing religious doctrines, heathen, pagan and Christian.

In 1969 the folk-rock supergroup Crosby, Stills & Nash would boast that their close-knitted harmonies possessed the mystical power to 'move the air'. But the same could be said of The Watersons and The Young Tradition. However, their approach to singing was in turn strongly influenced by the Copper family of Rottingdean, Sussex, for whom unison vocalising had been an ingrained way of life for more than a century, and whose unique, intuitive multipart harmonies now emerged as a much-imitated influence on the *sound* of British ensemble folk singing.

'Life has changed so drastically in the last few decades', wrote Bob Copper in the early 1970s, 'that it must be almost impossible for anyone under the age of thirty to imagine what it was like in the days when these songs were still being sung in the ordinary course of events and not as the result of a folk song revival.' In the 1920s, when Bob Copper was a boy, he regularly felt the years rolling away as 'old-timers' sang songs they had learned when they were themselves boys back in the 1840s and 50s. 'I became aware at an early age that I was witnessing the very last chapter of a long story and that what I was seeing and hearing would quickly be finished and gone for ever.'⁶ The Copper family is a rare instance of a Victorian working-class dynasty that cared for and archived its own store of folk songs and singing styles, rather than leaving the job to a more privileged middle-class collector. Discovered by the Folk-Song Society's Kate Lee in 1898, patriarchs James 'Brasser' Copper, born in 1845, and his brother Thomas were made honorary members and encouraged to write down their own songs, which had been a constant in their everyday life since the mid-1850s. That legacy was upheld throughout the upheavals of the twentieth century by a further four generations. Brasser's son John and grandchildren Ron

Three generations of the Copper family, stewards of a 150-year-old rural folk tradition. Clockwise from bottom left: Bob, John, Jill and Ron Copper, photographed in the mid-1970s.

and Bob all appeared in Alan Lomax's *Song Hunter* TV series in the 1950s and were frequent guests of Peter Kennedy on *As I Roved Out*; Bob made field recordings for the BBC in the south of England. The Coppers' repertoire spanned a period in English history with a clearly etched trajectory of an agricultural paradise destroyed by the creep of modernity and the huge losses of the First World War. 'The world those old-timers lived in always seemed to me to be more exciting', wrote Bob Copper, 'and more colourful and the men themselves more highly individual . . . They ploughed their land with teams of oxen, sowed their seed by hand, reaped the corn with sickles and threshed out the grain with flails as their Saxon ancestors had. Their lives were hard but uncomplicated and through living and working close to nature they had a clearly defined and well-balanced sense of values. In the main they were content and were aware when they sang, in the words of one of their songs, "Peace and plenty fill the year", that it was not so far from the truth.

'They knew peace. The Crimean War was a distant and shadowy memory that had long since ceased to ruffle the village calm and the Boer War was yet to come. Although they still sang in praise of heroes . . . their immediate horizons were unclouded by wars or threats of war.'[7]

In the mid-1960s that tough oral memory resurfaced among the generation of folk musicians born during the Second World War. Martin Carthy's duo with fiddler Dave Swarbrick, singer Anne Briggs, the urban troubadour John Renbourn (and, to a partial extent, his sparring partner Bert Jansch), and the prototype Incredible String Band duo from Edinburgh, Robin Williamson and Clive Palmer, rejected the spartan industrial dogma of the Ewan MacColl circle and blew the dust off a pile of much older tomes. The pre-Christian atmosphere was most tangible in the 'new routes' taken by Shirley Collins and two young all-vocal ensembles, The Young Tradition and The Watersons. With these clans, who had access to the wider markets being opened up by the pop industry and matched a love of the music with a more relaxed attitude to its historical and social provenance, the sound of British folk music began irrevocably to change. The ruling spirit of folk song needed to be sacrificed, and a new one rebirthed, in order for the form to survive.

The Watersons were a four-piece vocal group from Kingston-upon-Hull. Based around three orphaned siblings – Norma, Mike and Elaine (Lal) – and one close family friend (John Harrison), the quartet had begun as teenage skiffle devotees in the mid-1950s but, following the example of MacColl's Ballads and Blues, from 1958 ran their own club – by 1965 it was a night called Folk Union One, based at Hull's Olde Blue Bell pub. Their reputation in the area was strong enough to command guest visits by Martin Carthy, Louis Killen, Anne Briggs and others, and they gradually phased out the American side of their material in favour of a strictly British, largely northern English, portfolio. Through examining archives, and via the long trek to significant folk events such as May Day at Padstow, Cornwall, they

The Watersons: (left to right) Mike Waterson, John Harrison, Lal Waterson and Norma Waterson, mid-1960s.

tapped into the serious heart of the tradition. The Watersons were all Catholics who had been raised by their grandmother, an Irish Gypsy. It was a potent heritage that imbued them with superstitious natures, fascinated by stories of death and ghosts.

Under the name The Waterson Family, they made their recording debut for Topic, one of four upcoming acts on the showcase compilation *Folk-Sound of Britain* (1965). Dispensing with guitars and banjos, they hollered unadorned close harmonies into a stark, chapel-like hush. The consensus was that they 'sounded traditional', but in a way no other folk singers did at the time. It was the result of pure intuition: there was no calculation in their art. When Bert Lloyd once commented joyfully on their mixolydian harmonies, they had to resort to a dictionary. Later in 1965 the quartet gathered around the microphone set up in the Camden Town flat of Topic producer Bill Leader and exhaled the extraordinary sequence of songs known as *Frost and Fire*.

In his capacity as an artistic director of Topic, Lloyd curated the album's contents. Focusing on the theme of death, ritual sacrifice and resurrection, he subtitled it *A Calendar of Ritual and Magical Songs*. The fourteen tracks are divided by calendrical seasons, and the four Watersons begin and end the album as midwinter wassailers, a custom popularised in the late eighteenth and early nineteenth centuries as groups of singers – 'waits' – made the rounds of the towns and villages, proffering a decorated bowl of spiced ale or wine and asking – in the form of a song, or 'wassail' – for a charitable donation. Midwinter comes shortly before the time of the first ploughing in preparation for the sowing of that year's new crop, and the waits' money, or food and drink, can be considered a form of benign sacrifice against the success of the next growth and harvest. The wassail-bowl's rounds were often associated with the singing of Christmas carols.

'The Derby Ram', for Lloyd, illustrated the phenomenon of rites pertaining to animal gods devolving over time to the level of burlesque and horseplay. The song describes an improbably well-endowed ram sighted at Derby Fair: '*This tup was fat behind, sir, / This tup was fat before, / His tup was nine feet round, sir / If not a little more.*' But the dance as it had survived was a pantomime, with the dancer no longer covered in the animal's skin but a costume patched together from a lump of old carpet. It's a reminder that the final resting place for lyrics that may have originated as magical nature invocations is the children's nursery rhyme.

Spring arrives with the heartily sung 'Pace-Egging Song', accompanying a 'trick or treat'-style custom in which gifts of eggs are solicited from doorsteps on Good Friday. The famous black-and-white Brian Shuel photo on the album's cover shows one of the Midgley pace-egg team, the 'Bugler', sitting alone with his drum, horn and elaborate, flamboyant headdress by a river running like molten gold in the spring sun.

'Seven Virgins (The Leaves of Life)' – sung in haunting solo by Norma Waterson – is a fine example of the interweaving of pagan and Christian elements: a tableau of Christ nailed to a yew tree. The perennial figure of 'John Barleycorn' makes an appearance as one of two summer songs. With its brutal treatment of an anthropomorphic rick of corn, it is one of the quintessential English folk songs, what Lloyd calls 'an unusually coherent figuration of the old myth of the corn-king cut down and rising again',[8] and covered by everyone from Martin Carthy and Pentangle to Traffic. Mike Waterson sings it solo, to the tune known as 'Dives and Lazarus' – also a favourite of Vaughan Williams.

The astounding harmonic grind of the autumnal 'Souling Song', with its gnashing bassline and three-part melodic lines that shiver up against each other, is appropriate to the song's location in Halloween and All Souls' Night. A long way from the sugary harmonising of The Beach Boys or The Hollies, the melodic lines cleave tightly together, clash and vibrate. The Watersons' particular talent was the innate ability of each member to jump around, improvising the harmonies, one singer handing the harmony to the next and dropping down or springing up to catch the next roll of the song. The voices might converge on a unison line, then suddenly split apart into a myriad of colours as if refracted through some sonic lens. Lal Waterson once claimed that the secret of their sonic friction consisted in having two voices singing and two making 'noises' – herself and brother Mike creating a screech element. Sometimes no single Waterson would follow the central melody all the way through; instead, it was tossed from voice to voice, touched on by each of the quartet at some point on their own respective melodic paths through the song. There was a sense of plainsong about it, emphasised by Leader's production, which daubed a hint of stone-chamber reverb onto their chants.

The Watersons' polyphonic austerity refreshed the sound of modern folk in Britain to the extent that publications as diverse as *Sing*, *Melody Maker* and *Gramophone* all praised *Frost and Fire* to the stars, while BBC Two commissioned a documentary on the group, *Travelling for a Living*, aired in 1966. It's a rare visual record of the folk scene at that moment. Fly-on-the-wall cameras inveigle themselves into The Watersons' terraced house in Hull, where mountains of books jostle for space with LPs by The Beatles and The Rolling Stones. What's most interesting is the musicians' awareness of their own position as pretenders to an established tradition. The film shows the group visiting Cecil Sharp House and studying various old cylinder recordings, reinforcing their entitlement to be seen as 'authentic' singers because they seek this connection with the older revivalists. 'A group', observes Norma, 'is not a traditional thing to do.'

'We are in fact playing at a game that was theirs completely naturally,' says Mike at one point during a filmed discussion between the group and some friends. Anne Briggs, visiting the group from London, makes a perceptive comment: 'We're all solo singers, we're conditioned to sing in clubs, to be club performers, which was never the role of folk singers before. The thing is, what we've done is we've picked up the threads of a tradition – but other than a few old recordings we've not got anything else to go on.'

'They seem to have captured a sort of harmonising that would be called traditional,' adds Bill Leader, 'but at the same time, all the popular music they've ever heard – Ella Fitzgerald, The Rolling Stones – one can feel this edging into everything they do.'

Two more Watersons albums emerged from their researches before the family came apart in 1968. John Harrison moved to London and learnt traditional Irish fiddle with Michael Gorman, and later appeared with husband and wife duo Dave and Toni Arthur. Norma made an unexpected move to the Caribbean, working as a DJ on the sunshine island of Montserrat. She returned to Britain in early 1972, and promptly married Martin Carthy, creating another powerful folk dynasty that survives into the twenty-first century through their daughter Eliza. Working as a duo, Lal and Mike began writing the songs that ended up as *Bright Phoebus* (1972). Featuring guest musicians Martin Carthy, Maddy Prior, Ashley Hutchings and Tim Hart from Steeleye Span, and Fairport Convention drummer Dave Mattacks, *Bright Phoebus* is a curious response to the new directions in folk-rock that were taking place at the time: apart from the clumping 'Rubber Band', with its unexpected musique concrète-style twangs, these are chamber pieces with an uncanny twist, such as the child sacrifice implied in 'The Scarecrow', or the fate of the unhappy 'Winifer Odd', smashed by a car as she bends down to pick up a lucky star from the road. From intimate guitar and voice arrangements to the Nick Drake-like strings of 'Never the Same' and the country rock of 'The Magical Man', the tracks are as unpredictable as English weather. Shades and sunny intervals dominate the lyrics, and the clouds part spectacularly for the closing 'Bright Phoebus', where the triumphant sun beams down with the full force of a spiritual awakening.

Lal and Mike Waterson recording *Bright Phoebus* with
producer Bill Leader (left), 1972.

The Young Tradition was originally the name of a folk club running
weekly in the basement of the Scot's Hoose pub, which sat in the
heart of London between Soho and Covent Garden. The club was
hosted by Bruce Dunnet, literally a tub-thumper and soapbox
preacher for the Marxist folk enclave: he booked the Royal Albert
Hall for Pete Seeger's 1961 tribute and gave Ewan MacColl's
Singer's Club its name. He could often be seen handing out political
leaflets in Stamford Hill, ran various clubs around the city, and once
refused an option to manage The Rolling Stones on the grounds
that their repertoire was too rooted in American rhythm 'n' blues.

Ironically, the figure who would shortly become his principal
protégé was a small-'c' conservative. Peter Bellamy, a twenty-one-
year-old art student from Norfolk, was one of Dunnet's stable of
regular singers. He was in London to study at the Royal College
of Art, where his teachers included Peter Blake. In this fashionable
environment Bellamy had adopted the strident Mod dandyism

of Carnaby Street, a hedonistic approach to leisure time and an appreciation of Warhol's screenprints – all complemented by his profound admiration for the writings of Rudyard Kipling. With his blond bowl hairstyle, he looked like a chorister-turned-dandy miscegenation of Warhol and The Rolling Stones' Brian Jones. He brandished pince-nez and lace cravats for photo shoots, wore a floppy Amish hat bought in Massachusetts and made his own clothes out of brocade and velvet. On his wall at home hung a naval cap worn by his ancestor, a surgeon-commander who had served alongside Admiral Nelson at the Battle of Trafalgar. Sometimes it appeared Bellamy's psychic radar was permanently attuned to that era, which produced such a range of sea shanties and popular song. William Morris had come back to the folk movement, only this time he provided the fabric of Peter Bellamy's Carnaby Street slacks.

Bellamy met a thirty-year-old blade called Royston Wood while they were both sleeping on the floor of a mutual friend, and quickly discovered a natural blending of their voices in close harmony. Bellamy was familiar with Norfolk farming, fishing and drinking songs nurtured by singers like Sam Larner, Harry Cox and Walter Pardon, but in London he was listening to their records in a cloud of hashish. This was the kind of material Bellamy and Wood were performing at the Scot's Hoose when Heather Wood, a twenty-year-old redhead, walked into the club in April 1965, was captivated by the combination of Bellamy's nasal vocal chords and Royston's deep, piping bass, and from the audience spontaneously joined in as a third harmoniser. Within weeks, Bellamy ditched his art course and the trio, now calling themselves The Young Tradition, moved into the upper floor of the house in west London occupied by Bert Jansch, John Renbourn, Anne Briggs (occasionally), various friends and a rotating *galère* of itinerant folkies.

The Young Tradition (1966) and its successor, *So Cheerfully Round* (1967), both released on Transatlantic, are rustic tapestries of ballads, carols and street cries from the late eighteenth and early nineteenth

Keep on Kipling: Peter Bellamy in an early-1970s Argo Records
promotional shot. Note William Morris waistcoat.

centuries; a parade of serving-maids, poachers, fishermen, cunning
foxes, bold dragoons, pretty ploughboys and hungry children. An
exception was their monumental setting of the 'Lyke Wake Dirge'
(on the first album), a song chronicled by the writer and antiquarian
John Aubrey in 1686 but certainly of far earlier provenance. The
'Lyke' of the title is an ancient Briton word for 'corpse', and the text
outlines a dead soul's preparations for a journey into the underworld,
passing through unforgiving spiritual terrain, such as 'Whinny-muir
[moor]', 'the Brig [Bridge] o'Dread' and 'Purgatory'. The song was
birthed in the north of England; it speaks of the reparations required
for a soul to be at peace after death. Those who were charitable in

life shall receive comforts and pleasures. If not, torments await: '*The fire will burn thee to the bare bone.*' The Young Tradition's setting, where the harmony moves in parallel fifths, produces a chilling dirge, the rites of a black ceremonial.[9]

Where the Carnaby Street chic adopted by The Stones, Jimi Hendrix et al. around 1966–7 offered a raffish take on the Regency-era dandy highwayman, Bellamy genuinely seemed to inhabit that lost world in his mind – while remaining thoroughly conscious of the impact of the pop scene. The front cover of *The Young Tradition* is a moody, tenebrous head shot in the manner of The Stones' *Aftermath*, half faces looming out of black shadow. For *So Cheerfully Round* they became more theatrical, indolently lounging on haybales with a pitchfork.

Even more than The Watersons, who had evolved as an acoustic vocal group in a predominantly live setting, The Young Tradition's sharp vocal attack was all the keener for its proximity to a microphone. Hearing these recordings conjures mental images of a trio of carved wooden organ pipes, their mouthpieces mechanically flapping open to emit the notes. For the four years of the group's existence, The Young Tradition rolled up their sleeves and pitched in wherever their services were needed, which included an appearance (as a 'rabble') on Judy Collins's 1967 album *In My Life* and on Shirley Collins's 1967 LP *The Sweet Primeroses*. Just before their final concert at Cecil Sharp House, in

The Watersons, *Frost and Fire* (1965); The Young Tradition, *So Cheerfully Round* (1967); Peter Bellamy, *Merlin's Isle of Gramarye* (1972).

October 1969, they made an album's worth of Christmas carols with Shirley and Dolly Collins, which was only released in 1995 as *The Holly Bears the Crown*. Their demise was brought about mainly due to a lack of financial comeback for their efforts and amicable disagreements about where they should go next with the music. In 1968–9 Bellamy made the first three of around fifteen solo albums: *Mainly Norfolk*, *Fair England's Shore* and *The Fox Jumps Over the Parson's Gate*, concentrating his attentions on the East Anglian country songs and shanties of the Napoleonic era. *Oak, Ash and Thorn* and *Merlin's Isle of Gramarye* – featuring settings of songs from Rudyard Kipling's children's books *Puck of Pook's Hill* and *Rewards and Fairies* – followed in 1970 and 1972: the beginning of a Kipling obsession that lasted until the end of Bellamy's life.[10]

The Young Tradition's third and final album, *Galleries* (1968), was an epic of time-banditry, whizzing through the seven ages of English folk song, from field to ballad to seventeenth-century Puritan hymns. It boldly juxtaposed music by Renaissance poet Thomas Campion and Methodist preacher Charles Wesley, making one daring leap forward to blues singer Robert Johnson's complaint of stones in his passway, and with a pastiche 'Medieval Mystery Tour' copped from Bert Jansch and John Renbourn. A staple diet of English folk was also included in the shape of 'John Barleycorn', 'The Husband and the Servingman' and 'The Bitter Withy'. But the most eyebrow-raising element was the instrumental ensemble that made its guest appearance on two songs, Campion's 'What If a Day' and the traditional 'Agincourt Carol'. The Early Music Consort's David Munrow, Christopher Hogwood and Roddy and Adam Skeaping were among the first of a new breed of authentic instrumentalists, avid collectors of medieval rebecs, shawms and hurdy-gurdies, reviving a medieval Gothic and Renaissance repertoire all but lost to the classical mainstream. Their approach was at once scholarly and populist; in what was to prove a short life, Munrow managed to raise the profile of Early Music significantly, with around fifty recordings

David Munrow, Early Music pioneer and vital element in Shirley
and Dolly Collins's classic Harvest albums.

and plentiful appearances on TV and radio. Munrow and Bellamy
had this in common: neither was afraid to tilt quixotically at a canon.

Munrow was eighteen in 1960, when he took a year off in Peru
before going up to study English at Cambridge University. At
school he had become a proficient pianist, bassoonist and choral
singer, and as a teaching assistant in the Andes he was captivated
by the sounds of local folk musicians playing flutes, pan pipes and
ocarinas. Shortly afterwards, at Cambridge, he noticed a medieval
crumhorn hanging on the wall at a friend's digs and began to
seek out – and teach himself to play – examples of every type
of instrument that time had consigned to oblivion: crumhorns,
sackbuts, sorduns, shawms, rebecs, tabors, viols, citole, organetto,
racketts and chalumeaux, and all the senior and junior members of
the recorder family. Instruments he couldn't find he commissioned

to be made by master craftsmen, who used engravings and paintings as their guide. While affiliated to the University of Birmingham in 1967 to research seventeenth-century bawdy songs, he met Christopher Hogwood, a specialist in Baroque harpsichord; together they formed the Early Music Consort, which became a focal point for Britain's vintage instrumentalists. At the same time, Munrow joined another ensemble dedicated to period-instrument performance and historical salvage – Musica Reservata.

1968 and 69 were exceptionally busy years for Munrow. Not only did he take part in the Musica Reservata albums *To Entertain a King*, *Music from the 100 Years War* and *Music from the Decameron*, and make the debut Early Music Consort LP *Ecco la Primavera: Florentine Music of the 14th Century*, he also embarked on an extensive tour of mainland Europe, during which time he and his cohorts eagerly snapped up new instruments at flea markets and antique shops.

Munrow combined his academic interest in his field with a commitment to popularising it as far as he could. No purist, he allowed himself to be roped into a bizarre 1969 hybrid studio project by Ken Barnes, a zeitgeist-surfing in-house producer at Decca Records who had recently enjoyed a small measure of success with a fusion disc he'd cooked up called *Curried Jazz*. Now an impossibly rare curio, The Roundtable's *Spinning Wheel* LP partnered Munrow and his merry men with a bunch of jazz session-players including Kenny Baker, Don Lusher, John Marshall and drummer Kenny Clare. The songsheet of this testcard-jazz/minstrel-gallery confection included compositions by Lennon and McCartney, Bacharach and David and American folk siren Laura Nyro, and also the Simon and Garfunkel hit (via Martin Carthy) 'Scarborough Fair'.

Munrow reached a mass audience via the Early Music Consort's soundtracks to the 1970 BBC television series *Elizabeth R* (starring future Labour politician Glenda Jackson) and *The Six Wives of Henry VIII*. In 1971 director Ken Russell selected the group to create appropriately medieval musical interludes for his film *The Devils*

(Peter Maxwell Davies was the featured composer). Munrow transported radio audiences on a merry dance through musical history in a series called *The Pied Piper*, and provided incidental music for a 1973 adaptation of Tolkien's *The Hobbit*. A review of a 1971 London concert indicated the 'astonishingly wide cross-section of the public' that could be attracted to such an event in that era of broad-minded arts consumption: 'scholars and antiquarians . . . jazz-types and orientals . . . leather-clad avantgarde composers looking for material for dadaistic parody; TV pop-music producers in search of with-it new sounds and images; recorder groups from girls' convent schools . . . and a whole Chaucerian band of laymen pilgrims . . . uni-sex students; priests and politicians; bishops and actresses; dukes, duchesses and hippy children; individuals one hadn't met since far-off Oxbridge days; and even critics straying furtively from the well trodden Brahmsian paths'.[11] Crucially, though, David Munrow also played a decisive role in the battle to liberate folk music from its conventions in the late 1960s.

The Early Music movement as we know it today began in practice with the efforts of Munrow, and it had the effect of blowing the dust off centuries of music-making, both uncovering brand-new repertoire and refreshing the experience of more familiar historical music that had hitherto been heard through the prism of the Romantic orchestra. Munrow hated hearing pre-Romantic music sung with

John Renbourn, *Sir John Alot of Merrie Englandes Musyk Thyng & Ye Grene Knyghte* (1968); Shirley Collins, *The Power of the True Love Knot* (1968); Shirley and Dolly Collins, *Anthems in Eden* (1969).

operatic vibrato, for example, and pioneered the use of vocalists whose voices didn't wobble. Neither did he harbour any sentimental illusions about the music's role in contemporary life. 'Like the whole antiquarian business,' he told an interviewer in 1974, '[Early Music] is a twentieth-century phenomenon. After two world wars, we're not very keen on looking into the future. We prefer to look back at what, superficially at any rate, look like brighter and simpler times. Of course, that's a vast illusion. We like to enjoy our early music in a world that has lavatories and central heating, don't we?'[12]

The more progressive bucks of the folk scene – Shirley Collins, The Young Tradition and John Renbourn – were after a similar means of restoration. Prior to The Consort's appearance on The Young Tradition's *Galleries* in 1968, Munrow had anonymously played recorder on Renbourn's *Sir John Alot of Merrie Englandes Musyk Thyng &Ye Grene Knyghte*. Recorded in January of that year, the record successfully clothed the bedsit guitarist in doublet and hose. Renbourn emerged from the affable marijuana fug of his previous folk-blues records to prove himself a serious musician of the order of a Julian Bream or John Williams, tackling an arrangement of a William Byrd fantasia, 'The Earle of Salisbury', and following through with another nine pieces that sounded cut from the same cloth, but which in fact were mostly the guitarist's own compositions. Renbourn pasted his own face into the cover image of a brass rubbing of Sir Roger Trumpington, and the way the album was framed as a tongue-in-cheek historical fragment recalled American folk guitarist John Fahey's fictionalising of himself and America's blues mythology as 'Blind Joe Death'.

The record's release came just as Renbourn's new group The Pentangle released their debut album and were gearing up to record two more. As we will see later, the group gave him the platform to explore these techniques with an improvisational looseness. Meanwhile, on his subsequent solo albums Renbourn continued his journey into Early Music with increasing dedication and seriousness of purpose. On 1970's *The Lady and the Unicorn* he applied his filigree technique to a procession of courtly dance tunes from across medieval Europe, including an old English tune, 'Trotto', and an Italian one, 'Saltarello', given a folk-drone feel by Renbourn's use of an unusual tuning and double-tracked with a sitar. He adapted two fourteenth-century Italian pieces for acoustic guitar, 'Lamento di Tristan' and 'La Rotta'. Pentangle's drummer Terry Cox, Fairport Convention violinist Dave Swarbrick and several others contributed, adding a folk-chamber vibe with hand-drums, glockenspiel, strings and flutes: a period music for the hippy generation that conjured visions of East–West meetings in the ages of Marco Polo and Sir Francis Drake. The sleeve was adorned with the famous fifteenth-century tapestry from Paris's Cluny Museum, *La Dame à la Licorne*, a vermillion world bursting with floral vigour, fruiting trees and mythical beasts. He continued to dip into pavans, galliards and other sounds of the Middle Ages on records like *The Hermit* (1976), *The Enchanted Garden* (1980) and *The Nine Maidens* (1985).

David Munrow hanged himself at home in 1976, depressed after the recent deaths of both his father and father-in-law. Obituaries convey a measure of the self-criticism, perfectionism and workaholism that may have been contributing factors, mentioning his 'manic energy . . . he would stay up most of the night preparing parts, and then be at the session an hour before it started, putting out the music stands. We had to restrain him from putting out the microphones as well. He would never spare himself during a session, and usually ended up pop-eyed with exhaustion.'[13] As one of the first true Early Music revivalists, he helped set in train a movement that is still vigorous more than forty years later. His colleague Christopher Hogwood went on to found the Academy of Ancient Music in 1973, which remains one of the world's leading period-instrument orchestras. Many Early Music Consort recordings from this period remain in print, notably the *Music of the Crusades* (1970), evoking martial fury with visceral force; the set of crazed dances by seventeenth-century music theorist and composer Michael Praetorius; and the groundbreaking body of musical archaeology, *The Art of the Netherlands* (1976). 'Very much a man of the gramophone',[14] Munrow believed records offered possibilities unlike the concert hall for presenting the music, carefully selecting his own artwork and compiling meticulous sleeve notes. His rendition of Elizabethan composer Anthony Holborne's 'The Fairie Round' is inscribed on the 'Golden Record' installed in the two *Voyager* spacecraft launched in 1977, drifting through interstellar space for eternity.

The growing interest in medieval-period reconstruction is vividly legible in the music, cinema listings and television schedules of the late 1960s and early 70s. Besides the BBC Tudor series mentioned earlier – which led to a spin-off cinema version, *Henry VIII and his Six Wives*, in 1972 – there was *Anne of the Thousand Days* (1969), centred on Henry's first wife Anne Boleyn, starring Richard Burton and Geneviève Bujold; the Thomas More biopic *A Man for All Seasons* (1966); Peter O'Toole as Henry II in Anthony Harvey's *The Lion in Winter* (1968); David Hemmings as *Alfred the Great* (1969); the hysterical convent of Russell's *The Devils* (1971); and future singer Murray Head in a melodramatic retelling of *Gawain and the Green Knight* (1973). In the same period HTV West made a series of often repeated mud-and-guts episodes of *Arthur of the Britons* (1972–3), and visionary Italian director Pier Paolo Pasolini unveiled his earthy adapations of the *Decameron* (1970) and *The Canterbury Tales* (1971). From the time of the English Civil War, Ken Hughes cast Richard Harris in his erratic portrait of *Cromwell* (1970); and the twenty-three-year-old doomed genius Michael Reeves made his *Witchfinder General* in 1968, in which the East Anglian farmland becomes a transfigured backdrop to a tale of superstition and violent religious persecution in 1645. Period reconstruction, whether in film, television or music, has been a staple of British culture, innate to a mindset that always finds its identity in the grain of the past.

Since the very earliest world literature, the idea of 'pastoral' has always offset the unwanted changes in the present against a perceived lost world of ancestors. Even Hesiod's *Works and Days*, one of the earliest surviving ancient Greek poetic cycles, from the ninth century BCE, speaks of a golden age of ease in the distant past. William Cobbett's *Rural Rides*, written up in 1831 at the end of the Regency age, sought for signs of an older way of life among the villages and towns he visited on horseback. In the 1830s and 40s poet John Clare traced his own growing sense of alienation and outsiderdom onto a vision of town life and mechanical progress having disturbed local flora and fauna and disrupted natural cycles and processes that had lasted an eternity. The second half of Victoria's reign was, for William Morris, a period of horrendous progress and defilement of the intrinsic decency and dignity of the rural way of life. Thomas Hardy, writing between the 1870s and 1890s, set his characters in the previous half-century, describing a symbiosis between humans and nature that had only just vanished. By the 1960s, the years in which Hardy had been active had themselves come to resemble an uncomplicated agrarian idyll: the sweet, harmonious England of collective memory and desire.

Shirley and Dolly Collins's upbringing was steeped in this dialectic of progress versus continuity. Hastings, where they grew up, lies about thirty miles down the coast from Rottingdean, and they intimately knew the same lanes, hills and woodland haunts – and songs – as the Copper family. In the 1930s and 40s there was still just enough of the Sussex Weald preserved as raw countryside to qualify it as one of those hallowed and rare spots in Britain that can feel like an unspoiled Arcadia. 'The field I'm in is where music evolves and it's not imposed on you overnight,' Shirley told me during an afternoon I spent at her home in Lewes.

The innocent pre-war age, and the looming shadows of experience and modernity, formed the principal dynamic of the music Shirley Collins made between 1967–70. The America Collins had so comprehensively traversed with Alan Lomax was now a closed book, and she would not see Lomax again until a brief meeting in 1993. Her emphasis therefore shifted towards a more exclusively English repertoire. 'I had lost my romantic view of America and American music,' she has said.[15] On 'Dearest Dear', the leave-taking song that closed her Davy Graham collaboration *Folk Roots, New Routes*, Graham's guitar sounded as brittle as a harpsichord, which unconsciously gestured towards the turn her music would take next: towards an archaeology of English song that fused contemporary folk with a drift of archaic instrumentation. Shirley spent much time rummaging around in the dustiest corners of Cecil Sharp House, unearthing broadsides, documents, wax-cylinder recordings and folk-song collections in books, boxes and unsorted shelves.

Her voice was uniquely suited to this purpose: not heavily accented, but with enough flattened vowels to indicate her provenance in the south-east. But the main quality was its clarity and neutrality. Sometimes accused of coldness, her voice was in fact an ideal folk voice, sounding as though it was grappling with the words for the very first time, and yet equally as though it was so inured to the pain and suffering so often portrayed in the songs that it had insulated itself from them. These songs, collected from sources with strong regional accents, are sieved through Shirley's vocal and strained of their coarseness, whitewashed pure. 'I didn't ever change my vocal style,' Collins tells me, 'because I couldn't, I didn't know how to anyway. It sounds vain, but I always knew that this music had been born in me. I knew what I was doing, I knew how to sing it, and I wasn't going to veer away from that. The songs kept their integrity and acknowledged where they had come from.'

Released in 1967, *The Sweet Primeroses* marked Shirley's reunion with her sister Dolly, who had studied modern composition with Alan Bush and was now leading a faintly eccentric existence installed with a piano in a double-decker bus in a field outside Hastings,

Eden's anthemist: Shirley Collins, *c.*1966.

attempting to reconnect with what she believed were the Collins family's Irish Gypsy ancestry (their mother was camped nearby in a painted wagon). In accompanying her younger sister, Dolly chose the portative organ, also known as a pipe or flute organ, a contraption dating back to the thirteenth century that consists of squared-off upright wooden pipes. Dolly's sparse, reedy organ tones placed the music in a more temporally distant realm than the contemporary guitar arrangements – we are transported back to the tiny stone candlelit chapel at Telham, Sussex, where the sisters attended services with their family.

Shirley's five-string banjo returned on 1968's *The Power of the True*

Love Knot, a collection of songs of love – impassioned declarations, tragic yearnings, separations, couplings. The producer was Joe Boyd: American Elektra employee, veteran manager of the early-1960s blues-boom tours in the UK, and in 1967 one of the chief agitators for Britain's psychedelic underground. 'He didn't like my singing,' Shirley remembers, with characteristic frankness. 'Because he was used to Sandy [Denny], a bit more apparent emotion in the singing. It was a more modern singing than mine, and Joe thought I was too flat and pale. "Put a bit more life into it . . ."' Boyd brought in the court jesters of folk's medieval banquet, Robin Williamson and Mike Heron of The Incredible String Band, to supply the tootle of a tin whistle and a feather-light battery of Japanese sticks, finger cymbals and African drums. During the sessions, Collins recalls, 'Robin wanted to give Dolly some drugs, and he said, "You've never seen a tree until you've taken LSD." She rounded on him and said, "I know perfectly well what a tree looks like!" So there was always this distance between us, I guess, because they were taking so much stuff. But we loved them and they were charming.'

Despite that cultural distance, Boyd's credentials led to Shirley and Dolly's next two albums, *Anthems in Eden* and *Love, Death and the Lady*, being issued through Harvest Records, one of the most iconoclastic labels of the burgeoning underground. In 1969 Harvest was already home to artists such as Pink Floyd, Deep Purple, Kevin Ayers, Third Ear Band, Michael Chapman, Roy Harper, Forest and The Edgar Broughton Band. These two records are among the crowning glories of English folk's Indian summer, fusing all the elements of Copper family harmonies, Early Music instruments and modern arrangements of traditional songs around an overarching conceptual thread. While their labelmates frolicked in a hemp-smoke paradise in the Hundred Acre Wood, noses deep in Tolkien, the *Mabinogion* and Lewis Carroll, the sisters channelled England's ancestral spirits in song.

> Today's England has a special generation; from
> grammar schools and housing estates, from techs
> and universities are coming enough young men and
> women with a clear historical and prophetic vision
> of themselves, enough now to continue the story; no
> propagandist is going to fool them, or government
> coerce them: They know that they will inherit the
> best of their tradition, and to them this record is
> fondly dedicated.
>
> Austin John Marshall, sleeve note to
> *Anthems in Eden* (1969)

The Adam and Eve of Genesis were cast out of the Garden as penance for a sin of their own making. Britain's twentieth-century Fall consisted of a haven-homeland obliterated by the deaths of the Great War – Paradise removed. But rather than leading to mankind's condemnation to a life of toil and suffering, as in the biblical account, *Anthems*'s sleeve note pointed towards a sense of empowerment of the people: from the 'innocence' of a deferential underclass that would blithely allow itself to be conscripted to fight its masters' wars, to the 'knowledge' of a classless modern society that wouldn't get fooled again. During the First World War the military press gangs, so often the subject of eighteenth-century folk songs, were replaced with willing or coerced conscription. In place of the ceremonies of life and springtime, villages across the land ended up with stone memorial centrepieces on which the deaths of their sons were indelibly engraved. The album's working title was *Anthems Before the Fall*, and it tells of the agricultural calendar of pre-war working-class life – birth, growth and death – interrupted and converted into an unnatural cycle of birth, parting and loss.

'At one time,' says Shirley Collins, 'folk was the music that represented the people of this country, because it came from a whole swathe of labouring-class people, and it had done for

October songs: Shirley and Dolly Collins (right, in shadow) with Mike Heron and Robin Williamson of The Incredible String Band, Queen Elizabeth Hall, London, 1967.

centuries until progress speeded up so much that nothing evolved any more – things just stopped overnight. You can change a whole system and the way people listen to music. When the radio and gramophones came, it slammed down the drawbridge, really, for some music, and it wasn't going to be able to leap across that, because people just wanted to listen to the modern stuff.

'It's all bound up with history as well, after the [eighteenth-century] Enclosures Act, when people lost all their grazing rights, their common land, their gardens; and with the move from the land, after the wars, when industrialisation came in and machines came into the farm. What were those farm workers going to do except move into the towns? I think once they'd gone there, they were going to take on the music hall – the songs couldn't have been relevant to them any more. What's interesting to me is that you get masses of songs about country lads press-ganged away to war, but you don't get songs about getting pressed away from the country to the towns – so maybe they'd given up.'

Anthems in Eden is characterised by what Dolly Collins called a 'natural orchestra', the songs costume-dressed in an unusual and occasionally ramshackle guise of organ and period instruments. Fresh from his contribution to Renbourn's *Sir John Alot*, David Munrow was invited in as musical director, and the small ensemble drawn from the Early Music Consort dappled the record with crumhorns, sackbut, cornett (a wooden ancestor of the trumpet), rackett, recorders, viols, harpsichord, etc. 'David was just incandescent, really,' Shirley Collins says. 'He had so much energy that you really did feel if you put your finger on him you would get an electric shock. I've never met anybody like him for absolute focus, and this energy crackling out of him.' Munrow zapped the album with an arsenal of period instruments from a period unknown.

Side one of *Anthems in Eden* retitled songs like 'Searching for Lambs', 'The Blacksmith' and 'Our Captain Cried' as 'A Meeting', 'A Denying' and 'A Forsaking', to weave a patchwork 'Song-Story'. The first half of this medley is classic English pastoral: peasant courtship songs spiced up with the unrequited lust of 'The Blacksmith'. The music then shifts into a melancholy minor key and the cycle lapses into a dream: 'Lowlands', a gorgeous call and response between Shirley and the six-man chorus, finds one of the forsaken wives dreaming of her husband's loss in the unspecified Lowlands – in this context, though, unmistakably referencing the First World War battlefields of Belgium and Flanders. 'Pleasant and Delightful' describes the final, tearful farewell, as the male lover/soldier pledges to return from the front, but the 'Whitsun Dance' that follows leaps fifty years into the future, with the woman still wearing her bridal gown with green ribbons at each year's Whitsun dance, in memory of her dead fiancé. Over Dolly's funereal pipes, Shirley concludes, '*There's a fine roll of honour where the maypole once was/ And the ladies go dancing at Whitsun*'. The 'Song-Story' ends with the intrusion of the chorus belting out the 'Staines Morris', a maypole fertility dance that ends on a formal yet festive note.

The second side contained a selection of other folk songs that didn't fit the song-story, plus a version of The Incredible String Band's 'God Dog', delightfully accompanied by Munrow's piping treble recorder, Christopher Hogwood's harpsichord and Dolly's organ fanfaring a little triumphal flourish between verses. On 'Rambleaway', Rod and Adam Skeaping's viols and Hogwood's harpsichord glow with the woody warmth of English consort music.

They repeated the trick on *Love, Death and the Lady* (1970). It may begin with the time-honoured folk line '*As I walked out one morn in May*', but Collins hardly sounds full of the joys of spring. In fact, although John Marshall was again producing, their marriage was on the rocks, and the album's maudlin mood is clouded with doomed love, betrayal and suicide. The arrangements – Dolly's spiralling piano chords on 'Are You Going to Leave Me?', Peter Wood's mewling accordion on the devastating 'Go from my Window' or the martial tattoos on 'Salisbury Plain' courtesy of Pentangle drummer Terry Cox – are like nothing previously heard in British folk but suspend the songs in a strangely ageless sonic time zone somewhere between *Dido and Aeneas* and *Rubber Soul*.

'What the songs do,' Shirley confides, 'is take me into that world [of the past]; they take you back centuries. In a twelve-verse song, you can be transported, and I think that's such a strength in a song, that it can take you on a journey. Sometimes you don't even know what sort of journey you've gone on, because a lot of the meanings have eroded over the years, and you just get glimpses of lives. Not through the words of a great playwright or poet or author, but just through the minds and mirrors of ordinary people. I think one of the reasons the country's in such trouble is that nobody's connected to it, to their ancestors or what's gone before. And if other people's lives aren't important, I don't know how your own can be.'

Shirley and Dolly Collins's Harvest LPs were the high-water mark of the 1960s' traditional folk tendency. The Young Tradition, and the massive growth of folk clubs around the country (from thirty or forty in 1964 to an estimated 400 by the end of the decade), proved that folk and fashion could go hand in hand. Anne Briggs, Bert Jansch, the Carthy/Swarbrick duo and their disciples had popularised the image of the bohemian folk singer, with an eclectic enough remit to include both British and American songs, original compositions and transcriptions from jazz and classical music. John Renbourn's interest in Early Music had added another temporal dimension to the feast, permitting scope for the kind of sonic fictions also used by Americans John Fahey, Sandy Bull and Buffy Sainte-Marie. By the winter of 1969, when *Anthems in Eden* was being recorded over a hasty two days, folk music was already in the midst of another giant mutation. And it was Jansch and Renbourn, as the nucleus of the group Pentangle, who would begin to shepherd British folk towards its new grass.

7

Air

How do you know but ev'ry Bird that cuts the airy way,
Is an immense world of delight, clos'd by your senses five?
William Blake, 'A Memorable Fancy', from *The
Marriage of Heaven and Hell* (1790)

Jump baby jump
Spread your wings out and float away.
Pentangle, 'Jump Baby Jump' (1972)

A posse of medieval travellers gallops through the ferny brushwood
of the Pilgrims' Way towards the spiritual magnet of Canterbury.
An armoured knight unhoods his falcon, gazing skywards as the
bird takes wing on the updraught. The scene cuts abruptly; the
falcon transforms into a Hurricane fighter plane swooping low
over the fields, and we see the same knight's face in the same
attitude, now clad in a 1940s military beret.

Michael Powell and Emeric Pressburger's 1944 film *A Canterbury
Tale* is one of the most concentrated fictional examinations of the
'English condition' produced during the war years. The scenery of
rural Kent is the constant backdrop, and the action is played out in
a village where a blacksmith still plies his trade, timber is lopped
and prepared according to time-honoured methods and the mail
is delivered by horse and cart. There is continual reference to the
persistence of historical memory throughout the film, and many
shots are composed in such a way that the scene might be set at any
time in the 800 years between the age of Chaucer and the twentieth

century. The opening sequence described above makes explicit play with the notion of collapsing temporal distance, as well as anticipating the famous opening of Kubrick's *2001* by twenty-five years. Throughout the film the attitudes of young and old to time and historical memory are contrasted and questioned. There's a moment at the film's end when a young British sergeant enters Canterbury Cathedral and tells the organist that he is 'urgently' looking for someone. The organist gives him a quizzical glance, an admonition wordlessly implying that the concept of urgency no longer applies in a monument so massively freighted with age. And the character of Alison Smith, played by Sheila Sim, is teased by the village blacksmith for not understanding the ancient jargon of his trade, while a visiting American serviceman, who grew up in the lumber territory of Oregon, finds the terminology almost identical – just as the folk revival under Cecil Sharp had found its songs retained intact in the Appalachian mountains.

As we have seen, the collapsing of time between past and present recurs time and again in the British imagination. The lure of the Middle Ages exerted its pull on Byron, Shelley and Tennyson, the architect A. W. N. Pugin, the Pre-Raphaelite painters and Stanley Spencer, all of whom reconstituted the medieval epoch for their own times – and that particular silver chain was also picked up by certain exploratory musicians in the late 1960s.

> And why the pentangle is proper to that prince so noble
> I intend now to tell you, though it may tarry my story.
> It is a sign that Solomon once set on a time
> To betoken Troth, as it is entitled to do;
> For it is a figure that in it five points holdeth,
> And each line overlaps and is linked with another,
> And every way is endless; and the English, I hear,
> Everywhere name it the Endless Knot.
>
> Anonymous (trans. J. R. R. Tolkien), *Sir Gawain and the Green Knight* (c. 1400)

The swimmer arches her back, bobbing between dreaming and waking, just as her face rises and sinks at the liquid threshold of air and water. Sunbeams dazzle the surface, dilating into the sleeper's vision as if through a fisheye lens. Up on the riverbanks, on each side, she is lazily aware of '*Moonflowers bright with people walking/ Drinking wine and eating fruit and laughing . . . Death alone walks with no one to converse with.*'

The gracious paradise evoked in Pentangle's song 'Pentangling' might be a vignette from the Thameside of William Morris's *News from Nowhere*. The sunlit hippy dawn meets Morris's bucolic medieval Arcadia. The weather is perpetually hot, the sky clear, ownership is banished, and a carefree, effortless existence is

Pentangle in a London park, June 1968. Left to right: Bert Jansch, Danny Thompson, Jacqui McShee, Terry Cox, John Renbourn.

nourished with an abundance of good things to eat and drink. It is, in Donovan's words, a 'land of doesn't have to be' – a flower child's utopia where the only thing missing is a big rock candy mountain. '*You know I fished just a little to ease my body and soul / Just sit and dream on the riverbank / Let my mind relax and let my consciousness be easy and free.*'

Pentangle's theme song first appeared on their debut album, *The Pentangle*, released in May 1968 and recorded during the previous month and a half. The arrangement fits the soft-focus vapour of the lyric: Jacqui McShee's spritely trill blurs and elides certain words, making 'swimmer' sound almost like 'summer'. The song's evolution over the ensuing half-decade provides an index of the freedoms opened up by this mercurial unit. The seven-minute version on *The Pentangle* includes a short instrumental break, but by 1970 'Pentangling' was being routinely protracted to twenty minutes or more, with a lengthy acoustic-bass solo by Danny Thompson at its core, bowing, sawing and plucking in a manner that recalled Jimmy Garrison's deep lacunae in John Coltrane masterworks such as *A Love Supreme*. Propelled on Terry Cox's air-pockets of brushed drums, the twin guitars of Bert Jansch and John Renbourn fill out the rest of the tableau, pruning back to reveal Renbourn's long, probing lines of enquiry into the tune before an invisible collective nod heralds a synchronised dive back into the main theme.

The group grew organically out of the mulch of acquaintances, collaborations, workaholic Tin Pan Alley sessioneers and friendships that fertilised the London folk/blues/jazz milieu of the mid-1960s. As mentioned in the previous chapter, for a year from around the spring of 1965 Jansch and Renbourn both lived at 30 Somali Road in north-west London's Cricklewood district. The large, rented, semi-detached house was also occupied by the three members of The Young Tradition, and quickly became a kind of unofficial folknik drop-in centre, both for London musicians or wandering minstrels rolling through town. Anne Briggs frequently crashed there on her trips away from Ireland, where in 1966 she was living with her lover Johnny Moynihan, the bouzouki-strumming singer of Sweeney's Men. Renbourn was in a duo with Californian singer Dorris Henderson, holding down a regular slot on the TV show *Gadzooks! It's All Happening*, a topical, gossipy, pop shop window. Portraying itself as a programme with its finger on the swingin' pulse, the first series featured guests such as Lulu, Marianne Faithfull, Peter Cook, Tom Jones, Sandie Shaw and Davy Jones and the Manish Boys – the first-ever television appearance by the man later known as David Bowie (promptly banned for wearing his hair too long). Alexis Korner led the house band, convening the future rhythm section of The Pentangle, bassist Danny Thompson and drummer Terry Cox.

Over the sweltering, dusty summer of 1966, as England basked in the glorious aftermath of its World Cup win, Jansch and Renbourn's parallel careers made a decisive gear shift. Renbourn recorded his great second LP *Another Monday* in the makeshift studio at Bill Leader's Camden Town flat. Four songs featured the voice of Jacqui McShee, a regular folk singer since 1960 who by the middle of the decade was running her own folk club in Sutton, near Kingston upon Thames. She booked the Jansch/Renbourn duo for a gig, an engagement that led to her working the folk clubs in partnership with Renbourn in the latter half of the year. The two guitarists relocated to a new flat in St Edmund's Terrace, on the edge of Primrose Hill, and there recorded two watershed albums that took the decisive step towards the loosening up of the conventions of folk-music presentation. *Bert and John* was taped in the living room of their new flat, and presumably stands as an accurate record of the casual, freewheeling ambience of their shared lives at the time. It's the apogee of the breed of eclectic, pan-cultural guitar collections proposed by Davy Graham, but even as Graham spent the rest of the 1960s diluting his repertoire for his albums in a misguided bid for popular acceptance (his singing never up to the standards required to handle Lennon–McCartney tunes and jazz standards already owned by the great entertainers), *Bert and John* sounded lean and hungry, the tracks' elaborate narrative tapestries stitched fluently and, occasionally, with a note of urgency. After the rollick of Charles Mingus's 'Goodbye Pork Pie Hat' and the complex twelve-bar 'Tic-Tocative', Jansch and Renbourn's compositions become concentrated to a degree that we might define as a more British register – less concerned with a sense of widescreen expansiveness, more of a close huddle, a smallness and focus on detail and rhythmic attack. To those qualities 'Stepping Stones' adds a frisson of melancholy. And in their dignified rendering of Anne Briggs's leave-taking song 'The Time Has Come' – its first recorded appearance – was the intimation that fresh pastures beckoned.

Jansch's *Jack Orion* – recorded at almost the same time as *Bert and John* – consolidated the approach he had nurtured informally in tandem with Anne Briggs: eight songs cast in a setting that was pure Albion. With the dying banjo strains of the opening Appalachian-tinged 'The Waggoner's Lad', all echoes of an Americanised hobo music faded away altogether. Using the Davy Graham DADGAD tuning to sustain a driving, minor-key Celtic drone feel throughout, Jansch remorselessly broke down tunes like 'Henry Martin', the hardy perennial 'Nottamun Town', the Briggs discovery 'Black Water Side' and 'Jack Orion' itself, in a version which was effectively custom-built for him with the aid of Bert Lloyd, who adapted it from 'Glasgerion', one of the Child ballads of genuinely medieval Scottish origin. The erotically deceived harper of the earlier lyric becomes a fiddler who instigates a bloodbath that ends in the slaying of his servant boy, a princess and himself. The tune became a signature for Jansch, Pentangle and beyond: in 1970 the folk-rock group Trees turned 'Glasgerion' into a romping Grateful Dead-style freakout. But in the incredible string tangle of the 1966 take Renbourn's interjections on second guitar careen off Jansch's circular picking, like a roulette ball bombing off the sides of the wheel. He even has a crack at Ewan MacColl's 'The First Time Ever I Saw Your Face', sieving its uncharacteristically glutinous sentiment through the retuned guitar strings and reconstituting it as an under-two-minute sigh of downcast yearning. *Jack Orion* staked out the cardinal points of the Pentangle sound.

Immediately south of St Edmund's Terrace, where this music was clawed into shape, the paths criss-crossing the western half of Regent's Park form the shape of a rough but unmistakable pentagon, whose sides are extended to form five star-points. The pentangle has ancient origins, traceable back to Babylonian sorcery and Greek hermetic philosophy. Linked to the motions of the planet Venus, it has been adopted as a magical symbol by pagans, Christians, Satanists and even Freemasons. In 1967 its universality across denominations and continents chimed with the inclusive spirit of the age. Renbourn complemented his own fascination for medieval and Renaissance pavanes and galliards by reading Arthurian literature, and chose the name Pentangle 'to protect us from the evils of the music business,' he jokes. 'I don't think we spent an awful lot of time thinking about names, but that one seemed about right. And when we visited America, the lighter side of the occult was being revived by the hippies, and the pentangle was the sign on the Tarot cards, and it all seemed to link up nicely.'

The five bold straight lines that forged the shape corresponded to its five chevaliers. From the end of January 1967 the loose round table of Jansch, McShee and Renbourn initiated a residency at the Horseshoe Hotel, a giant, late-Victorian mansion building at 264–7 Tottenham Court Road in central London. Upstairs, the establishment had a 400-seat concert hall complete with domed ceiling painted with stars – a relic of the decade after the war, when the space had been used as a Lodge by the Wood Green chapter of Freemasons. For the next year, on a weekly basis, The Pentangle stamped its imprint in improvised sessions, building a large, enthusiastic audience. By the beginning of March Renbourn had called up his old TV sparring partners Danny Thompson and Terry Cox as the regular rhythm section.

Cox and Thompson's modern-jazz pedigree puffed a mercurial lightness into Pentangle, a lightness elemental as air. The buoyant group sound is partly a product of the dynamic of their recordings, in which (at least until more recent digital remasters) Thompson's bass sounds thinned out in favour of the acoustic guitars and drum brushes. Small rhythmic cells bubble up in repetitive cycles around interlocked bass and drums that flex with the elasticity of jazz. When I hear a track like 'Bells', the instrumental second track of their debut album, I visualise an ephemeral game of prismatic coloured light. Cox, ever fleet around his drums, coaxes the tune onward, his squally solo pattering like butterflies trapped in a balsa-wood box. 'Hear My Call', which starts up immediately after, is a close cousin of Miles Davis's 'All Blues', the quintessential modal-jazz number which also underpins Tim Buckley's contemporaneous 'Strange Feelin'' (Danny Thompson stood in as Buckley's bassist when the Californian played London's Royal Festival Hall in 1968). The briefly flickering 'Mirage' achieves a lazy, lysergic euphoria in which the narrator pleads with a lover to take her *so far from here . . . to the end/ of a rainbow dream'*.

Indeed, precisely while The Pentangle were keeping things locked down at the Horseshoe Hotel, the dusky browns and greens of the summer of 1966 were being daubed with acidic primaries as a technicolour tidal wave swept across London's music scene. On 23 December 1966, a few blocks down Tottenham Court Road at number 23, UFO opened in the basement of the Blarney Club. Run by Joe Boyd and John 'Hoppy' Hopkins, the early weeks of the club acted as an experimental workshop where the formality of British pop was methodically broken down with immersive baths of acid rock by the likes of Pink Floyd, Soft Machine, Tomorrow and The Crazy World of Arthur Brown. As Pentangle's music developed at the Horseshoe – and they too added a chromatic lightshow similar to Mark Boyle and his wife Joan's oil-wheel projections at UFO – a British version of the Monterey Pop Festival love-in was being enacted in weekly instalments. Unlike Fairport Convention, Pentangle never performed at UFO, and couldn't be described as psychedelic, but their light-dappled music is touched with a British pastoral response to the Summer of Love. And of all the British folk-rock groups that began to spring up in their wake, it was Pentangle whose success brought them closest to the American psychedelic wunderkinder – in their time they shared bills with Jefferson Airplane and The Grateful Dead, and during one memorable trip to the Laurel Canyon home of Warner Brothers chief Mo Ostin, while torrential thunderstorms dissolved the manicured backyards of the valley's charmed children to mudslides, they consumed a drunken brunch with Laura Nyro, Joni Mitchell, Phil Ochs and Randy Newman.

The Pentangle was released on 17 May 1968, on Transatlantic Records. The modish black-and-white graphics on the sleeve resemble nothing else from that time; if anything, they're closest to the TV logo of *The Avengers* crossed with the famous side-on silhouette used by Miles Davis since the late 1950s. Nevertheless, coupled with a curious woodblocky font for the title, it provided one of the enduring images of the folk-rock flowering – the black, cut-out shadows reducing five individuals to a homogenous cult, bringers of an adventurous new sound, anonymous heralds of a new folk–jazz fusion era.

On this album, too, for the first time in history, a rock drum kit can be heard backing English traditional songs. Terry Cox can claim that distinction, although he plays in muted fashion, with brushes, not steering the songs but taking a subordinate role to the group's guitarists (on 'Let No Man Steal Your Thyme' and 'Bruton

Town'). The folk songs and ballads apparently conspire to keep the rhythmic aspect backgrounded. Cox tends to shade in behind with rumbles and fills, unable to take possession of the material. The first instance of a drum kit being played with sticks on a folk song in what might be called a rock 'n' roll style came the following spring, when Fairport Convention recorded *Unhalfbricking*.

The Pentangle was the product of a new era of work-intensiveness for the group, who had been adopted in February by manager Jo Lustig, a hustling New York svengali who had built up a formidable reputation as a PR guru for Miles Davis, Dave Brubeck and Nat King Cole, had made a successful chart act out of folk singer Julie Felix, managed a number of progressive folk artists including Roy Harper, and was worming his way into the film and TV business. Lustig turned the relaxed inner dynamics of Pentangle into a workaholic unit and a profitable enterprise, with a high degree of exposure via some eleven BBC sessions, a theme tune for a TV series and, from 1969, an international touring schedule that kept them on the road almost incessantly for the next four years. The crossover folk stars of the late 1960s, such as Harper, Ralph McTell and Al Stewart, were still men of the people, having worked their way through small city venues, feet away from their peers in the audience. Lustig's methods included building up a fourth wall of performer mystique, creating an artificial distance between artist and public. At one rainy outdoor festival, when one of his protégés climbed out of a Mini to assist a group of fans who were pushing it through the mud, Lustig reportedly ordered him back inside, saying, 'You're the star; they've paid to see you, let them do it!'[1]

By 29 June 1968, when they recorded the live set at the Royal Festival Hall that made up one half of the *Sweet Child* double album, they had corralled that looseness into a professional yet very engaging package of English traditionals ('So Early in the Spring', 'Bruton Town'), tunes arising out of Renbourn's Early Music jag (a medley of Renaissance dances and a setting of John Donne's poem

'Goe, and catch a falling starre') and the odd curveball like 'Moon Dog', Terry Cox's turn on the bongos, accompanying himself on a croaking paean to the legendary blind American street musician/ avant-garde composer Moondog, in which Cox is transported deep into the reverb chamber to ear-boggling effect. Such was their cachet by this time that, fresh from his triumph with The Beatles' *Sgt Pepper* jacket, British pop artist Peter Blake supplied *Sweet Child*'s cover, a solid-edged pentagram speckled with red and blue and burnished with flecks of gold.

Although possessed of one of the most lithe rhythm sections of their era, Pentangle could never be described as 'heavy'. Especially when Jansch and Renbourn's twin acoustic guitars are rolling and tumbling in a froth of leaping and teasing melodies, sheathed in the woody twang of the bass, Cox's scudding brush-drum gambols and McShee's faerie siren call, the cumulative effect is of an aerated play of light, a sonic mirage in which fragments of styles jump in and out of focus, drawing a curly line between a courtly medievalism and the enlightened foolery of Haight-Ashbury. Theirs was, perhaps, a music that could only have emerged at that particular moment: an uncalculated synthesis of musical disciplines, rock and folk inflated by modern jazz's zephyr breeze.

'Tha' won't get me down t'pit.' For Billy Casper, the fifteen-year-old hero of Barry Hines's 1968 novel *A Kestrel for a Knave*, his intended future of working down the local coal mine promises only a black hole to swallow childhood dreams, the annihilation of idealism and working-class aspirations to learning, literally a preserver of ignorance and Dark Age values. Instead, Billy looks to the sky. He teaches himself the rudiments of falconry from a stolen library book and succeeds in taming a wild kestrel, whose soaring flights become a symbol of the possibility of freedom from his proscribed life.

The eagle, the vulture and the 'merloun', or merlin, are hawks proper to the office of emperor, says the *Boke of St Albans*, a catalogue of writings on gentlemanly pursuits printed in 1486. The author of the section on falconry, one Dame Juliana Berners, lists fifteen types of birds of prey in descending order of rank, from the 'Falcon Gentle and Tercel Gentle' appropriate to princes, right down to the lower orders: a hobby for a young man, a goshawk for a yeoman, a sparrowhawk for a priest. At the very bottom of the list, at number fifteen, is the poor kestrel: suited only for servants, children and knaves.

Harold McNair, whose free-spirited folk-jazz flute lifted everything from Donovan hits to the *Kes* soundtrack.

'It's a bird for the riff-raff of the world,'[2] said Ken Loach, whose adaptation of Hines's novel, *Kes* (1969), proved to be a landmark in his career as a director. As Billy crosses from the residential precincts into the natural habitat, through woods to the open meadows where he lets Kes fly, Chris Menges's cinematography renders the scenery in misty, damp leaf greens and umbers. And then Pan emerges onto the soundtrack: the wind pipes through an eerie alto flute, echoing the bird's upward thrust. In Billy's moments of communion with Kes, the flute's rasping exhalations spiral upwards towards open skies: a 'Kestrel Ascending' offering an image of hope, freedom and escape.

Kes's theme was created by jobbing composer John Cameron, but the flute was played on the soundtrack by Harold McNair, a mixed-race Jamaican jazz flautist and reedsman who had moved to Britain from the Bahamas in 1960 and become a regular face at venues such as Ronnie Scott's in Soho, as well as contributing tenor saxophone to the theme tune of the 1962 James Bond film, *Dr No*. His 1965 album *Affectionate Fink*, cut with a British vibraphonist and Ornette Coleman's rhythm section David Izenzon and Charles Moffett, came out on Island Records, at a time when Chris Blackwell's label was more closely associated with Jamaican pop, calypso, jazz, rhythm and blues, and early soul.

McNair was already John Cameron's flautist of choice by the mid-1960s. A jazz pianist and Cambridge graduate, Cameron had stepped into the world of 1960s 'mood music', later known as Library Music, recording exotically tinged pieces for the KPM company such as *Afro-Rock* and *Jazz Rock*, drawing on a small coterie of available session musicians, including percussionist Tony Carr, with horns by Henry Lowther, Dick Heckstall-Smith (later of blues-rock outfit Colosseum) and others, while the bass stool was warmed by Herbie Flowers and the ubiquitous Danny Thompson. Around the axis of the sought-after Cameron, knots were tied binding a small coterie of musicians bridging the worlds of folk, blues, jazz, rock 'n' roll and light orchestral music. Thompson first encountered Harold McNair in September 1965, when the two of them took part in the recording of Donovan's 'Sunny Goodge Street' at Peer Music in Denmark Street. In January 1966 Donovan's manager Mickie Most hired Cameron to provide keyboards and arrangements for his protégé's hit single 'Sunshine Superman' at Abbey Road Studios (the date also featured Jimmy Page on guitar). The same ensemble continued to appear on Donovan's sessions throughout the summer and autumn of 1966, with The Beatles taping *Revolver* in the adjoining studio; McNair was called back in October to tootle on the Cameron arrangement of 'Writer in the Sun'. McNair's distinctive flute style, which also graces Donovan's singles 'Catch the Wind', 'Mellow Yellow' and 'Hurdy Gurdy Man', as well as many of his album tracks, helped to position the instrument as a trilling signifier of dreamy flower-power indolence. On 'Writer in the Sun', which came out on the 1967 album *Mellow Yellow*, the flute etches the thoughts of the 'retired writer' as they flutter and pirouette above his prostrate form. The arrangement, with its lazy summer mood enhanced by a small chamber group of woodwinds, anticipates Nick Drake's 'Thoughts of Mary Jane', another time-standing-still song that encapsulates the desire to relax and float downstream.

Thanks to these imaginative arrangements and the interplay of seasoned, eclectic, open-minded, professional musicians who could step from a full-blown jazz session to a pop or folk context with practised ease, British folk-rock was aerated with a looseness that carried it beyond its one-man-and-a-guitar roots. 'I think those kind of musicians at the time were the most flexible,' commented Cameron many years later. 'The early rock musicians were sometimes not as flexible as they should be. The classical musicians were totally inflexible, so you needed someone with a large amount of musicality but who could think on their feet. People like Danny Thompson, of course, came into their own. Danny was one of the first of those musicians who said, "I don't want any boundaries, I'll play what I damn well like," and it was those kind of musicians who were great to use. Harold was very similar.'[3]

McNair is one of the more interesting figures floating around in the crowded world of mid-1960s Soho, and his trajectory reveals much about the musical fluidity of the times. In the closing years of the 1960s McNair released his giddy flute to fly across John Martyn's second album *The Tumbler*, Davy Graham's *Large as Life and Twice as Natural* (1968), Magna Carta's self-titled progressive-folk debut from 1969, and *Hello* (also 1969), an album of introspective, symphonic folk-pop by Marc Brierley. His presence on the *Kes* soundtrack stemmed from a 1967 session at Olympic Studios with Donovan, Cameron, Danny Thompson, Tony Carr and a string quartet, when the singer recorded the opening theme he had written for Loach's debut movie, *Poor Cow*. Though he's uncredited, I'm convinced it's McNair's flute trilling through Tim Hollier's *Message to a Harlequin* of 1968, another portfolio of mellow, hemp-clouded inspiration concocted under Cameron's wing. One song in particular, 'Bird of Paradise', compresses the wistful folk-jazz of Pentangle and Tim Buckley with the orchestral nuances of Scott Walker. '*Take wing, bird of paradise, and fly / follow whichever star may catch your eye,*' croons Hollier, a twenty-one-year-old protégé of Simon Napier-Bell, as McNair's flute flaps its ornamental feathers between the lines. '*Don't let me clip your wings now / You gotta find your paradise somehow . . .*' The link between the flute and an ideal of flight is firmly established.[4]

Five years after *Affectionate Fink* the musical landscape was vastly altered, and McNair could make an album like *The Fence*, featuring free pianist Keith Tippett, Tony Carr, Traffic's Steve Winwood and Ric Grech, and Pentangle's Terry Cox and Danny Thompson. The same year (1970) he also turned out the Ellingtonian cocktail jazz of *Flute and Nut* with John Cameron, and appeared in Ginger Baker's hard-driving Air Force supergroup, featuring the same

Traffic members plus Denny Laine of Wings and Graham Bond. On his final cue on *Kes*, a thirty-eight-second, rain-sodden lament as the bird is buried, he blows a murmuring, unresolved line loaded with trepidation. The cancer that had been killing him since the late 1960s finally finished its work on 7 March 1971.

By that time, British jazz, folk, rock and pop were well stirred into a powerfully strange brew. The Canterbury artists – Soft Machine, Caravan, Kevin Ayers – blended surrealism and woozy psychedelia that owed as much to the freewheeling exploits of John Coltrane and Miles Davis as to their UFO club compadres like Pink Floyd and Tomorrow. Parallel to his productions for The Incredible String Band, Fairport Convention and Nick Drake, Joe Boyd was also producing fiery albums by the South African expatriate jazz group led by pianist Chris McGregor, where the cacophony of Mongezi Feza's and Dudu Pukwana's exiled horns and Louis Moholo's polyrhythmic drumming produced some of the most 'out' moments in jazz in Britain of the late 1960s. Boyd mediated various conversations between the fields of jazz and folk-rock: for example, placing McGregor's piano on Nick Drake's 'Poor Boy' (on 1970's *Bryter Layter*) and hiring Danny Thompson to supply bass for McGregor's Septet (on a 1969 session finally released in 2008 as *Up to Earth*). Saxophonist Dudu Pukwana blew on John and Beverley Martyn's *Road to Ruin*, and Richard Thompson blasted his guitar into the first recording by Assegai, Pukwana's Afro-jazz spin-off, in 1969.

Such outernationalist fusions were also the province of another West Indian expatriate. A former schoolmate of Harold McNair back at the Alpha Boys School in Kingston, Jamaica, bebop saxophonist Joe Harriott migrated to Britain in 1951. Around 1960, the year of American bandleader Ornette Coleman's breakthrough album *Free Jazz*, Harriott began referring to his own music as 'abstract' or 'free form'. The late 1960s saw him forming an unprecedented partnership with Anglo-Indian violinist and composer John Mayer, who had come to Britain on his own as a teenager on the boat from Bombay. Integrating a double quintet of Harriott's jazz group with an ensemble of Indian instrumentalists assembled by Mayer, they recorded *Indo-Jazz Suite* in 1966, followed by the more successful two volumes of *Indo-Jazz Fusions* (1967/8). *Indo-Jazz Fusions* made enough impression to earn the group an appearance at the August 1969 Isle of Wight Festival, an event whose 150,000-strong crowd – drawn by major attractions such as Bob Dylan and The Band, Free and The Who – was also treated to some of the United Kingdom's most intrepid genre border-crossers: Pentangle, Mighty Baby, Family, Aynsley Dunbar, Third Ear Band and Eclection, featuring Sandy Denny's future husband Trevor Lucas.

Very much on the scene at the same time – present at the recording of Mighty Baby's debut LP, and a friend of Jackson C.

Acid-folk outlander: Welshman Meic Stevens.

Frank and Syd Barrett – was a Welsh singer-songwriter called Meic Stevens, influential in his home country for founding psychedelic labels Sain and Wren and singing mystic troubadour songs in his native Welsh tongue. In autumn 1969 Stevens took part in an event playing alongside the ten-piece Indo-Jazz Fusions, and the following year the group's sitarist Diwan Motihar and tabla player Keshav Sathe recorded parts on the Welshman's Warners LP *Outlander*, with arrangements on that record's standout tracks, 'The Sailor and Madonna' and 'Yorric', credited to John Mayer.[5] 'Yorric' is in fact one of the triumphs of its age, one which dramatically extends the 'Celtic crescent' – eight and a half minutes of savage acoustic raga-folk whose drones and modes resound in a rough arc from Scotland, Wales and Ireland, via Brittany and the Iberian peninsula towards Morocco and North Africa, to join hands with the Indian subcontinent. Stevens's verses – a lysergically altered extrapolation on mortality taking Hamlet's famous soliloquy as a subliminal starting point – are interspersed with whirling improvisations, as the tabla, sitar and flute leap up into buzzing flurries of activity.

But even by the time it appeared there was (on the same record label) already a strong precedent for a track like 'Yorric', with its long, uninterrupted stream-of-consciousness lyrical flow, its judicious combination of acoustic and free-flowing instruments and trained jazz musicians, and its sense of the mythopoetic enchantment of the Celtic imagination: an album whose opening lines appear to be sung from the vantage point of a bird in swooping free flight: '*If I ventured in the slipstream/ Between the viaducts of your dreams . . .*'

Recorded over two days in 1968 in New York and released in November of that year, Van Morrison's *Astral Weeks* marked a significant turning point in the evolution of rock into a serious art form. The garage rock and rhythm 'n' blues of Morrison's youthful

Van Morrison, *Astral Weeks* (1968).

group Them were left far behind, as the freedom principle of modal jazz was applied to a method of songwriting which allowed the track to breathe or blossom organically. The form is appropriate, as Morrison was channelling the spirit of the boundless Beat writing of Jack Kerouac, as well as keeping visionary poets like Keats and Yeats at his side. 'Astral Weeks' itself, for example, coasts for seven minutes on an even keel of two see-sawing chords, knitted together by a constant shaker pulse. The song, which feels longer than its seven minutes, is an introspective odyssey that begins on the edge of a town '*where immobile steel rims crack/ and the ditch in the back roads stop*', via scenes of paranoia and unease and the realisation that '*I'm nothing but a stranger in this world*', to a utopian desire '*to be born again/ In another world/ In another time*'.

'Cyprus Avenue' literally enacts that slippage from reality into another place, another time. The avenue in question is a real location in Morrison's native Belfast, a tree-lined residential street in one of the city's affluent neighbourhoods whose tranquil atmosphere prompted childhood reveries and visions in the young Morrison, who grew up with his parents in the more deprived east side of

Belfast. Memories of visiting the hallowed spot exerted a powerful influence on the artist's consciousness many years after he had left Northern Ireland. '*I may go crazy*,' confides the song's narrator, as he finds himself ensnared in his own deceptive memory of the place. '*And wait a minute*,' he interjects, as if grabbing your arm as the horse-drawn parade of apparitions appears, '*Yonder comes my lady/ Rainbow ribbons in her hair . . .*'

Astral Weeks takes its title from a painter friend of Morrison's youth, the eccentric Irish artist Cecil McCartney, whose abstract canvases were guided by an obsession with interdimensional travel. For Morrison, the album was also a means of slipping out of time present. Cyprus Avenue – or his retrospective mental reconstruction of it – provided the key to unlock his imagination and catapult him into the visionary state that characterises his best work, like Alice popping the substance marked 'Eat me' and entering a new and unfamiliar dimension. The album's other memorable set piece, 'Madame George', also takes place on Cyprus Avenue, whose nostalgic images of soldier boys marching, perfumes drifting and children collecting bottle-tops prompt Morrison to '*fall into a trance*'. Speaking from Woodstock in upstate New York, where he was living in 1970, Morrison emphasised the local specificity of 'Cyprus Avenue': 'Just imagine . . . [if] we got on a plane and we went from here to Belfast, and we hung out and came back, then you would know the song. But I don't think I could tell you about the song if we didn't do that. But it's part of the opera. Like I said, Cyprus Avenue is a real place, with definite people, and it's true.'[6]

Unfolding according to the contemplative logic of their lyrical orbits, *Astral Weeks*'s songs unhooked themselves from pop's dependence on verse/chorus structure, coasting on idling rhythms, raging and subsiding with the ebb and flow of Morrison's soulful scat. The soundworld – a loose-limbed acoustic tapestry of guitar, double bass, flute, vibraphone and dampened percussion

– was unmistakably attributable to the calibre of the musicians convened for the session: Richard Davis, whose formidable bass talents had shadowed Eric Dolphy on the mercurial Blue Note classic *Out to Lunch*; guitarist Jay Berliner had previous form with Charles Mingus; Connie Kay was drummer with The Modern Jazz Quartet; percussionist/vibesman Warren Smith's sessionography included Miles Davis, Aretha Franklin, Nat King Cole, Sam Rivers and American folk mystics Pearls Before Swine. Morrison reputedly barely exchanged a word with the personnel, retreating to a sealed sound booth to record his parts and leaving it to their seasoned expertise to fill out the space. It is a music quite literally snatched out of the air.

Belfast itself would rarely be evoked in such halcyon imagery again. The unrest that led to the beginning of the Troubles in Northern Ireland had already begun with the foundation of loyalist paramilitary group the UVF; even while Van Morrison was preparing the material for *Astral Weeks*, Northern Ireland's Civil Rights Association, campaigning for greater Catholic equality in government, was experiencing peace marches brutally broken up by gangs of Protestant Unionists. As the violence peaked with the formation of the Provisional IRA in 1969, Belfast's old magical tableaux began to be transformed into a concrete battleground decorated with militant pro- and anti-Loyalist murals. Tellingly, at the end of 'Slim Slow Slider' – the album's closing seconds – the poise suddenly crumbles, and the record/vision fades away even as the song degenerates into a free-form scrapple. The spell is broken, but not before *Astral Weeks* has conjured an idealised notion of an Ireland, impressed upon a child's eyes, before the Fall.

Pentangle's endless knot was also a lashing-together of discrete musical worlds. Bert Jansch, Jacqui McShee and John Renbourn drifted together from the freewheeling bohemia of the London folk scene; for all their maverick spirit, Danny Thompson and Terry Cox were seasoned, disciplined professional musicians from the demanding and competitive arena of modern jazz. These disparate elements knitted together on the group's final three albums, *Cruel Sister* (1970), *Reflection* (1971) and *Solomon's Seal* (1972). The Who producer Shel Talmy had produced 1969's *Basket of Light*, but for *Cruel Sister* they turned to Bill Leader, whose transparent, non-intrusive recording method would simply capture the group in its raw state. In the event, *Cruel Sister* is an odd record to emerge from a group at its commercial zenith. It contains a mere five tracks, all of them English ballads. Among these, 'When I Was in My Prime' is sung unaccompanied by McShee; the title track seethes and twists under Renbourn's sitar lines; and the eighteen-minute jam on 'Jack Orion' occupies the whole of side two. Reflecting the group's increasing bent towards improvisation, on this masterfully handled epic they dramatically frame the action in three 'acts'. Beginning with Jansch alone, singing of how Jack Orion could '*fiddle the fish out of salt water*', by the seventh verse the whole group have finally joined the game and Renbourn's electric guitar develops an acid-fuzz halo. Once the fiddler's pageboy Tom has deceived his way to sleeping with the princess who had originally promised herself to Jack, the song shifts into a recorder/pavane-like interlude with ominous bowed bass from Thompson, as if butter wouldn't melt in Tom's mouth as he sends his master off to his assignation. When the princess stabs herself in front of Jack, Jansch soberly plucks the original riff on his acoustic, and Terry Cox picks out a mournful, glowing solo on a dulcitone – a nineteenth-century keyboard instrument in which hammers strike a range of tuning forks. A brief hard-rock section follows, with Renbourn at his most electrifying, before Jansch and McShee – harmonising in a manner that recalls the Neil Young/Stephen Stills axis in Buffalo Springfield – sing through the tragedy's violent denouement. The eclectic flow of this version of 'Jack Orion' shows a group firmly in control of its myriad generic impulses.

Pentangle may have prized the longevity of ballads and traditional music, but when they came to write their own material, many of the songs describe illusory, insubstantial worlds; all that is solid melts into air. 'Light Flight', the lead-off track on *Basket of Light*, describes the familiar retreat from '*the city's race*' to '*a better place*' where someone is lying in the sunshine '*marking time*'. But in a strange middle verse the reflective solitude is shattered by a sudden perception of eternity: '*how it rushes by, / Now a thousand moons are about to die/ no time to reflect on what the time was spent on.*' The song reached the ears of millions in 1969 when it was used as the theme tune to the BBC drama *Take Three Girls*. The programme's opening sequence showed the titular 'girls' – three young flatmates with contrasting social backgrounds attempting to create independent lives in the heart of London – adrift in the bustle of London traffic, standing still while cars, buses and taxis flicker in front of them. The same year, Nick Drake was portrayed in similar fashion – mutely watching a blurry world pass by – on the sleeve of his album *Five Leaves Left*.

The title track of 1971's *Reflection* describes a dream-like vision in which McShee '*saw the whole world take flight*'; a room becomes mystifyingly emptied, and the devil flashes into view, representing some kind of disappointment or evaporation of an ideal: '*I've searched for satisfaction, disillusion is his guise.*' In the midst of a commercial success achieved by nearly three years of continuous touring and recording, by 1971 disillusion was gaining the upper hand. In his contribution 'When I Get Home', Jansch sings of reaching the point at a drunken party where the temptations of the night pull against his guilty need to rejoin his wife and home comforts – should he spread his wings or acknowledge they are now clipped? After three years, all of Pentangle were confronted by this dilemma, and the recording sessions for *Reflection* were reportedly fractious affairs, with every

Bert Jansch, *Jack Orion* (1966); Pentangle, *Cruel Sister* (1970) and *Solomon's Seal* (1972).

member apart from McShee threatening to leave by turns. Jo Lustig's punishing schedule had holed them below the waterline; a massive world tour taking in Australia, Scandinavia and the US in early 1971 took its toll on the group's personal lives (as if to compensate, the record sleeve is a family-album montage of photos of group members, and takes pains to include a few snaps of assorted children and partners/wives/boyfriends, as well as studio and live shots). It was a long time since Jansch and Renbourn's flatshare days, too: Jansch now lived in the Sussex village of Ticehurst; Renbourn lived in Surrey but by the end of the year decamped to Devon; Danny Thompson owned a large house in Suffolk; McShee lived in Reigate; Terry Cox had a family on Minorca. For Jansch's unpredictable, free-spirited muse in particular, the situation was intolerable. On a holiday tour of Ireland with Renbourn in summer 1971, they found themselves perched on the edge of the Cliffs of Moher, passing a wine bottle between them and imagining launching themselves into 700 feet of vertiginous air, floating above the seagulls, soaring on eagle's wings and circling round a ship's mast. Jansch turned this sozzled, reckless speculation into a song, 'Jump Baby Jump', which featured on the final Pentangle album, *Solomon's Seal*.

Chris Ayliffe's woodcut-style illustration on the cover of *Solomon's Seal* (1972) depicts a pentangle of woven twigs, knotted together with a vine wreath, in which each one of the triangles within the pentangle contains a pictorial cipher for each song. If *Reflection* was the product of the group's high summer, this wintry swansong was musically and technically less ambitious. But Pentangle in fact sounded more focused than before, and their instrumentation coheres in a way they had not previously managed. A modest, earnest summation of their achievements, it collects five common English folk tunes, including 'The Cherry Tree Carol', 'Willy of Winsbury' and 'Lady of Carlisle', plus Jansch's 'Jump Baby Jump' and 'People on the Highway', a poignant song of resignation and moving on: '*For it's better to be going / Better to be moving / Than clinging to your past.*'

Transience recurs many times in Jansch's songwriting: when the going gets tough, cast off the problem, let it melt into air. *Rosemary Lane*, the solo album he released in May 1971, was a reminder of how much of his technical tracery was getting subsumed in the eddies and swoops of Pentangle in full flight. Recorded with Bill Leader at Jansch's country retreat in Ticehurst – a postcard Sussex village which does indeed possess a Rosemary Lane – this is Jansch at his most English, reflecting in solitude in the womb of his country home. The final 'Bird Song' contains telling lines that speak of his unwillingness to face the spotlight. Birds laden with golden, jewelled plumage have trouble getting off the ground, while the humble wren '*has nothing, but he can fly / Anywhere beneath God's sky*'. Jansch identifies with the wren's humility, relishing the freedom that comes with few possessions or responsibilities and getting down to building its nest.

As young heirs to the folk tradition, the Pentangle generation's treatment of British folk tunes was severely scrutinised, and often criticised for what seemed like roughshod trampling on a delicate heritage site. Ewan MacColl and Peggy Seeger, and their Critics Group, kept a dignified distance, apart from isolated visits to clubs like Les Cousins. Significantly, it was a British, not American, audience member – a folk singer named John Cordwell – who hurled the iconic accusation 'Judas!' at Dylan, at Manchester Free Trade Hall on 17 May 1966. As Ian MacDonald has demonstrated, Cordwell's objection was not based on knee-jerk Luddism – as a progressive left-winger, he actively welcomed Dylan's move from the overtly political troubadour songs to the more personal, psychedelic confessional mode on *Bringing It All Back Home* and *Blonde on Blonde*. The betrayal was not specifically because Dylan had electrified his sound; rather, that the resultant messy and indistinct sound and Dylan's apparently cavalier, contemptuous attitude while performing electrically caused his texts to whirl away in a gust of mush. Dylan's performance that night, says MacDonald, 'ended the traditional relationship between artist and audience: listeners became implicitly demoted to passive spectators. To the morally serious folk community, this wasn't just anti-social; it was tantamount to counter-revolution. Dylan had done a Napoleon: declared himself electric Emperor.'[7]

In this context – communication blowing away in a hurricane of bombastic, chaotic noise – the aerated, transparent soundworld Pentangle created the following year begins to make strategic sense. Karl Dallas, in *The Electric Muse*, picked up on Marshall McLuhan's thesis that electronic media prompted a return to oral culture: 'If it is true, as McLuhan says, that "today we come to the oral condition again via the electronic media" then electronic culture ought to satisfy the same criteria as folk culture and, in time, become undistinguishable from it.'[8] But this, in turn, was complicated by the need for commercial music, in a crowded marketplace, to promote and develop artists as individual, larger-than-life personalities – a significant break with the anonymous collective transmission of folk music. Dallas creates a useful distinction between purely pop performers – cogs in the capitalist music machine – and pure folk traditionalists such as Harry Cox, by denoting in-between, post-Dylan 'rock poets' as 'Byronic'.

Internationalist to the core, A. L. Lloyd's response to the modernisation of folk music was more nuanced. Conceding that 'The easily identified, water-pure, guaranteed authentic folk song beloved of the scholars is dying everywhere,' he noted, 'in sophisticated urban surroundings it is rising again and entering on a second existence . . . Whether this "second existence" is ephemeral or not, it is artificial, with the repertory at once protected as a conscious portion of "heritage", and exposed to the winds by being shifted onto the plane of mass entertainment, divorced from its natural setting and the function it fulfilled in its former folklore milieu . . . For all that, we have to realize that many revived folk songs today, in their "second existence", are probably enjoying a more vigorous life than they did in their first, restricted time, even if they are bent to different purposes.'[9] Folk music had been set free to soar like the kestrel. Two years after this was printed, Lloyd was playing 'Deep Throat' consultant to Fairport Convention's revamping of folk on *Liege and Lief*.

More recent critics of the folk revival have suggested that the entire body of work considered 'British folk', from the Victorian age onwards, has been nothing more than carefully staged illusion, the product of a wholesale middle-class appropriation of working people's culture. Dave Harker's *Fakesong*, published in 1985, used detailed deconstruction of Sharp's collecting and publishing strategies to suggest that the folk canon was nothing but a house of cards. Sharp's selective collection methods, he argued, led to a misrepresentation of working-class culture, and his bias towards an idealised 'rural peasantry' which effectively no longer existed meant that the true identity of working people's songs was pushed to the background. Harker's research was largely based on statistical analysis of Sharp's collections, but his arithmetic, it has subsequently been proved, does not always add up – ignoring, for instance, the fact that Sharp often discovered the same songs in different villages when calculating the total number of tunes.[10]

Harker's research was begun in the early 1970s, when the issue of co-option of 'the people's music' by the mass media was still a hot potato. There's no question that the waters were muddy by that time. The likes of John Renbourn, Bert Jansch and Jacqui McShee were among the last generation who might have been directly influenced by the introduction of folk singing to the school curriculum, and to have been regularly exposed to the BBC's coverage of folk culture. This was the inevitable outcome of the wider exposure garnered by the second folk revival: the 1960s middle class, comfortable with the new 'aural/oral' transmission via the phonograph, filleted out what they wanted from folk music, self-consciously taking fashionable, marketable elements, but not necessarily for cynical self-serving purposes. The term 'folk music' slipped its moorings, took a jump off the cliff edge; now it was a floating signifier, to be plucked from the air and appropriated by anyone who could find a suitable framework. Bob Dylan, as the most visible example, had given widespread permission for individualism and modern poetry to be presented in a 'folk music' context, and the expanding pop industry opened up a global campfire around which what had begun as an intimate social form of music could be sung.

The magical switch between the hawk and the hurricane reflects the very British experience of living in the past simultaneously with the present. Pentangle's music, in its swirling vortex of referents, the galliard shading into the raga, the ballad transmuting into the acid jam, unwittingly reflects these contested territories. For all the academic sweat expended in the ensuing decades to prove that the folk idea is a wilderness of mirrors, the music survives where otherwise there would be none. Like the Green Knight, the force of nature who lays down the challenge to the pentangle-festooned Sir Gawain, you can swing your axe and decapitate it, but it will simply pick its own head up, repeat its challenge and ride off into the night.

8

Earth

> What is song's eternity?
> Come and see
> Melodys of earth and sky
> Here they be
> Songs once sung to Adam's ears
> Can it be?
> — Ballads of six thousand years
> Thrive thrive
> Songs awakened with the spheres
> Alive.
>
> John Clare, 'Song's Eternity', 1830s

I stand at the corner of two residential roads on Muswell Hill in north London, my finger tracing the outline of Gothic letters carved into a section of log that also features a sculpted, twin-masted fishing boat. The 'log' is actually a piece of carefully disguised pottery, and the letters spell out 'Fairport', the name of this huge residence with its teetering mock-Tudor brick chimneys, built at the height of the 1920s suburban housing boom.

In the mid-1960s the house was the dwelling of young men lured away from dreary futures by the sirens of rock. The sessions they convened there gave their name to one of the most enduring franchises in British popular music. While it's famous for being a 'folk-rock' group, Fairport Convention neither began nor is currently trading under that description, although for several years it acted as a catalytic converter within the folk-rock scene, a breeding ground and research vehicle whose members took what they learned there and applied it outside the group across the broader field of British rock. *Liege and Lief*, the 1969 LP that went a long way towards redrawing the map of British folk music, was described in its own advertising copy as 'Documenting a (very brief) era'. It was an experimental side project that turned the folk world upside down, recasting it in a musical syntax that could be understood by a generation already schooled not in the 'authenticity' of folk music, but the complex intermeshing of song and fashion that attended the pop scene.

Think of Fairport Convention as an old country mansion, its entrance and exit doors permanently open to successive tenants who have passed through, stayed, abandoned it and returned. Some have lived there for most of their lives, some are new, some come knocking on the door again after a turn of travelling out in the world. Each new set of inhabitants may refurbish the rooms; the exterior might become a little shabby sometimes; but it's never quite allowed to tumble in ruins. And the house has now been standing so long that a whole community has sprung up around it.

But to return to Muswell Hill, and the brick-and-mortar house that inspired the name. In the early 1960s the huge house was home to the Nicol family, whose son Simon was born in October 1950. His father ran a medical practice on the ground floor, but after his death in 1964 the family moved down the road and rented out the two upper floors as flats and bedsits. A nineteen-year-old trainee journalist, Ashley Hutchings, was one of the first tenants. Born in the nearby suburb of Bounds Green, Hutchings was the son of a pianist who worked in a dance band, Leonard Hutchings and the Embassy Five; his mother committed suicide when he was five. By his mid-teens Hutchings had acquired the nickname Tyger, a Blakean moniker attesting to his combative sportsmanship. A debonair sense of personal style combined with an interest in skiffle and the early blues boom; he was an early aficionado of the fledgling Rolling Stones. After moving into Fairport he graduated quickly from reporting for magazines such as *Furnishing World* to acting as personal assistant to Alfred Morgan, president of Haymarket Publications. There, under the directorship of a young Michael Heseltine and working elbow to elbow with future radical Tariq Ali, Hutchings combined the day job in Waterloo with evenings playing electric bass with assorted blues and rhythm 'n' blues groups, and exploring London's after-hours rock 'n' roll clubs. After witnessing the stupendous technique of Bert Jansch at the Prince of Wales Feathers in Soho in January 1965, he stepped into the parallel universe of London's folk scene, from Ewan MacColl's fundamentalist bastion to the new thing at Bunjies and the Scot's Hoose.

Hutchings and his landlord's son, Simon Nicol, began fooling around with guitars and washboards as a kind of jug-band duo, scoring regular gigs as Dr K's Blues Band at private parties and social functions. The turning point arrived on 6 July 1966, when the duo met up with another local boy, Richard Thompson, in a Muswell Hill pub and discussed forming a folk-rock group. Thompson, born in 1949, already had a reputation for his guitar technique around the north London scene and had filled in as guitarist in Dr K's. Hutchings immediately recognised the free-form genius of Thompson's playing and improvising and wanted that chemistry full-time. The first Fairport Convention gig as a four-piece (with original, short-lived drummer Shaun Frater) took place on 27 May 1967 at St Michael's Hall in Golders Green. Even in that momentous year for rock music, the date was auspicious: *Are You Experienced?* had been on the streets for a week and a half, and *Sgt Pepper's Lonely Hearts Club Band* was five days away.

As they performed to the growing 'head' community of London's underground, the group gained new drummer Martin Lamble and two extra vocalists, Judy Dyble and Ian MacDonald, later known as Iain Matthews. In their first two years they harboured the spirit of West Coast soft psychedelia, incarnated among middle-class north Londoners. The vocal harmonies are carbon replicas of the

Byrds of *Turn! Turn! Turn!*, The Lovin' Spoonful, Richard and Mimi Fariña, and The Mamas and the Papas; the set lists an amalgam of Dylan, Jefferson Airplane, Paul Butterfield, Joni Mitchell, Phil Ochs, Tim Hardin and Love. Mirroring The Byrds' gradual shift in 1968 from the acid pilots of *Fifth Dimension* to the lysergic hillbillies of *Sweetheart of the Rodeo*, The Flying Burrito Brothers and Gram Parsons, as well as Dylan and The Band's rediscovery of American primitivism, Fairport's desire, held especially by Hutchings and Matthews, was to travel further down this country-rock route. But there was another side too, more aligned with the unfettered, fanciful flights of The Grateful Dead, where Fairport's instrumentalists would play ten-minute extemporisations on tracks like 'Reno, Nevada'.

With the haste typical of those formative times, the group found themselves in front of the UFO audience on 28 July 1967 supporting Pink Floyd, and were signed – with Joe Boyd as manager – to Polydor Records. *Fairport Convention*, recorded in November 1967 and released in the summer of 1968, is largely Californian in flavour but contains traces of an experimental bent. 'The Lobster' set a poem of that name by the eccentric Proust scholar George D. Painter, anthologised in *The Penguin Book of Sick Verse*, a favourite of Thompson's. 'M1 Breakdown' – a title that would shortly come to gain tragic resonance for this particular group – begins with the sound of a Transit van before its Jew's-harp shuffle takes hold. In 'It's All Right Ma, It's Only Witchcraft', an approaching hurricane becomes a metaphor for the dawning of a new era. And what group of the period would come up with a title like 'Portfolio'? Such unexpected details carried over onto the blues rocker 'Mr Lacey' on their second album, *What We Did on Our Holidays*. Dr Bruce Lacey was an inventor of robots and automata who lived next door to Hutchings in the mid-1960s, and the hoover-like whooshing noises that take a 'solo' in the song's middle eight are made by three of Lacey's robots, which he transported down to the studio in south London, their inventor gleefully prodding them into life while dressed in a space suit.

Holidays is a transitional record. With the group signed long-term to Island Records, Dyble was asked to leave in the late spring of 1968, and Boyd put forward as her replacement Sandy Denny, a regular frequenter of clubs like Les Cousins who had recently served an apprenticeship with London folk outfit Strawbs. The twenty-one-year-old was well established as a singer of traditional folk songs, and from this moment such material begins to creep into the group's songbook. Matthews stayed for another month, but with Denny around there was no room for a second singer. 'Nottamun Town' was their first recorded version of an English folk song, taped for a John Peel session on 2 June 1968. Like Pentangle, Fairport's earliest adoptions of folk tunes were weighted in favour of mood rather than drama. The recording that appeared on *What We Did on Our Holidays* featured drummer Martin Lamble only at the very end, on a pair of bongos – they hadn't yet worked out how to fit the group format into the trad zone. On 'She Moves through the Fair' (an Irish folk song with lyrics added in 1909 by its collector Padraic Colum), Denny can be heard tapping her autoharp, while Lamble conjures an atmosphere of stilled rapture with bongos, cymbal shimmers and light cracks on the snare. If the vocal harmonies on the first album aped Jefferson Airplane, on Richard Thompson's composition 'Meet on the Ledge' they took on the closer unison singing that can be recognised as a peculiarly British style. Matthews – just before his departure – and Denny trade the verses of this mournful, wise-before-its-time anthem, loaded with premonitory rumblings about deaths past and to come, and the reunion of the dead at some unspecified level of enlightenment.

Walter Scott's 1816 novel *The Antiquary* is set in a remote, fictional Scottish town called Fairport, the ancestral seat of Jonathan

Oldbuck, which proves to be loaded with ancient provenance, from Roman ruins to mysterious torture implements, all unearthed by an enthusiastic young amateur historian and antiquarian named Lovel. It's an appropriate parallel, because Fairport Convention was shortly to be turned into the site of the group's own antiquarian delvings into the loam of old English music.

The first inkling comes four tracks into *Unhalfbricking*, with 'A Sailor's Life'. Recorded in the spring of 1969, the track features Dave Swarbrick on the fiddle, and over the course of the track's eleven minutes – improvised on its first take – you can actually hear the group develop a new confidence, and something erupts into being that has never quite been heard in British music before. All the elements that we might associate with English electric folk are switched on. Its abstract, beatless opening verses, with a tidal spray of cymbals and rippling electric guitars, are parted after three minutes by Nicol's repetitive guitar riff, one that will carry throughout the voyage. Lamble beats a martial tattoo on his tom-toms, until at seven minutes the swell bursts its banks and a muscular riff is joined, with simultaneous raga-rock soloing by Thompson and Swarbrick. Between this moment and the music's final, gentle abatement come a historic few minutes: the first recorded use of drumsticks and drum kit on a rendition of an English folk song.

It was also the first time Swarbrick had ever amplified his fiddle. 'Richard was the first electric-guitar player I ever worked with,' says Dave Swarbrick, remembering how recording 'A Sailor's Life' brought him into contact with electricity for the first time. 'We didn't have any pickups in those days, we used a telephone mic. We smashed a telephone open and elastic-banded it to the fiddle.'

'We were coming from different worlds,' says Richard Thompson, 'and attempting to meet in the middle. On "A Sailor's Life", you hear us listening to each other and looking for common ground – inventing a middle language as we go. I think it worked because Swarb was ready for something else, and I was ready for something else.'

Swarbrick was already well ensconced in the folk-music circuit, having been a member of the Birmingham-based Ian Campbell Folk Group, and accompanied Bert Lloyd on several of his Topic recordings of the mid-1960s. At the same time, in 1966 he forged a successful duo with guitarist Martin Carthy. They had just released their third album, a collection of bleak, astringent ballads called *Prince Heathen*, when the call came from Boyd. The duo's repertoire favoured the picaresque, the tragic and supernatural. One of the highlights of *Prince Heathen* is 'Reynardine', a tale of a savage, malevolent werefox which Swarbrick brought with him to Fairport. 'Salisbury Plain', sung unaccompanied by Carthy, depicts the rough coupling of a brigand and a maiden; 'Seven Yellow Gypsies' is about the abduction of a noblewoman; 'Prince Heathen' is the devil himself taking violent revenge on a woman who refuses to submit to his advances. These are songs that speak of a lawless land, with forces more powerful than societal factors at large.

Unhalfbricking's sleeve is unbearably poignant. We'll examine its front cover later in the book; the reverse is a suburban Last Supper. The group's five members are arranged awkwardly around Denny's family dining table, holding half-chewed slices of white toast. Within a month or so of this photo being taken, Martin Lamble would be dead, killed in an 'M1 breakdown' more horrific than anything they could have imagined.

The cataclysm strikes around four in the morning of 12 May 1969, near Scratchwood Services, just south of Watford on the M1 motorway into London. One minute the Transit van is roaring down the tarmac on its final stretch before dropping off at the six occupants' various homes. The next it's cartwheeling off the verge, spewing guitars, drums, speakers and amplifiers from its burst back doors. Martin Lamble dies instantly in the crash, as does Richard Thompson's girlfriend Jeannie Franklyn, a promising clothes designer who has outfitted many of London's fashionable musicians. Ashley Hutchings is hurled out of the vehicle, and comes to his senses staggering on the hard shoulder with blood streaming from a broken nose and cheekbone. Simon Nicol is least harmed, but if the equipment had toppled *into* the van instead of out of it, he would have been crushed to death. Fortunately for Sandy Denny, she has taken a lift back to London in her boyfriend Trevor Lucas's car. The van's driver, roadie Harvey Bramham, later receives a six-month jail sentence for causing death by dangerous driving.[1]

Fairport Convention's dreams of becoming a British equivalent to The Band or The Byrds should have been crushed on that stretch of motorway in 1969. But what happened in the next five months was one of the most remarkable recuperations in British rock. By the end of October the group had created *Liege and Lief*, a glorious mixture of melancholic Fairport-penned originals, turbocharged jigs and reels, and electrified, magical ancient ballads, and which asked the question: could traditional folk song be claimed and owned by the rock generation, and what could rock learn from the process?

Following his discharge from hospital, and after Lamble's funeral, Hutchings emerged as Fairport's driving force, repositioning the group according to a growing obsession with the traditional ballads, pagan folk songs and musical heritage of Britain that had been a substantial part of Sandy Denny's pre-Fairport songbook. He began worshipping at the temple of the Ralph Vaughan Williams Memorial Library in Cecil Sharp House, and rolled up at many of the nation's folk festivals. Via Swarbrick, he also made the acquaintance of Bert Lloyd, whose comprehensive book, *Folk Song in England*, was published in a popular paperback in 1967. Lloyd became Fairport's oracle for the next few years and was even, in the early 1970s, briefly considered as a potential member. In regular consultation with the veteran folklorist, Hutchings began piecing together workable texts from the myriad extant versions that existed in the collections of Cecil Sharp, Francis Child, Lucy Broadwood and others. All his contemporaries recall the fervour with which he embarked on his homework, but even forty years later, talking to me backstage before a concert by his new ensemble Rainbow Chasers, he is at a loss to explain exactly why he was seized with this new passion.

'All through my youth', he muses, 'I loved Westerns, cowboy films. So what with cowboy films as a kid, the blues as my first real love, and then the West Coast thing that happened in the mid-1960s with The Byrds, who I adored, and Dylan, and Buffalo Springfield and so on . . . inevitably, knowing my personality, there was going to come a time when I would swing the other way. It was obvious that we had to go back to our own roots to form our own brand of music. And I've always been the archivist, the person who roots around and tries to find obscure material. That summer of the crash, I just went to as many folk festivals as I could, stayed up late talking to traditional and revival musicians, cramming a lot of knowledge into my head in a very short time. Maybe the others were a bit amused by it, I don't know – I suspect they might have been.

'Very soon after we got out of hospital, we weren't certain that we were going to carry on at that point, whether we had the will to. So we called a meeting, and we decided there and then what the future was: we would get a new drummer in place of Martin, we would ask Dave Swarbrick to join us, and we would concentrate on this new direction which had been started on *Unhalfbricking*. We were all agreed on it, there was no problem, and very quickly it came together.'

If there had been no crash, it's likely Fairport would have

continued with the cross-purposed mix of material to be found on *Unhalfbricking*. 'A Sailor's Life' and Denny's wistful 'Who Knows Where the Time Goes?' are the exceptions on a record which also contains no less than three Bob Dylan covers and the country-tinged Thompson song 'Cajun Woman'. With their hearts somewhere in the mid-Atlantic, Fairport would have just kept on pedalling in their American heroes' slipstream. By Simon Nicol's own admission, the core of the group were 'uptight, buttoned-up, middle-class kids'. Their slightly awkward default setting needed the alchemy of Sandy Denny, 'a wild child and free spirit', and the mischievous, mercurial figure of Swarbrick, to spark into new life. Plus, in one important respect, they were about to follow in the footsteps of the group that was the closest model for Fairport at that moment: The Band.

Summer 1968 saw the release of The Band's *Music from Big Pink*, a record that indelibly marked the Fairport psyche. After backing Dylan on his 1966 tour – the last before the motorbike crash that put him out of commission for most of 1967 – The Band sought out a rural 'cultural detox' at a house in Saugerties, near the bohemian upstate New York town of Woodstock, where the wooden boards were painted a pale shade of pink. Here, sequestered away from the twists and turns of the American Summer of Love, The Band developed a rootsy group sound, the grainy wholefood alternative to psychedelia's fancy feast. One writer has called their singing 'like lost souls capering slowly round a campfire under a deep, dark evening sky in the backwoods',[2] and Dylan himself painted the naive-art cover, in which an elephant invades a Band rehearsal in the great outdoors. *Music from Big Pink*'s reconnection with rural Americana effectively shut the door to impetuous foreign wannabes like Fairport, outsiders who could never hope to 'own' such material so convincingly. But Fairport would shortly be packed off to their own equivalent of Big Pink: a remote country manor where they could regroup, recuperate and indulge in some musical therapy.

Joe Boyd's Witchseason Productions began in 1967, when the American producer/manager was introduced to the business team of Chris Stamp and Kit Lambert. Stamp was the brother of film actor Terence; Lambert the troubled, addictive-personality son of the composer Constant Lambert. Together they worked under the banner of Track Records, headquartered in Soho, steering The Who to their enormous success. Enamoured by what they had heard of Fairport, they gave Boyd enough money to open his own office and finance the group's first single on Polydor. By 1969 The Incredible String Band, John and Beverley Martyn and Nick Drake were all on Boyd's books, and the deals he brokered for most of his artists with Island Records helped to cement the label's underground credentials. Fairport's Island contract obliged them to deliver two albums a year. *Unhalfbricking* was half the battle, but there was no time to lose: it was July by the time Hutchings was discharged from hospital and felt ready to work again. Meanwhile, Boyd's office had come up with an idea to help the band move forward out of the horror of their accident. Witchseason employee Anthea Roberts (the former runner of the Troubadour folk club in Earl's Court) found the advert in the back pages of *The Lady*: Farley House, deep in the Hampshire countryside, to rent for the summer.

If you had no knowledge of the existence of Farley House, you could never run into it by accident. On a sopping wet March weekend, thirty-eight years after Fairport's residency, I turn off the M3 south of Winchester and find myself in an older England: the chain of villages, hamlets, sleeping country churches, fields and hedgerows remain strung together by twisting lanes invisible under their canopy of dripping leaves. The hamlet of Farley Chamberlayne was hacked out of the Hampshire forest nearly a millennium ago, the ancestral manor of William the Conqueror's chamberlain. Nearby rises the prehistoric round barrow known as

Getting back to the garden: Fairport Convention frolic on
the lawn at Farley House, Hampshire, summer 1969.

Farley Mount; on its summit is a curious folly built of white stone
– a chapel with a pyramid roof. It's a shrine to a horse that fell into
a chalk pit in 1733; a year later it recovered enough to win the
Hunter's Plate in a race on Worthy Downs, using the name Beware
Chalk Pit. For anyone coming to this place for healing or to recover
their potency, the landscape is studded with good omens.

The signpost to Farley House, carved into a halved log, is easy
to miss. It directs the observant traveller down a muddy driveway,
lined with cow pastures, before the seventeenth-century Queen
Anne facade is revealed, painted the same creamy buttermilk
yellow as it appears in Eric Hayes's photographs on the sleeve of
Liege and Lief. The building is a shell, gutted in preparation for major
refurbishment. A ditch for new wiring and pipes moats the building's
periphery. The floors have been stripped out, leaving a skeletal grid
of beams and joists. Plastic sheeting flaps in the window frames.
Diggers and cement mixers lurk in the driveway. The wisteria that

Fairport rehearsing material for *Liege and Lief*. Left to right: Ashley Hutchings, Dave Swarbrick, Sandy Denny, Richard Thompson, Simon Nicol, Dave Mattacks.

flung itself over the back of the house in 1969 is still there, although pulled off the wall and lying in a tangled clump until the rear facade is repainted. Best preserved is the back garden: just like in the forty-year-old photographs, the massive fir tree still presides over the flat lawn like a protective guardian; the rope swing in which Richard Thompson was pictured cradling a restorative mug of tea dangles from one of the lower boughs. A small detail like this suddenly shrinks nearly four decades of history. From July to September 1969, in a room overlooking this lawn, Fairport Convention reconstituted themselves, and in the process piped fresh air into a stagnating tradition. Farley Chamberlayne was a crucible of change whose remoteness forced a strenuous dedication to the task in hand.

As well as hiring Swarbrick, Fairport needed a replacement drummer. After a series of auditions, they found their new recruit. Dave Mattacks had worked his way through various underdog rock 'n' roll outfits like The Pioneers and Andy and the Marksmen, and had been playing with a professional dance band in Ireland and Scotland for the previous couple of years. As it turned out, though, he was not only rhythmically a safe pair of hands, but an inspired musician waiting to break new ground. From a relatively unglamorous career, Mattacks was about to become indelibly associated with the classic rhythms of English folk-rock. His deceptively unfussy style was to be the heartbeat through the life of Fairport, Hutchings's subsequent line-ups of The Albion Band, as well as countless sessions for artists indelibly associated with this era: Steeleye Span, The Incredible String Band, Shirley Collins, John Martyn, Nick Drake, Richard Thompson, Mike Heron, Spirogyra and others. In his hands, the beats fall with a heaviness that seems to gouge at the earth itself, fleet-footed enough to avoid getting bogged down. He was fortunately named: the mattock was a medieval tool, part hammer, part digging implement, sometimes brandished as a crude weapon. The funky plod of Mattacks's drumming proved the ideal foil for the mushy instrumental palette of English electric folk, propelling its accordions, fiddles, abrasive guitars and astringent harmonies forward without denying their bulk and grit.

'It was purely a case of responding to the best of my abilities to what was going on around me,' says Mattacks, who now lives in Boston, Massachusetts. 'I didn't really get it until I'd been in the band about a year. I didn't really understand the aesthetics of what they were doing. And then when I did, it had quite an effect on how I then perceived music, and my approach to my instrument and the kind of music I wanted to play.' Mattacks was sympathetic to the 'four-squariness' inherent in British folk tunes, but 'the danger with the worst of folk-rock is that it can sound ploddy, no matter the tempo. So the thing is to have that four-square thing to it, but make it swing.'

🦋

'A little football on the lawn, kite-flying on Farley Mount, busking in Winchester Cathedral Close to pay the milk bill . . . happy

English folk-rock's safest pair of hands: drummer Dave Mattacks.

times,' eulogises Richard Thompson. 'We were only a few months after losing Martin Lamble, and I think we were still in shock, so this was a healing time. The environment was perfect, and the mission kept us sane.'

The photos that exist of Fairport at Farley Chamberlayne have taken on the mantle of the ultimate English idyll, an artistic exploration undertaken in tranquillity, with the group dawdling on the lawn of the magnificent seventeenth-century Queen Anne-style house in the golden sunlight of late summer; or rehearsing in their oak-floored, brocade-curtained music room, with amplifier lights winking through the fug of cigarette smoke and bronze sunbeams diffusing in the swirling dust inside the French windows. Nevertheless, this was a group in shock, its collective pain buried deep in the earth. Hayes's photos can't quite conceal the bruises

257

on Ashley Hutchings's broken nose, while the bereaved Thompson appears white as a sheet. In such therapeutic seclusion there was nothing for it but to knuckle down to several months' hard work. Although no actual recording took place there, they wrote new material and selected and adapted folk tunes such as 'Matty Groves', 'Reynardine' and the serpentine twists and turns of the epic ballad 'Tam Lin'. 'We had a music room,' recalls Swarbrick, 'and we went into it every day, from early in the morning to late at night. And others were away practising in their own rooms. We religiously worked very hard. I'm talking twelve, fourteen hours a day, to get this together. We knew that we didn't have Farley Chamberlayne for ever – it was an expensive place to rent. We had a project; everybody was, dare I say, young and well fired-up – hormones all over the bleeding place!'

Hutchings adds: 'We just came down for breakfast and then wandered into the room one by one and then eventually a rehearsal would start. Someone might come downstairs and say, "I was thinking last night what we should really do is such-and-such." But there was a great deal of fun around. I can imagine that the way we worked was totally different to, say, the Critics Group, who discussed in a very earnest and academic way how songs should be sung. We still had the rock 'n' roll attitude, and it was a whole different way of working to the old guard.'

As well as The Band's *Big Pink*, another favourite at Farley Chamberlayne was the self-titled debut by Sweeney's Men, which accommodated Irish traditional tunes in a contemporary acoustic setting. This drumless group featured Anne Briggs's partner at the time, Johnny Moynihan. If Fairport listened to the radio at all, they would likely have caught that summer's surprise smash hit, David Bowie's 'Space Oddity', with its zero-gravity drum part played by none other than Pentangle's Terry Cox. The single had been rush-released to coincide with the *Apollo 11* moon landing, which took place on 20 July. A few days after that giant leap for mankind, Eric

Hayes turned up in Hampshire with his camera and snapped the iconic images of Fairport at work and play.

'It was a magical time,' confirms Hutchings. 'And there's a lot of magic on that album. There was a special feeling in the house, in the room, and also a lot of hidden magic and weirdness on that album. Well, the past is weird, you know, our ancestors did a lot of weird things.'

After spending one more week rehearsing at Swarbrick's home in Pembrokeshire, Fairport re-emerged from their retreat on 24 September 1969 with a grand comeback concert at London's Royal Festival Hall through one of the biggest PA systems the venerable venue had ever hosted. Also on the bill were Witchseason colleagues Nick Drake and John and Beverley Martyn, whose acoustic songwriting, though now referred to as 'folk-rock', stood in marked contrast to Fairport's melting pot of old and new. Following their rapturously received (and reportedly deafening) show, the group went into south London's Sound Techniques studio on 16 October with producer Joe Boyd and engineer John Wood for the first of six sessions that gave birth to the eight tracks that finally appeared on *Liege and Lief*.

Released in December 1969, *Liege and Lief* retains a coherence and integrity shared by very few British folk-rock records. It may have had the Island palm-tree logo imprinted on its pink central roundel, but an oak would have been far more appropriate, for the atmosphere it evokes is English to its core. There is a feeling of ideas and emotions still being absorbed. Though it's neither deliberately, studiedly archaic or quaint, an accommodation with the past is made that seamlessly suits the electrified rock arrangements. There is a self-consciousness about the project, but not so much that the group can't fully abandon themselves to their new sound as it flowers into being.

Mere and Mete was the alternative title considered, the significant factor being that both options were rooted in Saxon etymology. Embedded in the meaning of 'liege' is both the feudal lord and the vassal that owes him allegiance. Adjectivally, the word also refers to the relationship that binds them – the medieval contract in which the land was the mutual interest, with serfs and bondsmen farming the soil which made up the lord's estate. The archaic adverb 'lief' stems from an old German word for 'love' and means 'gladly', 'willingly', as in the Shakespearean 'I had as lief the town crier spoke my lines'. Liege and lief is a voluntary surrender to the spirit of old Britain.

It begins with 'Come All Ye', whose swinging motion backs Sandy Denny as she lays out the group's wares with a pocket description of each band member. The song can be read as a wider invocation, a summoning of Britain's dormant musical powers: '*Together we shall try / To raise the spirit of the air / And move the rolling sky.*' Significantly, the 'roving' minstrels of countless traditional tunes are now 'rolling', and Swarbrick now plays '*a violin of solid wood*' – i.e. one that is amplified like a solid-body electric guitar. And when Denny mentions her own role – '*the high notes come from you and me / For we will sing so clear*' – there is an implied inclusiveness. The communal feel is reinforced when the entire company joins in the choruses.

'Reynardine', 'Matty Groves' and 'Tam Lin' are three ballads that deal with murder or mysterious transformations, the former creeping stealthily through thickets of seething cymbals and menacing rumbles from the rhythm section. 'The Deserter' is the picaresque saga of an unwilling army conscript in the Napoleonic Wars. The theme had topical resonance: 15 October, the day before the track was recorded, was the day of the Moratorium protest in the US – one of the biggest anti-war demonstrations in American history, involving millions marching against Nixon's Vietnam campaign, in which the draft, literally run as a lottery, was cutting short many young people's counter-cultural dreams. Following a medley of high-octane instrumental jigs and reels – complex, but played with palpable relish – comes the LP's greatest achievement. The epic ballad 'Tam Lin' is compressed into seven minutes, governed by a slippery, mercurial rhythm. The centre of its pulse shimmers and shifts almost from bar to bar, its verses broken into periods slipping in and out of three–four and four–four time. The weird narrative climaxes as Janet saves Tam Lin, the faery father of her child, from being sacrificed as a tithe to Hell, and as he is held in her arms other fairies try to make her drop him by changing his shape into a succession of fierce beasts. The ballad's scenic jump cuts and shape-shifting content is suitably set off by Fairport's magical construction, which goes into a kind of tumbling freefall between each stanza.

Among these sit three songs written by the group. As well as 'Come All Ye', there are two Thompson compositions pointing to the recent tragedy that none of them were discussing openly over the Farley House breakfast table. 'Farewell, Farewell' is addressed to the nameless dead; the phrase *'and will you never cut the cloth'* probably alludes to Jeannie Franklyn's career as a fashion designer. 'Crazy Man Michael', credited to Swarbrick and Thompson, closes the record with a bitter tale, sung with pitiless understatement by Sandy Denny, of a man deranged by visions ever since he shot a raven, only to discover that the bird was his own lover, with a bullet hole through the heart. It is a devastating end to the record, but its formal language and pastoral-mythological setting fits the mood of the older folk songs. Most remarkable of all, of the album's eight tracks 'Come All Ye' is the only song that has a chorus that can easily be joined by an audience. The rest wander deeper into their respective narratives; unlike a pop song with refrains, hooks and totemic, easily assimilable recapitulations, these songs hold the attention with the persistence of a tale-spinner.

Despite its gestation in the Hampshire summer, the prevailing climate of *Liege and Lief* is similar to the transitional seasons – there is spring here, but an autumnal veil also; mild, but overcast with the blank white clouds that signal a disturbance in the season's round. Fate is exacted; English balladry displays its full menace and mystery; and there's tentative reflection upon pain and loss, tainted by hard experience.

Visually, the LP was presented as a hobbyist's portfolio of antiquarian interests. A hand-drawn, leafy cartouche sits upon a background wash of smoky calamine, like the untreated plaster in a forgotten attic room. Apart from Hutchings, who is seen in profile, the group members stare out from violet-tinged oval frames: Edwardian keepsakes prepared for a locket. Except that one of these Edwardians, Dave Mattacks, has somehow travelled forward in time and brought back a pair of aviator shades. On the reverse, a leering, gap-toothed idol, crudely whittled from a block, leers from the centre of an ovoid floral wreath. This carved homunculus was, according to Hutchings, found by Swarbrick under a pile of leaves in a churchyard; Swarbrick himself only says that it belonged to his Danish wife Brigitta, 'and I'm afraid I can't tell you any more about it than that'.

The gatefold sleeve opens to reveal an archaeology of English customs in digested, pamphlet form – predominantly relating to death. As well as sepia photos of folklorist forefathers Francis Child and Cecil Sharp, and engravings of turn-of-the-century

Fairport Convention, *Liege and Lief*, front and inner gatefold (1969).

morris dancing, rural songsters and weird folk mannequins like the Burry Man of West Lothian, there's the Padstow Obby Oss (which Fairport had witnessed on May Day that year, a fortnight before the fatal crash), with reference to its May death dance and its supplicatory reappearance the following day, begging for alms. Pace-egging, coupled with an accompanying mummers' play about a hero fighting evil, being killed and revived by a mock physician, draws attention to the death of winter and rebirth of life at springtime. In the Celtic 'hunting of the wren' custom, the tiny bird is hounded out of hedgerows and killed; a caption reads: 'In remote areas boys playing instruments plead for money for the burial of a wren.' Other artefacts include John Dyer's poem, 'Down among the Dead Men', and a postcard (discovered in the Farley House attic) of the gravestone of Thomas Thetcher, a grenadier whose preserved tombstone is situated in the churchyard of nearby Winchester Cathedral. Savage death and ritual resurrection: upon these lodestones was *Liege and Lief* erected.

Fairport received both praise and condemnation when the album appeared. Purists might have objected to their cavalier mismatching of tunes and texts, and a certain slapdash approach which led to, for instance, the 'Lord Arnold' of the 'official' 'Matty Groves' becoming 'Lord Darnell', thanks to Hutchings mishearing Bert Lloyd's voice down the telephone. But such misreadings and distortions are in the nature of the oral tradition, and it threw into question the spurious 'authenticity' of the folk versions studiously set in stone by the Victorian and Edwardian collectors. Fairport's electrifying act preserved and restored the guts and spontaneous vigour to the folk continuum.

'There were certain people in the hardcore traditional or revivalist folk movement who saw us as perhaps encroaching on their territory and taking liberties with "their" music,' says Simon Nicol. 'It's a preposterous attitude, because they're just songs, they don't exist under glass, they're not exhibits in a museum that you have to preserve in amber.' In any case, remembers Swarbrick, the English folk circuit was in a pretty stagnant state by the end of the decade. 'I used to go out with Ian Campbell to pubs and all you could hear was the dominoes clinking. It was an effort to get things going.'

'It was radical from top to bottom,' emphasises Hutchings. 'We had respect for tradition and the material, respect for the people that had gone before, and the legacy, so we weren't just blithely kicking out what had gone before, we were radically building on it. So much of the developments in traditional folk music are academically driven, but for us it was a natural thing. There would always be earnest, dry sleeve notes on any traditional album saying exactly where a song came from, how many years old it was, and so on. Whereas we just leapt in and did this in a rock 'n' roll kind of way. For example, "Tam Lin" was pieced together: the tune doesn't go with the song. Same with "Matty Groves", actually, the tune comes from another source. We weren't concerned with being historically accurate, it was rock 'n' roll. And it blew a lot of cobwebs away. We were on a kind of crusade.'

Thompson amplifies the dawning realisation, within the group, of the importance of this project. 'Nothing resonates like an old song. To sing something beautifully written, and then refined over hundreds of years, that still has meaning and urgency, that still creates vivid pictures in the mind, is a deeply rewarding thing. I think we hoped the band would achieve some mainstream popularity, so that we could bring the tradition a little closer to people's lives. This has happened more in Ireland and Scotland, but the English still seem to see their own culture as an embarrassment or a novelty – it's that post-empirical confusion. I think it was a blueprint for indigenous reconnection that could be applied elsewhere.'

Liege and Lief was a high-water mark for Fairport Convention, and for the whole notion of British folk-rock. And yet its very influence meant that, because it would be imitated and diluted so many times in the future, it also marked the beginning of the genre's long, slow decline into the 1970s, as legions of lumpen labourers ploughed through jigs and reels at breakneck pace. The line-up didn't even survive until the album was released. Both Sandy Denny and Ashley Hutchings quit in November. As Dave Mattacks observes, they had reached opposite poles of the group's internal dynamics. 'Ashley's left of centre – "English folk music is the holy grail" – and he wants to go completely in that direction. Sandy's already done the traditional thing and is really getting into pursuing her own writing. And there's this group of people in the middle who like the marriage of the two extremes. One minute we're doing all these great gigs and everything seems to be going really well, and then the next minute they're both gone.'

Hutchings, by his own admission, 'had a bit of a breakdown, at the time of the release of *Liege and Lief* – a delayed reaction to the crash, no question about it. And I still believe that Sandy and I should have stayed, could have stayed, and maybe with a stronger person at the helm other than Joe, who would have knocked our heads together and said, "Don't be stupid, you've started something here – keep it going." But there was a laissez-faire attitude, and it was "OK, well, if that's what you want to do, off you go." But deep down, I really think Sandy and I could have resolved everything and should have stayed, actually. But it was other forces. Sandy was hyped up at that period, and I was having dizzy spells and breaking down to some degree. The pain had all gone – it was all mental.'

Even as *Liege and Lief* was appearing in the shops, Ashley Hutchings was already striking out on his own. 'The story of the 1970s for me', he sums up, 'is largely of obsession with traditional English music, getting deeper into it, marrying Shirley Collins, living in the countryside away from everything, going back to playing acoustic bass guitar, and then at the end of the 1970s going to the National Theatre providing music for plays.' Hutchings has ploughed his own deep furrow through English music and folk culture, his bass guitar churning up the bedded-in turf of morris and country dance, rural folk song and balladry, exposing them to the air, sometimes to ridicule, at other times to a celebration of a national folklore that was left to rot or had the highway of American popular culture bulldozed through its centre. If a huge amount of pop and rock in the 1960s and 70s effectively ended up taking American rock back to America, Hutchings has set his life's work to pushing British music in the opposite direction.

That journey began with the formation of Steeleye Span, a group that, like Fairport Convention, seldom kept the same personnel for more than a year at a time. The seeds were sown at the Keele Folk Festival in June 1969, when Hutchings shared a ride back to London with Tim Hart and Maddy Prior. Still in their late teens, this duo had made their mark in the folk clubs of St Albans since they got together – professionally and romantically – in 1966, performing crystal-clear guitar/vocal renditions of the ballads and troubadour songs of yore that they unearthed with the help of ubiquitous mentor Bert Lloyd. For their two volumes of *Folk Songs of Old England*, from 1968 and 1969, representing their repertoire of that period, they were photographed in front of Hampton Court Palace, and there was an echo of Tudor polyphony in the way their voices intertwined around arrangements of 'Adam and Eve' and 'Earl Richard'. These were songs from Merrie England's springtime, and later, on *Summer Solstice* (1971), they would much better capture the mood of sun-kissed medieval Arcadia. Lloyd was sitting in the car that summer night as they sped back to London from Keele, nodding his approval of an all-night conversation which left Hutchings with the distinct impression that the duo were desperate to break out of the folk mould.

Half a year later Hutchings summoned Hart and Prior to a
meeting with another young folk-music couple who had become
his protégés, Gay and Terry Woods. Fresh from Ireland, Terry
Woods had been a member of Sweeney's Men, the Irish trio
whose self-titled 1968 LP had been such a favourite of Fairport
Convention. At the close of 1969 the group was on the rocks –
bouzouki player Johnny Moynihan and Woods couldn't stand to
be in the same room. A couple of weeks after the *Liege and Lief*
sessions had ended, Gay and Terry Woods, Moynihan and third
member Andy Irvine were at Hutchings's north London home,
trying to patch up their differences in a last-ditch rehearsal, though
relations broke down irretrievably and Moynihan slunk back to
Ireland. Hutchings and the Woods duo struck up a favourable
working relationship, however, and secured a record deal with
RCA via new manager Sandy Roberton, a veteran publisher of the
blues boom who was now managing and producing British folk
acts. Hutchings brought together the two couples, with himself
as ringleader, and used the RCA advance to rent a bungalow in
Winterbourne Stoke, an exquisitely preserved Wiltshire village
next door to Stonehenge, for three months in an attempt to repeat
the enriching, healing sojourn of Farley Chamberlayne. *Liege and
Lief*'s autumnal north wind inexorably shaded into the winter of
the first Steeleye Span.

For Hutchings the wintering at Winterbourne Stoke was less
a rock group's country get-together, more a literary retreat in
the mould of Thomas Hardy or Edward Thomas. In the group
photos taken at the time, Hutchings has changed his appearance
considerably: no longer the thickly maned bass lord of Farley
Chamberlayne, six months later he looks like a small-town
undertaker, a bearded, peacoat-clad eccentric, pottering down the
lanes with his cane, bowler hat and chequered, skintight trousers.
One image in particular suggests temporality in freefall: the group
are walking past a thatched cottage, carrying instrument cases,

Hutchings tapping his way with his stick, Prior holding a bodhran drum. Time travellers stalking the deserted streets of a medieval village, but from which age did these travellers originate?

Rehearsals were interspersed with further folkloric research. Maddy Prior and Gay Woods spent the long dark evenings in the freezing bungalow teaching each other Irish step-dancing and clog-dancing, crocheting and embroidering, 'looking for all the world like two medieval ladies sewing silken seams', as Prior recalled it.[3] Hutchings discovered a new fascination for gardening, and sallied forth for occasional stints with spade and hoe. But underneath the pastoral bonhomie, the atmosphere was very different from

Time-travellers, but from which time? Steeleye Span at Winterbourne Stoke, 1970. Left to right: Terry Woods, Gay Woods, Ashley Hutchings, Maddy Prior, Tim Hart.

the leisurely consensus at Farley Chamberlayne. Hutchings found himself the peacemaker in the middle of a war between two chalk-and-cheese couples, bickering over domestic trifles and mealtime arrangements. The antagonism spilled over into their first recording sessions – a week at Sound Techniques in late March 1970 which gave birth to the first Steeleye Span album.

The first three Steeleye records, *Hark! The Village Wait* (1970), *Please to See the King* (1971) and *Ten Man Mop* (1971) – the ones with Ashley Hutchings as the group's driving force – are textured with a loamy, atavistic grit. On the first of these, the mix of amplified and acoustic instruments (including concertina, harmonium, five-string banjos and Tim Hart's customised electric dulcimer) rub up against each other like a shedload of rusted, notched and pitted farm implements. Electric guitars are tuned with a coarse sawtooth edge, as though the amplifiers need a drop of easing oil. Terry Woods uses the mandola and banjo as percussion, running in circles around the solid tea-chest drums of the LP's two drummers, Gerry Conway and Dave Mattacks. The group's close-harmony singing draws a line from the Coppers/Young Tradition/Watersons, hovering exhilaratingly at times on the cusp of major and minor keys. On 'One Night As I Lay on My Bed', the electric dulcimer – which Tim Hart would arrange flat on his knees like a lap-steel guitar – spreads a ring of bright water behind the percussive union of Terry Woods's banjo and Mattacks's rhythm. 'Copshawholme Fair', discovered during the 1960s on a seventy-eight rpm record in Cumberland County Library by a Leeds song collector, is an exuberant imagistic pageant, listing the colourful characters and wares at a market-town 'mop' fair – a folk counterpart to the celebratory, descriptive Beatles of 'Penny Lane'.

But the knees-up didn't last. The squally weather between the Irish and English couples almost rained off the entire recording session, and almost as soon as it was in the can the Woodses left the group in high dudgeon. They briefly joined the quirky, London-based Irish folk group Dr Strangely Strange, and then returned to Ireland, where they spent several years as The Woods Band, writing their own folk-rock material.

Meanwhile, at Tim Hart's insistence, Martin Carthy was inducted into the Steeleye line-up, along with classically trained violinist Peter Knight. Carthy ended up exerting a strong influence on this second iteration of the group. It was, in fact, Carthy who had suggested the name Steeleye Span – a miserly character from the folk song 'Horkstow Grange' – to Hart when the group was starting out. And Carthy suggested not bothering to hire a drummer for the second album, *Please to See the King*, allowing the group a greater degree of fluid interplay: 'you shouldn't use the percussion like a club'.[4] Instead, Hutchings's bass crook confidently shepherds the tunes along. Carthy used his new position to experiment for the first time with an electric guitar and massive Fender amplifier, generating a thunderous peal that rings out of the record's grooves. Maddy Prior, singing alone, introduces giddy microtonal swoops and sways. Songs such as the rerun of 'The Blacksmith', 'The Lark in the Morning' and 'Female Drummer' are clothed in silken finery, with tart, modal close harmonies meshing exhilaratingly with the layers of skirling mandolin, electric-guitar chimes and Knight's skittering violin. On 'The Lark' in particular, Carthy's middle-eight chops with his guitar are fantastically weighty, cutting across Hart's weaving dulcimer like heavy, compacted sods of clay. 'Boys of Bedlam' features Carthy's psychedelic-phased guitar and a spooky, moaning choir who sound as if they have their heads buried in a hurdy-gurdy. Paradoxically, the amplification on Peter Knight's violin is what gives this LP such a grainy, coarse ambience, a kind of aural sepia tone bleeding through the body of the music.

Please to See the King is a piercing, keen-edged record, perhaps the closest a British act has come to what Bob Dylan, speaking of his own recordings of 1965–6, called 'that thin, that wild mercury sound . . . metallic and bright gold'. The title, taken from the song 'The King' that Carthy introduced to the album sessions, was spoken, according to custom, by 'wren-hunters' who went knocking on doors and requesting money in return for a peep at the slaughtered bird in a coffin, bound with a ribbon. And like the wren-hunters of yore, the early Steeleye found themselves in the midst of a difficult economy, hawking their wares around the country at a succession of student-union gigs, in the community which was most receptive to this new incarnation of folk music.

On the cover of their third LP, *Ten Man Mop, Or Mr Reservoir Butler Rides Again*, released at the end of 1971, the band members pastiched themselves as old-time labourers: Hutchings in collarless shirt clutching a rake; Knight next to a fishing boat; Carthy propping up a market cart; and Prior on a churchyard wall. 'A "mop",' Tim Hart has explained, 'was a mop-fair, a hiring fair, the implication being that we, and the five codgers also on the sleeve, were looking for work.' But if the fivesome were seeking their fortune, they were going the wrong way about it. *Ten Man Mop* was packaged so extravagantly – in a gold-leaf box set – that they lost money on each copy sold. Likewise, apart from the two magnificently solemn drone ballads, 'When I Was on Horseback' and 'Captain Coulston', much of its contents suffer from falling stock. The largely Irish-flavoured jigs, reels and roister-doistering songs like 'Marrowbones' and 'Four Nights Drunk' are beginning to sound like earnest reconstructions rather than the glorious new idiom of the previous two records. Once Steeleye began to treat the material with more respect, the magic seemed to dissipate. Hutchings appeared to feel the same way, and left the group at the end of the year. Carthy also walked out – he objected to Hart and Prior's desire to replace Hutchings with bassist Rick Kemp – and, shortly afterwards, married Norma Waterson, lately returned from her stint as a DJ in the West Indies.

Because of the subsequent commercial impact of Steeleye Span – sell-out American tours, their own TV series and two enormous hit singles – it's easy to think of the group as representing all the crass aspects of British folk music. But the pizzazz of the 1970s has eclipsed the raw thrills of *Hark! The Village Wait* and *Please to See the King*, two hungry-sounding albums that held out a tantalising vision of a potential pan-British music that never materialised.

Ashley Hutchings has been beating the bounds of English traditional music ever since. When he first heard Shirley and Dolly Collins's *Anthems in Eden*, just after quitting Fairport back in 1969, he broke down in body-shaking sobs; the suite finally unlocked and articulated all that he loved about English music. 'It evokes the countryside and it evokes the healing . . . I imagine it defined the whole of the rest of my career.'[5]

He had fallen in love, and not just with the music. Months later he went to see Shirley Collins perform at Cecil Sharp House, and invited her to the local pub in the interval. Coming back from the bar, he put down the cognac he'd bought her, leaned forward and kissed her. Collins had just separated from her husband John Marshall, and Hutchings could see an end to his involvement in Steeleye on the horizon. Their new partnership signalled a change in both their fortunes and their lifestyles. They moved to Red Rose Cottage, a Tudor property deep in the Sussex countryside in the village of Etchingham, and were married nearby on 6 August 1971, surrounded by auspicious omens: the registrar was called Mr Tree, the assistant was Daisy Field.

The fifteenth of February 1971 was D-Day – the date decimalisation was introduced in Britain. On that day the ancient monetary system of twelve pence to the shilling, twenty shillings to the pound was replaced with a decimal system, at last setting Britain on course to join the Common Market. With its roots in the Roman occupation, the old coinage system had entered the very fabric of the English language – 'the king's shilling', 'I don't

Albion dreaming: Shirley Collins and Ashley Hutchings at Etchingham, Sussex, 1971, around the time of their marriage and completion of the Albion Country Band album *No Roses*.

give tuppence', 'bent as a nine-bob note', etc.

The insecurities of changing times can be detected in *Corunna*, an experimental historical drama that Steeleye Span took part in during the summer of 1971. The play was set in the Napoleonic Wars, specifically the English retreat from Spain during the Peninsular Wars of 1808. Director Keith Dewhurst took a Brechtian approach, breaking the fourth wall between players and audience; as well as integrating songs from *Please to See the King* and *Ten Man Mop* into the action, the group took speaking roles in the story, with Ashley Hutchings acting as a narrator (photos of the show depict Martin Carthy, barefoot, adjusting his towering Fender amplifier as grenadiers in tricorned hats parade in the foreground). The play concluded with the lead character returning to a Manchester turned into an unrecognisable wasteland after the Industrial Revolution. 'I can't remember what the England we fought for was like,' he complains. 'What was it like?' Steeleye Span provided the response, launching into 'The Lark in the Morning', with electric guitars pealing like carillons in a country church. 'Song of the Advertising Copywriter' followed, sung by Hutchings and Tim Hart, ushering in a new post-industrial consumer society in which community was threatened by manufactured desires ('*In my Polaroid glasses/ I despise the masses . . .*').

Hutchings's theatrical project fed into *No Roses*, the album he was busy making at the same time with Shirley Collins, which was assembled piecemeal over several months and ended up featuring twenty-six different musicians in various combinations. The group was billed as The Albion Country Band, marking the start of what would become an institution in the UK's folk and folk-rock scene, which has hosted a transient population of musicians and has veered from electric work to renditions of traditional morris-dance tunes.

Albion is the most venerable, ancient name by which the British Isles have been known, of such antiquity now that its usage evokes the mythological aspects of British nationhood. Throughout the 1970s and 80s the various incarnations of The Albion Band explicitly acted as a conduit for waking up slumbering English indigenous music, its latent power released from dormant energy sumps.

The sleeve of *No Roses* features two English lions: a stone carving from Eltham Palace on the front; on the reverse, a photo taken by Cecil Sharp of a hirsute farm worker from whom he had collected a tune in 1906. Inside, the newlyweds explore their patch of English Eden, wandering the fields immediately behind Red Rose Cottage. Hutchings wears leather jodhpurs he found at Farley House; Collins is up to her neck in a cornflower dress. We have made our home on the land, they seem to say, and this is the music of the homeland. And yet the title – lifted by Collins from a song popular with the Copper family – signals that all is not cosy there. The advertising blurb summed it up neatly: 'Nine songs of love, death, transportation, ritual and custom from the English tradition'.

The core line-up of *No Roses* effectively reunited the old Fairport: Hutchings, Richard Thompson and Simon Nicol on electric guitars, Dave Mattacks drumming on some tracks. Producer Sandy Roberton weaves a rich, coarse-knit broadcloth from an instrumentarium that includes concertina and hammered dulcimer (played by Cecil Sharp House librarian Dave Bland), saxophone (avant-gardist Lol Coxhill), accordion (folk traditionalist John Kirkpatrick) and Northumbrian small pipes, Jew's harp, bassoon and collectable brass instruments the serpent and ophicleide. The album consolidates the convergence of folk music and rock that had been taking place since the mid-1960s, and, appropriately, influential figures such as Lal and Mike Waterson, The Young Tradition's Royston Wood, Maddy Prior and northern fiddler Barry Dransfield took part. A significant contribution is made by pianist Ian Whiteman and drummer Roger Powell of psychedelic-mystic rock group Mighty Baby.

The record hinges on two songs about dead women. 'Murder of Maria Marten' is a piece of folk reportage about a real-life 'Red Barn murder' in Suffolk in 1828; Percy Grainger recorded Joseph Taylor singing one verse in Lincolnshire in 1905. Hutchings's arrangement takes creative liberties with its substance for dramatic effect. We fade in on the band rocking in full spate, Mattacks heaving at the drums, as Collins plunges us into the thick of the action. A murderer, William Corder, arranges to meet his lover, and takes along his gun, pickaxe and spade. The music then fades out, and Francis Baines's hurdy-gurdy sets up an ethereal, mournful

Tim Hart and Maddy Prior, *Folk Songs of Old England Vol. 1* (1968); Ashley Hutchings et al., *Morris On* (1972); Steeleye Span, *Please to See the King* (1971).

wail. Over this, Collins sings Corder's confession of his part in the crime. And in order for his gruesome story to begin, the group crunches into its riff again as Collins describes the body being dug up; Nic Jones doubles her voice like a phantom on the verses about the murdered girl coming back as a ghost to communicate her fate to her parents. Finally, we return to the guilty hurdy-gurdy theme, with the condemned man pleading for understanding of his tale. As the banshee noise fades away, a horse-drawn trap speeds across the stereo field on its way to the gallows pole. By cutting up the text and using concrete sound effects, Hutchings acknowledges the fragmentary state of Britain's folk archive, and its potential for constant pruning, shaping and reinvention.

'Poor Murdered Woman', closing the record, travels with a stately carriage, a dignified beat reinforcing the unfussy report of a body discovered on Leatherhead Common in 1834 by a local hunt. Here, and throughout the album, the unprecedented instrumentation caused Shirley Collins to rise to the finest vocal performances of her career.

No Roses was recorded between June and November 1971. In the same period Hutchings was carrying out the last of his engagements with Steeleye Span and developing the other major work of that year – assembling a group with Richard Thompson, Dave Mattacks, John Kirkpatrick and Barry Dransfield to perform a sonic folly entitled *Morris On*.

To those who actually practise it, morris dance has an elemental quality, an ancient ritual magic comparable to the whirling dervish dance of Sufism, the Native American ghost dance or the spiritual movements developed by G. I. Gurdjieff. Its gestures are designed to act as a lightning conductor for spiritual energies to unite the universe with the earth and replicate the seasonal cycles of growth, death and rebirth. Morris dancers' tatter jackets act as symbolic antennae; clogs dash against the ground, awakening slumbering earth gods. The EFDSS had gentrified the dance in the

1930s and 40s, slowing the pace and draining its erotic vigour. More recently, morris has become the anvil round the revival's neck, its boisterous moves, outlandish costumes and trite musical accompaniment treated as a national joke. To dive into the music of this much-ridiculed custom shows how giddily Ashley Hutchings had fallen under the spell of English traditional music. Morris was the last locked cupboard of the entire post-war folk revival. By unsealing it, he was prepared to stake a hard-won reputation and credibility on a music that appeared to be unredeemable.

The trigger for the project came when he heard tapes of William Kimber, a concertina player with the Headington Quarry morris who not only turned the head of Cecil Sharp but survived to be recorded by Peter Kennedy in the 1950s. Enthralled by Kimber's frenzied squeezing, Hutchings sought out John Kirkpatrick, a genius accordionist who had been plying his trade in north London folk clubs and was barely aware of the folk-rock movement.

From the good-natured spirit of *Morris On* (morris sides use the terms 'morris on' and 'morris off' for their entrances and exits) you'd hardly think these issues were troubling him too much. Its grass-green sleeve frames a photo that's pure pantomime: the five players line up in fancy dress on the lawn at Red Rose Cottage, folk archetypes à la Bonzo Dog Doo-Dah Band. John Kirkpatrick is a soot-soiled chimney sweep who's traded his brushes for a vacuum cleaner. A po-faced Hutchings, in white morris costume modelled on extant photos of Jinky Wells of Bampton, wields a futuristic Gibson Flying V festooned with ribbons. Richard Thompson is a clean-shaven Robin Hood in Lincoln green packing a modern steel crossbow, cocked and ready. Barry Dransfield is tarted up as a moll, and Dave Mattacks, in bowler hat and black tails, sits astride a chopper bike against which leans a hobby horse. Cidered-up rude mechanicals living their own midsummer night's dream.

Compared to the vinegary minor chords and drones of Steeleye Span and *No Roses*, with their grey seas, muddy ditches and murder scenes, Hutchings's electric morris parts the clouds and sends shafts of sunlight streaming across the landscape. The record is relaxed, preserving false starts, studio backchat, laughter. Dancers from the Chingford morris rattle sticks in 'Lads A'Bunchum/Young Collins', and their bells can be heard jangling as they shoulder awkwardly out of the cramped studio. On the 'WillowTree/Bean Setting/Shooting' medley, repetitive concertina loops combine with Mattacks's traction-engine drumming, racking up the intensity. 'The Cuckoo's Nest' is the kind of lusty romp Cecil Sharp wanted to censor, with its lyrics circling predatorily around the female sex. The mood is hearty, slightly blokeish, brimming with an undisputed vitality.

With decimalisation and an increasingly disordered Northern Ireland promising profound shifts in the British state of mind, it's perhaps not such a coincidence that the years 1969–72 witnessed the summit of the electric folk movement, which clung to the certainties offered by a historical music that spoke out of a supposedly more stable past. Pentangle, Fairport Convention and Steeleye Span all achieved a high level of visibility and respectable sales, and beneath the radar a network of artists occupied the niche between pub folk nights and college gigs. Those four years were an Indian summer of unprecedented musical connections, cross-pollinations and fortuitous meetings – traditionalists and modernisers, superstars and underground outsiders, acoustic and electric. Fairport, Steeleye Span and The Albion Country Band effectively defined the keynote sound of English electric folk: phantoms of the agrarian past are channelled via an electrified present, chipping out the Anglo-*paysan* poetry of the countryside with blunt axes. Like the crafts-based society envisioned in *News from Nowhere*, this branch of electric folk made its choices based on instinct backed up by long reflection and earnest research. And, inspired by their example, many others followed their inward exodus to England's garden sanctuary.

9

Orpheus in the Undergrowth

Of all the trees that grow so fair,
Old England to adorn,
Greater is none beneath the sun,
Than Oak, and Ash, and Thorn.
Sing Oak, and Ash, and Thorn, good sirs,
(All of a Midsummer morn!)
Surely we sing of no little thing,
In Oak, and Ash, and Thorn!

Rudyard Kipling, 'Oak, Ash, and Thorn' (1906)

In Rudyard Kipling's classic Edwardian children's book *Puck of Pook's Hill*, a faery apparition casts a spell over two children by brushing a clump of oak, ash and thorn leaves across their faces. They enter a time-travelling trance in which historical figures – Romans, Domesday-era knights, feudal barons – manifest themselves and spin rambling yarns of their exploits, battles, treachery and derring-do, all of which have taken place across the very land that now forms the kids' adventure playground. This vertical exploded view of England's pastures is Edwardian psychogeography, designed to instil a sense of the heroic history that has cut its furrows deep in the soil, sowing the seeds of a national psyche. Ushered there by Puck's cunning wood magic, the greenwood becomes the gateway to an idealised England where the imagination runs naked and free, until the time comes to swish the oak, ash and thorn twigs once more, awaken from the English dreaming and return to . . . well, in Kipling's children's case, no doubt a piping hot tea of crumpets and scones, lavished upon them by a servile nanny.

The English Orpheus: Nick Drake.

Kipling died in 1936, but had he remained alive another twenty-seven years he would have heard Harold Wilson's words to the Labour Party Conference of 1963, a wake-up call to a nation in danger of sleepwalking into global obsolescence. 'The Britain that is going to be forged in the white heat of this [technological/scientific] revolution will be no place for restrictive practices or for outdated methods on either side of industry . . .' Uttered at the beginning of the year in which The Beatles released their first number-one single, the speech signalled a new British self-consciousness as a metropolitan society whose successful destiny lay in skewing the balance towards its urban population and industrial prowess.

The disconnect between country and city forms the basis of some of Britain's most deeply entrenched schisms. For all the migration of the nation's rural workforce into British cities as a consequence of the Industrial Revolution, the landscape retains its grip on the collective imagination, offering the promise of tranquillity, open space, freedom from responsibility; a rustic souvenir of permanence and stability. Britons treasure their shrinking countryside like a family heirloom wrapped in silk, locked away in the secret compartment of a writing table, protected from foreign invasion for most of a millennium. Britain's natural habitats are especially fragile; truly unpopulated wildernesses are few and far between. But there exist several contrasting versions of what the countryside means. For the aristocracy, the country estate is the rightful inheritance, a patch of Edenic acreage whose ancestral ownership is an inalienable right sanctioned by history and blood. But for the middle-class offspring who reached maturity in the mid-1960s, brought up in the garden cities, suburbs and leafy districts of post-war Britain, the pull was often felt in both directions. The city was where middle-class professional aspirations were mostly realised. But for anyone doubtful about the prospect of becoming a wage slave or civil servant and encouraged towards the life of the imagination by art, literature and music, retreating to the countryside – still, in the 1960s, hardly transformed from its turn-of-the-century appearance by industrial-scale agriculture, where there was still enough darkness to view the stars, hear birdsong and wake to the distant tolling of rural church bells – was the most desirable way to drop out. These were people for whom Joni Mitchell's 'Woodstock', with its exhortation to get back to the garden, was not yet a hippy cliché, but a genuinely workable alternative. Breaking out beyond London's green belt was, and remains, like crossing the border into another country altogether.

Certainly, in the immediate aftermath of Donovan's *A Gift from a Flower to a Garden* of 1968, the landscape of British rock blossomed under a wave of reforestation. Simply listing group names from the period 1968–72 builds up a composite image of this Arcadian topography, native woodnotes running wild in a putative pre-industrial time zone. Forest, Sunforest, Silver Birch, Fuchsia, Oak, Trees (second album: *The Garden of Jane Delawney*). The Strawbs' psychedelic folk masterpiece, *From the Witchwood*. Magna Carta's yellowed *Seasons*, packaged with mock-medieval illuminated script and a posy of evergreen leaves and summer flowers. There was a group called Midwinter, and another called Oberon, public schoolboys who made one obscure album of eldritch folk called *A Midsummer Night's Dream*. Folk-inflected medievalists traded under names like Dulcimer, Parchment, Madrigal, Caedmon, Amazing Blondel, Wooden O and The Druids. Lindisfarne placed themselves on the mystical isle off the coast of Northumberland; Irish duo Tír na nÓg summoned the mythical Celtic land of eternal youth; their fellow countrymen Loudest Whisper invoked Celtic legends on *Children of Lír*, as did Deep Purple on *The Book of Taliesyn*. In this sylvan setting, where Tim Hart and Maddy Prior celebrated *Summer Solstice*, groups ran amuck like mythical beasts: Chimera, Gryphon, Comus, Mr Fox, unicorns (on the third album by Tyrannosaurus Rex, as well as John Renbourn's *Lady and the Unicorn* LP). Through the trees, glimpses of a quaint antiquarian architecture: Tudor Lodge, Kippington Lodge, Fairfield Parlour, Tintern Abbey, Fotheringay. The rustic vibe was also perpetuated by record labels adopting names like Harvest, Dawn and Dandelion. As a memento mori, there was even a duo called Fresh Maggots.

The nurseries of the late-1960s folk-rock boom may have been predominantly city-based – London, Birmingham, Edinburgh, Canterbury, Cambridge – but the young blades that grew there all inclined towards the country sun. Their songs read like a recipe book for rural enlightenment with elemental ingredients: summer, autumn, winter, spring; sunshine, rain, water, snow, trees; seas stormy and becalmed; rivers stagnant or in full spate. Cities bleed the soul, inhabited by squares, losers, clockwatchers, The Man. The city scythes away humanity, nature replants it. Sandy Denny's 'The Pond and the Stream', which speaks of the city screening out the natural world, encapsulates the mood. These observations are not original, but they recur insistently throughout folk-rock's infant years, affecting everything from the lyrical content to the staging of photo shoots, part of a mass experiment to propagate an organic alternative to Wilson's white heat.

With *Liege and Lief* unveiled but Sandy Denny and Ashley Hutchings gone, Fairport Convention's remaining members – Dave Mattacks, Simon Nicol, Dave Swarbrick and Richard Thompson – dusted themselves off and continued the mission. They hired Birmingham bassist Dave Pegg, who had spent much of the 1960s crossing between Midlands rock and blues-boom outfits and playing in Swarbrick's former troupe, The Ian Campbell Folk Group. At the end of 1969 this five-piece Fairport moved into The Angel, a disused pub near Ware in Hertfordshire, along with their families and road crew, where they would remain for the next two years. There they produced several of the best albums under the Fairport franchise – *Full House* (1970), *Angel Delight* and *'Babbacombe' Lee* (both 1971). *Full House* features some incendiary playing from the ensemble, from the ragged, monumental Thompson solo on 'Sloth' to the St Vitus jigs and hyper-reels of 'Dirty Linen'.

Conditions at The Angel were less salubrious than at their previous dwelling. 'It was an amazing place,' remembers Dave Pegg. 'There was only one toilet in the entire building, and a tin bath, so you had to get up really early because there were about fourteen people. Everybody had their own hi-fi, and the walls were lath and plaster, and with the hi-fis all going at the same time occasionally you'd hear *Music from Big Pink* phasing, because you'd hear the same track from several different rooms.'

Various events at The Angel have passed into Fairport legend. The local newspaper at first ran scare stories about an invasion of hippies, but the police were soon knocking on their door asking them to play a charity gig, for which the group received a dishwasher as payment. Their music room was occupied by the road crew, who built a dividing wall out of antique furniture they found in a barn next door; some of it ended up on their Guy Fawkes-night bonfire. 'It was higher than the house,' says Pegg. When a lorry collided with the pub in the early hours one morning, smashing through the outer walls into Swarbrick's bedroom, it was one more incident that might have destroyed a less hardy group (Richard Thompson left to pursue his solo career not long after). So it was appropriate that, for an outfit that had received so many stays of execution, their next project should be a concept album about a real-life convict who cheated the hangman's noose three times.

The Devonshire labourer John 'Babbacombe' Lee, the original 'man they couldn't hang', was let out of jail in 1907 after serving a twenty-three-year sentence for murdering his employer, and immediately sold his sensational story to the press. Swarbrick found a sheaf of press cuttings about Lee while rooting around in an antique shop. 'The lyrics are taken from his memoir, lifted straight out,' he says. At a time when group morale was low, the process of creating *'Babbacombe' Lee* prevented Fairport from disintegrating altogether. 'It unified the band and [Swarbrick] delegated, he said we've all got to get involved in the writing of this,' recalls Pegg. Nicol adds: 'It was a huge jump in the dark, because it had to be played from start to finish, there weren't any breaks between the tracks, it was a story, like a radio play or an opera.' The record stands up well today, even though Swarbrick's vocals were criticised at the time. The highlight is 'Dream', where the narrator creeps into Lee's head on the eve of his planned execution and witnesses a vision telling him he will not be harmed.

Even before Fairport's months in the country, though, one of the first to try the rural life was Traffic, the group which grew out of

Out to grass: Traffic at the White Horse, Uffington, 1967. Left to right: Dave Mason, Steve Winwood, Jim Capaldi, Chris Wood.

informal improvised rock sessions at a club called the Elbow Room in Birmingham, convened by guitarist Dave Mason and drummer Jim Capaldi, later joined by flute player/saxophonist Chris Wood and the nineteen-year-old Hammond organ prodigy from The Spencer Davis Group, Steve Winwood. In spring 1967 the group began working up material through rural jamming sessions at The Cottage, a remote dwelling near the Berkshire hamlet of Aston Tirrold.[1] Tucked away up a muddy lane that became impassable in heavy rain, on an estate owned by a local racehorse magnate, they enjoyed total isolation, with not a house, road or pylon in sight. The group adapted the property to the needs of a contemporary psychedelic unit. They laid down a concrete forecourt overlooking the garden – a sound stage for incessant jamming sessions which, especially on warm summer nights, could easily maintain their intrinsic momentum until the dawn chorus took over. Freed from the rigour of studio bookings, the group recalibrated their musical calendar to the rise and fall of the sun and moon, living in a kind of elongated, unregulated time zone that wouldn't have been possible in London, where the streetlight glow shut off the stars. The mantric quality of Traffic's grooves – what Winwood called at the time 'a constant flow of writing, playing, well, just a flow'² – certainly derives its self-perpetuating power from this arrangement – not for nothing did 'Houses for Everyone', the third track on *Mr Fantasy*, replicate the sound of a clockwork mechanism being wound up, as if Traffic were a spring-driven motor that would keep on chugging until the energy was used up (or the drugs wore off). During their nocturnal jams they projected a complicated liquid lightshow onto the outside of the house, with different colours triggered by particular ranges of the harmonic spectrum. The thick, candlelit air on *Mr Fantasy*'s front cover sets the tone perfectly, as the band cluster in the womby glow of the cottage's blazing hearth. To borrow the phrase later used by Steeleye Span, Traffic lived in the original 'Rocket Cottage', a rustic launch pad for voyages to inner space.

Most important, though, was the freedom the isolation gave them to design a total hallucinatory ambience around themselves. While the town they had left behind was full of '*People like sardines all packed in a can / Waiting for Christmas that's made in Japan*' ('Berkshire Poppies'), Traffic existed in an opiated trance. On *Mr Fantasy*'s inner gatefold, an oneiric episode is played out in a field, as the group are confronted by a Gothic lady in an outlandish feather headdress materialising out of a dry-ice cloud. Winwood hacks at logs with a hatchet, and Mason practises sitar in an austere bare-boarded bedroom cell. On 1968's *Traffic*, the foursome appear as psychedelic rangers of the Berkshire Downs, passing a joint on a hillside overlooking the strange prehistoric earthwork at Uffington Castle.

The combination of timeless bucolic existence and plentiful hallucinogens made for a potent brew. On walks across the neighbouring fields, a parade of red-coated aristocratic huntsmen, bee-keepers and poachers shooting birds with bows and arrows would pass before their eyes. The weird atmosphere certainly touched one journalist dispatched to the scene in 1969: 'The afternoon is suspended in time and place. There are no bearings; no roads, no houses, no cars, no telephone poles, no indications of place or direction, our destination is simply the miraculous, the signs and markings of ancient cultures, tumuli, Stone Age encampments, burial mounds, a site where a dragon was slain, a magical landscape that has remained intact for 2000 years.'[3]

On tracks like 'Dear Mr Fantasy' and 'Hole in My Shoe', Chris Wood's flute was given a prominent role (as it was in Jethro Tull, another of Island's key progressive acts at the same time – who also worked up a palimpsest of England's past), as though Pan was delighting to see such bacchanals in the heart of England's pastures green. The pagan echoes did not stop there. With a copy of The Watersons' *Frost and Fire* on repeat play in the house, Winwood latched onto the 'John Barleycorn' story as the pillar of the 1970 album *John Barleycorn Must Die*, a temporary reunion of three out of the original four members (Mason stayed out) after they had parted company at the end of 1969.

Although recordings were done in London, Winwood confessed he preferred the sound of the cottage: 'Every room has its own character, and the room in the cottage where we do rough takes of the songs has its own special quality, because it is an old house and you can tell what kind of room the sound was recorded in when you listen to the tape.'[4] Instead of the airless precision of modern multitrack studios, artificially aged acoustics were the way to go.

'Are you the farmer?' growls a drunken Richard E. Grant, lost and bedraggled in a field, in the middle of Bruce Robinson's *Withnail & I* (1986). The film's tale of two unemployed actors haring off to the Lake District to escape their London squat and stagnant, stillborn careers dramatises and satirises the incongruities of the young middle-class dream of the countryside in 1969. Such scenes are brought to mind when considering the example of Heron, a Berkshire semi-acoustic quartet whose two surviving albums from the dawn of the 1970s were both recorded by a mobile unit *en plein air*. Frustrated with their experience of taping a single in Pye Studios in summer 1970, the group made their way to a farmhouse in Appleford, Berkshire (the residence of vocalist Tony Pook's parents, and only a few minutes' drive north of Aston Tirrold), and settled down in a circle of chairs

Heron, *Twice as Nice & Half the Price* (1971).

in a meadow at the back of the house to play the thirteen songs of their first album, *Heron* (1970), as Pye engineers set up microphone booms around them. A separate mic was positioned some distance away, specifically to capture the ambience of the great outdoors. As a result, twittering, trilling blackbirds and larks and swishing foliage fill the spaces between tracks, and the gaps are longer than average, as if urging the listener to slow down and tune in with the spirit and rhythm of the place. This incarnation of the group – vocalists Tony Pook and Gerald G. T. Moore, guitarist Roy Apps and keyboardist Steve Jones – had no bass and drums; instead, a leafy blend of acoustic guitars, Moore's mandolin, Jones's electric piano and accordion, and rainbow-hued harmony vocals lend it an organic breeziness. A Wordsworthian hippy mood prevails throughout their lyrics. Many are songs of goodbye: relationships melt away like the snow or fall like autumn leaves, etc. But they did achieve an exceptional harmony with the countryside on 'Lord and Master', a reverie sung by a pantheistic nature-god whose being is entwined with the seasonal cycles he describes: '*I am the maker of everything and I soar with the birds in the sky.*'

One year later, after distribution problems had stymied their chances of success, the group trucked down to West Emlett Cottage, near the village of Black Dog in deepest Devon, with an extra drummer, electric guitarist and bassist in tow. Also present was slide guitarist Mike Cooper, a Dawn labelmate whose folk-jazz LP *Trout Steel* featured Heron on backing vocals. The sprawling sessions, again recorded out in the open, were collected on the double LP *Twice as Nice & Half the Price*, a less focused collection than Heron's debut. When the outdoor recording began to be interrupted by low-flying RAF jet fighters, a phone call persuaded the local base commander to halt the sorties. The album's cover photo – snapped by Cooper – is an iconic image of folk-rock's newfound paradise. The ochre-washed, two-storey cottage nestles in a lush, sunlit hollow, a sheet dangling out of an upper window. The musicians are in mid-flow, ranged along a low bank immediately outside the front door, as friends and partners loll on the grass. John Constable has become court photographer to the counter-culture.

The folk clubs of the 1960s produced an unprecedented number of singer-songwriters, unleashing a solo genre which, purists complain, is herded under the umbrella of 'folk music', even though their repertoire was largely of their own invention and dealt with personal, not communal, subjects. The man (or woman) with the guitar provided a significant fraction of pop music's core repertoire in the late twentieth century. In Britain, Anne Briggs, Jansch and Renbourn, Bridget St John, Roy Harper, Donovan, Al Stewart, Sandy Denny, Cat Stevens, Ralph McTell, Al Jones, Ian A. Anderson, Andy Roberts, Shelagh McDonald, Steve Ashley, Keith Christmas, John Martyn, Kevin Ayers, Marc Brierley, Beverley Martyn, Gillian McPherson, Kevin Coyne, Van Morrison, Meic Stevens, Linda Peters, Bill Fay, Nick Drake, Tim Hollier and Robin Scott delivered songs reporting on the state of the world or the vagaries of their own interior lives, from the political harangue to the intimate confessional. Some, such as Harper and Ayers, could be laconic and sceptical; while others – Christmas and Scott – played the role of lovestruck troubadour to the hilt. Robin Scott's *Woman from the Warm Grass*, released in 1969, is an album-length serenade to his girlfriend at the time, Penny Lamb. Some tracks are couched in a Leonard Cohen bedsit ambience; others benefit from the presence of members of Mighty Baby, a psychedelic outfit discussed in a later chapter. Scott's romantic, dreamy evocations of his lover in the rain, on the beach and in the grass are a small step away from the courtly love sonnets of a Philip Sidney or Thomas Campion.

For there *was* already a tradition in Britain that anticipated the music of these 1960s minstrels. These kind of artists are often dubbed 'troubadours' with good reason: the earliest recorded 'trouvères', dating from the twelfth-century court of Eleanor of Aquitaine, were likewise singing songs that dealt with the emotions – love, lust, betrayal, joy, loss, revenge – or with the unpredictable sides of human nature, or were using complex symbolic codes to reflect current affairs. The medieval troubadour tradition developed out of the secular folk universe, as an alternative to the music that was heard in church, but often retained its devotional aspect – directed, instead, towards the lover. Troubadours, who reached the court of the music-loving British king Richard the Lionheart in the late twelfth century, would sing their poetry, mostly unaccompanied, to small, private gatherings across the courts of Europe. By 1536, when the first printed book of accompanied solo songs appeared (by Luis Milán of Valencia),[5] there existed a well-established tradition of songs sung to the strain of the vihuela or lute. The preface to that book aligned the modern vihuelist with the 'primero inventor' of this genre: Orpheus. In Greek mythology, Orpheus's lute caused gods and nymphs to weep, and provoked the sympathy of Hades and Persephone in the Underworld. The death of his beloved Eurydice gave him a lifetime of inspirational material, and he ended his days in disfavour with fellow mortals by worshipping the sun god Apollo to the exclusion of all others. In Orpheus lies the mix of ecstasy, melancholy and Icarus-like ambition that has informed the work of composers and musicians from myth-time to the present.

In England, the accompanied song or 'ayre' reached its apotheosis in the age of Shakespeare. Lutenist John Dowland published his three books of *Songs or Ayres* between 1597 and 1603, followed two years later by his masterwork, *Lachrymae*: 'seven passionate pavans', including 'Flow, My Teares', whose falling notes literally drip with grief. The lute songs of Dowland and his contemporaries – including Thomas Campion, John Danyel, Anthony Holborne, Robert Johnson and Philip Rosseter – set the melancholic tropes of the age into downcast minor keys: love, weeping, jealousy, the victory of time over mortality, constancy of nature versus the inconstancy of lovers, the torments of unrequited love, women's vanity, decaying beauty, loss, death and mourning. The Orphic legacy displaces all the world's grieving onto the shoulders of these sensitive souls with their ageless guitars.

A lesser-spotted troubadour of the late 1960s, Bill Fay, is waiting for the rain to anoint him and for the frost to awaken his soul. He has been sitting on that park bench so long in contemplation that the tumbling autumn leaves have begun to settle upon his jacket. He sits cross-legged, donkey jacket crumpled around him, head drawn back warily on the neck, his eyes pointed off to the left of the cameraman's shoulder. The eyes drink in the shrubberies and herbaceous borders, gaze deep into the bole of the trees, trying to feel, if only for an instant, the ages they have been rooted there.

The image is reproduced on the back cover of the album *Bill Fay*, released in 1970. On the front, in black and white, Fay advances tentatively towards the camera, placed almost at ground level. It seems Fay is gliding across a stretch of water – a miracle occurring on a grey afternoon in Hyde Park. But look closer and the miracle is a prosaic accident. He is standing on a concrete platform in the middle of a large puddle of rainwater.

Fay's first two albums remained the stuff of rumour until their first-time reissue in 2005. *Bill Fay* offers a peculiar but evocative mix of character vignettes and horticultural reverie. Fay was acutely sensitive to the suburban impact of the post-war generation gap. In British households of the 1960s, wartime memories affected the fabric of family life – younger, pop-inculcated youngsters rubbing shoulders with veterans of two world wars – in occasionally surreal ways. A suburban dreamer with a penchant for 'heavy conversations' about philosophy and the state of the world, Fay found himself caught between both tendencies. His late-1960s song 'Parasite Child' is told from a junkie's viewpoint. The drug aspect is not autobiographical, but it expresses the dilemma of the misunderstood. '*Ain't no use surrounding me*,' he chides an uncle who accuses him of having a head like a sieve. '*It seems to me I just can't be what you want me to be.*'

'Planting myself in the garden': Bill Fay.

Fay taught himself piano as a teenager during the early 1960s. In 1962 he went up to Bangor University in Wales to study electronics, and took summer work experience at the Ministry of Defence's Royal Radar Establishment at nearby Malvern. While companions were drafted into top-secret work plotting electrostatic fields around missiles, Fay was banished to the library to read up on 'something to do with radio transmission', a task he refers to, in a rare interview he granted me in 2005, as 'a miserable experience'. For solace the city boy headed for the countryside. 'I used to walk up the hills and remember regularly stopping at a pig farm – watching them and taking in their simplicity.' Later that summer of 1964 he shared a cottage with some friends and bought a harmonium, on which he began to write songs. His demos found their way into the hands of Peter Eden, the manager of Donovan and Mick Softley, who signed the singer to Decca's underground imprint, Nova, in 1970. With Eden producing and Fay on piano, a group was put together from the ranks of the capital's jazz/pop/folk crossover scene – guitarist Ray Russell, drummers John Marshall and Trevor Taylor, bassist George Bird – and progressive jazz arranger Michael Gibbs was hired to write orchestrations for a twenty-seven-piece jazz ensemble. *Bill Fay* is peopled with characters from an England still in its post-war throes, valiantly soldiering on, living with their dreams, memories and private griefs. Mundane exteriors can shelter deeper hurts, stranger notions. Old May lost her boy in the Great War, but could still belt out sentimental tunes down the boozer, '*the ones we know so well*'. Stan, '*an innocent soul in a vastly changing world*', scuttling home from the allotment at night with only a watering can to protect himself from being abducted to Mars, '*or was it Jupiter?*' And Gentle Willie, who went to war, deserted his platoon, built a tower to protect himself, and found himself on his battlements with a ringside seat over even more carnage. These were the damaged, who had fought to preserve England's green and pleasant land, but felt excluded from the Aquarian Age.

As well as the thumbnail portraits, Fay displayed an organic songwriting mode. The album opens with 'Garden Song': '*I'm planting myself in the garden, believe me / Between the potatoes and parsley.*' Fay's delivery has an eerie purpose – he couldn't sound *less* stoned. '*I'm looking for lasting relations with the spider, the greenfly, or maggot /*

They're telling me something I don't know.' The song has the quality of reverie and awakening all at the same moment, as Fay attempts to synchronise his mind with the 'long now' of organic time: 'Trying to place myself in a true, not shadowy reality, to wake up to something not just going on around in the world, but a deeper reality. But the starting point would be the natural world – the trees, living things.'

But Fay's music wasn't happy-go-lucky enough for the Luv Generation to make it a hit. He augmented a paltry income from music by packing fish in Selfridges and 'hoeing the beds, edging, mowing' in a London park. To invoke *Withnail & I* once more, it was the beginning of the greatest decade in the history of mankind, and there would be a lot of refugees.

'A black eyed dog he called at my door / A black eyed dog he called out for more.' I picture the singer of those words, Nick Drake, barricading his basement from the inside, as the dealer rattles the lock – perhaps the same one who roars *'Let me in'* in John Martyn's song 'Dealer'. With his hollow eyes and barked demands, he assumes the terrifying appearance of a hellhound.

The final recorded testament of Nick Drake, 'Black Eyed Dog' is a bolt of abject fear clenched into a three-minute song. Recorded in July 1974, four months before his death, it is a feral cry of inner torment marking the closure of an extraordinary trajectory.

Drake began as a Keatsian troubadour in the hazy, Shangri-La summer of 1967, dropped out of Cambridge University to pursue a music career, but crashed to earth in London in a mess of melted wax and feathers. He scored his drugs from (and played card games with) Bob Squire, a Cockney friend of Joe Boyd with hazy London underworld connections. Some of those drugs were consumed at parties with one of several separate groups of friends, most notably at the Chelsea residence of an upper-class set that might be called the psychedelic aristocracy. Central to this world of 'posh hippies' were the teenage children of David Ormsby-Gore, the former Ambassador to the United States, aka Conservative peer Lord Harlech. Jane, Alice, Victoria and Julian Ormsby-Gore lived in a luxury flat with walls daubed a blinding shade of silver. Drake had met Victoria through her boyfriend Julian Lloyd during his gap year. Her sister Jane – the reputed inspiration for The Rolling Stones' 'Lady Jane' – was married to Michael Rainey, owner of the Hung on You fashion boutique. 'We were very influenced by Byron,' Jane Ormsby-Gore explained years later, 'those Byron shirts with frilly fronts and big sleeves. And literature: Spenser's *Faerie Queene* . . . that sort of mood, rather romantic.'[6] Several of Drake's songs indicate that he was repelled and yet strangely absorbed by this parliament of doomed, super-rich romantics – and indeed, like himself, many of these bedraggled, deathly refugees failed to adjust to the 1970s. Another satellite of this group was the Guinness heir Tara Browne, whose suicide was the inspiration for the '*he blew his mind out in a car*' verse of The Beatles' 'A Day in the Life'. Alice Ormsby-Gore spent the first half of the 1970s hooked on heroin and engaged to Eric Clapton; in 1995 her body was discovered dead from an overdose in a run-down Bournemouth bedsit.

In countless reminiscences, Nick Drake appears as a black-clad, wordless wraith, and yet the mystery is that somewhere underneath the excruciating awkwardness, at first, was an ambitious driven force that made connections in the music business, arranged his own introductory meeting with Island Records' Chris Blackwell in late 1967, and talked his way into his first public performance, supporting Country Joe and the Fish, Fairport Convention and others at a Vietnam Solidarity Campaign concert at the Round-house in Camden Town in December of that year. (Something about that gig arrested the attention of Fairport's Ashley Hutchings, who took Drake's phone number and urged Joe Boyd to call him.) Later, haunted by his lack of success – Island simply couldn't shift his albums – Drake became a strange, spidery ghost at the centre of a web of connections across society, class and celebrity. Once, in a Marrakesh restaurant in 1967, he was persuaded to serenade Mick Jagger, Keith Richards, Brian Jones, Anita Pallenberg and Cecil Beaton, seated at a neighbouring table. Recently departed Velvet Underground founder John Cale moved into his Hampstead flat for two days in 1970 to work on arrangements for several tracks on *Bryter Layter*; he had several silent meetings with Françoise Hardy in preparation for a songwriting appointment that never occurred. There's even a tragic 1971 vignette of Drake visiting Tittenhurst Park, the Ascot mansion of John Lennon and Yoko Ono, while they were away (the wife of an old college friend worked as the couple's assistant). One pictures the long, translucent fingers bitterly running over the keys of Lennon's white 'Imagine' piano. At Drake's final meeting with Joe Boyd in 1974, the producer reported he was subjected to an angry tirade, in which the singer held Boyd accountable for the fact that he had never made a living from his music, and that all the glowing reviews never translated into a solid career. His emotionally undernourished, disembodied state was perfectly encapsulated in the lines John Martyn wrote for him in 1973: '*You've been getting too deep, you've been living on solid air / You've been missing your sleep and you've been moving through solid air.*'

The Nick Drake that emerges from the two extant biographies is a lost, inchoate genius that you sometimes wish you could grab by the shoulders and shake. But what if his detachment – which some remember as mere aloofness, others as a black hole slumped in the corner of a room – was a genuinely *other* way of being; the only way to preserve the innocent state from which he derived a sense of truth and honesty? For in the hushed, enchanted circle of Drake's finest music, it's possible to hear the Blakean attempt to 'Hold infinity in the palm of your hand / And Eternity in an Hour.'

There's a photograph by Keith Morris, reproduced on the back cover of Drake's first album *Five Leaves Left*. Drake is backed against a brick wall in an awkward stance, clutching his belt and crossing his ankles, dispassionately observing a City gentleman blurring past on the pavement. The image of an artist living outside time, rejecting the speed of contemporary existence for a life of solitude and contemplation, is repeated on the back of *Bryter Layter*: Drake is perched on the hard shoulder of the A40 Westway above Paddington – in 1970, a newly built escape route out of west London – presenting the back of his head to camera as he gazes at a speeding car's streaking headlights. (Another set of pictures from the same Keith Morris session shows Drake positioned next to an *Evening Standard* billboard blaring the headline: 'Budget Speech'. Drake stands detached from political events; at the same time, the phrase mocks the singer's own notorious verbal parsimony.)

Like Hamlet's monologues, Drake was always at his most articulate when engaged in deeply private dialogue with his own brain. In song he achieved a clarity and honesty he could never translate to his encounters with people, existing in an internalised state incompatible with the world of schedules and organised events. '*If songs were lines in a conversation,*' he sang (on 'Hazey Jane II'), '*the situation would be fine.*'

On the cover of *Bryter Layter*, shot by Nigel Waymouth of Hapshash and the Coloured Coat, Drake is a hippy Hamlet, a melancholic bard rendered as twentieth-century troubadour, exchanging the lute for a Guild six-string acoustic. He shrinks from the lens, sicklied over with the pale cast of thought. Many of his songs dramatise the numbness of the private soul when confronted with the whirling material matter of life. At the same time, the Cambridge which allowed him so much time to read, think and write music also cocooned him from the world he wanted to break into: the London of Joe Boyd, record deals, concerts, and the chance to have his message broadcast to the wider world.

At Cambridge, where he studied English Literature at

Outside of society: Nick Drake in an outtake from a *Five Leaves*
Left photo session, Hampstead, 1969.

Fitzwilliam College between 1967–9 (dropping out before his final examinations), Nick Drake would have been keenly aware of the hallowed former alumni, the ghosts of Britain's cultural history who had walked the compact streets, inhabited the panelled lodgings, meditated in the libraries, observed the lilac blossom dripping into the River Cam in springtime. He shot the breeze on Trinity Street with the avant-garde poet J. H. Prynne, and took tea with the eighty-nine-year-old E. M. Forster. Being an undergraduate at Cambridge can be a disorientating experience, living among, and through – and yet apart from – the traditions that linger in an academic hothouse nearly a thousand years old. In daily life Drake would have encountered a privileged student *galère* of fledgling authors, poets, playwrights, broadcasters, entertainers, politicians, entrepreneurs and scientists. He would have been made acutely aware of the conflict between ancient assumptions (about class, knowledge, power, tradition, continuity)

299

and the drug-lubricated liberation theology of his own generation. He was an honorary member (the 'Oddefellowe') of a breakfast club at Gonville and Caius College called The Loungers, which also included Robert Kirby, string arranger of *Five Leaves Left* and *Bryter Layter*. One condition of membership was to 'lounge at the gate of humility [the college's main entrance] once a week at 1pm for 5 minutes and "observe how strange creatures ye Lord hath made"'.[7] Drake remained an oddefellowe, an aloof observer, for the rest of his short life.

Accordingly, he summoned a music that delicately cradled the two sides in a fragile equilibrium: the poise and grace of Elizabethan chamber/instrumental music, its mechanisms intricate as a clock or music box, and the Zen/visionary poetry adopted as instruction book by the counter-culture – a mystical concoction of Blake, Yeats and Buddhism, coloured in the sea-green, slate-grey and sky-blue hues of the Romantic nature poets – and equally profoundly attenuated to conditions of transience and mortality. Above all, Drake's body of work is a long, imploring quest for a love he knows is unattainable, a love that is often indivisible from an enlightened or satori-like state. '*Oh, if you would and if you could,*' he whispers to the idealised other in 'Northern Sky', '*Straighten my new mind's eye.*'

A former friend and musical partner, Ross Grainger, described Drake as a 'modern pagan' long after his death, recalling conversations about Gaia theory, Stonehenge, ley lines and supernatural forces.[8] Drake's songs may be full of natural images – rain, sun, moon, sky, ocean, sand, trees, roses, thorns, etc. – but nature was no panacea either. It was part of the trap, forging a new set of manacles for the mind. For Drake, human fate was linked to the relentless round of the seasons – summer bliss must shade into autumnal age and regret; then comes the killing winter. His songs trace eternal cycles, natural revolutions, the turning of the year and the seasons, but with an awareness that repetitive motion can become a treadmill. Drake, whose reading touched on Buddhism as well as English literature and – at his death – Camus's *Myth of Sisyphus*, would have been acutely aware of the cycle of fate, the Buddhist Wheel of Becoming as well as Boethius's wheel of fate, which informs the Chaucerian English poetry he would have read as part of the Cambridge English tripos.

For someone so reportedly shambolic and disorganised, his guitar technique – which he taught himself in two years – is staggeringly precise. As much a percussion instrument as a melody generator, Drake's guitar spins a rhythmelodic web in which fretboard hammer-ons and a supple right hand pluck and weave rippling cross-rhythms, from the early 'Cello Song' and 'Three Hours' right through to 'Rider on the Wheel', one of his wretched 'five last songs'. His chord sequences trace melodic coils, their interlaced spirals splayed out with arachnoid fingerwork. His singing, in turn, inhabits a third temporal plane. Words and phrases are not locked to the end stops of the musical lines, but worm their way freely across beats and bar lines.

At the home where he spent his childhood, Far Leys House in Tanworth-in-Arden – a chocolate-box village midway between Coventry (industrial town) and Stratford-upon-Avon (birthplace of Shakespeare) – he spent his formative days in the huge sheltered garden, a silent haven untroubled by the noise of traffic. While the family often engaged in communal music-making, Drake's songwriting proper began during a gap year (1966–7) spent in Aix-en-Provence in the south of France with a group of schoolfriends from Marlborough College. There, under the pretence of learning the language, they indulged in a life of relaxed drinking, smoking, meeting girls, imbibing music and carefree philosophising. Drake wound up performing at local folk clubs and met an American girl singer, Robin Frederick, with whom he seems to have formed some kind of (platonic) connection. It is this idyllic world, a lost domain he never recaptured, which forms the backdrop to the first of his three albums, *Five Leaves Left*.

Although his Cambridge friend Robert Kirby had never worked in a recording studio before, his string arrangements left the initially sceptical Boyd and engineer John Wood 'absolutely stunned'.[9] Often lazily described as 'Baroque', Kirby's orchestrations are actually much closer to the string music of certain English twentieth-century composers, especially Butterworth, Delius and Warlock.[10] But Kirby's contribution to *Five Leaves Left* – from the 'first cuckoo in spring' of 'Thoughts of Mary Jane' to the nimbus stripes of 'Way to Blue' – shows an intuitive empathy with Drake's sensibility. 'Day Is Done', as bleak as The Beatles' 'Eleanor Rigby', already contains the sense of darkening futility that comes with the quotidian setting of the sun, a daily reminder of all the desires unfulfilled, goals unachieved, paradises lost. Drake's composition is a downward spiral of minor chords, sucked in a vortex towards each line's desolate ending. As if casting a spell to determine his own posthumous rehabilitation, 'Fruit Tree' bitterly dissects the entertainment industry's harvest of souls. The tree '*will never flourish/ Till its stock is in the ground*': the play on 'stock' as both upright stem and as human investment is a particularly poisonous metaphor.

There's nothing on *Five Leaves Left* to match 'River Man', which finds Drake at his most transcendent. The song's complex metaphysics describes three orders of being. There is the River Man himself, a demigod presiding over the stream of material, sensual life; there is the song's 'I' (Drake), a satyr-like servant or acolyte, fated to remain bankside observing human activity and reporting back to the River Man ('*going to tell him all I can/ About the ban on feeling free*'); and there is 'Betty', a mortal torn between the divine and the life of sensation which inoculates humans against the pain of mortality. For this one track, Kirby relinquished the arranger's quill to Harry Robinson, a Scottish aristocrat who regularly composed incidental music for Hammer Films. Robinson's strings bathe the track in numinous light, swelling and bursting their banks as Betty is dragged back into the river of life. Drake's water-milling guitar, in a five-four time signature, occupies a parallel but disconnected plane from the strings, washing across the beat in rills against the bank. And there he is fated to remain, watching souls emerge on their momentary grasps at enlightened bliss: '*Oh, how they come and go,*' he intones twice as the song fades out over dissonant chords from both the guitar and Robinson's strings – an uncomfortable, irresolute coda.

Somewhere between 1968 and 1969 Drake's own leaves turned, from the hedonistic student of 1967 to a withdrawn, solipsistic, shrunken seer, 'beaten senseless by the negative parts of [his] own sensitivity', as John Martyn once expressed it.[11] Once *Five Leaves Left* sessions were wrapped up in July 1969, its creator had barely as many years left to live.

Most of *Bryter Layter* was written during the final months of 1969, while Fairport Convention were recording *Liege and Lief*. Drake appeared as the catatonic opening act at Fairport's 'homecoming' gig at the South Bank in September; then, in the middle of 1970, he visited them at The Angel. While failing to charm the worldly Fairporters with his reticent manner, he introduced his new material to Dave Pegg and Dave Mattacks, who acted as the album's core rhythm section (Richard Thompson also contributed guitar to 'Hazey Jane II').

Bryter Layter is a curious concoction of fluid, jazz-tinged folk-rock – melancholy with a desperate edge – and test-card instrumentals. Hip stars and sessioneers from the worlds of Soho jazz and American pop – pianist Chris McGregor, flautists Lyn Dobson and Ray Warleigh, backing singers Doris Troy and P. P. Arnold – popped in at Joe Boyd's behest to ornament various tracks with textural nuances. The rhythms fluctuate between a rock-solid Dave Mattacks and the feathery swing of The Beach

Boys' resident percussionist, Mike Kowalski. Robert Kirby tries his hand at some brass arrangements which sound decidedly out of character for Drake, like the unworn brothel creepers on the cover. As this cosmopolitan stew implies, it's Drake's city record, his response to his new London life, a round of lonely street wanderings, drop-ins at folk clubs like Les Cousins, and attendance at drug-ins with the aristocratic Chelsea set. 'Fly' marks an Icarus tumble towards low self-esteem: *'I've fallen far down the first time around/ Now I just sit on the ground in your way.'* In the self-mocking 'Poor Boy', he's the *'Sonny boy/ With smokes for sale/ Went to ground with a face so pale.'* 'At the Chime of a City Clock' is a misanthropic response to urban alienation. Drake's exceptional sensitivity left him prey to the dehumanising effect of the Great Stink, and he evolved into a malnourished ghost that briefly spooked friends' houses, wordlessly accepted cups of tea and silently drifted away. For the *'city man/ Who leaves his armour down'*, showing his hand – revealing all his emotional cards, opening himself via his songs – merely resulted in Drake falling further and further adrift.

There is one moment, the album's penultimate song, when the clouds briefly part, Drake sloughs off his despond and we are afforded a glimpse of his leaping soul. A love song couched in pagan exultation, 'Northern Sky' benefits from John Cale's magic dust, as he multitracks a triple keyboard layer of organ, twinkling celeste and pianistic flourishes. Mike Kowalski's spry rimshots lend the track a mercurial fleet-footedness. The song's narrator, in the first flush of new love, experiences a bolt of joy akin to the parting of clouds. The euphoria leads to piercing insight into the heart of nature, a knowing that manifests itself sensually.

If 'Northern Sky' had been the album's final track, it would have signed off with an epiphanic, hopeful conclusion to an otherwise agitated, restless record. Instead, perversely, the (anti)climax is 'Sunday', an instrumental flute salad perched somewhere between Love's 'Orange Skies' and the theme tune to an Open University programme about pond life. *Bryter Layter* failed to sell more than a few hundred copies, and Drake all but abandoned thoughts of playing live to promote his work. His devastation at the album's failure was compounded by a feeling that his intentions had been taken over and distorted by Boyd's musical direction. Despite a brief, unconsummated fling with Linda Peters (soon to marry Richard Thompson) during 1971, and an ongoing affair with a woman called Sophia Ryde, the singer was feeling '*weaker than the palest blue*'. The songs he buffed up on a writing retreat at Chris Blackwell's Portuguese villa in summer 1971 are cursed with a malign lunar influence, loaded with contempt, self-loathing, longing for an end. Joe Boyd sold up Witchseason and headed back to Los Angeles that year, so Drake made a private arrangement with John Wood to record the songs on his third and final LP, *Pink Moon*.

The two sessions that produced the album's eleven tracks occurred in the dead of two October nights. The story goes that Drake turned up, played the songs straight (with a single piano overdub), and returned wordless to the dark. For a record of one voice and an acoustic guitar, it is an exceptionally intimate, hypnotic experience, as though Sound Techniques became a sounding chamber for Drake's thoughts, the dark socket housing his mind's eye. The urban blight of *Bryter Layter* is abstracted into a generalised sense of hypocrisy unpunished; Drake is now a lonely, nomadic entity wandering '*the road that'll see me through*' in a nocturnal landscape irradiated by the gloaming of an ominous moon. Veering from accusatory to visionary, Drake is a world-weary ancient mariner laying a curse on his listeners: '*None of you stand so tall/ Pink moon gonna get ye all.*' His psychological state was becoming clear: no lover was able to gear down to his vegetable speed of thought; no one could join him on the Arcadian riverbank. The role of sensitive soothsayer he had cast for himself was becoming incompatible with achieving any kind of material existence at all. He described himself as he believed others saw him

– '*the parasite of this town*'. And while the guitar accompaniments are beautiful and stark, the stellar technique has given way to a desultory strumming that suggests a water-wheel impotently churning a dried-up stream.

Drake tossed the tapes through the door of Island Records, then went to ground in Tanworth-in-Arden, where he spent most of the remaining three years of his life, an uncommunicative black hole in the bosom of his uncomprehending family. In July 1974, encouraged by a phone call with Joe Boyd, Drake began the slow process of manufacturing a comeback. He taped his 'five last songs', a damaged, sometimes autistically finicky suite that includes the psychotic menace of 'Black Eyed Dog'. Here, his voice decouples from his usual tenor murmur, producing a cramped whine of abject terror. Along with the minimal, tambura-like drone of the guitar line, the effect is disquieting and voyeuristically sad.

Like 'Free Ride' on *Pink Moon*, 'Rider on the Wheel' may allude to Sophia Ryde, one of the fashionable west London set, who described herself as Drake's 'best (girl)friend',[12] the ambiguity no doubt reflecting Drake's own discomfiture in the face of romantic encounters. 'Hanging on a Star' appears to be a direct message to Joe Boyd, or to a public that refused to listen to his message: '*Why leave me hanging on a star / When you deem me so high?*' In 'Voice from the Mountain', Drake has utterly capitulated to some invisible aural presence in nature; he has become an empty vessel through which a vocal urge is being channelled.

On the morning of 25 November 1974 his mother Molly found his dead body, overdosed on the antidepressant Tryptizol, spread across his childhood bed, his sole testaments a letter to Sophia Ryde and a neatly handwritten exercise book containing his collected lyrics. It's easy to view these documents as a combined suicide note, and the verdict of the local coroner backed that up: 'Acute Amitriptyline Poisoning – self administered when suffering from a depressive illness (suicide)'. But that conclusion – reached with no post-mortem, and two weeks after Drake's body had been cremated – now appears unreliable.

Prescribed to steer him out of the deepest trenches of his depression and help him sleep, Tryptizol was one of many such drugs routinely administered by doctors in the early 1970s, following a concerted marketing drive from medicine manufacturers. 'Doctors were pimps for new anti-depressants,' believes the music writer Nick Kent, who used the drug himself around the same time and found that 'it turned you into a zombie'. Much stronger than valium, Tryptizol produced no discernible highs or lows; it merely turned the habitual user into a barely functioning cabbage. The symptoms perfectly fit the many descriptions of Nick Drake's wilted, asocial demeanour in the last years of his life. It is not a drug that produced mental clarity; neither is it an obvious choice if you want to take your own life. As Kent pointed out in a 1975 tribute, 'there were bottles full of aspirins and barbiturates on hand for such a task . . . the tryptasol [*sic*] he was prescribed were so potent that, were even one to be taken over the prescribed limit, death could easily follow in purely accidental circumstances'.[13] And there were several factors, that November night, that might have been preoccupying him. He had already been dismayed by the suicide the previous spring of a musical hero, Graham Bond, the troubled sax and keyboard player who had lately drifted into paranoid dabblings with the occult before throwing himself under a train. On 5 November his old friend Alice Ormsby-Gore discovered the body of her elder brother Julian lying where he had shot his own head off in the blood-spattered silver-walled flat. And, finally, Drake had just received a letter from his female companion, Sophia Ryde, gently announcing that their relationship, unconsummated as it was, was over. With spirits lowered and senses blurred, it might well have been easy to reach for the bottle again: just one more, to shoo the black-eyed dog away.

Drake was actually on the verge of a more positive future when he died. He had, after all, re-established contact with Joe Boyd and

John Wood, recorded his first new material for three years, spent a tranquil summer living on a barge on the Seine, and occasionally even considered fanciful new careers in computing or the army. But he also appears to have maintained some insalubrious acquaintances in the city. In 1980, while Nick Kent was interviewing John Martyn for an article in the *New Musical Express*,[14] the singer took him to an address in west London which, Martyn claimed, would explain a great deal about Drake's final months. Kent remembers that it seemed to be a drug squat inhabited by a heroin-using couple in their forties, 'older than the average druggie'. They were pleasant, he recalls, but spoke with a vague, washed-out demeanour. He questioned the woman there, who told him that Nick Drake had visited them about a month before his death, and that he used to sit with them, like a tranquillised vegetable, for hours at a time (Kent does not believe Drake himself used heroin). But there was one occasion, presumably when his tranquillisers wore off, when he broke out of his trance and screamed, 'What's happening to me?' That his all-too-brief surfacings from the comatose state were so traumatic indicates the depth of his chemical depression. Undrugged reality was a rare thing now, and hardly a luxury.

When I asked John Martyn to clarify who these friends of Drake's were, he would only reply, 'Well, they both committed suicide, using heroin to do so. It was a couple – they had two sons, I've no idea what happened to them. She was a prostitute and he was a villain. Actually, he didn't have the balls to be a villain – he was a hound.' At every turn, the black-eyed dog appeared on Drake's trail.

What is this voice anyway, the voice that chose to sing through Nick Drake? Although he's often conveniently classified as a folk singer, the term can only be applied in a contextual sense: he played in folk clubs, associated with folk musicians. But his was not the voice of the folk, the declamatory voice seeking to communicate universal truths to a wider community. It is the voice of the one who sits beside you, a little too close, the confiding whisper of someone uncomfortable addressing more than one person at a time (just as Drake kept his groups of friends compartmentalised). The soothsayer is the speaker of truth, and sooth is one letter away from soothe, which is exactly how Drake's voice works on you. Limned with a misty husk, Drake's voice never embellishes or ornaments his lines. He impresses himself upon you by his reticence, absenting himself even as he grasps your attention.

While Nick Drake was recording *Five Leaves Left*, revolution and violent dissent was sweeping around the world, from the streets of Paris to the plazas of Mexico City. But in all the published recollections, no one remembers Drake showing any interest in world events or politics. It seems that rather than fight for a better world, he preferred to seek enlightenment in isolation from it. At the core of Drake's world is a mental garden whose seclusion and protection grants an inkling of infinity. His songs in a sense *are* the English landscape: a haven in which the national psyche eternally seeks refuge. It is not the Little England hymned and condemned in The Kinks' 'Village Green Preservation Society', but the garden of the English mind, defended for a thousand years, jealously staked off against invaders and improvers.

Cynics mock the hippy dream of 'getting it together in the country', but the reason for Nick Drake's growing popularity so long after his death, as the planet enters an age of ecological despair, must have something to do with his refusal, at the end, to allow the serpent of cynicism into his garden. To be arrested by Nick Drake's music is to acknowledge that if we all abandoned the calendar of industry, fashion and routine, slowed down to the magical time, stepped far beyond the chime of a city clock, took more time to hear what the trees whisper, what the sea sings and the moon brings, dusted by oak, ash and thorn, we might yet be granted a glimpse of Paradise.

10

Water

Yes, I saw the ocean, said of it
'Nothing's bigger than this.'
John Martyn, 'The Ocean' (1970)

Fall and listen with your ears upon the paving stone.
Is that what you hear? The coming of the sea?
Sandy Denny/Fotheringay, 'The Sea' (1970)

The barge's windows are blacked out; candles unburned for years
gather dust on the ledges. But despite the musty air and cramped
conditions, Theo Johnson's Folk Barge, moored at Kingston,
south-west of London, has, by 1967, nurtured a vibrant little
community – a 'Thames delta' – of singers, bohos, students and
curious outsiders.

One of them is a young man, Iain McGeachy, a Glaswegian who
discovered the barge while spending summer holidays with his
mother on a houseboat near Thames Ditton. Leaping erratically
between a thick Glasgow brogue and a Jack the Lad Cockney accent,
he steps up to the rickety stage to play puckish songs and lullabies
overrun with goblins, pixies, magic fairy rings and sugar fish,
menacing gardeners, golden girls and streams meandering through
his mind. One night, Theo Johnson comes right out with it: he knows
how to make the young Iain a star. Johnson makes the necessary
introduction to Chris Blackwell of Island Records, who promptly
grooms McGeachy for success. First to go is the name: adopting a
new surname after his favourite brand of guitar, McGeachy is reborn

as John Martyn. His first two Island albums, *London Conversation* and *The Tumbler*, which feature the chirruping flute of Harold McNair, are saturated with the innocence and young love experienced in these indolent, bucolic days on the river. Reminiscences of his carefree childhood on the houseboat surface on 'Knuckledy Crunch and Slippledee-Slee', where Martyn describes his amazement when he first saw another motorboat chugging past, with its promise of freedom, travel, escape. Other numbers such as 'Fishin' Blues', 'The River' and 'A Day at the Sea' continue the liquid theme.

We will rejoin Martyn later, further down the river. Meanwhile, here on stage is another of the barge's guitar-toting regulars: Jackson Frank, the American author of one of this crowd's favourite songs, 'Blues Run the Game', which has already been taken up by a few of the other regular performers and floor singers. Here he is, in 1965, singing one of his most mournful songs, accompanying himself with a plangent melody at the high end of his guitar fretboard: 'I Want to Be Alone', also known as 'Dialogue'. Some of its lines seem located right here, in the depths of the barge itself. It is effectively a break-up song; a message from one who cannot deal with close contact to a lover who cannot bear to face a night alone. As he sang the song on the river, Frank might well have been directing his intense gaze into the very eyes of Alexandra 'Sandy' Denny, the eighteen-year-old to whom the song was addressed.

Denny, who in the summer of 1965 was working as a trainee nurse at Brompton Chest Hospital, biding her time before entering Kingston School of Art, had realised that this west London folk milieu was her ticket out of the conventional expectations held for her by her parents, both of whom had military backgrounds. As early as 1964 she was hanging out with another of the art school's alumni, John Renbourn, and his student friends at the Prince of Wales Feathers pub in Wimbledon, and through them discovering clubs like the Troubadour and Bunjies, where she tentatively began stepping up and performing whenever she could pluck up the courage. She became a regular at the house in Somali Road inhabited by Renbourn, The Young Tradition and Bert Jansch (with whom she also had a brief affair). These mid-1960s years, as Denny gradually developed in confidence and picked up paid singing work, were formative; between 1964 and 1968 she upgraded her life's licence from the black and white of her family's expectations to the vibrant colour of music, alcohol, parties and the liberated socialising of her peers. Her first recordings were made with folk artiste Johnny Silvo, then as a short-lived member of Strawbs in 1966–7, with whom she introduced one of her signature compositions, the wistful 'Who Knows Where the Time Goes?'. In this period, during which she dated Pentangle bassist Danny Thompson and befriended Linda Peters (later married to Richard Thompson), she became adept in a repertoire that ranged from covers of favourite American folk singers, like Joan Baez, Bob Dylan and Richard Fariña's 'Quiet Joys of Brotherhood', to traditional British ballads such as 'Polly on the Shore'. 'Who Knows Where the Time Goes?' reached the ears of Judy Collins across the Atlantic, who recorded it in 1968 and even used it as the title of an album that year.

Inevitably, Denny met Joe Boyd in 1967, and her previous experience and connections led her inexorably towards the job of replacing Judy Dyble as lead singer of Fairport Convention in the spring of 1968. By the time she and Fairport came to record 'A Sailor's Life', the electrified folk song that radically altered their course, Denny felt finished with the folk-music canon even as Ashley Hutchings was accelerating their rate of knots in that direction. She was already flexing her own songwriting muscles, drawing upon the folk tradition's natural backdrops and tragic inevitabilities, while spinning her own insecurities, self-analysis, dream images and metonymic character sketches into the mix. As Jackson Frank's 'Dialogue' had implied, she could not bear solitude, and the shape of her career reflects that: as well as the four LPs in

Sandy Denny enjoys an idyll moment, 1970.

her own name, her songs are refracted through Fairport in its *Liege and Lief* phase; Fotheringay, the group she formed immediately after quitting; and Fairport again in their 1973–5 vintage, when she rejoined the group for their albums *Rosie* and *Rising for the Moon*. Equating solo with '*so low*', Denny's neediness left her despondent whenever she had to embark on solitary tours, and she was even known to sack managers who tried to dissuade her from the costly nightmare of paying a group on retainer.

In 1971, on 'Next Time Around', opening side two of her album *The North Star Grassman and the Ravens*, she glanced backwards at the vanished days on the river, the Folk Barge and her introverted lover in a cryptic portrait. '*The house it was built by some man in a rhyme*,' she sings, meaning 'Jack'. '*But whatever became of his talented son?*' – Jackson – '*who wrote me a dialogue set to a tune/ Always you told me of being alone.*' Finally, Denny contributes her own side of the 'Dialogue'. The second verse intimates Frank's own disfiguring accident when he was caught in a fire at his school, after which the building's designers were held to account for its collapse. '*Because of the architect the buildings fell down,*' runs Denny's song, '*Smothered or drowned all the seeds that were sown.*' Although the real-life incident that inspired these lines was a blaze, Denny can't help transforming the disaster into a flood.

The best of Sandy Denny's music inhabits the shore or the riverbank, or drifts upon the sea in the company of its dislocated sailors. Songs like 'Late November', 'The Sea Captain', 'The Sea', 'The Pond and the Stream', 'The North Star Grassman and the Ravens', 'Winter Winds' and 'All Our Days' are beset by gusts of wind stirring up the summer's dusts, rumbling clouds and approaching squalls. The season is typically autumn or early winter; there is frequently a restless imagistic play of ill omens; the bailiffs are calling in the debt on summer's lease. '*My dreams were like the autumn leaves,*' she sings in 'No End', '*they faded and they fell so fast.*' '*And a cold wind it blows/ Through good fortunes of time,*' 'The Music Weaver' chimes in.

Like Mary, Queen of Scots (whose imprisonment in Northamptonshire's Fotheringhay Castle held such a strong fascination for Denny that she named her first group after the stronghold), she held her own secrets prisoner, as if afraid of the damage they might wreak if set free. Both Sandy Denny and John Martyn began their careers in London's layabout folk community; both soon harboured a scepticism about certain aspects of traditional music-making. Between them, they did more than most to cause the permafrost of tradition to melt into a more liquid consistency.

Within a month or so of walking out on Fairport Convention in November 1969, Denny was forging ahead with Fotheringay, her new group with her current boyfriend Trevor Lucas. Born in 1943 in Melbourne, the hirsute, ginger-whiskered Lucas had made a small reputation for himself as an Australian folkie, cutting a solo album of convict ballads and Dylan covers in 1964. Many contemporaries remember him as competent but with little musical talent; a good-time guy who latched onto his wife's talents as a way of furthering himself. Whatever the truth of these opinions, Lucas certainly proved himself an able and cunning networker from the moment of his arrival in Britain in 1965. He appeared on Bert Lloyd's Topic album of whaling songs and shanties, *Leviathan*, in that year, and took part in the label's collection of pioneer and sheep farmers' lays, *The Great Australian Legend*. In 1967 he guested on the soundtrack to John Schlesinger's Thomas Hardy movie *Far from the Madding Crowd*, which was liberally doused in Wessex folk music (Lucas sings a 'Tinker's Song' and 'I Sowed the Seeds of Love', the song that first burrowed its way into Cecil Sharp's ears back in Hambridge). With a group of international expatriates, Lucas formed Eclection in late 1967, a fairly pedestrian beat group with shades of Jefferson Airplane and The Byrds. Eclection fell apart in the autumn of 1969 after one album which failed to incite huge sales for Jac Holzman's Elektra imprint, by which time Lucas and Denny had been a couple for almost a year.

Fotheringay on stage, 1970. Left to right: Jerry Donahue, Trevor Lucas, Gerry Conway, Sandy Denny, Pat Donaldson.

By April 1970 Fotheringay, featuring guitarist Jerry Donahue, bassist Pat Donaldson and Eclection's drummer Gerry Conway, had recorded their first album and completed a short UK tour. Produced by Joe Boyd, *Fotheringay* is effectively the first proper Sandy Denny record, heaving and tossing with briny swells. 'The Sea' casts the salt water as '*a joker, a deceiver*', biding its time before it joins forces with eternity to bring all human endeavour to nothing: '*Sea flows under your doors in London Town, / And all your defences are broken down.*' 'The Pond and the Stream' fail to materialise in the verses of that song, but Denny explicitly refers to '*Annie*' – i.e. the free-spirited folk singer Anne Briggs, a friend of Denny's from the Somali Road days – as the one who '*wanders on the land*' and '*loves the freedom of the air*'. Briggs's transient presence is the stream to Denny's lily pad in London's giant pond: '*I live in the city,*' she sings, '*And imagine country scenes.*'

Fotheringay's mix of slow-rocking English and Scottish ballads and windswept Denny originals made for a beguiling songbook. Occasionally the mood-shifts were a little too crude, from Denny's husky damsel croon to Lucas's fruity drawl on material such as his 'Ballad of Ned Kelly' or The Band's *Basement Tapes* track 'Too Much of Nothing'. In addition, Lucas had invited his own sister to paint the front-cover artwork, a flagrantly embarrassing group portrait of four phallocentric paisley troubadours strutting and preening around their demure flaxen-haired songbird clad in an elaborate Elizabethan costume. Joe Boyd found working with Fotheringay a permanent headache, exasperated by Lucas's extravagant spending of the group's A&M Records advance on a Bentley and a sound system whose monolithic speaker stacks were nicknamed 'Stonehenge'.

Work started in late 1970 on a follow-up album that never materialised (until completed by the surviving members in 2008); this eventually morphed into sessions for the first album bearing Sandy Denny's name, *The North Star Grassman and the Ravens*. The

Trevor Lucas and Sandy Denny hold court at their flat in
Parsons Green, south-west London, *c.* 1971.

group's members still provided the core personnel, and Denny
added Richard Thompson (on the verge of leaving the Fairport
stable) as producer and electric guitarist. The ever reliable Ian
Whiteman of Mighty Baby played most of the piano on the album,
and backing vocals on the anti-war epic 'John the Gun' were
sung by The Young Tradition's Royston Wood and the Dransfield
brothers Barry and Robin. Following his triumphant work on Nick
Drake's 'River Man', Harry Robinson was drafted in to arrange
string parts for two tracks.

The North Star Grassman is a composite portrait of the artist in a
transitional stage in her life and career, bobbing on an unruly sea
of friends, lovers, dreams, journeys and trepidations. 'Next Time
Around', 'Wretched Wilbur' and 'Crazy Lady Blues' are cryptic
portraits of specific friends and acquaintances. 'Late November'
and the title track conduct an uncanny, enigmatic self-analysis.

Even the more Americanised, earthy cover material is thematically appropriate: Bob Dylan's 'Down in the Flood' extends the deluge imagery with its high tides and swollen levees, while Denny's boogie-woogie take on Brenda Lee's 'Let's Jump the Broomstick' can perhaps be heard as an early proposal to future husband Trevor Lucas, with the '*My father don't like it, my brother don't like it*' refrain reflecting her family's private disdain for her worldly partner.

Slapstick Tragedies was the record's working title, which may have indicated Denny's own self-image but which would have been inappropriate for the slow tempos, sweeping string passages and ebbing tidal lines. Never again would her music achieve such a thalassic swell. The thematic tension between country and city now yaws towards the counterpoint of land and sea, symbolic of Denny's yearning for a stable home, which was continually upset by the migrations enforced by her work (as well as her fears that Lucas was directing his amorous attentions elsewhere while she was gone). The sea is anarchic, unmapped; sailors are artists and dreamers. 'When I write songs,' she told an interviewer in 1973, 'I often picture myself standing on a beach or standing on a rock or a promenade or something. I just put myself there sometimes and without even realising it I find myself describing what I'm looking at and often it's the sea. I keep promising myself I'll put myself somewhere else when I'm writing songs but I really can't think of anywhere that's nicer than that.'[1] Denny's lyrics return to the waterside, but there is no mention of a destination: the Sea Captain '*loved the ocean*' for its own sake, and merely '*deserted*' in order to '*cross the wide sea*', but perishes alone in a blazing vessel.

The record launches with the stately piano chords of 'Late November', a song in which Denny spreads out her cargo of weird omens and morbid visions – a compilation of her prophetic dreams about the fate of Fairport Convention. The first lines convey the finality: '*The wine it was drunk, the ship it was sunk/ The shot it was dead, all the sorrows were drowned.*' The moment when she took to the lifeboats occurred in late November 1969, when she refused to take a promotional flight to Denmark. On 21 February of that year she had recorded a dream in her diary about the group's roadie Harvey Bramham, who was driving the van that crashed on the M1 on '*the ill-fated day*' a couple of months later. '*As we drew south the mist it came down,*' she sings, and the entry in her dream diary placed her in the passenger seat of Bramham's van, holding the steering wheel while the roadie tinkered with a sound system to play music while on the move. 'On the right hand side of the road was the sea and we were driving along the edge. The sea was black and choppy. The sky was stormy grey . . .' It is the desolate coastline of *North Star Grassman*. Later in the same epic dream she wanders on a lonely beach and finds some unidentifiable entrails; a cow tells her these are the last remaining vestiges of the human race. She then senses another presence behind her, and turns to see two tall, brown-skinned people with grey eyes and brown robes who escort her to their dwelling, which is populated by many more. Several months later, in real life, she found herself on the beach she had dreamed of, near Eden Mouth in St Andrew's Bay in Scotland, paralysed as she watched a jet fighter swoop low over the sea and then vanish. The dream vision and the air disaster feed into 'Late November''s final verse.

'Late November', then, is a record of two premonitions: of the demise of Fairport Convention and an air crash. The superstitious seam continues in 'The North Star Grassman and the Ravens', one of Denny's most curious and impenetrable songs. With a sonic underlay of washing waves and a chiming ship's bell, it begins with an image of a boat's crew ranged on a deck, pulling away from the shore and watched by a crowd who '*wonder what the sailor knows*'.

The 'they' Denny leaves behind view her only as a wanderer, a deserter, or the kind of free-roaming spirit she admired in Anne Briggs. In the second verse Denny turns to an image of stability and continuity: the Tower of London. Like Fotheringhay Castle, the

Tower is another prison that has played a significant role in English history for nearly a thousand years. The ravens who famously inhabit its grounds may be a link to a legend from the fourteenth-/ fifteenth-century Welsh *Mabinogion*, which tells of the head of an ancient king of Britain, Bran the Blessed (the name translates as 'Crow', but is often rendered as 'Raven'), being buried in London as a talisman to ward off invasion from France – the land would be safe as long as the head remained in its resting place. That legend was later mapped onto a superstition that if the ravens that colonise the Tower ever abandon their habitat, it will collapse, and with it the monarchy and the nation itself. At least that's what was confided to Charles II, when his Astronomer Royal John Flamsteed, based at the Tower of London, requested that the birds should be removed to prevent their droppings from soiling his telescope lenses. When the king refused, Flamsteed moved his observatory to its present site at Greenwich – a place where astronomers and sailors rubbed shoulders, as the Maritime College was situated nearby. These details seem to lie in the distant background of Denny's song, although the real subject – the 'Grassman' of the title (never referenced in the song) – remains elusive. Introducing the song at the 1971 Lincoln Festival, she announced it was 'about a friend of mine who used to be a sailor'. Whoever this character was, he appears to have met his doom while on his voyage: Denny ponders whether the ravens deserted the Tower one day without anyone noticing, '*To circle over ships at sea*' with the intention of '*claiming yet another son*'.

Two further 'portrait songs' appear at the end of the album: 'Crazy Lady Blues', an unambiguous tribute to Denny's best friend, Linda Peters, the '*always yawning*' woman then involved in a fumbling, sexless relationship with Nick Drake. 'Wretched Wilbur' is more enigmatic; perhaps a composite of men such as Ashley Hutchings ('*with roses in his hands*' alluding to the just-released Albion Country Band album *No Roses?*), Strawbs' Dave Cousins and Bert Lloyd, who kept '*ploughing up the land*' of an idea of traditional music after Denny had moved on.

There's only one remnant from Denny's traditional roots: 'Blackwaterside', in a stunning, terse electric version. Anne Briggs, who had introduced the song (also known as 'The False Young Man') to Denny after Bert Lloyd played her a recording of the Irish traveller Mary Doran, released her own rendering of the song in the same year, but it had already been recorded by Briggs's other friend (and Denny's former lover) Bert Jansch on *Jack Orion*. Thus, the song connects Denny's earliest musical life with her present one, five years later. Tellingly, though, she alters Briggs's version in the final verse to add her own apocalyptic twist: where Briggs sings '*Sure it's fishes they'll fly and the seas run dry / 'Tis then you'll marry I,*' Denny changes it to '*And when the sky does fall and the seas will run dry / Why, it's then you'll marry I.*'

For the sleeve art, photographer Marcus Keef located a magnificently cobwebbed apothecary's shop, lined with wooden drawers, grinding pestles and dusty grimoires. Denny, the grasswoman at the counter, measures out dried herbs next to a pair of marble-and-brass scales. She looks as though she has just awoken from a hundred years of paralysis – the teacup she is pouring from has left its circular mark on a countertop covered in dust. The clock stands at nearly twenty minutes to six; the lanterns are already lit, and an early autumn sun flares in the diamond-latticed window panes. Its golden blaze floods across a vase of dried flowers, filling Denny's corner and lighting up a barometer whose reading, we must assume, is falling from 'Fair' to 'Change'. The dried flowers are honesty (*Lunaria annua*), so called because it reveals its seeds through thin, translucent, coin-shaped pods. These give it its alternative names moonflower and money plant; the placement here is appropriate to the record's lunar, tidal influence. In a pink pot next to her left hand is a posy of gypsophila, commonly known as baby's-breath. Honesty and children: the language of flowers was speaking loud and clear.

Herbal remedies: Sandy Denny poses for the sleeve of
The North Star Grassman and the Ravens (1971).

Her next record, simply called *Sandy*, picks up the nautical thread
with its very first lines: '*Oh it's like a storm at sea/ And everything
is lost.*' Produced, like all three remaining solo albums, by Trevor
Lucas, and released in 1972, *Sandy* finds the tempests of the
previous year beginning to abate. Lucas's influence was felt ever
more strongly, especially on *Like an Old Fashioned Waltz* (1973) and
Rendezvous (1977), which made liberal use of brass and orchestral
arrangements, sometimes erring on the side of schmaltz or simply
sweetening the songs' bitter sentiments too much.

Multitracking her own voice, Denny delivers a show-stopping
version of 'Quiet Joys of Brotherhood', the Richard Fariña lyric
she had kept in her repertoire since the mid-1960s, grafted onto
the tune of the Irish air 'My Lagan Love'. Its idyllic opening stanzas,
describing nature at peace and thriving on interconnectedness, are

rent asunder in the final verse, a bleak environmental message in which man's efforts tear down the oaks, enslave the stallions and even put the sand to work in hourglasses.

When her mid-1970s reunion with Fairport Convention failed to realign the group as a world-beating rock outfit, Denny's life strayed down an increasingly self-destructive path. She and Lucas installed themselves in a country cottage in the diminutive Northamptonshire village of Byfield – where several Fairport members had also established their base – but, faced with alcoholism, a serially unfaithful husband and to all intents and purposes an open marriage, Denny's behaviour took a wayward turn over the next three years. When two of her closest friends and confidants, Richard and Linda Thompson, disappeared from her life to secrete themselves in a Sufi commune, Denny took a Scientology audit (undercutting the solemnity of the occasion by making a grab for the counsellor's crotch). Finally, it was long-awaited motherhood that sent Denny into her final, fatal tailspin. During her pregnancy in early 1977 she kept company with The Who's notorious hellraiser Keith Moon (she had previously harboured a secret, unconsummated love for Pete Townshend). Her daughter Georgia was born by caesarean section in July, two months premature, but, as various Fairport members reported afterwards, her behaviour was erratic and she seemed to have failed to establish a strong bond with her baby – on one occasion she drove her Volkswagen Beetle into a ditch with the carry-cot loose on the seat.[2] In a small hamlet such as Byfield, such behaviour could not go unnoticed, and even friends started to ignore her calls. 'No More Sad Refrains', the last track on her last album, *Rendezvous* (1977), promises that *'when these winter days are over / I mean to set myself upon my feet,'* but barely had the winter days of 1978 passed than her feet, catastrophically, let her down.

Unhalfbricking was one of the first, if not *the* first, album covers of the 1960s to display an image only, barren of text to indicate the artist or album title. The scene is the garden of Sandy Denny's family home in Arthur Road, Wimbledon. The tree branches have only just sprouted their spring leaves; the flowerbed is full of freshly hoed earth ready for the new season's planting; the spire of St Mary's Church spikes upwards into a sky of minty blue.

The garden gate is propped ajar, and Neil and Edna Denny have briefly stepped outside the perimeter of their home to face Eric Hayes's lens. They stand rooted to their domain, with mouths clamped in sceptical smiles, clad in browns, creams and greys. Edna's hands are clasped, awkwardly protective, across her camel-coloured woollen skirt. Neil's fists are on his hips, with a hint of passive aggression. Behind them, heads serendipitously framed in a noughts-and-crosses board of creosoted trellis, we can make out their daughter Sandy, aged twenty-two, and the four boys from Fairport Convention, variously standing, sitting or crouching around a tea table. The whole scene is eerily frozen. The five auteurs of the album appear only as tiny figures framed in one of the fence panels, resembling those Renaissance frescoes where the subject of the painting – the flagellation, or a holy miracle – is viewed casually in the background, through a window frame or in a distant field.

'We had no concept,' recalls Eric Hayes, a twenty-three-year-old Canadian photographer and music fan who fetched up in London in 1968 while travelling the world. He was matched up with Fairport after he dropped a portfolio into the Witchseason office, and was dispatched, with no brief, to shoot *Unhalfbricking*'s cover. 'No idea what we would do, so I suggested that we should get together and see what might happen. So one morning the band and their van picked me up and all of us drove around London

Fairport Convention, *Unhalfbricking* (1969).

looking for inspiration. It was Sandy who eventually said, "Why don't we go and visit my parents in Wimbledon? They have a nice house and a lawn and maybe we can shoot something there." And we all thought that was a great idea.

'I don't know how Sandy's mother felt about the whole band, complete with a photographer and his wife, showing up unexpectedly, but she very graciously served us tea on the lawn. I recall working on that idea for a while, with Sandy in the foreground pouring a cuppa and the rest of the band as supportive compositional elements behind her. At some point I must have tired of that and backed away entirely, when the idea came up to put Sandy's parents in the foreground and the entire band taking tea on the lawn behind the latticework fence. Many people have asked me how hard it was to get each person's head in a different hole of the fence, but in truth it was a lucky accident. The cover was cropped to fit the square format of the vinyl album cover. I don't know who did the graphic layout, nor do I know who chose that particular frame as the cover shot.'

The omens of Sandy's fate are already here, loaded into this single photograph.

Sandy stands behind Martin Lamble, who would be dead within a few weeks. Nine years later, almost to the month, on 4 April 1978, Sandy was discovered in a heap at the bottom of the stairs at her friend Miranda Ward's London flat. This fall is usually cited as the cause of her death. But whatever happened on the stairs that caused her to black out, it was the end result of another serious fall and head injury she had sustained several weeks earlier, while staying at her parents' holiday cottage in Cornwall. The tragedy is compounded by the knowledge that the parents outlived both their children: her beloved brother David, who had accompanied her on several of her British and American tours, was killed a year later in a road accident in Colorado.

Neil and Edna Denny were military folk. They met each other while serving in the Second World War – Neil in the Royal Air Force, Edna in the Women's RAF. Decent people who had successfully defended their country against Nazi invasion, endured food rationing throughout the war and for nearly ten years afterwards, and felt pride in the coronation of a glamorous young queen. They loved, nurtured and sheltered their children. But they were utterly unprepared for the bomb culture of pop. A hard-drinking, cocaine-ingesting, emotional wreck of a daughter and an indolent rock-star wannabe of a son-in-law were not among the roster of problems they had so far had to deal with in life.

When Sandy Denny began releasing her own records, there was no precedent in British popular music for a woman writing a large body of her own material on her own terms. She wanted to write great songs, but she was no calculating manipulator of her own career. Doing all the peripheral promotional stuff around the music – the business of being solo – was a painful process. It was lonely out on that beach.

In her best-known song, 'Who Knows Where the Time Goes?', probably the first she ever wrote, in 1966, she's on a '*sad, deserted shore*' watching migrating birds quitting their habitat according to some invisible signal, just like her '*fickle friends*'. The home that was protected by the presence of a lover is left barren by his absence. When she wrote these lines, the twenty-year-old Sandy could still hope: '*So come the storms of winter and then the birds in spring again . . . I have no fear of time.*'

Neil and Edna did not approve of Trevor Lucas, and they rarely met him face to face. In March 1978 Sandy Denny's marriage, professional life and her ability to cope with the day-to-day necessities of mothering an eight-month-old baby were all disintegrating fast. She tumbled down the rickety stairwell at her parents' Cornish holiday cottage, smashing her head on the stone floor. She was drunk, and possibly holding her baby daughter, when it happened. Concerned with keeping up appearances, her parents refused to take her to the local hospital. Afterwards, she told her friend Philippa Clare that her mother had said, 'I'm not having you seen drunk.'[3] An X-ray at the local casualty ward might well have revealed the damage to her skull that showed up over the following three weeks as blinding headaches, culminating in the brain haemorrhage that left her dying at the bottom of another set of stairs. Her husband, she had found out three days beforehand, had decided he could not share her burdens any longer, and had covertly flown back to Australia, taking their daughter with him.

On *Unhalfbricking*, in her parents' garden, before the slapstick tragedies struck, she appears happy, content, surfing on the promise of a wide open future. When she embarked on the stormy seas of the rest of her life, she took the journey from the tranquil garden to the outer limit of the British imagination: to the shore, the liminal threshold where the nation's identity dissolves into the lowering mist. Pining for home but condemned to stand eternally on the beach, waving to the departed or to a vision of herself poised upon the rolling deck, Sandy Denny never kept peace between all the warring factions in her music. The only way to make the storms abate was to imprison them in her art. Years after Fotheringhay and the Tower of London, prisons continued to overshadow her writing. In 'The King and Queen of England', a song demoed at home in December 1974 but not included on any of her official albums, she casts herself as the jailer of her own songs, the repositories of all her love and of pain. '*But I can't find the key*,' she informs them. '*You may never be free.*'

The silver chain glints once more, winding back in space and time through the meadows of Richmond and Surrey, to the slippledee-slee, lazy hazy days on the Thames delta, where John Martyn spent most of that psychedelic 1967 summer crooning his mercurial, tongue-tripping confection of sprites and fairy fables to the stoned incumbents of the Folk Barge. Martyn was born to the McGeachy family on 11 September 1948, in New Malden, Surrey. His Glaswegian father and English mother (he also described her as 'a Belgian Jew') both sang light opera for a living, but separated not long after the birth of their son, who stayed in the paternal home. Martyn's upbringing in the hard-knock life of the Glasgow ports – where his grandfather had owned a small fleet of trawlers – was given a flip side by his annual two-month visits to his mother in Surbiton, Surrey (he and his stepfather didn't see eye to eye, so Martyn tended to stay with an aunt at Thames Ditton, across the river from Hampton Court). He picked up his fascination with the guitar from Scottish folk singer Hamish Imlach, and from watching Davy Graham, Bert Jansch and Robin Williamson up close in his local Scottish folk clubs; while his annual trips to England introduced another world of visions to his artistic sensibility: 'London was like a dream to me [. . .] even the Southern line, the green trains, and the journey from Waterloo to Surbiton [. . .]. You see I come from Glasgow which is a very stroppy part of town and you don't have any choice up there – either you're violent or you're a weed. And I haven't got the capacity for being trodden on. I'm a natural born coward just like everybody else, but I don't like being taken advantage of. I'm probably still the same now. But at the time it was just either eat or be eaten and it was just such a pleasant change to come down here. There were fights in school all the time and knives were bandied about, and it always seemed more civilised to be in England, especially round the Kingston way. It was just a very civilised part of my life.'[4]

Martyn spent the summer of 1967 living at Theo Johnson's Richmond flat. A revolving cast of characters lived or crashed

Beverley and John Martyn before the clouds gathered, around the release of their duo album *Stormbringer!* (1970).

there, including Johnny Silvo (Sandy Denny's first employer), Diz Disley and Hamish Imlach on his trips south. Robin Frederick, the young female American traveller who had entertained a crush on Nick Drake in Aix-en-Provence earlier that year, came to stay. She journeyed to London at the invitation of Bridget St John, another musically inclined English teenager who had been staying in Aix (though she apparently never met Drake there) and who went on to record several albums of her own beguiling material for John Peel's Dandelion label. Exploring London's folk-club scene, Frederick met John Martyn at Bunjies in Soho, and spent much of the Summer of Love in the Richmond flat.

'You couldn't really call it "furnished",' she says. 'There were a couple of rooms with beds on the floor. A couch and stereo in the living room. That was it. The first Incredible String Band album was released right then, and John had gotten hold of a copy. We listened to it over and over for hours, sitting on the bare wooden floor in the living room. You can hear the same naive, childlike quality in The Incredible String Band that you hear in John's songs. I know John has been very critical of his early work, really distancing himself from it. The simplicity and natural wisdom of childhood – and folk music – was very much in vogue during that time, culminating in The Beatles' "Yellow Submarine" in 1968. It had an appeal that may be hard to recall now.'

In the moments when the needle was lifted off Martyn's copy of *Sgt Pepper*, and he left off practising on his newly acquired sitar, the pair would pick up their guitars and trade songs. Frederick brought a souvenir from France: 'Sandy Grey', a song she had written inspired by her feelings about the indistinct, in-between colours of Nick Drake's elusive persona. '[Drake] asked me to meet him one evening at La Rotunde, a cafe where we all used to hang out,' recalls Frederick, over forty years later. 'I showed up and waited for him but he never turned up. One of his roommates was there; whether Nick sent him or he just happened to be there,

I don't know. I remember him making excuses for Nick – "Oh, that's just the way he is" – but I wasn't having any of it. I waited for a long while at the cafe and then left when I decided he wasn't coming. My pride was hurt. I remember being quite upset about it. In "Sandy Grey" I cast Nick in the role of wandering, rootless, fatherless boy.' Martyn had not yet met Drake, and Frederick never told him about the origin of the song, but some aspect of it clearly touched Martyn's nerves, for he recorded 'Sandy Grey' on *London Conversation*, the LP he made as the first white solo performer Chris Blackwell contracted to Island Records. 'Those were the days of the dancing, whirling dervish,' Martyn recalled. 'I breezed through them.'

Between 1967–8 that breeze was more like a whirlwind, as Martyn suddenly found himself at the epicentre of the folk-jazz scene, the aloof underbelly of the rock industry. Robin Frederick sums up his character at that time in two words: 'Angelic, self-destructive. These two things co-exist uncomfortably. At the time I knew him, I think he was on the genuine high of having a record deal with Island, getting recognition at really a very young age. Everything was possible. Back in 1967, love was something a lot of people were trying on for size. John wore it like his own skin and kept it on.' At Les Cousins he reacquainted himself with his Incredible String Band associates from Scotland; he shared stages with his guitar idols; and at the Folk Barge he befriended Jackson C. Frank, with whom he undertook what he later called 'fake Leary Acid Tests', occasionally on swimming trips. 'We just used to sit there and take loads of acid, or mescaline or whatever hallucinogenic was going,' Martyn recalls. 'And have a look and see what happened. It was always cool.' 'There was one night when he dropped acid and tried to fly out of a second-storey window,' adds Robin Frederick. 'Is that a reflection of what acid does to your brain or is the acid triggering something that's there inside? I don't know. I just remember how hard it was to stop him and how scared I was.' Accompanying Frank one evening to a show at Chelsea College of Art, Martyn spied on stage 'this very sexual lady, with a big hooter and great big brown eyes'.[5] It was the woman who would not only become his wife and the mother of two of his children, but would also become the subject of many of his songs over the ensuing decade.

A year younger than Martyn, Beverley Kutner had already racked up three years' more experience as a professional musician. In the mid-1960s she was courted by both Donovan and Bert Jansch, and she is the chic lady with the black piled-up hair and Chelsea boots sprawled on Jansch's floor on the sleeve of 1965's *It Don't Bother Me*. Her jug band, The Levee Breakers, released a George Martin-produced single on Parlophone in 1965, and the following year, known simply as 'Beverley', she cut 'Happy New Year', backed by London sessioneers Jimmy Page, John Paul Jones and Nicky Hopkins, which inaugurated Deram, the new underground imprint set up by Decca. She guested on Simon and Garfunkel's *Bookends* album and, at their invitation, appeared at Monterey Pop in 1967. John Martyn arrived in her life just as Joe Boyd had swept her up with his Witchseason broomstick and brokered a solo album deal with Warner Brothers. 'She made me aware of the idea of laying myself a bit naked,' Martyn told an interviewer. 'She just loosened something in my head.'[6]

They married in 1969, and in April began taping four of Beverley's tunes in London. With a Warners deal confirmed, and with typically immaculate timing, Boyd shipped them out to Woodstock, the sleepy upstate New York town that had suddenly become Olympus for a handful of reclusive rock gods. There the Martyns found their next-door neighbour, Jimi Hendrix, flying in and out in a purple helicopter, Van Morrison enjoying post-*Astral Weeks* paradise with Janet Planet, Bob Dylan in residence nearby having just wrapped the recordings for *Nashville Skyline*, and The Band still occupying Big Pink. In fact, The Band's drummer

Levon Helm and bassist Harvey Brooks joined the ensemble that helped the Martyns complete *Stormbringer*. For Beverley, though, things turned out different than planned. Her husband ended up dominating the creative sessions, and eventually the album was released as a duo, with herself only credited as writer of three of the ten tracks. By the time they returned to London in September, Nick Drake had completed *Five Leaves Left*, and Fairport Convention were packing up to leave Farley Chamberlayne. All three appeared at the Royal Festival Hall on 24 September at Fairport's comeback gig.

The John and Beverley Martyn duo only released one more album together, 1970's *The Road to Ruin*, a collection of urbane stone-in-love folk-rock songs such as 'Give Us a Ring' and 'Sorry to Be So Long', reading like lovers' scribbled notes and memos left in the hallway. After that, Beverley took a background role. By the start of 1971, when she gave birth to their daughter Mhairi, she already had a two-year-old son, Wesley, from a previous relationship, whom John had adopted as his own.

Watching footage of Martyn playing live can be an unsettling experience. After a tortured, deeply emotive passage or song rendition, Martyn instantly snaps out of character, undercutting the intensity of the moment with a cheery 'Awright!', the 'Eyethangyew!' of a pompous music-hall entertainer, or a crude joke. It's a refusal to admit that these oceanic statements of love, these precarious weighings of head and heart might come from some mysterious, deeply buried seam of pain. 'I like that contrast,' he told me, reviewing his career several months before his death in January 2009. 'It's not a conscious thing, but I have discovered that myself, yeah, I get carried away during the actual performance, and then when I'm talking to people I try to talk to them on a lighter level, because otherwise we'll all go home fucking crying . . . or laughing, depending on which way you take it.' His conversational voice was likewise wracked with the duality of his origins: he nonchalantly slips from Sarf England drawl to Scots (b)rogue, ironic Lord Snooty sniff to brimstone Baptist preacher man. 'I'm above nationality,' he declared.

None of his contemporaries leave you flying so high or (d)riven so deep, nor so colourfully bruised, as Martyn's music in the 1970s. While earlier records like *London Conversation* and *The Tumbler* are invested with wide-eyed, innocent wonder, as his work matured it manifested a powerful struggle between the male ego and its opposite, the feminised, domesticated husband yearning for romantic monogamy. Glaswegian John, his father's son, harboured violence, adultery, the weight of male expectations, and electricity. London John, nurtured by the river, was his mother's boy, the childlike innocent, the romantic lover, the acoustic merman who finished his sets with 'Singing in the Rain' because it 'conveys such a love of life'.[7] The problem was that both places had been his home.

The portrait on the sleeve of *Bless the Weather* (1971) has a straggly-locked Martyn as a decapitated John the Baptist, with his head hanging disembodied between a flaring sunset and a locust clinging to a thick blade of grass. Martyn, a keen amateur photographer, snapped the picture himself. 'I got into this thing of taking shots of blades of grass, and insects interested me. It's actually a fly, but it looks a bit menacing. I like the idea of double exposure, so I put one across the other, and it came out in sepia. I was a pretty boy in those days as well, I could get away with it.' 'John the Baptist' was also a song he had contributed to *Stormbringer*, in which he pictured his own severed head grinning at his wife from the plate, in an image which seemed to reveal ambiguities in his own mind about the prospect of domesticity and fatherhood.

On 'Bless the Weather', Danny Thompson's chocolatey double bass sidles up to Martyn's glittering, harmonic-flecked guitar tumble for the first time. The Pentangle stalwart would become Martyn's regular bass anchor, his elegantly volatile low-end lope helping to guide Martyn through the modal folk fusion of *Solid Air* and *Inside Out*. At the end of *Bless the Weather*'s appetising plate of acoustic cold cuts, like 'Go Easy' and 'Head and Heart', Mighty Baby's pianist Ian Whiteman and drummer Roger Powell join in for the seven-minute instrumental 'Glistening Glyndebourne'. Here, Martyn and the group can be heard scrabbling towards freer forms. It begins in neutral gear, with an eddying preamble not unlike the limpid opening to Miles Davis's modal milestone 'So What'. After almost two minutes appears the first-ever sighting of the delay-drenched acoustic guitar that became John Martyn's textural hallmark, and the group pick up their pace and rhythm from the audio shower of notes and flashing harmonics, flickering through the improvisation like petals on a wet, black bough.

On 'Glistening Glyndebourne', Martyn was still using a WEM Copicat echo machine, but he soon acquired a state-of-the-art Echoplex machine. 'I had a WEM Copicat which I was using to try and extend the sound of the fuzztone on the guitar so I could play the same note for half an hour if I felt like it, and twitch it now and again,' Martyn explained. 'And of course it broke, as they do, and I bought the Echoplex and it sounded very nice, and completely by chance I found out you could make rhythmic noises with it. I was actually looking for sustain. I wanted to sound like Pharoah Sanders . . .'

Designed by Mike Battle, an Illinois electronics buff, the Echoplex first appeared on the market in 1959, and had undergone several refinements by the time John Martyn got his hands on one. The rectangular chrome box had a loop of tape fitted on top, and a sliding system of record and playback heads altered the delay in real time. Sustain and volume could be controlled separately, and, appropriately for Martyn, there was an additional effect labelled 'wet/dry mix'. Around 1971 Martyn began to dismay folk puritans by hooking up an array of foot pedals, Echoplex, fuzzbox, volume and wah-wah. The Echoplex gave an elasticity to his guitar, set up a rippling pond of ricocheting waves into which Martyn would chop new pulses, as if tossing pebbles into the mazy mirror. 'I just like the idea of making a machine human in that way,' he said, 'and I like impressing the humanness of yourself onto a machine rather than the other way round.'[8]

With his next record, the magnificent *Solid Air* (1973), Martyn managed to turn the opposed polarities of his Scottish and English upbringing to his artistic advantage. He steeped folk music in acid; made it vulnerable, open to all kinds of foreign invaders – cosmic jazz and improvisation, the ad infinitum of dub echo, the ghost of electricity. It was made in the receding tide of a tumultuous sea change in modern jazz, one that Martyn had been following with great interest. In the wake of Miles Davis's forays into oceanic electric music, beginning around 1969–70 with *In a Silent Way* and *Bitches Brew*, alumni of his groups furthered the advance into what became known as jazz fusion. Martyn especially admired Weather Report, the virtuosic ensemble started by Davis's saxophonist Wayne Shorter and keyboardist Joe Zawinul, who augmented the brittle percussive attack of the Fender Rhodes electric piano with distortion and volume pedals. Meanwhile, Martyn's hero Pharoah Sanders, a former colleague of the late John Coltrane, was immersing himself in oriental mysticism, offsetting passages of screaming atonal ecstasy with ruminative reveries like 'Astral Traveling', from 1971's *Thembi*. As late as 1998 Martyn was claiming never to have heard that track, but his song 'Solid Air' is remarkably similar, both in its chord progression and its throbbing, twinkling Rhodes washes. Martyn also consciously modelled his vocal style on Leon Thomas, an African-American singer whose moaning ululations appeared on Sanders's 1969 album *Karma* (which also featured Richard Davis, bassist on Van Morrison's *Astral Weeks*). Martyn referred back to this record time and again in interviews throughout the 1970s, claiming he wanted his guitar to sound like the sonic rivers he heard emanating from Sanders's hornbell.

Solid Air may not sound like a piece of free-jazz 'fire music', but its electric pianos and clavinets, vibes and congas add up to a potent bastard's brew stoked up by a man militant for love. 'You know when Pharoah Sanders screams with his horn, that's not anger, it's just a depth of emotion, it's a cathartic release,' he confessed to an interviewer after the album's release. 'It's an energy thing, it's better than fighting! You see music could be a force, the Indians have recognised that for years . . .'[9] The cover – again designed by Martyn – is a field of black interrupted by a circular photograph by the British pioneer of heat-sensitive and holographic imaging, John Webster. The image is deceptively tranquil: most people assume the spectral, iridescent ripples are caused by fingers brushing through water, but in fact it's a literal snapshot of a hand passing through solid air. 'You're seeing the heat the skin generates,' affirmed Martyn. 'It's what you see if you put your hand up in front of a fan, or even a breeze – using the correct film you will get that effect. The army use it to detect terrorists at night . . .' Inside, the tracks are a Jekyll-and-Hyde collection of tender acoustic balladry ('Over the Hill', 'Go Down Easy') and belching electric funk/rock stew, such as Skip James's possessed blues incantation 'I'd Rather Be the Devil' – here revisionist rather than reverential, reconstituting British folk as a glittering slew of mud flecked with gold dust. The devil rides out in 'Dreams by the Sea': an idyll is shattered by paranoid suspicions of infidelity; barking clavinets, *Shaft*-style wah-wah pedals and superbly funky drumming from Dave Mattacks throw jumpy, nervous shadows across the song. 'May You Never' is a catalogue of advice and admonishments dedicated to his two children, which could easily have been born of his own experiences: '*May you never lose your temper if you get in a bar-room fight/ May you never lose your woman overnight . . .*' By this time Martyn was sharing tour buses – and hotel beds – with teenage singer and Island labelmate Claire Hamill, to whose early albums he contributed guitar. 'It put an awful lot of strain on the family life, being a musician. You get trapped: there's a devil in me that definitely comes out now and again. No question. Same as in everybody, I suppose. I was a bit more upfront about it. I don't know why. Without being a songwriter, I think I'd have been a lesser person.'

Inside Out, released the same year, confirmed that monsters were hatching in the idyll. The real, darkling story is illustrated in the artwork: on one side, Martyn's silhouetted head is filled with a thunderstorm, while outside the sun blazes. On the back, the weather is reversed: sun in the brain, outside it's rain. Martyn turns in some of his most distinctive guitar playing so far, and a thicker, more spontaneous group sound is achieved with the addition of Traffic's Steve Winwood, Chris Wood, Bobby Keyes and percussionists Keshav Sathe and Remi Kabaka. With its suggestion of chopped-out cocaine, 'Fine Lines' alludes to the chaos of life on the rock 'n' roll road, '*Making the bread, going mad in the head*'. When he repeats the stanza about calling up his friends to '*talk about the love that I know is in us all*', you're no longer sure if he really believes in it. 'Ain't No Saint' is a drunken slur: '*Just get it together,*' he snaps, with no mental energy left for reasoned argument. The instrumental improvisation titled 'Beverley' sounds restless, uncentred. On *Sunday's Child* (1974) Martyn's cast as a wandering star, revolving far from the stable centre of his domestic life. He sends bulletins back home from hotels 2,000 miles away ('Root Love'), professes his undying commitment ('One Day Without You'), and on 'Clutches', in his now frequent 'devil voice', he proclaims how sweet it is to remain in the possession of his '*residential woman*'. He also dedicated 'Spencer the Rover' and 'My Baby Girl' to the children, Wesley and Mhairi (the couple's own son, Spenser, was born soon afterwards in 1975). 'Quite literally,' he confided to Ian MacDonald, 'the most important things to me are my children's smile and my woman's love.'[10]

If Martyn's home life was cracking up, musically he was pushing the envelope. His brushes with experimental and free music are rarely mentioned, but in the winter of 1975 he toured Britain with Danny Thompson and a mighty figure from the world of British improvised music – drummer and percussionist John Stevens. Free's Paul Kossoff was nominally part of the same group, although, in the throes of narcotic self-destruction, he barely made half the dates (Martyn had guested on Kossoff's solo LP *Back Street Crawler*). Martyn, Stevens, Thompson – this is the trio captured on *Live at Leeds*, privately released in 1975 by Martyn himself in an edition of 10,000 copies, sold by mail order from Hastings. Kossoff's erratic playing had to be cut from the finished master.

Live at Leeds is about as far out as Martyn ever soared. John Stevens is a massive presence at the centre of this maelstrom, simultaneously propelling the songs forward and chiselling their foundations apart. Melting in the inferno, 'Inside Out' stretched to eighteen minutes of convulsive, chewy energy. Stevens only worked sporadically with Martyn after that, cropping up on several tracks on 1977's *One World*. Martyn, for his part, sang and played guitar on 'Anni', a single by Stevens's more rock-influenced group Away, and engaged in a couple of Stevens's Spontaneous Music Ensemble big-band scream-ups, which employed the drummer's philosophy of 'search and reflect', a studied, democratic approach to collective improvisation.[11] What footprints did Stevens's methods leave in Martyn's own music? 'The things I learnt from John Stevens weren't things you'd "learn", as such,' Martyn told me. 'There were thousands of things you learnt with John Stevens. A complex character. I liked him because he had a spiritual thing about him. The last time I worked with him, he said, "We'll all sit down and sing a note – the note that you're most comfortable with." Some of us sang better than others. And we came to this

The electric lyre: John Martyn on stage, late 1970s.

chord that we all liked. "Right – that's the chord we're going to write the piece about." Spontaneity is what I learnt from John Stevens.'

He learned more during the busman's holiday he took in

Jamaica in the first half of 1976. Carousing with the likes of Max Romeo, Burning Spear (Martyn guests on their *Man in the Hills* LP of that year) and the legendary dub producer Lee 'Scratch' Perry, his 'raving' side was encouraged to come to the fore. Like the spiritual jazz players Martyn had formerly revered, he was now exploring the other side – the male ego rampant. 'I find out they're all fucking ravers,' he exploded, 'selling junk to each other – pissing up and down the bars and beating their missuses up. It came as a bit of a shock, really.

'There was only three ways to get paid by that boy,' remembered Martyn of his days with Perry at the Black Ark studio. 'Dodgy dollars, hookers or blue movies. So eventually I just started doing it all for nothing. We were mostly doing the same thing at the same time. I wobbled in and brought an Echoplex, and he'd never heard one before.'

Perry collaborated on the dub-rock number 'Big Muff', a double homage to the distortion pedal and the female anatomy, written after Martyn saw Perry playing ribald games with Chris Blackwell's animal-shaped breakfast crockery. The track appears on 1977's *One World*, the final bright bloom in the garden of British folk-rock. With its luminous, glassy production – credited to Blackwell himself – and contemporary flourishes such as drum machines, Moog synthesizer and Yamaha organ, plus tablas and a couple of orchestral backings courtesy of Harry Robinson, it's a signpost towards a possible future for Martyn's music that never quite materialised. Martyn's Echoplex guitar is used almost symphonically in places, in an 'infinite' repeat that would resurface in later post-punk guitar groups like The Durutti Column and Felt. As foils to Martyn's kaleidoscopic echo guitar, Steve Winwood's gum-pot synths and John Stevens's muscular funk drumming are the record's lifeblood, but despite the sonic vitality, the theme of the record is exhaustion. 'Dealer' and 'Smiling Stranger' thumbnail-sketch the less salubrious characters from the rock 'n' roll circus. 'Couldn't Love You More' is a last peal of unconditional love, and 'Dancing' giddily special-pleads for the singer's domestic absence. The title track is usually assumed to be a utopian call to unity, but it's actually an existentialist, outsider's plaint: '*Most of us . . . don't know what it means to take our place in one world/ To make our peace in one world*' . . . a world that's, in the final analysis, '*cold and lonely*'. When I put that interpretation to Martyn, he admitted it was 'a difficult question', but concluded, 'It was definitely meant to be a positive thing – it was supposed to be a unifying thought, but it is a cold and lonely world for some – that is a fact. And I think that's a compassionate thing, more than a grieving thing – I'm saying, some fucker's far worse off than you are, baby. It's difficult to perform because it's very emotional, and it's kind of intense.'

One World was partly recorded at Island's Basing Street Studios, but portions were also taped on a mobile unit at Chris Blackwell's Berkshire estate, Woolwich Green Farm, which was ringed on three sides by an ornamental lake. One morning, between three and six o'clock, the engineers set up a pair of amplifiers on floating pontoons, spaced widely apart on the water. Martyn set up a drum machine and his effects pedals in an outdoor spot overlooking the lake, plugged in his guitar and taped the extraordinary instrumental 'Small Hours'. Over a programmed electronic heartbeat, and picking up the ambient sound of geese honking on the shore and the distant rumble of a goods train, Martyn practically breathes through his guitar pickup, squeezing stained-glass chords through his tenderly applied volume pedal. Time seems arrested; the music is the still centre of a turning world of surging waves and intermittent bird calls.

The torrential spate of the post-war British folk-rock impulse dries up here, with this monumental, deeply elegiac leave-taking. It had been a long voyage from 'Back Down the River' via 'Dreams by the Sea' to 'Small Hours', but Martyn's transformation of the acoustic guitar into a boiling electric lyre was complete. He had never had much time for the earthier reinventions of traditional folk tunes in any case. 'I don't like when they put a 4/4 against a lovely traditional tune,' he said in 2008. 'It's horrible, it sounds wrong. Fairport Convention, Steeleye Span, go away! It's not relevant to anything – it's a hybrid, like a cross between a swan and a duck, the rhythm section being the duck. As soon as you put that bass and drums on it, it coarsens it and changes the nature of the music and makes it into something quite unacceptable to me. I love proper folk music – Martin Carthy, Dick Gaughan, Eliza Carthy, The Watersons and all that stuff, but as soon as they put a fucking 4/4 on the back of it, it's no good at all.'

On 'Small Hours' and on live versions of 'One World' which he performed throughout 1978, the chords spread out in oceanic wrinkles, flowing into one another and undulating like water finding its equilibrium. The surf lapping peacefully at the shore knows nothing of the tempest in the middle of the ocean. John Martyn's most beloved songs are like this: rollers breaking innocently at our feet, gentle backwash from the thunderheads, hurricanes and typhoons raging in the distant sea. 'Obviously one loses one's innocence as one gets older,' he confessed in the late 1990s, by then a confirmed Buddhist, 'but I think innocence really is permanent. It *is* permanent. And whether it can be regained once lost, I don't know. I would probably believe so. Depends how thoroughly you look at yourself, and how thoroughly you examine your internal mental processes. I think if you do that to a strong enough extent, and with a good will, then you could recover your innocence. And, as I say, recovery is not the point really; it's to work with innocence – it's just like the well of life, isn't it? I'm a great believer in that. I believe we all come from one great pit of life, and we zip back. Might come back as a piece of grass, or a microphone, or a bullshitting Scotsman.'

The pain that lies so forcefully behind Martyn's music may well lie in that strange family divide that slashed through his childhood, the same rift that gifted him his unsettling plural voices and the fatally errant behaviour that made him both family man and adulterous rocker. 'It's always been there, a mainstay, really,' he admitted. 'My emotional condition will always predicate and pre-dictate . . . It will always drive the music, my own state, if I'm happy or sad or indeterminate, or, Heaven forfend, spiritual. It's very direct. I don't try – it's just the way it happens. I've never tried in my life – honestly I haven't.' Most of all, it is the pain of separation from an innocent belief in the power and permanence of love, believed in because he did experience it, in those far-off, late-1960s days, the days of all heart and no head, before the Fall.

11

Fire

None could have other than natural or organic thoughts if he had none but organic perceptions.

William Blake, *There Is No Natural Religion* (1788)

Effort and contrariness change the directions of time.

The Incredible String Band, 'The Eyes of Fate' (1967)

At the heart of the earliest civilisations glowed the fire. Its warming blaze enabled humans to extend their social time into the darkness of night; it flooded an otherwise cold, dark area with heat, light and protection from wild beasts. Its flickering circle defined a social space that could include an entire community, and the golden ring became a focus for entertainment – storytelling, communal singing, conversation, magic or religious ritual. As primitive societies altered their behaviour from nomadism to arable farming, that social space became fixed, and the fireplace was the hearth of the village. Smoke could be transformed into a prehistoric telegraph system, and blazing hilltop beacons could relay simple communications from coast to coast.

The global village sprang up in 1962. In the 1960s the combined electronic media of radio, telephony, television and computers acted as a new string of blazing beacons, conveying messages around the planet's rim. The anthropologist of the global village was the American thinker Marshall McLuhan. The phrase was coined in his book *The Gutenberg Galaxy* (1962), and has achieved widespread currency in the age of the worldwide web.

In McLuhan's global village, the modern equivalent of the campfire was the light bulb. 'It creates an environment by its mere presence,' he wrote.[1] Eventually the light bulb would become

Bards of the global campfire: Robin Williamson (left) and Mike Heron of The Incredible String Band, 1967.

central to his famous notion of the medium as the message: the light bulb is a blank medium which holds no intrinsic content, but without it certain human experiences, architectures, etc., would not have been possible. Electric light has facilitated certain social interactions – allowing people to remain awake and active, at work or play, throughout the night without the need to forage for stocks of firewood – and its nature has contributed to new conditions for living, from high-rise towers to streets where lighting alone potentially deters attacks in otherwise dangerous zones.

If the 1960s were now the age of the global village, where were the bards making merry around the global campfire? Rock 'n' roll played its part in the phenomenon identified by McLuhan: the sounds of The Beatles, Dylan and The Rolling Stones sweeping around the world via international corporate distribution networks and world tours. But the group that, to a far greater extent, captured that elemental essence of music as an intimate rite in the flickering light, imparting sacred mysteries to rapt ears in the sapphire deep of night, was The Incredible String Band. The music of its prime movers, Robin Williamson and Mike Heron – stoned Noël Cowards preaching dropout gospel in the sapient tongues of the mystic Beats – burns at its own pace, smouldering and erupting into showers of rhythmic and lyrical sparks. Flickering between tempo changes and vocal registers, over a blistered surface of alien instrumentation imported from expeditions in far-flung regions – testimony to the global momentum of the McLuhan generation – the music consumes everything thrown into it in a blaze of inspiration. With their polyphonic parley of exotic instruments, they even *sound* like the music you'd expect to hear at a world village corroboree. Wilfrid Mellers – the English classical-music critic who analysed The Beatles with the seriousness of a musicologist – referred to the group as the 'now familiar "global village" folkies' in a 1969 album review.[2]

In the unique symbology devised by William Blake, the visionary poet and artist whose work has ever exerted a strong influence on Robin Williamson, fire (as the characteristic feature of Hell) illuminates the path to an instinctive understanding of the divine. Blake insisted that the sacred was located within humans, not fenced off and curated by the Church or other external institutions. Blake harboured a deep distrust of formal learning and blind common sense that froze up the imagination; the sentiment, if not the metre, of the lines '*His twilight words may melt the slush / Of what you have been taught,*' from The Incredible String Band's 'You Know What You Could Be', is Blake redrawn. In the Blakean cosmos, sense and sexuality, pleasure and pain, grace and sin are all part of the continuum of the divine – none are considered transgressions. Prometheus, the thief of fire – who appears in 'The Mad Hatter's Song' as '*the problem child, still juggling with his brains*' – was a kind of saint, for attempting to grasp the forbidden elemental energy. Finally, fire, in the shape of the sun (Blake's Sol), is the common element that unites Heaven with Hell. In the wider scope of world mythology, fire is a symbol of earthly light and interior vision; also of transformation and ritual purification. In alchemy, relentless heat reduces impure matter to its base elements. The Hindu goddess Shiva, notes Joseph Campbell in *The Power of Myth*, is depicted cradling a flame designed to scourge away the veil of time and open the mind to eternity.

The subtitle of McLuhan's book *Understanding Media* was *The Extensions of Man*. It's a phrase that comes to mind when contemplating the graven images that Blake etched around his writings. The scratchy lines delineating the tiny human figures that punctuate *The Marriage of Heaven and Hell*, and even the very letters themselves, frequently extend into snaking flames, like arrows of energy darting into some spiritual dimension. Elsewhere Blake takes his lines for a walk, with grapevines of text twining out of their stanzas. Forms that resemble vegetable growth patterns and shapes found in nature are known as phytomorphic (from the

Greek *phyto*, meaning plant). The music of The Incredible String Band was equally *phytosonic*. With no drum kit to lock down the tempos on their earliest albums, the pace of the songs minutely accelerates or slows down, growing odd tendrils of melody or budding out fresh stamens. Just as the totality of a flower is composed of root, stem, leaf and petal, so String Band songs such as 'My Name Is Death' or 'A Very Cellular Song' each contain differently styled passages, as if viewing different components of a poetic thought through successively stronger lenses. The multifarious instrumentalism – Heron and Williamson multitrack tin whistles, flutes, harpsichords, ethnic drums, fiddles, lutes, gimbris, ouds and sitars, as well as their own guitars – is brilliantly inventive, while the refreshed palette of each song, flicking between Bahamian calypso, lurching bar-room blues, folk–raga fusion, Celtic psychedelia and Jacobean minstrelsy, eludes the concept of a fixed 'String Band sound'. Strings and voices occasionally veer out of tune, but the effect is not the ramshackle musical jalopies of The Holy Modal Rounders or The Bonzo Dog Doo-Dah Band; when Williamson improvises dhrupad-like vocal swoops on 'The Mad Hatter's Song', it is a clutching after notes, the visionary's probing towards the unknown regions of his own capability.

Blake wrote of 'fire seeking its own form'.[3] Visualising the sound-shape of a plucked sitar or oud note suggests a leaf or a flame: beginning with a sharp pluck, its elliptical duration swells in the centre and decays to a sharp point. Incredible String Band music has its roots in the ground but extends its tendrils, seeking the sun's life-giving force. 'In those days, before the Moog synthesizer had really got going, the only way to make interesting sounds easily was to get interesting instruments,' Robin Williamson once explained.[4] As their fellow explorers Pink Floyd, Soft Machine and Jimi Hendrix were discovering in the late 1960s, the jolt of electricity sustains, distorts and mutates the materiality of sound. But until the early 1970s The Incredible String Band's music was almost entirely constructed from acoustic materials played and sung in real time, the only artificiality or 'weirdness' arising from their extensive use of overdubbing to build up a phantasmagorical junk orchestra of obscure, fabulous instruments: idiophones, aerophones, singing membranes and free reeds; or the serpent, the shofar and the lur, the ophicleide and the tárogató, the bombarde and the gayageum; and even more improbable contraptions, such as the tambang, kalipac and tittibuk of Lord Dunsany's sumptious, decadent fictions.

In the summer of 1967 millions may have been halted in their tracks by the sonic fictions of *Sgt Pepper's Lonely Hearts Club Band*, but The Incredible String Band's *5000 Spirits or the Layers of the Onion*, released one month later in July, was an infinitely more intimate and disorienting happening, a perky potlatch of ideas and space shanties that teased and eluded interpretation as deftly as the White Rabbit of Wonderland. The previous summer, steered by Joe Boyd, Robin Williamson and Mike Heron had released *The Incredible String Band* on Elektra as a trio with English banjoist Clive Palmer: what Williamson later described as a 'gypsy vaudeville jug band Celtic mixture'.[5] Photographed for the cover holding exotic string instruments – a gimbri, a tromba marina and a Ukrainian bandura – in Harold Moores classical-record shop in Soho, these three musicians wore their outsider status with confidence. Growing up in Edinburgh, Williamson left school at seventeen to join the bohemian, shoestring local community forming around folkies like Archie Fisher and Hamish Imlach, hanging out in nicotine-wreathed coffee shops and folk clubs, reading an extensive, visionary mix of Jack Kerouac, William Blake, Robbie Burns, Dylan Thomas and D. T. Suzuki.

Through the likes of Fisher, and his own researches, Williamson discovered 'an existing [local] tradition going on that was neglected enough for it to be quite wild, you know, like a wildflower? Because the tradition hadn't been tampered with at all in Scotland . . . So the folk scene in Scotland wasn't a revival, exactly. It was all still there. As it was in Ireland. It had never gone away. So when we came in with a new take on it, we were taking it right from the source, rather than from the revival.'[6] In 1962 he found a musical partner in Clive Palmer, strongly influenced by American interwar figures such as Uncle Dave Macon (a one-man repository of old-time music, vaudeville, jug band, blues, gospel and comic songs) and the nostalgic banjo music of the Edwardian music hall.

Born in north London during the Second World War, Palmer's itinerant teenage lifestyle took him to Scotland in 1962, where he met Williamson, by this time sharing a flat with Bert Jansch. Palmer moved in, too, and the 'three dreamers' (as Jansch later memorialised them in a song of that name) shared their lives until Jansch hot-footed it to London in 1964. One fateful night in May 1965 producer Joe Boyd wandered into a bar and was immediately seduced by Palmer and Williamson's duo, playing a weird mix of jug-band jigs and woolly folk standards, or, as Boyd later remembered it, 'Scots traditional music as if it had taken a journey to the Appalachians and back via Morocco and Bulgaria'.[7]

Mike Heron was drafted in shortly afterwards, escaping from Edinburgh rock 'n' roll and blues groups with loser names like Rock Bottom and The Deadbeats and a day job as a cost accountant. In May 1966 Palmer and Williamson started Clive's Incredible Folk Club, a tempestuous after-hours folk shebeen above a department store on Glasgow's Sauchiehall Street that attracted a host of folkies, freaks and local gangsters. When the plug was understandably pulled on the club after a few months, the trio adapted the name for their own ensemble. They recorded their first Elektra album, *The Incredible String Band*, but Palmer and Williamson were restless spirits, and for them, at the time, the album was the closing of a chapter. In July 1966 both of them separately bought one-way tickets out of Scotland. Palmer struck out with a friend on an epic hitch-hike that took him from Dover to Delhi. Williamson spent four months in Morocco with 'Licorice' (aka Christina McKechnie, the deceptively quiet schoolgirl who had recently become Williamson's girlfriend, and who eventually would become a member of the group), intending to study the local music and to make a permanent life there. 'I didn't intend to come back to Britain at all,' he tells me. 'When I went to Morocco I intended to stay there. I was going to learn the flute, the ney flute. And of course I was fascinated with the Sufi tradition. And there was the Gnaoua. I did see some of their ceremonies, and it profoundly impressed me.' After running out of funds, he returned to Scotland in the autumn, his knapsack stuffed with the gimbri, oud, shenai and bag of ethnic flutes he'd bartered for in the bustling souks of Fes.

Something marvellous happened during those blissful months in North Africa. For Williamson, as for so many other Western visitors at the time, opening the hotel doors onto the streets of Fes or Marrakesh was like stepping back hundreds of years to a medieval market town throbbing with exotic life and tinged with sensuality. 'It was like going back to the Middle Ages, yes,' he agrees. 'Particularly the Arab towns, the medinas. They had no cars, just donkeys and camels, and little tiny alleyways. Except for the radio – the radio was everywhere. Wonderful music on late at night. The royal band singing songs at one, two o'clock in the morning.' Later Williamson would vividly describe the Moroccan panorama in writing: 'legless beggars in carts and minstrels with drums and *hrittas* like ancient oboes or shawms with reed hard as an oyster. Buzzing flutes, and barbers plucking tunes on gimbris with mirrors on the back of them to show the customers the back of their shaved heads. Stoned, you would faint at the beauty of the king's walled garden. Reflections beyond reflections and jasmine buds pressed would perfume your finger for a whole day. Cool sour milk and hard black bread and figs and goat meat and the red-hot soup called *hrira*. Tea houses where *kif* smokers sat inviolate months at a turn; clapped to the music one hand against the breast, then both hands together in the air of God.' Riding around in horse-drawn carts, indulging in the pleasures of steam baths, observing the occult trance rituals of the Gnaoua drummers and steeped in hallucinatory kif smoke, the sheer vitality of the culture stoked up a new determination in Williamson. 'There was a glimmering of a way forward forever and it involved the casting of bread upon the water, the facing up or towards danger or through hubbub or the humdrum or humiliation and indignity of the human state or the century of the fuming west.'[8]

Within a few months of Williamson's return, he and Heron were staying at Temple Cottage in Balmore, north of Glasgow, working on the extraordinary set of songs that make up the first of The Incredible String Band's great albums, *5000 Spirits or the Layers of the Onion*. It was recorded during the early spring of 1967 at Sound Techniques in London. Joe Boyd, acting as producer, introduced the ubiquitous Danny Thompson on bass on many of the tracks. Other musicians made fleeting guest appearances: UFO club and *International Times* founder John 'Hoppy' Hopkins cranks out the honky-tonk piano on 'The Mad Hatter's Song'; Soma, aka Nazir Jarazbhoy, plays sitar on the same; and Licorice supplies several squeaky vocal interjections.

5000 Spirits begins with a few short bars of ruminative acoustic guitar before the remarkable sound of Robin Williamson sawing a

The Incredible String Band, *5000 Spirits or the Layers of the Onion* front and back covers (1967); *The Hangman's Beautiful Daughter* (original UK sleeve, 1968).

double-bass bow across the strings of a gimbri, a primitive North African lute with a crude rectangular body. Its insouciant, almost casual entry belies the otherworldliness of the sound here: a sense of the marvellous served up without fuss, like a starfruit placed next to a dish of bacon and beans. Then comes the opening line, '*The bent twig of darkness grows the petals of the morning . . .*', which brilliantly evokes two overlapping unfoldings in a mere eleven words – dawn's advance and spring's encroach. Much of The Incredible String Band's themes deal with the instant of becoming, the cusp moment when the cycle of growth sheds its slough and enters a phase of regeneration. The title of the following year's *The Hangman's Beautiful Daughter* is the most prominent example: Heron and Williamson claimed at the time that it represented both the 1960s generation taking over from their parents and a new phase for the group as individuals. ('The hangman is death and his beautiful daughter is what comes after,' claimed Mike Heron to Karl Dallas just before the LP's release in 1968. 'Or you might say that the hangman is the past 20 years of our life and the beautiful daughter is now, what we are able to do after all these years.')[9] There's a similar paradox – minus the temporal element – in the title of the final String Band studio album, *Hard Rope and Silken Twine*.

Very little of *5000 Spirits* occurs during the ordinary hours of daylight. There are repeated references to the dawn and the early morning, to events in the middle of the night, and to the internal day–night of dreams. Impressionistic memories of unwelcoming city streets occasionally surface, many traceable to specific locations in Edinburgh. Social and economic pressures melt away in the countryside's decelerated speed of life, accompanied by a lysergically heightened awareness of the moment: '*Gently tender snowdrop grows,*' sings Heron, '*See the past tense quietly go.*' The songs paint the surreally threadbare conditions in which they existed: farmyard animals intrude, gambolling mice kick footballs in broad daylight. Daffodils are placed between toes, pails hang on nails, nights end before they've even begun. In Heron's more fanciful, Edward Lear-ish numbers, a 'little cloud' points the way to '*distant lands wondrous and fair*', while a talking hedgehog's therapeutic mottoes are a jolt to a self-pitying lover: '*You know all the words and you've sung all the notes but you never quite learned the songs you sung.*' 'The Hedgehog's Song''s spiky injunctions to imbibe the music fully extend the moral into a life lesson. 'No Sleep Blues' details the dishevelment of Edinburgh and Glasgow squats, a '*delirium no-sleepum*' of post-acid comedown and feverish small-hours creativity.

The days at Balmore were quieter, and organised vastly differently from those of most working people; long after their clocks had unwound, these were people living a timeless life. 'Those were wonderful times,' Williamson reminisces. 'Balmore was actually much more tranquil [than the city]. "Waltz of the New Moon" was composed at Balmore. In an old railway car that had been dumped in a field, and I used to go up there and write. It was a great place to write, nice and quiet.' Being surrounded by nature was 'comforting', as Williamson puts it; the gates of Eden could be allowed to swing open in their own time, not be forced apart by narcotic callipers. 'In those days, people were trying to gatecrash Paradise by using drugs, often with disastrous results on their own psyche,' Williamson observes. 'And there were many casualties, some of whom I knew quite well. I suppose "The Mad Hatter's Song" is sort of about that. Because there clearly is something to be learned about the mystery of being alive, but whether you can do it by all-out assault . . . Societies which have used shamanic mysteries have got a backup built into the society to support people who undertake these voyages into the unknown. But the 1960s had no backup, and no preparation for these people, who were chucked out without a parachute.' And why, at the foot of the Campsie Fells, would the Mad Hatter have been on his mind? Because in

Lewis Carroll's Wonderland, the Hatter and the March Hare exist in a stopped-clock world: hosting an eternal tea party, endlessly shuffling around a table of dirty cups. The Hatter enjoys such an intimate relationship with Time that he has learnt to control it. 'Suppose it were nine o'clock in the morning, just in time to begin lessons: you'd only have to whisper a hint to Time, and round goes the clock in a twinkling! Half-past one, time for dinner!'[10]

As if to compensate for the lack of sunlight, *5000 Spirits* is loaded with obsessive recurrences of eyes, seeing and looking – attempts to perceive the radiance of ordinary things. '*My eyes are listening to some sounds that I think just might be springtime*' ('Painting Box'); '*you must have to see clear sometimes*' and '*I will set my one eye for the shores of the blind*' ('The Mad Hatter's Song'); '*Oh who can see in the eyes of fate / All life alone in its chronic patterns?*' and '*All is in the eye and in its blink of seeing*' ('The Eyes of Fate'). There is the sense of trying to transmute a colourless present into a rainbow of synaesthetic revelations. 'Chinese White' takes its title from a shade of paint: the '*cloud-cream lapping*'. Amid images of inertia and entropic decay (a dying plough, a mouldering book), the duo intensively double their voices to urge, '*Will your magic Christmas tree be shining / Gently all around?*' The song is an awakening of the spirit, from the whitewash of routine to a tinsel illumination of the soul.

If the album's side one is largely set in the morning of consciousness, side two is its twilight. 'The Hedgehog's Song' and 'First Girl I Loved' are gentle, oddly comic mullings over innocence and experience (the passage of time making the former lover '*a grown-up female stranger*'). Their whimsical sense of regret takes a harsher turn with 'My Name Is Death', a mordant dirge that could have been intoned from the Reaper's black hood in *The Seventh Seal*. '*You must come to clay*,' the figure beckons, and 'clay' is also the last word of the next song, 'Gently Tender', whose nervous, panting rhythms act out the shadows and serpents flickering in the '*green bush trees*'. Arcadia may have been attained, but the miracle is simultaneously undone: '*All my wine is water*,' '*All my pearls are clay.*'

If The Incredible String Band's mission was to deliver 'a crash course in the transformation of an entire culture',[11] then 'Way Back in the 1960s' imagined the revolution already long in the past, and its perpetrators left befuddled by subsequent developments. As a piece of reverse sci-fi, it's a mind-boggling riposte to Paul McCartney's 'When I'm Sixty-Four', which essentially imagines cosy retirement in a world unchanged. Williamson's song, by contrast, takes place after a '*wild World War Three*', with a grizzled nonagenarian, hoarding '*real food tins*', reminiscing to his grandchildren ('*I can't even understand you when you try to talk slow*') about times when 'making your own entertainment' involved going to the cinema, and when travel was hard because '*we still used the wheel*'. Hilarious, prescient and cheekily derisive of the group's contemporary audience: the song embodied everything that made The Incredible String Band simultaneously of their time and hovering gloriously above it.

Organic forms in graphic art can be traced from William Morris's prints and textiles, via the *fin de siècle* art nouveau movement, to the distinctive artwork of late-1960s counter-culture artists like Hapshash and the Coloured Coat and The Fool, whom Joe Boyd commissioned to paint the cover art for *5000 Spirits*. The Fool – a Dutch couple, Simon Posthuma and Marijke Koger – embraced the group's panoramic vision with gusto. 'If you want to get really deep about it,' Robin Williamson once reluctantly confessed to a 1979 interviewer, '[the title] seemed to be a symbol of consciousness. You know, you either think of it as layers and layers and layers of onion or thousands of voices.'[12] The sleeve is a psychedelic schematic with the all-seeing eye at its dead centre. All four elements are layered: earth, with its root systems visible in cross-section; air, giving life to the emerging plants and flowers; water, in the shape of curling waves at the top of the sky;

and on the reverse side, the names 'Robin Williamson And Mike Heron' are delineated in flames. Above the elements soars a winged hermaphrodite Janus, wearing the planet Earth as a pendant and presiding over the rotation of the heavenly bodies. In fertile loam at the foot of the sleeve lies the onion, its shoots sprouting from a bulb bisected to reveal its irregular concentric layers. As well as being a common denizen of the domestic vegetable patch, the onion has a powerful position in myth and lore: the ancient Egyptians buried it with their dead as a symbol of eternal life, while it is a popular image in modern psychology to dispute the idea that a personality has some terminal inner core; instead, the heart of the onion represents just another layer of a complex and unfinished personality.

These visionary ramblers cloaked their imaginations in the dark stole of rural sanctity. Solemnity and studiousness bedded down next to tweeness and wit; a song like 'The Eyes of Fate' could be profound and still mock its own pretensions. '*Do what you like,*' insists 'The Mad Hatter's Song', recalling arch mage Aleister Crowley's 'Do as thou wilt.' A moment's hesitation, as if adjusting expectations, then the line modulates to a resigned nihilism: '*Do what you can . . . My poor little man / For Jesus will stretch out his hand no more.*'

In the summer of 1967 The Incredible String Band travelled to the United States to perform at the Newport Folk Festival. Passing through Elektra's New York offices on their way back, they helped themselves to as many LPs as they could carry from the famous Nonesuch International Series, which was part of Jac Holzman's record-company empire. In the wake of Alan Lomax's pioneering Columbia World Library, Nonesuch was one of the first off the block to market the indigenous music of non-Western cultures with professionalism and integrity. Their world-music releases had been available for a few years, but in 1967 producer David Lewiston and field recordist Peter K. Siegel initiated the Nonesuch Explorer Series, recordings from far-flung regions marketed at a sophisticated younger listenership assumed to possess the intelligence to join the aural dots between ancient ethnic musics, modern folk and psychedelic rock. Robin Williamson and Mike Heron walked away with albums of kabuki theatre from Japan; of Bulgarian choirs; Greek bouzoukis; an album of guitarists from the Bahamas – Brucie Green, Frederick McQueen and Joseph Spence; and one of the first widely available glimpses of Balinese gamelan, *Music from the Morning of the World*. Steadily imbibed along with hallucinogenics over the following autumn, this grand bazaar of non-tempered noises would play its part in steering the direction of the album The Incredible String Band created in December 1967. It's the album that remains their best known, one that took them to a high placing in the British charts: *The Hangman's Beautiful Daughter*.

There is a story told by Thomas Butts, a friend and patron of William Blake, who visited the artist's Lambeth dwelling one day to find the front door unlocked and no one answering his knock. Passing through the empty house, Butts eventually discovered Blake and his wife Catherine sitting in a summer house in the back garden, 'freed from "those troublesome disguises" which have prevailed since the Fall'.[13] By way of explanation, Blake told him that they were playing at being Adam and Eve in the Garden of Eden, reciting passages of Milton's *Paradise Lost*. In 1968 The Incredible String Band were playing a similar kind of game (although they kept their troublesome disguises on). 'The only way to make the world into a paradise is to behave as if it WAS paradise,' contended Williamson just after *The Hangman's Beautiful Daughter* came out.[14] Now, he explains, 'I think everyone in the 1960s believed the world was about to change for the better – that was the thing about Woodstock. Everyone thought the world was about to change, right away, for the better. I think I probably seriously believed at that point that money would become obsolete, and that war was a thing of the past, and the global village would . . . it certainly seemed that it was going to happen, and it was a shame, but there you are.'

On the front cover of the original British edition of the LP, Heron and Williamson are silhouetted against a crisp, ultramarine sky: shepherds of the delectable mountains in thick woollen cloaks, striding the snow-dusted Scottish moor with visionary radars tuned to the ether. On the back, in the chestnut light of a Caledonian December afternoon, the skysailors have rejoined their ragged community for an informal portrait at the fringe of Lennox Forest.[15] Iain Skinner's photo, taken on Christmas Day 1967, has become one of the iconic images of British counter-culture. Licorice squats on the right, cuddling Williamson's dog

The Incredible String Band, *The Hangman's Beautiful Daughter* (1968), an iconic image of British folk-rock.

Leaf with an inscrutable, faraway gaze. In the centre, Heron's new girlfriend Rose Simpson peeps coyly round long black tresses (both partners would be officially inducted into the group about a year later). Five of the children of Mary Stewart – landlady at the Balmore house which was The Incredible String Band's base – stare at the lens wearing a variety of eccentric costume hats. At the back, two male friends from Balmore, Roger Marshall and Nicky Walton, overlook the scene like stray attendants from the fringes of a Holbein family canvas. The two artists submerge themselves within this motley band. Heron loiters to one side holding a curious child's monkey mask; Williamson crouches low in the centre, brandishing a toy Chinese red dragon. The wristwatch worn by the young girl in the foreground is the only detail that places the scene in the twentieth century.

The photo communicates the idea that whatever the 'Incredible String Band' consisted of at that stage, it was an entity more than the sum of just two musicians: it's a nomadic family of lovers, confederates and acolytes. Using so many foreign instruments reinforced the sense of inclusivity. There was no place for the virtuoso – anyone could pick up a harmonica or a pair of finger cymbals and join in. The pair peppered *Hangman's* with more varied textures than on *5000 Spirits*: Heron plays sitar, Hammond organ, guitar, hammered dulcimer and harpsichord; Williamson guitar, gimbri, penny whistle, percussion, pan pipes, piano, oud, mandolin, Jew's harp, shehnai, water harp and harmonica. They may have been dilettantes on many of these instruments, but *Hangman's* is a great deal tighter and denser-sounding than the previous release, and less sweetened with frivolity.

Most of *The Hangman's Beautiful Daughter* has the cluttered, disjointed aura of a dream. Side one is more vaudevillian, from the mocking Gilbert and Sullivan chorus line of 'The Minotaur's Song' to the campfire spiritual sections of 'A Very Cellular Song'. Meanwhile, after Mike Heron's rejection of urban life in 'Mercy I

Cry City', the duo spend the remainder of side two meandering down a winding Lethean waterway of dream and fantasy. The genre-shifts across the whole LP, from Bahamian spiritual to Indian hymn, Elizabethan lament to acid raga, smoggy industrial blues to abstract neo-gamelan improv, act as scene changes for a living theatre peopled by an alternative Tarot deck of increasingly bizarre archetypes: the Minotaur, the Witch, the Monkey, the Emperor of China, the Wizard of Changes, the City, the Woman with a Bulldozer, the Amoeba . . .

The first song on the record, 'Koeeoaddi There' (its meaningless title created by rolling a letter-covered dice), was, according to Williamson's later recollection, 'a dream from start to finish, the dream I had put to music, so it has the same logic that the dream has, which is not much logic'.[16] With no musical overture, his words raise the curtain on a scene already teeming with movement and growth: '*The natural cards revolve, ever changing/ Seeded elsewhere, planted in the garden fair/ Grow trees, grow trees . . .*' 'Natural cards' suggests a hand shuffling the Tarot pack, whose suits are divined according to their 'natures'. Then comes a riddle: '*Earth, water, fire and air/ Met together in a garden fair/ Put in a basket bound with skin . . .*' A basket bound with skin must be the human form, composed of the four elements, or humours, and placed on Earth (the 'garden fair'). Then Williamson, the impish tease, casts this red herring back into the waters: '*If you answer this riddle you'll never begin.*' Much later, pressed about these lines, he commented: 'If you answer the riddle you'll never begin; there's no answer to the riddle . . . There are bits and pieces about early memories in Edinburgh and so forth, but it's a collage song with bits of this dream, bits of early childhood, and it's basically the fact that I consider that life is pretty much an unanswerable riddle, with not really much of an answer to it some of the times. I think that's its magic.'[17]

'Koeeoaddi There' primes listeners for the organic development of most of these songs, with startling internal changes of pace and mood, ranging from childhood memories to fairy tales and fantasies, philosophical ramblings, supernatural apparitions and Dr Seuss-style semantic conjuring tricks. Conscious use of random operations played a part too; Williamson admits that he was using chance 'all the time' during this period. The centrepiece is 'A Very Cellular Song', a thirteen-minute cluster of disparate musical molecules culminating in an amoeba's love song (*'If I need a friend I just give a wriggle / Split right down the middle'*). Over the song's duration it splits into seven distinct segments and even ingests two other songs whole. One is 'Bid You Goodnight', a joyful Caribbean call-and-response song by The Pindar Family which itself lifts lines from the Old Testament and the Psalms. The other is 'May the Long Time Sun Shine upon You', a Sikh farewell blessing used in kundalini yoga. Here, Heron beams it out as a holistic hymn, a blissed-out cosmic canon while *'the energy projection of my cells / Wishes you well'*. 'Part of "Cellular Song" was written on acid actually,' recalled Heron afterwards. 'Most of it on one trip, kind of through the night, before the dawn. It wasn't personal though. I was writing a song for the world while on acid.'[18]

Such complete communion becomes the driving force of the second side, which travels from the *'brick and noise and rush'* of a city that's *'trying to steal my soul'* towards mental and spiritual renewal. In 'Waltz of the New Moon', the album moves into its lunar phase. Nature reveals itself as a crowd of deities: the new moon's sliver is perceived as the eyelid of God and the ring of Krishna; a storm breaks, the waters rise, bearing Williamson's gnomic questioning of reality: *'Ask the snail beneath the stone, ask the stone beneath the wall / are there any stars at all?'* Williamson then bids the Fire King's daughter bring water; its trickling is heard coursing into 'The Water Song', a Buddhist meditation on transformation: *'O wizard of changes, teach me the lesson of flowing.'* The deluge gathers force, white-watering into the whirlpool of 'Three Is a Green Crown'. And amid this sitar / bouzouki / gimbri

Death and regeneration: the Hanged Man and his beautiful daughter
the Empress, from the 1909 Rider Waite Tarot deck.

drone, the hangman's daughter begins to reveal herself.

The key to the code is in the song's title, which indicates the third
card in the Tarot's Major Arcana: the Empress. 'I've always been
interested in the Tarot,' Williamson tells me, 'not as a fortune-telling
tool, but as something which tells you more about the present. And
more about yourself in the present. It's also a wonderful book of
pictures. The song is an evocation of that card.' In the most common
Tarot artwork, the so-called Rider Waite set, the Empress is
depicted wearing a crown wrapped in a green laurel wreath, sitting
on a stone seat surrounded by a field of wheat, a green wood and
a waterfall: she is, in short, Mother Nature. Her crown is a cluster
of twelve stars: the wheel of the year. In the biblical Revelation
of St John, a woman with a crown of twelve stars is 'the Earthly

Paradise': the Empress is thus associated with the Garden of Eden. 'In another order of ideas,' adds A. E. Waite in *The Pictorial Key to the Tarot*, 'the card of the Empress signifies the door or gate by which an entrance is obtained into this life, as into the Garden of Venus; and then the way which leads out therefrom, into that which is beyond, is the secret known to the High Priestess . . .' – a reading explicit in Williamson's invocation in 'Three Is a Green Crown': '*Oh second self, oh gate of the soft mystery.*'

In the numerology of the Tarot, the Empress is strongly linked with the Hanged Man, the dying god who perishes at the winter solstice and is reborn with the spring. The Hanged Man is sacrificed upside down on a tree or cross of living wood: resurrection is implicit in his death. His immolation sets the eternal cycle spinning once more, ready to give birth to his beautiful offspring. Williamson's contemplation of the Empress concludes not too far from the '*Love is all and love is everywhere*' of The Beatles' cosmic epic 'Tomorrow Never Knows': '*Vibrating light, forever one the sun / The book of life is open to us / There'll be no secrets left between us.*'

'Swift as the Wind' is one last aside from Mike Heron, describing the apparition of an ancient pagan warrior in his childhood bedroom, while the adults scold his fantasising brain: '*You must stop imagining all this, for your own good / Why don't you go with the rest and play downstairs?*' The disquiet is matched by a weird, arhythmic vocal delivery that Heron would repeat on later songs, as if the words are trying to punch their way out of a sack.

At the last, 'Nightfall' descends, '*washing thoughts of the day on your waters away*'. Guitar, sitar and skittering mandolin eddy lightly around each other in a becalmed lagoon, as sleep, '*night's daughter*', projects dreams through cinema-screen eyes, with the prospect of the blank page of dawn looming ahead. The rumbling, tumbling rickshaw of time deposits us back at the cloud-cream lapping first light of 'Chinese White' on *5000 Spirits*. The hangman is hooded, his eyes deliberately blinded; his daughter is born at sunrise. Here, as the curtain falls, is the final manifestation of the hangman's beautiful daughter: the emergence from the murk of ignorance into a radiant rebirth of Gnostic consciousness.

The Hangman's Beautiful Daughter was released in March 1968, before the snows of winter had entirely melted in the Highlands. The sonic wizardry made heads smoke; the pantheistic fusion flared like a bonfire of religions, fuelled by the duo's ecstatic scrying games. From this elevated position, The Incredible String Band were incapable of going downstairs and playing with the rest. There were few maps at the time to navigate the waters the duo were sailing; no one fused the enlightenment of existing in the landscape so powerfully with the luminous effects of acid. To quote that great hippy philosopher, Winston Churchill, the album is a riddle wrapped in a mystery inside an enigma. It embodies the dream of starting anew in a paradise of free love and altered consciousness without forsaking the wonderment that drives the quest for understanding.

With the album reaching number five in the national charts, their influence began to vibrate beyond the confines of their immediate circle. Paul McCartney had already claimed *5000 Spirits* as his most treasured album of 1967; The Rolling Stones' *Their Satanic Majesties Request* is notably studded with String Band-isms, especially in its use of exotic ethnic instruments. The Stones entertained hopes of signing the String Band to their record label, and, perhaps inspired by the group's commitment to incorporating world-music elements, Brian Jones headed off in the summer of 1968 to Morocco's Rif Mountains to record another 'music from the morning of the world': the pan pipes and trance drumming of The Master Musicians of Jajouka.

On stage, the String Band appeared to emanate from a distant time zone. 'The stage takes on the form of a recently raided music shop when Robin and Mike are performing,' wrote one contemporary critic. 'They themselves move around the instruments like two wandering minstrels somehow reincarnated into the 1970s. At one time I just could not visualise either of them in a twentieth century setting. It was beyond my imagination to conceive of them travelling in a train or eating a Wimpy. For them I pictured woods and water, trees and little stone cottages with smoke twisting into a sky.'[19]

During 1968 the line-up of The Incredible String Band changed. In April they performed a big concert at London's Royal Festival Hall, supported by Tim Buckley, to introduce the *Hangman* album. Two American tours (one in May, another in October–November) accelerated the doubling of the group's amoebic cells, as Heron and Williamson included girlfriends Rose Simpson and Licorice in the line-up (Simpson took a crash course in playing the bass guitar). Meanwhile, the group's cellular structure was boosted by a chance meeting with two British dancers they met while rooming at New York's Chelsea Hotel in June. Malcolm Le Maistre and his partner, Greek-born Rakis (aka John Koumantarakis), were members of The Exploding Galaxy, a dance and mime troupe who had entertained London's hippy throng at UFO, Middle Earth and the Arts Lab. They were listening as The Incredible String Band performed 'Maya' live on local radio station WBAI, and bumped into the group as they returned from the studio to their hotel. A late-night conversation led to the proposal of an extended collaboration (which began with the dancers romping about on stage at the String Band's June Fillmore East gig). Returning to Britain, Le Maistre rented a disused farmhouse in West Wales, large enough to house an artistic colony. Sited between the fishing village of Newport and a small settlement called Velindre, Penwern sits on a hill near the spot where Stonehenge's bluestones were supposedly quarried. Robin Williamson and Licorice moved in soon after, although Heron and Simpson kept their distance, visiting only occasionally from Scotland. An ever-swirling host of visitors and hangers-on descended on the place over that summer and autumn, including Ivan Pawle of Dr Strangely Strange, an Irish group whose ramshackle, surrealist folk owed a debt to the String Band but rarely matched it. The clan sucked up vibrations from the nearby Pentre Ifan, a megalithic cromlech spreading its energies across the nearby villages and farms and out over Newport Bay. Over the spring, summer and autumn Heron and Williamson cut the double album *Wee Tam and The Big Huge*; cast themselves and their friends in a home-made film that was eventually incorporated into the documentary *Be Glad for the Song Has No Ending*; toured America again; and joined the Church of Scientology.

> What is it that we are part of?
> And what is it that we are?
> > The Incredible String Band, 'The Half-Remarkable
> > Question' (1968)

Wee Tam and The Big Huge, written and recorded intermittently between April and August 1968, was first released as a double album, although Elektra's American office shortly afterwards split it in two, a catastrophic decision not least because it diluted album sales, but also because the four original sides clearly form a single thematic continuum. It would take many more pages to wrestle with the entire rich and vast span of allusion, mythopoetics, connective leaps between the earthly particulars and the universal generalities (implicit in the title itself), and red herrings at play. To summarise, though, the gist of the record is a wholesale cognitive clear-out, in which Heron and Williamson toss their accumulated religious baggage on the bonfire.

Wee Tam unfolds at a slower and more reflective pace than *Hangman*, as if, following the flaming winter jamboree of the previous record, the seers are now left alone through a long, hot summer, contemplating the dying embers of their revelations. Heron's contributions, 'You Get Brighter', 'Greatest Friend' and 'Air', are anthems soaked in benign light, while 'The Mountain of God' is composed entirely of lines cherry-picked from the biblical books of Isaiah and Hebrews, the *Book of Common Prayer*, *The Church of Scotland Hymnal* and a dash of A. A. Milne. Williamson's songs, especially, combine the oceanic and Ossianic: flowing odysseys of thought in which sheaves of biblical and religious quotation are stacked athwart lyrical, bardic utterances. Guitars and keyboards hang light as thyme sprigs next to the saffron buzz of a sitar. There is a pervading theme of marshalling forces for a spiritual quest. '*Mariners, mariners, gather your skills,*' exhorts Williamson, a twentieth-century Noah, in 'Maya'. '*Come let us build the ship of the future/ In an ancient pattern that journeys far*' ('The Circle Is Unbroken'). The mariners, spiritual and religious leaders and mythical beasts assemble over the whole record in myriad references: Lazarus, the Lion and the Unicorn, Merlin, Maya (Hindu goddess of illusion), Hitler (in two separate references), Richard the Lionheart, the Three Kings, Moses, Cleopatra and Jesus. The byzantine fusion of global instruments now held court with a Babel of world religions.

Many of the songs refer to a state of wandering in hostile, barren wilderness, saddled with a bulging sack of religious baggage that needs to be discharged. In 'Lordly Nightshade' Williamson is loaded down with '*a big bag of coal on my head . . . vaguely seeking some fire to burn*'. '*I asked the ice, it would not say/ But only cracked and moved away,*' '*I ain't got no home in this world any more*'; '*I wear my body like a caravan/ Gypsy rover in this magic land*' ('Ducks on a Pond'); '*Island I remember living here/ Wandering beneath the empty skies*' ('Maya'). Man is a vulnerable mouse, a sweetmeat for the '*hawk of truth*'. 'Job's Tears' confronts the moment of Christ's Passion, laying the events of Golgotha on top of Robert Graves's assertion, in *The White Goddess*, that the dying Messiah manifests the universal archetype of the king sacrificed to appease the gods to perpetuate the natural cycle. The symbolic landscapes recall Christian mystic poets like Thomas Traherne or John Bunyan, whose every step of his *Pilgrim's Progress* is peopled by an archetype or a signifying tract of ground. In Mike Heron's 'Douglas Traherne Harding', the singer describes paying at a toll gate to cross a river to where he '*enjoyed the world aright*', but when he sneaked across to avoid the toll, '*cold I was, no crown did I wear*'. The song betrays a dissatisfaction with the easily won freedoms of his generation. Can freedom really be achieved so cheaply, with no personal sacrifice? If there is any conclusion to be drawn from *Wee Tam and The Big Huge*, it is that enlightenment must come at a higher cost than most of their contemporaries were prepared to pay. The passion with which the String Band addressed the quest made the mystical pretensions of other contemporaries merely sound like the honeyed crumbs of those who had no bread.

Perhaps the real clue as to why the group embraced organised religion lies in the album's very first lines, on 'Job's Tears', a kind of 'welcome back' message to their listeners: '*We're all still here, no one has gone away/ Waiting, acting much too well, and procrastinating.*' 'Procrastinating' is the key word: they may have let time slip by in the past, but now is the time to put away childish things. Spiritual gurus of questionable integrity were 1968's must-have accessory in the pop world. The Incredible String Band actually had a meeting with the Maharishi Mahesh Yogi in mid-January 1968, in Lund, Sweden, several months before The Beatles' famous visit to the ashram at Rishikesh, although they were disillusioned by the financial commitment required by the yogi. With oriental mysticism fast becoming part of the repertoire of fashion, The Incredible String Band seemed to be asking, is enlightenment any more than a rummage through the dressing-up box of the world's religions?

'*All this world is but a play / Be thou the joyful player,*' runs the chorus of 'Maya', and *Wee Tam and The Big Huge* is peppered with references to players, acting, even film-making and projection (likely inspired by the presence of Peter Neal shooting *Be Glad for the Song Has No Ending*, which was made while the current crop of songs were in progress). 'In the end,' comments Williamson, 'it seemed to me Buddha was right: the world is basically an illusion caused by the senses. It appears to be getting truer and truer as physics progresses.' 'The Iron Stone', a song Williamson has continued to perform regularly into the twenty-first century, enacts the vision that flames into being when the narrator grasps a lump of alien rock found on a beach. The stone acts as a portal to hidden dimensions: in a puff of smoke, the colourful denizens of a vanished Atlantean world rise up before him, and he joins the cavalcade in the guise of a dragon. 'I still have the iron stone,' Williamson reveals. 'I found it on the beach at Cramond, near Edinburgh. I think it is a meteorite. No one's actually authenticated it, but it certainly looks like one. It's a mysterious and intriguing thing. It's about eight inches long, but very heavy. It stands up, it's got a flat end, like a standing stone. It had come from so far away, from outer space, and it seemed to be carrying this atmosphere of parallel worlds and possibilities.'

With its resident dancers and costumed chinoiserie, The Incredible String Band began to present itself as a magical revue by a troupe of wise jesters, whose insights and wit were as preposterous or as revelatory as you wished to make them. The hijacked BBC documentary that eventually surfaced as *Be Glad for the Song Has No Ending* degenerates into various piratical pantomime sequences around the beaches of Newport Bay and the mystic dolmen of Pentre Ifan, with Mike Heron and Robin Williamson the gold-skinned gods weighing souls in the balance. The Victorian-amateur-dramatics look became a trademark of subsequent live appearances. One of the first American critics to grapple with the Incredible String Band spectacle, on the Boston date of their autumn 1968 tour, chronicled their stage presence:

'Festooned with colorful rugs and cluttered with instruments, the stage on which they appeared had the aura of gypsy encampments. That aura was heightened by an occasional waft of incense and by the presence of two girls known as Licorice and Rose [. . .] who live, travel and perform with the band. Resplendent in beads, braids, silks and velvet, Robin and Mike wandered about, sipped tea, and spent interminable intervals tuning up. But once they started singing, they wove a trance. Their lyrics connect the natural and supernatural, transmuting homely details into talismans of the beyond. An ordinary object like the stone in "The Iron Stone" evokes a vision of Atlantis, of a divine jester called "Sir Primalform Magnifico", of "forests and centaurs and gods of the nights". The meandering songs, some of them 25 minutes long, contain dreamlike cascades of cryptic imagery . . .'[20] One of these might have been 'Creation', a sixteen-minute epic which closed the otherwise disappointing album *Changing Horses* (1969). With multiple scene changes, a marvellous passage emulating a stormy sea, and a clutch of false endings, it's the last taste of the *Wee Tam* soundworld before their music entered a more problematic phase.

Showmanship and multi-instrumentalism was on display at a 1969 show at the University of York: 'They showed a strong, modest pleasure in being close to instruments. The four of them – Liquorice [*sic*] of the missing tooth and big dipper hemline being fourth – got through bass guitar, acoustics, electrified acoustic lead, violins, sitar, mandolin, organ, tin whistle, piano, ocarina, bongos, tambourine, triangle, harmonica and big bass gong. And between each song, a big shuffle-round, a big hunt-the-next-instrument, a big fight with the mikes. A good performance in itself. Rose is just great with a microphone: charmed and wary like a child close to a bumble-bee.'[21]

In the harsh winter of 1970, in the group's new artistic community at Glen Row, a terrace of cottages on the Glenconner estate in Peebleshire, south of Edinburgh, the String Band and their dancers, renamed Stone Monkey, dreamed up *U*, a lengthy multimedia

The Incredible String Band at Glen Row, Scotland, 1971. Left to right: Mike Heron, Robin Williamson, Rose Simpson, Licorice McKechnie.

parable for the stage. Opening as a ten-night run in April 1970 at the Roundhouse, north London, *U*'s digression-heavy plot narrated the conceptual birth, death and reincarnation of a soul. Robots, prostitutes, highwaymen, pirates, levitating mermaids and cosmic beings popped up along the route. After London, the whole show was airlifted to New York for another five nights at the Fillmore East. Despite large and enthusiastic audiences, *U* proved to be a financial sinkhole. In an attempt to recoup some of the losses, the four String Band musicians shed their dancers and trappings and played the show as a music-only affair along the West Coast, dropping into a San Francisco studio to rush-record the *U* songs, which Elektra released as an autumn double LP.

Fans adored *U*, critics wriggled uncomfortably; and The Incredible String Band's comet began its long, slow descent towards its eventual 1974 break-up. *U* and the attendant theatricals were much more Robin and Licorice's bag; Rose Simpson left shortly afterwards, and Mike Heron reconnected with his rock roots by making the solo album *Smiling Men with Bad Reputations*, produced by John Cale and featuring members of The Who. The theatrical side of the String Band was part of their charm, but the substance lay much more in the religious investigations of their earlier work.

In a printed songbook from 1968,[22] each member was asked to scribble a short profile, including date of birth and details of their education. 'Music is prayer,' Williamson stated in his entry, adding, 'everything else is interesting in an infinite sort of way.'

By the end of 1968, with this latent religious tendency whetted by the creation of *Wee Tam and The Big Huge*, the foursome were ready to jump off the rumbling, tumbling rickshaw of time and rest a while on the steady, heady boulder of truth. Their minds were cleansed and open to offers. At a vegetarian restaurant in New York in November, Joe Boyd left the group sitting with an old acquaintance from his student days, David Simon, a former member of Jim Kweskin's Jug Band. Unknown to Boyd, Simon had joined the Church of Scientology, and signed up Licorice and Williamson the very next day. Heron and Simpson enrolled in London shortly after their return home.

The immediate effect of crossing L. Ron Hubbard's 'bridge to total freedom' in The Incredible String Band's music was that the lyrics became less cryptic – the urge to communicate directly and with clarity came to the fore. The positivity of an album like *I Looked Up* (1970) may reflect their experience of Scientology's 'going clear', a process designed as a 'release from all physical pain and painful emotion'. The strongest changes were felt on an organisational level. Joe Boyd recalls that he 'began to notice interesting changes in their personalities. They had always avoided discussions about money; now they eagerly convened meetings about group finances. Touring schedules and recording plans were sorted out quickly and efficiently . . . Internal jealousies seemed to evaporate overnight. They stopped taking drugs or alcohol . . . The results seemed to be a happier, saner group of people who had become a pleasure to deal with.'[23]

'I wouldn't try to trace [Scientology's] influence in my music, because my music has always pursued pretty much its own course, you know, almost independent of my life,' commented Williamson in 1979. 'It's actually a very practical philosophy. It enables you to live slightly better, get on with your fellows slightly better and feel a bit happier about things. That's the reason that I'm interested in it – it's very usable and practical. I've been rather romantic and spiritually inclined. It's probably been helpful to me because of its practicality.'[24] Perhaps they simply needed to give that toll keeper his due, as if the mental effort to juggle all the unresolved 'contraries' (the word was a favourite of Blake) in their music was beyond human endurance.

Rose Simpson left the church around the time she left the group, eventually becoming involved in Welsh local politics and becoming Lady Mayoress of Aberystwyth in 1994. Mike Heron, who has continued living at Glen Row ever since, left the church in 1983; Williamson appears to have made a final separation around the mid-1990s. Licorice, who remained in the group until 1972 even though Williamson was now married to the group's American manager Janet Shankman, spent the 1970s initially as a member of U-Boat, a group led by David Bowie's former drummer Woody Woodmansey (also a Scientologist), then in California as a member of The Silver Moon Band. She married Brian Lambert, the guitarist in Williamson's Merry Band, and spent some years living in the Hollywood Hills. From the early 1980s onwards, when she supposedly divorced Lambert, information on her life turns to illegible blotches, water spilled on the watercolour. One rumour has it that she was seen living homeless in the streets of Los Angeles, moved to one of California's desert cities in the late 1980s, wrote a letter, postmarked Sacramento, to her sister in Edinburgh in 1990, then walked off into the Arizona Desert, never to return. Long after her final communication, many are still waiting to see if she crosses back over the bridge, while fearing that she may have turned to clay.[25]

The intention behind the early String Band repertoire is to see the world whole, with its physical and metaphysical components interconnected. Named gods have vanished, but God is everywhere. If their methods can appear occasionally whimsical, childish even, it is because, like William Blake, they forced themselves to divine a plane beyond the material realities of their time and preserve the state of innocence that is necessary for belief, keeping at bay the 'experience' that introduces doubt. Vision, as in visionary art, is a form of whole sight that restores the imagination, the state that the world of common sense tries to annihilate. And like their music, vision is a synthesis of contrary elements, a marriage of Heaven and Hell whose purpose is – *pace* 'The Circle Is Unbroken' – to find the '*light that is one, though the lamps be many*'.

At the close of *The Big Huge*, on the magnificent 'The Circle Is Unbroken', the sitars and ouds are faded down in favour of more distinctively Celtic elements: pan pipes and harp. It anticipates the development of Robin Williamson's art in later years. In 1975 he moved to Los Angeles, playing low-key dates in bars and making occasional albums with his Merry Band, including *Journey's Edge* (1975), *American Stonehenge* (1976) and *A Glint at the Kindling* (1979). In America, this native of Scotland with Northern Irish ancestry was paradoxically pulled back towards his own Celtic roots. 'Like looking through a telescope backwards,' he laughingly recalls. 'Well, America in general prompts one to do that, because of, say, the Irish community in Chicago – it was where [the 1850 "bible of Irish music"] *O'Neill's Music of Ireland* was written. The first Scottish Gaelic translations of the Bible were done in

North Carolina, in the mid-nineteenth century. And so there was a big longing back towards kind of an imaginary Celtic roots in America. And I got the idea: wouldn't it be nice to write songs in that vein – new Celtic songs? And after that I got into storytelling, and I was one of the first people to use the harp in storytelling, and developed the harp as a piece of bardic equipment, to try to deliver spoken word with improvised, spontaneous music.'

In the early 1990s Williamson returned to live in Cardiff with his new wife, Bina, an East African Asian raised in the Sikh tradition. Together they developed a permanently touring, seasonally adjusted musical and spoken-word project that spun a new rainbow thread of religions and folklores – Sikh, Christian, Celtic, Jewish and beyond, 'trying to present the extraordinary fact of being alive, without any sort of dogma'. Adopting the harp as his main instrument, he took on the role of global-village bard: a mobile repository of oral history, a shamanic (re)teller of folk tales and Celtic sagas such as those found in the *Mabinogion* and the *Book of Taliesin*. In his fifties Williamson also emerged as a singer of devotional poetry, setting mystic verse by William Blake, Dylan Thomas, Henry Vaughan, John Clare, Walt Whitman, Thomas Wyatt – all writers who in their own ways perceived a truth transcending the physical world and intensified by the immersion of the self within it.

The global village, in its original context in McLuhan's *The Gutenberg Galaxy*, was not an example of gleeful futurology. It was a warning. The global village would become, as real villages often are, a society suspicious of outsiders and intolerant of out-of-step behaviour. McLuhan foresaw with horror the approaching end of print culture, with its privileging of the individual conscious voice. If print and books were the technologies that nurtured individualism in world culture, the return to the oral culture of the electronic age held the potential for a new form of worldwide tribalism in which, metaphorically speaking, the drums that beat loudest would command the strongest influence over the public domain, thus opening the door for totalitarianism and rule by terror. But the global village in the digital age is a more utopian community: the democracy of interconnectedness exemplified by the early virtual community, the WELL (Whole Earth 'Lectronic Link), founded in 1985. As one of the last surviving entities which preserves something of the liberation theologies of the late 1960s, the early internet promoted popular holism that surfed the wave of economic globalisation that surged through the early 1990s.

A belief in the interconnectedness of all things, the web of life, is one of the key tenets of the modern-day Druid. The pre-Christian origins of the original Celtic Druid priest-caste remain largely a mystery, although it is interesting to note the etymology of the word, which is of highly antique origin. The component parts, filtered up through Celtic, Greek and Latin from distant Indo-European roots, are '*deru*' ('oak') and '*weid*' ('see', and by extension 'vision, knowledge'). Thus, a Druid is a wood enchanter who acquires vision and wisdom through an innate understanding of the natural world. But the popular image of a Druid – bearded, white-robed, partial to mistletoe – is merely fallout from the antiquarian 'Druidical' revival of the eighteenth century. William Stukeley linked Stonehenge and Avebury with Druidic rites in his sensational studies of the monuments in the 1740s, which triggered a splurge of Albion studies and literature: scholarly works like Jacob Bryant's *A New System of Ancient Mythology* (1774), Edward Jones's *Musical and Poetical Relicks of the Welsh Bards* (1794), Edward Davies's *Celtic Researches in the Origin, Traditions and Languages of the Ancient Britons* (1804) and the unreliable patchwork of myth and poetry of Welshman Iolo Morganwg, founder of the bardic Gorsedd ceremony which survives to this day. A neo-Druidical society, The Ancient Order of Druids, was founded in 1781. This revival posited that the ancient Britons were direct descendants of Noah, and therefore that the British people could trace their language, faith, traditions and even bloodlines directly back via Adam to God Himself: a lineage highly attractive to William

Blake, who was then in the throes of writing such masterpieces as *The Marriage of Heaven and Hell* and *Jerusalem*. 'Adam was a Druid, and Noah,' wrote Blake, 'also Abraham was called to succeed the Druidical age, which began to turn allegoric and mental signification into corporeal command, whereby human sacrifice would have depopulated the earth. All these things are written in Eden . . .'[26]

So Druidry as it appears today is not a direct survival of a pre-Roman priest cult, but the occult companion to the reawakening of interest in 'the Matter of Britain' dating from the dawn of the industrial age. Prominent Britons, from Walter Scott to Winston Churchill, have been members of Druid orders; Queen Elizabeth II and the Prince of Wales are both honorary members of the Wales Gorsedd. The Order of Bards, Ovates and Druids is a post-war organisation set up in 1964 which has a custom of appointing an Honorary Chief Bard every ten years. A previous incumbent of that position was John Michell, an expert in mythology, sacred geometry and earth mysteries, and whose book *The View over Atlantis* came out in 1969, inspiring, among others, the founders of the Glastonbury Festival. In 1998 the position was given to Robin Williamson. It is largely a ceremonial role, and he is not himself a member of the Order: 'It doesn't involve anything other than giving me a rather nice ivy wreath,' he says modestly, though clearly moved by the recognition.

What is it, then, to be a bard in the twenty-first century? 'Well,' declares Williamson, 'it's clear that the tradition of being a travelling performer, or storyteller/singer kind of thing, particularly at the level that me and Bina are doing – village halls, arts centres, getting around the country – that's a very ancient tradition that goes back thousands and thousands of years. It's one of the last nomadic lifestyles that have survived into the twenty-first century.' Does he still believe, as he wrote all those decades ago, that music is a form of prayer? 'I do still feel that, yes. I also feel that music is a kind of teacher, because as you travel about following music, you do tend to learn a thing or two.'

Meanwhile, Williamson continued to refine his reinvention of his 'bardic equipment', the Celtic harp. 'A magic instrument', as he calls it, 'because it has all the connotations of the ancient stories, and rumour has it that angels play the harp. But in a way that's also its difficulty, because it's such a beautiful-sounding instrument, it's hard to make it sound harsh. It does sound sweet no matter what you do to it, so I'm trying to give it a certain amount of oomph.' The coarsened timbre of his harp can be heard to fine effect on the third of his albums for German label ECM, *The Iron Stone* (2007), containing scintillating updates of the perennial ballad 'Sir Patrick Spens' and a revisitation of his own 'The Iron Stone' – a song that continues to blaze, like a beacon, from a hilltop way back in the 1960s.

'What I wanted to do when I was seventeen was to write like Jack Kerouac,' explains Williamson, musing on his relationship to the word 'visionary', 'who I thought was able to write spontaneously. I thought that was a wonderful thing. And then I found out that Kerouac had some leaning back towards people like Walt Whitman and William Blake. And looking at William Blake, I found that he had quite a leaning towards the Druid tradition of Britain – certainly the notion of an inspired voice had a lot to do with the Druid tradition. And I think I'm trying to tap into that source of inspiration in that sense – that's visionary, and that's what I'm still interested in doing.

'The Druids today have reformed in a variety of takes, but presumably long ago, when the Romans first encountered them, they were the spiritual guardians of this particular island, and Gaul. And whatever they were about, I think human beings who want to be true to themselves and to their own inner nature are always going to follow the same sort of path. The word "God" isn't as interesting to me as the word "life". Because life, and being alive, is the extraordinary thing; even though "God" is a wonderful word, it's such a tangle of meanings people attach to it. Whereas life – everyone can agree that we're actually alive at the moment. We can't actually argue about that too much.'

A Collection of Antiques and Curios

'Sixteenth-century, if it's a day,' said Roger. 'Fresh as new.
How's it survived under that lot?'

Alan Garner, *The Owl Service* (1967)

The more you cut it back, the more it grows.
Anthony Shaffer, screenwriter, *The Wicker Man*[1]

Ghosts are memories with a stubborn will to survive; their
haunting is a refusal to be forgotten. Ageing objects carry with
them an accumulated charge of significance, with the potential
to unleash visitations from the past. Alan Garner's novel *The Owl
Service*, published in 1967, is a classic of young-adult literature that
mines the landscape of a remote Welsh valley, Celtic myth from the
Mabinogion, adolescent eroticism and buried familial transgressions
for dramatic value. It's set in a house near Garner's real-life home,
on the north side of the Cader Idris mountain in Gwynedd, north-
west Wales, a 900-metre-high rock already rich in superstition
without the need for fiction. Its name means 'the seat of Idris', and
the peak is held to have Arthurian associations; furthermore, locals
warn that anyone spending the night on the haunted mountaintop
may wake up either insane or gifted with a poetic muse.

Garner described Bryn Hall, the real building that inspired his
story, as 'a house among dark trees, a house without electricity, but a
house with more electricity than most people found comfortable'.[2]
The action in *The Owl Service* is let loose by the discovery of a pile of
antique crockery, concealed in a boarded-up attic. The distinctive owl

Strawbs, *Just a Collection of Antiques and Curios* (1970).

pattern on this dusty dinner service is traced by the teenage Alison onto sheets of paper and folded into origami owls, which causes the pattern to disappear from the plates. Lumps of pebble-dash mysteriously crumble away from a wall, uncovering a Renaissance fresco of a spring goddess. At the book's terrifying climax, Alison is attacked by a swirl of folded-paper owls that claw and tear at her body. Similar experiences, we learn, have occurred to previous occupants of the house as myth has persisted to play itself out in an unbroken chain. Long-buried memories continually reassert themselves in a series of ghostly correlations between past and present.

A creepy, bird-like automaton also appeared in the opening credits of the long-running BBC series *Going for a Song*, which ran from 1965–77. Framed as a quiz show in which contestants tried to assess the age and provenance of various items of pottery, furniture and paintings, it was a forerunner of the immensely popular *Antiques Roadshow*. These programmes' persistence indicates the special place in the British heart for old stuff, an impression reinforced by the presence of an antiques shop in almost every city, town and village the length of the land. Encountered in the tiniest hamlet, the bric-a-brac emporium acts as a time capsule, the swept-up repository of uninherited heirlooms, obsolete farm tools, chairs worn smooth by anterior posteriors, discarded medals and keepsakes in glass cases. The browser in an antique shop is confronted with the everyday domestic practical devices utilised by our forefathers. They are melancholy places: stockrooms where a nation warehouses its unclaimed losses. Turnover in such places is frequently slow; prosaic objects wait patiently to be resurrected as curios and ornaments.

'Going for a song': the phrase, first recorded in Shakespeare's *All's Well that Ends Well*, is redolent of its origins in an earlier age when music was less in thrall to market forces or publishing restrictions. Up until the 1960s, when it achieved a totemic power often out of proportion with its content, the popular song was the repository of cheap sentiment and romantic cliché, while folk songs were generated and regenerated as freely as the air we breathe. In early-twentieth-century America, the cross-nation traffic of accumulated cultures coalesced around the hillbilly sound of Appalachia to form what we now call 'country music'. Early practitioners like The Carter Family and Jimmie Rodgers managed to boil down the sprawling mulch of influences into a shellac-friendly popular-song format: songs that still retain a fragment of the root-tip of collective folk memory. Over the years, the term 'country music' has hardened into a tight genre,

Fresh Maggots, *Fresh Maggots* (1971); Dr Strangely Strange, *Kip of the Serenes* (1969); Synanthesia, *Synanthesia* (1969).

especially in the wake of the modernised country rock of the late 1960s and onwards, where the music's centre of gravity shifted from the Appalachians to Nashville and Texas, and finally to Laurel Canyon: the gold rush in the Rhinestone Hills.

The most creative and revisionist period in American country – when cosmic cowboys such as The Byrds, Gram Parsons, The Flying Burrito Brothers, Mike Nesmith et al. modernised a roots music that was already becoming Vegas-friendly – came exactly simultaneously with the folk-rock movement in Britain. Even in the UK, there were certain artists – former Fairport vocalist Iain Matthews among them – who embraced American country-rock styles even as the group he had just left were steeping themselves in Caledonian jigs and reels. There are echoes of US country in certain tracks by Sandy Denny's group Fotheringay. But although it's difficult to separate the idea of country music from the spangly image of Dolly Parton and Kenny Rogers at the Grand Ole Opry, it's tempting to rescue the term to describe the singularly British music that flourished immediately after the frontiers were opened by the elemental pathfinders – Pentangle, Fairport, The Incredible String Band and John Martyn. Artists such as Clive Palmer's COB, Strawbs, Forest, Trees, Mr Fox, Dr Strangely Strange, Trader Horne, The Albion Country Band, Bread, Love and Dreams, The Woods Band, Tír na nÓg, Mellow Candle, Moonkyte, Steve Ashley and others made music that fell into an uncategorisable ditch, somewhere between the better-travelled roads of pop, psychedelia, folk and progressive rock. Like American country, their material was composted from a variety of musical residues, but here the elements stretched further back in time. Pagan chant and Christian hymns; medieval, Tudor and Restoration secular sounds; the nature-worshipping verse of the revolutionary Romantics; and an occult communion with the British landscape were all factors spun into the sonic web, along with the requisite dusting of foreign and exotic instrumentation.

This 'British country music' tapped indigenous roots, while fashioning the sound in modern tailoring. It tends to play up the atmospheric effects that make the countryside seem most transcendent – offering an organic experience as far removed as possible from the urban. Time runs slower in the country; magic, myth and murder intertwine and have not yet been swept out of its mysterious corners. If some of it verged on easily satirised tweeness, such as the self-conscious debut of Dr Strangely Strange, at its best it retained the tumbledown hardiness of a drystone wall. Running away from the city can bring ecstatic highs and inner peace, but it can also place the refugee face to face with nature at its most forbidding and alien. The poet Edward Thomas, reviewing his 'Georgian' contemporaries' verse in 1913, could have been describing British country music half a century in the future: 'It shows much beauty, strength and mystery, and some

COB, *Moyshe McStiff and the Tartan Lancers of the Sacred Heart* (1972);
Bread, Love and Dreams, *The Strange Tale of Captain Shannon and the Hunchback of Gigha* (1970); Trees, *The Garden of Jane Delawney* (1970).

magic – much aspiration, less defiance, no revolt – and it brings out with great cleverness many sides of the modern love of the simple and primitive, as seen in children, peasants, savages, early men, animals and nature in general.'[3]

In a pair of English hands – those of George Formby, or Tommy Steele in *Half a Sixpence*, for instance – the banjo and ukulele are instruments whose very sonic properties reek of nostalgia and musical trivia. The banjo's staccato clucks cue up mental images of toy towns, cheap laughs and holiday variety shows. Banjos, mandolins and hammered dulcimers are all over the incidental music of 1960s BBC children's series *Trumpton* and *Camberwick Green*, whose stop-motion puppetry embodied English small-town and village life at its most parochial. *Bagpuss*, another BBC animation from the mid-1970s, was set in a crypt-like antiques shop whose dusty denizens come alive to invent stories and songs about bits of discarded dross that appear in the shop window. The folk-singing ragdoll Madeleine was voiced by Sandra Kerr, and her banjo-plucking frog accompanist was John Faulkner, both former alumni of Ewan MacColl and Peggy Seeger's Critics Group.

Clive Palmer, one of the three original members of The Incredible String Band, got his first sniff of a banjo at the age of ten, when he acquired an old Cammeyer model built in the age of King Edward VII. He taught himself to play using an instruction book dating from the same period, and for ever afterwards Palmer retained a particular penchant for Edwardian folk and music-hall tunes, an end-of-the-pier nostalgia. Palmer is an elusive fish in British folk, a single-minded individual content to catalyse then move on; a happy-go-lucky musical antiquarian with an undoubted gift and an idiosyncratic ear, but whose wilful lack of ambition kept his career in a perpetual state of arrested development. His claim to fame will always rest on his founding role in The Incredible String Band, but his actual contributions to the trio's first, self-titled Elektra album are relatively modest. Of the sixteen tracks, the group only play three as a trio ensemble. As for the rest, Palmer contributes one solo song and partners Williamson on one further track, and the remainder is Robin and Mike's show. Between leaving The Incredible String Band in 1966 and his 'retirement' from music in 1974, he was a peripatetic figure whose life at the time was lived on the fringes of society, in a breadline blur of low-rent cottages and caravans, pubs and folk clubs.

His greatest act of nomadism was the epic journey he made in late 1966, crossing Europe and continuing via Beirut, Damascus and Kuwait to Kabul; then, via Baghdad, across Iran to Kathmandu, the Kashmir and into the Indian subcontinent. In a stroke of weird luck that would typify his later life, he was invited to appear on a Delhi TV show by two girls he met in the street. But if Williamson's North African sojourn laid the foundations for the String Band's forward-looking, pan-global soundworld, Palmer's next move, in 1967, was to relocate to London, team up with folk guitarist Wizz Jones and record an album of nostalgic music-hall tunes produced by Donovan's manager Peter Eden. *Banjoland* remained unissued until 1995: Palmer couldn't sell it to any labels at the time, and no wonder, as its genial, dryly recorded Edwardiana like 'The Boy I Love Is Up in the Gallery' and 'Smiling Through' must have felt crazily out of sync with the progressive, flamboyant flower-power pulse of 1967. In retrospect, that historical context is what gives *Banjoland* some of its charm. Heard alongside *5000 Spirits or the Layers of the Onion*, *Sgt Pepper's Lonely Hearts Club Band*, *Disraeli Gears*, *The Piper at the Gates of Dawn*, *Odessey and Oracle*, *SF Sorrow* or any of the other defining albums of the period, it offers a peaceful backwater, with Palmer and Jones bathetically picking away like a neglected sideshow in some poorly attended seaside concert hall while the glittering attractions parade their wares elsewhere.

With no takers for his antiquarian musical vision, Palmer moved to Cornwall in early 1968 and set in train a period of several years of wilful outsiderism. In this far-flung and relatively poor county – England's very own Wild West – the residue of the Cornish folk scene discovered by the likes of Donovan, John Renbourn and Mick Softley back in the early 1960s was still stumbling on, with a nominal focal point at the Folk Cottage club in Mitchell,

Music of the ages: COB, 1971. Left to right: Clive Palmer, Mick Bennett, Genevieve Val Baker, John Bidwell.

near Newquay. The landscape of relaxed frugality, rural solitude and cheap accommodation suited Palmer and co.'s somewhat ramshackle approach. He passed through four groups – The Famous Jug Band, The Stockroom Five, The Temple Creatures and Burning Bush – in the space of two and a half years. Then, in early 1971, while he was squatting in a caravan near Falmouth, word reached Palmer that Jo Lustig, the go-getting manager of Pentangle and Julie Felix, was on the lookout for new talent to sign to the Transatlantic label. Ralph McTell, an old friend, had recommended Palmer to Lustig, and offered to produce any new venture he might care to come up with. Palmer hooked up with Mick Bennett, a bookish free spirit who had wandered down to Cornwall in 1967 and never left, and Cornish guitarist John Bidwell. Bennett read poetry widely and all three were immersed in books on oriental philosophy, Buddhism and 'the search for meaning'. They called themselves COB (Clive's Original Band, pronounced 'cob') and hunkered down in the caravan to write a new set of songs. 'I used to go for long walks – it was easier then, there were less fences up – and dream them up as I went,' Bennett later recalled.[4] In a daze of hunger, living off a pauper's diet of biscuits, potatoes and cups of tea, the trio concocted the set that was recorded in May of that year as *Spirit of Love*. It's an understated collection, hymnal and solemn even on the more gospelised numbers like 'Wade in the Water' and the title song, with its '*Spirit of love move in thee/ Spirit of love set you free*' refrain. Palmer made a new version of 'Banjoland', laying the choppy notes over a field recording of an English seafront, sharpening the piece's Margate Sands reverie. But for the most part COB constructed mantric, hypnotic songs from acoustic elements – drones from harmoniums, massed voices and Bidwell's dulcitar, a customised dulcimer with a widened neck, causing it to sound like a lute superimposed on a sitar. 'Music of the Ages', 'Serpent's Kiss' and the Scots bothy ballad 'Scranky Black Farmer' are cast as vernacular plainchants. '*Time entwines my very soul / The tangled briar kills the tree,'* laments Palmer in 'Music of the Ages', the album's eeriest piece. He squints for *'the glimmer of an ember / Dwelling in the ashes here'* that will summon a manifestation of ancient ghosts, recalling John Ireland's Arthur Machen-inspired visions of dancing children on the Sussex Downs. Except that the theme of the song is the *failure* to keep the 'music of the ages' in view: he's confronted instead by a devastating void, *'the silence of a million tongues'*. It is the lament of the antiquarian, straining to visualise the past but losing the connection.

COB's next and final record, *Moyshe McStiff and the Tartan Lancers of the Sacred Heart*, extended the group's creative anachronisms, with more acoustic folk instrumentation gently augmented with Middle Eastern flourishes. Paul Whitehead's cover art set the scene: a pastiche of an Uccello-style Florentine painting of three armoured crusaders spearing a dragon in a windswept desert. Old and New Testament references abound in Mick Bennett's lyrics, a reminder of the confrontation of cultures as medieval Crusaders entered the lands of the Saracen or sought the Ark of the Covenant in the faraway African kingdom of Lalibela. 'Sheba's Return – Lion of Judah' opens with Palmer unfurling a snake charmer's sinuous lines on a clarinet; Danny Thompson (who had popped in to show his son what went on in a recording studio) grinds out shadowy vales of bowed double bass.

The esoteric-sounding album title is actually a composite of the group's nicknames: Bennett's Jewish / Scots ancestry led to the name Moyshe McStiff, while Palmer and Bidwell styled themselves the Tartan Lancers (the name of Ralph McTell's local off-licence). In more recent comments Palmer has downplayed its content: 'I think people are drawn to it today because of its sad, faintly religious atmosphere, but at the time that might have been what held us back. It's Middle Eastern, it's contemplative, and it's about quite serious subjects. There was no religious intention – it just came out that way. A lot of the time we felt like painters, making pictures with no definite purpose.'[5]

'*This life is nothing more than waiting for the sky to open*,' declaims Mick Bennett on 'Heart Dancer' at the close of the record. Poor and scrawny but demanding nourishment for their hermit souls, COB's home was the wilderness. On principle, these latter-day St Jeromes refused to draw state unemployment benefits, and busking was often their main source of income. There was little take-up for their two records (plus one misplaced 'reggae' single, 'Blue Morning'), and despite touring with Pentangle, COB split in March 1973 after one too many arguments between Palmer and Bennett. Palmer made little impression on the musical sphere afterwards, and spent most of the 1970s living off his skills as a carpenter and craftsman, from building a staircase for Ralph McTell to assembling woodwind instruments and making dental and medical appliances. After moving to Brittany at the end of the 1970s, he surfaced occasionally to reunite with both Mike Heron and (separately) Robin Williamson in the 1990s. He has remained a perpetual nearly-man, whose undeniable proficiency never quite translated into a career that would sustain him.

In 1970, while Clive Palmer was eking out his frugal existence in Cornwall's 'Cannabis Creek', Dave Cousins of Strawbs was, by contrast, somewhat overemployed. As one of the most highly regarded folk guitarists in Britain, he was in demand as an accompanist to visiting American artists like Joni Mitchell, Leonard Cohen and Arlo Guthrie. Cousins ran a weekly folk club and arts lab at the White Bear pub in Hounslow, south-west London, booking the likes of David Bowie and Edgar Broughton, and was working as a freelance producer for Denmark Radio (during the 1980s he was managing director of Devon Air in the south-west of England). His publishing company, Strawberry Music, administered Strawbs' own music and retained the rights

Antiques roadshow: Strawbs' *From the Witchwood* line-up, 1971. Left to right: Richard Hudson, Dave Cousins, John Ford, Rick Wakeman, Tony Hooper.

to Sandy Denny's song, 'Who Knows Where the Time Goes?', a nice earner thanks to Judy Collins's 1968 cover version.

Cousins was born David Hindson to a north London Catholic family in 1945. His father died when he was eight months old and his mother remarried, this time to a Protestant man with whom she had another son – a situation that would inform his song 'The Hangman and the Papist'. By the time Strawbs cut the live album *Just a Collection of Antiques and Curios* in 1970, the group had been through many incarnations. Cousins and guitarist Tony Hooper formed The Strawberry Hill Boys in 1964, inspired by bluegrass and American hillbilly music. (Appropriately, Strawberry Hill was also the name of the Twickenham castle/mansion built in the eighteenth century by author Horace Walpole, which kicked off the Gothic taste for pastiched architectural follies.) In the early autumn of 1966 Cousins, renamed after the Soho folk club, heard

Sandy Denny performing an early set of folk tunes at south London's Troubadour, and invited her to join the rechristened Strawbs. Peter Kennedy heard them rehearsing in the basement at Cecil Sharp House (with Trevor Lucas tapping out rhythms on a guitar case) and invited them to appear on his BBC *Folk Song Cellar* radio show. Denny unleashed her signature composition 'Who Knows Where the Time Goes?' on the group, who taped it in July 1967 during a two-week residency in Copenhagen.[6] Denny transferred to Fairport Convention twelve months later, before *Strawbs*, their first official LP, emerged in 1969. A&M Records threw a handsome sum of money at this slice of folk-pop, chambered-up with a small string section imported from Edward Heath's orchestra and featuring a group of Arabian oud players, plus John Paul Jones and Nicky Hopkins in backup instrumental roles. Indications of future directions came with the last track, 'The Battle', a blood-and-guts yarn set at the ramparts of a besieged castle. *Dragonfly* (1970) includes 'The Vision of the Lady of the Lake', a ten-minute epic fluttering with Arthurian emblems. Producer Tony Visconti helped Cousins engineer the weird, sibyl-ant vocal phasing that would play such a strong role in the group's music over the next few years.

The Queen Elizabeth Hall concert at which they recorded *Just a Collection of Antiques and Curios* saw Cousins and Hooper expand to a five-piece electronic folk-rock unit, with the addition of Rick Wakeman on keyboards, bassist John Ford and drummer Richard Hudson. Wakeman, a recent graduate of the Royal Academy of Music and then still a largely unknown session player, took centre stage with 'Fingertips', a postmodern-*avant-la-lettre* medley of pianistic styles ranging from Chopin, Jacques Loussier and lounge schmaltz to silent-movie melodrama. The twelve-minute 'Antique Suite' was a medley featuring distinctively scurrying harpsichord and lyrics inhabited by a tray of medal ribbons, a choirboy's cassocks, an unused wheelchair and Coronation teapots that '*bring about a sense of loss*'. As Cousins surveys this dusty collection of antiques and curios, it's clear a departed relative's memory is commemorated in this bric-a-brac. The record was wrapped up in a sleeve showing an assemblage of a lute, pottery, a tabla, sheet music and other trinkets, in the manner of a seventeenth-century Dutch still life.

In February and March 1971, with Visconti producing again, this quintet attempted to recreate the greenwood in Air Studios, whose windows ironically overlooked London's commercial epicentre at the junction of Oxford Street and Regent Street. A spectral, silverised photograph of a gnarled tree spreads its spidery twigs across the front cover; opening up the gatefold revealed the hermit St Jerome in a surprisingly lush wilderness populated with fishermen, an owl, a family of deer and a sourpuss lion. *From the Witchwood*'s textural weave is as crammed as that tapestry, a queer chiaroscuro patchwork of acoustic and electric colours, Mellotrons and organs, amplified dulcimers and haunting vocal special effects. While recording *Witchwood*, Cousins ran into one of Visconti's protégés at the time, Marc Bolan, who had recently converted his Tyrannosaurus Rex to T.Rex and was preparing to record *Electric Warrior*. Bolan frequently invented composite words ('starhide', 'diamondstar', etc.), lending his lyrics a gaudy, sibylline surface, and he encouraged Cousins to use similar techniques. Cousins, who by this time owned a house and weekend caravan in Devon, often writes as if he is lifting a distorting lens to his eye, resulting in scenes half-observed, half-imagined. '*A string of diamonds formed a stream / That tumbled down the daunting cliff to sparklebright on the beach*,' he marvels in 'A Glimpse of Heaven'. 'I used to walk along the deserted beach looking up at the cliffs with little streams trickling down, and at the patchwork fields, and to me, it was a glimpse of heaven, having lived in London all my life,'[7] he says. From this rapturous opening we descend into the darkness of the Witchwood itself, a place whose strange unearthly music focuses and intensifies the heightened state of awareness, while trapping the unwary into becoming the forest's '*bidden slave*': '*My fingers grew like branches/ I stood rooted to the ground.*' Finally, the trees supply the wood for the narrator's coffin. The song, Cousins later admitted, was written as a cautionary tale to his LSD-using road crew, 'who were well into mind-expanders, the Floyd and liquid lights'. Nature, implies Cousins's lyric, can get you higher than pharmaceuticals.

'The Shepherd's Song' recounts a day Cousins spent with his girlfriend in a hayfield near Box Hill. As they enjoy a post-coital dawdle in the long grass, a shepherd blows away the rain with his silver trumpet: for a brief moment Surrey has become the poetic Arcadia of Philip Sidney or James Thomson. But there's an atavistic streak to the album that refuses to be cowed by such blissful interludes. 'The Hangman and the Papist' is a moral fable, histrionically sung, of a Protestant boy chosen to wear the hangman's hood to execute a condemned Catholic, who turns out to be his own brother. As well as referencing Cousins's own family situation, the song alludes to the deepening Troubles in Northern Ireland, which were intensifying as the album was being written. 'Sheep''s pacifist message is played out in the scenario of animals being led to slaughter in a market town. A boy watches '*Row after row of raw carcasses/ Their blood runs in the gutters*', and then vows to '*Plant seeds of love/ And harvest peace*' when he is older.

The album's wuthering, windswept mood is mirrored in the arrangements: celeste, dulcimers and clarinets tumble around Wakeman's liberal Moog synthesizer and Mellotron, while the rockier rhythms strain forward against the pulse like a hound tugging at a leash. Cousins's voice has the tremor of one who is attempting to weave a spell; the diction often slips into archaisms, helping to position this music firmly apart from the Americanisations which had infiltrated mainstream pop, stamping it with a markedly British voice.

Groups that sounded 'folky' on the surface derived their feel because the tradition had been ploughed up, its furrows lying raw and exposed to new influences. Trees were a group of five Londoners who pushed the 'electric pastoral' sound further than most of their contemporaries. Guitarist David Costa had been one of those polo-necked attendees of the capital's folk clubs, and was especially taken with the pagan austerity of the Martin Carthy and Dave Swarbrick Topic albums.

Trees only produced two LPs, both in 1970; the first, *The Garden of Jane Delawney*, grafted limber, leafy rock explorations onto more formally clipped borders. Barry Clarke was a formidable Richard Thompson-influenced electric guitarist whose arsenal of feedback and effects shepherded older ballads like 'Glasgerion' and 'She Moved through the Fair' much further into organic rock pastures than Fairport ever ventured. They also took a worthy crack at 'The Great Silkie of Skule Skerry', an Orkney folk tale of a supernatural aquatic beast. Harpsichord provides a virginal twist to the macabre title track – the 'garden' being a cluster of savage fantasies inside Ms Delawney's Gothic dreams, including a river stained crimson with her lover's blood – while Celia Humphris's earnest, cut-glass choirgirl vocals inhabit a shaded arboretum whose formality places it beyond time. Bassist Bis Boshell wrote the song while still at school in 1965. 'I can't explain anything about it,' he admitted in 2007. 'I don't know who Jane Delawney is, what it means, or what influenced me in writing it. It just appeared as if from nowhere.'[8]

A young girl – Jane Delawney, perhaps – stands in a garden (actually Golders Hill Park in north London), rendered magical by Hipgnosis's treatment, on Trees' second and final LP, *On the Shore*. This is a curiosity cabinet of tunes old and new, from the thirteenth-century troubadour update 'Adam's Toon' to folk tunes 'Streets of Derry', 'Geordie', 'Sally Free and Easy' and 'Polly on the Shore', stoked up by Boshell's chunky bass injections. There are also modern facsimiles like 'While the Iron Is Hot', a song about nineteenth-century machine-breakers, and 'Murdoch', written at Boshell's family home in North Wales, just the other side of the Cader Idris mountain where Alan Garner wrote and set *The Owl Service*, and just as heavy with the forbidding landscape of awakened legends and imposing heights.

Trees were lopped off before achieving their full height, but the silky voice of Humphris (now Celia Drummond, wife of BBC radio personality Pete) exerts a continuing subliminal presence on the British populace, as she became a prolific female voice-over artist, playing the parts of bored housewives advertising chocolate bars or warning travellers on London's Northern Line to mind the gap.

The Lincolnshire Wolds contain some of the most historically charged landscape in Britain. Dividing the cities of Lincoln and Grimsby in a south-east-to-north-westerly sweep, this area has been occupied by various ancient invaders. The B1225 road is a remnant of Caistor High Street, built by the Romans to speed their legions between London and Hull. Several centuries later, Viking marauders made their homes here too, fresh off the longships that beached at what is now the windswept seaside resort of Cleethorpes. The locality has one of the highest concentrations of lost and deserted medieval villages in the country, settlements abandoned after the life was literally farmed out of the soil. The name 'Wolds' itself – derived from the Teutonic '*Wald*', or wood – flags the area as heavily forested. And so it is appropriate that the town of Walesby, which lies at the very edge of what is now an officially designated Area of Outstanding Natural Beauty, produced the group called Forest at the end of the 1960s. Brothers Martin and Adrian Welham, together with Derek Allenby, came together as a folk trio, The Foresters of Walesby, in 1965, with a similar range of rural folk songs to The Watersons, who lived not far north

Tanglewood tales: Forest, *c.*1970. Left to right: Adrian Welham,
Derek Allenby, Martin Welham.

in Hull. Martin and Derek moved to Birmingham to attend the
local university, and younger brother Adrian joined them in order
to make the group a going concern. By 1969, encouraged by their
heroes and friends The Young Tradition, they were writing their
own material on a small range of acoustic instruments, guitars,
mandolins, recorders and pan pipes, organ and harmonium.
Moving to London in 1969, they camped for a few weeks at
John Peel's flat, and the influential DJ's recommendation secured
them a place on the Harvest label alongside Pink Floyd, Deep
Purple, Third Ear Band and Shirley and Dolly Collins. They found
themselves recording their debut album at Abbey Road, parking
their old estate car between John Lennon's psychedelic Rolls-
Royce and George Harrison's stretch Mercedes, and adding the
studio's array of instruments – including the harmonium The
Beatles used on 'We Can Work It Out' – to their own mix.

Forest's entire oeuvre – two albums on Harvest, plus the early
single 'Searching for Shadows' – appears to take place inside a pre-

urban, pre-industrial *mise en scène*, a mental glade damp with dew and festooned with cobwebs. In sharp contrast with the impish dalliances of Dr Strangely Strange, Forest's tanglewood tales are maudlin and macabre. This is no Arcadia of lazy shepherds and obliging goatherds, but the emblematic landscape of Bunyan's *Pilgrim's Progress*, with its Hill Difficulty, By-Path Meadow, Enchanted Ground and Valley of the Shadow of Death.

The first album, *Forest*, with its faux-art-nouveau trees metamorphosing into wood-sylphs making music on pipes and lutes under a bright full moon, conceals odd flashes of American country stylings, with lap steel guitars. But by the time of *Full Circle* (1970), the group's gossamer orchestration of faerie instruments is more confidently realised, with clusters of harmonised flutes adding a plaintive chorus. *Full Circle*'s cover is another painting, this time a blustery heath with an abandoned church tower, straggly thorn bushes and a young woman with a swaddled bundle apparently sheltering in a pile of leaves. Inside the gatefold, the same scene is gruesomely transfigured: a gibbet with a hanged figure has appeared next to the tower; ominous bird-like forms loom out of the clouds; skulls and bones emerge from what was previously a pile of rocks and scrub; and the woman's baby looks like a corpse. The spectre of Arthur Machen's uncanny fictions casts its sickly shadow over this forsaken scenery. The church is actually a representation of All Saints' Church at the top of the hill above the Foresters' home village of Walesby, in which the fledgling group used to rehearse. Known as the Ramblers' Church, it was built in the twelfth century on Anglo-Saxon foundations near a national beacon site, and nearly a millennium's history is cemented into its stonework.

Appropriately enough for a group on a label called Harvest, there is a sustained autumnal mood across both records. It is a deathly seasonal interlude, that period between the cremation of the crop stubble and the witching hours of Halloween and All Soul's Night. Forest's last recorded track is called 'Autumn Childhood',

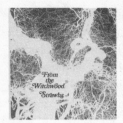  

Strawbs, *From the Witchwood* (1971); Trees, *On the Shore* (1970);
Black Sabbath, *Black Sabbath* (1970).

an eerie extended piece in which the smells and visual sensations of autumn trigger childhood fears and a sense of mortality: '*The dust and cobwebs left a pain/ That ploughed the furrows of the dead/ And burning woodsmoke filled my head.*'

Other songs described peasants dying of hunger ('Famine Song'), a ritualistic execution ('The Midnight Hanging of a Runaway Serf') and pagan animism ('Bluebell Dance'). 'Graveyard' is sung by a wandering phantom under a '*sharp moon*', recognising the body it formerly inhabited. 'I did genuinely have a dream,' says writer Adrian Welham, 'where I was looking at myself dead, basically. The moon was out that night, and if I'm conscious there's a full moon I never sleep well, even now.' Forest's music took a walk in Britain's ancient groves and stirred up the makeshift graves, undead warriors and spooky folk memories that had lain preserved among the toadstools and moss on the windless woodland floor.

As we've already seen, the Irish group Sweeney's Men had been among the first to map modern instruments onto traditional folk tunes around 1967 – though, with Andy Irvine mixing a Greek bouzouki in with bodhran and tin whistle, it was far from 'authentic'. A little later, Dublin offered up its own small but stir-crazy alternative scene, with a flurry of Celtic acid folk – Mellow Candle, Tír na nÓg, Loudest Whisper, The Woods Band (Terry and

Gay Woods's post-Steeleye Span folk-rock outfit) and Dr Strangely Strange, a puckish gang whose minstrelly arrangements and zonked magic realism epitomise the weird and woolly halcyon days of acid folk – or, as the group preferred, 'psychedelic lounge music'.

Tim Booth, a local folkie, formed Dr Strangely Strange with English rock 'n' roll guitarist and fellow Trinity College student Ivan Pawle. A number of players passed through the group's revolving door until Booth's friend, artist and keyboard player Tim Goulding, was piped aboard. If the 1960s wouldn't come to them in monochrome Ireland, they realised they would have to invent them for themselves. 'Nineteen sixty-six was the fiftieth anniversary of the 1916 rising,' says Booth. 'It was a patriotic and jingoistic time with lots of military parades and dramatic re-enactments and born-again Republicans running around self-righteously – not a good time to be a proto-hippy. Being in a band meant concentrating on creativity and escaping from that hoopla.'

Their two albums, *Kip of the Serenes* (1969) and *Heavy Petting* (1970), were lysergic pageants of waking dreams summoning an Ireland of wonders, populated with a gallery of eccentric characters drawn from history, mythology, fiction and the recesses of their own imaginations – a kind of *Ulysses* in pantaloons. When The Incredible String Band's Robin Williamson swung by their commune, The Orphanage, he and Pawle struck up a friendship

Forest, *Full Circle* (1970); Mellow Candle, *Swaddling Songs* (1972).

that resulted in the group signing up to Joe Boyd's Witchseason management. In January 1969, to commence work on *Kip of the Serenes*, they moved to London, occupying a shared house in Dalston, round the corner from their friend and former Trinity alumnus, the writer Iain Sinclair (another frequent visitor was Sinclair's friend Tom Baker, screenwriter at the time on Michael Reeves's *Witchfinder General*). The record is marked by a relaxed, giggly informality, offset by the chapel-like tones of Goulding's organ and harmonium, and the intrusion of a jazz solo played on Baroque flute. 'I remember most of the *Kip* session being recorded live with us sitting around as if playing a gig,' recalls Tim Goulding. 'The whole thing was recorded in a few days.

'Looking back at it now,' he continues, 'it certainly appears like magic realism. Many of [the characters in the songs] are drawn from Irish literary, political and musical sources.' On 'Donnybrook Fair', a parade of figures from Ireland's revolutionary past are worked into a vibrant tableau, observed by an enigmatic unicorn representing 'the Outsider, and to some extent myself', affirms Tim Booth, the song's author. 'The song was a chance to get my own back on what I regarded as the philistine Republican ethic that governed the country. The song went down well there, but there was a certain right-wing poet who attempted to assault me after one gig. I've no idea what happened to the poet, but I still sing the song.' Recording spontaneously in a campfire-style circle, the group recreated the hubbub of Dublin's streets, evoked the weird country of 'On the West Cork Hack', and rang misty bells on 'Ship of Fools'.

The casual vibe continued on the rockier *Heavy Petting*, released on Vertigo in November 1970 in an elaborate die-cut tree sleeve. 'That was partially recorded in a ballroom in Dublin where the studio was wheeled out of a cupboard by day and put back for the evening entertainment,' explains Goulding. Friends dropping in to contribute to the mix included the young Gary Moore, guitarist at the time with Dublin rockers Skid Row, mandolinist Andy Irvine of Sweeney's Men, and Fairport Convention drummer Dave Mattacks.

The Strangelies' cosmography was presided over by Doctor Strange, a hybrid of the Marvel Comics superhero Dr Strange and the curatives in Robert Burton's seventeenth-century *Anatomy of Melancholy*. The medicinal references clearly reflected the group's consumption of enlightening hallucinogens. 'LSD could be characterised as one of the sacraments of the 1960s revolution,' confirms Goulding, 'and was often a precursor of further exploration using meditation. The lyrics of those songs were extremely visual and related to the skyscraper clarity that acid appeared to furnish. Looking into the heart of a blackberry bush or observing the stubble growing on the chin of the local sergeant were heady catalysts.' Struggling to make ends meet, the group disbanded in mid-1971, but all remained living within reach of each other in the west of Ireland, reuniting at erratic intervals.

Dublin's acid-folk scene also threw up Mellow Candle, whose one album, *Swaddling Songs*, sounded the least 'Celtic' of all their contemporaries like Tír na nÓg, Horslips and The Woods Band. Formed in 1968 around two fifteen-year-old girls, Clodagh Simonds and Alison O'Donnell, their first single, 'Feeling High' / 'Tea with the Sun', was released on Simon Napier-Bell's SNB label, whose principal investor was the actor David Hemmings, who had just accepted the starring role in Clive Donner's film *Alfred the Great*. The duo were later joined by guitarist David Williams, bassist Pat Morris (later replaced by Frank Boylan) and drummer William Murray, and signed to Deram in 1971, recording *Swaddling Songs* at the end of that year. Simonds's piano, and the tight but free-ranging rock ensemble, ensure the songs meander unpredictably like sheep tracks on a windswept moor, and rock hard, as on 'The Poet and the Witch', 'Break Your Token' and 'Lonely Man'. Mellow Candle's songs are riven with crepuscular pagan atmospheres, birds of ill omen, fabular creatures, coffins and crows. For Mellow Candle, the wilderness offered an enchanted antidote to the crushing enervation of city life. The last track contains just two lines of text: '*I know the Dublin pavements / Will be boulders on my grave.*' The group broke up in 1973; O'Donnell married Williams, moved to South Africa and formed Flibbertigibbet. Clodagh Simonds ended up guesting on several mid-1970s Mike Oldfield albums and worked for a time as Richard Branson's personal assistant. In the 1990s she came out of the woodwork with a folk-influenced ambient electronic project, Fovea Hex, and collaborated with Current 93.

Back in England, another short-lived group, Synanthesia, active at exactly the same time, dredged up more specific echoes of the islands' pagan roots: their one and only album was originally planned as a series of tributes to the Roman deities. Singer, vibraphonist and guitarist Dennis Homes grew up in London's East End, but had an epiphany after seeing Bert Jansch perform at Les Cousins and was enchanted a second time, shortly afterwards, when he heard Harold McNair's flute on Donovan's *A Gift from a Flower to a Garden*. The acoustic trio he put together in 1968 with Leslie Cook (guitar) and Jim Fraser (saxophones, flutes and woodwinds) was named after a 1962 Cannonball Adderley jazz tune, and the flutes and bongos lent a Pan-centric flourish to their literate emanations. *Synanthesia*, their only record, came out in September 1969; it began with an invocation to 'Minerva', goddess of light and wisdom: '*Apathetic blindfold you cut down / Ignorance you force below the ground.*' On 'The Tale of the Spider and the Fly', Fraser's multitracked oboe and noseflute (which he occasionally played simultaneously) lend an appropriately exotic touch, and their hymn to the goddess of memory, 'Mnemosyne', is streaked with Electric Prunes-style distorted wah-wah. The group fell apart in early 1970, but like the everlasting flame hymned in 'Vesta', or the eternal thread spun by the 'Fates', the spell endures.

Synanthesia's three heads appear on their only record sleeve as extra nodules on the wrinkly bole of a gnarled tree trunk, mossed and knobbled with undateable age. The scene is shrouded in a misty, winter-dawn half-light that casts a thin, smoky patina over the image. This artificially aged grain is a common device in the film stock of this period. It is most effectively utilised on one of the best-selling rock albums of all time, which dates from the epicentre of the period discussed in this chapter: Led Zeppelin's 🜂 🜚 🜛 🜜.

The famous layered image, which uses the gatefold format to intensify its play of close-up and distant zooms, is also a near-perfect visual counterpoint to the opening of T. S. Eliot's *Four Quartets*, where the poet meditates on time past and time present being both perhaps present in time future. No textual clues, just a haggard, bowler-hatted Victorian labourer in a field, stooped with the weight of the faggots bundled on his back. He rests for a moment on a gnarled staff, the ghost of a vanished rural peasantry, now the subject of a kitsch painting that's nailed to layers of faded, peeling wallpaper on a damp cottage wall. With the wings of the gatefold spread open, we see that the cottage wall is half demolished, and it now stands on a vacant lot overlooking a grimy row of deadbeat, red-brick terraced houses, over which a dove-grey tower block stands monolithic. The unknown photographer has captured one of those English summers where the clouds never quite let the sun through; even though the bushes are clearly in leaf and flower, the sky is stained with the threatening pink of impending hail. The tower block is Butterfield Court in Dudley, one of Birmingham's many suburban outcrops. Birmingham is a creation of the Industrial Revolution, a massive manufacturing city planted in the heart of what was rural England, and which sucked the agricultural workforce into its factories and cramped housing. Positioned on a hillock, Butterfield Court's twenty storeys can, on a clear day, be seen thirty or forty miles away, from the tranquil meadows of Worcestershire and Shropshire: an ever-present symbol of urban encroachment. ⟨⚇⚇ ⚇ ⚇⟩'s cover illustrates an ongoing social, historical and environmental process. 'Someone dies from hunger nearly every day', reads the faintly discernible text of a billboard poster for Oxfam, plastered on the side of a terraced house. Elsewhere in the world, famines and hardships continue to blight the lives of millions of feudal workers, even as the fungus of new towns extends its gentrifying footprint. The cottage, the terrace and the tower block: three generations of workers' housing. Even here, the dialogue between country and city, progress and conservation, hangman and daughter is being perpetuated – a 'battle of evermore' – in a single, mass-marketed image.

⟨⚇⚇ ⚇ ⚇⟩ embodies the moment when Led Zeppelin's early blues-rock began to redraw itself along more folky and fantastical lines. Even before their debut in 1968, Led Zeppelin's members had contributed to a significant chunk of British folk-rock's development in their session-musician days, culminating in the 1967 unification of Jimmy Page, John Paul Jones and John Bonham on Donovan's 'Hurdy Gurdy Man' (Robert Plant later sang backing vocals on Donovan's 'Barabajagal'). Their very public tip of the cap to progressive folk singer Roy Harper ('Hats Off to (Roy) Harper') led to Jimmy Page (aka S. Flavius Mercurius) guesting on Harper's *Stormcock* album of 1971. A much-cited quote from 1990 has Plant admitting that much of their inspiration came when they 'just bought an Incredible String Band album and followed the directions'.[9] It's worth focusing on the double meaning to this apparently throwaway remark. Sure, Zeppelin used *The Hangman's Beautiful Daughter* as a recipe book; but also, they duly noted the different, eclectic 'directions' in which that group's music was pulling, bedding their mossy mythopoetics in perfumed gardens of Celtic and Indian modes and exploring esoteric magic such as the Tarot and Crowleyan ritual. Their previous two LPs, *Led Zeppelin*

II and *III*, contained references to Tolkien characters, Arthurian legend and fairy-tale monarchs. *III* leavened the hard-rock bite with a mouthful of acoustic reverie on 'The Bron-Y-Aur Stomp', named after the Welsh cottage to which Page and Plant repaired to write (which, like Trees' rehearsal home, also lay less than ten miles distant from the Cader Idris of Alan Garner's *Owl Service*).

As songwriters, Page and Plant's immersion in the remote borderlands was wound up in their exploration of Albion's landscapes of legend and the occult. Page had purchased Boleskine House, the Loch Ness residence of Golden Dawn founder Aleister Crowley, in 1970, and had attempted an abortive soundtrack for Kenneth Anger's satanic-themed film *Lucifer Rising*. The area around Bron-Yr-Aur (Page and Plant's spelling ended up slightly off) was becoming popular with moneyed hippies looking for a rustic second home. For Plant, who bought a working sheep farm in 1973 a few miles away, the site offered convenient access to the National Library of Wales at Aberystwyth, which houses ancient manuscripts like the *Book of Taliesin* and *The Black Book of Carmarthen*. While ⬡ ⬡ ⬡ ⬡ wields some of the densest rock formations of all time in 'When the Levee Breaks' and 'Black Dog', the archetypally fey opening of golden-hour chestnut 'Stairway to Heaven' – at over one million copies, the biggest-selling sheet music in rock history – as well as the mandolins of 'The Battle of Evermore' and 'Going to California', are of a piece with the sylvan acoustic shimmer of Forest, The Incredible String Band and the nixie-land stomp of the new British country music. The lyrics of 'The Battle of Evermore' are a slightly confused hybrid: folk memory of medieval border skirmishes between English armies and raggle-taggle Celtic or Pictish villagers are jumbled up with scenes from the climactic battle royal at Pelennor Fields in Tolkien's *The Return of the King*. The rallying 'come-all-ye' from the ramparts, calling for the defenders to '*Sing as you raise your bow/ Shoot straighter than before*', is voiced by Sandy Denny, who briefly joined the revels at Headley Grange, the Hampshire country house where Zeppelin recorded the album, in the interim months between the disbanding of Fotheringay and the making of her own *North Star Grassman and the Ravens*. Yet for all the references to Ringwraiths and magic runes, its point about the oppressed banding together to fight off the militaristic machines of the besieger and preserve a way of life linked to the soil and the seasons remains in tune with the rural fantasies of the underground scene at the time.

The cocktail of hermetic magic, runeology and riffage that was part of 's package would become a much imitated cliché of the blacker subgenres of heavy metal. Jimmy Page's obsession with the black arts was paralleled in the early work of Led Zeppelin's Black Country fellow travellers at the dawn of metal, Black Sabbath. Named after a Boris Karloff horror movie, Sabbath lapped up books by pop occultist Dennis Wheatley and wrote their own signature tune based on the tritone, or 'Devil's interval', castigated and forbidden by medieval theologians as satanic harmonics. Their first LP, *Black Sabbath* (1970), came wrapped in another iconic image. A witch prowls the fungal banks

Led Zeppelin, ⚯ (1971).

of a river in front of Mapledurham Watermill, the ochre pallor of her face as sickly as the coral-pink dawn air. The photographer who engineered this uncanny apparition was 'Keef', also known as Marcus Keef (but whose real name was Keith MacMillan), a young artist who supplied many photos and layouts for progressive labels of the day, including Vertigo, Neon and Nepentha. He made a speciality of shooting with infra-red stock, which created the 'false colours' of the Black Sabbath sleeve. Developed as a Second World War reconnaissance tool for detecting military presence under camouflage, infra-red film renders leaves and grass – anything containing chlorophyll – as magenta; blood, and therefore human skin, is rendered in green. But Keef didn't rely on that gimmick alone. He was at his best contriving ambiguous, eerie tableaux and forlorn still lives: Sandy Denny in her herbalist's den (on *North Star Grassman and the Ravens*); a transvestite David Bowie reclining in silk (*The Man Who Sold the World*); the sword-brandishing ghost-warrior of Black Sabbath's *Paranoid*; the bookish composer stewing in a dusty garret (Fairfield Parlour's *From Home to Home*); a woman and child, chalk-white in an ivory room (*Local Anaesthetic* by UK psychedelicists Nirvana); sunlight beams glimmering upon a graveyard of carousel steeds (Dando Shaft's *Dando Shaft*). Keef's interiors are characteristically dirty, dusty and lit with pale yellow streaks of wintry sun; roughly caulked walls have the creakiness of stage sets. Bleached landscapes are populated by clowns, circus performers, high priestesses, broken dolls' heads, flaming busts. These images are the polar opposite of the fabulistic fantasies Roger Dean was beginning to make for progressive artists of the same period. This is 'progressive' seen in negative: jerry-built absurdism assembled from the detritus of remaindered past lives. In the aftermath of pop's enlightened late-1960s supernova, the papery brown layers of the onion barely concealed a mouldering core.[10]

That 'look' – a nostalgic richness of colour viewed through a misty gauze, familiar from myriad coffee-table photo-books of 'disappearing Britain' – reached its apotheosis in two very different films made in the first half of the 1970s: *Akenfield* and *The Wicker Man*. Based on the 1969 book by Ronald Blythe, *Akenfield* was shot by Peter Hall around eight different Norfolk villages, and cast with real-life inhabitants who improvised the entire script. As in Shirley and Dolly Collins's *Anthems in Eden*, the First World War marks a turning point for the English way of life. A young boy, Tom, attends the funeral of his grandfather, who never left his village after he returned from the war. Tom is subjected to comparable pressures and dilemmas: should he stay or should he go, and will he suffer the same failures as his ancestor if he abandons his rural home? Shot over the duration of a whole year, the passage of the seasons is embedded within the film's grain. Hall and cameraman Ivan Strasburg, together with a soundtrack comprising Michael Tippett's *Fantasia Concertante on a Theme of Corelli* and folk songs arranged by Dave and Toni Arthur, 'capture[d] a part of England in a way that few films have done since the death of Humphrey Jennings', observed one newspaper critic.[11] 'A rare work of art, as perfectly composed as a Constable painting,' crowed another.[12] Screened both on television and at cinemas in 1974, the film's exquisite, unsentimental period tone made a strong impression on audiences in the midst of the oil crisis, attracted to simpler alternatives to modern life.

The *Battle of the Field* LP, made in 1973 by Ashley Hutchings's Albion Country Band, contained a tapestry of songs in a similar rural register. Hutchings, trowelling garden muck in jodhpurs and rolled-up sleeves, could have been an extra in the movie. Richard Thompson, Dave Mattacks and Martin Carthy punch with more weight than on the previous year's *Morris On*, harrowing the grooves into deep furrows. But even as the mixed electronic and acoustic group attempt to wrestle this Albion country music into a future form of hayrick 'n' roll (there's even some squelchy Moog synth bass at one point), it's impossible to shake the sensation of flailing

Back to the land: Ashley Hutchings on the sleeve of Albion
Country Band's *Battle of the Field*, 1973.

to revive a feeling for a senile England whose vision is starting to
grow dim. '*The faded flower of England will rise and bloom again*,' goes
the hopeful line in Richard Thompson's 'Albion Sunrise'. A year
later, Hutchings and Shirley Collins were forced to create their
acoustic Etchingham Steam Band as a direct result of the power
cuts plunging British homes into pre-industrial candlelight.

Instead of Tippett, it would have been an interesting exercise
to invite The Albion Country Band to soundtrack *Akenfield*. The
creators of *The Wicker Man*, on the other hand – screenwriter
Anthony Shaffer and director Robin Hardy – recognised the potent
connections between paganism and the new folk music. Made for
the British Lion company, it was initially released as a double-bill
with Nic Roeg's *Don't Look Now* – which must have made for a fairly
intense evening at the pictures. After its initial butchered studio cut
was restored by the director in 2002, *The Wicker Man*'s reputation
increased dramatically. Starring Christopher Lee as the magus-like
Lord Summerisle, and with Hammer's cinematographer Harry
Waxman behind the viewfinder, it pushed British horror towards
a folkloric *film fantastique*. Unlike most squarely generic horror
movies, Shaffer's script refused to delineate clear divisions between
good and evil. In north-west Scotland, police sergeant Howie

(played by Edward Woodward) is lured to investigate a missing girl on the remote, privately owned Summerisle. We might expect audience sympathies to remain with this representative of upright rationalism and mainland law. But Howie is made to appear uptight and unsympathetic – his very first line is a gruff instruction to a colleague to get his hair cut – and one of the main conflicts of the movie is the crumbling of his piety and his lawman's logic when exposed to the alternative ritual universe on Summerisle.[13]

For, like the 'forward into the past' utopia of William Morris's *News from Nowhere*, Summerisle is a speculative Other Britain: a meticulously researched, exquisitely designed microcosm of what sacred and profane life in a village might be like if Christianity had never been imported to the Isles. In addition, we are strongly invited to consider Summerisle as an Eden. After Howie, in his seaplane, has soared beyond the forbidding rocky landscapes of the Hebrides in the film's opening minutes, he finds himself swooping over a self-sustaining island oasis patterned with apple-bearing orchards and tropical palm gardens. Later he stumbles upon couples flagrantly rutting on the village green, organised sexual initiations of virgins, and naked fertility rites being performed by a group of women in a megalithic stone circle. The islanders teach sex magic on the school curriculum, practise folk remedies, believe in reincarnation and make sacrificial offerings to the nature gods to ensure their crops' increase. The film's back-story tells of a nature religion being imposed on the island population in the mid-nineteenth century by the grandfather of the current Lord Summerisle; churches have been deconsecrated and left to ruin, and the island's main source of income comes from exporting its famous apples. Howie's mistake is to assume he is on a murder hunt. As he grows to understand more about the religion of this community – and to realise that the previous year the island's fruit yield was barren for the first time – he suspects the missing girl Rowan Morrison is still alive, but being held in secret to be used in a sacrificial slaying. In fact, Howie discovers during the film's final, chilling twenty minutes, it is he all along who – as a king (a representative of the law) who arrived of his own free will, a virgin and a fool – has been destined to appease the gods, by being burned alive along with sundry farm animals in a giant basket-weave effigy as a sacrifice to the god of the sun and the goddess of the orchards.[14]

This could so easily have turned into a generic zombie movie, with the islanders acting as if held in the trance of the ritual. But it is here that the film's moral centre becomes so intoxicatingly unsteady. So far as the island pagans are concerned, sacrifice is not made to satisfy bloodlust. Nowhere in the film does any character do or say anything out of evil or malevolent motives; everyone Howie interrogates is thoroughly polite and courteous to him, and truthful according to their own beliefs. Their propitiatory belief system holds that to sacrifice another human being for this cause is the highest honour they can bestow, and, as Lord Summerisle reminds Howie, as an unreformed Christian he will die a martyr's death. In an extra stroke of directorial genius, the outcome has been implicit since the very first intertitle that prefaces the action: 'The producer would like to thank The Lord Summerisle and the people of his island . . . for this privileged insight into their religious practices and for their generous co-operation . . .'. In fact, there *was* no Summerisle: the locale was constructed by editing footage from around twenty-five different locations all over western Scotland. The prefatory thanks is therefore part of the fiction, implying a complicity with the practices of the pagan population of the island.

Midway through the action, Lord Summerisle explains how his upbringing taught him to 'reverence the music, and the drama and the rituals of the old gods'. Music, in a style very much in keeping with the prevailing early-1970s climate of rural acoustic folk, takes a crucial role in the production, although curiously they hired an American theatre director and playwright, Paul Giovanni, to construct the soundtrack. Giovanni composed all the songs and sang many of them himself, in a breathy, seductive Scots burr, abetted by three recent Royal College of Music graduates: Peter Brewis (recorder, bass guitar, Jew's harp, harmonica), Michael Cole (concertina, harmonica, bassoon) and Gary Carpenter (piano, recorders, fife, ocarina, lyre). Carpenter convened a group from members of his folk-rock outfit, Hocket, featuring Andrew Tompkins (guitar), Ian Cutler (violin) and Bernard Murray (percussion), forming a one-off ensemble specifically for *The Wicker Man* which he christened Magnet. The name was well chosen, as music is the film's lodestone, an integral part of the lure that drags Howie to his doom. Most of the soundtrack was pre-recorded under Giovanni's direction and played back later on set. Giovanni and his musicians appear all over the film itself, playing in the Green Man pub, sawing out the breathless, cyclic maypole dance, and capering alongside the climactic May Day procession. Carpenter stood off-camera, banging a drum to keep time while Britt Ekland cavorted naked to 'Willow's Song' in the hotel room adjoining Sgt Howie's. If Howie only had ears to hear, the songs offer clues to the nature of the island's religion, couching flagrant eroticism and nature worship in cotton-lined, hypnotic acoustic folk. As the wicker man blazes in the final scenes, the clash of belief systems is conducted through music: Howie breaks into Psalm 23, 'The Lord Is My Shepherd', in a desperate counterpoint to the villagers' 'Sumer Is A-Cumen In', the medieval round generally considered the oldest of its kind in Britain. The songs grate against each other, but the Christian is consumed by fire. In the final shot, incredibly achieved in real time, the wicker head topples in flames to reveal the setting sun, Bright Phoebus, streaming eternal across the sea. *The Wicker Man* daringly broaches the casket of Anglo-Saxon tribal memory and, in the Battle of Evermore between the old gods and the Judaeo-Christian cult which supplanted them, with the music of the ages calling on the spring, it declares the pagans victorious.

13

We Put Our Magick on You

Stand in a church where the village choir once sang
And roll along the pathway where the dead man used to
hang.

Mr Fox, 'The Hanged Man' (1970)

A teenage boy enters a country church, lifts the organ lid and pumps out several passages from Elgar's *Dream of Gerontius*. Rich in Catholic pomp and mystery, the oratorio was the composer's most visionary flight, describing the passage of a dead soul towards a judgemental encounter with a fiery God. Finally, the boy arrives at the score's epicentre: a gigantic discord that rips a terrible, divine grimace across the entire gamut of the orchestra. A mighty crack splits the floor of the church aisle, bodily rending the building in two. King Penda awakes . . .

Penda's Fen, a ninety-minute film made for BBC Television's *Play for Today* series in 1973, is a complex meditation on the matter of Britain. Written by David Rudkin (who was involved in the adaptation of Stephen Weeks's film of *Gawain and the Green Knight* in the same year) and directed by the inspirational Alan Clarke, it was created at exactly the same time as *The Wicker Man*, and deals with a similar theme: the lingering pagan presence in the British landscape, and by extension, in the soul of the nation.

While *The Wicker Man*'s pagan community consciously isolates itself from the jurisdiction of mainland Britain, in *Penda's Fen* the buried presence of paganism is treated as a force for national redemption, although in an unexpected way. The young hero, Stephen Franklin, is a misfit public schoolboy living in remote Pinvin, a hamlet in the heart of Worcestershire. It's Elgar country, and Stephen is obsessed with the composer's music. He begins the film as a conservative Christian prig who's nevertheless wrestling with guilt over a slowly surfacing, latent homosexuality. His father is the local vicar, whose outward calm and stoicism conceals a secret heretical past. During a long heart-to-heart talk, as they ramble through the country lanes near Bredon Hill, his father muses upon the old meaning of 'pagan' – 'belonging to the village'. 'The village is sneered at as something petty. Petty it can be. Yet it *works* – the scale is human. People can relate there. Man may yet, in the nick of time, revolt, and save himself. Revolt from the monolith; come back to the village.' He then goes much further, invoking Penda of Mercia, a seventh-century warrior and 'a king of Midland England – the last of his kind, last pagan king of England, fighting his last battle against the new machine. That battle in which he is to fall. King Penda . . . what mystery of this land went down with him for ever?' Gradually Stephen unpicks the secret locked up in the local place names: Pinvin (which actually exists) derives from Pinfin – Pendefen – Penda's Fen. He is living right on top of the burial ground of England's last pagan ruler. His dream visions increase along with his understandings – he meets the wheelchair-bound ghost of Elgar, who whispers the solution to his *Enigma Variations*; and finally, on Bredon Hill, Stephen comes face to face with Penda himself, who instils a sense of anarchic purpose and selfhood in the boy: 'We trusted you, our sacred daemon of ungovernableness. Cherish the flame; we shall rest easy. Stephen, be secret; child, be strange; dark, true, impure . . . Cherish our flame, our dawn shall come.'

The vision of Albion in *Penda's Fen* ends far from the comfortable Middle England complacency of its beginning: the country is embraced, by its oldest pagan spirit as well as by its younger radicals, as a chaotic, revolutionary, mongrel nation. The pattern under the plough, the occult history of Albion – the British

Dreamtime – lies waiting to be discovered by anyone with the right mental equipment.

The loamy colour schemes and macabre settings of Marcus Keef's photos, as well as some of the early work of Hipgnosis (whose first commission was the 1967 book jacket of A. L. Lloyd's *Folk Song in England*), took their cue from the visual style of contemporary British horror films. Arthur Grant, Hammer Films' chief cinematographer from the late 1950s until his death in 1972, stripped away the cobwebbed, studio-lit, Gothic expressionist noir that had dominated horror since German silents like F. W. Murnau's *Faust* and *The Cabinet of Dr Caligari*, or James Whale's 1930 *Frankenstein*. Instead, Grant used real outdoor locations, and exploited natural light to depict the land in muddy terracotta and dismal greys. He was behind the camera for 1967's *Quatermass and the Pit*, in which an ancient spacecraft is excavated from beneath the London Underground and the swinging capital is terrorised by a dormant alien race. *Quatermass and the Pit* was unusual in the Hammer oeuvre in being set squarely in the present, as the majority of horror scripts were set in the past, inheritors of the nineteenth-century macabre established by Mary Shelley's *Frankenstein* and Bram Stoker's *Dracula*. Young director Michael Reeves set his *Witchfinder General* (Tigon Films, 1968) in a Stuart-era Suffolk rendered in dirty realist style. Although centring on Matthew Hopkins's Puritanical witch hunts, which channelled the religious paranoia of Civil War England into the demonisation of innocents, the sorcery is only in the minds of the accusers; the horror is in the lives ruined by the perverted justice meted out by a sadist acting under legal authority. Another Tigon film set in the seventeenth century is Piers Haggard's *Blood on Satan's Claw* (1971).[1] Like the *Quatermass* series, the plot turns on a sinister object churned up from underground: a gruesome skull unearthed by a farmer's plough that turns the young people of the village into a wood-dwelling pagan witch cult with a penchant for erotic blood sacrifices. There is a genuinely malevolent magic at work here, but like *Witchfinder General*, it is presented as no fairy tale, but an eruption of terror in a community of working people.[2]

A fox slinks through two of the best British horror films of the mid-1960s. *The Tomb of Ligeia* (directed by Roger Corman, 1964), based on an Edgar Allan Poe story, features a succession of English heritage sites, from the ruined abbey of Castle Acre Priory to a country-church wedding and a red-coated fox hunt in full pursuit. Hammer's *The Plague of the Zombies* (directed by John Gilling, 1966) caricatures the English capitalist aristocracy as voodoo-practising slave-masters, zombifying their workforce to increase the production rate in a Cornish tin mine. The film includes a hounds-and-redcoats pursuit of the young heroine, Diane Clare.

Fox hunting in Britain, officially declared illegal in 2004, has traditionally been a focal point for the class politics of progress and conservatism. Scruffy hunt saboteurs from the anarchist left, facing off against stallion-mounted, landowning squires, make for televisual gold that perpetuates centuries-old societal chasms. But spare a thought for poor, exhausted Reynard. Ages before he begins to turn up in written fables of the twelfth century, the fox has been the wily trickster, or the hounded victim, of European legends and lays. He is sighted in Chaucer's *Nun's Priest's Tale*, and symbolises the hero's predicament in *Sir Gawain and the Green Knight*. As well as in folk songs such as 'Bold Reynard', 'Reynard the Fox', 'Tally Ho, Hark Away' and 'The Robber Bridegroom', he appears all over English literature and music, from Beatrix Potter's *The Tale of Mr Tod* to Roald Dahl's *Fantastic Mr Fox*, and from Peter Warlock's song 'The Fox' of 1930 to Julian Cope's 'Reynard the Fox' of 1984. The fox popped up again in one of the most frequently performed 'old' songs in the 1960s folk-rock repertoire: 'Reynardine'. The song has a sinister tone, telling of a woman who encounters a fox-man at large in the hills. Although she resists his advances at first, she appears hypnotised into submission by his piercing stare and '*teeth that brightly shine*'. The supernatural suggestion that this outlaw is half beast seems to place it in the deep antiquity of fairy tale and legend. But the tale of how this song was reinstated by Bert Lloyd and came to be covered by everyone from Anne Briggs and Martin Carthy to Shirley Collins and Davy Graham, Fairport Convention, Archie Fisher, Bert Jansch, Maddy Prior and others says a great deal about how 'tradition' was frequently refurbished to suit modern tastes and expectations.

The text familiar from 'Reynardine' does not appear in any written form until the early nineteenth century. Variants of 'The Mountains High', a printed broadside ballad from around 1814, contain a character called Rinordine, Ranordine, Ryner Dyne and other alternatives. These early versions make no particular reference to Rinordine as having foxy characteristics, and it's likely that the name is actually an orally transmitted corruption of a name like 'Randal Ryan'. In these songs he's simply an armed bandit up in the mountains with a seductive eye for a passing wench. Jumping forward to the beginning of the twentieth century, Joseph Campbell and Herbert Hughes, two poets collecting folk songs in Ireland, come across an old lady who sings them the song and chills their marrow by confiding that Rinordine is a magical beast. On this single recollection of an eighty-year-old woman in faraway Kilmacrenan, both Campbell and Hughes separately produce rewritten versions, now titled 'Reynardine', in which we're told the protagonist is a 'fairy fox' (in Campbell's *The Mountainy Singer*, 1909) and that 'His eyes did brightly shine' (Hughes's *Irish Country Songs*, also 1909). The new title and these descriptive details – not at all present in the earlier broadsides – collectively emphasise the lycanthropic dimensions of the story.

Fast forward past two world wars. Bert Lloyd performs 'Reynardine' on his late-1950s folk-song album, *The Foggy Dew and*

Other Traditional English Love Songs. He sings the 1909 addition, '*eyes did brightly shine*', in this 1956 version of the song, and writes, on the reverse cover, that the song 'puts its fingers to its lips and preserves the mystery, letting the enigmatic text and dramatic tune hint at unspeakable things'. By the time he records it again, on the 1966 LP *First Person* (Topic), the song's text is the familiar one used later by Anne Briggs and Fairport Convention, with the line about shining eyes changed to the even more sinister '*His teeth did brightly shine*'. In his sleeve notes, Lloyd leaves no doubt about his belief that Reynardine is 'A vulpine name for a crafty hero', and that the 'horrific' dimension of the material is uppermost in his mind: 'The dread uncertainty is whether he is man or animal. Similar unease broods within this song. Some commentators have thought it concerns a love affair between an English lady and an Irish outlaw, and have set its date in Elizabeth I's time. Others believe the story is older and consider Reynardine, the "little fox", to be a supernatural, lycanthropic lover.'[3] Lloyd claimed to have collected the song from a 'Tom Cook' in The Eel's Foot at Eastbridge, Suffolk, but no one has managed to trace this mysterious source. Almost certainly, he did not exist. Lloyd, it seems, wrote or remodelled 'Reynardine' to fit his own taste for an ambiguous supernatural quality, and invented a third-party source to give credence to the notion that it resided in a long-held folk memory. Like Marcus Keef's 'false colour' photography, Lloyd used a folkloric infrared filter to distort and intensify whichever shades of meaning he wished to emphasise. In the small print on Anne Briggs's 1971 LP *The Time Has Come*, he all but admitted his own intervention: 'Words and tune of this version,' reads the confession, 'are adapted by me from an Irish original.'[4]

Why should anyone care about these apparently minor corrections and tinkerings? For one thing, they connect right back to Cecil Sharp's description of the folk tradition as an organic growth, replenishing itself through adaptive mutation. For another, they warn the listener, browsing in the Old Curiosity Shop of culture, to look out for fake modern reproductions. And finally, it reveals a strong urge, in the modern folk revival, to zoom in on the creepy and the uncanny, the Gothic, the strange and the magical.

Black magic and white magic, healing incantations, forbidden harmonies, secret trysts and grisly crimes accumulate, ghost-like, in the eaves of Britain's 'country music'. Scoundrelly Reynardine incarnated himself once more, this time as the short-lived Mr Fox, a folk-rock group founded by husband-and-wife team Bob and Carole Pegg, who wrote all their own material and occupied a unique stronghold between folk music's bread-and-butter 'source musicians' and the electrified roots of Steeleye Span. Bob and Carole modelled the group's instrumental palette on the combinations of strings, woodwinds and wind organs found in the village harvest-home and church bands of the Yorkshire Dales, where Bob had conducted folklore research and field recordings in the mid-1960s. Mr Fox's Gothic guignol concentrated the energy of Dalesmen's country dances and the spookiness of British lore within convincing reproductions of antique song. Their name was provided directly by Bert Lloyd, visiting the folk club run by the Peggs at The Royal Sovereign, Kirkstall, who unforgettably recited a yarn from Halliwell's book of popular Victorian rhymes and nursery tales, featuring a serial-killing 'Mr Fox'.

When Carole Pegg first clapped eyes on her future husband, he was sixteen, and appearing as Hamlet in a school play in their home town of Nottingham. It was 1960, and Carole had been aping Joan Baez at the local Folk Workshop and at singers sessions at local coffee bars. 'I saw him on stage, and I thought, "Well, yes . . .",' laughs Carole. Within a few years they were 'local celebs' in Nottingham, as she recalls it, after they scored a slot performing folk-song summaries of topical news items on *Midlands at Six*, a

Mr Fox's Bob and Carole Pegg, 1970.

local television programme. 'People were following us in the town centre and we were racing to the loos to escape, and all that.' They published their own magazine, *Abe's Folk Music*, which aimed to apply in-depth critique to the burgeoning folk-music scene. 'That established me in my early twenties as a troublemaker,' admits Bob Pegg, 'it got me a reputation. People when they met me would immediately be looking for some kind of contentious statement – which I was often quite happy to make.' In 1962 he took a place at Leeds University's Institute of Dialect and Folk Life Studies, researching the folk music of the Yorkshire Dales. 'Something in me wanted to go to a rural area and try and find music and song that came from a wellspring, if you like,' explains Bob, 'that had roots in a real place. So, rather like the early folk-song collectors, I kind of knew what I wanted to find before I went out there. And I did find it, you know, I found these fiddle players who played very similarly to the way Carole plays in Mr Fox – in fact, they were a great influence on her fiddle playing, I would say.

'My notion', he continues, 'was that the Yorkshire Dales had music and song which went back centuries, unaffected by the world outside. Which is, of course, complete nonsense. The peacefulness of the Dales in the 1960s, when I was doing fieldwork there, was something quite recent.' Carole cut short her studies at Southampton University to join Bob in Yorkshire, and they instigated a club at nearby Kirkstall, in the Ballads and Blues mould. Among many artists who appeared there, Ewan MacColl and Peggy Seeger held a two-day seminar on folk-singing technique. MacColl and Seeger's ideas about locality and authenticity certainly rubbed off on the duo: 'We actually banned guitars from the club as a result of their weekend seminar,' recalls Bob. 'He brought along recordings of traditional singers from England, Ireland and Scotland, and also places like Azerbaijan. So he was playing us Muslim melismatic singers, and saying, "Look, this guy can really use his voice," and that we should really be thinking

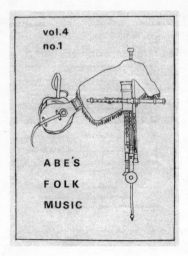 

Two editions of *Abe's Folk Music*, Bob Pegg's unconventional folk 'zine, early 1960s.

about doing this sort of thing with the English songs.' Later in the decade the Peggs visited MacColl and Seeger in Beckenham, and were invited to join the Critics Group. 'All the blokes, apart from me and another guy, had these little Ewan MacColl beards,' recalls Bob. 'They wanted us to go down and live in London . . . just as well we didn't, as it ended up with lots of people at each other's throats.' At the meeting, radio ballads producer Charles Parker showed up selling tapes of *The Song Carriers*, a radio series which had only been broadcast on the BBC's Midlands station, featuring field recordings of British and Central Asian traditional singers with a commentary by MacColl. 'We bought them,' says Bob, 'and they were very, very important in our listening and our thinking about singing, narrative song and local technique.' Bob and Carole Pegg kept their distance from MacColl and Seeger, as they were tuning in to a parallel thread of folk culture that the Critics Group had bypassed. 'It was represented by people like The Spinners,' explains Bob, 'who were kind of "good ol' boys" entertainers: they'd sing a bit of calypso and a bit of sea shanty, and a ballad. There was also another kind of hardcore traditional movement, led by Reg Hall and a guy called Mervyn Plunkett, who ran a magazine called *Ethnic*.[5] It was just like *Abe's Folk Music*, and it was just full of ideas about real hardcore traditional music. What Reg Hall and Mervyn Plunkett were saying was, "This MacColl taking our folk music is just bollocks, when all you've got to do is go to one of these pubs in East Anglia and you'll hear all kinds of stuff – fantastic singers, amazing melodeon players, great step dancers!" It's all part of a community as well, that's what makes it real. It doesn't exist in isolation in a recording: you can go there, have a pint, you can join in. The public face of the Reg Hall contingent was [folk singer] Bob Davenport – he represented the ethos of this anti-MacColl thing, anti all the artiness that he and Peggy Seeger stood for. So this was kind of the antidote to MacColl, and we really started to be pulled in that direction.'

'I don't know if nationally there was some kind of crisis of identity, but we felt like we had to say, "Hang on, we're English rather than American" – that certainly came into it,' says Carole. 'Why should we sing a song in an American accent, even if it's American? We felt that we were making English music, we wanted to be making English music, but we wanted to be more adventurous than just reproducing something.' Accordingly, the Peggs stopped accompanying themselves with guitars and tried out flibbertigibbet combinations of penny whistles, concertinas and Carole's fiddle. By the end of the 1960s they had amassed a solid national reputation and were performing at clubs all over the country.

Bob Pegg transferred to a teaching post at Stevenage College in 1969, which brought the Pegg family within striking distance of London. Fresh from the grizzled hills and valleys of the North, they needed an imaginative project to screen out the dispiriting concrete new-town surroundings and lecturers' wife-swapping key parties. Producer Bill Leader approached them after a London folk gig, offering them a recording session for his new Trailer label. *He Came from the Mountains*, which they recorded as a duo in Leader's Camden flat/studio (in 1969, but not released until 1972), is still largely guitar-driven and more than a little tinged with rustic Americana, including a Phil Ochs cover. But several tracks feature overdubs by the musicians they recruited from the Stevenage music scene at the beginning of 1970 and enrolled in Mr Fox.

Bob and Carole had known Fairport Convention for some while, having met the group on a previous tour that took in Leeds and Sheffield. In the autumn of 1969, during the production of *Liege and Lief*, Bob had submitted some illustrations for the album's sleeve art, three of which were used. In the spring of 1970 the Peggs invited Fairport's departed bassist Ashley Hutchings, in free fall after the disintegration of the first incarnation of Steeleye Span, to spend a month's recuperation in Stevenage. Hutchings perused Bob's folk archive and the tapes he had made in Yorkshire, and for a few weeks it even appeared Hutchings would be joining the newly fledged Mr Fox. 'Over the course of some weeks we played these to Ashley,' recalls Carole with some rancour, 'and basically Ashley pissed off and formed [the second] Steeleye Span, and Bob was not a happy man. He definitely did the dirty because he listened to all our stuff and talked about it, and he took the option that was best for him. But we decided that we'd do it anyway.'

'He was putting together a band,' clarifies Bob, 'and we were under the impression that we were going to be in it, and we co-wrote [the Mr Fox songs] "Mr Trill's Song" and "Salisbury Plain". He was playing bass and we were playing melodeon and fiddle, and at the end of it all he told us that he had formed Steeleye Span. He offered us the possibility of working with him on something along the lines of Etchingham Steam Band, but we told him to sling his

Mr Fox, *Mr Fox* (1970).

hook, because we wanted to be *famous*! He was always asking us what did we think of so-and-so, Barry Dransfield, Martin Carthy . . . He was canvassing any opinion he could. I don't feel bitter, because I don't feel like Steeleye were doing anything remotely like what we were trying to do.' That's as may be, but listening to Mr Fox's version of 'House Carpenter' (1971) next to The Albion Country Band's 'Poor Murdered Woman' (same year), or their 'Ballad of Neddy Dick' (1970) and 'Dancing Song' (1971) back to back with Hutchings's electric versions of country dance on *Morris On* (1972) and *The Compleat Dancing Master* (1974), it's easy to understand why the Peggs might have been aggrieved at the time.

Mr Fox, issued on Transatlantic in 1970, invited audiences to 'Join Us in Our Game', a sprightly, come-all-ye-style prologue that compiled a medley of images from the album: frozen streams, the gay goshawk, the hanged man, the green man and the villagers who relieved their hard-working burden with joyful clog dances. This was a 'game' indeed, dressing fictional songs from the costume-chest of folk memory. The instrumental mix set it quite apart from the rock-solid thump of Fairport Convention. Where Dave Mattacks would hold down a solid, four-square drumbeat, Alan Eden – who previously played with marching pipe bands – rolled and clattered around his tom-toms, a bone-rattling tattoo that chivvied rather than set the pulse. Instead, Barry Lyons's electric bass did the timekeeping, while Andrew Massey's cello and John Myatt's oboe, pipes and recorders daubed gravelly and fluted notes across the sound field. Bob and Carole Pegg tag-teamed the vocals in distinctively Midlands accents, and folded electric organ and fiddle respectively into the masquerade.

'I was interested in a polyphonic idea of things,' explains Bob, 'different melodic strands working together. In the villages, the same musicians would often play for a village dance on a Saturday evening and then for a chapel on the Sunday. I loved that idea, and really wanted a sound that reflected what that might have sounded like. It made you feel like you were eating a good steak, musically. I'm very influenced by hymns as well, because I was brought up a Methodist. Great tunes. It's a bit like coming home musically: the idea really chimed in with a lot of very basic feelings, along with the rawness, the acousticness of the cello and the clarinet.' The Peggs understood the sources that had fed the folk tradition, the symbolism of landscape, and the way types morphed into archetypes and took on non-human forms. Songs such as 'The Gay Goshawk' and 'Salisbury Plain' were intricate replicas of source songs, and yet Mr Fox was craftily aware of how that tradition had been reinvented and mediated. Bob Pegg: 'We were very influenced by Wordsworth and Coleridge – the idea of plain speech that informs *Lyrical Ballads* is behind a lot of the songs. In fact, I was pursuing an illusion, and I did come to realise this eventually, but that was part of the attraction of the Dales, this kind of innocence, this rawness, this unslickness in the music, and the fact that this music is also rooted to a place. And was functional, so the fiddle player didn't just stay at home and play for their fire, or for folk collectors like me; they were out in the village halls. And that was good somehow, the link with the community.'

'Aunt Lucy Broadwood', controversially bearing the name of the Victorian folk collector but based, according to Bob, on an eccentric relative, makes a cameo on their second album, *The Gipsy* (1971), in a dream-like narrative delivered by Bob in a curious, proto-rap stream of consciousness. 'I claim to be the inventor of English folk rap,' jokes Bob. 'Well, the rap thing came out of "the dozens", which was American prison poetry. "Aunt Lucy Broadwood" is based on my Auntie Mabel, who lived alone in a big house, slept in the kitchen even though she had a bed, used to wander the hedgerows collecting herbs and things which she would brew in a big pot on the stove into some kind of vile liquid – I think it cleared her bowels out. And she was our Lucy Broadwood – not the folk collector, I just took the name. In Stevenage, around midnight one night, there was a hammering on the door and it was a deputation of local folkies, howling about how dare I write a song like that about Lucy Broadwood?'

And yet, as a trained folklorist, Bob Pegg had possibly the most sanguine take on the imitative aspect of British folk at that moment in time. He took a broad, historically informed view of the jumble of sources and interventions, and even made the case for including lewd shanties and rugby songs in the canon of folk culture, while finally concluding that the path is there to be rambled by anyone. Four years after the demise of Mr Fox, he published an illustrated book, *Folk*, that celebrated the eccentricities and irregularities of traditional music and those singers and instrumentalists who had preserved it, while critiquing Edwardian collectors who panned the peasantry for flecks of gold. Even people who rail against the use of electric guitars and drums in folk, Pegg observes, accept concertinas and melodeons, which were barely one hundred years old themselves. 'I think we have to face the probability', the book concludes, 'that folk music is an illusion created unconsciously by the people who talk about it, go out looking for it, make collections of it, write books about it, and announce to an audience that they are going to play it. It is rather like a mirage which changes according to the social and cultural standpoint of whoever is looking at it. From a distance it looks distinct, almost tangible. The closer you get the more uncertain its outline becomes, until you merge with it, and it disappears entirely. What remain constant are the conditions that produce the mirage . . . In the past, the folk-music collector and scholar has been free to pick and choose from a vast body of material whatever items suit the particular point he wishes to make – and he has been equally at liberty to ignore anything that does not fit into his general scheme. This vast body of material is the repertoire of the man, or woman, the scholar calls folk singer and musician. It has no historical unity, for individual items can be as old as pre-Christian ritual or as fresh as this morning's radio show. It has no thematic unity, for its subjects may range from mild erotic allegory to blood-curdling adventure . . . The only thread that runs through the whole of the folk singer and musician's repertoire is orality.'[6]

For Pegg, the definition of orality could stretch to include taping folk songs off the TV or radio, or imbibing traditional music via the record player. In the following passage, you can almost make out the sound of decades of ice beginning to melt: 'Once we have abandoned vague notions of "folk", and have begun instead to look quite specifically at orally transmitted music, our preconceived notions of what we thought were archaic forms begin to break down. We can begin to see the links between the music of the old village bands and the rock and roll band, the country fiddler and the electric guitarist, the nineteenth-century farm worker and the rugby-club songster. Social situations and cultural influences have changed . . . but the principles that created what we call folk music are still alive today. They have just been too close for us to notice them.'[7]

On 'Mr Fox' itself, the group give Reynardine the sucker punch. Carole's description of Foxy, her fiancé, beating and abusing another woman, and slicing off her hand, attains a degree of graphic detail that the old ballads usually coyly abstracted. Here Reynard finally gets his comeuppance, when the fox is confronted with his crimes against women, in scenes that recall the bloodthirsty sensationalism of Hammer movies, as the hounds *'tore him limb from limb, they tore him hair from hair / And his flesh it was eaten by birds of the air'*.

Mr Fox only lasted for two years, their demise coinciding with the collapse of the Peggs' marriage. Bob Pegg unwisely seduced the couple's nanny, who happened to be the girlfriend of Barry Lyons. During the gig which turned out to be Mr Fox's last, the bassist poured beer into Pegg's electric organ, resulting in a 'very public fight' in which Pegg 'ended up under a mound of people and my wrists got broken'. Mr Fox, though, left two flawed albums which, at their best, told stories that summoned a powerful sense of place. The narrator of 'The Gipsy' plots a desperate chase after his departed Romany lover through the potholed moors around the Langstrothdale Chase of North Yorkshire, detailing names of rivers, villages and landmarks along the route that bespeak a deep personal knowledge of the region, including references to the Wensleydale cheese manufacturers of Gayle. A reference to a *'white lady'* walking into a stream alludes to a ghostly sighting by some relatives of a friend of Pegg's. The song is embedded in terrain whose names connect the land with pre-Christian times: the rivers Deepdale and Wharf, for instance, are linguistically connected to the pagan goddesses Diva and Verbena.

They closed *The Gipsy* with 'All the Good Times', a leave-taking song whose anthemic regret falls between 'Auld Lang Syne' and 'Meet on the Ledge'. But the track that focused and concentrated their supernatural sensibility was Carole's composition 'Mendle', a vision of a seductive sorceress meeting her doom on a tempestuous hilltop, which – with its fuzz guitar, overdriven Hammond organ and hailstorm of drums – opened *The Gipsy* on a note of hysterical intensity. 'Mendle' was written while Carole was reading *Mist over Pendle*, Robert Neill's 1951 novel about Lancashire witches. Mr Fox found themselves performing near the Manchester suburb of Prestwich, where the book was set: 'There's a hill there called Pendle, I've always been slightly psychic, you know, seeing things . . . and I was reading *Mist over Pendle* . . . and we'd done this gig and we went up Pendle and we were pissed, so it became "Pissed over Mendle" and then "Mendle". I thought that I would drop that other bit of it.'

Bob locates the germ of 'Mendle' in the true mystery of Netta Fornario, a thirty-three-year-old member of a branch of the Golden Dawn who was discovered dead on a 'fairy mound' on the remote island of Iona in 1929, apparently killed during some occult ritual. 'Her death was never explained,' he says, 'but there were obviously very mystical, very black-magic motives imputed to it but nobody ever got to the bottom of it.' The group attracted uncanny experiences at the time. 'We were staying in Lancashire in one of the mill towns there,' he continues. 'One of the people we stayed with, Kath was her name, had been down to Bristol to work for these antique dealers who used to rob graves, and one day she'd been robbing a grave, or a crypt, and the guy she was with popped out for a sandwich. She thought she heard him coming back, but it was the police. Eventually she was put back on a train back to Chorley or wherever, and then one morning, after being back for a bit, she woke up on the train pulling into Bristol station. She had no idea how she'd got on the train, but the black magicians were waiting on the platform for her. She had no mirrors in her house, because she said that whenever she looked into a mirror she saw a black magician, a wizard – one of the antique dealers she'd worked for.'

'I've always seen ghosts,' explains Carole Pegg, 'which in those days used to disturb me hugely. I remember sleeping on Bill Leader's floor when we were recording *He Came from the Mountains* and seeing these faces in the room, in the corner, which came and floated in front of me, and I screamed and Bill came running. I've always seen these things. I think that I can sense place, so if there's something there, I can sense it. I've written songs after I've seen something in a place, for instance. For me, it projects me into song.'

Following Mr Fox's break-up, Carole became Carolanne Pegg and recorded one album, *Carolanne*, under her Transatlantic contract, in 1973. It's a more rock-based release (guitarist Albert Lee makes a blistering guest appearance), even though there's still liberal use of fiddle, melodeon and other elements familiar from the Mr Fox days. A theme of emotional recuperation runs through it, as well as an explicit vein of talismanic magic and dream logic. In 'Sapphire', the blue gemstone is attached like a third eye to her forehead – a charm to cool her anger. 'My Lady in the Well' and 'Wycoller' are inspired by ghostly sightings, the former a woman on Glastonbury Tor. These themes intertwine on 'A Witch's Guide to the Underground', in which Pegg reclines in the branches of an elder (a tree that figures strongly in magical lore), daydreaming '*about the man I fancy*'. As with Mr Fox, the enchantment is in the lyrical specifics: she names the wild flowers from her favourite meadow, for instance, which lifts the song from the clichéd floral imagery of a thousand other pop songs. These songs about strange phenomena, with their vivid detail, coupled with a singing style in which she exaggerates consonants and leaps up and down the scale, make *Carolanne* an uncanny pre-echo of Kate Bush.[8]

In a coda to this phase of her musical career, Carole briefly formed a working association with the volatile keyboardist and saxophonist Graham Bond during 1973. Depressive and drug-dependent,

Bond had been a prominent motivator in the British blues boom of the early 1960s, playing his Hammond organ and Leslie speaker set-up with Jack Bruce, Ginger Baker and John McLaughlin, and later Dick Heckstall-Smith and Jon Hiseman, in The Graham Bond Organization – the seed group for later progressive units Cream and Colosseum. By the early 1970s Bond had become obsessed with the occult. His albums *Holy Magick* (1970) and *We Put Our Magick on You* (1971) transposed the ornament of ritual onto steamy rhythmic workouts heavily infused with ritual magic chants and mantric voodoo, like Traffic under the hypnotic spell of some juju fetish. Bond's voice of sanded papyrus utters Crowleyan invocations, Thelemic gumbo and Arthurian blues. He began 1973 in recovery from a nervous breakdown, but began talking to Carole Pegg after she had performed at London's Roundhouse. They spent several months rehearsing a group called Magus in a spine-chilling country house in the middle of a wood. 'The first time I went,' she recounts, 'there was this terrible thunderstorm and lightning going up this track, with leaves blowing onto the car. In the kitchen there was a well that, if you looked in, there was this clear blue water right at the bottom. Then there was the main room, all oak-panelled, snooker room, open fire, grand piano, and windows through which you could see all the lightning and rain. And then the lights went out. And the phone didn't work. Lightning on the axe in the corner . . .

'It was inspiring to work with Graham. He was quite a strong man who was already a very established musician. But it was fun, we were making some funky kind of sounds, but we were running out of money. There was just one very cranky cassette tape of those rehearsals we did . . . I split the band because I had been separated from my daughter, and I had this moment of elucidation, that here I was looking after all these grown men in this band – and where was my daughter?'

Bond fell further into confusion, believing he was the son of

Aleister Crowley and performing exorcisms on Long John Baldry's cat, before throwing himself in the path of an underground train at Finsbury Park station in May 1974. Carole Pegg began a Cambridge University PhD in the folk music of East Anglia, during which time she lived in Suffolk near the traditional music communities that gathered in The Eel's Foot Inn at Eastbridge and The Ship at Blaxhall – where she discovered many of the floor singers who had stimulated Ernest Moeran, Peter Kennedy and Bert Lloyd at the dawn of the post-war folk revival still holding court in their old age. In 1987 she extended her anthropological field studies to the opposite side of the planet, becoming an authority on the shamanic and nomadic cultures of Mongolia and Inner Asia. 'I feel I'm trying to help these little societies that are struggling with the colonial Russian scenario,' she comments now. 'Post-Soviet period, they wanted to say, "This is who we are, and this is our music that expresses who we are," and that's what Mr Fox was trying to do. In the 1960s things were changing, because we were all "turning on", and all of that, but if I look at the Soviet Union and the big change from Soviet times to a different political system, the reaction was not that they wanted to hang on to it, but actually to leap over that period that they had been so unhappy in and suffered terribly in, and go back to who they thought they were in their deep past. It's something I'm deeply into now, working with these indigenous peoples in the Altai Mountains, how their music relates to who they are, the sense of identity, the sense of place and the sense of landscape, and where they are spiritually and all that kind of thing. And it seems to me that's what I was up to all those years ago, although I hadn't thought of it in that way.'

After Mr Fox met its messy end, Bob Pegg fled from Stevenage to lick his wounds in a remote cottage north of Huddersfield. The rest of the 1970s were productive: he channelled his earlier anthropological research into two books, the aforementioned *Folk* (1976) and the later *Rites and Riots* (1981). Both added up to a 'secret

The old, weird Albion: Neddy Dick of Swaledale with his 'rock band', 1920s.

museum of Albion', highlighting the oddities and eccentricities of the country's folk musicians, dancers and customs that belonged to a tradition while preserving their uniqueness within it. For instance, *Folk* contained remarkable photos of the reclusive, maverick instrument builder Neddy Dick of Swaledale, proudly displaying his 'rock band', 'a collection of big, rough stones laid out in a line, from which Neddy Dick would beat primitive tunes with two mallets'. Neddy Dick, who died in 1927, was celebrated in a Mr Fox song on the first album, and the village of Keld, where he lived, is the climactic location of Pegg's song 'The Gipsy'. 'He loved music, said he could hear it in the air,' writes Pegg. 'He took a harmonium and nailed an old tree branch to it, then screwed clock bells to the branch. With a long stick in his left hand, he could play bells and harmonium at the same time.'

Bob Pegg's own musical projects over the same period abounded in a similar desire to explore the undocumented strangeness of the British people and tap into the magic powers locked in the land.

A new partnership with Nick Strutt, who had acted as Mr Fox's guitarist and mandolinist in the group's final months, led to the duo releasing *Bob Pegg and Nick Strutt* (1973), awash with Fortean mysteries, folk rumours of beasts abroad in the Lancashire hills, and space operas – songs that forced Britain's surface to yield up its long-held secrets. In 'Jesus Christ Sitting on Top of a Hill in the Lake District', 'those feet' are briefly glimpsed among England's pleasant pastures green. Describing his song 'Wildman' to an interviewer in 1973, Pegg explained: 'The voice has a chill edge to it – it's a sexless, androgynous voice. It's as if you walk into a dark wood, it's green all round. You come to a dead end, cut off by bushes. You pull the bushes back, and there on a wall is a white statue, blind, and it starts to sing. That's the kind of voice I'm after.'⁹

The Ship Builder (1974), which Pegg described as 'straight out of an early Romantic opium dream',¹⁰ began life as a thematic folk opera, with parts intended for Shirley Collins and even Fairport Convention (who had released their own folk concept album, *'Babbacombe' Lee*, some years before). *Ancient Maps* (1975) features a procession of one-eyed merchants, hermits, treasure hunters, grail questers and wildmen of the hills criss-crossing the ley lines that lie in a pattern beneath the motorways and new towns of modern Britain. With attendant jazz musicians and contributions from the Bath Festival Orchestra, some of the arrangements have a lightness at odds with the dark characters roaming the text. By 1978 events in the seedy underworld of Leeds were catching up with Pegg's increasingly caustic visions. Officers from West Yorkshire police, under pressure to deliver results in their investigation of the Ripper murders, somehow got wind of Pegg's grungy single 'The Werewolf of Old Chapeltown', which mentions not only the evisceration of a prostitute, but even the Hayfield Hotel, where many of Peter Sutcliffe's victims used to drink. Pegg was briefly brought in for questioning, but naturally eliminated from enquiries in an instant. In 1989 he moved to the Scottish Highlands, where he resides, near the Cromarty Firth, in a landscape rich with superstition, folklore and magic: close by are Boleskine House, the former residence of Aleister Crowley and Jimmy Page, and Dornoch, where, in 1727, Janet Horne became the last person in Britain to be executed for witchcraft. 'What really attracts me to this place', he concludes, 'is the stories. It's just full of stories, and the stories are still here.'

Mr Fox were not the only group tuned in to the enduring presence of the supernatural in the British folk tradition. Anyone of a certain age exposed to BBC children's television during the 1970s will recall Toni Arthur: the enthusiastic, female, polo-necked co-presenter of toddler show *Play School* and its all-singing, all-dancing big brother *Playaway*, plus the folksy round-Britain travelogue series *Take a Ticket to* . . . But would parents have been so keen on exposing their little ones to the acoustic guitar-wielding wrangler of Big Ted, Humpty and their stuffed chums had they known that Toni had recently attended naked pagan ceremonies conducted by Britain's self-styled 'King of the Witches'?

By the time Toni Arthur began her television career, in September 1971, she and her husband Dave were established figures on the traditional folk circuit. Bert Lloyd acted as artistic director of their

Dave and Toni Arthur, *Morning Stands on Tiptoe* (1967), *Hearken to the Witches Rune* (1970); Graham Bond, *Holy Magick* (1970).

Transatlantic album *Morning Stands on Tiptoe* (1967), on whose sleeve Toni stands bathed in a dewy golden dawn in front of the White Horse at Cherhill, Wiltshire, and *The Lark in the Morning* (Topic, 1968). They had met in the early 1960s when Toni strolled into Dave's central London coffee bar, The Twelve-Stringer; by the end of the decade they were living in Lewisham, part of a babysitting circle with Shirley Collins, who lived across the heath, and Pete Maynard and Marian Gray of Martin Carthy's former skiffle group The Thamesiders. Dave Swarbrick lived nearby, and they were visited by Bob and Carole Pegg whenever the Mr Fox duo were gigging in London. Like the Peggs, and the Tim Hart/Maddy Prior duo, they were a couple drawn together in a romantic and professional quest through their country's folk heritage. 'We were interested in the fact that folk music, the popular culture, involves song, dance, storytelling, a whole range of things,' Dave Arthur tells me. 'Everything impinges on everything else in traditional culture . . . Dancers tell stories, singers dance, it's all mixed in.' The Arthurs devoured the whole gamut of English traditional culture, fraternising with the Hammersmith Morris and learning clog-dance steps from champion Johnson Elwood. 'I had to feel this music,' insists Toni, 'feel it and understand it with its total intensity. I could see how the "airy fairy" Irish traditional dance went exactly with the skipping, sliding, slurring sound of traditional Irish folk song. But I couldn't feel English music with my body. I needed to feel the rhythms through my feet. I tried morris dancing and country dancing, but that did little. Then I met Johnson Elwood in County Durham and learned the north-east style of clog dancing from him. Supposedly, Jimmy Elwood, Johnson's father, had taught Dan Leno, who had taught Fred Astaire, and thus tap-dancing began. And boy, did I understand the music more through this clonking, jumping, heart-pounding dance.'

'It seemed logical that if you could dance, you felt innately the rhythms, particularly the English rhythms, then it must affect your singing and the songs,' adds Dave Arthur. 'If you play a melodeon, you must imbibe somehow this English rhythm thing that I was looking for. So we were morris dancing, clog dancing, playing instrumental music, singing ballads and songs, researching, going off to manuscript collections and working on material, original stuff that nobody else was working on. And there was nobody else doing it then, we were really the only people mixing these things up at folk clubs. I would do a morris jig in the first half, Toni would do a clog dance on the table in a pub, and we'd play a couple of instrumental tunes, we'd sing songs. We'd talk about magic, as we'd got into witchcraft and studying it, to find out how witchcraft was reflected in traditional song – if the magical ballads were anything to do with what was perceived then as the Wicca, the witch covens that were going round in England, and whether they were actually related or whether it was a separate thing. And so we started going to meetings of witches and going through their ritual books and things, and we were invited as guests to all sorts of coven meetings, and then we were stuck in "Tam Lin" and all these magical ballads and somehow trying to relate them to what was going on in the occult world and find out what the connections were.'

In terms of their status in popular understanding, British pagan witchcraft and folk music are strikingly similar. Both are believed, even by many of the people who practise them, to afford a link to the distant medieval past or pre-Christian antiquity, but many of their identifying features are actually relatively modern inventions. A vastly simplified timeline of modern pagan witchcraft would go something like this: the art had kept a low profile since the witch hunts of the English Civil War and its aftermath. As we have seen, the revived Druidry of the late eighteenth and nineteenth centuries preserved certain aspects of hermetic lore in a relatively benign form. The highly influential late-Victorian Hermetic Order of the Golden Dawn, which included authors such as Bram Stoker, W. B. Yeats, Arthur

Machen, Algernon Blackwood, E. Nesbit and Aleister Crowley among its membership, set off a chain of organisations around the country which combined practising Thelemic magic and personal development with Masonic-style hierarchies, most prominently the OTO (Ordo Templi Orientis).

Gerald Gardner, acknowledged as the founder of modern Wicca, was an OTO initiate. A civil servant who had spent much of his working life based in Malaya and who collected magical artefacts, Gardner retired to a dozy village near the New Forest and was inducted into a local witch coven around the beginning of the 1940s. The details of who exactly provoked who to do what over the ensuing fifteen years are sketchy and much disputed, but by 1954 Gardner had become the most prominent leader among Britain's nationwide network of pagan witch covens, and had authored a book, *Witchcraft Today*, that described the modern Wicca movement as a resurgence of pre-Christian religion, a direct continuation of European pagan cults. Would-be initiates to what became known as 'Gardnerian Wicca' were required to make their own handwritten copy of the *Book of Shadows*, a workbook of spells, incantations and ritual instructions which had to be borrowed from another coven member.

In the early 1960s Alex Sanders, a young member of his local Manchester Gardnerian coven, became his group's High Priest, and through a charm offensive towards the media (tipping off tabloid reporters and TV stations about forthcoming 'secret' coven meetings, taking care to alert them to the likely presence of telegenic nude virgins) contributed to a huge surge in coven membership across the UK. For this reason, his followers nominated him King of the Witches, which was also the title of a biography of Sanders which added to the movement's notoriety on its publication in 1969.

By that time, Sanders and his wife Maxine were living in London's Notting Hill. One day he took a phone call from a researcher wanting permission to borrow Sanders's own *Book of Shadows* as part of a study of English folk-song origins. The caller was Dave Arthur. 'Alex Sanders, the King of the Witches, gave me his copy,' remembers Arthur, 'and I sat there for bloody weeks, copying by hand. And then I started going through it, and there's all these bits and snippets of rhymes and things, and one of them appears in the horn dance: "Take thou no scorn to wear the horn/ It was a crest ere thou wast born/ Thy father's father wore it/ And thy father bore it." And of course, that came from a Shakespeare play,[11] someone had found that and said, "Oh, that sounds authentic," so they dropped that into it. Then I was reading things like Charles Leland's book *Aradia*,[12] the gospel of the Italian witch cults that Leland collected during the nineteenth century. And I found all these rituals in there that were identical, they had just been lifted piecemeal and dropped into the *Book of Shadows* as authentic English rituals, and I also found a couple of things I had read in Crowley manuscripts and W. B. Yeats.'

'King of the Witches' Alex Sanders, on the sleeve of his 1970 album *A Witch Is Born*.

The cobbled-together nature of the *Book of Shadows* sharpened Dave Arthur's scepticism about the origins of many of the folk songs in the English tradition. 'So then we were looking at things like "Tam Lin" and these various ballads, "Thomas Rhymer", "Alison Gross", "John Barleycorn" of course, which at that point everyone was thinking was some kind of ritual song, the spirit in the barley and all of that, and of course it was just a drinking song in print in the 1700s. The conclusion I came to was that it was a completely made-up thing, by Gerald Gardner, primarily in the 1950s when the witchcraft laws were repealed. He put all this stuff together and made a religion from it.'

Legend of the Witches, a documentary made by Malcolm Leigh in 1970, shows the Sanders coven as Dave and Toni Arthur would have found it on their frequent visits to the basement flat in Notting Hill Gate. Intriguingly, the coven can be seen to have adopted some of the technology of modern psychedelia, using stroboscopic lights and flickering Op Art circles reminiscent of the hypnotic 'dreamachines' invented by William Burroughs and Brion Gysin. Sharp cuts between interior and exterior shots draw a clear connection between the ancient use of fire as a ritual focus and these artificially induced flicker effects. In one ceremony, shot in what looks suspiciously like a cheap television studio and soundtracked with fashionably muzzy sitar and tabla, an initiate is brought, unclothed, towards a stroboscope. 'His senses are constantly switched from one extreme to the other,' narrates the voice-over, 'so that he may come to the [scrying] mirror with all normal preconceptions swept from his mind.'

'In this particular group,' recalls Toni, 'Alex had a lot of mentally disturbed people. Especially those who heard voices and saw things. In the normal world they would have been considered ripe for ECT or very strong medication. However, he told them they were privileged to have contact with the other world. That they must learn to know when the "visitors" should invade their lives and to learn to live quietly with them. And it seemed to work remarkably well – at least they were happy, did no one any harm, and were able to live in society and without drugs.'

'We went down for rituals occasionally when he invited us,' continues Dave Arthur. 'There was a particular one where a German TV company went down to film. And he asked us as a favour to sing "John Barleycorn" and he would do a John Barleycorn ritual. We must have worn cloaks – we weren't naked, all the others were. I don't *think* we were . . . We sang "John Barleycorn", and Alex had just invented this bizarre ritual where he got this girl from the coven and threw flour over her, and then they tipped beer over her, and then it got so out of hand it was ridiculous. And the Germans who were filming it thought it was unbelievable, it was wonderful. He just went through the song as we sang it and made it up: the cutting down of the corn, the springing up, the threshing, and at the end of it this big libation with the beer and flour thrown everywhere.'[13]

Toni adds: 'Of course, Alex, the great showman that he was, told us we had to attend his coven meetings to truly "understand". With fear and trepidation we did this. Yes, we stripped naked and danced round in a circle. But this was surprisingly unsexy. We went about four or five times – and every time the magic seemed less and less plausible. I had a problem with religion of any kind. Wicca seemed perfectly harmless. It's not to be confused with black magic. It's not the purposeful reversing of Catholic ceremonies in order to gain power over others. It's just a sweet nature-revering religion. As one of the main premises is "anything you do you'll get back threefold", it's hardly given to evil work.

'What finished any involvement for me was when we took our dog Bess with us one time we were visiting. Alex leaned mysteriously over and felt her stomach and said, "Yes, the pups will come in about seven weeks." Magic indeed – she'd just been sterilised!'[14]

Hearken to the Witches Rune, which Dave and Toni recorded for Bill Leader's Trailer label in 1970, is one of English folk's great lost recordings, if only because it's been out of print since its first pressing. Far from the mystical sunrise of their 1967 image, on *Witches Rune* they are abroad in the thick of night, squinting out of the midnight shadows, as if about to disrobe for a black mass. This collection of the magical ballads they were steeped in at the time – 'Alison Gross', 'The Standing Stones', 'The Cruel Mother', 'The Fairy Child' et al. – has the raw spontaneity of what they might have been like if incorporated in magic rituals. Fans have long been baffled by the verse printed on the sleeve, under the title 'Hearken to the Witches Rune', even though there's no song of that name in the set list. In fact, Dave Arthur reveals, it's Sanders's own adaptation of the 'Witch's Chant', written by Gerald Gardner's High Priestess, Doreen Valiente, which has been adopted as a kind of supernatural 'come-all-ye' by successive Wiccans: '*Darksome night and shining moon/ East South West then North/ Hearken to the witch's rune/ Here I come to call thee forth.*'

If Wicca is a patchwork invention, shaped by the likes of Alex Sanders to fit the permissive mores of his time, then Dave and Toni Arthur's conclusions should equally be applied to our understanding of folk music – that its authenticity cannot be trusted. But should that completely invalidate Wicca as a modern religion, or discount the music? As we have repeatedly seen, there is no fixed origin, no one-and-only author, only a transmission process from mouth to mouth, age to age. The version of 'The Cruel Mother' on *Witches Rune* is substantially different, textually, from the one in, for instance, Geoffrey Grigson's *Penguin Book of Ballads*. But the story is essentially the same: a young woman gives birth in secret, stabs the baby (or twins in some versions) with a penknife, and buries it by moonlight. Later, the dead child appears to the mother in the porch of a church, cursing her and reminding her that eternal damnation awaits. It is a song that has been collected in many parts of the country over the decades; academics will wrangle for ever over the urtext, but in reality there is no 'correctness'. The cruel mother will continue to be haunted by the guilt-inducing spectre of her child, because, whether sung by a Highland crofter, an acoustic duo in a folk club, an electric rock band at an outdoor festival or in a home studio with an electronic ambient backing track, the song itself is undead, a ghost that refuses to be forgotten.

14

The Million-Volt Circus

To fathom hell, or soar angelic, take a pinch of psychedelic.
Dr Humphry Osmond, letter to Aldous Huxley (1955)[1]

'Curiouser and curiouser!' cried Alice (she was so much
surprised, that for the moment she quite forgot how to speak
good English); 'now I'm opening out like the largest telescope
that ever was!'
Lewis Carroll, *Alice's Adventures in Wonderland* (1865)

On 28 December 1966 the spirit of English psychedelia took its first breath. That evening, BBC television transmitted *Alice in Wonderland*, a specially commissioned seventy-two-minute adaptation of Lewis Carroll's celebrated children's fable. Directed by Jonathan Miller in black and white, and starring the likes of John Gielgud, Peter Cook, Alan Bennett and Peter Sellers, the production took a strikingly different tack from the famous Technicolor flora and fauna of Walt Disney's 1951 cartoon. Miller opted not to rummage in the BBC costume department's animal-head cupboards, but instead depicted all the inhabitants of Wonderland – including the March Hare, White Rabbit, Mock Turtle and Dodo – as human characters, denizens of a bureaucratic, doddering and occasionally vicious mid-Victorian milieu. This was Wonderland rerouted via Czech expressionism with a dash of Ingmar Bergman; Alice as defiant, hair-tossing Kafka heroine, patiently yet sullenly negotiating a sequence of excruciating encounters with eccentric bores and psychotic egoists. Alice's perambulations mostly emphasise the child's perspective on a stupefyingly dull, hidebound and repressive institutional culture. And in Miller's setting, the boredom is counterpointed by the unending, sultry, dusty summer afternoon in which it takes place, accentuated by a magnificently languid soundtrack, composed for the programme by the Indian sitar master Ravi Shankar.

Miller's *Alice* is particularly adept at bringing out the central unspoken theme of Carroll's novel: the fact that the heroine is undergoing the uneasy throes of puberty. Trick photography, vertiginous angles and outsize props recreate her growth spurts and shrinkages when she consumes mushrooms or bottles marked 'Eat me' and 'Drink me'. At the conclusion of Carroll's sequel, *Alice Through the Looking-Glass*, she eventually crosses to the far side of a chessboard and becomes Queen – in other words, she becomes a responsible adult. The Victorians prized and preserved children's innocence as long as it could hold out: the jump to adulthood was absolute, the crossing of a clearly marked line. Lewis Carroll, for all his fascination with mathematics, logic games and linguistic riddles, was a Romantic manqué, insisting on seeing with the child's eye. The kaleidoscopic journey of his Alice serves to show up the absurdity of an adult world that claimed responsibility and the moral high ground, but was more often bogged down in meaningless ritual and hollow etiquette. At the end of Miller's adaptation, Alice recites lines from Wordsworth's *Intimations of Immortality from Recollections of Early Childhood*:

> There was a time when meadow, grove, and stream,
> The earth, and every common sight,
> To me did seem
> Apparelled in celestial light,
> The glory and the freshness of a dream.
> It is not now as it hath been of yore; –
> Turn wheresoe'er I may,
> By night or day,
> The things which I have seen I now can see no more.

The intensified vision of childhood, and the mourning of its loss, are the defining characteristics of both Romanticism and English psychedelia. For the technicolour dreamers of the 1960s, the tone had already been set back in the mid-1950s, in some of the first newspaper reports on LSD use in Britain. 'Science Has Alice-in-Wonderland Drug', blared the headline to the *News Chronicle*'s article on the psychiatric research taking place under Dr Ronnie Sandison at Powick Hospital in Worcestershire.[2] Another report mentioned that, after ingesting the new drug, 'The patient acts, speaks and thinks like a child and in this state is led step by step through buried memories until the incidents which may be causing his mental condition are reached.'[3] Dr Sandison himself noted his subjects' 'change to an infantile body image'.[4] Some of The Beatles' first LSD-inspired music, twelve years later, was a therapeutic magic-carpet ride to childhood's pleasure gardens. The group had already wrapped up the sessions for 'Strawberry Fields Forever' just before Christmas 1966. The morning after the transmission of Miller's *Alice*, they entered Abbey Road Studios to commence recording 'Penny Lane'. Six months later, Lewis Carroll would take his place, sandwiched between Marlene Dietrich and T. E. Lawrence, on the sleeve of *Sgt Pepper's Lonely Hearts Club Band*.

Early morning, 30 January 1967: exactly one month after the *Alice in Wonderland* transmission. The four Beatles pull up in their limousines at the gates of Knole Park, near Sevenoaks in Kent. Swedish film director Peter Goldmann is already here, supervising his camera and lighting crews and marshalling the gathering crowd of onlookers, mostly uniformed lads from the local public school. They are here to shoot a promotional film – one of the first of its kind – for The Beatles' new single, 'Strawberry Fields Forever', which has been gestating along with its flip side, 'Penny Lane', for most of the previous autumn. The track has turned out to be the group's second successful experimental creation since 'Tomorrow Never Knows', the backwards-guitar-drenched closer of the previous year's *Revolver*. But where 'Tomorrow Never Knows' was saturated in quasi-Buddhist mysticism and Jungian psychology, 'Strawberry Fields' is the first example anywhere of what Ian MacDonald called 'a sort of technologically-evolved folk music'[5]: an innately English psychedelia.

What makes 'Strawberry Fields Forever' psychedelic, and what makes it English? It's the outcome of a magic trick in itself, having been craftily constructed from two out-of-tune takes. The quartet are heard in the first minute or so playing with a sleepwalking, woozy gait; then the EMI engineers spin in the second section featuring what sounds like the monumental swoops of a symphony orchestra, but in fact is just three cellos and four trumpets. The splice is clearly audible: the dreamy pace is given an electric shock as Ringo Starr cranks the tempo into a rolling panjandrum and the ploughing strings gouge vertiginous troughs. Towards the end of the song, cymbals are played backwards and two distinct drum tracks appear to be overlaid, slightly askew, like drawings on overlapping sheets of tracing paper. The song progresses through distinct 'movements', beginning with the reedy stripes of a lonely mellotron – its recordery tones anticipating the prevalence of woodwind instruments in many folk-rock records of the next few years. The conventional distinction between verse and chorus is blurred into an asymmetric pattern of dissolves. Ringing out between the scene-shifts, in a delicate falling cadence, are the taut, hammered strings of a svaramandal, an Indian dulcimer-type instrument anglicised as 'swordmandel' – the obligatory 'exotic' tinge of the psychedelic aesthetic. 'Strawberry Fields Forever' is pregnant with whole futures of music; an underground bulb in its winter-long sleep.

The song is radical lyrically, too: impressionistic and syntactically perverse in places, the text alone resists confining itself to one specific subject, mood or experience. In fact, the lines enact *non-specificity*: it contains conversational evasions such as '*that is, you can't, you know, tune in*', '*always, no sometimes*' and '*I mean, er, yes*' – hesitations unprecedented in pop lyrics of the time. Repeated references to knowing and not knowing, misunderstanding, living with eyes closed, agreeing and disagreeing, are offset against the one certainty, the one thing that is 'forever': Strawberry Fields. And that certainty is based not on anything in the present, but on a memory.

To locate the key to this remarkable piece of experimental pop – and to the enigma of English psychedelia – you need to examine the song at the moment of its conception. There is a wobbly bootleg in circulation of John Lennon taping his earliest fumblings with the idea in the summer of 1966, while staying at Santa Isabel, a house in Almeria, south-eastern Spain. There to film his starring role as Musketeer Gripweed in Richard Lester's *How I Won the War*, Lennon spent six weeks in exile, his first change of pace since the group had retired from live performance and Lennon had been persecuted in America for his notoriously inflated 'bigger than Jesus' remark. The exile's thoughts naturally turned towards his distant home, and to the childhood he had barely had a moment to ruminate upon during the past five years' Beatlemania. 'It did me a lot of good to get away,' he told *Playboy* many years later. 'I was there six weeks. I wrote "Strawberry Fields Forever" there, by the way. It gave me time to think on my own, away from the others. From then on, I was looking for somewhere to go, but I didn't have the nerve to really step out on the boat by myself and push it off.'[6] So the song is dominated by this loss of nerve, and the lyrical evasions previously noted are mental gear-slippages that are held in check by a nostalgic memory.

Strawberry Field was a romantically named Salvation Army orphanage near Penny Lane in Liverpool, a Gothic pile with wooded grounds where Lennon and his friends would play cowboys and Indians in its bushes and scale its trees (something of that clambering spirit survives in the promo film, which is centred on a gnarly oak tree in the middle of Knole Park). By adding an 's', Lennon transferred a real place to a timeless and ethereal plane, like 'Elysian Fields'.

In those Santa Isabel demos, Lennon is obsessing around the phrase '*No one is on my wavelength*' – a relatively trite expression of the misfit's condition. Then he extends the cliché, musing that his wavelength must be too high or low – the ambiguity that pervades the song is already present. On a later sketch, Lennon's free association has converted the technological metaphor into an organic one: now, it is not the wavelength that is too high or low, but the tree he is in. Thinking about being up a tree leads him directly to the first memory that comes to mind: the long-gone larks in Strawberry Field. Another line, that all this uncertainty is nothing to get mad about, then becomes '*nothing to get hung about*'. This is the voice of his aunt and stepmother Mimi, who reportedly threatened to 'hang' the young Lennon whenever he committed a misdemeanour.

In Knole Park, an upright piano has been gutted and its strings disembowelled, woven up into the branches of a withered tree: an Aeolian harp of fish bones. The film cuts between dawn mist and night shots spotlit with red and green gels. Like the track, the video is composed of exaggerated focus-pulls and haunting double exposures. The handheld camera gets in The Beatles' faces, as they visibly shiver in the morning freeze. The group are disconcertingly lifeless: much of the film consists of close-ups of their blank, newly moustachioed faces gaping at the lens, or side-on tracking shots as each one plods, apparently chilled to the bone, around the tree. What action there is centres on the gutted piano; John, George and Ringo gather round it like some sonic altar as Paul, having tiptoed in reverse and 'dropped upwards' into the tree, fine-tunes the strings on tuning pegs that resemble a television aerial. The film, then, captures both the 'wavelength' origin of the song and its final form. The last forty-five seconds – the back-masked 'false ending' – both demystify and intensify the enigma: The Beatles banter as they trudge off to the set; the piano is pulled over, crashing into two film lanterns.

The two-day shoot for 'Strawberry Fields Forever' acted as the gateway to the group's next historic move. Between takes, Lennon purchased a Victorian circus poster at a nearby antique shop, from which he lifted the complete lyrics to 'Being for the Benefit of Mr Kite'. The day after they completed filming, they were back at Abbey Road, where they recorded the theme tune of *Sgt Pepper's Lonely Hearts Club Band*. The spontaneous underground began shooting its tendrils towards the light.

> . . . fairy stories held me high on
> Clouds of sunlight floating by.
> Oh Mother, tell me more . . .

> Pink Floyd, 'Matilda Mother' (1967)

John Lennon's line about 'tuning in', of course, also linked to Timothy Leary's phrase 'Turn on, tune in, drop out', invented at the behest of Marshall McLuhan as the buzz line of America's counter-culture. It's unlikely Lennon would have been conscious of the slogan when he wrote the song, as Leary only first used it in public during a New York press conference in September 1966: 'Like every great religion of the past we seek to find the divinity within and to express this revelation in a life of glorification and the worship of God. These ancient goals we define in the metaphor of the present – turn on, tune in, drop out.' Far from being intended to mean 'Get stoned and abandon all constructive activity' – the interpretation of thousands of hippy camp followers – Leary's injunction was a Pied Piper's clarion call to the young people of tomorrow to search for a meaningful spiritual path out of modernity's misery factory. The late-1960s love-in would be an unexpected bonus.

English psychedelia emphasised not so much turning on and tuning in, but turning back and tuning in to echoes of the past. The British never 'did' free love to the same extent as the Californians: the courtly, medieval flavour of much acoustic folk and rock of the late 1960s and early 70s carries an air of unworldliness. Implicit in this more remote mien was the yawning difference between post-war British and American youth. In the United States, affluence and an ingrained constitutional classlessness laid the seedbed for a vigorous counter-culture. For Britons, the austerity years of the 1950s were a memory too recent to shrug off easily, while a class system still visibly and audibly in force made indolence a luxury. When Joni Mitchell sang of getting back to the garden, you felt she pictured a host of naked longhairs disporting themselves in love games on the cliffs of Big Sur. For Brits, the image that springs to mind is a cheeky reefer in the potting shed before getting back to work on the allotment.

History has made *Sgt Pepper* the foundation stone of the English psychedelic revolution, but it was very much part of a tidal wave. Throughout the spring of 1967 The Beatles – who had already claimed to have enjoyed a sneaky toke in the Buckingham Palace lavatories – found themselves creating the album in studios sandwiched between other emerging groups who were labouring over two more significant experimental rock albums of that year: The Pretty Things' thematic *SF Sorrow*, and Pink Floyd's *The Piper at the Gates of Dawn*. As we've already seen, Pink Floyd's chief songwriter Syd Barrett named the record after the seventh chapter of Kenneth Grahame's *TheWind in theWillows*, the perennial Edwardian children's favourite embodying the whimsical life of the woods. The chapter features a dream-like encounter with the Great God Pan himself, an experience Barrett believed he had shared in his lazy afternoons in Grantchester Meadows near Cambridge, according to Pink Floyd's manager at the time, Andrew King: 'He thought Pan had given him insight and understanding into the way nature works.'[7]

Pink Floyd's Barrett period (1966–9) is all about escapism. Several of Barrett's songs are shaped as fairy tales populated with a Grimm cast of kings, princesses and gnomes. His songs, from the earliest writings to his post-Floyd solo work, are a colourful parade of gingerbread men, mice called Gerald, buttercups and dandelions, terrapins and octopi, candy, currant buns and ice cream, dream dragons and unicorns. Pink Floyd's music of this period is strangely pushed and pulled between nostalgia for the secret gardens of the child's imagination and the space-age futurism of interstellar overdrive. Binning the operating manual for spaceship Earth, they set the controls for an accelerated oblivion. But that sunburst could equally merge into the endless summer memories of childhood.

If there's one word that sums up the spirit of the English Summer of Love, it would have to be 'carnivalesque'. Fairgrounds, circuses, open-air markets, musical halls proffering 'amusements' of a predominantly comical and light-musical character, pavement theatre, broadside ballads, the roadside songs of street hawkers and sweeps, the songs and stories of nomadic pedlars and Gypsies all provided an outlet for shared enjoyment but formed the 'underground' of their day, part of a vernacular public culture that was largely overlooked by the arbiters of Victorian artistic taste. As industrial labour pressurised and organised the working population along mechanical lines, such unsanctioned culture was the distant forerunner of post-war popular music. The difference was that in the 1960s there was an industry ready and waiting to exploit it as soon as it rose up from the streets, bundling it into the impeccably managed carnival of 'Swinging London'. *Sgt Pepper's*

Lonely Hearts Club Band, the flagship album of the era, is a carousel of styles hawked by a group of fairground barkers clad in gaudy Victorian satins and clutching brass instruments. They remained in character from the start of the year, when they recorded the avant-garde 'Carnival of Light' – a fifteen-minute collage of dissonance and shouting that remained unreleased for more than four decades – until the end of the year, when they exhorted TV viewers on Boxing Day 1967 to roll up for what turned out to be a rather drizzly, underwhelming magical mystery tour.

With the wireless dial locked to John Peel's buccaneering pirate-radio show *The Perfumed Garden*, adherents of this new cult reached deep into history's dressing-up box. Wrapping themselves in the floral prints of William Morris and the crushed velvet, lace cuffs and cravats of Oscar Wilde, the Mod-Edwardian dandy lions progressed in the late 1960s towards the out-and-out fancy dress visible on, for instance, The Young Tradition's *Galleries* or The Rolling Stones' flawed riposte to The Beatles, *Their Satanic Majesties Request*. At the UFO Club, Arthur Brown would effect acrobatic entrances worthy of a music-hall conjuror, popping through trapdoors, swinging in on a trapeze or materialising in a pyrotechnic puff of smoke. It's no coincidence that when The Stones chose to close 1968 by filming a multi-act TV extravaganza (never actually broadcast), they constructed a big top over the sound stage and called it *The Rock 'n' Roll Circus*. And with the conversion of Camden Town's former covered railway turntable into a giant performance venue called The Roundhouse, the movement had its own circus tent. The ringmaster of The Roundhouse's rehabilitation was Arnold Wesker, the playwright who had founded the influential left-wing theatre and folk-music initiative Centre 42, which now owned the building's shell. Wesker hoped to make it 'a workers' fun palace and a mecca for the socialist arts', but was stymied by lack of funds.[8] *International Times* hosted its launch party there in 1966, with sideshows including a giant jelly moulded in a bathtub.

As declared on *IT*'s strapline, the prime concerns of the newly energised underground movement included 'Culture, Space, Love and the Invisible Insurrection of a Million Minds'. The insurrection switched into overdrive from around May Day of 1967, that moment in which spring fertility rites coincide with the communist-backed workers' public holiday. In 1967 it was also the moment when the gateway to the Summer of Love swung open. On 29 April the 14 Hour Technicolour Dream at north London's Alexandra Palace became the first event of its kind to attract more than 10,000 people. *IT*'s team of hustlers, including Barry Miles, John 'Hoppy' Hopkins and Mick Farren, were behind this one, too. With art installations and performances such as Yoko Ono's *Cut Piece*, geodesic domes and styrofoam igloos, a helter-skelter ride and stalls selling trinkets and toys, this was a Great Exhibition for the costumed peacocks of Swinging London, under a blanket of electric cacophony. Groups such as Tomorrow, The Crazy World of Arthur Brown, Pink Floyd, The Soft Machine, The Pretty Things, Graham Bond, John's Children, Alex Harvey, Champion Jack Dupree, The Move, The Deviants and The Giant Sun Trolley performed – often in a simultaneous soundclash – on twin, facing stages. 'What the hell was going on here?' asked Mick Farren, singer with The Deviants, in a later memoir. 'Was it merely a vast fashion aberration, or were we seeing a brand-new mass art movement, like the Pre-Raphaelites or the Aesthetes, only quantum multiplied by the vast numbers of the baby boom? The idea that seemed almost dangerous to entertain was that Miles' abstraction of an alternative society was actually coming to pass, but at a frightening and uncontrolled rate, like a viral culture growing exponentially, each cell dividing and reproducing over and over again.'[9]

The festivities continued thirteen days later with Pink Floyd's

Won't you join the dance? Donovan in Jacques Demy's *The Pied Piper* (1972).

Games for May, a 'space age relaxation for the climax of spring' at the Queen Elizabeth Hall. Blasting through one of the first quadraphonic amplification systems, The Floyd improvised their work-in-progress *Piper* album as a rock Rite of Spring. The foyer resounded with canned birdsong, and front-row ticket holders were showered with bubbles and daffodils tossed by someone in an admiral's costume. July found The Beatles premiering the flower-power anthem 'All You Need Is Love', with its music-hall brass-fanfare introduction, taking the spectacle to a global level via a live international TV link. Meanwhile, Donovan removed all traces of his Woody Guthrie-influenced past, peeled the sticky-tape legend 'This guitar kills' off his acoustic guitar and replaced it with spangly silver stars, as part of his reinvention as pot-headed Pied Piper come to spirit off the children of Albion to a hidden land of perpetual fried picnics. After hymning the 'Mellow Yellow' saffron cake he used to buy at a baker's shop in St Ives during his beatnik hikes to Cornwall, Donovan spent most of 1967 as a man-child magus hosting a technicolour tea party. A promotional film made for a medley of songs from that year's *A Gift from a Flower to a Garden* shows Donovan in florid wizard's robes holding court on the lawn of a Cornish cottage that's been transformed into a clotted-cream Camelot. Graham Nash juggles oranges, clad in beads and a shawl, and other youthful friends in elfin attire tootle bamboo pipes and swat wooden tambourines. Much of *A Gift . . .* was aimed at his audience's inner child. He appended lines from Lewis Carroll's 'Lobster Quadrille' to 'Under the Greenwood Tree', and the second disc of the double LP was subtitled *For Little Ones*, an acoustic collection of gentle child-friendly tunes for what he called 'the dawning generation'. Between July 1968 and early 1971 Donovan recorded a children's album that surfaced as *HMS Donovan*, mostly new music settings of existing poems and lyrics. It was the kind of child's garden of verse that recalled Victorian nurseries or the youthful protagonists of E. Nesbit stories, a fantastical and nonsensical songbook including Lewis Carroll's 'Jabberwocky' and 'The Walrus and the Carpenter', Edward Lear's 'The Owl and the Pussycat', Yeats's 'Song of the Wandering Aengus', even the deathless 'Twinkle Twinkle Little Star'. Donovan's own composition, 'In an Old Fashioned Picture Book', was a sentimental tapestry of seafront nostalgia, as yellowed photos of a little girl called Patience found in an old album stir up *'Faint sounds of a distant brass band, who rides the donkey today? / Will our visions of tomorrow mingle with those of yesterday?'* His attempt to set up a commune on his private Scottish islands Isay, Mingay and Clett – the goal of Vashti Bunyan's year-long pilgrimage – came to nothing, as he vanished into tax exile shortly after. But in 1972 Donovan was actually cast in the lead role of Jacques Demy's film *The Pied Piper*.

The attempt to reclaim a lost childhood was an inevitable response from the urban generation born in the mid- to late 1940s who had made their playgrounds in the rubble-strewn aftermath of a world war. Britain's blues boom of the early to mid-1960s was an attachment fantasy to an America that appeared, by comparison, to be a land of plenty. But as the decade wore on, and Britons could get to witness the glory of Bob Dylan's performances at first hand, the Anglo version of American music was shown up as a cheap imitation. The native Dylan was intimately entangled in the language of the Beats, Burroughs and Ginsberg in a way the English pretenders would never master. So the authenticist diktats of Ewan MacColl and co. had, perhaps, sunk deeper than expected; the challenge now was to redraw rock and psychedelia in a British vernacular. Not so much a distorted Americana, more a warped Victoriana: pastoral myths for the smoke-bound consumer, hallucinatory trips to the country and a rebirth in the secret gardens of childhood. Not for nothing did Michael Horovitz title his 1969 anthology of underground and counter-cultural poetry *Children of Albion*, with William Blake's painting *Glad Day* emblazoned on the front cover. And lest we forget, the working title for The Beatles' 1968 'White Album' was *A Doll's House*.

Music typical of the born-again Avalonians could be found on records like The Zombies' *Odessey and Oracle*, a reverb-soaked sunshine-pop record which fed Watersons-style close harmonies through The Beach Boys' beatific solar filter, and whose songs like 'Time of the Season', 'Brief Candle' and 'Changes' obsessed on the passage of time and the wheel of the year. Or there was *Children of the Sun* by The Sallyangie, an admixture of starlight, golden innocence, dreamy idealism and lightly narcotised surrealism. The Sallyangie were the teenage brother–sister duo of Mike and Sally Oldfield. The future begetter of *Tubular Bells* appears as a fifteen-year-old pageboy to his elder sister's swan-singing Ophelia. For all the tales of sweet princes and feeding cream cheese to doves on the lawn, Mike Oldfield's backcloth of tender acoustic guitar and primitive percussion provides a beguiling accompaniment to Sally's oddly mannered delivery.

Mike Oldfield later turned up as electric guitarist on the early solo albums of Kevin Ayers, the founder of Canterbury's The Wilde

Flowers, who later became UFO regulars The Soft Machine. Ayers's 'Girl on a Swing', from 1969, is just one example of the way Lewis Carroll's child-woman Alice recurs – under a variety of different names – as an unattainable, mysterious archetype in many of the English psychedelic songs of this period: The Beatles' 'Lucy in the Sky with Diamonds', The Rolling Stones' 'Child of the Moon', King Crimson's 'Moonchild', Pink Floyd's 'See Emily Play' and 'Julia Dream', Syd Barrett's adaptation of James Joyce's poem 'Golden Hair', Donovan's 'Jennifer Juniper', The Zombies' 'A Rose for Emily', Tyrannosaurus Rex's 'Debora', Kaleidoscope's 'Jenny Artichoke' . . .

Kaleidoscope were among the quickest off the mark at the dawn of 1967, having simultaneously arrived at their own version of *Sgt Pepper*'s florid celebratory circus. A west London four-piece fronted by songwriting duo Peter Daltrey and Eddie Pumer, they evolved from a mid-1960s beat group into paisley-clad, sculpturally coiffed nabobs of the new pop. Resplendent in Edwardian lace cravats, velvet frock coats and Annello & Davide Cuban heels, they looked as if they had just stepped off H. G. Wells's time machine to confront the Morlocks of the modern age. The garishly lit 'Kaleidoscope' and 'Holiday Maker', recorded in February, pre-dated the release of *Sgt Pepper*, and their album, *Tangerine Dream*, released in November, was being made all through the Summer of Love. Like a nanny demanding hush before the telling of a lengthy tale, *Tangerine Dream* begins by stilling its listeners with a hypnotic mantra: *'Relax your eyes/ For after all, we can but share these minutes . . .'*. The song 'Kaleidoscope' itself, and 'Dive into Yesterday', are vivid synaesthetic festivals of colour and sensation: *'Satin sounds, lots of million-coloured lights/ Some vermillion'*; *'The Mardi Gras at midnight, the songs tumbling in sound/ While Shakespeare floats with wild roses in his head.'* 'Flight from Ashiya', their first single, released in September, describes a turbulent, chaotic aeroplane trip. But, like Jonathan Miller's *Alice in Wonderland*, Kaleidoscope were also brilliant at painting still, ageless interiors;

the mothy romance of dusty attics and the long, quiet continuation of routine lives such as 'Mr Small the Watch-Repairer Man'. 'A Lesson Perhaps' is a spoken-word parable, a Mervyn Peake-style vignette of a '*king of the forest*' withering away in a Gothic throne room of dust and flies. Their songs were written in the attic of Pumer's family home in Acton, immortalised in '(Further Reflections) in the Room of Percussion' – a lofty creative oasis where, behind rain-beaten windows, and under the influence of ruby wine, joss sticks and an ouija board, '*The crooked faces of clocks appear and die in nightmare dreams*'.

The group made one more album as Kaleidoscope, *Faintly Blowing*, released in the spring of 1969. Executioners, magic zoos, ladies on trains offering intoxicating liquids, snapdragons and imprisoned cowboys pass through in a phantasmagoric parade; Donovan's collaborator John Cameron contributes orchestral arrangements for the lavish 'If You So Wish' and 'Black Fjord', the latter a whip-cracking cavalcade of Norse and Saxon gods. The song's Vikings, as well as Tudor and medieval minstrels, a demure milkmaid and a green-hooded Pierrot, all materialise out of the woodland mist that creeps around the group on the album sleeve. The photo was shot next to an ancient blasted oak trunk in the middle of Burnham Beeches, an ancient tract of Buckinghamshire woodland popular as a fantastical film location, from a 1952 *Robin Hood and His Merrie Men* to twenty-first-century adaptations of King Arthur and Harry Potter. The group stand despondent and funereal among their misty memories, as if aware that their 'Sunnyside Circus' will soon be striking camp and moving on without them. A Beatles-style pop supernova was intended for Kaleidoscope by its managers, which never quite occurred. Later in 1969 they changed their name to the quaint Fairfield Parlour, made one flawed album, *From Home to Home* (Vertigo), appeared at the second Isle of Wight Festival and then faded away. *Faintly Blowing*'s final track, an experimental, proto-progressive freakout called 'Music', is loaded with an awareness that the ancestral spirits their music tried to protect were being displaced by the noise of modernity: '. . . *the organ-grinder's ghost is changing key / The rock 'n' roll crusade has crucified the past / Leaving only shadows of electricity.*'

'We seek to stimulate our own inner gardens if we are to save our Earth and ourselves from engulfment.' Thus wrote Muz Murray in the introduction to his independently produced magazine *Gandalf's Garden*, which ran to six issues between 1968–70. *Gandalf's Garden* was the name of Murray's shop on the King's Road in Chelsea, a proto-New Age comfort zone which housed a commune of enlightened heads and soul gardeners, distinctively eschewing drugs in favour of the more natural highs of incense, meditation, yoga and emergent eco-consciousness. With cushions, beanbags and honey tea on tap, the shop was a cocoon equipped to

Kaleidoscope, *Faintly Blowing* (1969).

isolate fragile hippy sensibilities from the big, bad world outside, clouding their heads with the kind of alternative information found in the house journal: Earth mysteries, the lost continents of Mu and Atlantis, speculations about Jesus's links with the Druids and Glastonbury, and philosophies from the ancient Greeks to Hare Krishna. 'Oh, To Be in England' was the sarcastic title of one regular section, lampooning parochial cuttings from newspapers and journals. But one had to wonder whether the bulk of the magazine's other content betrayed an equally strong yearning for a lost country: an appeal to a dormant Arthur/Albion archetype to awaken and offer balm to a broken land.

Thus enlightened, much of Gandalf's Garden's clientele would have regularly slouched towards Middle Earth, the underground club started by John 'Hoppy' Hopkins in November 1967 in the basement of a Covent Garden warehouse, and which later moved to the Roundhouse. Like Hopkins's previous club, UFO (which had recently shut down), Middle Earth provided a total immersive environment in sound and light. The psychedelic slide shows and lava-lamp projections by Mark Boyle, Binder Edwards and Vaughan, Jo Gannon, Ken Hughes and Mike Leonard added amoebic backdrops to the very cellular songs of The Soft Machine, Pink Floyd, The Nice, Tomorrow, The Crazy World of Arthur Brown, Fairport Convention, Eclection and The Alan Bown Set. In fact, the glutinous warp of ambiguous, morphing forms – which simultaneously suggested deep-space telescopy and a womb with a view – was the gimmick that inspired the likes of Pink Floyd to abstract and stretch out their instrumental sound, rather than vice versa.

Like the anti-materialistic Victorian Pre-Raphaelite artists they modelled their looks on, English hippies invoked the sleeping King Arthur as a shield against a venal, plastic age. But Middle Earth and Gandalf's Garden confirmed the centrality of the novels everyone was reading – or at least checking the back-cover blurb of – in the British underground: J. R. R. Tolkien's three-volume

Front cover of the second edition of *Gandalf's Garden* (1968).

legendarium, *The Lord of the Rings*. Completed in 1955, the monumental trilogy compressed the Oxford philologist's interests in Northern European language, myth and racial memory into a new form of high-register fantasy writing. With hindsight it's easy to understand the appeal of Tolkien's Middle-earth to the British generation of Hobbit heads. Britain *was* Middle-earth: a conflicted cluster of kingdoms and languages, with a very aged ancient history that was written in scattered fragments and dialects across its map. The Shire, homeland of the Hobbits, is a caricature of the Anglo-Saxon ideal of Merrie England, all rolling downs, village greens and easeful plenty. The weed that is smoked in Hobbits' clay pipes, it's even hinted, is a mild narcotic that triggers their love of spinning epic yarns of distant yore. In Middle-earth, the counterforce is the dark land of Mordor to the south-east. With its engines of war and the fiery, white-heat technology of Mount Doom, Mordor is a military-industrial complex gearing up to wage a battle of evermore, forever disrupting the stability of the rest of Middle-earth. As a rough, fantastical mapping of the previous twenty years of world history, Tolkien wove a convincing enough analogy, and it certainly spoke to the children born in the middle of the real-life conflict who now just wanted to retreat to the Shires to do their own thing in peace.

In the closing months of 1967 the young Marc Bolan handed copies of *The Hobbit* and *The Lord of the Rings* to producer Tony Visconti with the words, 'If you're gonna record me, you gotta read these.'[10] Bolan had recently split from his freakbeat group John's Children and had scaled down operations to an acoustic duo, Tyrannosaurus Rex, with percussionist Steve Peregrine Took, whose name marked him as yet another denizen of Tolkien's universe. Visconti produced Tyrannosaurus Rex's first album, which appeared in the summer of 1968 under the Rococo title *My People Were Fair and Had Sky in Their Hair . . . But Now They're Content to Wear Stars on Their Brows*. 'Tyrannosaurus Rex rose out of the sad and scattered leaves of an older summer,' read the album's somewhat precious sleeve notes. 'During the hard, grey winter they were tended and strengthened by those who love them. They blossomed with the coming of spring, children rejoiced and the earth sang with them. It will be a long and ecstatic summer.' The lines were penned by John Peel, whose radio presentations were tightly entwined with Bolan's manoeuvres during the Tyrannosaurus Rex years. The early autumn of 1967 marked an interim period for Peel: he had lost his job at the pirate station Radio London, where he had ruled the private fiefdom of his legendary *Perfumed Garden*, and had not yet moved to the BBC, where he would live out the remainder of a four-decade career. On *The Perfumed Garden*, Peel had developed a very English-whimsical form of radiophonic anarchy, replicating the indolent vibe of the average middle-class music fan's herbal, hedonistic bedroom. 'We're going to have to buy an island somewhere, or make one, and all go and live on it together, and have hundreds of dibblers, and sparrows, and all the other nice things wafting around, and nobody would bother us,' he might improvise, between a sitary Donovan track and a slice of swampy Memphis blues.[11] 'Wander through in our midst and

Tyrannosaurus Rex, *Prophets, Seers and Sages, the Angels of the Ages* (1968).

pick out a flower from the Perfumed Garden and plant it in your mind.'[12] With its idle, surrealistic speculations, mock-florid links, extracts from the *International Times* and indirect encouragements to attend political demonstrations, the show preserved the last, carefree days of adolescence, the age of dreaming rather than doing. It was a brief, charmed interlude, for the Garden was boarded up by broadcasting authorities, along with the rest of Radio London, in August 1967.

Peel's DJ slot at the Middle Earth club put him in close touch with the freakier end of Britain's folk-progressive scene, and when he began his tenure at the BBC with *Top Gear* on the first day of October, he commissioned many of the regular performers to record 'sessions' exclusively for the programme – which accumulated over his lifetime to become an institution. Within a month, his buddies Tyrannosaurus Rex became the first unsigned act to receive the BBC shilling (they went on to tape six sessions in eighteen months, prompting accusations of favouritism). From January 1968 Peel returned to the midnight slot where his intimate, conspiratorial style worked best, presenting *Night Ride*, a barely more professionalised continuation of *The Perfumed Garden*. Until its closure in summer 1968, Middle Earth cradled a brief interlude of innocence in the British scene, which Peel and Bolan embraced to the full. They went record shopping together and enjoyed questing days out with their respective partners (Bolan with June Child, the former lover of Syd Barrett) to Glastonbury Tor and Stonehenge. Peel even narrated Bolan's *Wind in the Willows*-ish woodland fable on 'Romany Soup', from 1969's *Unicorn*. One Tyrannosaurus Rex concert advertisement from the same year promises 'John Peel proving the existence of fairies'.[13] And when Peel set up his own record label (home to Bridget St John, Principal Edwards Magic Theatre, Kevin Coyne and others), he named it Dandelion – in honour of a hamster Bolan had given him as a gift.

For Marc Bolan, the Tyrannosaurus rex was a dragon that science had proved to have walked the Earth, justifying the existence of the other mythical beasts – centaurs, unicorns – that cantered through his songs. A typical Tyrannosaurus Rex happening consisted of the strumming 'Warlock of Love' and his bongo-batting scullion – 'A couple of rough gnomes bashing each other with toadstools', as Chris Welch memorably described them in *Melody Maker* – sitting cross-legged on an Afghan carpet, with Bolan bleating in a Larry the Lamb tremolo. Compared to The Incredible String Band's contemporaneous spirit odysseys, Bolan's songs sound like an unbearably overspiced cod-Celtic gumbo, a kitsch antique store stuffed with onyx dolphins, marble satyrs, astrakhan chaises, ostrich feathers and elkhorn trumpets. Just as the duo ostentatiously crammed the back-cover photo of *Unicorn* with the trappings of mystic learning – Kahlil Gibran's *The Prophet*, a *Children's Shakespeare*, volumes of Blake and Yeats, and a photo album of the fake Cottingley fairies – they might dedicate an album to 'Aslan and the Old Narnians' or adorn their live sets with poetry readings about elves, gorgons or Greek or

Inca gods. If there was any narrative arc to Bolan's songwriting between 1967–9, it could be found in the recurring characters of the 'Scenescofs', who corrupt the youthful hippy idyll with age, cynicism and barbarity. 'I don't want to know about society as it is – it brings me down,' Bolan told *Circus* magazine. 'I wish I could get away to another place where mountains rise unspoilt to the sky and you could ride horses as far as the eye could see.'[14]

Towards the end of the 1960s a growing number of artists gravitated towards psychedelia's glittering colour wheel to escape the monochrome hues of the blues boom. By the time he became an elfin hippy minstrel, Marc Bolan had plotted a changeling path through the decade's youth subcultures, beginning as a sharp-dressed Mod. By 1968, when Middle Earth moved to The Roundhouse, the sharpest Mods in the toolbox – The Creation, The Action and David Bowie (whose mime act featured at some of the last Middle Earth nights) – were gleefully alienating their skinhead fanbase and trying to seduce the longhairs instead. The Action went further than the rest. After a few years reproducing Motown and Stax soul hits such as 'Land of a Thousand Dances' alongside their own upbeat material, the edges of their three-minute single format began to stretch into longer free-form modes, including forty-minute versions of John Coltrane's 'India'. According to guitarist Martin Stone (who joined The Action in late 1968), the group's collective head was blown by the emergent marriages of free-form rock and space-age country coming from the US West Coast. 'We supported The Byrds at Middle Earth just when they were on the verge of going country,' he recalled. 'I remember Richard Thompson was backstage, mouth hanging open. I was hooked, I wanted to be a country and western musician. Fuck pop music! So we changed our name to Mighty Baby and eventually we turned country rock, although not really enough for my tastes.'[15] If

Mighty Baby was country-and-western, it was of a unique, cosmic, jazz-fuelled kind, and certainly no slavish lil' brother imitation of Americana. If anything, they channelled the lysergic modern cowboy stance of Buffalo Springfield and the elongated space–time continuum of The Grateful Dead, culminating in their appearance at the 1971 Glastonbury Fayre, which lasted a full three hours. A kaleidoscopic fifteen-minute extract of their set, released on the triple album of the event, shows an exhilarating future free rock that the group didn't survive long enough to pursue.

Coltrane's extended outer-space explorations, which became ever more searching and outlandish towards the end of his life, were literal attempts to reach an elevated plane where he might commune with the gods. Taking their hero's cue, his acolytes in Mighty Baby put initially vague spiritual leanings into practice. In 1971 Martin Stone – already awakened to the occult by readings of Aleister Crowley, G. I. Gurdjieff and the *I Ching* – became drawn into a newly formed Sufi order in London, taking drummer Roger Powell, then saxophonist Ian Whiteman and bassist Mike Evans with him on trips to Morocco to experience the ecstatic trance music of the Sufi ceremonies at first hand. The group fractured shortly afterwards, as singer Alan 'Bam' King showed no interest in his colleagues' religious vocation. Whiteman, Evans and Powell (together with Californian Sufis Conrad and Susan Archuletta) cut one further album as The Habibiyya, *If Man but Knew* (Island, 1972), a devotional, ascetic 'world fusion' record *avant la lettre*, based on the group's first impressions of the Moroccan devotional sounds they had picked up during their explorations in North Africa. They tossed together a sonic salad of whatever 'exotic' instruments they could lay their hands on: Japanese shakuhachis and kotos, zithers, piano, banjo, oboes and lightly stippled drums and percussion, in a manner that offers an intriguing, spontaneous parallel to West Coast composer Terry Riley's mantric minimalist piece *A Rainbow in Curved Air*.

Significantly, at exactly the same time, Mighty Baby had become one of the seed groups for many folk-rock sessions of the early 1970s. Together or separately, Ian Whiteman, Mike Evans and Roger Powell clocked up credits on, among others, John Martyn's *Bless the Weather*, Richard and Linda Thompson's *Pour Down Like Silver* and *Hokey Pokey*, The Albion Country Band's *No Roses*, Sandy Denny's *North Star Grassman and the Ravens*, Robin Scott's *Woman from the Warm Grass*, Keith Christmas's *Stimulus* and *Pigmy*, Shelagh McDonald's *Album* and *Stargazer*, Bridget St John's *Thank You For . . .*, Andy Roberts's *Home Grown* and Iain Matthews's *Tigers Will Survive*. Martin Stone went on to play in London pub-rock outfit Chilli Willi and the Red Hot Peppers with Phil Lithman of The Residents, later becoming a celebrated antiquarian book dealer (he once sold Crowley's *I Ching* to Jimmy Page, and was enshrined as the character Nicholas Lane in Iain Sinclair's novel *White Chappell – Scarlet Tracings*). Mike Evans and Ian Whiteman, meanwhile, were instrumental in the conversion of Richard and Linda Thompson to the Sufi faith in 1973, and they all attended the same Islamic commune in Suffolk.

When it was set up in 1969 as the experimental, underground wing of EMI, Harvest Records briefly became the repository of the legacy left by Pink Floyd's and Soft Machine's fluid spatial explorations. The Floyd – regrouping after the departure of Syd Barrett, whose LSD excess altered his personality to an unmanageable extent – were the label's flagship group, and their free-form *Ummagumma* (1969), *Atom Heart Mother* (1970) and *Meddle* (1971) stirred elements of tone painting, collage and musique concrète into an increasingly concentrated mix. On *Ummagumma* they were aided by underground poet, singer and instrument inventor Ron Geesin, as a square-peg replacement for Barrett's madcap genius. Even in the group's most experimental phase, Pink Floyd's music was still directed towards an Arcadian England: 'Grantchester Meadows', from *Ummagumma*, and the proto-ambient drift of *Atom Heart Mother* (its bovine sleeve recalling Peter Warlock's denigration of Vaughan Williams's music as 'a cow in a field on a foggy evening'). Through the madness and amplification of the technicolour dream, they still kept a peaceful sliver of Cambridge's eternal summer inside their heads, where the kingfisher darted and the green brook swirled beneath the willows.

Harvest was also home to The Third Ear Band, who pursued a rarefied version of Pink Floyd's abstract music of this period. They were a loose conglomerate of occult-minded instrumentalists that had its origins in The Giant Sun Trolley, one of the many acts appearing at the 14 Hour Technicolour Dream. Percussionist Glen Sweeney, the group's one constant member, began his career by seizing the bandstand in London's Hyde Park with several freaky friends, and playing even after the police informed them that music was banned from the park. (They politely asked whether that rule applied to the birds.) After Sweeney and oboist Paul Mimms took part in a December 1968 multimedia event at the Royal Albert Hall called The Alchemical Wedding – at which John Lennon and Yoko Ono conducted a forty-five-minute bag-in – The Third Ear Band sculpted an esoteric chamber music from acoustic elements; their first album was duly titled *Alchemy*. With track titles such as 'Druid One', 'Stone Circle', 'Dragon Lines' and 'Egyptian Book of the Dead', these were incantational songs-without-words, a ritualistic consort music whose atonal tinctures sometimes recalled the European folk-chamber music of Béla Bartók and the terse reductionism of Anton Webern, sometimes the free play of John Stevens's Spontaneous Music Ensemble. John Peel even turned up to play Jew's harp on 'Area Three'. 'I called the music alchemical because it was produced by repetition,' explained Sweeney,[16] whose muted battery of hand drums shaped hypnotic hymns to the fearful symmetry of the elements and the heavenly rotations. This was not cultish window dressing, though: the group made connections with Druid orders and accompanied their dawn solstice ceremonies. *Third Ear Band* (1970), often referred to as *Elements* because of its four lengthy improvisations 'Air', 'Earth', 'Fire' and 'Water', found the group – now a quartet with the addition of Ursula Smith (cello) and Richard Coff (violin, viola) – propagating a fungal acoustic music with spores of pan-European folk, Early Music and oriental drone dynamics. Their meditational medievalism found its way into two film soundtracks they created in 1970 and 1971: for a German television film about Abelard and Heloise, and for Roman Polanski's dark-age rendering of *Macbeth*. The Third Ear Band's arcane, absorbing music stands as one of several unexplored lanes leading away from the psychedelic garden that remains neglected and overgrown.

At the beginning of this chapter I suggested that 'Strawberry Fields Forever' contained the seeds of future musics. The vertiginous trippiness and cracked-mirror Anglicana of psychedelia is there, as is the structural complexity of prog rock. But even more distantly – faintly discernible in *Sgt Pepper*'s alternative personae, elaborate costumes and media manipulation – was an embryonic glam.

From Strawberry Fields to Grantchester Meadows, the enchanted demesne of English psychedelia blossomed for around three years. But the naive freshness of vision which brought it into being began to wither under the darkening skies of the new decade. A September 1968 BBC documentary on the scene, *The Sound of Change*, intercut live footage of Pink Floyd playing 'Sisyphus' with scenes from the recent riots in Paris of May 1968. Vietnam, the Bomb and the growing troubles in Ulster – to name only a few – demanded a heightened response: not fey innocence, but knowledge, cynicism and direct action, reflected in the rise of the new urban underground of Mick Farren's Social Deviants,

Hawkwind, *Oz* magazine and the militant bombers The Angry Brigade.

It took an Englishman to call Bob Dylan out as Judas. Such vitriol was never hurled with such resonant force at a British artist. The inclusion of a song called 'Iscariot' on Tyrannosaurus Rex's *Unicorn* might have offered a clue, if anyone still actually cared about such betrayals by the end of the 1960s, that the comfort and stability of the folk/psychedelic Wonderland was not going to last for ever. For, in one way of looking at it, Britain's Judases were Marc Bolan, who Trojan-horsed the faery forest as a tourist dandy in the underworld, and David Bowie, the wild-eyed boy from Freecloud who morphed into the urban spaceman. As Electric Warrior and Ziggy Stardust, Bolan and Bowie were far more effective Pied Pipers than Donovan, transporting their young listeners from immersion in a speculative, mythological past, and repositioning pop music in a future of plastic, glitter and tin. And as if to cement the deal, the first time they appeared on stage together – Bolan strumming along to Bowie's galactic ballad 'Space Oddity' – was in January 1969, at Manchester's Free Trade Hall, the very scene of Dylan's momentous, controversial appearance two and a half years earlier. If folk, folk-rock and its tributaries were, however subconsciously, believed to spring from collective, stable racial memory, glam tipped music into a wilderness of masks and mirrors, divided selves refracted through a succession of grotesque invented facades. Bowie's 'Cygnet Committee' gave the kiss-off to a sham underground society that drained the resources of genuine idealists: '*I ravaged at my finance just for those, / Those whose claims were steeped in peace, tranquillity.*' With one crushing stomp of its platform soles, glam wiped out the market value of British rock's Arcadian dreams. From now on, the direction of time travel would point relentlessly towards the future.

And what becomes of the oaken-hearted? Before twilight descended on Electric Eden, the first half of the 1970s brought various attempts to bring folk and rock music, alternative lifestyles, grass-roots commerce, earth magic and utopian scheming – the entire stark, staring panoply of the Albion Free State – out into the fields and under the stars, in the age of the great British outdoor festival.

Paradise Enclosed

The sun machine is coming down, and we're gonna have a party.

David Bowie, 'Memory of a Free Festival' (1969)

ENTRANCE IS EVERYWHERE.

Slogan painted on perimeter fence, Isle of
Wight Festival (1970)

'The Glastonbury landscape', wrote Geoffrey Ashe, one of the mid-twentieth century's pioneering historians of the mythical terrain of Wessex, 'is weird.'[1] As an opening sentence, it was hard to beat: terminology that tapped hippy lingo as well as containing the tincture of strangeness. For all its current over-use as a signifier of oddity, the word 'weird' derives its power from ancient Germanic roots. '*Wurthis*' meant 'to turn' or 'wind'; the word's inherent sense of movement led to the modern German '*werden*', 'to become' (literally, 'to turn into'). From '*werden*', Old English derived the word 'wyrd', meaning 'destiny' or 'fate': in other words, the condition to which your becoming brings you. The 'Weird Sisters' of Shakespeare's *Macbeth* are the three Fates, prophets and even controllers of human destiny.

With its high street crammed with astrologers, crystal-peddlers and New Age bookshops, Glastonbury has made itself a concentration of the latterday 'weird Albion'. And yet, in the parallel dreamtime of alternative British history and legend, Glastonbury is, in a more literal sense, the focus of Albion's 'wyrd'

– its destiny. For overshadowing this small Somerset town, with its ruined abbey, holy wells, thorn tree reputedly planted by Joseph of Arimathea, stands the Tor, an ancient earthwork capped by a more recent Gothic church tower. Beneath the Tor – according to one of the myriad legends attached to this veritable junction-box of myth – Arthur, the once and future king, slumbers through the ages, to awaken in Albion's hour of need and fulfil the nation's destiny. Ever since Glastonbury was first consciously associated with the story of King Arthur – by no means the only such location in Britain – around the time of the Norman Conquest, the town has become the strange attractor of Albion's spiritual energies, enhanced by its proximity (and ley-line connections) to those other southern England monuments, the stone circles of Avebury and Stonehenge.

Once a year, around the summer solstice, international attention focuses on a small cluster of fields at Pilton, several miles down the road: the site of the Glastonbury Festival. Mainstream it may have become, several decades after its small-scale beginnings, but at its fringes it preserves the vestiges of its founding principles: a serious attempt to stake out and remake Utopia in an English field. The temporary tented villages of Britain's outdoor festivals represented a practical attempt to live out the dream of Albion: getting back to the land, to a simpler way of life that pushed modern convenience into the background (with the exception of electricity to power the PA system), in a temporary autonomous zone where unconventional behaviours and attitudes could be exercised without restraint.

Shakespeare's Weird Sisters hold fate in their hands, but – like many of Glastonbury's inhabitants – they are also strange Others, practitioners of pagan magic, outsiders from society. By the early nineteenth century, 'weird' begins to enter the language with the specific meaning of odd-looking or uncanny. In 1960 the sense of otherness was directly applied to the infant counter-culture in Britain, when a review in *Melody Maker* accused unruly members of the audience at the fifth Beaulieu Jazz Festival of being 'weirdies'.

It's hard to credit now, but the riot that gave rise to the *Maker*'s condemnation was a clash between fans of the trad-jazz star Acker 'Stranger on the Shore' Bilk and adherents of the foundation-shaking new thing of . . . Johnny Dankworth. The Beaulieu Jazz Festival, which took place on the private grounds of Lord Montagu's Hampshire estate between 1956 and 1960, began as a kind of alternative Glyndebourne for jazz, a summer garden party where attendees could scoff their picnics, camp overnight and experience music under open skies. When the 1960 event degenerated into a violent ruckus, with sheds set on fire and property damaged (in front of hastily unplugged BBC television cameras), Lord Montagu terminated the event. The following year, the president of the National Federation of Jazz Organisations of Great Britain, a former accountant named Harold Pendleton, inaugurated the 1961 National Jazz Festival at Richmond Athletic Grounds just outside London. Pendleton had already founded the Marquee Club in central London, a prime component of the British blues, rock and r'n'b circuit. His outdoor event, soon renamed the National Jazz and Blues Festival, proved an enduring formula, entertaining a world of music beyond the parameters of its title and establishing the annual meet as a subcultural Ascot. The crowd-baiting likes of The Who, The Yardbirds and The Small Faces brought an edginess to the event, and throughout the 1960s Pendleton weathered a succession of tribal clashes as his liberal programming policy attracted a hungrier, more hysterical breed of music aficionado. Moved along from Richmond, the festival transplanted to Windsor Racecourse in 1966, despite local residents' objections and police opposition that took an unpleasantly moral tone, focusing on the large mixed-sex marquee provided for the audience to spend the night. Pendleton, to his credit, stood up to the objectors and defended his ticketholders' right to behave as they pleased. The festival swung 180 degrees in 1967, reflecting changing times. The amphetamine beatniks of the previous year were replaced by a spliffed-up hippy crowd mellowing out to Donovan, The Nice and Eric Clapton, although Arthur Brown's fiery entrance – on a crane, with a blazing mask – and the no-show of Pink Floyd raised the temperature, and some unruly crowd elements set fire to a rubbish tip and attacked the fire services.

An Englishman's home might be his castle, but he prefers to do his feasting out of doors. Growing out of those 1950s jazz festivals, the British pop festival has moved, in the intervening half-century, from small, impromptu, mildly subversive gatherings to major landmarks on the British map of summer activities: media-sponsored calendar fixtures that draw together vast swathes of Britain's diverse population. At the same time, the chequered history of the music festival shows how, in microcosm, it has enacted many of the ancestral tensions in the relationship between the people and the stewards of the land, between commons and private ground. In many cases, the festival has provided the opportunity to test legal limits, flout property rights and set up encampments that permit a brief taste of alternative modes of living. Since the birth of the free festival, emotions have often run high between those inside and outside the enclosure; between those who have paid and those who feel entitled to participate freely.

The tone was established over the summer of 1968, when the Blackhill Enterprises management team, Peter Jenner and Andrew King, organised a monthly series of free rock concerts in London's Hyde Park. Breaking through initial opposition from the Ministry of Public Buildings and Works by securing the support of sympathetic Members of Parliament, Blackhill's stage was intended to promote their own stable of artists. The first, on 29 June, featured Pink Floyd, Tyrannosaurus Rex, Roy Harper and Jethro Tull. Over the next three months, the choice of artists –

Traffic, The Nice, The Pretty Things, The Action, Fleetwood Mac, Fairport Convention, Family, Eclection, Strawbs, The Move — combined with the sunshine and Arcadian layout of the park to create a Perfumed Garden in the heart of the Smoke, where fans could laze away the afternoon digging the pastoral rock while canoodling on the Serpentine in a hired rowing boat. So successful was the Hyde Park formula that the following year The Rolling Stones enlisted Blackhill to secure Hyde Park for their legendary 5 July wake for the recently departed Brian Jones, prefaced by Mick Jagger's Shelleyan eulogy and the release of white butterflies.

Seeing audiences of 150,000 thronging Hyde Park, promoters elsewhere inevitably seized on the outdoor gathering as an exploitable commodity. Complaints had already been aired about the rip-off prices charged to the hippy audience at 1967's Festival of the Flower Children in the august cloisters of Woburn Abbey. Between 1968 and 1970 there emerged several larger super-festivals, notably at Shepton Mallet, near Bath, and the Isle of Wight; miniature townsteads catering for more than 100,000 folks and therefore requiring heavy stewarding, security teams and supply lines of military complexity. At the 1970 Bath Festival of Blues and Progressive Music, Donovan played an impromptu two-and-a-half-hour acoustic set, chasing away Sunday morning hangovers and the bedragglement of the previous night's rain showers. Led Zeppelin played the epic three-hour set that effectively broke them as a live act in their homeland, having already convincingly squeezed America's lemon. And Pink Floyd premiered their proto-ambient pastoral suite, *Atom Heart Mother*, attended by a brass band and choir. Meanwhile, outside the festival precinct, The Pink Fairies — ex-members of Notting Hill outfit The Deviants, in the first of many appearances as ubiquitous loons of the British festival circuit — bashed out their primitive rock on a flatbed truck.

The Isle of Wight Festival, which had attracted a comfortable 10,000 to 1968's Great South Coast Bank Holiday Pop Festivity on the small Ford Farm, swelled to 150,000 in 1969, boosted by a rare British appearance from Bob Dylan and The Band.[2] At the behest of the local council, the third Isle of Wight Festival was shunted over to Afton Down on the western edge of the island. The promoters – local brothers Ray and Ron Foulk (who looked barely out of their teens), in partnership with Ricky Farr – could no longer strike private deals with local farmers happy for the extra income. Local opposition forced the hand of the council, who offered East Afton Farm as the only option. Suddenly they were well out of their depth: the event, eventually overrun with anything between 250,000 and 600,000 people (depending which account you believe), marked a watershed in British rock-festival history, a disastrous miscalculation whose practical failings struck a discordant note with the utopian ethics of the majority of its audience.

Much of the unrest that beset this festival, which was documented on Murray Lerner's film *Message to Love*, was amplified by the geography of the location. Afton Down was a wide, flat, grassy area nestling against the western edge of the island's downland, which meant that anyone arriving without a ticket was afforded a panoramic view of the enclosure from a naturally raked amphitheatre, dubbed 'Desolation Hill'. What they saw, though, was a rock 'n' roll carnival played out within a temporary fortress ringed by two layers of metal fencing. 'It's almost like a feudal court scene, this,' observes a festivalgoer captured by Lerner's camera, 'where you've got your royalty on the stage, and backstage you have the courtiers, the groupies and the managers, the people that keep the pop kings in power. And then you have your serfs out in the audience behind corrugated fences.' What looked like paranoid protectionism was in fact an ingenious solution to the problem of access around the site: the parallel fences created a sealed trackway to help food suppliers and emergency services bypass the crowds. But the hundreds of thousands in 'Canvas City'

Under siege: the Isle of Wight Festival 1970, as seen from Desolation Hill.

up on the hill, charged up with a sense of entitlement to the good things spread below them, laid siege to the barricades until, on the final day, the promoters announced their bankruptcy, let the fences fall and declared the event free, just in time for the hordes to witness star attractions Joan Baez, Leonard Cohen and a lumpen set from a sleepy Jimi Hendrix. Inside the compound, morale was unstable: White Panther security, cans thrown at a tearfully defiant Joni Mitchell, a tetchy Jim Morrison, a nervous Kris Kristofferson fearing for his life all contributed to a dark cloud that loomed over the proceedings. When Farr invited crowd members up to the microphone to air their grievances, one fried US festival veteran denounced what he saw as a 'psychedelic concentration camp'. By the time it was all over, the vibes had definitely been knocked out of whack, and there would be nothing on that scale again. As a nail in the coffin, Parliament passed an Act in 1971 banning unlicensed gatherings of more than 5,000 souls on the Isle of Wight until further notice. '*There'll always be an England*,' warbled the American alternative vaudeville star Tiny Tim, strumming his ukulele while dwarfed on the giant stage at sundown on the final Sunday. But whose England, exactly, was this legislation intended to protect?

For generations, access to land has been one of the most contested issues in British national life. Until the eighteenth century, farming tended to be practised in much bigger open fields than exist today, notionally divided into loose strips of land worked by assorted groups of labourers. Alternatively, huge tracts designated 'commons' were owned by a single individual but granted the right to anyone to graze livestock or cultivate crops.

Following the victory of anti-Royalist forces in the English Civil War, King Charles I's early-1649 execution spread post-revolutionary upheaval across the land. The religious, social, economic and legal yokes that had kept the poorest sections of society at bay, and aristocratic rule in place, were suddenly relaxed. Many took the king's riddance to mean the undisputed end of feudalism. At one extreme, lawless anarchy reared its head; at the other, communitarian altruism took hold. On 1 April 1649 a group of former soldiers of the Parliamentarian New Model Army and their wives and partners, led by William Everard and a Wigan merchant's son, Gerrard Winstanley, tramped up St George's Hill at Walton-on-Thames and set about planting crops and vegetables and constructing wooden dwellings on the plateau. Seeing Winstanley's folk hard at work with their spades and hoes, local people quickly christened them 'Diggers'. Winstanley, the nominal leader of this self-sustaining commune, originally called his people True Levellers, after coming under the influence of the radical London libertarians known as the Levellers, who agitated for religious freedom and the dissolution of Parliament. Scrutinising the scriptures for divine authority,

Winstanley preferred to create the conditions in which the earth could supply the grassroots needs of a united working folk: 'we work together, eat bread together' was his Christian communist credo, a sharing of the fruits of 'Mother Earth' underwritten by a 'universal law of love' and 'equity'.[3] The Diggers – who eventually appropriated unused common land in four counties during 1649 – looked to the England prior to the Norman Conquest of 1066 as a golden age, and their farming was intended to restore the land to that supposedly Edenic state. There would be no money and no private property in Digger Utopia; all possessions were held in a common treasury and available for the benefit of all. This was the anti-materialistic 'golden age republic' William Morris would imagine 250 years later in *News from Nowhere*. Unfortunately, the communes were broken up by local landowners and clergymen, who saw to it that the Diggers were attacked and dispersed within a year of their formation.

In the 1960s the Diggers reincarnated themselves at hippy Be-Ins in San Francisco – Robin Hoods-turned-urban guerrillas distributing pamphlets, free food and money – and their brothers turned up at British events, too. By 1971 *Gandalf's Garden* could include the following definition in a glossary of 'hip terminology': 'Digger: (Difficult to define) but basically one who believes in love, freedom and sharing as a way of life. Anything Digger, implies "that which is freely given, that which is self-reliant and that which is direct and to the point in a life-given situation".'[4]

The Inclosures Act of 1760 permitted landowners to divide up, fence off and exclusively use formerly common ground, thus creating the majority of the hedged fields and private estates in existence today. This land grab extended beyond agricultural zones to the wilder places, fenland, heath and moor, often commandeered by rich owners with government connections. Unseated from fields and meadows their families had toiled over for generations, the labouring classes were displaced into the newly expanding cities, just in time to take up new positions in the weaving factories of the Industrial Revolution. The village greens, parks and commons that survive today are the vestiges of what would have been wide open spaces for universal access.[5]

But the sense of entitlement lingers, lodged deep in the nation's psyche to an extent encapsulated by none other than Wordsworth, writing in his 1810 *Guide to the Lakes*, which he called 'a sort of national property in which every man has a right and interest who has an eye to perceive and a heart to enjoy'. Acceptable boundaries are complicated by the fact that, in British law, trespass is not by itself a prosecutable offence, and property owners may only use 'reasonable force' to evict interlopers. The well-publicised mass trespass on Kinder Scout in 1932 – for which Ewan MacColl composed his song 'The Manchester Rambler' – stimulated the national appetite for restoration of public rights of way. This direct-action movement culminated in the 1949 National Parks and Access to the Countryside Act, in which areas of open country were created by arrangement and negotiation with private landowners. In the restorative spirit typical of the post-war years, this was the era of newly created National Parks (such as the Peak District, Lake District, Dartmoor and Snowdonia), public footpaths and officially designated Areas of Outstanding Natural Beauty. And the issue of rural access was back on the agenda at the end of the 1960s, as the Countryside Act (1968) extended the bill towards a more active engagement with the landscape by 'encouraging the provision and improvement for persons resorting to the countryside of facilities for the enjoyment of the countryside and of open air recreation in the countryside'.[6] State permission to make free with Britain's green spaces came exactly at the moment when its youth movement was fully prepared to do just that – on terms which were not necessarily compatible with the mores and tranquillity of rural middle England.

By the mid-1970s there was a grass-roots movement to

persuade the state to provide sites dedicated to national music festivals. 'A permanent festival site must be chosen with care,' says one unnamed contributor to a book on the subject. 'It must not be a useless industrial site but a nice country site. The whole idea of a pop festival is to be out in the country, and I think every young person in Britain has this birthright. We know the land may be owned by farmers, by the Crown, by anyone and everyone else. But we're all taxpayers and I think we all have a right at some time of our lives to share this birthright. Anyway, what were our parents fighting for in the war? For England's green and pleasant land, so we were told.'[7]

The hermetic zone of the rock festival – a hotbed of radicalism, exploration of alternative lifestyles, and of alcohol and drug consumption – facilitated the convergence of city dudes and country dropouts, the rooted and the nomadic. The metropolitan ideal of the land was confronted by its realities – pleasurable more often than not, but there was always the risk of wet and windy weather, cold nights under disintegrating covers, petty theft, inedible food, unspeakable latrines and unpredictably intense drug trips to dampen the zeal.

In September 1968, on London's Hampstead Heath, Jefferson Airplane and Fairport Convention played at the free Camden Festival (a far smaller occasion than the Isle of Wight event the Airplane had played several days before). In June 1969 The Third Ear Band, The Deviants, The Incredible String Band, Mighty Baby, The Strawbs, Roy Harper, Family, The Edgar Broughton Band and the delightfully named Sir Charles Babbage's All Brass Computing Engine performed gratis at the Midsummer Pop Festival in Cambridge. And on Saturday 16 August – the same day that The Who, Jefferson Airplane, Sly and the Family Stone, Creedence Clearwater Revival and Janis Joplin were headlining at Woodstock – David Bowie's Beckenham Arts Lab hosted the Beckenham Free Festival on his local Recreation Ground in south London, with

Comus, Bridget St John, Keith Christmas and others, puppet shows, mime and theatre. Bowie's 'Memory of a Free Festival', with its anthemic, 'Hey Jude'-style coda, commemorated the emotional event: '*It was ragged and naive/ It was Heaven.*'

The raggedness and naivety of such grass-roots festivals – as opposed to the larger, profit-oriented ventures – made them an attractive form of pow-wow for the burgeoning Anglo-Saxon 'freak' underground. Mick Farren of The Deviants and satirical cartoonist Edward Barker were responsible for Phun City, which took place at the end of July 1970 on Ecclesdon Common, Worthing, in Sussex. Backed by *International Times*, Phun City was explicitly billed as a 'three day environment designed to the needs and desires of the freak', as one promotional flyer put it. The line-up comprised rock groups such as Detroit activists MC5, Free, The Pretty Things, The Edgar Broughton Band, Kevin Ayers, Mungo Jerry and Renaissance, plus a poetry gathering with Robert Creeley, Tom Raworth and Michael Horovitz, a sci-fi conference with William Burroughs, Alexander Trocchi and others, a pinball championship, cinema and 'guerrilla theatre'. There was even a Christian tent, and a bovver-booted, club-wielding alternative morris-dance team consisting of Hell's Angels and roadies called the Blackheath Foot and Death Men. With no perimeter fence erected, and the audience trusted to pay the £2 'entry' fee, Phun City's broad church opened its doors to scenes of barely restrained, orgiastic anarchy. The Pink Fairies stripped naked during their set, and the event's own flyers incited the crowd to 'fornicate' under conveniently strung-up polythene bivouacs in 'Narnia', the nearby twenty acres of woodland. The festival reportedly ended peacefully, although police busted the remaining hippies on the Monday morning, kicking over their cooking pots and making several drug-related arrests.

Phun City's atmosphere of bucolic, acid-fuelled disobedience set a precedent that contributed to the following month's riotous invasion at the Isle of Wight. The mischievous Mick Farren

Poster advertising the anarchic Phun City festival, 1970.

reconnoitred the Wight site ten days before opening time, correctly perceived that 'this IoW bash was going to be a black hole of decidedly negative energy', and released several thousand copies of a samizdat bulletin from the 'White Panther Ministry of Information' into 'the usual underground networks'. This pamphlet pointed out the site's structural weaknesses, advertised the alternative free festival that would be mounted immediately outside the fence, and accused the promoters of representing 'capitalist interests seeking to exploit the energy of the People's music'.[8] The siege, and eventual victory by the outsiders, was not the end of violence at outdoor festivals, as the Windsor (1970s) and Stonehenge (1980s) Free Festivals would show. But the civil war within the underground was over for the time being. Future skirmishes would take place between the people and the law. In any case, three weeks after the Isle of Wight fiasco, a small, peaceful gathering of 1,500 hippies assembled on a dairy farm in Somerset to try out a new model, one which would juggle the needs of security, commerce and utopianism beyond all expectations into the twenty-first century.

Michael Eavis inherited Worthy Farm on his father's death in 1958. Cutting short a projected career in the merchant navy, the twenty-three-year-old took over the running of the 150-acre farm at Pilton, a tiny rural hamlet on the road between Shepton Mallet and Glastonbury. In 1970, creeping through the bushes to gatecrash Led Zeppelin's mammoth set at the Bath Festival of Blues and Progressive Music just down the road, Eavis was inspired to create a small, practically free festival on his own turf, and began making phone calls the next morning. Two and a half months later he was in business. The Pilton Festival was a modest affair: the princely sum of one pound bought entrance to Worthy Farm, plus a ration of milk for the weekend. Headliners The Kinks were replaced at the eleventh hour by Tyrannosaurus Rex; and the rest of the bill was a relaxed array of agrarian folk-rock from the likes of Alan Bown, Steamhammer, Stackridge and Amazing Blondel. Though Eavis shouldered a small financial loss on the weekend, the event had attracted the attentions of a group of individuals, fronted by Arabella Churchill and Andrew Kerr, with a vision for the site that vastly transcended Eavis's casual enthusiasm. The following year, the event was repeated; this time, it was rebranded as Glastonbury Fayre.

One morning, while the Pilton Festival was under way, Andrew Kerr woke up to find himself lying on the summit of Glastonbury Tor. Gazing north-east towards the festival site, he was greeted with a near-holy vision: a rainbow touching Worthy Farm. Kerr read this as a symbol, a portent: his destiny was to be strongly connected to the wyrd of this special place.

Born in 1933, Kerr had already spent ten years, between 1958–68, as the personal and literary assistant to Randolph Churchill, son of Winston. Kerr steered Randolph through the writing of the first two volumes of his late father's biography, a task which came to an end when Randolph himself died in 1968.[9] Sir Winston, the old grandee, had died in his ninety-one-year-old dotage in 1965. For a country trying to get on with the business of escaping the shadow of the Second World War, the news initially came as something of an anticlimax. But there was a mythical, Arthurian aspect to the image of the king-like figure, on his deathbed for ten days, dying that the country might be born anew. 'Here, after all,' as Christopher Booker expressed it in his anatomy of the period's youth culture, *The Neophiliacs*, 'had been a man not only whose intimate links with history ran back to the last cavalry charge at Omdurman, in the year of the death of Gladstone [1898] – but whose life span connected the present with that of millions who had been contemporary with Palmerston and Peel and the Duke of Wellington, and even with hundreds of thousands, still alive well into his youth, who had lived in the time of Napoleon, Beethoven and George III. In Britain's last great crisis as an imperial world power, Churchill had stood out like Justinian in the twilight of Rome, as a man who derived his majesty from a sense of the imperial and military splendours of the past.'[10]

Churchill was eventually buried after an all-stops-out state-funeral procession through London, watched on live television by an estimated worldwide audience of 350 million. Much as Glastonbury Tor sticks out on Albion's folkloric skyline, Churchill's monumental frame dominated British politics through the tumultuous war years. As a Druid and Freemason, Churchill had his own connections to Britain's secret life. His famous 'Victory V' salute lived on as the favoured hippy gesture of peace. And a *Daily Mail* eulogy after his death, quoted by Booker, was tinged with a sentiment that would have appealed to the adherents of the 14 Hour Technicolour Dream two years later: 'When I get to Heaven, he said, I mean to spend a considerable portion of my first million years in painting. Tomorrow, perhaps, you will look up and there will be a rainbow in the sky. *Winston Spencer Churchill will be at work*.' Perhaps he was indeed brushing at his cosmic easel that 1970 morning on Glastonbury Tor, when Andrew Kerr received his vision of the future Glastonbury Fayre. Whatever, it was Churchillian blood – that of Randolph's daughter, Winston's granddaughter, twenty-one-year-old Arabella – that would take an equal share in the organisation. Once touted as a prospective bride for Prince Charles, romantically linked with a Swedish crown prince and named as 'Debutante of the Year' in 1967, her stars were lining up to make her a fully fledged member of the aristocracy. But in 1971 she very publicly rejected that destiny. She had been invited to travel to the International Azalea Festival in Norfolk, Virginia, an annual NATO-sponsored event, as that year's 'Azalea Queen' (chosen from one of the fifteen NATO countries). She refused, and wrote an open letter to the director of the International Azalea Foundation which was published in *Rolling Stone* magazine, throwing in her lot with the peace movement.

My Grandfather used the phrase 'The Iron Curtain'. It seems to me that what is facing us all now is the final curtain. I cannot support the idea of one nation inducing another nation to see its point of view by force of arms . . . I know you will say that NATO was established to deter aggression not to encourage it. I realise that when NATO was formed after World War

II there was probably a need for such an organisation, but now with ever increasing advances in science and technology the situation is growing out of hand. The gathering together of such masses of weapons surely negates the possibility of peaceful co-existence. It is, therefore, with deep regret I must inform you that I cannot participate in the Azalea Festival.

My decision is final. I will be out of London for the next three months.'¹

She joined forces with Andrew Kerr, who by now had embarked on an Avalonian exploration of alternative Britain, partnering Allen Watkins, son of *Old Straight Track* author Alfred, on ley-line hikes. Above all, Kerr had fallen under the spell of John Michell's *The View over Atlantis*, published in 1969, which chimed with and galvanised the underground interest in the awakening Albion.

Michell's book has since been called, by one of Britain's leading folklore historians, 'almost the founding document of the modern earth mysteries movement'.'² Its author, an Eton- and Cambridge-educated polymath, synthesised archaeology, mathematics, Holy Grail legend and New Age cosmology to propose a system of energies embossed upon the English landscape, intersecting at key spiritual sites in Wessex such as Avebury, Stonehenge and Glastonbury Tor, an area rich in sacred wells. The book connected the hidden patterns underlying the Albionic landscape with the navigation lines used by the Hopi and Australian Aboriginal tribes, and noted corresponding instances of sacred geometry at world heritage sites such as the Inca remains at Cusco and the Great Pyramid of Giza, and even suggested that flying-saucer sightings corresponded to the magnetic forces coursing through Avalon's power spots. For the mystic-minded Halflings of Middle-earth Britain, the leaves of Michell's book were wrapped around a stimulating portion of lembas for the brain.

Accordingly, nothing about the timing and siting of Glastonbury Fayre – which took place between 20–24 June – was coincidental. Kerr perceived that Worthy Farm was situated within the so-called Glastonbury Zodiac, an astrological pattern of fields surrounding the Glastonbury complex. The main stage – a scaffolding frame coated with plastic sheets – was designed, with Michell's consultation, as a one-tenth scale replica of the Great Pyramid, whose apex was situated over a blind spring (which Kerr located by dowsing) believed to lie on the 'spiral geodetic line' connected to the Glastonbury–Stonehenge ley. Kerr's site architect, Bill Harkin, had received ominous dreams of Worthy Farm, seeing the farmhouse sandwiched between triangular pillars of light. 'We discovered that the constellation Sagittarius, the Glastonbury Zodiac, the stage, the Sun and the central sun of the Galaxy would all be aligned at the time of the solstice on June 22, 1971.' From Michell's book, Kerr took the assertion that, at the summer solstice, astronomical alignments are at their most

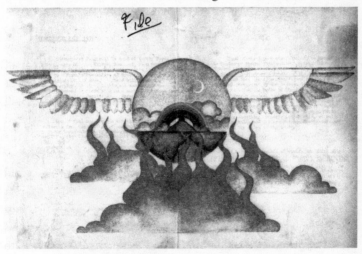

Cover sheet of the original proposal for Glastonbury Fayre, authored by Andrew Kerr and Arabella Churchill, January 1971.

energy-intensive, and that correctly proportioned and aligned buildings could suck down those energies to the planetary surface and accumulate them in wells, churches and monuments. 'What we were trying to do', Kerr explained shortly after the event, 'was to stimulate the Earth's nervous system with joy, appreciation and happiness so that our Mother planet would respond by breeding a happier, more balanced race of men, animals and plants. It was a fertility rite.'[13]

Entry to the festival was completely free, financed by donations, the sale of film rights (the Fayre was documented by Nic Roeg and David Puttnam) and income from the subsequently released triple LP, *Revelations*. Kerr himself sold off some old family-heirloom weapons; Churchill siphoned funds from her private income. There had been no media interest in Eavis's hastily arranged shindig the previous year; suddenly, though, the invocation of Glastonbury rather than Pilton lit up the title like a beacon. An estimated 12,000 turned up to hear a line-up including David Bowie, Hawkwind, The Pink Fairies, Mighty Baby, The Edgar

The Pyramid Stage at Glastonbury Fayre, 1971, designed to
stimulate the Earth's nervous system.

Songs of praise: revellers at Glastonbury, 1971.

Broughton Band, Fairport Convention, Quintessence, Melanie, Terry Reid, Gong, Arthur Brown, Brinsley Schwarz, Family and Traffic.

But more important than the music, for Kerr, was the small window of opportunity the festival afforded to experiment with an alternative, sustainable way of life that, for an all-too-brief few days, dispensed with worldly comforts and allowed focus on human interaction and cohabitation with nature. No alcohol was sold on site, and the only food served was vegetarian. Leaflets passed around the site urged festivalgoers to break bread with strangers, share and conserve water and food, refrain from damaging local crops and to clap more quietly to respect residents' desire for peace. In Jeremy Sandford and Ron Reid's illustrated history of British festival culture, *Tomorrow's People*, an uncredited organiser – very likely Andrew Kerr – described the Glastonbury ethic as: 'Caring for ourselves in conjunction with the environment; a consciousness of your effect on the environment while you're living in it, and of the effect of the environment on you.'

'Breaking bread' was no casually chosen phrase. Several Church of England vicars visited, and were filmed dancing, administering Holy Communion and even choking on spliffs. Appropriately for a site that contained the foundations of the Anglican Church as well as older traditions, Kerr's gospel was inspired as much by biblical descriptions of charity as by the hippy ethos. 'We had in mind a "fayre" like the old fayres of medieval Britain. I think that most people who were at Glastonbury were changed by it; changed by the knowledge that all of this was free and the result of people working for it because they believed in giving. We learned a sort of proximity in spiritual terms from Glastonbury; one lesson we learned was: we are the earth, the earth is us.'[14]

We have already seen how Glastonbury was colonised by radicals, artists and alternative communities in the early twentieth century, culminating in Rutland Boughton's operatic renderings of the Matter of Britain. Styling itself 'The Isle of Avalon', it's the place where the country's pagan and Christian religions overlap, thickly laminated with an abundance of unconfirmed legends. The tombs of both Joseph of Arimathea and King Arthur reputedly lie there, though neither has been found; it's the hiding place of the Holy Grail, the chalice containing Christ's Last Supper wine; and William Blake's 'Jerusalem' is predicated on a local belief that Jesus himself walked at Glastonbury. In his introduction to the revised *King Arthur's Avalon* in 1973, Geoffrey Ashe acknowledged that the site's 'real re-awakening' 'started with the discovery of Avalonian magic by junior seekers, so-called hippies or rather post-hippies, who were drifting into the district from the late 1960s onward'. Ashe also wrote in *Gandalf's Garden*, 'Britain will begin to be reborn when Glastonbury is. The Giant Albion will begin to wake when his sons and daughters gather inside the enchanted boundary, and summon him with the right words, the right actions, a different life.'[15]

Viewing the film *Glastonbury Fayre*,[16] and photographs of what went on inside that enchanted boundary, is like seeing some superimposition of William Morris's Earthly Paradise, a sanctuary for post-atomic war refugees, and the Glastonbury Zodiac remade as a gigantic bed-sitting room. A transient city of tepees, cellophane sheets and splayed guy ropes. Charred cauldrons bubble over blazing log fires; queues snake around outdoor soup kitchens; the Union Jack flutters with the yin and yang; women cradle kittens and hold wild flowers to their lips; babies crawl alongside basking dogs; couples shyly slink to the edge of a copse. Hell's Angels sport mirror-sheen Wehrmacht helmets; flowers are tucked into headbands or drawn on torsos; spliffs are puffed and passed around; Hare Krishna devotees chant over tamburas; pipe-puffing or denim-clad Anglican vicars join throbbing circles of Jesus-haired dancers. Impromptu spontaneous music ensembles band together and march through the site with fifes and drums. Baked revellers clatter empty Coke cans together, bash tambourines, blow recorders, tin whistles, ocarinas; greet the morning sun with yoga, ivy wreaths and hands clasped in prayer. A wrecked car lies half-buried in a makeshift grave. You can almost smell the mingled aromas of charred corn cobs, veggie burgers, natural body odour and humming latrines. Above all, there are outbreaks of decidedly un-English nudity and hedonistic dancing, whether to Fairport Convention's electric jigs, or to the 4/4 power stomp of Traffic's 'Gimme Some Lovin'', or the shamanistic space ritual of Hawkwind. Andrew Kerr's restrictions on alcohol meant little drunkenness; both the police and the Hell's Angels kept a low profile, and there was hardly any reported violence.

There was something beyond flower power at work: the momentary lifting of a veil that revealed a British society in a parallel universe; a fleeting social experiment and celebration that has never, despite numerous attempts, been repeated in quite the same way since. As one observer chronicled it, the Fayre 'constituted a last meeting of many tribes, a final potlatch before we all took our separate paths into a future few of us believed would be anything but inescapably darker. It was symbolic that we should come to this place, this land of our Once and Future King . . . because – whether you believed in the myths of Avalon or not – we'd soon need all the help we could get.'[17] Appropriately enough, the HTV series *Arthur of the Britons*, made in 1973, rejected the anachronistic portrayal of Grail tales with knights in shining armour; instead, its muddy settlements and feudal poverty were unthinkable without the scenes that had been witnessed two years before at Glastonbury Fayre. In this oasis of rock and rural retreat, myth and reality were becoming knotted together in a Gordian tanglewood.

The Glastonbury Festival did not officially take place again until 1978, but it has become one of the most prominent, and certainly best attended, events in the British social calendar. It's barely even 'alternative' any more: an inclusive umbrella for international pop culture and its disparate tribes to gather and celebrate themselves, rain or shine, in a giant campsite that mushrooms and contracts to accommodate at least 150,000 for several days in the middle of June. The (rebuilt) Pyramid Stage remains the central feature; John Michell's Atlantis myth has crystallised as a strong New Age presence; what's left of the travelling community is granted its own field two miles away. There is a Greenpeace field, and a 'Left Field' run by the South London Trades Union Congress. But what's most visible about the modern Glastonbury Festival is a perfect match for the age of public–private partnerships; a captive audience for advertising, sponsorships, handouts, flyers, services. Cashpoints, mobile-phone masts, wireless networks, 'proper' toilets: all part of the process of helping people forget they are camping in a field in the middle of Somerset. Andrew Kerr continued to live in a cottage near the site entrance, and founded the Whole Earth Show in 1992, an outdoor event highlighting organic and sustainable techniques. Arabella Churchill – married to Haggis McLeod, a juggler she met at Glastonbury in 1987 – founded the Children's World charity and continued to run the Children's and Theatre Tents until her death in 2007. Michael Eavis became the public face of the festival, a model of tolerance and charity (Eavis is famously teetotal, drug-free and a practising Methodist), donating hundreds of thousands of pounds to organisations ranging from the Campaign for Nuclear Disarmament to Oxfam, Greenpeace and WaterAid.

Glastonbury's supposed freedom actually takes place in a curated milieu that has always, even in 1971, been thoroughly *organised*. Anarchy is perpetually deferred. Other events provided a different order of experience for mental time travellers. Tapping into the enthusiasm for historical recreation typified by the foundation of military enactment society The Sealed Knot in 1969, the first of Suffolk's revitalised Horse Fairs took place at Barsham in 1972, which went even further towards trying to conjure up the atmosphere of Merrie England. Unlike Glastonbury, this pageant had no 'name' pop acts; it was even more purist in its recreation of a Renaissance fayre, with horse auctions, medieval costumes, folk theatre and mummers' plays, craft markets, appropriately rustic food and drink such as mead and whole roasts. In later years there were maypole frolics and country dancing till dawn, brass bands and buskers, 'bald hare racing'; even the mock trial of 'Black Bart', a knave on the run. John Peel, who lived with his family in nearby Stowmarket, attended the 1977 Faire held at Bungay, and wrote about it in his *Sounds* column, in the form of a reply to a correspondent who had enquired where all the Beautiful People had gone. 'I discovered only yesterday', replied Peel, in tones that suggested the heady aroma of the Perfumed Garden had long since dispersed, 'that they have survived – and as Beautiful People too

— in remote rural areas. With a gang of village layabouts and our district minibus I crossed down (or up) to a charming spot called Mettingham Castle, a tumbledown er . . . castle in the badlands of the Norfolk–Suffolk border for the Bungay Jubilee May Horse Fair. And there the buggers were. Hundreds of em. A veritable sea of velvet . . . They sat around fires, alongside beautiful Romany caravans, strummed out of tune guitars, and tapped incessantly on "hand crafted" "Indian drums" with a sharp disregard for tempo which was doubtless the result of remarkable inner cleanliness.'[18]

Such rigorously stewarded events resembled fancy-dress parties, with specified dress codes and clearly stated themes. At the other end of the scale came the spontaneous efflorescence of the mid-1970s free festivals. The first Windsor People's Free Festival took place in 1972 in the Great Park, where the National Jazz Festival had so outraged the local constabulary several years before. Its prime movers, Sid Rawle and Bill 'Ubi' Dwyer, were among the hordes tearing down the barricades at the 1970 Isle of Wight riot, and the experience hardened their resolve to harness people power by removing the boundaries and refusing even to set the parameters of how long the event should last. The first was attended by around 700 people, but the 1973 follow-up was closer to 7,000. Dwyer, a former civil servant converted to the idealist, hippy, anti-Establishment cause, printed up hundreds of thousands of leaflets which set out his demands in a mixture of evangelical rhetoric and anarchist tract: 'The festival . . . is a revolution . . . we want a new society . . . we want to replace, as a beginning, the family with the commune . . . We want to stop all rent paying. It is a feudal relic from the time of William the Conqueror . . . We want to bring God down out of the sky and put him where he belongs – the human heart.'

Kevin Brownlow and Andrew Mollo's vividly realist 1975 film *Winstanley*, a re-enactment of the Diggers' year in Surrey, shot over the course of a whole year using non-professional actors, cast Sid Rawle and his Windsor Free Festival gang as a mob of

Ranters, nakedly whooping it up and cussing inside the Digger enclave. Before the Windsor Free Festival could turn the world upside down, however, it was itself capsized by Thames Valley Police, violently invading the site and making a number of drug arrests. With Ubi Dwyer in jail for breaking a legal injunction on advertising another Windsor, Rawle became the figurehead for an

Poster for the second Windsor Free Festival, 1973.

extraordinary government-backed scheme, spearheaded by the Labour home secretary, Roy Jenkins, to create a state-sponsored free festival, which took place in August 1975 at Watchfield aerodrome, Oxfordshire. The event, which lasted nine days and attracted between 5–10,000, was under heavy scrutiny from all sides: by the media, police, civil servants, Watchfield's ultra-Conservative MP Airey Neave, and local residents.

But for hardcore anti-Establishment figures such as Ubi Dwyer, the idea of a state-sanctioned counter-cultural gathering was an unacceptable contradiction. In June 1974, the first of the Stonehenge Free Festivals had taken place, in a field and woodland adjoining the iconic megalithic circle. 'Wally Hope', aka Phil Russell, an orphan in receipt of a substantial private income, and with a penchant for sun worship, had hatched the idea, over a campfire at the previous Windsor bash, for a people's celebration of midsummer that would culminate in a colloquium at the stones. 'He wanted to claim back Stonehenge (a place that he regarded as sacred to the people and stolen by the government) and make it: a site for free festivals, free music, free space, free mind,' remembers Penny Rimbaud, who assisted in the festival preparations and later founded the anarcho-punk outfit Crass.[19] Hope was arrested and confined in a psychiatric institution later that year, where he was forcibly treated with anti-psychotic drugs, which reduced his mind to jelly and led to his death shortly afterwards. Thus martyred, a box of his ashes was ritually paraded around the stones at subsequent events. But he had started a new tradition at Stonehenge, which became the locus of largely peaceful events through the 1970s, notable for the way they provided one of the few spaces where the previous generations of hippy culture and the new urban punks – supposedly sworn enemies – would occupy the same camping space and idealistic territory, looking on as Druids conducted their officially sanctioned annual solstice ceremony. These assemblies were raggedly embroidered with faith, mysticism, LSD evangelism and national myth; populated by a rainbow coalition of subcultures eager to partake in the secret ritual life of Britain. As Wally Hope babbled to a newspaper after an overturned court appearance for illegal site occupation in August 1974: 'We are not squatters, we are men of God. We want to plant a Garden of Eden with apricots

Druid zone: poster for the second Stonehenge Free Festival, 1975.

Tepees at the 1976 Stonehenge Free Festival; the
megaliths are just visible in the background.

and cherries, where there will be guitars instead of guns and the
sun will be our nuclear bomb.'[20]

The National Trust and English Heritage, joint managers of the
Stonehenge site, passively tolerated these incursions until the mid-
1980s. The 'Battle of the Beanfield' of 1985 – when riot police
violently beat back a convoy of vehicles making its way to the
festival site – led to a barbed-wire exclusion zone being thrown
around the stones the following year. A battle for the right of
assembly at such places of national symbolism was being played
out once more, with the site stewards claiming that the party had
outgrown its capacity to manage itself, and that the revellers were
littering the area and physically damaging the stones. There would
be no more rock festivals held at Stonehenge until 1999.

'There are many among those who use festivals', comments a
voice from *Tomorrow's People*, 'who believe, extraordinary though

this may seem, that this is the way that much of Britain may one day be; that the life style provided and lived at pop festivals may be an indication of the way that society itself may be moving. Future social structures are seen as being more closely linked to the soil, to be more concerned with sharing, to take place in dwellings of a more improvisatory nature than we live in at the moment, and to contain more tribal togetherness than now.' But was this vision of levelled, sustainable living near the soil really a viable option? For many of these 'people of tomorrow', the unstated but nagging possibility behind the ideal of a pre-industrial utopia was as much a fear of having to survive a nuclear attack as a ticket to their ancestors' georgic golden age. The festival dream of building Eden in Avalon could not sustain itself against the political and social realities of Britain during the Thatcherite Conservative years. It was only ever accessible to an increasingly vilified minority, and the idea failed to ignite the wider imagination. The shout is raised every year, down the road at Pilton, but Glastonbury's slumbering wyrd remains unwoken.

The End of the Rainbow

There's nothing at the end of the rainbow
There's nothing to grow up for any more.
Richard and Linda Thompson, 'The End of the Rainbow' (1975)

The blossom came, but the fruit withered and died on the bough.
Lord Summerisle (Christopher Lee), *The Wicker Man* (1973)

The supreme depiction of the Earthly Paradise in English culture is *Paradise Lost*. Published in 1667, John Milton's religious epic presents a spiritual and planetary world in macrocosm; a topography of Adam and Eve's domain, Heaven and Hell, and the creatures that dwell in all three; a condensed history of civilisation, and visions of the distant future. Among all this, of course, Milton weaves his revolutionary spin on Temptation and the Fall. Written during the interim Commonwealth established by his hero, Oliver Cromwell, following the defeat and execution of Charles I, but only published after the Restoration of the monarchy, *Paradise Lost*'s account of mankind's fall from grace is subliminally loaded with the disappointment of a revolution that never delivered on its promises. Milton elevates Lucifer, the Fallen Angel, to heroic status, while Adam and Eve themselves are, by modern standards, worthy but dull. As William Blake later shrewdly observed, Milton was 'a true Poet and of the Devil's party without knowing it'.[1]

Paradise Lost was not the only one of Milton's works to deal with the loss of innocence. The piece properly entitled *A Maske Presented*

Comus, *First Utterance* (1971).

at Ludlow Castle, 1634: On Michaelmasse Night, etc., but usually known as *Comus*, enacts a battle of wills between debauchery and virtue. A lady, exhausted and abandoned in a forest by her brothers, is abducted by Comus, a beastly, depraved woodland denizen who uses sweet, intoxicating music and 'well-placed words of glozing courtesy' to charm and incapacitate his victims. The 'foul enchanter' hauls her off to his leafy lair, binds her to a 'marble venomed seat' with 'gums of glutinous heat', and tries to force the damsel to take a slurp from his 'liquorish baits'. Comus was reborn in one of the most singular English groups of the early 1970s, to deliver a threatening warning to the more docile, indolent ruminants of the underground's Earthly Paradise.

'I suppose it was a reaction to a lot of what was going on,' says Roger Wootton, lead singer and founding member of Comus, 'and I found things to react to in the hippy movement that annoyed me. It was all too sweet and nice, and I found it very limp and weak. It's funny, during the hippy period it was all "love and peace, man", and everyone mixing in. But what you actually had was a lot of people who didn't really fit together, and this would all come out of the woodwork later in the 1970s.'

Wootton formed Comus with guitarist Glenn Goring, whom he met while they were both students at Ravensbourne College of Art in 1968. (A contemporary was the trainee painter Robert Lewis, boyfriend of Vashti Bunyan, who had installed himself in a tepee in the college grounds.) Colin Pearson, a classically trained violinist, joined their informal music sessions, which consisted of acoustic renditions of Velvet Underground songs, and by the close of 1968 the three were renting a huge communal house in Beckenham, a London suburb so far to the south-east that it falls into Kent. The sixteen-year-old Bobbie Watson, girlfriend of another commune member, spontaneously started singing along in odd banshee harmonies with Wootton and became a formal group member, eventually transferring her affections to Goring. Finally, the group found a local champion in David Bowie, who gave them a residency at Growth, his Arts Lab at Beckenham's Three Tuns pub. Comus were among the artists at Bowie's Beckenham Free Festival in August 1969, and supported him at a prominent showcase gig at London's Purcell Room, apparently enraging him by blowing his own act off stage.

Comus are largely remembered today for one album, *First Utterance*, recorded in October 1970 and released in the winter of 1971 on the progressive label Dawn. Its striking gatefold cover, drawn by Wootton in black biro, depicts an emaciated homunculus, skin charred to a leathery black and gagging on its own bile, hauling itself by its elbows across a white backdrop. The self-loathing mannequin foreshadows the music's forbidding, often savage disquiet. Comus deployed mainly acoustic elements – guitars, violin, flute and oboe, bongos and percussion, plus electric bass – with a viciousness seldom heard in the pastorally inclined folk-rock of the time. Wootton wrote songs around a distinctive chopping, driving rhythm guitar. Colin Pearson's fiddle buzzed and trilled like a forbidden pagan jitterbug. Andy Hellaby's electric bass urged the music forward, occasionally locking into a Can-like

Comus, late 1971. Back row, left to right: Roger Wootton, Andy Hellaby, Colin
Pearson. Front row: Lindsay Cooper, Bobbie Watson, Glenn Goring.

mantric groove. Rob Young's flute cavorted like Pan gloating at the
revels. And then there are the vocals – Wootton swooping from
a saturnine soprano to guttural, lecherous goading, shadowed by
Watson's angelic counterpoints and milk-souring disharmonies.
Their repertoire was snarled tales of innocence corrupted, brutal
ravishment, clinical derangement and murderous gore.

Now a designer of computer flight simulators, Young remembers
the group's broad listening habits: 'I do remember Roger, Glenn,
Andy and I listening to King Crimson, Pink Floyd, and
the contemporary classical composers Takemitsu and Messiaen,
and they introduced me to a lot of quality music outside of my
knowledge, as did Colin, although I was then a great follower
of Stravinsky and Bartók. I'm not sure anyone in the band was a
great fan of conventional rock or pop music. I remember we had
a pretty common belief that we could achieve more original and
dynamically engaging performances with acoustic instruments

rather than the orthodox approach of ear-splitting high-decibel rock.' 'We used to go to Incredible String Band concerts,' adds Wootton, 'and The Pentangle, John Renbourn and Bert Jansch. This was our roots.'

Instead of brow-beating with high volume, Comus songs insinuated themselves under the skin. In 'Diana', Milton's beastly deceiver reappears ('*Lust he follows virtue close/ Through the steaming woodlands*'). 'The Herald' is a brief, peaceful interlude, a pastoral evocation of the dawn, featuring Hellaby's extended bass technique, using a metal guitar slide to generate an ethereal, eldritch whine. But with the sunrise comes the culling. The opening guitar strums of 'Song to Comus' strut like the creature stalking its prey through the forest ('*Hymen-hunter, hands of steel, crack you open and your red flesh peel*'). The monotonous, hammering four beats of each line replicate the meter Milton used for Comus's speech (the monster spoke in a primitive pulse, offset against the refined iambic pentameter of the 'civilised' characters). Wootton beats his chest while singing, to emit a breathless tremolo effect. In 'Drip Drip', a murderer lustfully contemplates his bleeding victim's corpse as he buries it in a forest. 'The Bite' mercilessly describes the lynching of a Christian.

Above all, it's the clenched hysteria, bordering on psychosis, of Wootton's vocals that dominate *First Utterance*. 'I think it's a character thing,' he says, 'because I can go there. The sort of manic, evil space that I can play around with, and you can get all this psychotic imagery. I came from a rural background in Kent, I had a very difficult upbringing with my parents – it put that anger and aggression in me. I hated my mother, so that was the anti-female things and the rape and murdering women – I don't want to psychoanalyse, but at the time it was much more instinctual than intellectually deliberate. I was on a roll with it. No one had done it before, so it was exciting to do, and no one else was doing anything like that, it was a complete contradiction to everything else.'

'I see Roger as a musical thespian,' says Goring, 'like an opera singer who plays a role. The Comus character is one he plays extremely well. Only a nutter could possibly believe that Roger's lyrics are his or the band's manifesto.'

The group feel, to this day, that *First Utterance* was a failure, poorly representing the full force of their live sound. 'It sounds tinny and thin compared to how we really sounded,' complains Watson. 'Most of it was done during a power workers' strike,' adds Goring, 'so blackouts were a common occurrence and dogged most of the proceedings.' Its impact was muted, thanks partly to a postal strike which held up its appearance in shops. Despite taking a few intriguing side trips – making music for and appearing in Lindsay Shonteff's voyeuristic groupie movie *Permissive*; Wootton drawing sleeve art for *Tone Float*, the debut album by Ralf Hütter and Florian Schneider's pre-Kraftwerk duo The Organisation – Comus didn't survive the reckoning year of 1971–2, a time of structural adjustment in the rock economy. 'Glam rock eclipsed us,' concedes Wootton. 'The irony is that David Bowie, who actually helped us off the ground, became our nemesis. Glam rock came in and suddenly the audience figures dropped right off, we got fewer and fewer gigs, and no one was interested. We couldn't get any work. Rob left because of the poverty and the hand-to-mouth existence – he couldn't take it any more.'

Though Comus officially disbanded in mid-1972, Wootton, Watson and Hellaby briefly convened two years later for a second album, *To Keep from Crying*, commissioned by Virgin Records. Featuring bassoonist Lindsay Cooper of Henry Cow and Didier Malherbe of Gong, it's an uncomfortable mix of commercial songwriting and experimental techniques. The album was bound to disappoint previous fans, and mystify newcomers, and it failed to sell. Comus retreated to hibernate under his mossy stone.

While all around them groups such as Amazing Blondel, Magna Carta and Renaissance perpetuated reassuring images of medievalist minstrelsy, Comus were nabobs of negativity, prophets disrupting the feast with unwelcome harangues. Other naysayers included Spirogyra, a left-field folk-rock group grappling with political realities that became harder to ignore during the early 1970s. Spirogyra (not to be confused with the late-1970s cocktail jazz-funk group) was the initiative of Martin Cockerham, who came down from his native Bolton, Lancashire, to the University of Kent at Canterbury in 1969. Within a year, Cockerham had formed a quartet with fellow students classical violinist/pianist Julian Cusack, bassist Steve Borrill and singer Barbara Gaskin. The earliest incarnation of Spirogyra narrowly missed out on a deal with Apple Records, but Sandy Roberton obtained their first LP, *St Radigunds* (1971), for his B&C imprint, recruiting Fairport Convention's Dave Mattacks as studio drummer and hiring Nick Drake's friend Robert Kirby as producer and string arranger. The album was named after the community house they occupied in St Radigund Street, in the centre of historic Canterbury, where their social circle included local luminaries, from Caravan and Gong to Ian Dury. On *St Radigunds* and its follow-up, *Old Boot Wine* (1972), long-form pieces such as 'The Duke of Beaufoot' and 'World's Eyes' squeezed acoustic rock into weird, amoebic shapes, while Cockerham's texts, sung by himself and Gaskin, covered an unusual array of subject matter: atomic theory, astronomy and the transience of beauty, tossing in consumerist critique, in stream-of-consciousness tirades. 'Disraeli's Problem', for instance, graphically referenced bleeding shoppers and children on the streets after a bomb attack in Northern Ireland, and called out the '*fool*' Home Secretary Reginald Maudling by name.

By 1973 Spirogyra was effectively a duo of Cockerham and Gaskin, now a couple. Cockerham was sharing a west London flat with Shirley Collins's ex-husband Austin John Marshall and folk musician Steve Ashley, who crops up on the third and final Spirogyra record, *Bells, Boots and Shambles* (1973). Mattacks was still present, and Dolly Collins waved her arranger's wand over an acoustic tapestry that included London Philharmonic Orchestra cellist John Boyce and jazz trumpeter Henry Lowther.

Five years before Joy Division, these songs are a philosophical response to a new sense of hopelessness, an existential angst that would resurface in the futurist pop of the end of the decade: '*I'm in a vacuum, a nameless statistical sea / My life's a number.*' Sequenced in four 'movements', the twelve-minute mini-suite 'In the Western World' broods on the place of a young idealist within the evolutionary machinery of industrial capital. The future is an atavistic succession of death traps, the pleasure garden evoked by so much bucolic folk has become a '*jungle fight*' for survival. The third section, 'Coming Back', pins hopes on the arrival of a saviour, a buried Christ / Arthur figure who will '*Give it back to the shores of Albion / Where the mills were first abused*'.

Half a decade earlier, Florida folkniks Pearls Before Swine stumbled on the formula for a kind of apocalypse folk on their album *Balaklava* (1968), couching cosmic awareness and veiled attacks on the Vietnam War and materialism in a vaulting studio ambience that crosswired galactic space shanties with wax-cylinder voice recordings from 1890 of Florence Nightingale and Trumpeter Landfrey, a bugler who had lived through the Charge of the Light Brigade.[2] In 1970 even Tim Buckley, the sun-blessed West Coast troubadour, was pushing his music into a disorientating, fractured avant-garde mode on albums like *Lorca* and *Starsailor*, which featured electronically distorted animal gibbering and the tragic merman lament of 'Song to the Siren', an anguished howl of loss that suggested a dark side to the Venice Beach dream of eternal summer. Folk music's discontents seemingly couldn't avert this slide towards the apocalyptic. In Britain, Bill Fay produced his second and final album, *Time of the Last Persecution*, in 1971, under the influence of the French Jesuit, palaeontologist and philosopher Teilhard de Chardin. First to coin the word 'Gaia' in relation to a notion of Earth as a single, conscious organism, De Chardin integrated Christian thought with modern science, and proposed that civilisation was approaching an 'omega point' – the dawn of a new age of globally altered consciousness.

'He was just one of many,' says Fay now, 'but he was just so optimistic and positive, and that definitely rubbed off. His thing was that life was important, and that it's only on the planet that life is reaching these kind of heights. The vastness of the universe and stars and all that, to him they were basically hydrogen, and I think it helped me in the sense that if I saw a butterfly flying by or something, I could actually feel the strangeness of that . . . I'd compare the blackness of outer space with this kind of . . . thing, flying about, and the complexity of it, and you think, blimey.'

If *Bill Fay* was his songs of innocence, *Time of the Last Persecution* was a collection of songs of experience. The album's recurring motif is a warning against false leaders, messiahs and prophets. Fay's breath is thick with imminent crisis, muttering on 'Plan D' about a secret conspiracy to make the seas rise and the skies open. One song is called 'Till the Christ Come Back'; 'Pictures of Adolf Again' explicitly refers to Hitler, Balthazar J. Vorster (architect of South Africa's apartheid regime), Christ and '*all the Caesars to come*'. The cover photo showed a heavily bearded Fay in an apparently dishevelled state, which has led to rumours that Fay was psychologically burned out. But the photo, taken by a friend, Jake Jackson, was taken in the studio while Fay's concentration was elsewhere. 'The dishevelled look,' chuckles Ray Russell, Fay's friend and guitarist on the album, 'I mean, I think we all looked like that. I think I had a few beads on. It's an anti-image, really.'

Fay is at pains to correct the impression that the album documented some kind of personal apocalypse. 'It was the problems of the world that I was talking about, not my own problems. The

Apocalypse soon: Bill Fay recording *Time of the Last Persecution*, 1971.

world was going through heavy times – or our view of the world was a heavy world.' 'Time of the Last Persecution' itself, attests Fay, 'was written immediately after the tanks rolling into the campus and killing students in America [at Kent State University, Ohio, in May 1970]. "Do not avenge these deaths, do not avenge them. Make for your own secret place," and don't get caught up in overthrowing things and all that. To me that wasn't the way to go. So I think I was trying to say that in the second album. And that you're entitled to come away from seeing riot police clubbing people, look at other things in the world as well, and not to get consumed and overcome by it.'

The end-time mood was growing contagious. On *Stormcock*, Roy Harper made reference to the riotous anti-Vietnam demonstration in Grosvenor Square, and talked of a state visit by

Cardinal Doomsday. The times were growing wild, and salvation had left no forwarding address.

Gambling on survival through the barrage of doom-mongering and the ever-present threat of Armageddon, some musicians decided to invest in some spiritual chips. The Digger/hippy philosophy of sharing the planet's common treasury effectively softened up a sizeable portion of youth culture to conversion to Christianity, as witnessed by the incursions of clerics into rock festivals like Glastonbury and Watchfield. And acoustic folk music provided the ideal idiom for rewriting the hymn book in a modern, gentle image. Beginning in America – notably with Billy Ray Hearn's Christian rock label Myrrh – and spreading to the UK in the 1970s on labels like Pilgrim, Dovetail, Grapevine and Reflection, the micro-genre known variously as 'Jesus music' or 'Christ music' brought a dash of 'Kumbaya' campfire togetherness to Anglican services. But inadvertently, there were a few groups – After the Fire, Caedmon, Canaan, Cloud, Bryn Haworth, Meet Jesus Music, Narnia, Nutshell, Parchment, Presence, Reynard, Trinity Folk, Water into Wine Band and 11.59 – which managed to make a music that has lasting value, a kind of Eucharistic-progressive sound that sits comfortably with the better acid folk of the period.

These were not doorstepping evangelicals, but they used the musical dialect and atmosphere of folk-rock to engender a tone of devotional contemplation. Scottish quintet Caedmon weren't afraid to throw in a trace of Latin percussion or a Celtic jig or two among their electric guitar, organ and cello. Live, they might include folk hymns like 'Swing Low' and 'Said Jesus to the Willow', and covers of Richard Fariña and American gospel folkie Larry Norman, alongside their own C. S. Lewis-inspired numbers like 'Aslan'. Their one album, from 1978, was a farewell recording, celebrating five years of existence. Caedmon, the earliest documented English poet, was a mystic seventh-century religious hermit; his name, plus the recurrence of St Columba in their song list, betrays an interest in the pagan-era arrival of Christianity to British shores – the age documented by the Venerable Bede. Nutshell, whose two mid-1970s albums came out on Myrrh, were originally known as Jesus Revolution. Parchment, formed in 1972 in Liverpool from the ashes of Trinity Folk, eventually set up their own label, Grapevine. The four-piece Water into Wine Band met at Cambridge University, graduated in 1974 and released *Hill Climbing for Beginners* on Myrrh that year. Christian or not, it's a marvellously soulful acoustic folk-rock suite, with a running theme of tribulation endured and epiphanies on the stony road to salvation. Their mellow, occasionally clashing harmonies and twelve-string guitars recall Heron's pastoral ambience, but they weren't averse to breaking into more agitated passages, as in the eleven-minute, multi-part epic 'Song of the Cross', an impassioned attempt to empathise with the pain of crucifixion.

Even Bob and Carole Pegg, just before the end of Mr Fox, teamed up with the folk poet, holy sceptic and iconoclastic theologian Sydney Carter to record *And Now It Is So Early*, an album of Carter's joyous hymns, (the Peggs' *He Came From The Mountains*, recorded in 1967, had included the one popular in school assemblies of the 70s, 'Lord of the Dance'). And Carter's music was also the subject of the first release on Reflection Records, which promoted the idea of an adventurous folk/acid rock-centred holy music – for instance *A Folk Passion*, a concept album on the last days of Christ's life which mingled church organ with a modern rhythm section. By far the strangest entry in Reflection's catalogue, though, was an uncredited compilation called *Sounds of Salvation*. Commissioned by the Methodist Missionary Society to be distributed at the Nineteenth General Assembly of the World Council of Churches, the LP is an uninterrupted sequence of songs in a variety of styles, from hard rock to blissful folk-rock and country-tinged acoustic balladry, linked by claustrophobic passages of musique concrète tape montages of multiple voices, as if caught on a roving microphone at several cocktail parties, and presumably intended to signify the godless babble of the modern age. No one has yet stepped forward to claim credit for this audio curiosity, and the album remains a cult collector's item. The Jesus-music movement may not have converted thousands to the cause, but it marked the modern church's new identification with a gentle, and at times mysterious, musical Anglicana that might appeal to younger ears. *The English Hymnal*, introduced with such vigour back at the start of the century by Ralph Vaughan Williams, now represented all that was stuffy and ceremonious about the Church of England. The time had come for Vaughan Williams to roll over.

In the Roman Catholic church of St Columba's in Upton-by-Chester, a spiky red-brick building consecrated in 1965, there are massive modern stained-glass windows designed by Hans Unger, a German artist who, among other commissions, designed many posters for the London Underground. At his workshops in Muswell Hill in north London, Unger's assistant on St Columba's windows – accomplishing the hands-on work of cutting the glass and assembling the mosaic – was the sixteen-year-old Richard Thompson. It was the apprentice's one and only experience of working in the 'real world' before he got down to the serious business of launching Fairport Convention.

In an omnivorous music career that has traversed decades and an impressively wide array of musical styles, Thompson has remained a practising religious observer – as a Sufi Muslim – but has managed to keep God out of his music. In fact, it's almost the opposite: his songs – especially during the 1970s, when he went out in partnership with his wife Linda – are much more humanist, unstinting and often harrowing in their confrontation with emotional desolation; he's a moralist who sees a stained world drained of morals.

At the point when he went solo, with *Henry the Human Fly* (1972), his philosophy was an untidy mess of New Age platitudes and cynical misanthropy. Thompson ceased taking part in Fairport Convention in early 1971, but kept his room at The Angel pub in Hertfordshire, where the group were shacked up, and worked on his own material, supporting himself with a marathon run of session work in London and playing odd gigs with Ashley Hutchings's Albion Band. Like many facing the brave new decade, Thompson feared the end of the world was nigh. 'Richard was convinced that 1975 was going to be the apocalypse year and that something terrible was going to happen,' stated one friend of Fairport.[3] In a 1970 interview, Thompson discussed astrology, vegetarianism, reincarnation, his belief in 'Karmic Laws', and the wider significance of his new hobby, archery: 'I wouldn't kill anybody, I just shoot at targets. But if there is anything left after a nuclear war, [a bow and arrow] would be very useful.'[4]

Henry set the end-time tone that would saturate his compositions of the 1970s. The first track, 'Roll Over Vaughn Williams', is a song of curious textures and cryptic lyrics. Thompson spills a spaghetti-skirl of guitar over it, like electrified uilleann pipes, and duets with himself on a coarsely amplified accordion. It's difficult to pick one single interpretation from his words, which don't even mention the (misspelt) composer, but there is an unmistakable air of confrontation about its prickly drone and repeated admonishment to '*live in fear*'. The song was written in the direct aftermath of *Liege and Lief* and *Full House*, and while Thompson was collaborating with Ashley Hutchings and John Kirkpatrick on the electric folk-dance project *Morris On*, and it's practically a manifesto for this earthy, electrified folk, which is not intended as a reassuring sop to bourgeois ears that all is well in the rural backwaters of the folk. 'It's kind of a mission statement,' he told me in 2009, 'a rallying cry, but at the same time a warning against stereotypes and labels.' The nearest we get to Vaughan

Williams is in the line *'Pencils ready, paper dry'*: the Edwardian folk-song collector poised to transcribe some villager's hoarse rendition of a long-lost tune. But Thompson's song wipes out any lingering sentimentality: the working-class singers who supplied the folk revivalists with their material were poor people enduring tough, hard times. And that's what the rest of the album mainly describes: 'The Poor Ditching Boy' toils in freezing storms, in a river too weary to flood, as he dwells on an unrequited love that's left him an emotional pauper. 'The Old Changing Way' is a low-life journey through the eyes of a travelling tinker; 'Twisted' the soliloquy of a self-pitying drunk; 'Painted Ladies' a misanthropic critique of the glamour industry.

In 'Wheely Down' (the name of a real-life historic village in Hampshire, about half an hour's drive from Farley Chamberlayne, which contains a blacksmiths' forge and artesans' workshops), the rolling English countryside yields only visions of futility: fools building houses on flooded ground, worms rotting the miller's wheel, rats eating the grain, ruined armies of deliverance, and a kestrel – symbol of the lowliest serf's falconry – wheeling forlornly in an empty sky. 'The New St George', which also appears on The Albion Country Band's *Battle of the Field*, is a war cry for a folk revolution, calling on workers to abandon factory and forge and flood the streets in a dance of freedom. Not the Aquarian awakening of middle-class idealism, but something more atavistic, unleashing the feral energy of a subjugated and exhausted populace.

Henry the Human Fly was recorded in a rush, but it has many of the hallmarks of Thompson's work later that decade: weary, sluggard beats, the crisp tremolo of Thompson's Stratocaster cutting across acoustic rhythm guitars, and the dignified wheeze of John Kirkpatrick's button accordion. Amid the sparkly circus of glam rock, Thompson's morbid disgruntlement made him appear, as the album title implied, a lowly sideshow freak. In financial terms, too, he was a mere insect: *Henry* was the lowest-selling release in the entire Warners record catalogue. Thompson ended the year by marrying Linda Peters, the beginning of a tempestuous musical and personal relationship that would reach a car-crash conclusion ten years later.

Linda Peters spent much of 1971 in America with Joe Boyd, to whom she was engaged. When that broke off at the end of the year, she returned to Britain alone, while her former fiancé developed film projects such as editing the music to *Deliverance* and *A Clockwork Orange*, and producing a feature-length documentary on Jimi Hendrix. As one of Sandy Denny's best friends, Linda was already well ensconced in the London folk-club scene, and a singer in her own right, much respected for her confident delivery. She had been chosen by Joe Boyd to work with Elton John on a showcase EP of songs by Nick Drake and Mike Heron, to publicise his Warlock Music publishing operation, and sang back-up on Albion Country Band records at the time. Following her short relationship with the beautiful but incoherent Drake, her whirlwind romance with Richard Thompson culminated in marriage within a matter of months. And in 1973 their fortunes seemed about to turn. The go-getting American manager Jo Lustig had just lost his former protégés Pentangle, who had finally split up after five years. Richard and Linda Thompson had already begun making an impact in British folk clubs as a trio with Fairport guitarist Simon Nicol, and Lustig signed them up as a husband-and-wife duo. Immediately they gathered new and familiar troops – Nicol, Pat Donaldson, Trevor Lucas, John Kirkpatrick, Royston Wood, Brian Gulland and Richard Harvey from progressive medievalists Gryphon, and members of the C. W. S. Manchester Silver Band – and set about taping some material. It was only due to a vinyl shortage – thanks to the global oil crisis – that *I Want to See the Bright Lights Tonight* was delayed until 1974.

As Thompson's biographer accurately summarised it, *Bright Lights* 'came as close as anyone to creating a uniquely pre-punk,

English rock 'n' roll'.[5] The song titles of *Bright Lights* tell a mournful enough story: 'Calvary Cross', 'Withered and Died', 'Down Where the Drunkards Roll', 'The Little Beggar Girl', 'The End of the Rainbow'. Timi Donald, the Island session drummer who had battered his way through *Henry the Human Fly*, had his feet firmly planted in the same earth as Dave Mattacks – anvil beats

Richard and Linda Thompson in a 1974 publicity shot
for their *I Want to See the Bright Lights* LP.

clunking with the coiled heft of a blacksmith's hammer. His contribution defines the album's clay-footed pace; the brass, accordion and antique woodwinds add Victorian streetwise whispers to the mix, appropriate to Thompson's Mayhew-like sketches of city lowlife. (They were touring under the group name Hokey Pokey at this time, a reference to the cries of the ice-cream sellers at Victorian funfairs.) 'The End of the Rainbow' is a profoundly depressing poem spoken over a cradle, warning the newborn of the perils and tragedies in store (the couple's first child had just been born). The end of the album leaves us hanging on an emotional high wire, as 'The Great Valerio' walks his tightrope, watched by hopeful '*acrobats of love*' in their ringside seats. As a glimmer of faith at the end of a powerfully faithless sequence of songs, it mirrored developments in the Thompsons' own lives. Because in 1973, following a chance conversation with Mighty Baby's pianist Ian Whiteman and a visit to a religious meeting on London's Euston Road, they discovered Islam. Shortly afterwards, the Thompsons bailed out of their spacious flat in Hampstead, gave away their material possessions and took up more frugal accommodation in a Sufi community in Maida Vale, west London, where men and women led separate lives for most of each day.

As prolific session men, Thompson had run into Whiteman many times in studios over the years. Whiteman's post-Mighty Baby project The Habibiyya, with its proto-New Age meditational rhythms, had just released its one and only album on Island's budget Help imprint, an outlet for more 'quirky' projects, including *Morris On*. Between those two records, a vast cultural gulf narrowed by a fraction. Hutchings was trying to summon up the earthy magic of the morris: 'Some of the movements of Morris dancing were designed to draw a power from the atmosphere, and the ground beneath them, and their bodies,' as he later outlined it.[6] In the same words, he could have been describing the secret, sacred dances of the Sufi Whirling Dervishes.

In retrospect, it's clear religion was waiting to happen to Richard Thompson. Commenting on 'Calvary Cross' in 1974, he said, 'It's about a drive that you might not want, but it's there, and you're a slave to it.'[7] Later, in a 1988 interview, he amplified, 'I'd always been interested in Zen and the Essenes and American Indians' spiritual traditions; I was just a young person trying to connect with reality somehow. I just realised that Sufism was where it was at. Intellectually I decided it was the thing to do, and when I met Muslims I recognised a quality in them that I wanted in my self.'[8]

Sufism represents Islam at its most rarefied and mystical: 'a pure version of Islam, the inner core of its teaching, the spiritual hub', as Thompson himself described it. 'It's derived purely from the Koran and the prophet Mohammed, in a direct line.'[9] Richard and Linda's appearance and behaviour altered in a number of ways. Live appearances at this time were austere and acoustic; Richard's Mullah had forbidden him to play electric guitar. Of the two LPs they released in 1975, *Hokey Pokey* is a notably more upbeat affair than *Bright Lights*, loaded with double entendres and rocked-up Victoriana. On the cover of *Pour Down Like Silver*, though, the impact of their faith is blatantly advertised: Richard has grown out his now familiar beard and his hair is wrapped in a turban. Linda gazes intensely at the viewer from within a sky-blue headscarf. The duo's religious commitments took them away from touring and recording between 1975–8, first in a brief, unfulfilling trial at running a couple of antique shops along with other commune members, then to another ascetic Islamic establishment in Hoxne, near Diss on the Norfolk–Suffolk border. On their last tour with a full group, their frequent prayer stops and air of difference left them increasingly isolated from former friends such as Simon Nicol, who recalled how 'they were beginning to draw away . . . from infidel society, and my feelings of being a trio with a rhythm section started to move towards a rhythm section accompanying a couple'.[10]

Most of the Thompsons' 1970s work struggles with a sense of hard-won knowledge, a literal dis-illusionment, a shattering of the rosy lens. It was as if the music permitted a wallowing in an imaginative world of filth from which Sufism might elevate and insulate them. 'Night Comes In', the song which supplies the title of *Pour Down Like Silver*, cuts closest to Sufi sensibility, with its references to drinking wine and dancing with feet hovering over the ground. The remainder of the record is martial and abrasive, with a despondency that would only intensify once the Thompsons returned to the stage in the late 1970s. Their final US tour in 1982, fulfulling a contractual obligation after they had agreed to divorce, has gone down in the rock annals as a legendarily bitter and destructive undertaking. But from the days of their first ventures, when they briefly called their group Sour Grapes, Richard Thompson has continually embraced a fatalism that was still in evidence three and a half decades later – perhaps with a little more irony than before – when he explained the reason for featuring a reclining chair on the sleeve of his album *1000 Years of Popular Music*: 'It seemed most accurately to represent Man's true relationship with the Cosmos – supine with mouth agape, perhaps in anticipation of the dentist's drill of eternal suffering.'[11]

Richard and Linda Thompson's decade-long career as a duo spanned the period when the hulking Avro Lancaster of folk-rock was shot down in a pall of smoke by punk's speedy Messerschmitts. After 1972, when the pool of musicians who had made up Fairport Convention, Fotheringay, The Albion Band, Mighty Baby et al. congregated for one final bash at Virgin Records' newly acquired Manor Studios to record an album of 1950s and 60s rock 'n' roll/ country favourites, the folk-rock blossom began perceptibly to wither on the twig. Virgin head Richard Branson had given Trevor

Lucas and friends bargain-rate access to the manor house in the prim Oxfordshire village of Shipton-on-Cherwell to fine-tune the freshly installed facilities. His construction team had just finished converting the historic pile into the world's first residential recording environment, a thirty-eight-bedroom retreat where artists could eat, sleep and record at leisure, with butlers, maids and cooks to satisfy their every whim. It was a streamlined 'getting it together in the country' philosophy that made sound business sense.

For the first unit off the Manor production line, Lucas convened Richard Thompson, Linda Peters, Sandy Denny, Ashley Hutchings, Dave Mattacks, Gerry Conway, Pat Donaldson, Ian Whiteman and others, including a horn section, collectively known as The Bunch. As John Lennon would do three years later on *Rock 'n' Roll*, The Bunch indulged a nostalgia for the pop music of their teens, at once a celebration and a putting-away of childish things. *Rock On*, the album culled from the week-long session, is a largely spirited compilation of oldies but mouldies, with highlights including Sandy Denny and Linda Peters's duet on 'When Will I Be Loved?', and Ashley Hutchings's hopped-up, drawling careen through Chuck Berry's 'Nadine'. For this Bunch, who had dedicated themselves to proselytising for an intrinsically British music, *Rock On*'s jukebox of guilty pleasures scribbled American graffiti on the walled garden. Robin Hood was riding a Harley. For one week only, this was folk-rock Babylon: Linda Peters recalled 'loads and loads of bedroom hopping' during the sessions; Thompson and Sandy Denny were throwing up in separate toilets while Lucas was recording 'The Locomotion'; and enough cans of beer were polished off that Lucas could knit an entire curtain of ring-pulls.[12]

The fun and games didn't last. At a New Year's party at the Howff club in London marking the end of 1972, Ashley Hutchings would yank out the plug when members of his Albion Country Band launched into a Chuck Berry riff. Just over a year later, Hutchings would be reduced to working as a postman in Etchingham, as the musical engagements dried up.

Sandy Denny also noted the feeling of emptiness in the folk fraternity around the same time: 'There don't seem to be any folk clubs like they used to be,' she told Jerry Gilbert. 'Since the Cousins closed down [in 1972] it was almost like a nucleus was taken away for some reason . . . In those days there was always a John Snow [pub] for the tradition people and then Cousins for the folkies with the harmonicas and it has always [been] buzzing around, the trads against the contemporaries. It's still going on, but it's such a sophisticated feud now and one doesn't enter into blatant ignoring of people. But there are these staunch ones left like Pete Bellamy.'[13]

Steeleye Span's Tim Hart identified the folk scene's problems of scale. When he started his original duo with Maddy Prior, they found they could exceedingly quickly reach the summit of what could be achieved playing folk music, in terms of workload, income, etc.: 'the crock of gold at the end of the rainbow on the folk scene wasn't difficult to achieve'.[14] The only way to progress, not stagnate, was to move on, resulting in the flash-in-the-pan stadium rock Steeleye of the mid-1970s.

Others, like Ashley Hutchings, identified fresh avenues in which to ply their wares. In 1978 his Albion Band supplied the live music for Keith Dewhurst's stage adaptation of Flora Thompson's rural novel *Lark Rise to Candleford* at London's National Theatre. The staging broke barriers between people and performers, with actors and musicians mingling in the auditorium. Thompson's fictional account of village life in the first half of the twentieth century plotted the same trajectory of British social history as Shirley and Dolly Collins's *Anthems in Eden*, observing the culling effects of the Great War and the migration of farm labourers to towns and cities to be transformed into a metropolitan proletariat. Thompson, a country girl who was a shrewd watcher

Electric Eden

Front cover of *The Electric Muse*, an attempt at a comprehensive survey of British folk music published in 1975.

of the alteration of national character, painted the rural past in shimmering, transfigured terms but harboured no lagging sentimentality for the vanished golden age. 'For myself I would desire a combination of old romance and modern machinery,' she wrote in her newspaper column, *The Peverel Papers*, a description which suited The Albion Band's robust electric folk-song tablature. The production, though, sent Hutchings's marriage to Shirley Collins crashing in flames. He had an affair with a younger member of the cast, and Collins was forced to watch them together as she sang her vocal parts – a traumatic experience which brought on acute hysterical dysphonia, a medical condition which removes the structural underpinnings of the singing voice (Sandy Denny and Linda Thompson were also afflicted). Shirley Collins – Alan Lomax's song huntress, Davy Graham's new route finder – never sang a concert or made a recording in her own name again.

Nineteen seventy-five was a year of retrospection in the music industry, a time for stocktaking and canonisation. British folk music's long, strange journey was compiled on the four-LP set *The Electric Muse*, which began with The Copper Family and Lead Belly and ended with Roy Harper and Traffic. The set accompanied a book of the same name, also published in 1975, co-authored by four writers with parallel but differing agendas. *The Electric Muse* attempted to survey the panorama of the folk revival, from the Victorian collectors to its American mutations through the twentieth century into industrial song and contemporary folk-rock, taking account of its inbuilt contradictions and problematic areas along the way. *The Electric Muse* concluded, somewhat hopefully, by surveying the surviving folk-rockers of 1975 – Fairport, Steeleye Span, Albion Country Band, etc. – as if urging them on to become as successful as the rock giants. Admitting that folk's golden age had come and gone, Robin Denselow concluded by putting a brave face on a predicament: 'The clubs are still there, and still provide one of the few openings for new performers. The audience for folk and folk-rock is still there. And so are the songs. Like rock, the folk revival could go almost anywhere next.'

Well, yes, it could; but not in the way Denselow apparently hoped. The Bunch's studio try-out smoothed the way for the symphonic rock epic that was recorded at Manor Studios in the autumn of 1972 which effectively put Virgin on the map and earned its first fortune: *Tubular Bells*. Its composer, Mike Oldfield – former teenage partner of his sister Sally in psych-folk duo The Sallyangie – followed it by retreating to his private studio at the Beacon, his Herefordshire country house, to compose the folky minimalism of *Hergest Ridge* (1974) and *Ommadawn* (1975), the latter an Afro-Celtic systems music with tribal drums, uilleann pipes by The Chieftains' Paddy Moloney and vocals by Bridget St John and ex-Mellow Candle singer Clodagh Simonds. At this fulcrum mid-1970s moment, Virgin (and its EG Records subsidiary) was releasing several examples of a shift in the way popular music could conjure pastoral moods.

But for the disaffected begetters of punk back in the mid-1970s, this abstract, context-free music was a pretty vacant indulgence, to be lumped in with the dinosaurs of rock that dominated the industry. In another irony, it was a former founder of underground progressive labels Harvest and Vertigo, Nick Mobbs, who struck EMI's fateful deal with The Sex Pistols in 1976. And it would be the home of Mike Oldfield and co., Virgin, that would eventually issue the Pistols' brazen challenge to the status quo, *Never Mind the Bollocks*.

It was a glorious time to be on school holidays in England, that summer of 1976. Britain was experiencing a drought, with parched lawns, tropical temperatures and baths limited to three inches of water. The adults didn't dig it too much, but for an eight-year-old with time on his hands it was an unforgettable, endless summer.

My family was holidaying on Langley Farm, an Elizabethan pile hidden down mazy country lanes and protected by cattle grids amid the rolling fields and terracotta soil of southern Devon. Surrounded by home-made cider, artery-clogging cream teas and fruity yeoman dialects, we were in prime Wurzel territory. The long drive from Bristol had been lightened by repeat-singing of a song riding high in the charts at the time: 'Combine Harvester (Brand New Key)' by 'scrumpy and Western' group The Wurzels.[15] Lead singer Pete Budd popped up regularly on commercial television all

Gurt big dollops of yokel folk: The Wurzels, *The Combine Harvester* (1976).

that summer in an ad for a popular dairy product: 'St Ivel Clotted Cream – arrrr, give 'em a gurt big dollop!' 'Dolloping' accordingly became the name of one of my favourite dangerous sports that summer: lying on my stomach on top of my Action Man armoured car and go-karting down the steepest hill on the farm.

One morning, curiosity overtook me and I decided to enter the one barn that had been forbidden when we first arrived. I approached the battened doors across the cobbled farmyard, cats and hens scattering in all directions. I stretch back through the years and lift the latch. The door creaks ajar. Hay motes eddy on fanned sunbeams. Straw bales exude a fermented whiff. But arranged in the middle of the barn are mysterious objects that are certainly not farm implements. I am familiar with these things, I know that they are the machines that make pop music, having glimpsed them on *Top of the Pops* and *Supersonic*, brandished by adults long-haired, leather-jacketed and raucous, spangled like Christmas and screaming like sugar-rushing kids. I even picked up some of their names – Suzi Quatro, Slade, Mud, The Sweet – before my parents clicked off the TV and whisked me off to bed. But here in this Devonshire barn, close enough to touch, is a sunburst Fender electric bass, a pile of sparkling drums and cymbals, a microphone stand and some electronic boxes covered with knobs and switches that my young mind can only compare to a control panel from Doctor Who's Tardis. Mystifyingly, I also distinctly remember a small trampoline.

I am called sharply out of the barn reverie, and a padlock is snapped on the door handle. Later that week the telephone in our self-catering cottage trills, and my mum is regaled with a woozy voice calling from Los Angeles, asking to speak to the guys from Yes.

I didn't know it then, but now I can check the history: it turns out Langley Farm used to rent out rehearsal space to rock groups at the time.[16] In 1976, when I stumbled in on Yes's stored instruments, the individual members of the prog super-group were taking a couple of years out between albums, indulging their own separate pretensions in solo projects that ranged from pompous oratorios to ramshackle meat 'n' spuds rock. Lead singer Jon Anderson composed the Tolkien-esque eco-folk fantasy album *Olias of Sunhillow*. Pursuing a concept first mooted on Yes's *Fragile*, Olias is a future-days Noah building a space ark to flee a disintegrating Earth. In the early twenty-first century the American group Animal Collective would derive a degree of hipness from replicating the vocal sound of this album, but in 1976 it encapsulated everything fey, unworldly and decadent that punk aimed to sweep away in its own wrathful deluge. Anderson's many-layered vocals and syntactically dubious lyrics are piled up like clotted cream on top of a syrupy confit of acoustic guitars and synthesizers. There's something over-ripe and faintly sickly about this gurt big dollop from the lead singer of the group that, more than most, symbolised prog rock's gluttonous pig-out.

In the ecology of music, in 1976 rock's brontosauri were enduring their own drought, and reacting to their imminent demise by dunking their heads in the bleached sand. At one extreme it was space opera or classical folly at its most bloated; at the other it clunkily tried to accommodate folkier strains. Gryphon made a valiant attempt to fuse prog's herky-jerky time signatures with a panoply of Early Music instruments, with decidedly mixed results. Anthony Phillips, a founder member of Genesis who left the group in 1970, befriended Harry Williamson, a twenty-one-year-old guitarist who had just moved from his native Devon to London and fallen in with The Windfuckers, a bunch of hippy heads from Andrew Kerr's Glastonbury Festival team. Williamson was the son of the prolific and unconventional author Henry Williamson, whose perennial children's books *Tarka the Otter* and *Salar the Salmon* had been succeeded by a fifteen-volume outpouring of memoir, *A Chronicle of Ancient Sunlight*, concluded in 1969. Williamson junior played a back-room role in the underground groups and free-festival culture of the 1970s, eventually turning up in groups such as Nik Turner's Sphynx, for whom he built a portable pyramid stage, and Mother Gong, part of Daevid Allen's extended family. In the early 1970s, when a film version of *Tarka the Otter* was mooted, Williamson took Anthony Phillips on a series of walks around the North Devonshire locations that had inspired his father's novel, and the pair began working up ideas for a folk-orchestral soundtrack. When the film eventually came out, in 1979, it was produced without the knowledge of the Williamson estate, and Phillips's Rodrigo/Debussyan suite was left unfinished (it was eventually completed and released in 1988, featuring Gong's Didier Malherbe and Henry Cow's Lindsay Cooper). Phillips's *The Geese and the Ghost* (1977) is all strummy Tudorbethan chamber pastiche as viewed from the other side of *Abbey Road*. The Tudor modernists – Vaughan Williams, Holst, Warlock et al. – were not ready to roll over just yet.

The inescapable truth was that if you were still making Albion-centric, historically resonant folk-rock after 1974, then the zeitgeist had deserted you. In the cash-strapped Britain of the mid-1970s, the unrepaired zones of inner-city London, Manchester, Glasgow and elsewhere were just as much of a wilderness as the great outdoors. The suburban children of that very metropolitan proletariat chronicled by Flora Thompson, faced with the choice of small-town stagnation or gravitation from town to country, chose to emigrate to the concrete centre of the circle. Old priorities were thrown into reverse. The photos of singers and groups dressed Gypsy-fashion, draped over oaks or reclining in long grass, begin to vanish from the music press and album sleeves; the backdrops to the new wave – and much after it – would be bricks, concrete, graffiti or the blank sheets of a photographic studio. There was a sense of historical fatigue: the whole recent genre of earnest medieval costume dramas (*Alfred the Great*, *Gawain and the Green Knight*, Bresson's *Lancelot du Lac*, *Arthur of the Britons*) was swept up and rumbustiously satirised in *Monty Python and the Holy Grail* (1975). 'It's only a model,' comments a hastily shushed Arthurian knight, surveying Camelot's plywood-and-canvas battlements. The film's conclusion reveals the whole enterprise as an elaborate charade by men in costume who should be locked up in a police cell.[17] Richard Lester's *Robin and Marian* (1976) eschewed swashbuckling deeds for melancholic middle age, casting Sean Connery and Audrey Hepburn as Britain's most enduring folk hero and heroine. The middle-aged James Bond and semi-retired Holly Golightly were transformed into tempered, philosophical, occasionally bickering pensioners. It all contributed to the feeling of Britain's defining mythologies slouching towards closedown.

Punk rock is frequently presented as an apocalyptic blast of raw anger that put all before it to the torch and instigated a cultural year zero. It certainly dragged pop culture back to the city and cemented its identity as an urban art form. The spectacular flurries of outrage whipped up by The Sex Pistols' svengali Malcolm McLaren were a necessary diversion, a sorely needed cattle prod to a body of music that had grown unhealthily fat. But punk's nihilistic, destructive urges sloshed the baby out with the bathwater. The vision of Albion, the unconscious collective dreaming of all the folk revivalists, troubadours, folk-rockers and psychedelic progressives, was too much of a distant ideal, of course, but at least it was an ideal. Punk refined its nihilism but proved unable to offer any alternatives. It's interesting to speculate what might have resulted had punk's musical cleansing spared some notion of folk – which was, after all, the culture of citizens, not aristocrats; a music for the levelled society.

With its blasphemous TV appearances, atavistic performances and Establishment-baiting song titles, punk was a tabloid spectacle that actually distracted from the aspects which united grass-roots punk and what remained of the Albion Free State. In Germany, France, Italy and elsewhere, punk was a way of life more associated with the peace movement, animal rights, squatting and environmentalism. In Britain, popular opinion was swift to cast such righteous communitarianism as the enemy within. The strongest link between the two cultures was the folk-punk-anarchist collective Crass. Penny Rimbaud (real name Jeremy Ratter) was an inmate of Dial House in Epping Forest, Essex, an anarchist 'reality asylum' set up in 1967. In 1974 Dial House was Wally Hope's base for organising the Stonehenge Free Festival. Hope's death was one of the driving events behind Rimbaud's foundation of Crass in 1977, along with Steve Ignorant, Gee Vaucher and Eve Libertine. Weathering the stormtrooper years of Thatcher's reign, Crass turned Dial House into an indie media powerhouse disseminating pamphlets and graffiti broadsides on anti-racism, anti-consumerism, feminism and religion, conceptual pranks, books and a string of political invective on singles such as 'How Does It Feel to Be the Mother of 1000 Dead?'. As critical of punk orthodoxy as of Establishment shibboleths, Rimbaud has claimed his music draws on a broad swathe of British art music, especially themes composed by Benjamin Britten. Crass's tub-thumping agitation was taken up by anarcho-punk-folk acts like New Model Army and The Levellers – who even took their names from the revolutionary period of English history – and Chumbawamba. Though musically stodgy, their puritanical anger drew strength from the mystic agrarian libertarianism of their ancestors, where the motivations of punk and historical people's resistance movements intersected. When John Lydon sang of anarchy in the UK, there were recent, visible examples to draw on: at the Windsor Free Festival of 1974, for instance, where – as reported in the national news – hippies, travellers and Hell's Angels fought the law, and the law beat them to a bloody pulp.

And by the mid-1970s there was a vein of nihilism in folk-rock too: the final tortured songs of Nick Drake, for example, or the alienating emptiness of John Martyn's 'One World'. But if there were affinities, the two sides refused to shake hands: The Pistols' Sid Vicious even insulted Martyn during a poker game in 1977 (Martyn took him outside and beat him up). There were other intriguing crossovers in the transition between old and new guard. Shortly before her death, Sandy Denny enthusiastically attended several gigs by punk romantics The Only Ones and considered inviting them to a recording session. Joe Strummer's pre-Clash pub-rock outfit, The 101ers, frequently played at free festivals, including Stonehenge. Rough Trade, the independent record store that formed the epicentre of London's punk and new-wave scene, was opened in 1976 on premises which had been a notorious Notting Hill hippy head shop. Richard Thompson himself had been a bandmate of The Stranglers' Hugh Cornwell in Emil and the Detectives during the early 1960s, when they both attended north London's William Ellis School. Keith Levene, iconoclastic guitarist with the early Clash, and then PiL, spent his adolescence as an awestruck guitar roadie for Steve Howe of Yes. Linda Thompson recollected Siouxsie and the Banshees making a demo next door at Olympic Studios – and being visited by John Lydon – while she and her husband were recording 1978's *First Light*; the two women went for a drink. 'When we finally got in, I said to [Siouxsie], "I thought you punks only did one take," which didn't go down too well. Our album, on the other hand, took two days to record.'[18]

At the 1973 Windsor Free Festival, a short-lived duo called Skyco sang their composition 'Tomorrow's Children', a piece of hippy gumbo whose fluffy celebration of '*Festivals in sunshine,/ Colour inside your mind, are you happy like you ought to be?*' provided the event's theme tune. Within six years, Skyco's Chris Difford and Glenn Tilbrook had changed their name to Squeeze and reverted to black and white in new-wave Cockney vignettes such as 'Up the Junction' (teenage pregnancy) and 'Black Coffee in Bed' (kitchen-sink adultery). And in the spring of 1979 Squeeze's 'Cool for Cats' shared Top Ten space with M's 'Pop Muzik', one of the first British future-pop hits. M was the alias of the romantic troubadour Robin Scott. When Scott recorded his *Woman from the Warm Grass* with Mighty Baby in 1969, he was taking art classes at Croydon College with Malcolm McLaren and Jamie Reid, and even shared a flat with McLaren and partner Vivienne Westwood. By the end of the 1970s Scott was working as a record producer in Paris and helped Julien Temple make a film about The Slits. 'Pop Muzik' celebrated and satirised the cookie-cutter global pop that was to fill dance floors in New York, London, Paris and Munich in the next decade; a bland, cosmopolitan internationalism that was the polar opposite of the local and national myths of the folk movement.

'It suited the middle class to consider rural life a "lost world",' wrote Raymond Williams, ruminating on twentieth-century nature idolatry in his 1974 study, *The Country and the City*. 'It is then not only that the real land and its people were falsified; a traditional and surviving rural England was scribbled over and almost hidden from sight by what is really a suburban and half-educated sprawl.' Set against the organic old guard, the Dada venom of punk, the angular edges of post-punk and new wave and the plastic seductions of New Romanticism resembled the artistic irruption of the 1920s, as the futurist Imagists and Vorticists such as Ezra Pound and Wyndham Lewis, and T. S. Eliot's *The Waste Land*, blasted away the nature mysticism of the so-called 'Georgian poets' – Edward Thomas, Rupert Brooke, A. E. Housman et al. As one literary critic of those turbulent times caustically put it, the Georgians were forever taking 'a little trip for a little weekend to a little cottage where they wrote a little poem on a little theme'.[19] Replace the word 'poem' with 'song', and it could have described the increasingly irrelevant, parlous state of folk music in the late 1970s. However frantically it tried to modernise its creaky little cottage, the results looked increasingly out of joint.

Rocket Cottage

This queer discursive essay-thing has come from remembrance
of natural beauty which has brought music, and of music that
opened suddenly a pathway through to show some picture,
long ago seen, it may be, but passioned, made mystic and far
more dear from the unexpectedness of the gift.

> Ivor Gurney, 'The Springs of Music' (1922)[1]

The songs that our grandfathers sung
We'll keep on singing true
But now it's time for me to say adieu.

> Peter Bellamy, 'Goodbye' (1975)

*The oars splash softer now, and the sculler noses its bow into the reeds.
The rower narrows his eyes against the stinging kiss of overhanging leaves,
ships his blades, and steadies the boat as he plants one foot on the bank.
An unseen hand, steadying his shoulder as he straightens, makes him swivel
with a start. A short fellow, pointed hat, clay pipe in hand. 'Greetings,
Guest,' says the dwarf. 'I wasn't sure if you were going to make it this far.
Just round yon bend is the source of your Thames. There's not much to see
— 'tis but a trickle.'*

'Your guest, you say?' says the rower.

*'Ay, all who trouble to visit me, by oak, ash and thorn, are Guests of
mine, leastways till they wrong me,' chirps the little one. 'Call me Puck, and
ask all the right questions, and I shan't be too much offended.'*

*The guest makes his boat fast to a willow root and follows Puck, who
is already skipping ahead. Nettles and knee-high grass indicate the glade*

path is seldom used. 'Where are we going?' the guest breathes, still tired from the row. 'First question — a good 'un, too!' twinkles Puck, revolving his head almost about-face.

They slip out of the trees, cross a dusty cart track, and the imp begins groping along a hedge until he grunts with satisfaction. 'Done this thousands of times, and still never quite hit the spot,' he murmurs, parting a loose spray of hedgerow to reveal a low iron gate, ridged with rust. He pushes it open and urges his guest in ahead of him. A gravel path winds through a pale lawn flecked with dry, black spots, between a willow and holly bush. Beyond the trees the guest discerns the black and white geometry of Tudor half-timbering. 'The grass hasn't quite recovered since our last, ahem, little conflagration,' Puck announces with a chuckle. 'But come through, come through — there now, and ain't she a beauty?'

The timbers, mullioned windows and roof thatch are certainly well preserved. A barrel, green with moss, stands to the left of the front door, and a honeysuckle twines over the red-brick portico. As Puck fumbles under the barrel and plucks out a huge brass key, the guest detects a faint vibration underfoot, a dry heat in the air. 'What's that rumbling?' he asks. 'We're just warming up the engines,' replies Puck, glancing towards the left corner of the house. Following his gaze, the guest spies a tall, dark yew tree hiding glints of post-office red. Puck must have noticed his curious face. 'Very well, very well, look if you must,' he admonishes, steering the guest towards the side of the house. There, tacked onto the brick chimney breast, almost as tall as the house itself, is a giant conical tube in metal, glossed in red, sticking out horizontally with a crown of yellow spikes painted around the end. At top and bottom, two protuberances — like hollowed-out fish fins. 'Don't stand in front of the burner, you'll get a blast,' warns Puck, who now appears to be skipping a little gleeful dance. 'Come, see the nose!' He prances to the other side of the house. Behind an identical yew, again affixed to the side of the cottage, is an enormous red bullet-head, sleek as a torpedo, curved and rising to a sharp point. 'The nose, the nose!' Puck is now singing to himself, spinning and jigging on the spot. 'Hey nonny no, and up she rises!' He lobs the key at his guest and collapses on the grass, clutching his sides. 'Come . . . it is time to keep your appointment with Rocket Cottage.'

From somewhere inside, the guest hears a faint, steady flitching noise: a series of arhythmic scratches. Elsewhere, possibly from a radio or tinny hi-fi, the sound of several nasal voices knotted in harmonic chant: a song he recognises as 'Gaudete'. He puts key to hole, and twists.

Of all the émigrés from the 1960s folk revival, Steeleye Span proved, for a fleeting moment, to be the most bankable franchise. Singer Maddy Prior remained the only constant presence since the group's foundation, in the winter of 1970, by a despondent Ashley

Steeleye Span at the height of their fame in 1975. Left to right: Nigel Pegrum, Rick Kemp, Maddy Prior, Bob Johnson, Tim Hart, Peter Knight.

Hutchings on the rebound from Fairport Convention. When he and Martin Carthy bailed out after the group's third album at the close of 1971, Prior and partner Tim Hart, with violinist Peter Knight, found new life as a harder-edged folk-rock ensemble, with guitarist Bob Johnson and bassist Rick Kemp. These new members had backgrounds in the world of rock but embraced the supernatural ballads and plainsong modalities of their new colleagues. This next, ramalama-infused Steeleye, which lasted for the next half decade, was a five-part-harmony powerhouse that pulled out all the stops to make folk-rock an international commercial splash.

At one of the last big British gigs played by this quintet, winding up a tour at London's Hammersmith Odeon in October 1976, the show climaxed with the group's entire fee for the night – £8,500 in used pound notes – raining down on their fans from specially drilled holes in the ceiling. Money, since their 1974 hit single 'Gaudete', a vivacious update of a sixteenth-century carol, had become a disposable commodity. In an interview shortly before the concert, Bob Johnson had stated: 'I used to wander up and down Muswell Hill when I was trying to write, singing to myself and bumping into things. Now I live in a seventeenth-century stone mansion in the country, with a great big cedar tree in the front garden; I can let my mind run free. In a corny sort of way, it's the right kind of atmosphere for writing murder ballads.'[2]

With manager Jo Lustig taking care of business, their sound was tightened further in 1973 when they hired their first permanent drummer, Nigel Pegrum, formerly of Gnidrolog. They were moving in higher circles in the entertainment firmament: Peter Sellers played ukulele on *Commoners' Crown*; David Bowie blew sax on the doo-wop standard 'To Know Him Is to Love Him', included on *NowWe Are Six*, which was produced by Jethro Tull's Ian Anderson; and during 1975 they hosted their own BBC television series, broadcast from six different historic houses around Britain. And their stage shows became increasingly flamboyant: the group sang the eerie, disembodied chant of 'Lyke Wake Dirge' wearing medieval space suits woven from priests' cassocks, and wore costumes and masks (nurse, boy scout, commando, deep-sea diver, etc.) for an entire mummers' play that was incorporated into the live sets. Adapted by Tim Hart, the mummers' play tried to reinstate the nature symbolism of the traditional version, which Hart believed had been watered down over the years. This was an electronic multimedia event, with back-projected films, exploding fireworks and backing tapes. Just as their mummers' play typified the spectacular but somewhat unwieldy fusion of multiplex dynamics and folkloric tradition, so too did 'All Around My Hat', their biggest-ever hit single, and the one by which so much British folk music has come to be measured. Cresting a nine-week stay in the Top Forty at number five in early December 1975, the song was a valiant stab at a Christmas number one, and saw them making a beribboned, acrobatic appearance on *Top of the Pops*. 'All Around My Hat' dated back to an early nineteenth-century broadside, a weeping song sung by a Cockney costermonger whose female convict lover is about to be placed on a transport ship to Australia. In remembrance of her, he vows to keep a sprig of willow, symbolic of mourning, tucked in his hatband. Peter Bellamy had included a version on his 1969 solo album *Fair England's Shore*, but Steeleye Span's rocked-up, triple-time version grafts a second song, 'Farewell He', onto the first to turn it into a folk-feminist dialogue on the (in)constancy of young men. Seventy years earlier, Cecil Sharp expressed the fervent hope that British folk music might reach the ears of thousands across the land. And here, at last, was Sharp's dream come true: bought by hundreds of thousands, heard by millions more, drunkenly danced to at a thousand nightclubs, weddings and office parties, and with a backbeat worthy of Status Quo.

The single and the album of the same name were produced by Mike Batt, whose track record with Family, Big Joe Williams and The Groundhogs was eclipsed, in the early 1970s, by the novelty children's records he made with The Wombles, the burrowing inhabitants of Wimbledon Common who had made 'Keep Britain Tidy' their mantra. Tim Hart bought a triple LP of Wombles tunes and was impressed with the clarity of its sub-glam power pop, and Batt was hired by Steeleye's new manager, Tony Secunda, the impulsive former manager of The Move, Marc Bolan, The Moody Blues and Procol Harum notorious for headline-grabbing promotional stunts (which included offering female fans a competition to win twelve hours with the male Steeleye member of their choice during a tour of Australia – without mentioning it to the group). It was Secunda, too, who drilled the cash holes in the Hammy-O roof.

'Gaudete', 'All Around My Hat' and extensive tours of Britain, America and Australia may have enabled the group to buy their little cottages (or mansions) in the country, but in 1976 no one wanted to come back to the fair. There would be no more chart entries, no more forty-date zigzags across the United States. It was the year of the drought, of punk's uprising. It was the year of *Rocket Cottage*.

You could tell *Rocket Cottage* was going to be clunky from the first glimpse of its sleeve. Within a tacky simulacrum of a green baize frame, the picturesque Tudorbethan dream-house, sandwiched between the upper and lower halves of a gaudy space rocket, with its climbing plant, thatched roof and group members peeping out of the windows, is in orbit around what looks like a carpeted planet. It's a ludicrous, comedy image, the kind of crude cartoon collage familiar from Terry Gilliam's Monty Python animations (its uncanny mismatch of old and new worlds pre-echoed by the title of Richard and Linda Thompson's song the previous year, 'Jet Plane in a Rocking Chair'). Either it's a piece of conceptual silliness dreamed up over a well-oiled pub table, or it's a genuine statement of futuristic folk intent. Either way, there's something so wrong about it, it almost comes out right.

Although, commercially speaking, Steeleye Span were riding a rapidly descending curve, the record itself isn't actually so bad. 'London' is clearly an attempt to repeat on the bouncy ensemble-vocal formula so successful over the past two years. There are production flourishes, again courtesy of Mike Batt – disco drumming on 'Orfeo'; dub weightlessness on 'Fighting For Strangers'; 'Shaft'-style wah-wah on 'Sligo Maid' – but there was flakiness too: 'The Camptown Races' was a studio false start, with production backchat, hillbilly fiddle and Maddy Prior corpsing on the lyrics. 'The Drunkard' sounds like a rehearsal: 'Do I detect undertones of "Everybody Must Get Stoned" somewhere in this stuff?' comments one of the group as the track tries to get itself in

Steeleye Span, *Rocket Cottage* (1976).

gear. There's a good chance the studio was 'kinda cloudy': it was recorded in Holland as a tax dodge. *Rocket Cottage* is the sound of a group forgetting its reason for being.

In an interview at the end of the year, Bob Johnson was asked if he was considering leaving the UK to become a tax exile. 'I would hate that absolutely. At my present level I would rather live on what I get in the country I love than go anywhere else. Everything I do and think is based on England. If I lived on the West Coast [of America] how on earth could I think about elves and fairies and goblins and old English castles and churches? I used to spend months looking at brasses in old churches. I'm just steeped in old England, as a hobby.

'My love of England doesn't stem from a nationalistic/political point of view,' he felt compelled to add. 'But as a human being I feel a great kinship with my country; I like the climate, I like the way the change of the seasons is a very obvious thing, I like the way you can travel from north to south and see as much a change in scenery as you probably could going from the East to the West Coast of America.'[3]

Johnson was so enamoured of elves and fairies and goblins that he and Peter Knight were already devising a separate venture, *The King of Elfland's Daughter*, based on a macabre romance by the *fin de siècle* writer Alfred, Lord Dunsany. Released in 1977, their inventive electric folk opera featured Mary Hopkin, Alexis Korner, P. P. Arnold and Frankie Miller, and was narrated by Lord Summerisle himself, Christopher Lee. Within a few months a shocked music press carried announcements that Johnson and Knight had left Steeleye Span and would be replaced by Martin Carthy and John Kirkpatrick. Employing these two stalwarts of the traditional folk circuit was seen as a retrenchment from electric supergroup to humble, traditional, acoustic roots. Meanwhile, Tony Secunda arranged for giant advertisements to be painted on the sides of several west London houses. One was for *The King of*

Elfland's Daughter. The other was a puff for Steeleye Span proper: another awkward juxtaposition to rival *Rocket Cottage*, featuring a mounted Hussar thundering into a booming cannon, rendered in Pop Art comic-book style, à la Roy Lichtenstein.

The gravy train had left the station. After a last British tour in early 1978, Steeleye Span voluntarily disbanded, and all went their separate ways, mostly burrowing back into the comparative obscurity of the traditional folk scene. The next time Hart, Prior, Johnson, Kemp, Knight and Kirkpatrick got together in a studio, it was in 1981, to record a collection of children's nursery rhymes.

'Look around you, Guest,' says Puck, leaning back in a rocking chair and propping his legs on an antique spinning wheel. 'Take your time, you've plenty of it.'

Walls roughly plastered, whitewashed, hung with country kitsch. Horsebrass vertically mounted on black leather thongs. A row of hooks with glass-bottomed pewter tankards. Dented copper bedpan dangling on a long mahogany shaft. A woodwormed spinning wheel, grey with dust, sulks in a corner. Framed repro engravings of the high streets of market towns, and yellowing photos of cheese-rollers, straw men, a nocturnal parade of flaming torches. Victorian circus poster: 'Extraordinary inducements!' 'Trained fleas', etc. Sundry extinct farm implements.

A click comes from the sideboard, and the guest watches the needle on a Dansette turntable lift off the 7" single that's been playing. He examines the label; it is indeed a scratchy copy of Steeleye Span's 'Gaudete'. Scattered around the record player are other singles in picture sleeves: The Wurzels' 'Combine Harvester', The Strawbs' 'Part of the Union', Fiddler's Dram's 'Day Trip to Bangor'. The guest gravitates to the bookshelf. The expected sun-blanched holiday readers: Agatha Christies, Barbara Cartlands, Alistair MacLeans; older editions of Walter Scott, Richard Jefferies, Hardy, Kipling, clothbound in floppy red leather. But higher up, necessitating a climb up a spiral set of teak library steps, there's a more eccentric shelf, assembled by a collector with a strong sense of purpose. Hilaire Belloc's History of England, *a first edition from* 1915. *A* 1970s *coffee-table book,* England – A Fortress Built by Nature, *by Ted Smart.* A Song for Every Season, *a memoir of a family of Sussex sheep farmers, by the folk singer Bob Copper. A row of volumes by journeyman folklorist George Ewart Evans –* The Pattern Under the Plough, Ask the Fellows Who Cut the Hay *and* Where Beards Wag All: *written in the* 1960s *in surefire conviction of the deathless wisdom of folk memory. Bob Stewart's* Where Is Saint George?, *skewing facts to fit an idea of ancient pagan survivals in English folk song. Henry Williamson's* Tarka the Otter, *and a complete set of the reclusive author's absurdly extended memoirs,* A Chronicle of Ancient Sunlight. *Roger Scruton's* England: An Elegy – *a High Tory's wistful lament. Edward Heath's books on* Sailing *and* Music, *the humanising hobbies of a dull politico bachelor-boy. A Betamax video cassette with a label, written in shaky pencil: 'The Changes,* 1975'. *The guest pulls down an unmarked picture album, its brittle leather binding beginning to crumble. Puck stands at his shoulder to look at the caramel-washed photographs of haymakers, waggoners, shepherds, poachers, saddled huntsmen ringed by steaming beagles. 'I remember when photographers started using sepia,' Puck is reminiscing. 'Heh heh, you know, Guest, when you see a sepia picture, you take it to be impossibly old – not that your notion of impossibly old is anything to touch mine. But how about this: why d'you reckon they squeezed the ink out of the old squidsack in the first place, eh? His natural tincture turned the silver nitrate to sulphur – gives you that yellow-brown tint, see. Master Cuttlefish died so your photos would be immortal. How do you like that? The printsmen of old thought sepia'd insure 'em against ageing. But when you look at these photos, age is all you see. Ain't that a pip?'*

As he gingerly replaces the album in its place on the shelf, the guest dislodges something slotted between Ted Heath's two hardbacks. Stained and crinkled with damp, it flutters to the floor like a flattened moth corpse. It is a cutting from the Daily Express *dated* 16 *January* 1973. *'Pop Fan*

Heath at Saucy Sailor Show', reads the headline, next to a photo of the prime minister's face, squashed into a smile. 'Oho,' says Puck, 'now there was a right royal night out.'

The United Kingdom's official induction into the European Economic Community (EEC) took place on the first day of 1973. In the middle of January a series of cultural galas commemorating the event took place under the banner Fanfare for Europe. Herbert von Karajan shipped his celebrated Berlin Philharmonic Orchestra over for a rare appearance at London's Royal Opera House, while an eclectic evening of British music at the Royal Albert Hall, attended by the likes of Princess Margaret and Lord Snowdon, included Steeleye Span on the bill. In a tip of the hat to Heath's maritime hobbies, Steeleye included the tune 'Saucy Sailor' in their set; the PM reportedly found it 'enormous fun'. It was probably the only amusing moment he enjoyed in that year of crippling geopolitical events.

Ten months later, on 6 October, a combined Arab military force led by Egypt and Syria attacked Israel's borders in revenge for the Six Day War of 1967. During the twenty-day conflict, Israel received material support from the United States. In a tactic prearranged before the first strike, Egypt and Syria mobilised the Arab members of OPEC to terminate crude oil supplies to America, and to any other countries that supported Israel, and prices were hiked up for the first time in many years. The UK actually escaped these sanctions: although Harold Wilson had supported Israel in 1967, Heath reversed the policy, denying the US access to British airfields and banning the supply of arms to either side. In November the EEC issued a collective policy that largely followed the British pro-Arab line, so most of Western Europe was permitted to continue importing oil from the Middle East, albeit at the higher rates. But, coupled with simultaneous rail and coal workers' strikes over the winter of 1973–4, Britain became, indirectly, the worst affected by the fallout, as the crisis impacted on energy supplies.

'*You don't get me, I'm part of the union, till the day I die*,' chorused The Strawbs on a single that rode the charts at number two for three weeks in February–March 1973. The lumbering folk-rock song – very unlike the group's previous, more sylvan acoustic-folk offerings – was a direct response to the effects of Heath's flagship Industrial Relations Act, introduced at great expense in 1971. The bill manoeuvred an Industrial Relations Court into play to resolve union disputes quickly and effectively. But the Trades Union Congress, the official umbrella for many of Britain's unions, found a loophole in the Act: individual unions were not actually compelled to register for the Court, and if they kept out of the system they could not be bound by it.

The Strawbs' barrel-housing ditty captured the mood in early 1973, but by the end of the year, when strike action began to exert tangible pressure on daily life, public opinion began to turn against union power. In the first three months of 1974 the three-day week was introduced to conserve electricity: businesses were restrained from opening more than three days in the week, and television stations blacked out at 10.30 every night. The *Wall Street Journal* waved 'Good-bye Great Britain' in April 1975, warning American investors to pull out of sterling. In the autumn of 1976 Labour prime minister James Callaghan was humiliated into the unprecedented step of appealing for aid from the International Monetary Fund. It had taken a mere three-quarters of a century for the United Kingdom to be reduced from a global empire to a Third World nation proffering a begging bowl. With the country brought to its knees by the butterfly effect of world events beyond its control, a new mood of self-sufficiency took hold. The promise of supplying its energy needs with its own reserves of North Sea oil and gas began to be realised in the second half of the 1970s, while ad breaks on national TV resounded with the thump of a rubber stamp bearing the screaming red legend 'SAVE IT'.

The EEC's Common Agricultural Policy actually benefitted British farmers. The market price of wheat increased by 250 per cent during the mid-1970s, and production of British wheat increased by half, above its previous peak levels in 1943. It was a long-awaited fillip for domestic farmers, but consumers paid the extra cost on top of spiralling inflation, adding to the sense of national depletion. As Britain's cities festered through to the end of the decade, its fecund cornfields bulged in the last great flowering of home-grown agricultural life. *'I've got twenty acres, and you've got forty-three,'* sang The Wurzels in their 1976 Wessex bumpkin rewrite of Melanie's 'Brand New Key'. The materialistic slant of its lyric attested to the growth spurt occurring in Britain's farmlands, while reinforcing age-old hayseed stereotypes.

Britain's folk-rock movement lost its way during these wan years, too, shedding its progressive impulse in favour of a conservative, insular presentation. There were exceptions: John Martyn produced his most thrilling work between 1973–7; and among other folk-rock records not previously mentioned in these pages, Steve Ashley's *Stroll On* (1975), Nigel Mazlyn Jones's *Ship to Shore* (1976), Miriam Backhouse's *Gypsy Without a Road* (1977) and Mandy Morton and Spriguns' *Time Will Pass* (1977) and *Magic Lady* (1978) are all infused with degrees of heady pagan mystery. Peter Bellamy's monumental ballad opera *The Transports*, conceived and recorded in 1977, looks almost like a wake for the death of the post-war revival: many of the key source and revivalist names were present (Bert Lloyd, Cyril Tawney, June Tabor, Martin Carthy, Dave Swarbrick, Mike and Norma Waterson, Dolly Collins, Martin Carthy, Nic Jones) in a tale about the convict ships bound for the far side of the world whose themes of loss, disappearances and final farewell resonated poignantly among this group of musicians. But the general trend in the mid- to late 1970s was a congruent slide back to the traditional folk repertoire of the previous two decades, when The Watersons, The Young Tradition and Ian Campbell ruled the roost. Ashley Hutchings and Shirley Collins's Etchingham Steam Band has been mentioned before, as a group formed of necessity in the power-cut winter of 1974. Hutchings's 1976 *Rattlebone and Ploughjack* continued his pursuit of an earthy, agrarian folk-rock form. Lindisfarne created pub rock as played in an Elizabethan inn. Folk-rockers like Green Man, The Druids and The Yetties fell back on traditional source material, often filtered through a sludgy, cheaply recorded acoustic. Groups sprang up with irritatingly parochial names that seemed drawn from the most distant ends of Britain's meandering country lanes: Hedgehog Pie, Figgy Duff, Pyewackett, The Celebrated Ratliffe Stout Band, Frogmorton, Bodger's Mate, Fiddler's Dram, Flibbertigibbet, Yorkshire Relish, Brandywine Bridge, The Whistlebinkies, Silly Wizard, Tickawinda. On the sleeve of Jethro Tull's *Songs from the Wood* (1977), Ian Anderson sat, a Robin Hood brewing a cauldron at his forest hearth; their follow-up, *Heavy Horses*, pictured shire horses harnessed for farm labour. The romance of time travel had tipped over into outright Luddism.

Puck is leading his guest down a narrow corridor off the cottage's living room. In the gloom the guest can make out a kitchen, the bodies of jugged hares and unplucked pheasants swinging from butcher's hooks. Puck stops at a panelled door, mottled with several layers of peeling gloss paint. The chafing noise the guest heard earlier comes from behind it. 'There's someone here I'd like you to see – though I don't know if he'd like to see you,' whispers Puck. 'For he trucks seldom with modern folk – Mods, he calls 'em,' he adds conspiratorially, tapping at the door with a twisted

knuckle. A grunt is heard from within. 'Ahoy there, Ned Ludd! Be ye about?' *calls Puck.*

The reply rasps like a sawblade through bark. 'Who rattles Ned's cage? Is it thee, scallion?'

'We have a guest, Captain — sharpen up,' *says Puck, and opens. The lower edge of the door brushes an arc through a sediment of woodchips and sawdust. A figure, wrapped in a striped bathrobe, squats on a skeletal wooden chair. On his head, above silvered mutton-chop cheeks, a sky-blue ribbon is tied lazily round a battered bonnet. He holds a pocket-knife in one hand and a section of tree branch in the other, halted in the middle of sharpening one end. The floor around him is piled high with curled woodshavings.*

'I give you Ned Ludlam,' *announces Puck.* 'Hard at work as ever, I see. Here's your guest from the future, Ned — won't you ask him the news?'

'Ned Ludd needs no news from nowhere,' *comes the gruff rejoinder.* 'I'll give you good day, Guest, and shan't want no more by return.'

Puck breaks the silence. 'Back in the age when the steam engines started to roll and the factories were coughing smoke, Ned here and his fellows took cudgel and axe to his stocking-frame — smashed it to firewood. Well, you can understand why — if one stocking-frame could weave the work of ten good men and women, how then should those ten earn their bread? There they were, arrived at the cities to work, with field and lane and forest all behind them, and there they were, starving in rows of grey houses, listening to the machines clacking away in the manufactories. Something broke, and they went to war against the machines. Oh yes, the King brought out his Redcoats to put a stop to Cap'n Ludd and his Luddites' mischief!'

Puck points to the fingers curled round knife and twig. 'See, those strong hands that broke the machines are good now only for whittling. What say ye, old Captain?'

'I sits and I thinks, and I whittles,' *grates the voice from the chair.* 'Would some Mod folks were minded the same, we might be spared a pot o' trouble in this world. Whittlin's whittlin', and that's all the truth,' *mutters*

Ned Ludd. 'Blunt a' come sharp, and sharp a' come blunt, and so the wheel turns.'

'We'll leave thee be, then, Ned,' says Puck, after a pause, withdrawing back through the doorway. 'I'll be back later to tend you; we shall have a bonny-fire this day, methinks.'

The whittling strikes up again behind the closed door. 'Set in his ways, would be a way of putting it. Come, let us watch a video.'

When the guest and his guide re-enter the front room, the Betamax tape from the shelf is lying on top of a cabinet in the corner. 'Open it,' suggests Puck, and the guest grasps the brass handles, pulls the cabinet doors aside, revealing a television set mounted inside, a 1970s Rediffusion model encased in walnut veneer. On a shelf underneath is a video recorder the size of a suitcase. The guest snaps the tape into the player's drawer, clunks it shut and leans his weight on the Play button. The screen wobbles into life: radiophonic electronic music bubbles over images of lorries streaming across the Severn Bridge, industrial machinery, a diesel train shooting out of a tunnel. The images freeze, and two words materialise in white block capitals: 'THE CHANGES'.

❦

In the global history of class struggle, revolutions are typically assumed to bring about fundamental changes, recasting political and social paradigms and remaking the world anew for a permanently altered future. That was true of *The Communist Manifesto* of Karl Marx and Friedrich Engels, just as it was of the Bolshevik revolution in Russia, the social engineering of Hitler's Nazis, Mao's Great Leap Forward, and the Pol Pot Khmer Rouge in 1970s Cambodia, to name a few. But revolutionaries are equally inclined to turn the wheel *backwards*, fighting to restore a perceived lost estate or denied birthright, rather than campaigning for a gleaming, high-technology future. From Winstanley and his Diggers, seeding rural Eden in Cromwell's Protectorate, to the Parisian Situationist sloganeers of the May 1968 disturbances, daubing walls with '*Sous les pavés, la plage!*' ('Beneath the paving stones, the beach!'), there has always been this desire to prise open the veneer of modern industrial society and reconnect with a fundamental mode of existence. Some took this as a cue for the onrush of barbarism: a return to an animalistic state of being, as reflected in Claude Faraldo's low-budget film *Themroc*, released in 1973 but deeply infused with a post-'68 aura.[4] French Situationism was rife with creative responses to the modern state's perceived intrusiveness into the individual psyche, the creeping realisation that the instinctual life of human beings had been corrupted and debased by the demands of work, capital and social manners.

In Britain, the distaste for modernism tends to look for solace in the dead certainties of a vanished but still idealised past. Published in 1970, Peter Dickinson's *The Changes*, a speculative fiction trilogy aimed at a teenage readership, imagined Britain suddenly, mysteriously plunged into a new Dark Age. Adults are seized with the compulsion to destroy machines and descend into a Luddite, agrarian way of life comparable with the seventeenth and eighteenth centuries, where any use or mention of machinery is punishable as heresy. The scenario chimed perfectly with the energy crisis of 1974, when the BBC filmed a disquieting adaptation for children's television. In a shift of emphasis from Dickinson's book, the first episode lingers over the onset of 'the madness' and the disorientating early days of the crisis, as eerily silent crowds of rioters bludgeon cars, bicycles, fridges and clocks in the streets, trains burn on tracks, water and electricity supplies are shut off and vicars preach apocalypse and damnation from pavement pulpits. The schoolgirl heroine Nicola Gore, separated from her parents, survives for a few days in her lifeless house, her candlelit nights an all-too-recent memory of real-life power cuts. As parts of the city become disease-ridden, she is advised to leave by a dying old man, who tellingly observes that the new, changed conditions are 'like when I was a kid – nicer really, more peaceful'.

'The Folkie', as satirised in *Viz* comic, 1988.

The public's collective hysteria is triggered by a cheese-wiry electronic whine created by Paddy Kingsland of the BBC Radiophonic Workshop. Nicola hears it too at first; every time she approaches a functioning vehicle or an overhead pylon, she is troubled by an audio hallucination similar to a pressure headache, though she later learns to resist it, and is eventually hunted down as a heretic. *The Changes* chillingly speculates about the latent tribalism that lies just beneath any belief in progress in Britain. Dickinson's book and the TV version include Nicola briefly falling in with a group of itinerant Sikhs who are immune to the Luddite madness and are suffering racist attacks from the English. The Changes seem to polarise the population along racial lines: 'Since the madness happened, we all seem to have become more Sikh,' one tells her. It's a strange detail, but it serves to emphasise that the techno-fear is an affliction peculiar to Britons with roots prior to the post-war period of increased immigration. Pull up the paving stones and disconnect the plugs, warns this dystopian fantasy, and you're left with a white nation desperate to retreat to the ancient shires and harvest its own potatoes.

And it's from precisely this discontented period in British history, these middle 1970s of want succeeded by drought, of decimalisation and unemployment, of European unification and rising immigration and what one modern historian has called 'unravelling implications about the identity of the United Kingdom itself',[5] that the surviving, predominantly negative view of 'folk' in Britain has been handed down. Two memorable satirical representations of the archetypal folk singer, one from the 1960s, the other from the 1980s, demonstrate the shift in mood. Just as the folk-rock movement swung into action, Kenneth Williams's Rambling Syd Rumpo radio character, who cropped up regularly on BBC radio's mid-1960s comedy show *Round the Horne*, was an affectionate tribute to the kind of oddball local 'characters' which the likes of Peter Kennedy and Bob Copper used to dredge up on their field-recording tours of the nation's pubs and villages: weird, rustic dialects barely masking clodhopping innuendo (typical titles: 'Green Grow My Nadgers, O!', 'The Grommet Tinker's Song', 'My Grussett Lies A-Fallowing-O'). By the late 1980s Syd had morphed into 'the folkie', a pathetic specimen who claimed to be a guardian of his national heritage: all chunky-knit woollen polo necks, spiky facial hair and nerdy National Health specs; a fondness for 'as I went out a-roving' balladry bellowed cacophonously out of tune with a finger in one ear; a pewter tankard and a kipper tucked into his belt; and a veneer of eco-friendly political correctness thinly masking unreconstructed sexism. From *The Folkie* strip in the satirical comic *Viz* to *The Fast Show*'s Bob Fleming, the folkie has become a highly mockable stereotype.

Syd Rumpo affectionately mocked a quaint, queer backwater of English culture. The *Folkie* strip was nastier, ridiculing folk music and those who clung to its customs, rituals and tuneless music as impossibly out of step with a modern and more cynical capitalist society. Under the Thatcher administration, which took over the reins of the country after a flailing Labour government collapsed in the face of the late-1970s Winter of Discontent, 'the Changes' were thrown into reverse gear. As society and culture became more metropolitanised, technologised and hardened to the growing climate of social unrest, reduction of public services and rising unemployment, 'folkies' numbered among the heretics, their music, appearance and customs such as the morris dance routinely lampooned as a convenient cipher for all the unknown, misunderstood aspects of British national culture. The morris clings onto life, carried into the twenty-first century by a dwindling but passionate community of folkloric survivalists. But it suffers a recurring image problem and remains very difficult to integrate comfortably with modern British culture – not that it feels it necessarily ought to.

Folk music in Britain survived in its own niche throughout the final two decades of the twentieth century, with its impact diffused; some found themselves out of step with new realities. Ewan MacColl died in 1989 with an unwritten project: the ninth and final radio ballad. He and Peggy Seeger had met and been entranced by an English sailor who had spent so much of his life travelling and spending time with non-English-speakers he had almost forgotten his own native tongue. MacColl envisioned a kind of modern-day *Pilgrim's Progress*, beginning at Cape Wrath and crossing the Atlantic to London, allowing a detached outsider's impressions of the way his country had been torn apart by 'Thatcher's vandals'. The despair surely mirrored MacColl's own conflicted feelings about the new England. Plagued by health problems, the old revolutionary found himself in a profoundly altered culture from the one he had tried to agitate from flatbed stages back in 1930s Manchester. 'His hatred of Thatcher almost kept him alive,' recalls his widow Peggy Seeger. 'He loathed her. He understood her position in the development of capitalism: it's the natural evolution of capitalism to have people like Maggie Thatcher and George Bush. He did feel that there was a dumbing-down of people. He remembered when an awful lot of the working class were concerned with learning to read and write, and the writings and political movements had a good juice to them. By the time the 1970s and 80s hit, you'd get an anti-fascist

march, and one of the famous bands would agree to play at the end
of the march, and people would come on the march just to hear
the band, and when the band played they'd leave. I think Ewan saw
a time when the working class drew together in the same way they
did in the American Civil War when they boycotted cotton coming
in from the United States, in Manchester. A lot of them starved,
in an industrial country, because of political principle. And a lot of
that seems to have disappeared in England.'

*The picture stutters for a second, then explodes in a sleet of static, as
the Betamax player gags on the crumpling tape. The guest realises he
is alone in the room, although he can hear Puck out in the corridor,
humming purposefully.* 'And if you come along with us, you're
numbered as a friend, and the faded flower of England will rise
and bloom again . . .' *With the television off, he becomes aware of a
changed ambience in the cottage: the room feels hotter, there's a thin veil
of misty smoke in the room, the rumbling sensation is more pronounced,
Ned Ludd's whittling now sounds like the frantic frottage of two sticks.
An embroidery sampler he hadn't noticed before hangs over the television
cabinet: where he would expect to read 'Home Sweet Home' or 'Bless this
House', a cross-stitched cartouche of daisies and marigolds encloses the
legend:*

> *You should make a Point*
> *of trying Everything once,*
> *excepting Incest and Folk-dancing.*
>
> Arnold Bax (1883–1953)

*The guest is interrupted by Puck, crimson-cheeked, breathlessly bursting
into the room.* 'It is time for you to leave us,' *he pants.* 'We don't have much
time now. You must get back on the river. I think you have seen all you need.
Did we answer your questions?' *Before the guest can answer, a booming*

instruction, chanted in a Gregorian four-part harmony, sweeps over the cottage.

COMMENCING COUNTDOWN. ENGINES ON.

'Make haste!' shouts Puck, bustling his guest along the hallway, knocking over a brass coal scuttle. Outside, white smoke is fogging up the garden, and the guest can feel an intense throb that seems to shake the very blackberry bushes. As he is hurried out of the iron gate, he takes a final glance backwards. Dimly visible through the haze, Rocket Cottage is raising itself creakingly to the vertical.

TEN. NINE. EIGHT. SEVEN.

Puck presses a brown paper package into the guest's hands. 'Packed lunch,' he confides. 'Ploughman's. You still have some way to go.'

SIX. FIVE. FOUR.

He steadies the oars and holds the boat against the bank as the guest eases himself onto his sliding seat.

THREE. TWO. CHECK IGNITION.

The noise has swelled to a Niagara rush. Sparks fizzle above the treeline. The bow is veering out into the river flow.

ONE.

'And may the gods' love be with you.' Puck, staring now at his guest with a face of stone, gives a last shove to the tip of the oar blade and watches for a moment as the hull drifts away from the bank.

LIFT-OFF.

Puck is gone.

The guest senses a flash searing across his vision before he hears it. The explosion cracks an instant later, coinciding with the puffball of black smoke, fringed with fire, that briefly surfaces above the trees. For a few seconds his boat is strafed with tiny plops. Flakes of ash and scraps of blackened paper flutter down around him. A mangled horsebrass flops into his lap. The guest grasps the handles and strains on his blades, leaning back as his sinews tighten into the stroke. As he gazes upwards, a clump of oak, ash and thorn leaves tumbles onto his forehead and lands with a soft crump on the stern of his sculling boat. Somewhere in the woods, blue smoke is *curling into the sky from a recently lit bonfire. From what sounds like miles away, the clang of a fire engine's bell slices through the early-evening air. The guest manoeuvres himself into the middle of the stream, leans forward over his blades and abandons himself to the ceaseless tug of the silver chain, bearing him back remorselessly to his own time.*

III

Poly-Albion

18

Gone to Earth

The sound of waves in a pool of water
I'm drowning in my nostalgia.
David Sylvian, 'Nostalgia', from *Brilliant Trees* (1984)

Ancient History – I can't contain ya
I got Megalithomania!
Julian Cope, 'Megalithomania', poem on
sleeve of *Jehovahkill* (1992)

One morning in the early phase of Margaret Thatcher's government, legend has it, ministers took their seats at a Downing Street Cabinet meeting to find a book dished out, one copy apiece. It was by an American economic theorist, Martin Wiener, published in 1981 and entitled *English Culture and the Decline of the Industrial Spirit, 1850–1980*. Thatcher's Secretary of State for Industry, Keith Joseph, also known as the 'Mad Monk', already fond of distributing reading lists to policy-makers and civil servants, designated Wiener as required reading. As the architect of a monetarist policy which exposed the British economy to the free market as never before, Joseph had been profoundly affected by Wiener's 'inquest on national failure'. To illustrate his study of progress in Britain since the Victorian era, he effectively psychoanalysed the English mental constitution. He noted the tendency, among conservatives and radicals alike, to locate 'the real England' in the idealised village, and drew on a wide range of examples from English literature – William Morris, Trollope, Hardy, Kipling, Gissing, J. B. Priestley,

John Betjeman – and on the writings of previous ministers and leaders, as well as the results of the 1940s Mass Observation survey, which revealed ordinary citizens' huge affection for the countryside. He drew attention to the root of the problem in the later nineteenth century, when the privileged offspring of first-generation Victorian entrepreneurs had been 'aristocratised' at public schools and universities. Classical education inculcated a distrust of money and the work ethic. In turn, these views were reinforced by respected intellectuals such as Carlyle and Ruskin, whose writings castigated progress, industry and technology as immoral and insupportable.

England's self-image, wrote Wiener, remained in thrall to such attitudes, embarrassed by big money and modernity, which hampered its ability to compete in the increasingly open global marketplace of the 1980s. Instead, it was a nation of pseudo-squires all longing for a 'haunt of ancient peace' on a manor they could call their own, which explained why 'the British found themselves becalmed in an economic Sargasso Sea'. Britons, Wiener argued, lived in perpetual fear of national life being eroded by progress: 'The nation that had been the mother of the industrial revolution was now uneasy with its offspring . . . the power of the Machine was invading and blighting the Shire.' Anti-industrial values, he concluded, reached into the upper echelons of the gentry and political class, and exerted a dampening effect on Britain's business and political life. 'At the end of the day', his book concluded, 'it may be that Margaret Thatcher will find her most fundamental challenge . . . in changing this frame of mind.' In his Westminster office, the Mad Monk of monetarism took this as a thrown-down gauntlet.

The music explored throughout this book embodies many of the qualities Martin Wiener was aiming at in his broadside, exemplifying the tendency, identified by one political observer, that 'Through a malign irony economic decline is a generator of parasitic growth industries.'[1] It's as true of cultural industries as any other. Coincidentally or not, folk music made little impact on the national consciousness during the 1980s, driven underground or associated with protest, vaguely aligned with a stymied left-wing opposition that occasionally appeared to identify itself with a 'Merrie England' view of class. Yet, quietly and doggedly, the likes of Martin Carthy, Norma Waterson, Fairport Convention, Dick Gaughan, Bert Jansch, John Renbourn, Maddy Prior, Ashley Hutchings and others soldiered on, well out of range of the music media's fashion radar. Peter Bellamy plied what remained of the UK's folk clubs with his misunderstood mix of Norfolk ballads and Kipling songs before killing himself with an overdose of tranquillisers and alcohol in 1991. John Martyn was pushed towards the kind of AOR success enjoyed by his friend and sometime band member, Phil Collins, but his music turned into an overproduced fusion soup. Fairport Convention played what was supposed to be their farewell concert in a field in Oxfordshire in 1979, but drew so many supporters they returned to Cropredy almost every year to stage an annual festival that has become one of the principal rallying points for the folk-music fallout in the next century.

The Les Cousins generation of folk-rockers might have been dispersed, but the spell was not entirely broken. In the changed, materialistic Britain of the 1980s, the ideas about myth and magic, memorial landscapes and nostalgia for a lost golden age were banished to internal exile, but scattered links of the silver chain glinted in the output of certain unconventional pop musicians of the time, most notably Kate Bush, Julian Cope, David Sylvian and Talk Talk. What linked all these artists was the fact that they had experienced some measure of commercial and popular success early on, but sought to kick their way free of expectations and create hybrid, idiosyncratic sound environments and, in a pop arena increasingly Americanised or homogenised for global consumption, maintain a distinctively British voice.

Searching for Peter Pan: Kate Bush, *Lionheart* (1978).

When the nineteen-year-old, leotard-clad Kate Bush erupted into the public eye in 1978, her early success owed much to the previous musical generation. Her EMI contract was secured thanks to the intervention of Pink Floyd's David Gilmour, who championed her after hearing her demos and made guest appearances on her later records. She took dance lessons with Lindsay Kemp, the performance artist who had not only taught the hippy David Bowie how to mime, but had also played the trickster pub landlord in *The Wicker Man*. And several of her early promo videos, including a concert film taken on her only tour, *Live at the Hammersmith Odeon 1979*, and clips for 'The Man with the Child in His Eyes' and 'Breathing', were directed by Keith MacMillan, the same 'Keef' who had created so many striking album covers for Vertigo and

Island in the early 1970s.[2] Her debut single, 'Wuthering Heights', channelled the thoughts of Cathy, heroine of Emily Brontë's celebrated evocation of the Yorkshire wilderness, and made her the first woman to achieve a British number one with a self-written song.

But for all her high profile as an international (if reclusive) celebrity, Bush's music has always been intriguing precisely because of the way she harnesses modern electronics and studio techniques to traditional instrumental textures and a lyrical sensibility that often invokes myth, fairy tale and magical transformations, and obliquely draws on the ballad canon. On the title track of her debut album, *The Kick Inside*, Bush sings of identifying with Lucy (or Lizie) Wan's story, a murder ballad that appears in the Francis Child collection. The tale of a neglected wife who disguises herself as a seductress to win back her husband in 1980's 'Babooshka' is a rewrite of 'Sovay', another ballad popularised in the 1960s by Martin Carthy and Anne Briggs. If occasionally her music sounds like a nouvelle cuisine buffet of disparate musics and feverish notions, British and Celtic sounds are an important seasoning on the feast. Her brother Paddy was a steadfast member of her musical inner circle, arranging and playing Irish traditional folk instruments, and her father has occasionally lent his voice to certain tracks. Her mother, who died in 1992, was half Irish, and as her career advanced, Bush increasingly played off her untamed Celtic streak against her decidedly comfortable Anglo-Saxon upbringing. Celtic musicians and instruments frequently occur on her records, and she has convened a number of significant players from the folk arena to add texture and colour to her compositions. Kate Bush's oeuvre has always remained a family affair, but it is laced with the pangs of losing home.

Her second album, *Lionheart*, is dedicated to 'Mr P. Pan whose tricks keep us on our toes'. It's an album whose tone veers between childlike earnestness and adolescent eroticism; on the sleeve she prowls suggestively over her attic dressing-up box, clad in a lion outfit. Like the psychedelic troubadours of the late 1960s, there was a part of Kate Bush that desired to cling to the child's imagination for ever. J. M. Barrie's immortal boy-sprite swoops across two songs: he's a token of wonder in a soul-destroying world in 'In Search of Peter Pan', and he's observed stealing kids from Kensington Park in 'Oh England My Lionheart'. The latter song is a piece of Bush's juvenilia which she later expressed some embarrassment about, but its plangent vignettes – apple blossom, shepherds, clover blooming on air-raid shelters, reading Shakespeare on the banks of the Thames, the ravens whose presence at the Tower of London are said to preserve the country's security – are classic images of English Arcady. Arranged for recorders and harpsichord, it shares sonic qualities with folk-rock groups such as Forest or Dr Strangely Strange. '*Give me one kiss and I'd be wassailing/In the orchard*,' sings this wide-eyed maid of Albion.

The presiding deity over *Never for Ever* (1980), and for most of Bush's work that followed it, would have to be Techne, the ancient Greek goddess of practical art or craft, with the nuance that 'craft' is also used to describe the practice of magic. The cover painting resembles the Gothic engraved style of Edwardian children's illustrator Arthur Rackham: Kate Bush lifts her skirt to unleash a horde of freakish beasts and monsters. Working with a Fairlight sequencing computer for the first time, courtesy of pop boffins John Walters and Richard Burgess of Landscape, Bush tailored her arrangements to a diverse array of musicians, demonstrating her capacity for fine detailing. On 'Breathing', Roy Harper adds backing vocals and John Giblin, soon to become a regular partner of John Martyn, plays bass. 'The Infant Kiss' features Early Music players Adam and Jo Skeaping, former associates of David Munrow who played with Shirley and Dolly Collins, Gryphon and Amazing Blondel in the early 1970s. The song was based on the disturbing tale of child sexuality in Jack Clayton's 1960 film *The*

Innocents, adapted from Henry James's story *The Turn of the Screw*, also a source of inspiration for an opera by Benjamin Britten. And another English composer was specifically invoked on 'Delius (Song of Summer)', which was in effect more of a homage to Max Adrian's stern 'ta-ta-taa'-ing portrayal in Ken Russell's 1968 BBC film about the pastoral composer's tricky relationship with his amanuensis Eric Fenby. Kevin Burke of The Bothy Band – former schoolfriend of Paddy Bush – contributed searing fiddle to 'Violin', an unhinged paean to the fiddle in its guise as demonic folk instrument, escaping from its buttoned-down role in the orchestra into the delirious trills of the folk dance.

Bush's music rose in parallel with the age of the pop video, and, as a studio artist who didn't play her music live, she enthusiastically embraced the form. The video for 'Cloudbusting', a song powered by Vaughan Williams/Frank Bridge-style string quartet strokes combined with sequenced drum tattoos, and one of the singles taken from 1985's *Hounds of Love*, was a miniaturised eco-conspiracy thriller, conceived by Bush with Terry Gilliam, and directed by Julian Doyle (Gilliam's special-effects man on his film *Brazil*). Bush had been reading the melancholy 1973 memoir *A Book of Dreams* by Peter Reich, son of renegade psychologist and scientist Wilhelm Reich, who designed the 'cloudbuster' during the 1940s as an extension of his research into 'orgone', or sexual energy. Reich's cloudbuster was intended to suck down the accumulated orgone in the atmosphere, thereby creating cloud formations and rainfall. Reich's meteorological experiments are widely viewed as crackpot physics by the scientific mainstream, and when his efforts to control the weather came to the notice of the FDA (Food and Drug Administration), they had him arrested.

Donald Sutherland plays the Reich/father figure and Bush plays his son (Sutherland played lead in Nic Roeg's *Don't Look Now*, apparently one of Kate Bush's favourite films). The film plays like a silent movie, with the pair hauling the rainmaker – a steampunk contraption of steel piping, handles and flywheels – up a grassy hillside and then joyfully operating its levers to make the clouds dance in the sky. With its windswept landscape, intense sunset lighting and the eccentric figures and machinery in the middle of it all, every frame looks like a Keef record sleeve. In particular, Donald Sutherland's laboratory, with its papers, apparatus, Foucault's pendulum and swirling dust motes, is as carefully constructed and stage-dressed as the apothecary on the front of Sandy Denny's *North Star Grassman and the Ravens*.

Hounds of Love was the high-water mark of Bush's discography, containing not only a clutch of successful singles ('Running Up that Hill (A Deal with God)', 'The Big Sky' and 'Cloudbusting'), but devoting a whole side to an experimental studio opera, *The Ninth Wave*, in which she put herself in the position of the survivor of an air crash, slowly freezing to death in the sea. Like her previous *The Dreaming* (1982), *Hounds of Love* featured the talents of more Irish musicians – Sean Keane of The Chieftains, and Planxty's Liam O'Flynn and Donal Lunny. Danny Thompson, the double bassist who had stamped his presence on Pentangle, John Martyn and so many other crucial early-1970s folk-rock recordings – also cameoed on both albums.

Named after a line in Tennyson's poem *The Coming of Arthur*, a verse of which serves as the album's epigram, *The Ninth Wave* allows Bush to give free rein to her internal chatter of disparate voices as she soliloquises from within the skull of a drowning woman. The suite plays tricks with time and space, too: 'Watching You Without Me', in which Bush's piano is backed up with Danny Thompson's lugubrious string bass, hovers over the shoulder of her future bereaved lover, while the 'Jig of Life' is a plea by the casualty's future self to survive the trauma and give her subsequent destiny a chance. Ambitious in scope, and a masterful exercise in studio psycho-acoustics, *The Ninth Wave* crystallised a theme of pining for the familiarities of home, for reinstatement within a firm identity, and of the imaginative powers unlocked during periods of isolation, that were common among other artists of this time.

When David Sylvian freed himself from his commitments to Japan, the New Romantic group he had formed in south London in 1974, he entered a period of splendid isolation in which he swerved aside from the angsty cosmetics of his former group. Dismayed by the

'Drowning in my nostalgia': David Sylvian in a promotional shot for *Gone to Earth*, 1986.

extent to which adolescent adulation could disrupt a lifestyle he preferred to spend in contemplation, the socially awkward singer, famous for his elaborate coif and patina of make-up, reinvented himself as peripatetic cosmopolitan rambler, attempting to engage with the spirit of place, beyond the facade presented to the average tourist. His solo music, beginning with the release of *Brilliant Trees* in 1984, featured an equally catholic assembly of musicians. In a similar fashion to the way jazz elements lubricated folk and rock in the late 1960s, Sylvian's solo albums were aerated by additives from beyond the pop sphere. Like Kate Bush, Sylvian composes what he can and convenes appropriate musicians to fill in the blanks; with Bush, he has even shared double bassist Eberhard Weber, trumpeter Kenny Wheeler, and Danny Thompson. Other key collaborators have been Robert Fripp, guitarist with progressive outfit King Crimson; Ryuichi Sakamoto, the founder of Japan's Yellow Magic Orchestra; and Holger Czukay, the bassist and producer of German krautrock group Can.

On Sylvian's final album with Japan, *Tin Drum* (1981), the song 'Ghosts' hinted at hindrances from the past foiling his present moves, set to an eerie, atonal electronic backing track. Sylvian later reflected that, during Japan's commercial peak, life 'seemed to be fun, but when you get older and realise the hollowness of the whole thing, you think you might as well do something of value or not bother'.[3] Sylvian's music began to buckle under the pressure of ambient, mood and tone poems, and his readings of Sartre, Mishima and Milan Kundera. *Brilliant Trees* contained two bony funk workouts, 'Pulling Punches' and 'Red Guitar', but the arty jazz pop of 'Ink in the Well' and 'Nostalgia', and the murky, ambient passages of side two, signalled new directions into an impressionistic, exploratory mode. 'Nostalgia' is a companion piece to 'Ghosts', with Sylvian's memories now frozen into tree-like shapes which he is ruthlessly pruning back to avoid '*drowning in my nostalgia*'. 'Brilliant Trees' itself accumulated hymnal, slow-burning power over a full eight minutes, building to a resonantly organic image of enduring love: '*There you stand making my life possible / Reaching up like a flower, leading my life back to the soil,*' followed by a gaseous coda with Jon Hassell's trumpet puffing steam over metallic percussion. The soil provided a rich metaphor for Sylvian's attempts to root himself following the years involved in the flighty pop world; the video for 'Red Guitar' even literally depicts him planted nipple-deep in baked earth.

What emerges from *Brilliant Trees* and the 1986 album with which it forms a pair, *Gone to Earth*, is the desire to move from faithless wilderness to spiritual homecoming. In later years, Sylvian would move to America and acquire a guru and a meditational discipline. 'There's a great deal more reverence in America to teachers of all kinds,' he told me in 1999. 'Some Americans are looked on as being very gullible because of that – but I enjoy the openness, the willingness to give something and someone a chance.' *Gone to Earth* alluded to a quest for metaphysical guidance, an acknowledgement of the stirrings of a new faith taking place under charged, totemic landscapes (it's no coincidence that a 1989 compendium of his solo work was titled *Weatherbox*). '*A little girl dreams of taking the veil,*' he croons on the opening track of *Gone to Earth*, whose title alluded to the 1950 Powell and Pressburger film of the same name (itself an adaptation of a tragic country novel by Mary Webb published in 1917), and whose cover painting by Russell Mills was based on an alchemical diagram by Elizabethan philosopher Robert Fludd. One song was even called 'River Man', and like Nick Drake's song of the same name, there is a holy man and a lover who appear to offer parallel, conflicting salvation. It's also possessed of an equally mystical, if slightly more oppressive atmosphere than Drake's song, Harry Robinson's strings replaced with Robert Fripp's 'sky saw' guitar. 'Silver Moon', with its sweeping piano-driven minor chords and lyrical references to waves and tides, has affinities with Sandy Denny songs such as 'Next Time Around' or 'Late November'. The album contained several spoken extracts from the lectures of J. G. Bennett, the well-travelled English spiritual teacher influenced by the mystic oriental philosophy of G. I. Gurdjieff. These recordings were no doubt sourced via Robert Fripp, a close follower of Bennett's courses and doctrines since the mid-1970s, and who was principal tape archivist at the late master's Dorset academy.

'Gone to Earth' was a muddy, atonal duet between Sylvian's voice – a crevasse at the song's heart – and Fripp's mangled-steel guitar. In an interview at the time, Sylvian spoke of 'the desire to understand, then a kind of anger at the inability to understand, the idea that if you're living your life and think you know what you're doing, you're sleeping on your feet, you've got no idea, you're not in control. That comes out in anger and frustration sometimes, which is just what . . . "Gone to Earth" is . . . it's about the fact that most of the things that I see of value in the world are trodden down, the value is not seen, aggression is always used against it. That track is the nearest I've got to what I've been aiming at all this time, just because it's so raw.'[4]

Gone to Earth contained a whole second disc of impressionistic songs without words; static music with an emotive core. His emotional and intellectual ups and downs continued to be a roller coaster that travelled slowly enough to make the danger of falling out seem real.

The most startling transformation, over the course of the 1980s, was the process by which Talk Talk metamorphosed from groomed and airbrushed New Romantics – all Simmons drum pads, elastic keyboard solos, guitar synthesizers, Fairlight sequencing and Athena-poster sleeves – to the avant-garde rock Passions of their celebrated final albums, *Spirit of Eden* and *Laughing Stock*. The conventional route in a pop career is to start out spiky and untamed, and let the machinations of the industry sandpaper

Talk Talk, *Spirit of Eden* (1988).

down all the elements that supposedly chafe against high sales. Talk Talk did things the wrong way round, making a late break out of the mould they'd been cast in. Their last two records constantly threaten heavy weather, like one of those early spring days when black clouds can share sky-space with dazzling sunlight. Where Kate Bush – Talk Talk's equally uncompromising labelmate – packed her tunes out with a sensual cornucopia of noise, sound effects, accents and textures, Talk Talk pared down their dynamics to extreme shifts from becalmed near-silence to torrential rock thunderclaps.

Even their early pop artifice was a misrepresentation of vocalist Mark Hollis's aims. As far back as 1980, Hollis was introducing his new junior partners to the delights of Delius, Satie, psychedelic garage by The Seeds and Love, and especially the modal jazz of Miles Davis and Gil Evans. In the early days, though, the pop artifice merely cloaked Hollis's confessional lyrics of anguish, injustice and hurt, struggling with notions of fate versus faith, with imagery swinging from the Bible to Luke Reinhart's *The Dice Man*.

When the singles for which they're best known – 'Life's What You Make It' and 'Give It Up' – hit the charts in 1986, they sounded like Cassandra baying in the wilderness – a lone, moral voice railing against the backdating of experience by mass-media saturation and the tragedies of drug addiction. (Not his own, it should be stressed: Mark Hollis has called heroin 'a wicked, horrible thing', admitting only to drinking to maintain the intensity of performing his songs on tour. But his elder brother Ed Hollis, former manager of Eddie and the Hot Rods, died shortly after the completion of *Spirit of Eden*, after a long battle with the drug.)

Spirit of Eden, which emerged from its nine-month pupation in September 1988, represented a wholesale re-evaluation, like a yuppie renouncing his financial career and taking off to live in a yurt. As well as the group's core players – Hollis with long-time friends, drummer Lee Harris and bassist Paul Webb – producer Tim Friese-Greene took a participatory creative role, playing harmonium, keyboards and guitar; and the sizeable budget EMI Records allocated paid for the Choir of Chelmsford Cathedral plus an eclectic thirteen-piece chamber-rock ensemble that included Nigel Kennedy on violin, Andrew Marriner (son of conductor Sir Neville) on clarinet, Danny Thompson on double bass, Henry Lowther on trumpet, Martin Ditcham on percussion and improviser Hugh Davies on his self-built 'shozygs' (contact-miked electronic devices installed in old encyclopedias).

Hollis equated the artificiality of modern studio techniques with the pervasive dishonesty of his times. Inspired by the rainbow-spectral arrangements and phenomenal technique in the classic Miles Davis / Gil Evans albums *Sketches of Spain* and *Porgy and Bess*, *Spirit of Eden* was a slight return to the environment at Sound Techniques created by John Wood and Joe Boyd: the studio as a wide-open sounding-space, throwing players back onto their own instrumental prowess. EMI's desperate marketing campaign was reduced to calling it 'An album for 1988'; in fact, it was much more an album for 1968, and yet had advanced further than almost all their contemporaries. A crucial addition to the team in this respect was Phill Brown, a veteran who had engineered records at Olympic Studios with Jimi Hendrix, Led Zeppelin, The Rolling Stones and others. Hollis hired him after a conversation in which Brown was asked to describe his overall memory of the Olympic days; Brown answered by describing an all-night Traffic session in 1967. This was music to Talk Talk's ears: Steve Winwood had played organ on *The Colour of Spring*.

You could call the 1980s-style close-miking of individual instruments the aural equivalent of air conditioning, allowing no ventilation around each constituent part of the stereo picture. Hollis and Friese-Greene preferred to throw the floor open and have an improvisational zone in which, according to Hollis, anyone could wander in and float an idea into the river of sound – even though there was a good chance it would end up deleted from the master tape. And like Traffic's endless jams at their Berkshire cottage, Hollis and Friese-Greene engineered the mood at Wessex Studios by plunging it into darkness, illuminated only by sound-triggered lighting around the drum kit and a psychedelic oil-wheel projector turning the control room into an isolation tank swimming with luminous, amoebic jelloids.

Secreted in this murky magic lantern for the best part of a year, Hollis created a sorrowing masterpiece, adrift in every way – from its fragile ensemble sound to its dejected, pining vocals – from the prevailing winds of the pop charts. The first sung line – after a tensed, dewy dawn of muted trumpet, sustained strings, tectonic rumbles and scraped ceramics lasting almost two and a half minutes – is '*The world's turned upside down*'. 'The Rainbow' arches across the whole of side one, the music inhaling and exhaling slowly through 'Eden' before breaking into an excoriating rasp in the middle of 'Desire'. Side two adds an extra measure of chagrined disgust with the injustices, needless deaths and materialism of his own time: Hollis as a modern-day Blake, bearing witness to London's dismal streets. With its luminous jazz-trio textures and Danny Thompson's double-bass figures, 'Inheritance' can be heard as a successor to John Martyn's 'Solid Air'. Particularly since the song's subject could conceivably be a thumbnail sketch of Nick Drake, a '*Nature's son . . . Burying progress in the clouds/ . . . Heaven bless you in your calm*'. Like Drake, Hollis is in communion with exquisite instants in the natural world: spring is broad-brushed in three words, '*lilac glistening foal*', and the lyrics, shaved almost to syntactical incomprehensibility, offset the simple joys of nature against lives governed by financial incentives. '*I've seen heroin for myself/ On the street so young laying wasted*,' sings Hollis on 'I Believe in You', a *cri de coeur* – with a choral section lifted from Sibelius's sixth symphony – that may be a warning to his brother at the height of his problems with the drug.

Hollis has a consummately un-rock vocal style, all whisper and no scream. At times, the voice is little more than a thin parting of the studio air; the words are stretched out, torn apart, boiled down to consonant acoustics. Even Hollis's clenched, left-sloping handwritten lyrics, reproduced on the inner sleeve, have something desolate about them, devoid of punctuation and cramped to the point of near illegibility, like fragments stuffed into a bottle and set adrift by a mariner marooned on his own island of despond.

At least on an island you have the Robinson Crusoe option to begin life anew. Like Talk Talk's earlier single 'Dum Dum Girl', *Spirit of Eden* pricked the bubble economy of the Thatcher years: their music was an exclusion zone where no postmodern irony or quixotic sampling would feel welcome. Between the lines lurked a vision of a world washed clean, where spring will inevitably cycle around bringing the new grass of renewal. During the creation of *Spirit* and *Laughing Stock*, Mark Hollis lived with his family on a farm near Bury St Edmunds in Suffolk, surrounded by a menagerie of eighteen animals. Images of the natural world recurred on the group's sleeve art, by painter James Marsh, and in several of their videos. For 'Life's What You Make It', the group set up in the small hours in a forest; their exaggerated clanging was intercut with stock footage of animals, reptiles and insects. Tim Pope's clip for 'Dum Dum Girl' was shot in the middle of an English green field with Hollis, Harris and Webb overdubbing the vocals live on camera.

Marsh's paintings – meticulous hybrids of Henri Rousseau and Roger Dean, with a nod to Tony Wright's merman-like illustration on John Martyn's *One World* – are indelibly associated with Talk Talk's music. On *Spirit of Eden*, a waterlogged mangrove, lonely in the middle of an ocean, provides shelter for a puffin, dragonfly and oystercatcher, along with various ornate seashells. The image of washed-up survivors of an ecological disaster, clinging to a threadbare sanctuary, was so important to the group that it occurred again on *Laughing Stock*; this time, a flock of exotic birds perches on a leafless tree, towering symbolically over the curvature of a drying-out planet, in an apparent reference to the song entitled 'After the Flood'.

In 1991, as Britain suffered its Black Monday plunge into recession, Talk Talk were rapidly approaching their own extinction. *Laughing Stock*, offspring of another protracted birth at Wessex Studios, was looser at the seams than *Spirit of Eden*, the stately circadian rhythms of Lee Harris signal-jammed with irruptions of static and noise and overlapping laminates of strings, guitars and organ. Bassist Paul Webb had already left the group, and in the face of the crumbling edifice, the album was a scorched-earth tilt at the finish line, again recorded in darkened chambers, that consumed musicians' and studio operatives' lives to the extent that 'marriages were collapsing, there were breakdowns, people resigning', as Phill Brown later recalled.[5] Hollis was barely communicating and his lyrics were increasingly cryptic, even biblical; musicians were given no map or context for what they were playing; and their manager had to break the news to their new label, Polydor, that the new record contained no singles.

But for all that, *Laughing Stock* is a brilliant achievement, building on the discoveries of *Spirit of Eden* but pushing towards hitherto unknown regions of fluidity, abstraction and hushed, tensed power. 'After the Flood' contains the masterstroke: with Lee Harris recreating the drum pattern of Can's 'Halleluwah', Hollis torched the centre of the track with a one-note, overtone-heavy Variophon solo. This was a German invention, a synthesized wind instrument shaped like a clarinet, with a blow control designed to allow greater expressive possibilities. Hollis's model was malfunctioning, and the deluge of noise he emits, lasting all of one minute fifteen seconds, jerks caustically between octaves, like a breaking voice bellowing in anguish. It is literally a purging flood of sound. Hollis stated that he visualised the jazz reeds player Roland Kirk, who was able to play two or three instruments at once in his mouth. 'It's one note, but you feel the note.'[6]

Drumless and intimate, 'Taphead' and 'Runeii' pointed the way to the minimalism of Mark Hollis's final statement, a self-titled solo record issued in 1998. It's been reported that Talk Talk had been contracted for another album, to be called *Mountains of the Moon*, and that *Mark Hollis* fulfilled that obligation. But by that time he had fallen out of touch with his former bandmates and with Tim Friese-Greene, though Phill Brown applied his magic touch to the recording, using just two overhead mics to capture Hollis's fragile, sparse chamber music. In the interim years, he had taught himself the clarinet and learnt to score for classical woodwinds; he had also pursued his own enthusiasms for the reductive minimalist musics of Erik Satie and Morton Feldman. 'I love sound. And I love silence. And in a way, I like silence more,' he stated on a press release accompanying the record, and much of this material aspired to its own self-erasure. Nothing on the album was electrified.

'The minute you work with just acoustic instruments,' he said, 'by virtue of the fact that they've already existed for hundreds of years, they can't date. When you're looking at writing music, the ideal must be: I'd like to make music that can exist outside the timeframe. So your biggest chance of doing that, I guess, is working with instruments that by their nature don't exist in a time period.'

These songs crawl at a snail's pace, and Hollis's vocal performance is a miracle of control. Elliptical verse is loaded with apocalyptic weight. As well as 'Watershed', which appears to refer to the glory days of Talk Talk ('*A song asale should have said so much/ Makes it harder the more you love*'), the timescale referred to in the album's centrepiece, 'A Life (1895–1915)', spans the turn of the twentieth century: twenty years in which Victorian imperial dignity was trampled into trench mud. 'The dates were taken from . . . the First World War . . . at the time I read a few books about that period, like *All Quiet on the Western Front*, *Testament of Youth*, and I think those dates – I might be wrong, but I've got a feeling they were [the lifespan of] Vera Brittain's boyfriend.' The theme of war also recurs on 'A New Jerusalem', which, Hollis informed me in 1997, in almost the last public statement he's ever made, was 'tied up with two things, when I thought about it: that was the way they talked about 1946; but equally I thought, whether you're back from Vietnam, or whatever, it's just that conflict between expectation and reality'.

That conflict is the key to the pain, and the moral anchor, that lies behind much of Talk Talk's later output. 'If I think of favourite films of mine,' Hollis explained, citing *The Bicycle Thieves* and *Les Enfants du paradis*, 'what they deal with is character and virtue, they don't deal with narrative. That's a very secondary thing.' The confession box on *Mark Hollis* is thick with purification, repentance, atonement and redemption. Coupled with several explicit references to Christianity on *Laughing Stock*, it might appear that

Hollis discovered religion, but, he assured me, 'I'm not a born-again Christian, but I would hope there's a humanitarian vision in there, for sure.'

And that's what Hollis has left us with: the 110 seconds of absolute silence that linger before the CD cuts out seem to be a pretty unambiguous statement of finality. Hollis has to all intents and purposes closed down as a public artist – the last glimpses, apart from producing an album by Anja Garbarek in 2001, were one tiny cameo on an album by beat sculptors UNKLE and (under the pseudonym John Cope) contributing hermetic piano lines to a very obscure CD by Phill Brown and Dave Allinson, *AV1*. Inevitably, Hollis is branded a recluse, though, as he wittily put it to me, 'I see things in terms of a pursuit rather than avoidance.'

Lee Harris and Paul Webb reunited after Talk Talk's collapse, built a studio in an industrial warehouse in north London, and squirrelled themselves away to create two fine records between 1994–6, little noticed at the time. The name .O.rang really encompassed Webb and Harris's protracted creation of grooves and atmospheres, working at their own speed, and, as with Talk Talk, inviting a host of extra talents – Matt Johnson of The The; Mark Feltham, Martin Ditcham and Phill Brown from the Talk Talk days; plus several new faces: Beth Gibbons, soon to be the retiring face of Portishead; Graham Sutton, guitarist of the oceanic rock group Bark Psychosis; Swiss singer Colette Meury; improv percussionist Paul Shearsmith; and keyboardist Phil Ramacon. *Herd of Instinct* (1994) sounded like Talk Talk gone *Lord of the Flies*: atavistic ethno-forgeries bristling with percussion, pipes and malletophones from South-East Asia, Africa and the Indian subcontinent. Harris and Webb namechecked the Nigerian bandleader Fela Kuti, the mantric music of Can, the innerspace dub of British reggae explorers African Head Charge and the crush-collision productions of Adrian Sherwood's On-U Sound label. If Mark Hollis had pursued calm, emptiness and silence in the 1990s, his former colleagues went the opposite way: .O.rang's music is an exhilarating and frequently claustrophobic jumble of parts, dragged in the same direction by Harris and Webb's lock-tight rhythm section. *Herd of Instinct*'s remarkable packaging made it feel like the product of some secret and esoteric anthropology, traces of shamanic visions and psychogeographic excursions boiled down to apocalyptic photomontages of gaping caverns, glowering volcanoes and lurid masks.

Fields and Waves (1996) was dressed up as an abandoned portfolio of undigested soundings, field recordings, surveillance photography and atmospheric measurements taken at urban and rural sites around Britain. An oscilloscope is photographed on the crumbling cliffs of Camber Sands in Kent; in the middle of London's busy Oxford Street and in a nearby underground station; being sniffed by a pig; placed in the hollow trunk of a tree; in the sewage outflow into an estuary; and being tweaked next to a mobile-phone mast. Labelled with map references and positional data in the manner of Richard Long's Land Art walks or Mark Boyle's 'earthprobes', the clues on *Fields and Waves* add up to a survey of the interstitial zone rarely explored by British music: the hinterlands where farmland and brownfields bump up against the grimy industrial O-ring encircling major conurbs. The ecological subtext of Talk Talk was here brought to the fore, in a way that now actively engaged with the polluted landfill wildernesses that were being superimposed on former arable land, and the factors that were reshaping the topography of Britain itself.

The project to perceive the British Isles whole, as an entire geographical entity or symbolic body, has been attempted in many forms down the centuries, in literature and art, as well as economic censuses such as the famous eleventh-century *Domesday Book*. Between 1598 and 1622 a history poet called Michael Drayton claimed to hear 'the sundry Musiques of England' flowing from its rivers and streams, and created 15,000 lines of a vast poem – divided into thirty 'songs' – which takes the reader on an epic overflight of the historic geographic sites of England and Wales. He called it *Poly-Olbion*, and it was published with accompanying maps in which each region was transformed into a human figure. *Poly-Olbion* stands at the source of the seventeenth century's great stream of antiquarian exploration, in which, as we have seen, such figures as John Aubrey, William Stukeley, John Leland and William Camden began to unearth relics and monuments from a forgotten, prehistoric civilisation on the isles. The surviving fragments were so disparate, their purpose so mysterious, that interpreting them could be achieved by arranging them in myriad possible permutations and imaginative fancies. The 'poly' in *Poly-Olbion* hints at a polyphony of versions of Albion's past, and the multiplicity of its contents, as well as being what Peter Ackroyd has called 'a recognition of the landscape as an organic being with its own laws of growth and change'.[7]

Much later, in cinema's silent age, Claude Friese-Greene set out in summer 1924 to film a motor-car trip from Land's End to John O'Groats. His father, the cinematographer William Friese-Greene, had invented his New All British Friese-Greene Natural Colour Process, one of the first attempts to create colour film. Claude's project, entitled *The Open Road*, was designed to show off his father's prototype technique, but survives as a tip-to-tip visual and social document of the British Isles between the wars. *The Open Road* was only ever exhibited at a 1920s trade convention, but was restored in the early years of the twenty-first century.[8] Coincidentally, a descendant of this film-pioneer dynasty was Tim Friese-Greene, the producer and sometime member of Talk Talk.

One of the items included in a reading list printed on the sleeve of .O.rang's *Fields and Waves* is *Journey to the Surface of the Earth*, a book of images and writings by Mark Boyle, published in 1970. In the conceptual-art climate of the late 1960s, Boyle — who regularly slathered oil-wheel and slide projections across the organic rock wrigglings of The Soft Machine and Pink Floyd at London's psychedelic hangouts — persuaded various blindfolded volunteers to throw darts at a giant wall map of the world. Boyle intended to visit the precise spots where the points of the darts fell and carry out 'a multi-sensual presentation of the site'. This involved marking out a small square in the landscape and filming it and the sky above, observing the animal and plant life within it, finding the nearest human settlement to the chosen location and 'treat[ing it] as a biological entity'. As the project developed, Boyle began including soundscape accompaniments to the visuals, recorded on site. One objective of Boyle's field trips was literally to lift out a portion of the ground — the surface coating of dust, stones, mud, grass, etc. — transfer it onto a board and chemically fix it, in order to exhibit it as a canvas, or 'earthprobe', in an art gallery. In the autumn of 1969 Boyle concentrated his efforts upon Camber Sands, a stretch of Kent coastline peculiarly sensitive to the transforming effects of wind, sea and other elements. Working in gale-force gusts, he made his *Tidal Series* of studies by fixing the top layers of sand from the beach in all its rippled, drift-marked and animal-scuffed variety. In *Journey to the Surface of the Earth*, Boyle elaborated his utopian theory of the human race as a biological entity: 'Maybe . . . there is a multi cellular animal called humanity and . . . when some atrocity happens or when anyone anywhere gets hurt we immediately feel the pain of it.' It was important that Boyle would actually take the trouble to get there — to find a truth in the physical reality of place.

One of the more unlikely grand surveys of the British mythical landscape was carried out in the 1990s, by yet another former pop star who had jumped the rails at the height of a promising career. As well as pursuing a diverse and unpredictable solo career since his early-1980s days as leader of The Teardrop Explodes, Julian Cope developed an obsessive interest in British prehistory, and as the turn of the millennium approached, he travelled from Cornwall to the Shetland Islands, from West Wales to the Yorkshire Dales, examining every significant megalithic stone circle, monument, cave, holy well, mound and Celtic cross, and chronicled his observations and conclusions in a monumental work of amateur archaeology he called *The Modern Antiquarian*. No dry objective study of site findings, this was a rock 'n' roll Poly-Albion that took its righteous tone from

The modern antiquarian: Julian Cope, 1992.

Cope's passionate advocacy of the lost religions and matriarchal cult of ancient Britain, which he saw as corrupted and debased by the importation of Christianity. It was the logical outcome of almost a decade during which such ideas had been drip-fed into his own music, spiking a cocktail of astro-archaeology, anti-establishment posturing, acid rock, cosmic metal and folky musing.

As lead singer of The Teardrop Explodes, Julian Cope was at the centre of the wave of Liverpool post-punk alternative music, among the likes of Echo and the Bunnymen, The Mighty Wah! and Big in Japan. By 1982 the group had found mainstream success with singles such as 'Reward' and 'Treason', but Cope buckled under the pressure of touring and the eccentric behaviour endemic to the group, which split up at the end of 1982. In his memoir, Cope recalls recovering from psychic burnout at his parents' home in Tamworth, and exploring the historic Midlands villages in the surrounding area. Meandering among the ruins of Alvecote Priory, he recalls playing there as a child: 'this was the swamp and its Anglo-Saxon funeral mound. It held great significance for my brother and me: we thought this ancient tract of land was inhabited by a spirit world and would tread carefully. Returning now, as a confused shell of an adult, the place seemed just as special.'[9] In the next few years Cope would return repeatedly to Alvecote, to celebrate his marriage and shoot videos and album covers, including the notorious sleeve of *Fried* (1985), where he crawls naked under a giant turtle-shell on the Mound beneath a sky 'classically English in its vague blue-grey cloudiness'. Describing the inspiration for that record in another memoir, Cope calls it 'the Saxon music of the Alvecote Mound. This was the music of Woden and the West Midlands'.[10] At the same time, Cope was developing an obsession with collecting model cars and toys dating from his youth, and his favourite film was *Back to the Future*. The psychedelic obsession with time travel and childhood were conflated as they had been in the late 1960s.

On *Fried*, the first inklings of Cope's focus on the past begin to appear, largely because he became exasperated by the exaggerated claims of novelty by many of the current pop artists. Looking to tradition, Cope picked up on the hundreds of incarnations of the wily fox, Reynardine. 'Reynard the Fox', the song that routinely climaxed his live shows at the time and for many years afterwards, selectively quoted from Thomas Gray's eighteenth-century poem 'The Fox', which mentions the animal's prodigious ability to keep on running. Cope's rendition found Reynard sprinting through the ages on a garage-punk riff and finding himself in the twentieth century, on Alvecote Mound with a plastic bag and a knife and a will to self-harm. Cope's own stage antics several times led to him slashing his own stomach in a bloody enactment of Reynard's own gut-spilling antics.

Vilified by the press and distrusted by the music industry, Cope reached his commercial apotheosis with 1987's *Saint Julian*. At this time, more and more of Cope's practice became charged with mystic resonance: the specially constructed microphone stand he used in concert, which allowed him to hang suspended above the front rows, he dubbed his 'Iggdrasil stand', equating it with the Norse Tree of Life. By 1992's *Jehovahkill*, his music was an eclectic mix of Teutonic hard rock and folky introspection; his lyrics a cocktail of mysticism, Norse and pagan legend, Gurdjieff, Jung and the revolutionary rock manifestos of MC5 manager John Sinclair. Sounding like a string of epiphanies, and emblazoned with photographs of stone circles, ancient serpents and engravings by William Stukeley, and with entreaties to 'Embrace the Cross, Reclaim the Cross' as a symbolic connection with the pre-Christian era, *Jehovahkill* signalled a decisive shift in Cope's outlook. The front cover features the Callanish in the Outer Hebrides, where four corridors of standing stones converge on a central stone circle. Seen from the air, it is a cross, constructed some 300 years before Christianity adopted the symbol. He had visited the site in the same year, and met with local visionary archaeologist and self-appointed custodian of the place Margaret Curtis, who inducted him into its mysteries. Callanish epitomises Cope's sense of injustice about the destruction of pagan religions by Judaeo-Christianity: 'The story of the Fall is vague and pious kaka written in the 8th century by anti-female churchmen,' he wrote in the booklet of *Jehovahkill*.

In the same year, Cope moved his family out of London to a farm in Wiltshire, a few miles down the road from Avebury and Silbury Hill, one of the focal points of England's megalithic network. Many of his subsequent activities took on a folkloric cast. Dropped by Island, he set up an independent label to release his own material, first called Magog, then Head Heritage, which continues as a label and website with a wealth of know-how for the modern-day heathen, from political direct action to alternative archaeology. His music has taken on multiple dimensions, from the ambient synthesizer musings of *Rite* to the cosmic krautrock of *Interpreter*, to the Odinist Metal of *Rome Wasn't Burned in a Day* and the crude 'fölk' of *Citizen Cain'd*. His amorphous collective, Black Sheep, formed in late 2007, invokes the rhetoric of English revolutionary movements and global anarchist factions, and makes spontaneous improvised chants and acoustic mantras, dotted with accordions, tub-thumping martial drums and psychedelic mellotron drones. It's also founded on a sonic fiction of time travel, forward to a 'post-Edisonian' future. 'I imagine it's 300 years from now,' Cope explained to me when I visited him in late 2009. 'Culture has finally come to a collapse, there's no electricity any more, and they are worshipping everything from this time – they are, let's say, post-post-post-Nine Inch Nails. They want that sound, but electricity's long gone, they don't even really know what it sounded like. All they can really do is run along touting solid-body Fender guitars, which have by now been repainted in various places where they have been battered, and in order to allude to rock 'n' roll volume, all they can really do is get a whole bunch of marching drums and go to the nearest gorge, which has fantastic acoustics, and bash the hell out of it.'

Back in 1993, from his new rural seclusion, and armed with Charles Hapgood's assertion that 'Every scientist is an amateur to start with', Cope embarked on his grand tour – or 'Gnostic odyssey' – of the surviving traces of Neolithic Britain. 'I saw that archaeologists were not even conferring between the various Ages (Neolithic, Bronze, Iron, Roman and so forth),' he wrote, 'and understood that, as a traveller by profession, I was ideally suited to perform this task of pilgrimage and sacred reconnaissance.'[11] Cope's own theory about the historic importance of the Neolithic age is that the setting up of standing stones is equivalent to the Fall – the moment when humanity, living in Edenic harmony and symbiosis with the rhythms of the earth, took its first steps towards living outside and apart from those rhythms. Raising a stone to commemorate a successful harvest, for instance, represents a kind of self-awareness. 'It was at this moment that humans first peeled themselves away from Mother Earth just long enough to feel a true Separation,' he writes. 'And it was here that the first feelings of "I" and "we" exploded in human consciousness.'

In speculating on the spiritual heritage of the ancient Britons, Cope effectively maps the Roman pagan and Christian invasions onto present-day political terrain: the Roman imperium becomes the modern-day Establishment. He is, as he has described it, 'one who writes only about that which he has visited'.[12] Like so many prior British utopians, his is an impossible but necessary dream: in this case, of a Britain remade as a lunar, born-again pagan society that has, in Blakean fashion, cast off its mind-forg'd manacles. Though often presenting himself as a jester or heathen Hell's Angel, Cope's learned research occupies a unique position, neither gonzo archaeology nor insular academic treatise. His holistic theories and insights into prehistory have been given credence by such institutions as the British Museum. Tapping complementary veins of attritional and introspective rock, Cope sings, speaks and writes in the voice of the heathen – the aboriginal 'people of the heath' who worshipped the earth as a mother goddess. But he disdains the comfortable, nostalgic option implied in the notion of 'heritage'. He told me about a study he had made of folk festivals around Britain that claimed to be several hundred years old. 'What amazed me about these so-called archaic festivals was, virtually none of them had anything pagan about them at all. They were kind of a bit lah-di-dah. You go to the Furry Dance in Helston in Cornwall, it's just a bunch of people dressed appropriately, running to one street corner; they do this dance, yell "Hail fellow, well met", and then charge off to the next street corner. Well, it's lovely, but there's nothing pagan about it. The only pagan one I've seen is the Obby Oss. To me, what makes it so pagan is, it's a bunch of totally drunken males staggering around, each one falling by the wayside; somebody else picks up the concertina and carries on playing it, with this demented tune . . . It took me two visits to even remember the tune, because it's clearly a tune that somebody else came along and went, "My grandad says it went like this, and we'll just play that bit on the end." Twenty years later, Uncle Cyril says, "That der-der-der that they play on the other side of the bay, that's actually the original – we'll integrate that." And all these dreadful tunes, which end up sounding great, because it's just so mysterious and tortuous – *that's* pagan. It's very important to go to these places to see what people mean by what is pagan and what is merely non-Christian.'

Cope's alternative, humane heritage movement made it abundantly clear that, for any Martin Wiener who might insist that the old Britain be cast off like a useless snakeskin, there would always be a resistance. No poetry without heretics.

19

Toward the Unknown Region

One chill March evening I walked into one of the many entrances to the underground station at London Bridge. For hundreds of years this was the only way across the River Thames. While the original stone bridge is long gone, the reverberations of all those millions of journeys – of the hopeful, the exhausted – still lingers in these precincts. Built in 1836, London Bridge railway station is the oldest in the city and continues daily to drag the hopeful in, and haul away the exhausted, in their thousands.

Following the underground entrance sign, I passed through a miniature shopping mall and halted ahead of the escalators. Here was my destination: a small, easily overlooked door in the brickwork, standing half open. Behind it, a makeshift ticket booth had been installed: table, chair and cash box. I held out my wrist to be stamped and walked on, into the black.

To enter the Shunt Vault is to be swallowed up in a cavernous relic of Victorian engineering: a vast cistern of stone arches that leap out of sight into nebulous gloom, way above your head. It's like some subterranean cathedral, stripped of decoration and drained of all spiritual function: an architectural abscess that has trapped and feasted on the dark of two centuries' nights.

As I walk down the central 'nave', peering through the gloom into deserted 'side chapels', my steps fall into glimmering patches of light from pairs of blue and red neons, placed at the foot of each brickwork arch. The nave is slightly too long, and somewhere in the middle I lose sight of the entrance. I'm not yet far enough inside to see anything further ahead. For a few moments I'm held in suspension, the damp air of ages past combining with the darkness to place a velvet barrier behind me, blocking the exit back to my own time.

But the experience is only momentary, because here, round a corner, is humming life: punters, friends, colleagues, sound system, video screens, a bar. The inner recesses of the vault have been converted into a performance space, and tonight it has been commandeered by Julian House and Jim Jupp, the two Englishmen behind the small boutique record label called Ghost Box. It began around 2004 as a small-scale, special-interest operation, and remains fairly obscure, but its cult appeal and following has certainly been acknowledged in magazine articles and newspapers and on national radio. Between them, House and Jupp make music under several aliases, including The Focus Group, Belbury Poly and Eric Zann, an unsettling amalgam of woozy audio samples. The fused worlds their imaginations inhabit are beautifully encapsulated in the witty title of a Focus Group CD: *We Are All Pan's People*. Tonight they are appearing in three dimensions, in a series of music performances and screenings from the Ghost Box video vault. And as I look up at the screen, I feel like I am being transported in time again, this time to the televisual world of my early childhood.

Everyone here, it seems, is a connoisseur of the uncanny. I wind up having a conversation near a cinema-sized screen on which is projected the 1973 television version of M. R. James's eerie tale *Lost Hearts*, part of an old BBC series of Christmas ghost stories. A leering child-spirit emerges into another boy's nightmare, strumming a hurdy-gurdy and grinning horrifically at his young observer alter ego, who is held transfixed in a waking dream before emitting a bloodcurdling scream. As the weird tinkling strains of the hurdy-gurdy trickle out of the sound system, the person I'm speaking to breaks off in mid-sentence and says, 'That's my ringtone.'

DJs are playing a continuous mix of the kind of music favoured by the Ghost Box team: a strange brew of samples from sources that, in themselves, rarely seem fashionable: cocktail jazz drums and marimbas; voice snippets from daytime TV or low-budget Hammer movies; analogue synthesizer burbles straight off an Open University physics lecture or wildlife documentary; the shimmering, abrasive textures of ramshackle musique concrète; snatches of Vernon Elliott's whimsical, folksy incidental music for Oliver Postgate animations such as *The Clangers* and *Pogle's Wood*; and naturally, *The Wicker Man* soundtrack. In the opening decade of the twenty-first century, there are a surprisingly large number of musicians, working underground, churning out similarly haunting and disquieting sonic fictions that chime with the notion of an alternative Albion: The Advisory Circle, Broadcast, The Caretaker, The Focus Group, Moon Wiring Club, Mordant Music, Mount Vernon Arts Lab . . . There's even a shadowy collective calling themselves English Heretic who undertake psychogeographic walks to install 'black plaques' at sites of occult significance, such as the grave of *Witchfinder General* director Michael Reeves.

From these sonic elements, the DJs are spinning an impromptu soundtrack to cult 1970s TV such as *Children of the Stones*, *The Stone Tape* and *Penda's Fen*. There's also a loop tape of short public-information films, which regularly cropped up in TV schedules between the 1960s and early 1980s. Viewed in retrospect, they offer a surreally exaggerated warning of potential domestic dangers or road hazards. A hooded, Bergman-esque Death stalks a group of children playing around a riverbank strewn with rusting junk; pylons loom over happy kite-flyers, threatening high-voltage electrocution; vintage Austins cheat tractor death on improbably empty country lanes. And I also spot old favourites of my own: 1970s adverts for the Countryside Commission, highlighting their trails of acorn-shaped waymarks painted on tree trunks and stiles to encourage the population to get out more and ramble away the weekends. Trackways are pounded by knapsack-toting hikers; then, to illustrate the deep heritage value of the countryside, we see the ghosts of a milkmaid and a cloaked minstrel materialising and fading away on the same paths. 'So you've seen them, too!' whispers Arthur Machen in my ear.

This entire subterranean experience tied in with a book I was reading at the time: *A Dream of Wessex*, by Christopher Priest. Published in 1977, it offers an unusual take on the time-travel genre. It's 1987, and a group are participating in a government-sanctioned experiment with time known as the Wessex Projection. The forty or so participants are pulled in and out of a hypnotic state in which, collectively, they visualise an imaginary Britain of 150 years in the future, the purpose being to understand how to fix the problems of the present day. While they are inside the projection, their bodies are held in suspended animation in a vault underneath the prehistoric remains of Maiden Castle in Dorset, the ancient earthwork and fortress that inspired John Ireland to compose his orchestral *Mai-Dun*. All the action in the projection takes place around the town of Dorchester, which, following an earthquake that separated the south-west of England from the mainland, is now one of the largest tourist destinations in the world, a Cannes-style resort on the island of Wessex. The USA has become an Islamic nation, and Britain has been annexed by the Soviet Union. But little of value has been gleaned from the experiment, and the projection has simply become a virtual reality in which the participants live out comfortable second lives in a perfect world of constant sunshine and surf. When another reality begins to pollute the consensual hallucination, the destabilisation effect flips the novel into an elegant lament for the mellower mores of the 1960s. Maiden Castle is the one anchor, a symbol of historical continuity and endurance, and the gateway through which the characters must be lured in order to disconnect from the projection and return to their own time.

While the Shunt Vault is nothing like as old as Maiden Castle, this event was also an experiment in consensual hallucination, and I felt the power of music to act as a portal between time zones. For anyone born between roughly 1965–75, these images have the quality of folk memories. Television and recorded music were our oral culture. The images and sounds that Ghost Box recombine have an effect at some primal level, and being exposed to them in these airtight conditions gave me an inkling of why. It's because they make Britain look good, and interesting, and mysterious and adventuresome. They show the countryside just before the worst effects of suburbanisation, agribusiness and gridlocked traffic took hold. But why is all this so emotionally affecting? It's because it's a country and an age that have now disappeared, but its aural and visual traces make us realise, too late, that we were once actually living there ourselves. The sense of loss creates pangs at some instinctual level; the only way to cancel it is to project into the collective hallucination, the dream of Electric Eden.

This book began with a consideration of the recurrence of the secret garden in British culture: the gate that swings open to reveal a time-locked pastoral haven. Latterly, the garden has become a joyously unruly tangle of exotic blooms, knotted roots and murky corners, overgrown to such an extent that it's hardly recognisable from the carefully planted bower of a century ago. What music fits these lost domains? Of all the musical accompaniments which spring to mind, the most immediate is a record called *From Gardens Where We Feel Secure*, made in 1983 by Virginia Astley. It doesn't 'go anywhere': it's a balmy, ambient suite of Delius-like piano and chamber-music vignettes that creates a timeless, hovering sensation. Church bells toll, garden birds twitter incessantly: it rolls on like an unending summer afternoon. Furtive music hiding in the shrubbery.

Birdsong and swishing waves became the benchmark sonic

signifiers of ambient electronica in the early 1990s, which evolved in the chill-out rooms of Acid House clubs. They are all over tracks like 'Loving You' and 'Little Fluffy Clouds' by The Orb, aka Dr Alex Paterson and Jimmy Cauty, who specialised in 'endless sound continuums'. Typically, they would fade out the drum machines and let amorphous synthesizer washes, pastoral sound effects and disembodied voice samples take over. With the guest appearance of former Gong guitarist Steve Hillage and his partner Miquette Giraudy, and the Photoshopped image of Battersea Power Station on the sleeve of their first album, there were connections being knitted here with the progressive pastoralia of the early 1970s. Hillage's sequence of solo space-rock LPs culminated in 1979's abstract guitar meditation *Rainbow Dome Musick*. With its gurgling water noises, languid whalesong and cryogenic synthesizers, *Rainbow Dome Musick*'s track 'Garden of Paradise' was a favourite DJ tool in Paterson's Monday night chill-out lounges at rave club Land of Oz, at London's Heaven, and a model for The Orb's ever-pulsating musical brainfood, which imported the sound of ascending larks and meadow-sweet ambience into inner-city techno Babylon.

During the 1980s Paterson had worked for EG Records, custodians of the music of Brian Eno – whose *On Land* (1982) is another would-be musical backdrop to the secret garden. This final release in his influential *Ambient* series was explicitly linked to a spirit of place, with synthesizer and treated-tape pieces evoking darkling presences and windswept moors. 'Lantern Marsh', 'Unfamiliar Wind (Leeks Hills)' and 'Dunwich Beach, Autumn, 1960' are all place names whisked from Eno's East Anglian childhood. '*On Land* is quite a disturbed landscape,' Eno commented. 'You get the pastoral prettiness on top, but underneath there's a dissonance that's like an impending earthquake.'[1]

Dissonance . . . the creaking gate. Thinking about music as a portal, I started to hear the creak in all sorts of unlikely places.

In the weird, uncanny beats of Boards of Canada, enigmatic Scottish brothers whose swimming, aqueous collage of hip-hop beats, disconcerting yelps of children's voices and obsession with numerology were honed at outdoor parties in the Pentland Hills. These were psychedelic barbecues: revellers cavorting round a blazing bonfire to backwards tapes and disorientating time-stretched samples blaring from a sound system strung up in the trees. Now they worked in geographical isolation, south of Edinburgh, not so far from where The Incredible String Band set up camp at Lord Glenconner's Glen Row estate. Their early music is a strong precursor of the Ghost Box aesthetic, with its BBC Radiophonic Workshop-style synth stings and stabs that triggered both rustic, youthful innocence and subliminal menace. Another portal revealed itself in certain tracks by Boards' labelmate Richard D. James, aka Aphex Twin, whose Cornish upbringing seeps through track titles like 'Cornish Acid', 'Redruthmix', 'Logan Rock Witch' (Logan Rock is a prominent feature of Cornwall's craggy, Arthurian coastline), 'Mt Saint Michel + Saint Michaels Mount'. I even found myself hearing, in the limestone crunch of the craggier end of Aphex's output – for instance his *Selected Ambient Works II* (1995) – a greatly magnified detail from Richard Thompson's Fairport-era electric guitar: the rattle of pickups and the humming glow of amplifier valves. And it was James's channelling of abstract, ambient Avalon that director Gideon Koppel picked up on when choosing Aphex Twin to soundtrack his film *Sleep Furiously* (2008), an elegiac, often transcendent portrait of a remote rural community in Wales. It was music out of time, for a place similarly far removed from urban time, where old farming ways and natural harmony are shown to prevail.

The common treasury of folk music, too, is undergoing transformations, in a wider context of 'world music' in which the indigenous music of individual nations has been fused with pop sensibilities and contemporary production values. The folk scene exhibits less of the old purism about roots and tradition. Violinist and singer Eliza Carthy, daughter of Martin Carthy and Norma Waterson, for instance, began dropping programmed drums and electronics into her music as far back as 1987, on *Red Rice*. While *Anglicana* and *Rough Music*, released on Topic, displayed a closer affinity with 'the tradition', Carthy was marketed as a crossover artist and her own songs fell squarely into a metrosexual confessional bracket. In 2007 Carthy was a key contributor to *The Imagined Village*, an album constructed by Afro Celt Sound System producer Simon Emmerson. The Imagined Village was also the name of the loose collective who contributed to the folk fusions across the record: Sheila Chandra with The Young Coppers; Paul Weller with Martin and Eliza Carthy; Billy Bragg; Tiger Moth; Transglobal Underground; and younger folk ensembles The Gloworms and Tunng. Taking the title from Georgina Boyes's revisionist history of the Victorian and Edwardian folk collectors, this was the tradition digitised, like Shakespeare in modern dress. Ballads and rural folk songs like 'John Barleycorn', 'The Welcome Sailor' and 'Cold Haily Rainy Night' were reclothed as trip-hop and organic electronica in a process of gentle sonic revisionism. The most ambitious track was Benjamin Zephaniah's retelling of 'Tam Lyn', with the supernatural love story transposed to a city nightclub of pimps and lowlife. Marketed as 'updating the tradition for a new generation', and with a sleeve facsimile of a hand-painted eighteenth-century tile showing a police officer inspecting a burnt-out car, *The Imagined Village* was never quite prepared to disclose whether it believed the English folk lineage was dead or alive.

In any case, the parameters of 'folk culture' in Britain are quietly being redrawn. Artist Jeremy Deller, who won the Turner Prize in 2004, curates an ongoing Folk Archive, a steadily amassing collection of photographs and artefacts which celebrate the creative life of Britain, showing the kind of spontaneous artwork, craftsmanship, and recently invented traditions that emerge at ground level. These include scarecrows, local parades, protest placards and leaflets, speaker stacks at Notting Hill Carnival, anti-McDonald's badges, novelty garden designs, customised lorry cabs, prison art, flower arrangements and painted food signs at seaside snack bars. The Folk Archive embraces a people's culture, rather than one prescribed by metropolitan taste-makers.

The Imagined Village is typical of the regular attempts to resuscitate British folk as an institution, to announce a new beginning for the music. But such grand claims and big budgets never quite seem to hit the mark. The musical underground had been tuning in to the reverberations of earlier folk revivals for a good while before that. In the diaspora from the industrial scene of the late 1970s, centred around the shamanic experimental music of Throbbing Gristle and PsychicTV, artists such as Current 93, Sol Invictus and Death in June pursued diverse interests in paganism, Gnosticism and alternative religions, European occultism and altered consciousness, via a genre dubbed 'neofolk', in which electronics and concrete music were augmented with acoustic and medieval instruments, drones and lyrics verging on the apocalyptic. The profile of Shirley Collins, who had remained out of the public eye since the late 1970s, was dramatically raised by the energies of Current 93's David Tibet, who issued a compilation CD of her music, *Fountain of Snow*, on his Durtro label in 1992. Tibet subsequently rehabilitated singer Bill Fay by putting out unreleased material from the mid-1970s, and Mellow Candle's Clodagh Simonds, now in ambient drone outfit Fovea Hex, became another Current 93 collaborator.

As for Tibet's own musical journey with Current 93, around the time of 1992's *Thunder Perfect Mind* his industrial rock swerved towards the earlier folk-rock age, in a plangent swirl of acoustic guitars, recorders, dulcimers and harps. Recorded at London's Topic studio, it featured a spoken introduction by Shirley Collins.

Current 93 has become a blanket name for an ever-changing stable of Tibet's friends and collaborators, including Nurse with Wound's Steven Stapleton, guitarist Michael Cashmore, Trembling Bells' Alex Neilson, Crass's Steve Ignorant, Tony Wakeford and Rose McDowall, and American artists such as Will Oldham, Ben Chasny and Baby Dee. Successive albums such as *Of Ruine or Some Blazing Starre* (1994), *The Inmost Light* trilogy (1995–6) and *Black Ships Ate the Sky* (2006) have chronicled obsessions with outsider artists, writers and painters (Thomas Ligotti, Louis Wain, Austin Osman Spare), the haunted writings of Arthur Machen and M. R. James, ancient European mythology and Buddhism. Tibet has framed his music as an ongoing exploration of mystical and Gnostic Christianity, in registers ranging from the whimsical to the apocalyptic, using The Incredible String Band and Comus as his musical models.[2]

In 1994 Martyn Bates, singer with post-punk group Eyeless in Gaza, embarked on an exploration of the Francis Child collection with *Murder Ballads (Drift)*. His sonic ferryman was Mick Harris, the former drummer with thrash-metal group Napalm Death, who had converted to a more introspective dark ambient approach in the early 1990s. A few years later, Bates teamed up with sound sculptor and improviser Max Eastley. Three decades before, Eastley had been a guitar-toting folkie and cohort of Donovan and John Renbourn on their visits to Devon and Cornwall; now he constructed delicate environmental artworks in wood, running water and wind. Bates blasts out the magical and transformational ballads, unaccompanied save for Harris's or Eastley's murmuring, menacing ribbons of electronic noise.

The granite bleakness and solemnity of murder ballads also lie behind the music of the much younger Scottish singer Alasdair Roberts. His songs hitch the solemnity and bleakness of tragic traditional songs to a visionary poetic diction that recalls Blake, Ted Hughes or David Jones, occasionally rising to bitter jeremiads worthy of a ranting Old Testament prophet. These sinister overtones were the factors most sought after by early-twenty-first-century practitioners of folk – and their audiences. A micro-genre of esoteric folk, resolutely underground in scale and economics, featured artists like Sharron Kraus and Andrew King, and groups with names like Alphane Moon, The Anvil, The Family Elan, Far Black Furlong, Hamilton Yarns, Nalle, Our Glassie Azoth, The Owl Service, Pantaleimon (led by David Tibet's wife Andria Degens), Plough Myth International, Pumajaw, Stormcrow, The Straw Bear Band, The Story (an acoustic duo featuring Forest's Martin Welham and his son Tom), Tinkerscuss and Trembling Bells, all sallying into the wildwood with dronal, rustic 'dark Britannica' and viewing the tradition through the retrospective prism of films like *The Wicker Man*.

Arising from the remains of Psychic TV and playing a major role in the post-industrial underground, Coil (John Balance and Peter Christopherson) devoted their creative lives to exploring the outer limits of the psychedelic experience, guided by a visionary and occult tradition that extended from the magus John Dee through William Blake to the magick legacy of Aleister Crowley and the subversive practices of William Burroughs. Much of their early output was an uncategorisable electronic music explicitly enriched by LSD use, but for the five years leading up to the death of Balance in 2004 (a drunken fall at his home in Weston-Super-Mare), their music was becoming more spacious, incorporating marimba, hurdy-gurdy and electric viola, as well as an array of analogue synthesizers and digital waveforms. Like Julian Cope – whose band member Thighpaulsandra they shared – they embraced the lunar influence and a pagan awareness of the processes of nature.

They ushered in this final phase with *Time Machines* (1998), four oscillating, buzzing analogue drones, to be listened to under the influence of psychotropic drugs, with the purpose of dissolving time. In the same year Coil embarked on a series of singles featuring pieces recorded at the exact moments of the spring and autumn equinox and the summer and winter solstice. Around the turn of the millennium they produced two volumes entitled *Musick to Play in the Dark*, in which, according to Balance, 'Coil are creating lunar consciousness musick for the foreseeable future . . . We are letting in things we shut out before. The feminine. The tidal. The cyclical.'[3] And the nocturnal. 'Broccoli', on Volume One of *Musick to Play in the Dark*, is sparse and slow, with rumbling sub-bass tones, deep as the grave, tendrils of electric piano and granular digital clicks resembling the fading embers of a smouldering fire. With its strange vocal performance by Peter Christopherson, like a disembodied voice from a pockmarked wax cylinder, here Coil acted as digital outlaws in intimate communion with a dead ancestor. '*Wise words from the departing*,' intones Christopherson, invoking the advice recalled from a deceased father, '*eat your greens – especially broccoli*.' Broccoli's fractal florets and high concentration of healing phytochemicals make it one of the most potent vegetables on the greengrocer's rack, and in herbal lore it is associated with the new moon. Coil's deceptively prosaic parental admonishments are transmuted into a trance-inducing mantra that commingle organic and digital, life and death, in an extraordinary, hypnotic nine-minute sonic spell.

Hack a path through the briars and push open the gate. The creak is a music that wakes the dead and gives them permission to keep haunting us.

Concealed behind these overgrown thickets of memory lies a patch of ground. Some call it Eden, others Arcadia; there have been many other names for dreamed-of places that offer a better world. We have glimpsed them, time and again, in this survey of the music of the British Isles. In doing so, we've seen the map of British music redrawn: away from the urban network of conventional history. The Malvern Hills, the mountains of Wales, the Yorkshire Dales, rural Scotland, villages in Essex, Kent, Sussex and Cornwall: this is a music that has come from the hinterlands, whether indigenously or from city people who have relocated to the country in pursuit of the myth of the natural life. Ever since the Enlightenment, and even to an extent prior to that, this superimposition of the biblical/Miltonic Paradise onto the golden age of the ancient Greeks has been a necessary survival mechanism for British culture – mental insulation against the changes wrought by industrial and agricultural revolution; against the huge losses of two world wars; against the sensation of loss and destruction of home. In these terms, an innate conservatism dwells deep in the soul of this music. And yet, as we've seen, many of its composers, agitators, innovators and stars have been radical spirits, aligned with the political left or just fundamentally unconventional and progressive in outlook. Politically, Britons don't 'do' great leaps forward, are uncomfortable with the idea of a year zero. In the context of eco-politics, an actual return to pre-Enlightenment agrarianism – the world of *The Changes* – can only lead to an unthinkable, brutish world in which the fittest survive and rule the weak. But on an allegorical level, to *think*, at least, in these terms is becoming the necessary response to the excesses of global capitalism, to the effects of trans-national corporatism, and to environmental disaster. To lose sight of the dream is to lose all hope for a better future.

Those who populate the British Isles are all, to some degree, of mixed race: the results of millennia of successive waves of immigration and foreign occupation, all slowly compacted into sedimental layers of accumulated culture, language and nationhood that has been known as many things, most recently 'British'. There's a strength in these tree rings. The process simply continues, following several generations of post-colonial immigration, and with economic migration across Europe's borders. That makes it impossible to predict what, exactly, Britain will be in the future and, more relevant to this book, how its music will continue to channel all the buried dreams, imaginative advances and desired utopias harboured in its people. Folk music derives its power from its connection with universals – the cyclic revolve of the seasons and the ritual year – and from archetypes that can be discovered and reinterpreted again and again across many of the world's legends. As populations and cities expand and the wilderness dwindles, to preserve the sense of enchantment with British landscape that is hard-wired into the national psyche it will become even more important to screen out modernity, to not quite see what's actually there, but to distort it through the antiquarian eye and the mental scrying glass.

But now it's time to ship oars, for the day is growing dim. Tie up at this bankside, or we shall be swept out to sea. Listen – there's the music, telling us we are coming home.

Notes

Quotes are taken from interviews with the author, unless indicated.

Prelude *The Silver Chain*

1 William Blake, 'A Vision of the Last Judgment', in *A Descriptive Catalogue of Pictures, Poetical and Historical Inventions* (London: D. N. Shury, 1809). Collected in Geoffrey Keynes (ed.), *Blake: Complete Writings* (Oxford: Oxford University Press, 1989).

2 Quoted in Robin Denselow, 'Folk-Rock in Britain', in Karl Dallas/Robin Denselow/Dave Laing/Robert Shelton, *The Electric Muse: The Story of Folk into Rock* (London: Methuen, 1975).

1 *The Inward Exodus*

1 Andrew Loog Oldham, *Stoned* (London: Secker & Warburg, 2000).

2 Derek Johnson, '"I'm Not a Rebel Anymore", Says Donovan', in *Hit Parader* (May 1967).

3 Johnson, '"I'm Not a Rebel Anymore"'.

4 The Romantic poet John Clare ended a period of incarceration at a mental asylum in Essex, and set out to walk northwards to his old village home in Helpston, Northamptonshire, in search of his (deceased) childhood sweetheart – essentially, a walk towards self-renewal.

5 Alfred Watkins, *The Old Straight Track* (London: Abacus, 1974/1925).

6 Robin Denselow, 'Picking Up the East', concert review, *Observer* (8 October 1967).

7 Robin Denselow, 'Round the U-Bend', *Guardian* (6 April 1970).

8 Denselow, 'Round the U-Bend'.

9 Quoted in Mary McCartney (prod.), *Wingspan* documentary (EMI DVD, 2001).

10 *Wingspan* DVD.

11 *Wingspan* DVD.

12 'Iris' refers to the fact that the words were written by Iris Mcfarlane, an English writer who was looking after Vashti's horse on Uist.

2 *An Orgy on the Green*

1 Ralph Vaughan Williams, 'English Folk Songs', lecture (10 January 1912), quoted

Notes

in Ursula Vaughan Williams, *A Biography of Ralph Vaughan Williams* (London: Oxford University Press, 1964).

2 Originally published as *News from Nowhere or An Epoch of Rest, Being Some Chapters from a Utopian Romance*, serialised in thirty-nine instalments in *Commonweal* (11 January–4 October 1890).

3 William Morris, 'Makeshift' (paper delivered 18 November 1894).

4 David Leopold, Introduction to William Morris, *News from Nowhere* (Oxford: Oxford World's Classics/OUP, 2003).

5 The phrase is spoken by Guest in *News from Nowhere*, Chapter XVI.

6 The 'poor man's heaven' in which all material needs are supplied in abundance without the need for labour to produce it. Versions have been recorded in European song, poetry and folk tales since at least the fourteenth century. See, for instance, A. L. Morton, *The English Utopia* (London: Lawrence & Wishart, 1952).

7 Octavia Hill, 'Colour, Space, and Music for the People', lecture subsequently published in the journal *Nineteenth Century*, vol. 15 (1884).

8 William Morris, 'Art and Socialism' (1884). Lecture collected in A. L. Morton (ed.), *William Morris: The Political Writings* (London: Lawrence & Wishart, 1984).

9 Gustav Holst, 'England & Her Music', lecture notes in Ursula Vaughan Williams and Imogen Holst (eds.), *Heirs and Rebels: Letters Written to Each Other and Occasional Writings on Music by Ralph Vaughan Williams and Gustav Holst* (Oxford: Oxford University Press, 1959).

10 Carl Engel, *An Introduction to the Study of National Music* (London: Longmans, Green, Reader & Dyer, 1866).

11 Oscar A. H. Schmitz, *Das Land Ohne Musik: Englische Gesellschaftsprobleme* (Munich: Georg Müller, 1914, my translation). The book is an extended character assassination of the English, covering attitudes and manners, artistic and cultural differences, imperialist arrogance and a perceived ignorance of other cultures (especially of Germany). He concludes that a fatal, unresolved mixture of Protestant individualism and Catholic formality means 'the English lack the Promethean drive ['*prometheushafte Schwung*'] of the German spirit'. Schmitz (1873–1931) was a prolific journalist and writer who travelled extensively around Europe, the British Isles, Russia and North Africa. He was a close friend of decadent writer Alfred Kubin, and a student of alternative culture and the occult, as well as the writings of Carl Jung. He is best remembered in his native land for his book *Haschisch* (1902), a study of fantastical literature with emphasis on eroticism, satanism, sadism, alternative religions, death cults and narcotics.

12 Gustav Holst, undated (1903) letter to Ralph Vaughan Williams in Vaughan Williams and Holst (eds.), *Heirs and Rebels*.

13 Peter Warlock, *Frederick Delius* (London: The Bodley Head, 1923).

14 Warlock, *Frederick Delius*.

15 Warlock, *Frederick Delius*.

Notes

16 Maud Karpeles, *Cecil Sharp: His Life and Work* (London: Routledge & Kegan Paul, 1967).

17 See, for instance, Dave Harker, *Fakesong: The Manufacture of British 'Folksong' 1700 to the Present Day* (Milton Keynes: Open University Press, 1985); and Georgina Boyes, *The Imagined Village: Culture, Ideology and the English Folk Revival* (Manchester: Manchester University Press, 1993).

18 Lucy Broadwood's uncle, John, had already published a collection of songs from the Sussex Weald in 1847, and following his lead, she began collecting songs from local people in the 1880s. Later, she was among the first collectors to use recording technology to gather her raw material, lugging wax-cylinder recorders around the lanes and village greens.

19 Cecil Sharp, *English Folk-Song: Some Conclusions* (London: Methuen, 1907).

20 Sharp, *English Folk-Song*.

21 Sharp, *English Folk-Song*. Compare Sharp's sentiments with Morris's future vision in *News from Nowhere*: 'Reformers would . . . revive the social life of the villages. Do what they will, however, it will not be the old life that they will restore. That has gone past recall. It will be of a new order, and one that will bear but little resemblance to the old social life of the "Merrie England" of history.'

22 Sharp, *English Folk-Song*.

23 Sharp, *English Folk-Song*.

24 Sharp, *English Folk-Song*.

25 Sharp, *English Folk-Song*.

26 Sharp, *English Folk-Song*.

27 The Grainger collection of wax-cylinder recordings is now archived by the EFDSS at Cecil Sharp House.

28 Published by Leonard & Co., 1890 (London) (originally private edition, 1847).

29 'Are We a Musical Nation?' in Ralph Vaughan Williams, *National Music and Other Essays* (London: Oxford University Press, 1963).

30 Vaughan Williams, 'The Influence of Folk-Song on the Music of the Church', in *National Music*.

31 Although Whitman was an American writer, Vaughan Williams adopted his visionary free verse as an honorary member of an English tradition that explored eternity, death and nature, in a line that included Blake, Keats and Swinburne. It's worth noting that Elgar had much poorer taste in poetry, setting worthy but dull poets like Cardinal Newman, Laurence Binyon and Arthur O'Shaughnessy.

32 Peter Ackroyd, 'English Music', in *Albion: The Origins of the English Imagination* (London: Chatto & Windus, 2002).

33 Vaughan Williams, 'The History of Nationalism in Music' in *National Music*.

34 Vaughan Williams rejected the king's offer of a knighthood in the early 1930s, though he did accept an Order of Merit in 1935 and was handed an Honorary Doctorate at Bristol University by Sir Winston Churchill in 1951.

35 Quoted in Ackroyd, 'English Music'.

36 The cheerful, rotund vagabond, a larger-than-life embodiment of 'Merrie England', was also a favourite of Vaughan Williams and Delius: the way Falstaff cleaved close to the king but ultimately was an outsider to the circles of power seemed to strike a chord with musicians at this time.

37 Imogen Holst, *Gustav Holst: A Biography* (London: Oxford University Press, 1969/1938).

38 Gustav Holst, 'The Mystic, the Philistine and the Artist', lecture published in *The Quest* (1920), reprinted in I. Holst, *Gustav Holst: A Biography*.

39 Letter to William Whittaker (1914), quoted in Paul Holmes, *Holst: His Life and Times* (London: Omnibus Press, 1997).

40 Letter to R. Vaughan Williams (March 1919), in Vaughan Williams and Holst (eds.), *Heirs and Rebels*.

41 In conjunction with Clifford Bax and his friend, the theosophist G. R. S. Mead.

42 Gustav Holst, 'The Mystic, the Philistine and the Artist'.

43 Quoted in Imogen Holst, *The Great Composers: Holst* (London: Faber and Faber, 1974).

44 I. Holst, *Gustav Holst: A Biography*.

45 Letter to Vally Lasker (1924), quoted in I. Holst, *Gustav Holst: A Biography*.

46 Letter to William Whittaker (1914).

47 Ivor Gurney, 'A Song of Pain and Beauty' (1917), in Gurney (ed. P. J. Kavanagh), *Collected Poems* (London: Fyfield Books, 2004).

48 Thomas Hardy, 'Channel Firing' (April 1914), in *Selected Poems* (London: Penguin, 1998).

3 *The Island Spell*

1 W. B. Yeats, *The Celtic Twilight* (London: A. H. Bullen, 1902/1893).

2 Yeats, *The Celtic Twilight*.

3 Arnold Bax, preface to *Nympholept* MS (London: Warner Chappell, 1912).

4 Bax occasionally inscribed the Irish struggle into the fabric of his music: the 1920 *Rhapsody for Viola and Orchestra* quotes the tune of 'A Soldier's Tale', the hymn of the Irish Republican Army.

5 Lewis Foreman, *Bax: A Composer and His Times* (Woodbridge: Boydell Press, 2007/1983).

6 A typical suburban 'Tudorbethan' house in north London's Muswell Hill, called Fairport, belonged to the family of Simon Nicol and gave his group Fairport Convention its name. *Mock Tudor* was also the title of a 1999 solo album by Richard Thompson, one of Fairport's founding members.

7 Quoted in Michael Hurd, *Rutland Boughton and the Glastonbury Festivals* (Oxford: Clarendon Press, 1993).

8 Hurd, *Rutland Boughton and the Glastonbury Festivals*.

9 Dion Fortune, *Glastonbury: Avalon of the Heart* (Newburyport, MA: Red Wheel/ Weiser, 2003/1934).

10 Muriel Searle, *John Ireland: The Man and His Music* (Tunbridge Wells: Midas Books, 1979).

11 John Ireland, letter to Clifford Curzon (undated). Quoted in Fiona Richards, *The Music of John Ireland* (Aldershot: Ashgate, 2000).

12 Arthur Machen, *The White People and Other Stories* (Hayward, CA: Chaosium, 2008/1904).

13 John Ireland, letter to Kenneth Thompson (23 January 1946). Quoted in Richards, *The Music of John Ireland*.

14 Ireland abandoned the island just before the German army began its occupation in 1940.

15 The Sussex Weald, which Ireland had visited regularly since the 1930s, was at the same time the base of a number of important figures in British occult history. At its centre was 'The Sanctuary', a secret community set up near the village of Washington in 1923 by Vera Pragnell, a Christian socialist influenced by the nature mysticism of Edward Carpenter. In 1931 Harry 'Dion' Byngham, a key figure in the Order of Woodcraft Chivalry, which believed in a 'Trinity' of Pan, Artemis and Dionysus, moved to Storrington, near the Chanctonbury Ring. Byngham's friend, the poet and clairvoyant Victor Neuburg, moved to nearby Steyning shortly afterwards. An associate of Aleister Crowley, in 1910 Neuburg had written *The Triumph of Pan*, a collection of ecstatic poems celebrating the god as a gay icon. Several ballads in his *Lillygay* (1920) were set to music by Peter Warlock. And his poem 'The Druids' was set on Chanctonbury Ring, a site which one occult historian has claimed as the site of the oldest pagan witch coven in Britain (Doreen Valiente, *Where Witchcraft Lives* (London: Aquarian, 1962)). John Ireland must surely have been aware of these presences, although unfortunately I have been unable to find evidence of any meetings between them.

16 Quoted in Barry Smith, *Peter Warlock: The Life of Philip Heseltine* (Oxford: Oxford University Press, 1996).

17 Smith, *Peter Warlock*.

18 Smith, *Peter Warlock*.

19 Smith, *Peter Warlock*.

20 In a curious parallel to Warlock and Moeran's rowdy tenure at Eynsford, on the other side of the country in North Devon the village of Georgeham had been intruded upon by another outside artistic presence. Novelist Henry Williamson moved to a cottage there in 1921 and proceeded to outrage local decency with a string of louche girlfriends, naked swimming displays, throwing apples at neighbouring farmers, dressing like a proto-hippy in loose clothing and bare feet. Best known as author of the children's book *Tarka the Otter*, Williamson's many books, including his fifteen-volume fictionalised memoir *A Chronicle of Ancient*

Sunlight, testify to a quasi-mystical relationship with nature and the English landscape, while his reputation was later severely tarnished because of his vocal support of the Hitler Youth and Oswald Mosley's British fascist movement. His son Harry, born in 1950, was destined to become an associate of hippy progressive rockers Gong in the early 1970s, and was part of the collective that organised the earliest free festivals at Stonehenge (see Chapter 16). Already, in the unconventional lifestyle choices of the likes of Warlock, Moeran and Williamson, the pre-echoes of a later British counter-cultural pattern are faintly detectable.

21 As a precursor to the 'real ale' image of folk fans of the 1970s and 1980s, Warlock was a beer connoisseur who campaigned for the drink to be kept free of unwanted chemicals.

22 Lionel Hill, *Lonely Waters: The Diary of a Friendship with E. J. Moeran* (London: Thames, 1985).

23 Geoffrey Self, *The Music of E. J. Moeran* (London: Toccata Press, 1986).

24 Hubert Foss, '"Peter Warlock" (Philip Heseltine)', in A. L. Bacharach (ed.), *British Music of Our Time* (London: Pelican, 1946).

25 Stanley Baldwin, *On England and Other Addresses* (London: Philip Allan, 1926).

26 Constant Lambert, *Music Ho!: A Study of Music in Decline* (London: Faber and Faber, 1934).

4 The Iron Muse

1 Maud Karpeles (1885–1976) was Cecil Sharp's amanuensis and ever-loyal apologist. She accompanied him on his collecting odyssey through the Appalachian mountains in 1916–17 and eventually wrote Sharp's biography in 1967. Her sister Helen was born in 1887, married Douglas Kennedy in 1914, and gave birth to Peter Kennedy in 1922.

2 The harshest critics of Sharp, particularly Georgina Boyes in *The Imagined Village*, castigate him for profiting from his activities, although they offer few alternative suggestions as to how revenue might be distributed. The question remains as to what claim even the source singers might have to any financial rewards according to this ideology. If singers are harbouring a piece that is 'common property', it is unclear why they should have any more right to profit from it than a collector. That would be the equivalent of a journalist paying an interviewee or source: a noble sentiment, but unworkable in practice. It is amusing to note the number of researchers happily working up such critiques while sitting in the Ralph Vaughan Williams Memorial Library at Cecil Sharp House, in facilities founded upon Sharp's entrepreneurism.

3 A. L. Lloyd, *Folk Song in England* (London: Panther, 1967).

4 John Grierson (ed. Forsyth Hardy), *Grierson on Documentary* (Berkeley, CA: University of California Press, 1966).

Notes

5 'The Moviegoer' (aka John Grierson), review of *Moana*, *New York Sun* (8 February 1926), quoted in *Sight & Sound*, vol. 17/9 (September 2007).

6 John Grierson, 'First Principles of Documentary', in *Cinema Quarterly*, vol. 1 (1932), reprinted in Kevin Macdonald and Mark Cousins (eds.), *Imagining Reality: The Faber Book of Documentary* (London: Faber and Faber, 1996).

7 In the 1990s it gave its name to a young Scottish electronic music duo – Boards of Canada – themselves profoundly affected by the curious hyperreality of its imagery and soundtracks (see Chapter 19).

8 Edgar Anstey (dir.), *West Country Journey* (Transport Commission, 1953). Collected on *See Britain by Train: The British Transport Films Collection, Volume Two* (BFI DVD, 2005).

9 Benjamin Britten, 'England and the Folk-Art Problem', in *Modern Music*, vol. 18 (January–February 1941).

10 Ewan MacColl, *Journeyman: An Autobiography* (London: Sidgwick & Jackson, 1990).

11 Phil Tanner (1862–1950), a farm labourer from the Gower Peninsula in Wales, was 'discovered' singing at a holiday camp in 1932 and first recorded by Maud Karpeles during his first visit to London in 1937. He sang 'The Banks of the Sweet Primroses', 'Henry Martin', 'Gower Reel' and 'Gower Wassail', issued as two 78 rpm discs on Columbia.

12 In Max Jones (ed.), *Folk: Review of a People's Music* (London: Jazz Music Books, 1945).

13 Interviewed on Mike Connolly (dir.), *Folk Britannia* (BBC Four, 2006).

14 David Attenborough produced several BBC folk-music programmes in this period, which accounts for his subsequent move into the nature programming for which he became world famous. While Peter Kennedy was posted to the Bristol branch of the BBC, he helped to develop a parabolic recording device to capture his folk singers, which became standard kit for the BBC's sound recordists on the Natural History Unit, based in Bristol. For a while the folk-recording and natural-history departments were merged, and the corporation's record label was issuing LPs of both local dialects and birdsong.

15 Published as Cecil Sharp (ed. Maud Karpeles), *English Folk Songs from the Southern Appalachians, Collected by Cecil J. Sharp; Comprising Two Hundred and Seventy-Four Songs and Ballads with Nine Hundred and Sixty-Eight Tunes, Including Thirty-Nine Tunes Contributed by Olive Dame Campbell* (Oxford: Oxford University Press, 1932).

16 Sharp, diary entry (19 August 1916), published in *Ballad Hunting in the Appalachians* (private pamphlet, undated).

17 Sharp felt contempt for Americanised music, describing John Lomax's book *Cowboy Songs and Other Frontier Ballads* as 'a volume which contains nothing but the dregs of literature and the garbage of musical phrase'. Sharp, letter to Mrs Storrow (6 December 1916). Correspondence held at Cecil Sharp House.

18 Now known as Smithsonian Folkways, the label released more than 2,000 albums of traditional, ethnic and documentary recordings before its acquisition by the Smithsonian Institution in 1986, the year of Moses Asch's death.

19 Alan Lomax, 'Saga of a Folksong Hunter', in A. Lomax (ed. R. D. Cohen), *Selected Writings 1934–1997* (New York: Routledge, 2003).

20 Lomax, 'Saga of a Folksong Hunter'.

21 Lomax, 'Saga of a Folksong Hunter'.

22 Alan Lomax, 'Skiffle: Why Is It So Popular? And Where Is It Going?', in *Selected Writings*.

23 Ewan MacColl (ed.), Preface to *The Shuttle and Cage: Industrial Folk-Ballads* (London: Workers' Music Association, 1954).

24 MacColl, *Journeyman*.

25 MacColl, *Journeyman*.

26 Ewan MacColl, promotional article for *Ballads and Blues* (BBC Written Records Archive, 1953).

27 MacColl, *Journeyman*.

28 MacColl's domestic arrangements were convoluted. He divorced Joan Littlewood in 1948 and married Jean Newlove in 1949, with whom he had a son, Hamish, in 1950. Neill MacColl was born to Peggy Seeger in March 1959; Newlove gave birth to Kirsty in October 1959. Seeger bore two more children (in 1962 and 1972); MacColl and Seeger did not actually marry until 1977 (his marriage to Newlove was not annulled until 1974).

29 MacColl, *Journeyman*.

30 MacColl, *Journeyman*.

31 In 2006 the BBC commissioned a new batch of six radio ballads, which, in the spirit of the originals, dealt with contemporary issues: HIV/AIDS sufferers, the pro- and anti-hunting lobbies, sectarian conflict in Northern Ireland, the declining steel and shipyard industries. If they did not stand out so sharply from the rest of the BBC's factual output, it was precisely because their dense narrative frieze of voices, noises and music, which the original series achieved by trial and error, had become standard practice.

32 MacColl, *Journeyman*.

5 Songs for Swingin' Survivors

1 Ray Horricks, sleeve note to *Folk, Blues and Beyond* (Decca LP, 1965).

2 Pete Seeger, sleeve note to *Nonesuch and Other Folk Tunes* (Folkways LP, 1959). This album, credited to Seeger and Frank Hamilton, was a collection of relaxed, informal renditions of folk musics from around the globe.

3 'Bob Dylan's Dream' and 'Girl from the North Country' appeared on *The Freewheelin' Bob Dylan* (Columbia LP, 1963).

4 *Madhouse on Castle Street* was broadcast as part of the BBC's Sunday Play series

on 13 January 1963. The telerecording was incinerated in 1968 and no copies
have been located. Much of the information was gleaned from a BBC *Arena*
documentary, *Dylan in the Madhouse* (BBC Four, 2007).

5 The enterprise was initiated in response to Resolution 42 passed by the
Trades Union Congress in 1960, vowing to combat the vulgarisation of mass
entertainment in the UK, which had corrupted 'classical and folk art in the name
of entertainment'. The project's musical directors were Ewan MacColl and A. L.
Lloyd. The nomadic caravan of jazz bands and folk musicians, actors, poets and
film screenings settled in different cities for a week at a time. Centre 42 was the
last significant union of music and mainstream politics until the late-1970s Rock
Against Racism festivals, and was an ideological precursor of Red Wedge in the
1980s. See Clive Barker, 'Report and Recommendations on the Policy of Centre
42' (CPA1/8/7/1, 1961); and (e.g.) Colin Harper, *Dazzling Stranger: Bert Jansch
and the British Folk and Blues Revival* (London: Bloomsbury, 2000).

6 Among the small coterie of people on this scene was Maxwell Helier-Eastley,
one of the nation's legions of young-men-with-guitars, who, as Max Eastley,
would transform into an environmental sound sculptor and instrument builder,
working with writer David Toop on *New and Rediscovered Musical Instruments*, for
Brian Eno's Obscure label (1975). In the late 1990s he revisited his folk roots
(see Chapter 19).

7 Pete Frame, 'Mick Softley', in *Zigzag* 1 (April 1971).

8 Frame, 'Mick Softley'.

9 The three records he made for CBS between 1970–2, *Sunrise*, *Street Singer*
and *Any Mother Doesn't Grumble*, assembled a crack squad of folk-rock
players: Barry Clark of Trees; Jerry Donahue, Pat Donaldson and Gerry
Conway of Sandy Denny's group Fotheringay; and Lyn Dobson, playing reed
instruments and sitar. On *Sunrise*, 'Time Machine' marries images of elfin
romps with suggestions of reincarnation. 'Ship' describes an evolutionary
ladder of transport, from a ship and train to a jet plane and a ship of the star-
cruising variety, each item delicately illustrated with evocative musical sound
effects, including a futuristic synthesizer and tremolo guitar as the spaceship
approaches Jupiter and Alpha Centauri (a mode of astro-pop already familiar
from David Bowie's hit of the year before, 'Space Oddity'). Softley floated
through a succession of groups and projects during the late 1960s and early
70s – including a hard-rock unit with Mac MacLeod called Soft Cloud and
an experimental outfit called the St Albans Spontaneous Music Ensemble
– and was briefly on the books of Ladbroke Grove promoters Clearwater
Productions. After a final album in 1976, *Capital*, where he returned to acoustic
guitar for a selection of powerfully cogent songs, Softley moved to Northern
Ireland and ceased all contact with the music industry.

10 MacLeod was initially invited to be part of a group Donovan was putting

together to tour the United States, and it was this crowd – MacLeod, his girlfriend Stella and her daughter, singer/poet Julian McAllister and long-time collaborator Rod Yallop, together with Mick Softley and his two children – who headed off to Donovan's Scottish island empire on Skye in the late summer of 1969 – the community Vashti Bunyan was also intending to join up with after her own peregrinations across Britain.

6 *Variations on a Theme of Albion*

1 A. L. Lloyd, sleeve notes to The Watersons' *Frost and Fire* (Topic LP, 1965).

2 A fourth volume, representing the fourth element, was released much later (Revenant CD, 2000).

3 Harry Smith kept up his activities until the end of his long life in 1991, the year the *Anthology* received a long-overdue Grammy award, having been openly acknowledged as a crucial influence by everyone from Bob Dylan to Patti Smith. At the award ceremony the frail, trembling Smith declared from the stage, 'I'm glad to say my dreams came true. I saw America changed through music.' Whether that change was for the better or worse, he gnomically declined to elaborate.

4 See G. B. Chambers, *Folksong-Plainsong* (London: Methuen, 1972).

5 Bob Stewart, *Where Is Saint George?: Pagan Imagery in English Folksong* (London: Blandford Press, 1977).

6 Bob Copper, *A Song for Every Season* (Newton Abbott: Country Book Club, 1972).

7 Copper, *A Song for Every Season*.

8 Lloyd, sleeve notes to *Frost and Fire*.

9 The 'Lyke Wake Dirge' has proved enduring. Benjamin Britten wrote it into his *Serenade for Tenor, Horn and Strings* (1943), a compilation of visionary spiritual texts; American folk singer Buffy Sainte-Marie rendered it on her *Fire & Fleet & Candlelight* (1967, the title taken from a line in the dirge). Pentangle included it on their *Basket of Light* album (1969), and in 1972 Steeleye Span performed it on tour as part of their 'mummers' play' (see Chapter 17).

10 Kipling lived in Rottingdean, Sussex, at the peak of his fame between 1897 and 1901 – the period in which some of his most famous writings were published, including *Captains Courageous* (1897), *Stalky & Co.* (1899), *Kim* (1901) and the *Just So Stories* (1902). Though there's no documentary record, it's tempting to imagine that Kipling heard the singing of the first-generation Copper family at Rottingdean around this time, which informed the cadences of the songs and verses included in these books.

11 Meirion Bowen, untitled review, in *Early Music* (January 1971).

12 Alan Blyth, David Munrow interview, in *Gramophone* (May 1974).

13 Christopher Bishop, David Munrow obituary, in *Gramophone* (July 1976).

14 Bishop, Munrow obituary.
15 Mike Barnes, 'Spirit of Eden', in *The Wire* 219 (May 2002).

7 Air

1 The Jo Lustig anecdote appears in Graham Hood, *Empty Pocket Blues: The Life and Music of Clive Palmer* (London: Helter Skelter, 2008). The musician in question was Steve Bonnett, guitarist at the time with Ralph McTell's group.
2 Graham Fuller (ed.), *Loach on Loach* (London: Faber and Faber, 1998).
3 Quoted in Lorne Murdoch, 'Mellow Yellow: The Mickie Most Years Part 2', sleeve notes to *Mellow Yellow* reissue (EMI CD, 2005).
4 The album also features the future drummer for Sandy Denny and Fairport Convention, Gerry Conway, and the songwriting duo David and Jonathan, whose first group in the early 1960s happened to be called The Kestrels.
5 Keshav Sathe subsequently played tabla on several notable folk crossover records, including Jan (Hendin) and Lorraine (LeFevre)'s *Gypsy People* (1969, including Terry Cox on percussion), Magic Carpet's *Magic Carpet* (1972), John Martyn's *Inside Out* (1973) and, as a member of the John Renbourn Band during the late 1970s, *A Maid in Bedlam* (1977) and *The Enchanted Garden* (1980).
6 Quoted in Happy Traum, 'Van Morrison in Conversation', in *Rolling Stone* (9 July 1970).
7 Ian MacDonald, 'Wild Mercury: A Tale of Two Dylans', in *The People's Music* (London: Pimlico, 2003).
8 Karl Dallas, 'Folk, Pop and the Electric Aesthetic', in Laing/Dallas/Denselow/Shelton, *The Electric Muse: The Story of Folk into Rock* (London: Methuen, 1975). The McLuhan quote is unsourced in the original.
9 A. L. Lloyd, *Folk Song in England* (London: Panther, 1967).
10 C. J. Bearman, 'Cecil Sharp in Somerset: Some Reflections on the Work of David Harker', in *Folklore*, vol. 113 (2002).

8 Earth

1 It has been suggested that Harvey Bramham was a heavy drug user and that he may have been taking part in a 'van race' between competing roadies, a common form of boredom relief – initiated by The Who's resident nutter Keith Moon – in the small hours on that particular stretch of motorway. See Alan Dawson, *Life on the Road: The Incredible Rock 'n' Roll Adventures of 'Dinky' Dawson* (New York: Billboard Books, 1999).
2 Ian MacDonald, 'The Band's *Music from Big Pink*', in *The People's Music* (London: Pimlico, 2003).
3 David Wells, sleeve notes to *Hark! The Village Wait* reissue (Castle/Sanctuary CD, 2005).

4 Brian Hinton and Geoff Wall, *Ashley Hutchings: The Guv'nor and the Rise of Folk Rock* (London: Helter Skelter Publishing, 2002).

5 Hinton and Wall, *Ashley Hutchings*.

9 *Orpheus in the Undergrowth*

1 County borders have since shifted, and Aston Tirrold is currently in Oxfordshire.

2 David Dalton, 'Traffic at Berkshire Cottage: Just Playing Together Was a Fantasy', in *Rolling Stone* (3 May 1969).

3 Dalton, 'Traffic at Berkshire Cottage'.

4 Dalton, 'Traffic at Berkshire Cottage'.

5 Luis Milán, *Libro de Música de Vihuela de Mano Intitulado 'El Maestro'* (Valencia: Francisco Díaz Romano, 1536).

6 Interview with Jane Ormsby-Gore in '1960s Fashion Interviews', on Victoria & Albert Museum website (vam.ac.uk, 2006).

7 Trevor Dann, *Darker Than the Deepest Sea: The Search for Nick Drake* (New York: Da Capo, 2006).

8 Dann, *Darker Than the Deepest Sea*.

9 Quoted in *Lost Boy: In Search of Nick Drake* (BBC Radio 2, 1998).

10 Robert Kirby's reputation soared after his engagements with Drake, and he went on to join The Strawbs in the mid-1970s, as well as providing arrangements for Ralph McTell, John Cale, Elton John, Shelagh McDonald and Vashti Bunyan, among many others, right through to Elvis Costello and Paul Weller in the 1980s.

11 Richard Howell, 'John Martyn Keeping Everything a Lot Less Rigid', in *Time Out* (1 October 1971).

12 Dann, *Darker Than the Deepest Sea*.

13 Nick Kent, 'Nick Drake: Requiem for a Solitary Man', in *New Musical Express* (8 February 1975).

14 Nick Kent, 'John Martyn: The Exorcism', in *New Musical Express* (29 November 1980).

10 *Water*

1 Jerry Gilbert, 'Sandy Denny in the Talk-In', in *Sounds* (8 September 1973).

2 Bruce Rowland and Dave Pegg both give versions of this story in Clinton Heylin, *No More Sad Refrains: The Life and Times of Sandy Denny* (London: Helter Skelter, 2000).

3 Quoted in Heylin, *No More Sad Refrains*.

4 Andy Childs, 'Talking with John Martyn', in *Zigzag* 41 (April/May 1974).

5 Richard Howell, 'John Martyn Keeping Everything a Lot Less Rigid', in *Time Out* (1 October 1971).

6 Howell, 'John Martyn Keeping Everything . . .'.

7 Howell, 'John Martyn Keeping Everything . . .'.

8 Childs, 'Talking with . . .'.

9 Andy Childs, 'A Happy Man', in *Supersnazz*, vol. 2 (October 1973).

10 Ian MacDonald, 'The Stormbringer Comes into the Sun', in *New Musical Express* (21 July 1973).

11 Some John Stevens Dance Orchestra recordings from 1979, featuring John Martyn alongside British improvisers Paul Rutherford, Lol Coxhill, Trevor Watts, Elton Dean, Robert Calvert and others, surfaced on *A Luta Continua* (Konnex CD, 1994).

11 *Fire*

1 Marshall McLuhan, *Understanding Media: The Extensions of Man* (Cambridge, MA: MIT Press, 1994/1964).

2 Wilfrid Mellers, review of The Incredible String Band's *Wee Tam and The Big Huge*, in *New Statesman* (17 January 1969).

3 William Blake, *The French Revolution* (1791).

4 Quoted in Ken Hunt, interview with Robin Williamson in *Swing* 51 (1979).

5 Quoted in *Retying the Knot* (BBC, 1997).

6 Hunt, *Swing* 51.

7 Joe Boyd, *White Bicycles: Making Music in the 1960s* (London: Serpent's Tail, 2005).

8 Robin Williamson, *Mirrorman's Sequences* in Tony Cohan and Gordon Beam (eds.), *Outlaw Visions* (Venice, CA: Acrobat Books, 1977). See also Robin Williamson, *Mirrorman's Sequences 1961–1966* Pig's Whisker Music spoken-word CD, 1997).

9 Quoted in Adrian Whittaker (ed.), *beGLAD: An Incredible String Band Compendium* (London: Helter Skelter, 2003).

10 Lewis Carroll, *Alice's Adventures in Wonderland* (London: Puffin, 1948/1865).

11 Ed Baxter, 'The Primer: British Folk-Rock', in *The Wire* 202 (December 2000).

12 Hunt, *Swing* 51.

13 Quoted in Peter Ackroyd, *Blake* (London: Minerva, 1996).

14 1968 *Disc* magazine interview, quoted in Hunt, *Swing* 51.

15 The front and back covers of *The Hangman's Beautiful Daughter* were switched on subsequent reissues.

16 Hunt, *Swing* 51.

17 Hunt, *Swing* 51.

18 Steve Turner, 'Incredible String Band', in *Beat Instrumental* (March 1971).

19 Turner, 'Incredible String Band'.

20 Unnamed writer, 'Talisman of the Beyond', review of The Incredible String Band at Boston Tea Party, Jordan Hall, 30 November 1968, in *Time Magazine* (13 December 1968).

21 Michael Gray, review of The Incredible String Band at York University, in *Rolling Stone* (9 August 1969).

Notes

22 Happy Traum (ed.), *The Incredible String Band Songbook* (London: Music Sales Corporation, 1968).

23 Joe Boyd, *White Bicycles*.

24 Hunt, *Swing* 51.

25 At the time of writing, it appeared that a Christina McKechnie, previously Lambert, was residing at an address in California. On balance, it seems likely that Licorice is still alive, although tact and respect for her privacy means that door has been left shut.

26 William Blake, *Descriptive Catalogue* . . . (1809). The extract forms part of a commentary on a painting, since vanished, called *The Ancient Britons*.

12 A Collection of Antiques and Curios

1 Shaffer's quote is taken from *The Wicker Man Enigma*, a documentary included in *The Wicker Man Special Edition* (Warner Home Video DVD, 2002).

2 Quoted in Stephen McKay, 'The Owl Service: The Legend Unravelled', sleeve notes to *The Owl Service* Granada TV adaptation, 1969 (Network DVD, 2008).

3 Edward Thomas, *The Daily Chronicle* (14 January 1913). Quoted in Raymond Williams, *The Country and the City* (London: Paladin, 1973).

4 Quoted in Grahame Hood, *Empty Pocket Blues: The Life and Music of Clive Palmer* (London: Helter Skelter, 2008).

5 Clive Palmer quoted in uncredited interview in *Moyshe McStiff and the Tartan Lancers of the Sacred Heart* reissue (Sunbeam CD, 2006).

6 The album's worth of material cut at the Tivoli was finally released as Sandy & The Strawbs, *All Our Own Work* (Pickwick LP, 1973).

7 Quoted in John Tobler, sleeve notes to *From the Witchwood* reissue (A&M CD, 1998).

8 Quoted in Stewart Lee, sleeve notes to *On the Shore* reissue (Sony/BMG CD, 2007).

9 Mat Snow, Robert Plant interview, *Q* (December 1990).

10 A key reference for Marcus Keef's photography would be the desperate Little Englanders of Richard Lester's post-nuclear film *The Bed-Sitting Room* (BFI DVD, 2009). The sole survivors of a nuclear blast search for usable teacups in the rubble of post-apocalyptic London and squabble about who's nearest in line to the throne. Released in 1969, it would be surprising if its mood and bleak cinematography did not directly inspire Keef's graphic vision. Lester's cinematographer was David Watkin, a former cameraman on the evocative 1950s and 60s British Transport Films, and Lester's colleague on *A Hard Day's Night*, *Help!* and the John Lennon vehicle *How I Won the War*. In 1969 he had just come off the set of Tony Richardson's *The Charge of the Light Brigade*, for which he tracked down an antique Ross lens, originally used to shoot Victorian postcards around 1850.

11 John Higgins, review of *Akenfield*, *The Times* (9 October 1974).

12 Unknown reviewer, *Cinema TV Today* (1 February 1975).

13 All descriptions of *The Wicker Man* in this chapter refer to Robin Hardy's ninety-nine-minute director's cut, which appeared on DVD in 2002 and restored fifteen minutes of missing material from the version that was on UK theatrical release in 1973. The sequence featuring Sgt Howie's exchanges with his fellow police officers did not appear in the early version.

14 The gods are named in Christopher Lee's speech as 'Nuada' and 'Avellenau'. In fact, Nuada is not the pagan sun god: Shaffer appears to have mistakenly cited Nuada Airgeitlám, a mythological king figure from Irish legend. The orchard goddess Avellenau has been lifted from a poem about Myrrdin (Merlin) in the *Afallenau*, part of *The Red Book of Hergest*, a late-fourteenth-century Welsh manuscript that also includes the text of the *Mabinogion*.

13 *We Put Our Magick on You*

1 *Blood on Satan's Claw* was released in the USA under the alternative title *Satan's Skin*.

2 The Arthur Grant-influenced cinematographer on *Witchfinder General* and *Blood on Satan's Claw*, John Coquillon, went on to work with Sam Peckinpah on *Straw Dogs*, the tense rape thriller set in a Cornish village, and the dusty, brutal Americana of *Pat Garrett and Billy the Kid*.

3 A. L. Lloyd, sleeve notes to *The Foggy Dew and Other Traditional English Love Songs* (Tradition Records LP, 1956).

4 For an exhaustive analysis of Lloyd's relationship with 'Reynardine', see Stephen D. Winick, 'A. L. Lloyd and Reynardine: Authenticity and Authorship in the Afterlife of a British Broadside Ballad', in *Folklore* (December 2004).

5 The magazine existed for only four issues, all published during 1959.

6 Bob Pegg, *Folk: A Portrait of English Traditional Music, Musicians and Customs* (London: Wildwood House, 1976).

7 Pegg, *Folk*.

8 Appropriately enough, since Bush's career-breaking single five years later, 'Wuthering Heights', is set in wild Brontë country, straight out of Mr Fox's desolate Yorkshire Dales.

9 Quoted in Fred Woods, Bob Pegg interview in *Folk Review* (April 1973).

10 Quoted in David Wells, sleeve notes to Bob Pegg, *Keeper of the Fire Anthology* (Castle/Sanctuary CD, 2006).

11 William Shakespeare, *As You Like It*, Act 4, Scene ii (1599/1600).

12 Charles G. Leland, *Aradia or the Gospel of the Witches* (London: David Nutt, 1899). Leland, an American folklorist, surveyed the rituals and beliefs of what he claimed was a surviving pagan cult in Tuscany. The book was a central tenet of Gardnerian Wicca in the 1950s.

13 For the record, Toni Arthur has no recollection of these particular events, nor of a German film crew.

14 Alex Sanders released an album under his name, *A Witch Is Born* (on A&M Records, home to The Strawbs, among others), which contained a recording of Sanders and Maxine leading a girl called Janet Owen through three successive degrees of initiation into their coven. Sanders's sense of theatre was compounded by his dramatic appearance on the LP sleeve, grimacing like a balding Vincent Price next to a floating ankh. In 1970 he acted as 'consultant' to Leicester-based progressive-rock group Black Widow, dabblers in occult trappings whose stage act included the simulated sacrifice of a naked woman. Their somewhat overwrought track 'Come to the Sabbat', from *Sacrifice* (CBS LP, 1970), purportedly bears traces of Sanders's hand.

14 *The Million-Volt Circus*

1 Michael Horowitz and Cynthia Palmer (eds.), *Moksha: Aldous Huxley's Classic Writings on Psychedelics and the Visionary Experience* (Rochester, VT: Park Street Press, 1999).

2 'Science Has Alice-in-Wonderland Drug', in *News Chronicle* (17 June 1954).

3 'Mrs Brown Comes out of the Shadows', in *Sunday Mercury* (23 August 1954).

4 R. A. Sandison, A. M. Spencer and J. D. A. Whitelaw, 'The Therapeutic Value of Lysergic Acid Diethylamide in Mental Illness', in *Journal of Mental Science*, vol. 100 (1954).

5 Ian MacDonald, *Revolution in the Head: The Beatles' Music and the Sixties* (London: Pimlico, 1997).

6 David Sheff, interview with John Lennon and Yoko Ono, in *Playboy* (January 1981).

7 Barry Miles, *Pink Floyd: The Early Years* (London: Omnibus Press, 2006).

8 Mick Farren, *Give the Anarchist a Cigarette* (London: Jonathan Cape, 2001).

9 Farren, *Give the Anarchist a Cigarette*.

10 Mark Paytress, *Bolan: The Rise and Fall of a 20th Century Superstar* (London: Omnibus Press, 2002).

11 John Peel, *The Perfumed Garden*, Radio London (16 July 1967).

12 John Peel, *The Perfumed Garden*, Radio London (24 July 1967).

13 Queen Elizabeth Hall, London (13 January 1969).

14 Quoted in Paytress, *Bolan*.

15 Quoted in Brian Hinton, 'Weighing Up the Mighty Baby', in *Ptolemaic Terrascope* (September 1995).

16 Luca Ferrari, sleeve note to Third Ear Band, *The Dragon Wakes* (unissued CD). Text published on ghettoraga.blogspot.com.

Notes

15 Paradise Enclosed

1 Geoffrey Ashe, *King Arthur's Avalon: The Story of Glastonbury* (London: Fontana, 1973/1957).

2 To get a sense of the scale of the influx on the island, the official recorded population figure for the Isle of Wight in 2007 (thirty-seven years after the event) was 138,000.

3 Gerrard Winstanley (ed. Christopher Hill), *The Law of Freedom and Other Writings* (Harmondsworth: Pelican Classics, 1973).

4 Unnamed writer, 'Define Your Terms, Young Man! A Short Glossary of Hip Terminology . . .' in *Gandalf's Garden*, vol. 6 (1971).

5 Oliver Goldsmith's poem *The Deserted Village* (1770) is one of the most enduring laments for the dispersal of the rural labouring class.

6 Section 1, Countryside Act (1968).

7 Jeremy Sandford and Ron Reid, *Tomorrow's People* (London: Jerome Publishing Company, 1974). The book is full of quotes from musicians, members of the public and festival promoters, none of them credited.

8 Farren, *Give the Anarchist a Cigarette*.

9 The project was taken over and completed by historian Martin Gilbert.

10 Christopher Booker, *The Neophiliacs: A Study of the Revolution in English Life in the Fifties and Sixties* (London: Collins, 1969).

11 Arabella Churchill, 'A Churchill Girl Says No to NATO', letter in *Rolling Stone* (1 April 1971).

12 Ronald Hutton, *Pagan Religions of the Ancient British Isles: Their Nature and Legacy* (London: Blackwell, 1995).

13 Andrew Kerr, 'Andrew Kerr explains the ideology that lay behind the setting up of Glastonbury', leaflet reproduced on ukrockfestivals.com (undated).

14 Sandford and Reid, *Tomorrow's People*.

15 Geoffrey Ashe, 'Glastonbury: Key to the Future', in *Gandalf's Garden*, vol. 4 (1969).

16 The feature-length film was eventually released two years later, in 1973.

17 Farren, *Give the Anarchist a Cigarette*.

18 John Peel, *Sounds* (21 May 1977).

19 Penny Rimbaud, 'The Last of the Hippies – An Hysterical Romance', in *A Series of Shock Slogans and Mindless Token Tantrums* (Exitstencil Press, 1982), a book of essays included with Crass, *Christ – The Album* (Crass Records LP, 1982).

20 'Garden of Eden with Guitars', *The Times* (13 August 1974).

16 The End of the Rainbow

1 William Blake, *The Marriage of Heaven and Hell*, in Geoffrey Keynes (ed.), *Blake: Complete Writings* (Oxford: Oxford University Press, 1989).

2 The bugler's real name was Martin Lanfried.

Notes

3 Kingsley Abbott quoted in Brian Hinton and Geoff Wall, *Ashley Hutchings: The Guv'nor and the Rise of Folk Rock* (London: Helter Skelter, 2003).

4 Roy Shipston, interview with Richard Thompson in *Disc & Music Echo* (22 August 1970).

5 Patrick Humphries, *Richard Thompson, Strange Affair: The Biography* (London: Virgin Books, 1996).

6 Quoted in Hinton and Wall, *Ashley Hutchings*.

7 Bob Woffinden, 'Richard & Linda Thompson: Life Without Fairport', in *New Musical Express* (15 June 1974).

8 Mat Snow, 'The Minstrel's Tale', in *Q* (December 1988).

9 Snow, 'The Minstrel's Tale'.

10 Humphries, *Richard Thompson, Strange Affair*.

11 'Questions & Answers' on Beesweb (richardthompson-music.com, 29 June 2006).

12 Clinton Heylin, *No More Sad Refrains: The Life and Times of Sandy Denny* (London: Helter Skelter, 2000).

13 Jerry Gilbert, 'Sandy Denny in the Talk-In', in *Sounds* (8 September 1973).

14 Quoted in Robin Denselow, 'Folk-Rock in Britain', in *The Electric Muse: The Story of Folk into Rock* (London: Methuen, 1975).

15 The Wurzels' version was a yokel take on Melanie's 'Brand New Key', a hit for the female singer in 1971.

16 In the late 1970s the barn was sold to a member of bombastic rock group Lone Star, who opened up a studio which was used, among others, by Hawkwind. The farm was later purchased by Steve Howe of Yes.

17 Although his 1978 attempt to adapt Lewis Carroll's *Jabberwocky* was a flop, director Terry Gilliam would later revisit the Grail/quest genre far more winningly in *Time Bandits* (1981) and *The Fisher King* (1991).

18 Steve Lafreniere, Linda Thompson interview, in *Index* 37 (February 2003).

19 Richard Aldington, *Life for Life's Sake: A Book of Reminiscences* (New York: Viking, 1941).

17 Rocket Cottage

1 Essay published in *Musical Quarterly*, vol. 8 (July 1922).

2 Bob Woffinden, 'Universalisation of Steeleye Span', in *New Musical Express* (13 November 1976).

3 Woffinden, 'Universalisation of Steeleye Span'.

4 In *Themroc*, Michel Piccoli flips out of his monotonous day job and smashes his apartment to smithereens, converting it to a twentieth-century cave dwelling, indulging in Stone Age grunts, cannibalism and incest with his mother and sister. Even a policeman gets dragged into the feral frolics.

5 Peter Clarke, *Hope and Glory: Britain 1900–2000* (London: Penguin, 1996).

18 *Gone to Earth*

1 Peter Hennessy, *Whitehall* (London: Fontana Press, 1990).

2 Keith MacMillan, formerly known as (Marcus) Keef, became a prolific music-video director between 1978 and the mid-1980s, working with Paul McCartney and Wings, XTC, Pat Benatar and others. He subsequently founded and produced the ITV programme *The Chart Show*, a pioneering format in which videos were shown with no presenter, and digital information flashed up at the bottom of the screen.

3 Quoted in Don Watson, 'Blonde on Blonde', in *New Musical Express* (23 August 1986).

4 Watson, 'Blonde on Blonde'.

5 Quoted in Jim Irvin, 'Talk Talk', in *Mojo* (April 2006).

6 Hollis speaking on promotional interview cassette for *Laughing Stock* (Verve, 1991).

7 Peter Ackroyd, *Albion: The Origins of the English Imagination* (London: Chatto & Windus, 2002).

8 *The Open Road: A Cinematic Postcard of Britain in the 1920s* (BFI DVD, 2008).

9 Julian Cope, *Head On: Memories of the Liverpool Punk Scene and the Story of The Teardrop Explodes (1976–82)* (London: Thorsons, 1994).

10 Julian Cope, *Repossessed: Shamanic Depressions in Tamworth & London (1983–89)* (London: Thorsons, 1999).

11 Julian Cope, *The Modern Antiquarian: A Pre-Millennial Odyssey through Megalithic Britain* (London: Thorsons, 1998).

12 Julian Cope, speech given at opening of Blake's Shadow: William Blake and his Artistic Legacy exhibition, Whitworth Art Gallery, Manchester (January 2008).

19 *Toward the Unknown Region*

1 Quoted in Don Watson, 'Man out of Time', in *Spin* (May 1989).

2 For a detailed account of Current 93's history and music, see David Keenan, *England's Hidden Reverse: A Secret History of the Esoteric Underground* (London: SAF Publishing, 2003).

3 Quoted in Rob Young, 'Worship the Glitch', in Rob Young (ed.), *Undercurrents: The Hidden Wiring of Modern Music* (London: Continuum, 2002).

Bibliography

Ackroyd, Peter, *Albion: The Origins of the English Imagination* (London: Chatto & Windus, 2002)

Bacharach, A. L. (ed.), *British Music of Our Time* (Harmondsworth: Pelican, 1946)

Bird, John, *Percy Grainger* (Oxford: Oxford University Press, 1999)

Blake, Andrew, *The Land Without Music: Music, Culture and Society in Twentieth-Century Britain* (Manchester: Manchester University Press, 1997)

Blythe, Ronald, *Akenfield: Portrait of an English Village* (Harmondsworth: Penguin, 1969)

Booker, Christopher, *The Neophiliacs: A Study of the Revolution in English Life in the Fifties and Sixties* (London: Fontana, 1970)

Boyd, Joe, *White Bicycles: Making Music in the 1960s* (London: Serpent's Tail, 2005)

Boyes, Georgina, *The Imagined Village: Culture, Ideology and the English Folk Revival* (Manchester: Manchester University Press, 1993)

Bunyan, John, *The Pilgrim's Progress* (Oxford: Oxford University Press, 2003 / 1678)

Carroll, Lewis, *Alice's Adventures in Wonderland* (London: Penguin Classics, 2003 / 1865)

Clarke, Peter, *Hope and Glory: Britain 1900–2000* (London: Penguin, 2004)

Collins, Shirley, *America Over the Water* (London: SAF Publishing, 2005)

Cope, Julian, *The Modern Antiquarian: A Pre-Millennial Odyssey through Megalithic Britain* (London: Thorsons, 1998)

Dallas, Karl / Denselow, Robin / Laing, Dave / Shelton, Robert, *The Electric Muse: The Story of Folk into Rock* (London: Methuen, 1975)

Dann, Trevor, *Darker Than the Deepest Sea* (New York: Da Capo, 2006)

Davis, Erik, *Led Zeppelin* ☙ 🜨 ♊ ⓘ (London: Continuum Books 33¹/₃, 2005)

Deller, Jeremy & Kane, Alan, *Folk Archive: Contemporary Popular Art from the UK* (London: Book Works, 2005)

Denselow, Robin, 'Born under a Bad Sign', in *When the Music's Over: The Story of Political Pop* (London: Faber and Faber, 1990)

Dickinson, Peter, *The Changes: A Trilogy* (New York: Dell, 1991 / 1970)

Dunaway, David King, *How Can I Keep from Singing: Pete Seeger* (London: Harrap, 1985)

Evans, George Ewart, *The Pattern under the Plough* (London: Faber and Faber, 1966)

Farren, Mick, *Give the Anarchist a Cigarette* (London: Jonathan Cape, 2001)

Ferrari, Luca, *Third Ear Band: Necromancers of the Drifting West* (Viterbo: Stampa Alternativa, 1997)

Bibliography

Foreman, Lewis, *Bax: A Composer and His Times* (Woodbridge: Boydell Press, 2007/1983)

Fowler, David, 'Rolf Gardiner, Cambridge and the Birth of Youth Culture between the Two World Wars', in *Youth Culture in Modern Britain, c. 1920–c. 1970* (London: Palgrave Macmillan, 2008)

Frazer, James, *The Golden Bough* (London: Penguin, 1996/1890)

Grahame, Kenneth, *Pagan Papers* (Teddington: Echo Library, 2006/1898)

—— *The Wind in the Willows* (London: Penguin Classics, 2005/1908)

Gregory, E. David, 'A. L. Lloyd and the English Folk Song Revival, 1934–44', in *Canadian Journal for Traditional Music* (1997)

—— 'Lomax in London: Alan Lomax, the BBC, and the Folk-Song Revival in England, 1950–58', in *Folk Music Journal*, vol. 8/2 (2002)

—— 'Starting Over: A. L. Lloyd and the Search for a New Folk Music, 1945–49', in *Canadian Journal for Traditional Music* (1999/2000)

Grigson, Geoffrey (ed.), *The Faber Book of Popular Verse* (London: Faber and Faber, 1971)

—— *The Penguin Book of Ballads* (Harmondsworth: Penguin, 1975)

Hamilton, Marybeth, *In Search of the Blues* (London: Jonathan Cape, 2007)

Harker, Ben, *Class Act: The Cultural and Political Life of Ewan MacColl* (London: Pluto Press, 2007)

Harker, Dave, *Fakesong: The Manufacture of British Folksong, 1700 to the Present Day* (Milton Keynes: Open University Press, 1985)

Harper, Colin, *Dazzling Stranger: Bert Jansch and the British Folk and Blues Revival* (London: Bloomsbury, 2006)

—— & Hodgett, Trevor, *Irish Folk, Trad & Blues: A Secret History* (London: Cherry Red Books, 2005)

Heylin, Clinton, *No More Sad Refrains: The Life and Times of Sandy Denny* (London: Helter Skelter, 2000)

Hinton, Brian & Wall, Geoff, *Ashley Hutchings: The Guv'nor and the Rise of Folk Rock* (London: Helter Skelter, 2002)

—— *Ashley Hutchings, Always Chasing Rainbows. The Authorised Biography Volume 2: 1974–1992* (Southampton: Stick It in Your Ear! Publications CD-Rom, 2007)

Hill, Lionel, *Lonely Waters: The Diary of a Friendship with E. J. Moeran* (London: Thames, 1985)

Hobsbawm, Eric, 'The Machine-Breakers', in *Uncommon People: Resistance, Rebellion and Jazz* (London: Weidenfeld & Nicholson, 1998)

Holmes, Paul, *Holst: Illustrated Lives of the Great Composers* (London: Omnibus Press, 1997)

—— *Vaughan Williams: Illustrated Lives of the Great Composers* (London: Omnibus Press, 1997)

Holst, Imogen, *Gustav Holst: A Biography* (London: Oxford University Press, 1969/1938)

Bibliography

Hood, Grahame, *Empty Pocket Blues: The Life and Music of Clive Palmer* (London: Helter Skelter, 2008)

Hoskins, W. G., *The Making of the English Landscape* (Harmondsworth: Penguin, 1985)

Housman, A. E., *Collected Poems* (Harmondsworth: Penguin, 1956)

Hughes, Meirion & Stradling, Robert, *The English Musical Renaissance 1840–1940: Constructing a National Music* (London: Routledge, 1993)

Humphries, Patrick, *Nick Drake: The Biography* (London: Bloomsbury, 1998)

— *Meet on the Ledge: Fairport Convention, the Classic Years* (London: Virgin Books, 1997)

— *Richard Thompson, Strange Affair: The Biography* (London: Virgin Books, 1997)

Hurd, Michael, *Rutland Boughton and the Glastonbury Festivals* (Oxford: Clarendon Press, 1993)

Hutton, Ronald, *The Druids* (London: Hambledon Continuum, 2007)

— *Stations of the Sun: A History of the Ritual Year in Britain* (Oxford: Oxford University Press, 2001)

— *The Triumph of the Moon: A History of Modern Pagan Witchcraft* (Oxford: Oxford University Press, 1999)

Jefferies, Richard, *After London, or Wild England* (London: Cassell & Co., 1886)

Keenan, David, *England's Hidden Reverse: A Secret History of the Esoteric Underground* (London: SAF Publishing, 2003)

Kennedy, Douglas, 'Policy, Programme and Practice', in *English Dance and Song*, vol. 9(4) (1945)

Kipling, Rudyard, *Puck of Pook's Hill* (London: Macmillan, 1937/1908)

Lee, C. P., *Like the Night: Bob Dylan and the Road to the Manchester Free Trade Hall* (London: Helter Skelter, 1998)

Lloyd, A. L., *Folk Song in England* (London: Panther, 1967)

Lomax, Alan (ed. Cohen, R. D.), *Selected Writings 1934–1997* (London: Routledge, 2003)

MacCarthy, Fiona, *William Morris: A Life for Our Time* (London: Faber and Faber, 1994)

MacColl, Ewan, *Journeyman: An Autobiography* (London: Sidgwick & Jackson, 1990)

MacDonald, Ian, *The People's Music* (London: Pimlico, 2003)

— *Revolution in the Head: The Beatles' Records and the Sixties* (London: Pimlico, 1997)

Machen, Arthur, *The Great God Pan and The Hill of Dreams* (Mineola, NY: Dover Publications, 2006/1916 & 1923)

McKay, George, *Glastonbury: A Very English Fair* (London: Victor Gollancz, 2000)

Matless, David, *Landscape and Englishness* (London: Reaktion Books, 1998)

Miles, Barry, *Paul McCartney: Many Years from Now* (London: Secker & Warburg, 1997)

— *Pink Floyd: The Early Years* (London: Omnibus Press, 2006)

Morris, William, *News from Nowhere* (Oxford: Oxford University Press, 2003/1890)

Morton, A. L., *The English Utopia* (London: Lawrence & Wishart, 1952)

Morton, H. V., *In Search of England* (London: Methuen, 1927)

— *I Saw Two Englands* (London: Methuen, 1941)

Bibliography

Morton Jack, Richard (ed.), *Galactic Ramble* (London: Foxcote Books, 2009)

Motion, Andrew, *The Lamberts: George, Constant and Kit* (London: Faber and Faber, 1986)

Munro, John Neil, *Some People Are Crazy: The John Martyn Story* (Edinburgh: Polygon/Birlinn, 2007)

Paytress, Mark, *Bolan: The Rise and Fall of a 20th Century Superstar* (London: Omnibus Press, 2002)

Pegg, Bob, *Folk* (London: Wildwood House, 1976)

— *Rites and Riots: Folk Customs of Britain and Europe* (Poole: Blandford Press, 1981)

Pirie, Peter J., *The English Musical Renaissance: Twentieth Century British Composers and Their Works* (London: Victor Gollancz, 1979)

Priest, Christopher, *A Dream of Wessex* (London: Faber and Faber, 1977)

Richards, Fiona, *The Music of John Ireland* (London: Ashgate, 2006)

Self, Geoffrey, *The Music of E. J. Moeran* (London: Toccata Press, 1986)

Sharp, Cecil, *English Folk-Song: Some Conclusions* (London: Methuen, 1907)

— & Karpeles, Maud, *Eighty English Folk Songs* (London: Faber and Faber, 1968)

Silkin, John (ed.), *The Penguin Book of First World War Poetry* (Harmondsworth: Penguin, 1981)

Smith, Barry, *Peter Warlock: The Life of Philip Heseltine* (Oxford: Oxford University Press, 1996)

Stewart, Bob, *Where Is Saint George? Pagan Imagery in English Folksong* (London: Blandford Press, 1977)

Vaughan Williams, Ralph, *National Music and Other Essays* (London: Oxford University Press, 1963)

— & Lloyd, A. L. (eds.), *The Penguin Book of English Folk Songs* (Harmondsworth: Penguin, 1959)

Vaughan Williams, Ursula, *RVW: A Biography of Ralph Vaughan Williams* (London: Oxford University Press, 1964)

Waite, A. E., *The Pictorial Key to the Tarot* (New York: Dover Books, 2005/1911)

Watkins, Alfred, *The Old Straight Track* (London: Abacus, 1974/1925)

Weston, Jessie, *From Ritual to Romance* (New York: Doubleday Anchor, 1957/1920)

Whittaker, Adrian (ed.), *beGLAD: An Incredible String Band Compendium* (London: Helter Skelter, 2003)

Wiener, Martin J., *English Culture and the Decline of the Industrial Spirit 1850–1980* (Cambridge: Cambridge University Press, 1981)

Williams, Raymond, *The Country and the City* (St Albans: Paladin, 1975)

Winstanley, Gerrard (ed. Christopher Hill), *The Law of Freedom and Other Writings* (Harmondsworth: Pelican, 1973)

Woods, Fred, *Folk Revival: The Rediscovery of a National Music* (Poole: Blandford Press, 1979)

Musical / Discographic Timeline

Arnold Bax, *A Celtic Song-Cycle*, voice & piano, words Fiona MacLeod (1904)
— *Cathaleen-na-Hoolihan* (1905)
— *Into the Twilight* (1908)
— *In the Faery Hills* (1909)
Frederick Delius, *A Mass of Life* (1904–5)
— *Brigg Fair: An English Rhapsody* (1907)
Edward Elgar, *The Dream of Gerontius*, oratorio (1900)
Gustav Holst, *A Somerset Rhapsody* (1907)
— *Savitri*, chamber opera (1908)
Roger Quilter, *Seven Elizabethan Lyrics*, voice & piano (1908)
Ralph Vaughan Williams, 'Linden Lea', voice & piano, words W. Barnes (1901)
— *In the Fen Country* (1904)
— *Norfolk Rhapsody No. 1* (1906, rev. 1914)
— *Toward the Unknown Region*, chorus & orchestra, words Walt Whitman (1906)
— *On Wenlock Edge*, voice, piano & string quartet, words A. E. Housman (1909)

Arnold Bax, *Rosc-catha* (1910)
— *Nympholept* (1912)
— *Piano Quintet in G minor* (1915)
— *Elegiac Trio*, flute, viola & harp (1916)
— *November Woods* (1917)
— *Tintagel* (1917, orch. 1919)
— *Folk-tale*, cello & piano (1918)
— *String Quartet No. 1* (1918)
Rutland Boughton, *The Birth of Arthur*, opera (1913)
— *The Immortal Hour*, opera (1914)
George Butterworth, *Two English Idylls* (1911)
— *A Shropshire Lad* (1912)
— *Bredon Hill and Other Songs*, voice & piano (1912)

— *The Banks of Green Willow* (1913)

Frederick Delius, *Summer Night on the River* (1911)

— *On Hearing the First Cuckoo in Spring* (1912)

Ivor Gurney, *Five Elizabethan Songs*, voice & piano (1913–14)

— 'Ha'nacker Mill', 'Sleep', 'The Cherry Trees', 'Orpheus', 'Under the Greenwood Tree', 'The Apple Orchard', 'All Night under the Moon', etc., song settings, words John Masefield, Edward Thomas, Wilfrid Gibson, W. B. Yeats, etc. (1913–37)

Gustav Holst, *Choral Hymns from the Rig Veda* (1908–12)

— *The Cloud Messenger* (1913)

— *The Planets Suite* (1916)

— *Six Choral Folk-Songs* (1916)

— *The Hymn of Jesus*, double chorus (1917)

John Ireland, *Decorations* ('The Island Spell', 'Moon-glade', 'Scarlet Ceremonies'), piano (1913)

— *The Forgotten Rite* (1917–18)

— *The Towing Path*, piano (1918)

Hubert Parry, 'Jerusalem', words William Blake (1916)

Ralph Vaughan Williams, *Fantasia on a Theme by Thomas Tallis* (1910, rev. 1913 & 1919)

— *Five Mystical Songs*, chorus, words George Herbert (1911)

— *Phantasy Quintet* (1912)

— *The Lark Ascending*, violin & orchestra (1914)

Peter Warlock, *Five Folk-Song Preludes*, piano (1918)

— *Corpus Christi Carol*, chorus (1919)

1920s

Granville Bantock, *The Great God Pan*, ballet (1920)

— *Pagan Symphony* (1927)

Arnold Bax, *Symphony No. 1* (1922)

— *Symphony No. 3* (1929)

Frederick Delius, *A Song of Summer* (1929–30)

Gerald Finzi, *By Footpath and Stile*, song set, words Thomas Hardy (1922)

— *Earth and Air and Rain*, song set, words Thomas Hardy (1928–32)

Gustav Holst, *Egdon Heath* (1927)

John Ireland, *The Land of Lost Content*, song cycle, words A. E. Housman (1920–1)

— *Mai-Dun* (1920–1)

E. J. Moeran, *String Quartet No. 1* (1921)

— *Rhapsody No. 1* (1922)

— *Two Legends* ('A Folk Story', 'Rune'), piano (1923)

— *Lonely Waters* (1924)

Roger Quilter, *Three Pastoral Songs*, song cycle, words Joseph Campbell (1921)

Musical / Discographic Timeline

Ralph Vaughan Williams, *A Pastoral Symphony (Symphony No. 3)* (1921)

—— *Shepherds of the Delectable Mountains* (1921)

—— *Sancta Civitas (The Holy City)* oratorio, words *Revelation of St John* (1923–5)

—— *Five Variants of 'Dives and Lazarus'* (1929)

Peter Warlock, *The Curlew*, voice & mixed sextet, words W. B. Yeats (1920–2)

—— *Serenade* (1921–2)

—— 'Adam Lay Ybounden', chorus (1922)

—— *Lillygay*, voice & piano (1922)

—— *Three Carols* ('Tyrley Tyrlow', 'Balulalow', 'The Sycamore Tree') (1923)

—— *Capriol Suite* (1926)

1930s

Arnold Bax, *The Tale the Pine-Trees Knew* (1931)

—— *Symphony No. 5* (1932)

—— *Symphony No. 6* (1935)

Gerald Finzi, *Dies Natalis*, cantata, words Thomas Traherne (1939)

—— *Before and After Summer*, voice & piano, words Thomas Hardy (1932–49)

Gustav Holst, *Hammersmith: Prelude and Scherzo* (1930)

John Ireland, *Legend*, piano & orchestra (1933)

—— *Concertino Pastorale* (1939)

E. J. Moeran, *Symphony in G Minor* (1937)

Paddy Ryan, 'The Man that Waters the Workers' Beer' / The Topic Singers and Band, 'The Internationale' (Topic 78 rpm, 1939)

Ralph Vaughan Williams, *Symphony No. 4* (1931–4)

—— *Fantasia on 'Greensleeves'* (1934)

—— *Five Tudor Portraits*, choral suite (1935)

1940s

Benjamin Britten, *Folk Song Arrangements* (1943–73)

John Ireland, *Sarnia: An Island Sequence* ('Le Catioroc', 'In a May Morning', 'Song of the Springtides'), piano (1940–1)

E. J. Moeran, *Violin Concerto* (1937–41)

—— *Sinfonietta* (1944)

—— *Cello Concerto* (1945)

Ralph Vaughan Williams, *Symphony No. 5* (1938–43)

—— *The People's Land*, film soundtrack (1943)

—— *Symphony No. 6* (1946–7)

1950s

Benjamin Britten, *Winter Words*, voice & piano, words Thomas Hardy (1954)

Musical / Discographic Timeline

Shirley Collins, *False True Lovers* (Topic 10", 1959)

Lonnie Donegan, 'Rock Island Line' (Decca 78 rpm, 1956)

Alan Lomax (compiler), *Columbia World Library of Folk and Primitive Music: Vol. 1 (England), Vol. 2 (Ireland), Vol. 3 (Scotland)* (Columbia, 1954, rec. 1951)

Ewan MacColl, 'The Asphalter's Song' / 'I'm Champion at Keepin' Em Rolling', etc. (Topic EP, 1950)

— with Al Jefferey, 'Dirty Old Town' (Topic EP, 1952)

— & Peggy Seeger, *The Shuttle and Cage* (Topic 10", 1957)

— & Peggy Seeger (feat. Steve Benbow), *Barrack Room Ballads* (Topic EP, 1958)

— & A. L. Lloyd (feat. Steve Benbow, Peggy Seeger, John Cole), *Bold Sportsmen All* (Topic 10", 1959)

Ewan MacColl / Charles Parker / Peggy Seeger, *The Ballad of John Axon*, radio ballad no. 1 (broadcast 1958; Argo, rel. 1965)

Chas McDevitt & Nancy Whiskey, 'Freight Train' (Oriole 78 rpm, 1957)

Ralph Vaughan Williams, *The Pilgrim's Progress*, opera (1909–51)

— *Ten Blake Songs*, voice & oboe (1957)

1960

Shirley Collins, *Sweet England* (Argo)

Ewan MacColl / Charles Parker / Peggy Seeger, *Singing the Fishing*, radio ballad no. 3 (Argo, rel. 1967)

1961

Ewan MacColl / Charles Parker / Peggy Seeger, *The Big Hewer*, radio ballad no. 4 (Argo, rel. 1967)

Various (coll. Alan Lomax with Seumas Ennis & Peter Kennedy), *Folksongs of Great Britain* (Caedmon, 10 LPs)

1962

Benjamin Britten, *War Requiem*, soloists, chorus & double orchestra, words Wilfred Owen

Davy Graham & Alexis Korner, *3/4 AD* (Topic EP)

1963

Anne Briggs, *The Hazards of Love* (Topic EP)

Davy Graham, *The Guitar Player* (Pye)

Ewan MacColl / Charles Parker / Peggy Seeger, *On the Edge*, radio ballad no. 6 (Argo, rel. 1968)

Various, *The Iron Muse: A Panorama of Industrial Folk Song* (Topic)

1964

Davy Graham, *Folk, Blues and Beyond* (Decca)
A. L. Lloyd & Ewan MacColl, *English and Scottish Folk Ballads* (Topic)
Ewan MacColl/Charles Parker/Peggy Seeger, *The Travelling People*, radio ballad no. 8
    (Argo, rel. 1968)

1965

Martin Carthy (feat. Dave Swarbrick), *Martin Carthy* (Fontana)
Shirley Collins & Davy Graham, *Folk Roots, New Routes* (Decca)
Donovan, *What's Bin Did and What's Bin Hid* (Pye)
— *Fairytale* (Pye)
Jackson C. Frank, *Jackson C. Frank* (Transatlantic)
Bert Jansch, *Bert Jansch* (Transatlantic)
— *It Don't Bother Me* (Transatlantic)
A. L. Lloyd, *First Person* (Topic)
John Renbourn, *John Renbourn* (Transatlantic)
Mick Softley, *Songs for Swingin' Survivors* (Columbia)
The Three City Four, *The Three City Four* (Decca)
The Watersons, *Frost and Fire* (Topic)

1966

Martin Carthy, *Second Album* (Fontana)
Donovan, *Sunshine Superman* (Epic, US only)
Incredible String Band, *Incredible String Band* (Elektra)
Bert Jansch, *Jack Orion* (Transatlantic)
Bert Jansch & John Renbourn, *Bert & John* (Transatlantic)
A. L. Lloyd/Anne Briggs/Frankie Armstrong, *The Bird in the Bush: Traditional Erotic
    Songs* (Topic)
The Young Tradition, *The Young Tradition* (Transatlantic)

1967

Dave & Toni Arthur, *Morning Stands on Tiptoe* (Transatlantic)
The Beatles, 'Penny Lane'/'Strawberry Fields Forever' (Parlophone 7″)
Marc Brierley, *Welcome to the Citadel* (Transatlantic)
Martin Carthy & Dave Swarbrick, *Byker Hill* (Fontana)
Shirley Collins, *The Sweet Primeroses* (Topic)
Sandy Denny & Strawbs, *All Our Own Work* (Pickwick, rel. 1973)
Roy Harper, *The Sophisticated Beggar* (Strike)
Incredible String Band, *5000 Spirits or The Layers of the Onion* (Elektra)

Musical / Discographic Timeline

Kaleidoscope, *Tangerine Dream* (Fontana)

John Martyn, *London Conversation* (Island)

Clive Palmer (with Wizz Jones), *Banjoland* (Sunbeam CD, rel. 2007)

Bob & Carole Pegg, *He Came from the Mountains* (Trailer, rel. 1971)

Pink Floyd, *The Piper at the Gates of Dawn* (Columbia/EMI)

John Renbourn, *Another Monday* (Transatlantic)

Traffic, *Mr Fantasy* (Island)

The Young Tradition, *So Cheerfully Round* (Transatlantic)

— *Chicken on a Raft* (Transatlantic EP)

1968

Dave & Toni Arthur, *The Lark in the Morning* (Topic)

Peter Bellamy, *Mainly Norfolk* (Transatlantic)

— *Fair England's Shore* (Transatlantic)

Martin Carthy & Dave Swarbrick, *But Two Came By* (Fontana)

Shirley Collins & Dolly Collins, *The Power of the True Love Knot* (Polydor)

Donovan, *A Gift from a Flower to a Garden* (Pye)

Eclection, *Eclection* (Elektra)

Fairport Convention, *Fairport Convention* (Polydor)

Archie Fisher, *Archie Fisher* (Transatlantic)

Davy Graham, *Large as Life and Twice as Natural* (Decca)

Roy Harper, *Come Out Fighting Genghis Smith* (CBS)

Tim Hart & Maddy Prior, *Folk Songs of Old England Vols 1 & 2* (Tee Pee)

Tim Hollier, *Message to a Harlequin* (United Artists)

Incredible String Band, *The Hangman's Beautiful Daughter* (Elektra)

— *Wee Tam and The Big Huge* (Elektra)

John Martyn, *The Tumbler* (Island)

Van Morrison, *Astral Weeks* (Warner Bros. US; UK rel. 1969)

Musica Reservata (dir. Michael Morrow, feat. David Munrow), *To Entertain a King* (Argo)

— *Metaphysical Tobacco: Songs and Dances by Dowland, East and Holborne* (Argo)

Pentangle, *The Pentangle* (Transatlantic)

— *Sweet Child* (Transatlantic)

Pink Floyd, *A Saucerful of Secrets* (Columbia/EMI)

John Renbourn, *Sir John Alot of Merrie Englandes Musyk Thyng and ye Grene Knyghte*
    (Transatlantic)

The Sallyangie, *Children of the Sun* (Transatlantic)

Traffic, *Traffic* (Island)

Tyrannosaurus Rex, *My People Were Fair and Had Sky in Their Hair . . . But Now They're
    Content to Wear Stars on Their Brows* (Regal Zonophone)

— *Prophets, Seers and Sages, the Angels of the Ages* (Regal Zonophone)

The Young Tradition, *Galleries* (Transatlantic)

Musical / Discographic Timeline

Peter Bellamy, *The Fox Jumps over the Parson's Gate* (Topic)
David Bowie, *David Bowie*, aka *Space Oddity* (Philips)
Marc Brierley, *Hello* (Transatlantic)
John Cameron, *Kes*, original soundtrack (Trunk, rel. 2001)
Martin Carthy & Dave Swarbrick, *Prince Heathen* (Fontana)
Shirley Collins & Dolly Collins, *Anthems in Eden* (Harvest)
Dr Strangely Strange, *Kip of the Serenes* (Island)
Nick Drake, *Five Leaves Left* (Island)
Fairport Convention, *What We Did on Our Holidays* (Island)
— *Unhalfbricking* (Island)
— *Liege and Lief* (Island)
Forest, *Forest* (Harvest)
Davy Graham, *Hat* (Decca)
Roy Harper, *Folkjokeopus* (Liberty)
Incredible String Band, *Changing Horses* (Elektra)
Kaleidoscope, *Faintly Blowing* (Fontana)
Mighty Baby, *Mighty Baby* (Head)
Pentangle, *Basket of Light* (Transatlantic)
Pink Floyd, *Ummagumma* (Harvest)
The Roundtable & David Munrow, *Spinning Wheel* (Jay Boy)
Bridget St John, *Ask Me No Questions* (Dandelion)
Robin Scott, *Woman from the Warm Grass* (Head)
Strawbs, *Strawbs* (A&M)
Synanthesia, *Synanthesia* (RCA Victor)
Third Ear Band, *Alchemy* (Harvest)
Tyrannosaurus Rex, *Unicorn* (Regal Zonophone)

1970

Dave & Toni Arthur, *Hearken to the Witches Rune* (Trailer)
Peter Bellamy, *Oak, Ash and Thorn* (Argo)
Black Sabbath, *Black Sabbath* (Vertigo)
Graham Bond, *Holy Magick* (Vertigo)
Bread, Love and Dreams, *The Strange Tale of Captain Shannon and the Hunchback from Gigha* (Decca)
Vashti Bunyan, *Just Another Diamond Day* (Philips)
Keith Christmas, *Fable of the Wings* (B&C)
Shirley Collins & Dolly Collins, *Love, Death and the Lady* (Harvest)
Dr Strangely Strange, *Heavy Petting* (Vertigo)
Nick Drake, *Bryter Layter* (Island)

Fairfield Parlour, *From Home to Home* (Vertigo)

Fairport Convention, *Full House* (Island)

The Famous Jug Band, *Sunshine Possibilities* (Liberty)

Bill Fay, *Bill Fay* (Deram Nova)

Forest, *Full Circle* (Harvest)

Fotheringay, *Fotheringay* (Island)

Roy Harper, *Flat, Baroque and Berserk* (Harvest)

Heron, *Heron* (Dawn)

Incredible String Band, *I Looked Up* (Elektra)

— *U* (Elektra)

Led Zeppelin, *III* (Atlantic)

Shelagh McDonald, *Shelagh McDonald Album* (B&C)

Harold McNair, *The Fence* (B&C)

Magna Carta, *Seasons* (Vertigo)

John & Beverley Martyn, *The Road to Ruin* (Island)

— *Stormbringer!* (Island)

Mr Fox, *Mr Fox* (Transatlantic)

Pentangle, *Cruel Sister* (Transatlantic)

Pink Floyd, *Atom Heart Mother* (Harvest)

John Renbourn, *The Lady and the Unicorn* (Transatlantic)

Alex Sanders, *A Witch Is Born* (A&M)

Mick Softley, *Sunrise* (CBS)

Steeleye Span, *Hark! The Village Wait* (RCA)

Meic Stevens, *Outlander* (Warner Bros.)

Strawbs, *Dragonfly* (A&M)

— *Just a Collection of Antiques and Curios* (A&M)

Third Ear Band, *Third Ear Band*, aka *Elements* (Harvest)

Traffic, *John Barleycorn Must Die* (Island)

Trees, *The Garden of Jane Delawney* (CBS)

— *On the Shore* (CBS)

Tyrannosaurus Rex, *A Beard of Stars* (Regal Zonophone)

Kenneth Williams, *The Best of Rambling Syd Rumpo* (EMI Regal)

1971

Graham Bond & Holy Magick, *We Put Our Magick on You* (Vertigo)

Bread, Love and Dreams, *Amaryllis* (Decca)

Anne Briggs, *Anne Briggs* (Topic)

— *The Time Has Come* (CBS)

Keith Christmas, *Pigmy* (B&C)

COB, *Spirit of Love* (CBS)

Shirley Collins & The Albion Country Band, *No Roses* (Pegasus)

Comus, *First Utterance* (Dawn)
Dando Shaft, *Dando Shaft* (RCA Neon)
Sandy Denny, *The North Star Grassman and the Ravens* (Island)
Donovan, *HMS Donovan* (Dawn)
Fairport Convention, *'Babbacombe' Lee* (Island)
Bill Fay, *Time of the Last Persecution* (Deram)
Forest, *Full Circle* (Harvest)
Fresh Maggots, *Fresh Maggots* (RCA)
Roy Harper, *Stormcock* (Harvest)
Tim Hart & Maddy Prior, *Summer Solstice* (B&C)
Heron, *Twice As Nice and Half the Price* (Dawn)
Mike Heron's Reputation, *Smiling Men with Bad Reputations* (Island)
Incredible String Band, *Be Glad for the Song Has No Ending* (Island)
—— *Liquid Acrobat as Regards the Air* (Island)
Bert Jansch, *Rosemary Lane* (Transatlantic)
Led Zeppelin, ⚭ 𖣂 ⊕ ① (Atlantic)
Shelagh McDonald, *Stargazer* (B&C)
Magna Carta, *Songs from Wasties Orchard* (Vertigo)
John Martyn, *Bless the Weather* (Island)
Mighty Baby, *A Jug of Love* (Blue Horizon)
Mr Fox, *The Gipsy* (Transatlantic)
Oberon, *A Midsummer Night's Dream* (Acorn)
Pentangle, *Reflection* (Transatlantic)
Pink Floyd, *Meddle* (Harvest)
John Renbourn, *Faro Annie* (Transatlantic)
Bridget St John, *Songs for the Gentle Man* (Dandelion)
Mick Softley, *Street Singer* (CBS)
Spirogyra, *St Radigunds* (B&C)
Steeleye Span, *Please to See the King* (B&C)
—— *Ten Man Mop, or Mr Reservoir Butler Rides Again* (Pegasus)
Strawbs, *From the Witchwood* (A&M)
Tír na nÓg, *Tír na nÓg* (Chrysalis)
The Woods Band, *The Woods Band* (Greenwich)

1972

Peter Bellamy, *Merlin's Isle of Gramarye* (Argo)
The Bunch, *Rock On* (Island)
Martin Carthy, *Shearwater* (Pegasus)
COB, *Moyshe McStiff and the Tartan Lancers of the Sacred Heart* (Polydor Folk Mill)
Dave Cousins, *Two Weeks Last Summer* (A&M)
Sandy Denny, *Sandy* (Island)

Musical / Discographic Timeline

Nick Drake, *Pink Moon* (Island)
Mark Fry, *Dreaming of Alice* (IT Dischi, Italy only)
The Habibiyya, *If Man but Knew* (Island/Help)
Ashley Hutchings et al., *Morris On* (Island/Help)
Incredible String Band, *Earthspan* (Island)
Mellow Candle, *Swaddling Songs* (Deram)
Parchment, *Light Up the Fire* (Pye)
Bob & Carole Pegg, *And Now It Is So Early – Songs of Sydney Carter* (Trailer)
Pentangle, *Solomon's Seal* (Reprise)
Mick Softley, *Any Mother Mustn't Grumble* (CBS)
Spirogyra, *Old Boot Wine* (Pegasus)
Steeleye Span, *Below the Salt* (Chrysalis)
Strawbs, *Grave New World* (A&M)
Richard Thompson, *Henry, the Human Fly* (Island)
Lal & Mike Waterson, *Bright Phoebus* (Trailer)
Robin Williamson, *Myrrh* (Island)

1973

The Albion Country Band, *Battle of the Field* (Island/Help, rel. 1976)
Anne Briggs, *Sing a Song for You* (Warner Bros., rel. 1991)
Sandy Denny, *Like an Old Fashioned Waltz* (Island)
Fairport Convention, *Rosie* (Island)
Paul Giovanni/Magnet, *The Wicker Man*, original soundtrack (Trunk, rel. 1998; Silva
    Screen, rel. 2002)
Ashley Hutchings, *Rattlebone and Ploughjack* (Island/Help, rel. 1976)
Incredible String Band, *No Ruinous Feud* (Island)
John Martyn, *Solid Air* (Island)
— *Inside Out* (Island)
Bob Pegg & Nick Strutt, *Bob Pegg & Nick Strutt* (Transatlantic)
Carolanne Pegg, *Carolanne* (Transatlantic)
Spirogyra, *Bells, Boots and Shambles* (Polydor)
Steeleye Span, *Parcel of Rogues* (Chrysalis)

1974

Steve Ashley, *Stroll On* (Gull)
Martin Carthy, *Sweet Wivelsfield* (Deram)
Shirley Collins, *Adieu to Old England* (Topic)
Fairport Convention, *Rising for the Moon* (Island)
Ashley Hutchings & John Kirkpatrick, *The Compleat Dancing Master* (Island/Help)
Incredible String Band, *Hard Rope and Silken Twine* (Island)

Musical / Discographic Timeline

John Martyn, *Sunday's Child* (Island)
Mike Oldfield, *Hergest Ridge* (Virgin)
Bob Pegg, *The Ship Builder* (Transatlantic)
Sounds of Salvation, *Sounds of Salvation* (Reflection)
Steeleye Span, *Now We Are Six* (Chrysalis)
Richard & Linda Thompson, *I Want to See the Bright Lights Tonight* (Island)
Water into Wine Band, *Hill Climbing for Beginners* (Myrrh)

1975

Peter Bellamy, *Barrack Room Ballads of Rudyard Kipling* (Green Linnet)
Etchingham Steam Band, *Etchingham Steam Band* (Fledg'ling, rel. 1995)
John Martyn, *Live at Leeds* (Island)
Mike Oldfield, *Ommadawn* (Virgin)
Bob Pegg, *Ancient Maps* (Transatlantic)
Steeleye Span, *Commoners Crown* (Chrysalis)
— *All Around My Hat* (Chrysalis)
Stone Angel, *Stone Angel* (Seashell)
Richard & Linda Thompson, *Hokey Pokey* (Island)
— *Pour Down Like Silver* (Island)
Various, *The Electric Muse: The Story of Folk into Rock* (Island / Transatlantic)

1976

Jon Anderson, *Olias of Sunhillow* (Atlantic)
Nigel Mazlyn Jones, *Ship to Shore* (Isle of Light)
Spriguns, *Revel Weird and Wild* (Decca)
Steeleye Span, *Rocket Cottage* (Chrysalis)
Water into Wine Band, *Harvest Time* (private press)
The Wurzels, *The Combine Harvester* (EMI)

1977

Peter Bellamy et al., *The Transports* (Free Reed)
Sandy Denny, *Rendezvous* (Island)
Jethro Tull, *Songs from the Wood* (Island)
Bob Johnson & Peter Knight, *The King of Elfland's Daughter* (Chrysalis)
John Martyn, *One World* (Island)
Tom Newman, *Faerie Symphony* (Decca)
Anthony Phillips, *The Geese and the Ghost* (Passport)
Spriguns, *Time Will Pass* (Decca)

Musical / Discographic Timeline

Mark Hollis, *Mark Hollis* (Polydor, 1998)

.O.rang, *Herd of Instinct* (Echo, 1994)

— *Fields and Waves* (Echo, 1996)

The Orb, *Adventures Beyond the Ultraworld* (Big Life, 1991)

Talk Talk, *Laughing Stock* (Verve, 1991)

Various, *Voice of the People: Traditional Music of England, Ireland, Scotland and Wales* (Topic, 20 CDs, 1998)

2000s

Belbury Poly, *The Owl's Map* (Ghost Box, 2006)

Black Sheep, *Kiss My Sweet Apocalypse* (Invada, 2009)

Boards of Canada, *Geogaddi* (Warp, 2000)

Broadcast & The Focus Group, *Investigate Witch Cults of the Radio Age* (Warp, 2009)

Vashti Bunyan, *Lookaftering* (FatCat, 2005)

Eliza Carthy, *Anglicana* (Topic, 2002)

Julian Cope, *Citizen Cain'd* (Head Heritage, 2005)

The Focus Group, *We Are All Pan's People* (Ghost Box, 2007)

Fovea Hex, *Neither Speak Nor Remain Silent* vols 1–3 (Die Stadt/Janet, 2005–7)

Sharron Kraus, *The Fox's Wedding* (Durtro Jnana, 2008)

The Owl Service, *A Garland of Song* (Southern, 2008)

Alasdair Roberts, *Farewell Sorrow* (Rough Trade, 2003)

— *No Earthly Man* (Drag City, 2005)

— *Spoils* (Drag City, 2009)

Scatter, *The Mountain Announces* (Blank Tapes, 2006)

The Story, *Arcane Rising* (Sunbeam, 2007)

Trembling Bells, *Carbeth* (Honest Jons, 2009)

Various, *The Imagined Village* (Real World, 2007)

Various, *John Barleycorn Reborn: Dark Britannica* (Cold Spring, 2007)

Robin Williamson, *The Iron Stone* (ECM, 2008)

Richard Youngs, *The Naive Shaman* (Jagjaguwar, 2006)

— *Autumn Response* (Jagjaguwar, 2007)

— *Under Stellar Stream* (Jagjaguwar, 2009)

Acknowledgements

I'm indebted to my agent, Neil Taylor, for responding positively to the idea of this book from the start. The endless enthusiasm and advocacy of my editor, Lee Brackstone, has made everything possible. Also at Faber, thanks to Ian Bahrami, Lisa Baker, Kate Burton, Eleanor Crow, Lucie Ewin, Silvia Novak and David Watkins.

I'm grateful to everyone that I interviewed for their time and their memories: Dave Arthur, Toni Arthur-Hay, Martyn Bates, Tim Booth, Vashti Bunyan, Shirley Collins, Gerry Conway, Julian Cope, Terry Cox, Peter Daltrey, Jerry Donahue, Pat Donaldson, Marcus Eoin, Bill Fay, Robin Frederick, Tim Goulding, Eric Hayes, Mark Hollis, Ashley Hutchings, Bert Jansch, Jacqui McShee, John Martyn, Dave Mattacks, Simon Nicol, Ivan Pawle, Bob Pegg, Carole Pegg, Dave Pegg, John Renbourn, Sandy Roberton, Mike Sandison, Keshav Sathe, Peggy Seeger, David Sylvian, Danny Thompson, Richard Thompson, Bobbie Watson, Adrian Welham, Martin Welham, Ian Whiteman, Robin Williamson, Roger Wootton and Rob Young (of Comus).

The following all contributed in innumerable ways, large and small, all equally valuable. For records and books lent, comments and conversations, vital info-snippets, contacts supplied, features and reviews commissioned, reading drafts and general encouragement, my thanks to: Daniel Barbenel, David Barbenel, Mike Barnes, Chris Bohn, Michael Bonner, Kevin Brice, Mike Cooper, Mark Coyle, Mark Fisher, William Fowler, Jason Gross, Tony Herrington, Julian House, Patrick Humphries, Charlie Inskip, Nick Kent, Richard King, John Mulvey, Mark Pilkington, Edwin Pouncey, Andy Roberts, John Robinson, Adrian Shaughnessy, Paul Smith, David Solomons, Andy Tait, David Tibet, Jonny Trunk, Derek Walmsley and Adrian Whittaker. Special thanks to Nathan Budzinski for assistance with interview transcriptions.

For supplying music, photos and images, useful materials, contacts and sundry help, I'm grateful to: Paul Adams at Fellside, Ian Anderson at *fRoots*, Nicolas Bell at the British Library, Joe Black and Azi Efterkazi at Universal, Ian Boughton at the Rutland Boughton Music Trust (rutlandboughtonmusictrust.org.uk), Phil Budden at Topic, Vashti Bunyan, Dorian Cope, Andy Farquarson and Stevie Horton at Iconic Music, Karen Fletcher at the Ralph Vaughan Williams Society (rvwsociety. com), Dick Greener at strawbsweb.co.uk, David Griffith at davidmunrow.org, Kirsty Hartsiotis at Cheltenham Art Gallery and Museum, Mick Houghton at Brassneck, Dorothy Howe at Sanctuary, Roger Hutchinson, Matthew Ingram,

Acknowledgements

Phil King at IPC, Stephen Jones of Heron, Dr Paul Long, Jean-Paul Margnac, John May at *The Generalist* (hqinfo.blogspot.com), Paul Misso (paulmisso.co.uk), Clare Morris, Richard Morton Jack at Sunbeam, Brian O'Reilly at Hux, Jim Page at the A. E. Housman Society, Bob Pegg, Bruce Phillips at the John Ireland Trust (musicweb-international.com/ireland), Jill Reading at the BFI, Fiona Richards, Harriet Simms at Glass Ceiling, Phil Smee, Barry Smith, David Suff at Fledg'ling, Malcolm Taylor at the Ralph Vaughan Williams Memorial Library, Neil Wayne and Nigel Schofield at Free Reed, Christopher Sykes, David Wells, Anne Wheeldon at the London Borough of Hammersmith and Fulham Archives, Reinhard Zierke at Mainly Norfolk (informatik.uni-hamburg.de/~zierke/folk). Thanks to Patrick Ward and Ben Weaver for eleventh-hour scanning.

For other research materials, thanks to the staff of the Barbican Music Library in London; Olav Nilsen at the Sølvberget Music Library in Stavanger, Norway; Barney Hoskyns and Tony Keys at rocksbackpages.com; Dave Barker at ukrockfestivals.com.

Finally, to Rod and Viv Young, and Arne and Aslaug Neset, thank you, as ever, for your love, generosity and support.

Axel and Mathilde, I never knew magic crazy as this. Anne Hilde, brightest in my northern sky.

In Memoriam

Two untimely deaths pushed me further towards writing *Electric Eden*. I always hoped that Ian MacDonald would write a book on the bigger picture of British music; sadly, he took his own life in 2003. I'm grateful to Trevor Manwaring for alerting me, in a conversation shortly before he died of an illness in 2004, to the music of Bill Fay, among others.

I'd also like to commemorate some who died while this book was being written: Syd Barrett, Steve Benbow, Arabella Churchill, Mike Evans, Davy Graham, Tim Hart, Peter Kennedy, Robert Kirby, John Martyn, John Michell, Nick Strutt and Rick Wright.

To my grandpa, Joseph Edgar Young (1898–1982), who fought for this.

Image Credits

3, 63, 66, 72, 114: Courtesy EFDSS.

14: Photo by Christopher Sykes, collection of Vashti Bunyan.

15: Drawing by Vashti Bunyan, collection of Vashti Bunyan.

18, 29, 166 (Crispian Woodgate), 177, 188 (EBA Studios), 190 (Folk Directions), 197 (Decca), 208, 211 (Weybridge Industrial Photographers), 217 (Topix), 285, 317 (George Wilkes), 340 (Island), 346 (Elektra), 373, 388 (Polydor), 522, 541 (Chrysalis), 573 (Virgin): courtesy IPC Archive.

47, 50: Hammersmith & Fulham Archives & Local History Centre.

57: Collection of Ursula Vaughan Williams, courtesy British Library.

Acknowledgements

75: Courtesy A. E. Housman Society.

83: Cheltenham Art Gallery and Museum Archives.

92: Illustration by Ernest H. Shepard.

95, 105 (top left): courtesy Rutland Boughton Music Trust.

98, 442: Savage Pencil Archive.

105: Courtesy John Ireland Trust, Barry Smith, Martin Anderson.

130, 138 (Bill Mencken), 143, 145, 149, 154, 161 (Hasted: Lawrence Photo), 182, 195 (John Bryan): courtesy *fRoots* Archive.

200: Courtesy David Griffith/davidmunrow.org.

202: Courtesy Reinhard Zierke (*Power of the True Love Knot*).

226: *Bradford Telegraph and Argus*.

254, 255, 257: Eric Hayes.

268, 273: Collection of Ashley Hutchings.

275: Hart/Prior courtesy Reinhard Zierke.

280, 299, 313, 329, 422: Keith Morris. Courtesy Clare Morris/Estate of Keith Morris (keithmorrisphoto.co.uk).

288: Courtesy Stephen Jones.

315: Tony Evans.

353: Courtesy Matthew Ingram (*5000 Spirits* back).

364: Artwork by Pamela Colman Smith.

382, 392: Courtesy Dick Greener/Strawbsweb.

398: Dave Hollis, collection of Adrian Welham.

401: Collection of Richard Morton Jack (Forest).

424, 427, 436: Reproduced by permission of Bob Pegg.

438: Collection of Jonny Trunk (*Witches Rune*).

458: Mirrorpix.

465: Collection of Andy Tait.

482: Jean-Paul Margnac.

488, 493, 501: Collection of John May.

494, 495: Paul Misso (paulmisso.co.uk).

503, 504: Roger Hutchinson.

509: Tony Kite, courtesy Comus.

515: Jake Jackson.

556: Artwork by Tony Harding, from *Viz* 30 (June/July 1988). Reproduced by permission.

588: Ian Dickson.

Index

Index

Index

Index

Index

Index

Index

Gong, 495, 511, 512, 533, 599

Gorman, Michael, 127, 132, 194

GPO Film Unit, 118, 119

Graham, Davy, 162–6, 171–4, 207, 219–20, 328, 419, 529

  3/4 AD, 163, 171; *Folk, Blues and Beyond*, 164; *Folk Roots, New Routes* (with Shirley Collins), 165–6, 170, 180, 207; *The Guitar Player*, 162; *Large as Life and Twice as Natural*, 229

Grahame, Kenneth: *The Wind in the Willows*, 88, 91–2, 454

Grainger, Percy, 3, 9, 61, 71, 275

Grant, Arthur, 417

Grant, Cy, 132, 142, 143

Grateful Dead, The, 220, 223, 246, 470

Graves, Robert: *The White Goddess*, 369–70

Grey, Marion, 167, 439

Grieg, Edvard, 58–9

Grierson, John, 118, 119, 121

Grigson, Geoffrey: *Penguin Book of Ballads*, 445

Groundhogs, The, 544

Growth Arts Lab, Beckenham, 486, 508

Gryphon, 282, 521, 533, 570

Guest, Roy, 171

guitars: acoustic, 160; early use in English folk music, 129–30, 160; electric vs. acoustic, 9, 161; flat-top, 159–60; tuning systems, 164, 165, 171, 220

Gurdjieff, G. I., 276, 470, 576, 590

Gurney, Ivor, 86, 539

Guthrie, Arlo, 174, 391

Guthrie, Woody, 123, 127, 133, 134, 144, 160, 167, 178, 458

Gypsies, 129, 153, 208, 455

'Gypsy Dave', 19, 24

Habibiyya, The, 470, 523

Haggard, Piers, 417

'Hal-An-Tow', 182

Hall, Peter, 410

Hall, Reg, 425

Hall, Robin, 132

Hamill, Claire, 338

Hammer Films, 302, 411, 417, 418, 431, 596

Hammersmith Morris, 439

Hammersmith Socialist Society, 56–7

Hapshash and the Coloured Coat, 298, 357

Hardin, Tim, 246

Hardy, Françoise, 297

Hardy, Robin, 411

Hardy, Thomas, 85, 87, 122, 206, 315, 565

  The Return of the Native, 79, 85, 107

Harker, Dave: *Fakesong*, 241

Harkin, Bill, 494

Harper, Roy, 8, 173, 209, 224, 290, 406, 480, 486, 529, 570

  Stormcock, 406, 515–16

Harriott, Joe, 230, 231

Harris, Lee, 578, 581, 582, 584, 585

Harris, Mick, 603

Harrison, George, 398, 452

Harrison, John, 190, 194

Hart, Tim, 45, 194, 266, 267, 269, 270, 271, 274, 527, 542, 543, 544, 547

Hart, Tim and Prior, Maddy, 439

  Folk Songs of Old England, 266; *Summer Solstice*, 266, 282

Harvest Records, 209, 214, 282, 398, 399, 472, 530

Hasted, John, 129, 130, 159–60

Hawkwind, 473, 494, 497

Haworth, Bryn, 516

Hayes, Eric, 254, 257–9, 324–6

Headington Quarry Morris Men, 64, 116, 277

Headley Grange, Hampshire, 407

Heart of England, The (documentary), 121

Heath, Edward, 548–9

Heckstall-Smith, Dick, 227, 434

Hedgehog Pie, 552

Hell's Angels, 488, 497, 536, 592

Helm, Levon, 332–3

Hemmings, David, 205, 403

Henderson, Dorris, 219

Henderson, Hamish, 131

Hendrix, Jimi, 174, 198, 245, 332, 349, 482, 521, 579

Henry Cow, 511, 533

Heron, 288–90

Heron, Mike, 28, 30, 45, 209, 256, 347, 349, 350, 351, 353, 354, 355, 359–63, 365, 367–72, 373–4, 375, 387, 391, 517, 521

Heseltine, Michael, 245

Heseltine, Philip *see* Warlock, Peter

Hill, Miranda, 55

Hill, Octavia, 55

Hillage, Steve, 599

Hines, Barry: *A Kestrel for a Knave*, 225–7

Hipgnosis, 396, 417

Hitler, Adolf, 514, 554

Hogwood, Christopher, 199, 200–201, 204, 213

Holborne, Anthony, 205, 291

Hollier, Tim, 229

Hollies, The, 192

Hollis, Mark, 577–85

Holst, Gustav, 6, 7, 56, 57, 58, 60, 74, 76, 79–85, 87, 104, 110, 533

  The Hymn of Jesus, 83–4; *The Planets*, 81, 85

Holst, Imogen, 80, 84

Holst, Isobel (née Harrison), 56, 81

Holy Grail, 94, 493, 496, 498

Holy Modal Rounders, The, 349

Holzman, Jac, 315, 358

Homer, 69

Hood, Robin, 126

Index

Index

Index

Index

Index

Index

Index

Index